Philip Pearsall Carpenter

The Mollusks of Western North America

Philip Pearsall Carpenter

The Mollusks of Western North America

ISBN/EAN: 9783743331419

Manufactured in Europe, USA, Canada, Australia, Japa

Cover: Foto ©ninafisch / pixelio.de

Manufactured and distributed by brebook publishing software
(www.brebook.com)

Philip Pearsall Carpenter

The Mollusks of Western North America

TABLE OF CONTENTS.

(iii)

INTRODUCTION.

AFTER the publication of my first "Report on the present state of our knowledge with regard to the Mollusca of the West Coast of North America," undertaken at the request of the British Association for the Advancement of Science, and printed in their Report for 1856, I visited America in order to arrange the first duplicate series of the great Reigen Collection of Mazatlan Shells which I had presented to the New York State Museum at Albany. It was one of the special objects of my visit to examine the types of previously described species in the United States, that I might compare them with those known in England. Having visited Washington to examine the types of the United States Exploring Expedition (Wilkes'), I was requested to spend the winter of 1859–60 in unpacking and arranging the shells belonging to the National Museum under its charge; and after my return to England I received from time to time the various collections sent to the Institution from the West Coast as they arrived; all of these were duly compared with the types in the Cumingian and other British collections.

Being thus in a position to correct a large number of unavoidable errors in my first Report, and to add a great deal of fresh information from American sources (chiefly obtained through the Smithsonian Institution), I was requested by the British Association to embody the material in a "Supplementary Report" on the same subject as the first. Knowing how difficult it is for American students to obtain access to serial publications, I obtained permission, in behalf of the Institution, to stereotype this second report, and the papers connected with it, which appeared in the "Proceedings of the Zoological Society," the "Annals and Magazine of Natural History," and the "Journal de Conchyliologie."

(v)

The present volume consists, therefore, of a reprint from these stereotype plates, with the original paging at the top, and the Smithsonian paging at the bottom; and of a general index of species.

The index was prepared (at the expense of the Smithsonian Institution) by Mr. E. Taylor, Student at McGill College. It includes not only the present volume but all my previous English publications on the subject, of which the principal are the First British Association Report and the British Museum Mazatlan Catalogue. All references to these works *not reprinted* have the page-number prefixed by a Roman Capital (O to X), by which they can be at once distinguished from the simple numbers which refer to the foot-page in this volume. Students who want an index to the First Report will fix the eye on the initial O; to the Mazatlan Catalogue on P.

In an accompanying list will be found an enumeration of all my papers published in European journals relative to American conchology, and for the most part reprinted in the present collection. In this, however, is not included any of the contributions to American serials, as the Journal of the Academy of Natural Sciences of Philadelphia, the Proceedings of the California Academy, or the American Journal of Conchology.

My principal object in the preparation of these works has been to make out and compare the writings of previous naturalists, so that it might be possible for succeeding students to begin where I left off, without being obliged to waste so large an amount of time as I have been compelled to do in analyzing the (often inaccurate) work of their predecessors.

As the work of previous writers, whether satisfactory or otherwise, is duly tabulated in my Reports, so that others may judge of its value as well as I, it is not fair (as is often done) to quote from these Reports as on my authority. I was simply the historian, not the original writer. In the First Report I was a novice in the scientific world, and rarely ventured on criticisms; in the second, I allowed myself with more confidence to state my own conclusions, because I found that others had not enjoyed the remarkable facilities of comparing types which fell to my lot, and which (in many instances) cannot be renewed. Since that time, Nuttall, Gould, Rich, Judge Cooper, and especially Hugh Cuming, have been called to another world; their collections have changed hands, and fresh causes of error have crept in. The present condition of the Cumingian Collection has been faithfully described by Dr. Gray in the Proceedings of the Zoological Society; and those who will take the trouble to compare his review of the *Calyptræidæ*, after the destruction of original labels consequent on Reeve's Monograph, with that which I gave in the Mazatlan Catalogue, while these labels were still fixed to the shells, will appreciate the advantages which I formerly enjoyed.

Readers who may discover any uncorrected errors in this volume, or in any of my other works, are urgently requested to apprise me of them (Box 193½ P. O., Montreal, C. E.), in order that they may be corrected in the Report of the Mollusca which Prof. Whitney has requested me to prepare for the California Geological Survey.

PHILIP P. CARPENTER.

Montreal, July 17, 1872.

LIST OF PAPERS

ON

AMERICAN MOLLUSCA

PUBLISHED IN EUROPEAN WORKS BY

P. P. CARPENTER.

REPRINTED.

A.

Supplementary Report on the Present State of our Knowledge with Regard to the Mollusca of the West Coast of North America. *Page* 1.[1]

> From the Report of the British Association for the Advancement of Science, for 1863, pp. 517—686. Published in August, 1864. Extra copies, with title-page, dated 1864.

B.

Review of Prof. C. B. Adams' "Catalogue of the Shells of Panama," from the Type Specimens. *Page* 173.

> From the Proceedings of the Zoölogical Society of London, June 23, 1863, pp. 339—369.

C.

Diagnoses of New Forms of Mollusks collected at Cape St. Lucas, Lower California. By Mr. J. Xantus. *Page* 207.

> From the Annals and Magazine of Natural History. Third Series, Vol. XIII., pp. 311—315, April, 1864. Ibid. (Nos. 15—36) pp. 474—479, June, 1864. Ibid. Vol. XIV. (Nos. 37—52), pp. 45—49, July, 1864.

D.

Contributions towards a Monograph of the Pandoridæ. *Page* 223.

> From the Proceedings of the Zoölogical Society of London, pp. 596—603, November 22, 1864.

---

[1] The references are to the bottom paging.

(ix)

E.

Diagnoses of New Forms of Mollusca from the Vancouver District. *Page* 233.

From the Annals and Magazine of Natural History. Third Series, Vol. XIV. (Nos. 5—37), pp. 423—429, December, 1864. Ibid. Vol. XV. (Nos. 37—56), pp. 28—32, January, 1865.

F.

Diagnoses of New Forms of Mollusca from the Vancouver District. *Page* 247.

From the Proceedings of the Zoölogical Society of London, pp. 201—204, February 14, 1865.

G

Diagnoses of New Species and a New Genus of Mollusks, from the Reigen Mazatlan Collection; with an Account of Additional Specimens presented to the British Museum. *Page* 253.

From the Proceedings of the Zoölogical Society of London, pp. 268—273, March 14, 1865.

H.

Descriptions of New Species and Varieties of Chitonidæ and Acmæidæ, from the Panama Collection of the late Prof. C. B. Adams. *Page* 263.

From the Proceedings of the Zoölogical Society of London, pp. 274—277, March 14, 1865

I.

Diagnoses of New Species of Mollusks, from the West Tropical Region of North America, principally collected by the Rev. J. Rowell, of San Francisco. *Page* 269

From the Proceedings of the Zoölogical Society of London, pp. 278—282, March 14, 1865.

K.

Diagnoses of New Forms of Mollusca, from the West coast of North America, first collected by Col. E. Jewett. *Page* 277.

From the Annals and Magazine of Natural History. Third Series, Vol. XV., pp. 177—182 (Nos. 373—386), March, 1865. Ibid. pp. 394—399 (*Mangelia variegata* to end), May, 1865.

L.

Diagnoses of New Forms of Mollusca, collected by Col. E. Jewett, on the West Tropical shores of North America. *Page* 291.

From the Annals and Magazine of Natural History. Third Series Vol. XV., pp. 399—400, May, 1865.

M.

Diagnoses des Mollusques nouveaux provenant de Californie et faisant partie du Musée de l'Institution Smithsonienne. *Page* 297.

From the Journal de Conchyliologie, Vol. XII. (Third Series, Vol. V.) pp. 123—149, April, 1865.

N.

On the Pleistocene Fossils collected by Col. E. Jewett, at Santa Barbara, California; with Descriptions of New Species. *Page* 319.

From the Annals and Magazine of Natural History, Third Series, Vol. XVII., pp. 274—278, April, 1866.

NOT REPRINTED.

O.

Report on the Present State of our Knowledge with Regard to the Mollusca of the West Coast of North America.

From the Report of the British Association for the Advancement of Science, for 1856, pp. 159—368. Published in 1857. Extra copies with title-page, list of plates with references to figures (4 pages), dated 1857. Not reprinted, but referred to under "O" in the general index.

P.

Catalogue of the Reigen Collection of Mazatlan Mollusca in the British Museum.

Each sheet dated: July, 1855—June, 1857. The Bryozoa, by G. Busk, Esq. Printed by order of the Trustees at the Oberlin Press, Warrington. 552 pp. First Edition, with Preface as arranged by Dr. J. E. Gray, on sale at the British Museum, price 8s. Second Edition, with Author's Preface, accompanying duplicate collections of the shells, published simultaneously.

A.

SUPPLEMENTARY REPORT

ON THE

PRESENT STATE OF OUR KNOWLEDGE

WITH REGARD TO

THE MOLLUSCA OF THE WEST COAST OF NORTH AMERICA.

BY

PHILIP P. CARPENTER, B.A., Ph.D.

From the Report of the British Association for the Advancement of Science, for 1863, pp. 517—686. Published in August, 1864. Extra copies, with title-page, dated 1864.

(1)

Supplementary Report on the Present State of our Knowledge with regard to the Mollusca of the West Coast of North America. By PHILIP P. CARPENTER, *B.A., Ph.D.**

THE object of the present Report is (1) to correct the errors which have been observed in the first Report ("Report &c." 1856, pp. 159–368); and (2) to point out the fresh sources of information which have been rendered available since that period. For convenience of comparison, the paragraph numbers refer to those of the first Report in the corrections, and are continued from them in the addenda. In the bibliographical portion, the criticisms by the writer of this Report are inserted in [ ]; a distinction not always attended to in the former volume, in consequence of which erroneous names and localities have been attributed to the reviewer, instead of to the authors quoted.

22. *Introduction.*—(Line 4 from bottom.) The river Willamette flows *northwards* (Gld.).

23. *Early Writers.*—The only Californian shell described by Linnæus is *Turbo sanguineus,= T. coccineus,* Desh.; v. Hanl. Ips. Linn. Conch. p. 334. The types are too much worn to decide whether they came from the North Pacific or (as is more probable) from the Mediterranean. In Gmelin's edition of Linnæus, *Lipsiæ,* 1788–1790,—which is, in great measure, a translation from a German work published a few years in advance [teste Hanley],—the following species are assigned to the "West Coast of America," probably on the authority of Martyn :—page 3529, *Murex foliatus :* 3702, *Patella pecten :* 3712, *Patella calyptra.* The last two seem exotic.

Many West-coast species had found their way into English collections during the last century, at a much earlier date than was expected at the time of the first Report. They were mainly derived from the voyages of Capt. Cook and other circumnavigators. Capt. Cook was accompanied by Solander, as naturalist, at the instance of Sir Joseph Banks. His shells passed into the hands of Mr. Humphrey, the dealer, at whose death the remainder, a thousand boxes, became the property of the elder Sowerby, and (in part) of Mawe [teste Hanley]. They took their chance of being figured or described by the early conchologists. The localities are (as might be expected) often interchanged, but have been quoted by later authors, who have not thought fit to avail themselves of more correct sources of information.

The first accurate delineations are by Thomas Martyn, in his 'Universal Conchologist,' London, 1784. Those who only know this book from Chenu's reprint, Paris, 1845, can form but a poor idea of the exquisite beauty of the original work. Of this, very few copies are accessible; but it may be consulted at the British Museum, the Royal Society, and the Royal College of Surgeons.

No.	Plate.	Fig.	
16	5	3.	*Patella tramoserica,* Mart. N.W.C. America, very rare. [N. Zealand.]
18	6	1.	*Patella calyptra,* Mart. N.W. Coast of America, very rare. [Not identified: resembles *Crep. adunca.* without deck. Hanl. considers it a *Hipponyx,* like *australis.*]
31	8	4.	*Trochus inæqualis,* Mart. Friendly Isles, common. [Does not closely resemble the Japan and Vancouver species,= *Pachypoma gibberosum,* Chemn.]
32	10	1.	*Trochus canaliculatus,* Mart. N. Zealand, rare.
33	10	2.	*Trochus annulatus,* Mart. N. Zealand, very rare.
34	10	3.	*Trochus costatus,* Mart. St. George's Sound, rare. [= *Calliostoma filosum, castaneum, ligatum,* and *modestum.*]

* In consequence of the expected arrival of fresh materials, this report has been corrected and continued up to the period of going to press.
Warrington Free Museum and Library, Aug. 1st, 1864.

3

Many of the figures of Martyn were reproduced by Chemnitz, in his comprehensive continuation of Martini's 'Conchylien Cabinet,' 1780-1795. Unhappily, though often quoted for generic and specific names, he did not adopt the binomial nomenclature (except in vol. xi.), but described each shell in two or more words, as it happened. For this reason he appears to have had no scruple in altering previous designations, as follows:—

Fig.

1538, 1539. *Murex Purpura alata*, "Mart. Conch. Un. vol. ii. f. 66, Leaved *Purpura foliata* from N.W. coast of America."

1634 .. *Murex Glomus cereus*, seu *Cereus conglomeratus*, "Mart. vol. ii. f. 43, Ridged *Buccinum liratum* from King George's Sound."

Vign. 21, f. A, B. *Buccinum compositum*, "Mart. Un. Conch. vol. ii. f. 44; Plaited *Buccinum* from King George's Sound."

Vign. 23, f. A, B. *Trochus gibberosus Novæ Zelandiæ*. "Forster's Cat. no. 1374; La Raboteuse de la nouvelle Zélande.—Mart. Un. Conch. vol. i. f. 31; Rugged *Trochus inæqualis* from Friendly Is."

1579, 1580. *Trochus doliarius*, "Mart. vol. i. f. 32, Fluted *Trochus canaliculatus* from N. Zealand."

1581, 1582. *Trochus virgineus*, "Favanne, Conch. pl. 79. f. 1. vol. ii. p. 342; id. Cat. Rais. no. 1352. p. 269; Le Sabot Magellanique.—Mart. Un. Conch. vol. i. f. 33; Ringed *Trochus annulatus* from N. Zealand.—Cab. Mus. Portl. no. 1240; the Purpled-edged *Trochus*; item, no. 1970, a large and fine specimen of the Purple-edged *Trochus* from the N.W. coast of America; rare." [= *T. cœlatus*, var. β. Gmel., teste Dillw. vol. ii. p. 800.]

1802, 1803. *Buccinum crispatum*. "The furbelowed Whelk." [=*B. plicatum*, Mart., non Ln.]

1841, 1842. *Murex amplustre*. N.W. coast of America. [This erroneous locality is copied from the Portland Cat.. The species is quoted from *Buccinum* (*Latirus*) *aplustre*, Mart., no. 3. pl. I. f. 3, where it is rightly assigned to the Friendly Is. =*M. argus*, var. γ. Gmel., teste Dillw. vol. ii. p. 735.]

The assignment of West American species to New Zealand, begun by Martyn, has continued a source of error to the present time. It occurs in Dr. Gould's 'Exploring Expedition Mollusca,' in the Cumingian Collection, and in the British Museum.

In the 'Travels in New Zealand,' by Ernest Dieffenbach, M.D., London 1843, vol. i. pp. 228-264, is given a "Catalogue of the Species of Mollusca and their Shells, which have hitherto been recorded as found at New Zealand," &c., by J. E. Gray. The author premises that some of the species [marked *] assigned by the older writers may be found erroneously placed. The following are probably from the West coast of North America, with the synonymy as understood by Dr. Gray:—

Page. No.
220 8. *Murex foliatus*, Gmel. 3329. = *M. purpura alata*, Chemn. x. pl. 160. f. 1538–9; Wood's Cat. f. 13. *Purpura foliata*, Mart. U. C. ii. 66.—*Hab*. N. Zealand, *Humphreys*. King George's Sound, *Martyn*. ["= *M. tripterus*, Kien.: non *M. tripterus*, Born et auct. = *trialatus*, Kien." teste Hanl.]

229 9. *Murex lyratus*, G nel. 3531. = *M. glomus cereus*, Chem. x. pl. 160. f. 1634.—*Buccinum lyratum*, Martyn, U. C. ii. f. 43.—*Hab*. N. Zealand, King George's Bay, *Martyn*.

233 43. *Purpura lamellosa*, = *Buccinum l.*, Gmel., Wood's Cat. f. 60. = *Buc. plicatum*, Martyn, U. C. ii. f. 41. = *Buc. compositum*, Chemn. x. 179, vign. 21. f. A, B. = *Buc. crispatum*, Chemn. xi. 84, pl. 187. f. 1802–3. *Murex cr.*, Lam. 174.—*Hab*. N. Zealand, King George's Sound, *Chemn.*, *Martyn*. Coast of Columbia.

237 *71. *Ziziphinus canaliculatus*. Trochus c., Martyn, U. C. pl. 32, = *Tr. doliarius*, Chemn. x. f. 1579–80; Wood's Cat. f. 96.—*Hab*. N. Zealand, *Martyn*. California, *Capt. Belcher, R.N.*

*72. *Ziziphinus annulatus*. Trochus a., Martyn, U. C. pl. 33. = *T. virgineus*, Chemn. x. f. 1581–2; Wood's Cat. f. 98. = *Tr. coelatus*, β., Gmel.—*Hab*. N. Zealand, *Martyn*. California, *Capt. Belcher*.

243 113. *Bulla Quoyii*, Gray, n. s. = *B. striata*, Q. & G., Voy. Astr. ii. 354, pl. 26. f. 8, 9, non Lam.—*Hab*. N. Zealand, *Quoy*, *Stanger*.

But the first authentic information on the molluscs of the North-western coast is given in the 'Voyage Round the World, but more particularly to the N.W. Coast of America,' by Capt. George Dixon, London, 1789: to which is added a Natural History Appendix.

Page 355, fig. 2. *Solen patulus**. Cook's River. [= *Machæra Nuttalli*, Conr.]

In the 'Conchology, or Natural History of Shells,' by George Perry, London, 1811, a work of no little pretension, yet singularly inaccurate, are figured the following species, but without authorities for the assigned localities:—

* As this extract is probably the first description on record of molluscs from the Pacific shores of N. America, by the original collector, and as the book is rarely to be met with, it may be interesting to quote the passage:—

"At the mouth of Cook's River [lat. 59°–61°] are many species of shell-fish, most of them, I presume, nondescript; and of all which I should have endeavoured to have got specimens, had business permitted. Among the bivalves we noticed some of a large species, of the *Cardium* or cockle-genus [*Cardium corbis*, Mart.], half-a-dozen of which would have afforded a good supper for one person; but, for a repast of that kind, our men preferred a large species of the *Solen* genus, which they got in quantity, and were easily discovered by their spouting up the water as the men walked over the sands where they inhabited: as I suppose it to be a new kind, I have given a figure of it in the annexed plate [*Solen patulus*; accurate external and internal views, size of life]. 'Tis a thin brittle shell, smooth within and without: one valve is furnished with two front and two lateral teeth [the 'laterals' are the nymphæ for the ligament]; the other has one front and one side tooth, which slip in between the others in the opposite valve: from the teeth, in each valve, proceeds a strong rib, which extends to above halfway across the shell, and gradually loses itself towards the edge, which is smooth and sharp. The colour of the outside is white, circularly, but faintly, zoned with violet, and is covered with a smooth yellowish-brown epidermis, which appears darkest where the zones are: the inside is white, slightly zoned, and tinted with violet and pink. The animal, as in all species of this genus, protrudes beyond the ends of the shell very much, and is exceeding good food.—A fine specimen of this kind is in the Collection of John Swainson, Esq., of the Custom House, London.—We saw also, on this coast, a kind of muscle, in colour and shape much like the common eatable muscle of Europe, but differed in being circularly wrinkled, and a great deal larger [*Mytilus Californianus*, Conr.]. One valve I saw at Queen Charlotte's Islands measured above nine inches and a half in length.—With pieces of these muscles, sharpened to an exquisite edge and point, the Indians head their harpoons and other instruments for fishing. They fasten them on with a kind of resinous substance."—*Dixon's 'Voyage.'*

Pl. Fig.
9 4. *Polyplex gracilis* [= *Trophon multicostatus*, Esch.]. N. Zealand.
29 5. *Melania striata.* New California. [All the figures of ' *Melania* ' on this plate
        represent large *Bulimi*, perhaps from S. America.]
35 4. *Cerithium reticulatum.* New California.
44 2. *Haustrum pictum* [= *Purpura planospira*]. East Indies.
44 3. *Haustrum dentex* [= *P. columellaris*]. Nootka Sound : only 2 sp. known.
44 4. *Haustrum tuberculatum* [= *P. patula*, jun.]. ?—
41 3. *Oliva Leveriana* [= *O. porphyria*]. ?—
47 2. *Trochus decarinatus* [= *Calliostoma canaliculatum*]. N. Zealand.
58 2. *Venus radiata* [= *Callista lupinaria*]. N. Zealand.

The common Californian *Haliotis* was, it seems, first described in the
' Zoological Miscellany,' by Dr. W. E. Leach, vol. i. 1814 *.
Page 131, pl. 58. *Haliotis-Cracherodii*, Leach. California.

Solander made use of the materials he had collected in Cook's Voyage, in
compiling a work on Conchology of considerable merit. Dillwyn made a copy
of it, and used it in preparing his own, allowing priority to its specific names ;
but it was never published. The types were lately parted-with by the Linnean Society, who had determined not to keep any collections except those of
Linnæus. The ' Descriptive Catalogue of Recent Shells,' &c., by L. W. Dillwyn : London, 1817, is considered by Dr. Gray to be the best conchological
work arranged according to the old system. The following are quoted from
the West Coast :—

Vol. Page.
i. 301. *Mytilus frons*, Linn. = *Ostrea frons*, Sol. Callone. Acapulco, *Humphreys*;
        West Indies, *auct.*
i. 469. *Cyprœa pustulata*, Sol. Acapulco.
ii. 617. *Buccinum plumbeum*, Chemn. California. [*Monoceros*, ?S. America.]

Following Dillwyn, and nearly eclipsing his fame through the originality
and excellence of his classification, appeared Lamarck's ' Animaux sans Ver-
tèbres,' 1818–1822. Coordinate with or preceding this work are his Articles
in the ' Annales du Muséum ' and the ' Encyclopédie.' The fresh sources of
his information are quoted in the first Report, p. 169.

In Delessert's ' Recueil,' 1841, are figured

Pl. 2, fig. 1. *Solen ambiguus*, Lam. [= *S. rudis*, C. B. Ad.] "Les mers d'Amérique."
Pl. 10, fig. 2. *Cytherea semilamellosa*, Gaudichaud [= *C. lupinaria*]. China Seas.

In Deshayes' invaluable edition of the ' An. s. Vert.,' Paris, 1835–45, are
quoted a variety of West Coast species which have already appeared under
their original authorities. The following may be added :—

Vol. Page.
viii. 252. *Bulimus Mexicanus*, Lam. = *Helix vittata*, Fér. Mexico.
ix. 33. *Haliotis Californiensis*, Swains. = *H. glabra*, Desh. California.
ix. 357. *Pleurotoma tuberculifera*, Br. & Sby. California.
ix. 584. *Murex radix*, Gmel. = *M. melanomathos* (pars), Dillw. Acapulco.
ix. 605. *Murex foliatus*, Gmel. = *M. tripterus*, Kien. N.W. America. " ? India."

The last of the early writers whose works should here be quoted, and whose
ideas on the relations of genera were considerably in advance of the age, though
somewhat fanciful, is Swainson, in his ' Zoological Illustrations,' 1820–1833 ;
' Appendix to the Sale Catalogue of Mrs. Bligh's Shells,' 1822 ; and ' Exotic
Conchology,' 1821–1835, reissued by Hanley, 1841. These works contain
the following West Coast species :—

* This work has been translated into French, and republished, by Chenu ; where the
same species is found on page 8, pl. 3. f. 2.

Bligh Cat. Page.

2. *Haliotis rufescens*, Swains. (Ditto in Exot. Conch. ed. ii. p. 34.) Galapagos [?] and California.
4. *Cassis* [*Malea*] *ringens*, Swains. ?—
5. *Cassis corrugata*, Swains. Native of the Galapagos.
5. *Harpa crenata*, Swains. ?—
8. *Strombus granulatus*, Swains. ?—

Exot. Conch. Plate.

86. *Conus princeps*, Ln. = *C. regius*, Martini, Lam. (C. P. var. β., Ln. = *C. ebræus*.) Asiatic Ocean.
97 (middle figure). *Marginella prunum*, Gmel., Martini = *Voluta plumbea*, Sol. MS. Africa. [The pinched W. Indian form.]
182. *Cypræa spadicea*, Swains., Tilloch's Phil. Mag. vol. lxi. p. 376. South Seas (*Mawe*).
80. *Haliotis Californiensis*, Swains. [Figured with 9 small holes.] 1821.
55. *Solen ambiguus*, Lam. N. America, 1820. [This shell is conspecific with the "*S. medius*, Alashka," of the B. M. Coll.; differing somewhat from the *S. ambiguus* as figured by Delessert. The B. M. locality is perhaps erroneous.]

24. *Valenciennes' Memoir on Humb. and Bonpl.*, 1833.—The following notes are from a study of the complete copy in the Libr. Roy. Coll. Surgeons.

Page.

221. *Donax radiata* [= var. of *D. punctatostriatus*, Hanl. 1843].
219. *Venus succincta* [= *Chione Californiensis*, Brod. 1835].
245. *Bulinus undatus*. [The Caribbean, not the Mexican, type is here figured.]
267. *Haliotis Californiana* [= *H. rufescens*, Swains., not *H. Californiensis*, Swains.].
267. (Add) *Haliotis interrupta*, Val. Tropical America. [The description accords with the young of *H. Cracherodii*, Leach.]
277. *Cerithium musica*. [Description accords with *C. maculosum*, Kien.]
278. *Cerithium granosum* [= *Cerithidea varicosa*].
279. *Cerithium fragaria* [= *Rhinoclavis gemmata*, Hds.].
282. *Cerithium varicosum* [= *Cerithidea varicosa*, Sby.].
308. *Strombus cancellatus*. Closely resembles *Rostellaria fissurella*, from Grignon. [Probably E. Indian.]
338. *Conus scalaris* [= *C. gradatus* (Mawe), Wood's Suppl.].
270. *Solarium bicanaliculatum*. Small species, like *S. Herberti*, Desh. Enc.
265. *Natica Bonplandi*. [The figure exactly represents *Neverita patula*, Sby.]
240. (Add) *Natica uber*, Val. Cumana.
317. *Purpura semi-imbricata*, Lam. [An. s. Vert. vol. x. p. 84, no. 39; not since identified from the brief description. Perhaps = *Cuma costata*, B'ainv.]
287. *Fusus turris* [= *F. Dupetithouarsii*, Kien.].
290. *Fusus Magellanicus* " = *Buc. Geversianum*, Pallas, = *Murex Peruvianus*, Enc. Méth."
295. *Ficula ficoides* [? = *decussata*].
296. *Pyrula spirata* [? = *Rapa*, jun.].

25. *Coquille.*—All the limpets quoted are South American.
26. *Eschscholtz.*—The following observations may be useful to the student:

Page.

10. *Murex ferrugineus* [= *Purp. crispata*, Chemn., var.; varices few, scarcely frilled].
11. *Murex lactuca* [= *Purpura crispata*, Chemn.].
11. *Murex multicostatus* [is not *Trophon clathratus*, as supposed by Midd.; but probably = *T. Gunneri*. It resembles *T. laciniatum*, Mart. (Falkland Is.) on a small scale; varices coronated, without spiral sculpture].
16. *Acmæa*. [Genus described in the Appendix to Kotzebue's Second Voyage, 1830 p. 350; somewhat before *Tectura*, teste Woodward.]
18. *Acmæa mamillata*. [The 'crowded tubercles' were perhaps due to nullipore.]
19. *Acmæa cassis* [if a northern shell, is perhaps the strongly ribbed var. of *pelta*; but the figure accords best with the Cape Horn species, *P. ænea*, Mart.].
20. *Acmæa digitalis* [is perhaps distinct from the variable *persona*; but passes into it by easy transitions].

7

Page.

21. *Fissurella aspera* [= *Glyphis Lincolni*, Gray, = *cratitia*, Gld. But *Gl. densiclathrata*, Rve, is probably distinct; Sta Barbara, *Jewett*, *Cooper*].

27. *Tankerville Cat.*, 1825.—The following species are also from the West Coast. The prices are added from the British Museum copy, as a record of their former rarity :—

No.	App. page.	Price.	
70		10s.	*Solen ambiguus.*
161		15s.	*Tellina operculata.*
162		5s.	*Tellina punicea.*
206		£10 10s.	*Lucina Childreni* [described by Gray in Ann. Phil.1824; v. also Zool. Journ. vol. i. 1825, pp. 221-2. There is no authority for the statement that it came from Brazil. The Br. Mus. specimens are from "Mus. Cracherode," and are probably West Coast. The only known locality is Cape St. Lucas.]
1203		30s.	*T ochus annulatus.*
1204		20s.	*Trochus doliarius.*
1690		10s.	*Murex crispatus.*
1842		15s.	*Purpura patula.*
1855		20s.	*Purpura planospira.*
1896		45s.	*Harpa crenata.*
2240		15s.	*Cyprœa spadicea.*
2251		2s.	*Cyprœa albuginosa.*
2330	xxxii	15s.	*O iva splendidula.* *Hab.?—*
2332	xxxiii	2s. 6d.	*Oliva biplicata.* West Coast North America.
2333	xxxiv	2s.	*Oliva columellaris.* ?—
2347		£5 5s.	*Conus regius.*

The „ in Rep., p. 174, should have been omitted, except at no. 808, p. vi. No. 1401 is described, on p. xii, as from Newfoundland. No. 1786 should have no page-reference.

In the 'Zoological Journal,' London, 1824–1829, appear descriptions of the following species :—

Pag.

Vol. i. March 1824, 60. *Natica patula*, Sby. "Brought from S. America by M. de Humboldt. 2 specimens only known."*

„   Oct. 1824, 309. *Cyprœa subrostrata*, Gray. Nehoue (Mus. Sby.). ['Probably fossil' (*Gray*): a white, smooth species, not to be confounded with *Trivia subrostrata.*]

„   Jan. 1825, 510. *Cyprœa albuginosa*, Mawe, pl. 7. f. 2; pl. 12. f. 2. California. Named, without description, in Mawe's Cat. (= *C. poraria*, var., Ducl.: Z. J. iv. p. 68.)

        513. *Cyprœa pustulata*, Sol. S. Coast of Mexico. China.

Vol. iii. Jan. 1827, 70. *Hinnites giganteus* (Sby.). ?— [= *H. Poulsoni*, Conr. Calif.] = *Hinnita gigantea*, Gray, Ann. Phil. Aug. 1826. = *Lima gigantea*, Id. in loc. cit. [non J. Sby.]

„   Sept. 1827, 363. *Cyprœa subrostrata*, Gray [bis, Trivia]. ?—

        364. *Cyprœa radians*, Lam. = *C. oniscus*, Dillw. = *C. pediculus*, β., Gmel. + *C. costata*, Dillw. W. Coast of Mexico, ? Adriatic.

        365. *Cyprœa Californiana*, Gray [Trivia]. California.

Vol. iv. Jan. 1828, 145–162. Monograph of *Ovulum*, by G. B. Sowerby, containing the species afterwards figured in the Spec. Conch.

28. *Beechey's Voyage.*—Increased study has supplied the following corrections :—

* At p. 511, note *, Dr. Gray states that the *Natica patula*, Barnes, Ann. Lyc. Nat. Hist. N. Y., Sept. 1824, i. 133, is "the shell described under that name by Sby. As there is another *N. patula* [? ubi], must be called by Mr. Barnes's MS. name of *N. helicoides*.' Also that *Dolium dentatum*, Barnes, loc. cit. = *D. ringens*, Sby.

8

Z. J. 372. *Naticea pallida* [= *Lunatia caurina*, Gld., + *soluta*, Gld.].
    372. *Natica otis*. [Var. = *Poliaices fusca*, Cpr.]
    372. *Natica clausa* [= *N. Beverlii*, Leach, MS. in B. M.].
    378. *Fusus lapillus* = *Buc. subrostratum*, Gray. [Resembles the smooth, stumpy form of *Purpura plicata*, Mart.: " perfectly distinct," teste Hanl.]
    379. *Conus arcuatus* [as figured in Z. B. V., is a very different shell from that in Mus. Cum. and the monographs; the latter is allied to *C. tornatus*].
    379. *Conus interruptus* [resembles the broad form of *C. mahogani*].
Z. B. V. 130. (Add) *Oliva semistriata*, Gray, pl. 36. f. 10. *Hab.* ? — [Panama, &c.]
    119. *Conus Ximenes* [scarcely differs from *C. mahogani*, var. in Mus. Cum.].
    132. [Should be] *Agaronia* [et passim].
    147. (Add) *Mouretia Peruviana*, Sby. (P. Z. S. 1835, p. 6) pl. 39. f. 6, 6'. [Also Margarita Bay, teste *Pease*.]
    148. *Patella Mazatlandica*. [This is the Sandwich Islands species, = *P. exarata*, Nutt., teste Hanl. The large specimens quoted are probably *P. talcosa*, Gld.]
    150. *Chama echinata*. [Further series of specimens make it doubtful whether this be not a distinct species from *C. frondosa*, var. The original sculpture has not yet been detected.]
    151. [Should be] *Cytherea biradiata*.
    152. (Add) *Cardita borealis*, Conr. (= "*Arcturus rudis*, Humphr.") pl. 44. f. 1. [Probably from near Icy Cape. Mus. Belcher.]

The types of the species described from this important voyage have been scattered. Some have been identified from Admiral Sir E. Belcher's Collection, which he kindly allowed me to examine for that purpose ; others are in the possession of Mr. Hanley ; but many appear hopelessly lost.

29. *Wood's Ind. Test.*—In Hanley's Revised Edition of this important work (London, 1856), several new localities are added from the writer's varied experience, and the synonymy is most carefully elaborated. No other book contains such a mass of trustworthy information on the old species in so small a compass. The following are quoted, either as original authorities, or for locality or synonymy :—

Page. Fig.
  2   10. *Chiton tunicatus*, Wood, Gen. Conch. 1815, pl. 2. f. 1 [= *Katherina Douglasiæ*, Gray]. Sitka.
  3   18. *Chiton lineatus*, Wood, Gen. Conch. 1815, pl. 2. f. 4, 5. Sitcha, North Calif. [Mr. Hanley believes that Sitka is the island in lat. 58°, and that Sitcha is in the district now known as Washington Territory, olim Oregon.]
  3   20. *Chiton sulcatus*, Wood, Gen. Conch. 1815, pl. 3. f. 1. Galapagos.
  19   16. *Solen maximus*, Wood, Gen. Conch. 1815, pl. 31. f. 3 [= *S. patulus*, Dixon. N.W. America]. Sandw. Is.
  21   8. *Tellina rugosa*, Born. Is. of Opara, New California. [Pacific Is.]
  27   73. *Tellina muricata*, Chemn. = *Lucina scabra*, Rve. Mexico.
  82   97. *Conus pusillus*, Wood : non Chemn. nec Lam. [nec Gld.] = *C. puncticulatus*, var., Lam. (quasi Brug.) Mexico.
  88   31. *Cypræa onyx*, Gray (quasi Lin.) = *C. adusta*, Chemn. [Pacific Is. The San Diegan shell is closely allied, = *Luponia spadicea*.] ' Calif.'
  99   35. *Voluta incrassata*, Dillw.; posterior to *O. angulata*, Lam. Centr. Am.
  183   14. *Haliotis Cracherodii*, Leach = *H. glabra*, Schub. 1829, non Chemn. et auct. Calif.
Suppl. 201   3. *Tellina lutea*, Gray = *T. alternidentata*, Br. & Sby. = *T. Guilfordiæ* Gray, in Griff. Cuv. pl. 19. f. 2. Icy Cape.
  202   1. *Donax scalpellum*, Gray, Ann. Phil. 1825, ix. 166; = *D. elongata* Mawe, Conch. pl. 9. f. 6, 1823. Calif.

9

Suppl. 202　2. *Donax stultorum*, Mawe, l. c. pl. 9. f. 7; = *Trigona st.*, Gray, Analyst, 1838. ? S. America [= *Tr. crassatelloides*, jun. Calif.].

204　5. *Chama crassicostata* = *Venericardia c.*, Sby., Tank. Cat. p. 4. = *Cardita Cuvieri*, Brod., P. Z. S. 1832. = *C. Michelini*, Val. Acapulco.

205　11. *Arca pectiniformis*, Gray (*Pectunculus*), non Lam. = *P. inæqualis*, Sby.

208　6. *Conus gradatus*, Mawe. Calif. [= *C. scalaris*, Val.] Pan.

211　25. *Voluta lens*, Mawe. Pan.

211　26. *Voluta harpa*, Mawe, Conch. Front. f. 2. 1823; = *V. nucleus*, Lam. S. Pacific.

211　33. *Voluta nux*, B. M. = *Oliva biplicata*, Sby., Tank. Cat. Calif.

212　38. *Voluta tenebrosa*, Mawe = *O. undatella*, Ducl. (Lam.) Pan.

212　4. *Buccinum tenue*, Mawe = *Cassis Massenæ*, Kien. Galapagos.

212　7. *Buccinum distortum*, Swains., Bligh's Cat. = *Columbella triumphalis*, Ducl. [*Clavella*]. W. Columbia.

213　10. *Buccinum brevidentatum*, Mawe = *Purp. cornigera*, Blainv. = *P. ocellata*, Kien. W. Columbia.

213　11. *Buccinum denticulatum*, Mawe ⎱ = *Monoceros lugubre*, Sby. Gen.
213　12. *Buccinum armatum*, Mawe　⎰　　　　Calif.

213　13. *Buccinum tectum*, Mawe = *Purp. callosa*, Sby. Gen., non Lam. = *P. angulifera*, Kien. (Ducl.) = *Cuma sulcata*, Swains. Mal. Pan.

213　15. *Buccinum planaxis*, Mawe = *Pl. planicosta*, Sby. = *P. canaliculata*, Duval, Rev. Zool. 1840, p. 107. Pan. [*Purp. canaliculata*, Ducl., is quite distinct.]

214　25. *Buccinum elongatum*, Mawe = *Terebra strigata*, Sby., Tank. Cat. = *T. zebra*, Kien. Pan.

215　15. *Strombus bituberculatus*, B. M., non auct. = *Str. Peruvianus*, Swains., Phil. Mag. 62. W. Columb.

216　3. *Murex rigidus*, B. M. = *Buc. nodatum*, Martyn = *Murex n.*, Gmel., Dillw. = *Turbinella rigida*, Gray. Pan. [Probably the Pacific sp.]

217　10. *Murex sanguineus*, Mawe = *Turbinella varicosa*, Rve. Galapagos.

217　14. *Murex salmo*, Mawe = *Fasciolaria granosa*, Kien., as of Brod., P. Z. S. 1832. Panama.

218　1. *Trochus undosus*, Wood = *T. undatus*, Mawe, Conch. no. 146 (not described); = *T. balænarum*, Val. Calif.

219　4. *Trochus pellis-serpentis*, Mawe = *Tegula elegans*, Less., Ill. Zool. pl. 50; = *Tr. strigilatus*, Phil. (quasi Anton) Abbild. pl. 2. f. 9. Pan.

225　45. *Turbo saxosus*, Mawe = *Marmorostoma undulata*, Swains., Zool. Ill. s. 2. Pan.

233　6. *Haliotis corrugata*, Mawe, Conch. no. 181. ? = *H. nodosa*, Phil. Abbil. pl. 2. Calif.

233　3. *Patella peziza*, Gray = *Dispotæa Byronensis*, Gray, Enc. Metr. Moll. pl. 4. f. 4 = [? *Crucibulum spinosum*, var.]. Chili.

31. *Voy. Beagle.*—The *Triton scaber* is rightly assigned to S. America: there is no satisfactory evidence for its appearance on the N.W. coast. The shells so quoted are probably either imported from the Magellan district, or are *Priene Oregonensis*, jun., or *Ocinebra*, var. *aspera*.

36. *Duclos.*—The original article is in the 'Annales Nat. Sc.,' May 1832, and contains the following species :—

104　1　1. *Purpura canaliculata*, Ducl., resembles *P. succincta* on a small scale. Cal.; very rare. [Figured with 10 principal and a few intercalary ribs. = *P. decemcostata*, Midd.]

105　1　2. *Purpura melones*, Ducl. ?—[Panama.]

109　2　8. *Purpura centiquadra*, Val. MS. [Ducl. states that Val. altered his own name to *speciosa* while the sheet was passing through the press. The latter, however, bears date 1833.]

111　2　10. *Purpura sphæridia*, Ducl. Cal. [A well-known *Sistrum* from the Pacific Is.]

10

The species quoted in the text from Guérin, which appear in the Mag. Zool. for 1844, also appear here with the early date. *Oliva polpaster*, a southern form, from Guayaquil, &c., is distinct from all varieties of the Gulf species, *O. Cumingii*; it bears date 1839. In the same vol. are described and figured—

Plate.

2. *Calyptræa (Calypeopsis) rugosa*, Less.   Payta, Peru.   [= *Cruc. imbricatum*, without pits.]

23. *Conus hieroglyphus*, Ducl.   Probably Cal.   [A Pacific form, like *C. abbreviatus.*]

27. *Cypræa eglantina*, Ducl.   Cal.   [A starved var. of *Aricia arabica*, Pacific Is.]

38. *Lady Douglas* (afterwards known as Lady Wigram).—*Placunanomia cepio.* [The type is an old shell, with faint ribs.]

Placunanomia alope. [The type is a young shell, with small scars and faint ribs.   The large series of specimens examined in the Smithsonian collections proves that these forms are among the many varieties of *P. macroschisma.*   The Indians have a superstitious dread of handling it.   Many more species have since been detected in the Brit. Mus., from the late Lady Wigram's valuable donations, including *Macoma inquinata*, Desh., described from her specimens ; but, as they are evidently from mixed localities, it has not been thought necessary to catalogue them.]

39. *Nuttall.*—The verification of Conrad's species being of considerable importance, I made diligent search for the original types during a recent tour in the United States.   The supposed collection at Harvard University, Cambridge, Mass., has not been discovered by Professor Agassiz.   The inquiries which Professor Longfellow kindly made at my request resulted in information that it was "in Dr. Wyman's Mus. Nat. Hist., in the granite building on Howard Street ;" but no opportunity has been afforded of collating it, or even of verifying its existence.   Dr. Jay rendered me every assistance in studying the types which he has catalogued in his collection, now rearranging in his residence at Memironeck, near New York, and gave such duplicates as could be spared for the Smithsonian Museum.   Several species, however, were not to be found, and some were clearly erroneous, as e. g. *Chama* "*exogyra*, Conr.," which proved to be *C. lobata*, Brod. ; W. I., teste Cuming ; China, Brit. Mus.   The most satisfactory information was derived from an interview with Mr. Conrad himself at the Acad. Nat. Sci., Philadelphia, where the honorary curator, Mr. W. G. Binney, afforded us all possible aid in eliminating types from the collections of the Academy and of private conchologists in the city.   Mr. Nuttall's death (the news of which was received soon after) prevented his revising the corrections thus obtained. As he had previously presented a duplicate series of his shells to the Brit. Mus., which had been incorporated with the general collection, and had signified to me his intention to leave the unique specimens to the nation, I at once communicated with the survivors and with Dr. Gray, who was fortunate enough to stop the intended sale, and to secure the shells, which were kindly presented by the executors.   They are now mounted, and kept in drawers adjoining the Reigen collection, the Vancouver collection, and the Stimpsonian typical collection of East Coast N. American shells.   The following is a *résumé* of corrections obtained from these different sources, numbered to correspond with the list, Rep. pp. 194–201 :—

2. "*Parapholas*" *penita* [is a *Pholadidea*].
3. *Platyodon cancellatus* [= *Cryptodonta myoides*, Nutt. MS.].
4. *Cryptodon Nuttallii*, Conr.   [The author, finding the generic name preoccupied changed it to *Schizothærus N.*: 1852, teste Bin. Bibl. ; 1854, Journ. A. N. S Phil. p. 199. = *Lutraria capax*, Gld. = *L. maxima*, Midd., = *Tresus maximus*,

Gray. Mr. Nuttall only brought home young specimens of this extraordinary shell. In its adult state it assumes either a transverse form (=*capax*) or the elongated condition, redescribed in a fossil state as new. Between these there is every gradation, as can be traced in the magnificent series in the Smiths. Mus. ; and a caskful of the animals in spirits, of various ages, has affiliated the large shells to the original Nuttallian specimens.]

10. *Pandora punctata* [is a *Clidiophora*. The series so named in the Nuttallian collection belongs, however, to the Atlantic *Cl. trilineata*].

11. *Solecurtus lucidus* [is almost certainly the young of no. 12. The amount of obliquity in the internal rib is extremely variable in the adult specimens].

12. *Solecurtus Nuttallii* [=*Machæra patula*, Dixon, =*Aulus grandis*, Gmel., teste Hds. in Mus. Cum. Mr. C.'s "*grandis*, var.," from Monterey, suits in its proportions for the adult of *S. lucidus*. The shell has been widely distributed by commerce, and appears to extend far in a northerly direction. The animal is very beautifully fringed].

14. *Solecurtus Californianus* [=*S. Dombeyi*, teste Mus. Cuming : non Hanl. MS.].

15. *Psammobia Pacifica* [is a *Heterodonax*, probably identical with the W. Indian *H. bimaculata*, which is found abundantly in its many varieties at Acapulco ;=*Tellina vicina*, C. B. Ad.].

17. *Sanguinolaria Californiana* [=*Macoma inconspicua*, Brod. & Sby., and is a northern species].

18. *Sanguinolaria rubroradiata* [is the young of a large species of *Psammobia*].

22. *Tellina alta* [=(from types) ?*Scrobicularia biangulata*, Cpr.].

23. [=*Macoma edulis*, Nutt.; a northern variety of *M. secta*, no. 25, and quite distinct from *M. edentula*.]

26. The locality is not confirmed, and is probably erroneous.

27. [Dr. Gould considers his *D. obesus* a distinct species; from a large series, it appears identical.]

28, 29. [These species of *Standella*, described from young specimens, were found of very large size by Dr. Cooper, with what may prove a third species, perhaps *S. nasuta*, Gld., olim.]

30b. *Petricola carditoides* [with *P. arcuata+cylindracea*, Desh., are varieties of *P. Californica*. The series preserved in the Smithsonian Museum connects all the extreme forms].

32. *Mysia tumida*, Conr. MS. [=*Diplodonta orbella*, Gld., and belongs to the section *Sphærella*, Conr. The label had been assigned by accident to a young valve of a *Chione*, probably from the Sandwich Is.].

33. *Tapes staminea*. [This is the extreme southern form of a widely diffused and very variable species, of which the normal condition is *Saxidomus Petitii*, Desh., =*Venus rigida*, Gld. pars. The principal varieties have been named *Tapes diversa*, Sby. =*Venus mundulus*, Rve., and *Venus ruderata*, Desh.]

34. [The Californian *Saxidomi* divide themselves into three groups : the large, southern, oval, grooved shells=*S. aratus*, Gld. ; the subquadrate, comparatively smooth, northern shells=*S. squalidus+giganteus*, Desh.; and an intermediate form, which is the true *S. Nuttallii*, Conr. Some of Mr. Nuttall's specimens were, however, the young of *S. aratus*, of which the adult was not known till very recently.]

35. [The young of this *Pachydesma* is "*Trigona stultorum*, Gray," Desh. MS. in British Museum.]

36. *Cytherea callosa* [=*C. nobilis*, Rve. It is not a *Dosinia*, but the type of a new subgenus, *Amiantis*, differing from *Callista* as *Mercenaria* does from *Venus*].

37. Plate 19, fig. 16 (not 14 nor 15). [The true *Venus Nuttallii* of Conr. (teste Conr. ips. and types in Mus. Phil. Ac. and Jav) is not the shell here catalogued, which generally goes by that name, but is a synonym for the *V. Californiensis*, Brod., =*succincta*, Val. The error was corrected in the Mus. Cum. in time for the right shell to be figured by Reeve in his recent monograph. It is doubtful what name Conrad intended for the shell here catalogued, which belongs to the group of *Stutchburyi, fluctifraga*, &c. If really distinct from the latter, it may stand as *Chione callosa*, Sby. jun. (non Conr.)]

38. *Venus Californiana* [(teste Conr. ips.) was intended for *V. Californiensis*, Brod. Not having access to the type, it could hardly be recognized by the

brief diagnosis. The name should therefore be dropped. The shell, pl. 19, fig. 15 (not 16)=*Chione simillima*, Sby., no. 39 ; a good Lower Californian species. It seems that the error was not in numbering of the figures, as Mr. Nuttall supposed, but in Conrad's identification of Broderip's species].

40. *Chione excavata* [is closely related to *Ch. succincta ;* the unique type, however, in Brit. Mus. displays characteristic differences of sculpture. It is singularly like the W. Indian *Ch. cancellata*, and may prove exotic].

41. *Cypricardia Californica* [= *C. Guiniaca*, Lam.,= *C. Duperryi*, Desh. Almost certainly from the Sandwich Is.].

45, 45b. *Cardium Californianum* [= *C. Nuttallii*, var. The species is named " *C. corbis*, Mart.," by Desh. MS. in Mus. Brit. and Cuming].

46. *Cardium quadragenarium* [= *C. luteolabrum*, Gld.].

51. *v. anteà*, no. 32.

56. *Modiola recta*. [Described from **very young** specimens. The broad form is *M. flabellata*, Gld.]

59. *Mytilus bifurcatus*. [The type is lost ; the figure and description would suit many species. It is allocated, in Mus. Cum., to the Californian *Septifer ;* but by Pease to a Sandwich Island *Mytilus*.]

60. [None of Conrad's species of *Isognomon* have been confirmed as from California. They are known to inhabit the Pacific Islands.]

62b. [Mr. Nuttall also brought an oyster, which he named in MS. *O. latecaudata*, = *O. lurida*, var. ; and *Hinnites giganteus*, Gray,= *H. Poulsoni*, Conr.]

64. [Dr. Gould states that *H. Nickliniana*, Lea,= *H. Californiensis*, Pfr., Chemn., Rve., but that *H. Californiensis*, Lea, is distinct.]

69. *Helix Townsendiana* [= *H. æruginosa*, Gld. MS.].

74. *Chiton Nuttallii* [is an *Ischnochiton*].

75. *Chiton acutus* [is an aberrant form of *Mopalia*. " *Chiton consimilis*," Nutt. MS. in Brit. Mus., appears to be *Mopalia Hindsii*, var. " *Chiton Californicus*" Nutt. MS.,="*Acanthopleura*" *scabra*, Rve.].

77. *Patella mamillata*, Nutt. [(non Esch.) is now **assigned in Mus. Cuming to** *Acmæa scabra*, Nutt., var. *limatula*].

83. *Fissurella ornata*, Nutt. [= *F. volcano*, Rve.].

84. *Glyphis densiclathrata*, Rve. [*V. anteà*, p. 522. The shell has been lost.]

86. *H. Californiensis*, Swains. [(not *Californiana*, Val., = *rufescens*), is an extreme var. of *H. Cracherodii*. The series in the Smithsonian Mus. have 5, 6, 7, 8, and 9 holes ; as soon as it has 10 and 11, it passes into *Californiensis*, which was figured in 1821 with 9 holes. When these are numerous, they are generally small in proportion].

91. *Calliostoma doliarium* [= *C. canaliculatum*, Mart. This and *C. annulatum*, Mart., are quite distinct from *C. filosum*, which= *C. costatum*, Mart.].

92. *Omphalius ater* [is the S. American species. The common Californian shell is]

94. *O. marginatus*, Nutt. MS. [=*funebralis*, A. Ad.].

97b. The collection contains one specimen of *Crepidula dorsata*.

103. [Is a *Serpulorbis*, without operc., teste Cooper.]

106. *Litorina tenebrata* [should be *patula*, Gld. (non Jeffr.). **Nuttall's MS. name** was published by Phil. in 1845].

107. *Natica ? maroccana*, var. *Californica*. [The varietal name **must be dropped.** The shell certainly came from the Sandwich Islands.]

† 108. [The shell is *Vitularia salebrosa*, jun., and not] *Ranella triquetra*.

109. *Mitra maura* [Swains., teste Rve. (? ubi)=*M. orientalis*, Gray, = *M.* " *Chilensis*," Kien.].

110. *Olivella glandinaria*, Nutt. [= *O. biplicata*, Sby.].

112, 113. *Purpura aperta* and *P. harpa* [are certainly from the Sandwich Islands].

114. *Purpura emarginata* [was described by Desh. from an immature specimen in which a half-formed knob caused an "emargination." The adult is one very extreme form ; *P. ostrina*, Gld., is another ; *P. fuscata*, Fbs., is a third. The normal condition is *P. lapillus*, Cooper (non Linn.),=*saxicola*, Val. Mr. Nuttall's collection also contains] *P. crispata*, var.

116. *Monoceros brevidens* [is an accidentally short-toothed form of *M. lapilloides*].

118. *Cerostoma Nuttallii* [with *C. foliatum* and *C. monoceros*, Sby., belongs to *Purpuridæ*].

13

The specimens numbered 2, 5, 8, 9, 19, 21, 28–31, 36, 44, 46, 49, 50, 52–54, 56, 59, 64–67, 70–72, 76, 84, 86–88, 98, 101, 103, 104, and 109 do not appear in the Brit. Mus. Nuttallian collection.

41. *Voy. Venus.*—Rev. Zool. and Guér. Mag.

Arca trapezia [= *A. tuberculosa*].
Saxicava legumen [= *S. pholadis*; ? from hole of *Lithophagus*].
Petricola arcuata [= the normal state of *P. carditoides*, Conr.].
Petricola cylindracea [= a short form of the same sp., developing ridges of growth, like *Tapes ruderata*, Desh.].
Venerupis gigantea [= *Saxidomus squalidus*, Desh.].
Cypricardia Duperreyi [= *C. Guinaica*, Lam., = *C. Californica*, Conr. A Sandwich Island species, twice quoted, but not confirmed, from Cal.].
Cardium Laperoussii [is an *Aphrodite*, like *Grœnlandicum*, but more transverse, and with lateral teeth less developed. This very rare and probably boreal shell has just been identified from Adm. Sir E. Belcher's coll.].
Cardium Californiense, Desh. [is not *C. Californianum* (= *Nuttallii*), Conr.; but = *C. pseudofossile*, Rve., 1844. The name of Desh. is unfortunate, as his shell is the Kamtschatkan form with strong ribs. The Californian form is smaller, with fainter ribs, = *C. blandum*, Gld.].
Purpura Freycinetii [is figured from a very extreme form of the Japanese species. *P. ostrina* passes into similar varieties].
Velutina Mülleri [probably = *V. lævigata*, which reaches Vancouver].
Lucina cristata [= *Tellidora lunulata*, Holmes; described from the Pleistocene of S. Carolina, and lately dredged alive by Dr. Stimpson; not *T. Burneti*].

The following may be added to Deshayes' list:—

Pl. 81. *Tellina ligamentina*, Desh., 1843. *Hab.* ?— [= *Macoma secta*, Conr.]
         Tellina Japonica, Desh., in Mus. Cum. [also appears to be *M. secta*, jun.].

In Valenciennes' plates to the Voy. Ven. have been recognized the following West Coast species and synonyms, in addition to those quoted in Rep. pp. 203–204:—

Plate. Fig.
3   2. *Trochus diadematus*, Val. [resembles *Pomaulax undosus*, jun., but the surface is faintly wrinkled all over; umbilical region not chiseled; and operc. not ridged. It is probably intended for *Pachypoma gibberosum*].
4   1. *Trochus rubiginosus*, Val. [probably = *T. annulatus*, Mart.].
     2. *Trochus pellucidus*, Val. [resembles *T. lima*, Panama].
6   3. *Buccinum Prevostii*, Val. [probably = *Pisania pagodus*].
8   1. *Purpura bufonides*, Val. [appears one of the many vars. of *P. biserialis*].
9   1. *Purpura rupestris*, Val. [probably = *Monoceros lugubre*, jun.].
10   1. *Murex aciculiger*, Val. [is represented with labral tooth and closed canal; but resembles *C. festivus*, Hds.].
     3. *Murex tortuus* (Brod.), Val. [resembles *Ph. princeps*, with a very poor operc., badly drawn].
16   1. *Venus Thouarsii*, Val. [? = *multicostata*, Sby.; figured with very broad, smooth, close ribs, scarcely indented, except in the middle].
     3. *Venus pectunculoides*, Val. [is probably *T. grata*, not *histrionica*].
17   2. *Cardium subelongatum* (Rve.), Val. [appears = *C. procerum*, jun.].
18   2. *Pecten comatus*, Val. (may be = *hastatus*, jun.; but, although figured without the red spot, it most resembles *Hin. giganteus*, jun.].
19   1. *Pecten excavatus*, Val. [= *Janira dentata*, Sby.].
     3.   „   *pomatia*, Val. [may be = *P. ventricosus*, jun.].
     4.   „   *rastellinum*, Val. [= *P. hastatus*, jun.].
21   *Ostrea gallus*, Val. ["Acapulco," with large plates, = *O. megodon*, Hanl.].
22   1. *Cardita arcella*, Val. [? = *Ven. radiata*, Sby.].
     2.   „   *modulosa* (Lam.), Val. [= *Lazaria affinis*].
     3.   „   *turgida* (Lam.), Val. [= *Ven. laticostata*].
     5.   „   *Michelini*, Val. [= *V. Cuvieri*].
23   2. *Nucula divaricata*, Val. [probably = *N. castrensis*].
24   1. *Penitella Conradi*, Val. [may be = *Pholadidea ovoidea*].

Plate. Fig.
2. *Penitella xilophaga*, Val. [may be the adult of fig. 4].
3. *Penitel a tubigera*, Val. [may possibly be intended for *Ph. penita*].
4. *Pholas rostrata*, Val. [is probably = *Netastoma Darwinii*, Sby. jun.].
5. *Ungulina luticola*,Val. [may be an extremely bad *Petricola robusta*].
6. *Corbula luticola*, Val. [is probably = *Sphænia fragilis*].
7. *Bornia luticola*, Val. [= *Kellia Laperoussii*].
8. *Saxicava clava*, Val. [= *S. legumen*, Desh., = *S. pholadis*, var.].

The identification of these species is attended with great uncertainty, as the types have not been seen, and the artist appears to have studied effect rather than accuracy.

42. *Voyage of Sulphur.*—The types of these species appear to have been scattered. Only a part are now to be found in the very valuable collection of Admiral Sir E. Belcher, in which most of the shells are, unfortunately, destitute both of names and of locality-marks.

Murex Belcheri [belongs to Purpuridæ, and may be considered the type of the genus *Chorus*].

Ranella Californica. [After comparing a series with the Cumingian specimens of *R. ventricosa*, it appears that the diagnostic characters are not constant.]

Marginella sapotilla. [The type in Mus. Cuming is much smaller than the ordinary condition of *M. prunum* = *cærulescens*, Lam., to which species the common Panama shells were referred by Mr. Cuming. In his collection, however, they stand thus:—Ordinary Panamic type "*sapotilla*, Hds.: 5–13 fms., sandy mud, Panama, *H.C.*" Another tablet of the true Panama shells "*Marginella*, n. sp., Panama,"—"San Domingo" having been crossed out. The small West Indian form, analogous to the typical *sapotilla*, is given as "*glans*, Mke." The large West Indian shells, with violet tinge behind the labrum, are "*cærulescens*, Lam., Panama," without authority. Another series of the W. Indian type is given as "*cærulescens*, var., Lam., 10 fms., sandy mud, Panama," without authority. Either habitat-errors have crept into the Cumingian labels, or else Mr. Redpath's observation will not hold, viz. that the Atlantic shells have a posterior pinch on the labrum, which is not seen in the Pacific. All the authentic series examined from the two coasts bear out his view. There will be two opinions as to whether this be more than a mere local distinction.]

Solarium quadriceps. [On comparing suites of *S. granulosum* from the Texan coast with series from the Gulf of California, it appeared that on each side of the Peninsula the shells went through similar changes in strength of sculpture, size of umbilicus, number of spiral granules, &c.; nor could any clue be obtained by which the coasts could be separated in a mixed collection. Hinds's shell stands at the furthest extreme of removal from *S. granulatum*.]

43. *U. S. Exploring Expedition.*—The shells of this collection were deposited in the Patent Office in Washington, D.C., where, notwithstanding the great care of Mr. Varden, the curator, they were not a little tampered-with. Dr. Gould laboured under great difficulties in his work of description; he had access only to that part of the collection which happened to be unpacked and exposed to view during the brief period that his professional engagements allowed of his visiting the capital; and his request to be allowed to take doubtful shells to Europe for identification was refused. The materials also were of an unsatisfactory kind, a large proportion of the specimens being much weathered, and many of the locality-marks being manifestly erroneous. If occasional errors have been detected in his great work, they may fairly be set down to causes over which the author had no control. Many of these

have been corrected by Dr. Gould himself, in his 'Otia Conchologica,' Boston, 1862, which contains the various papers in the 'Proceedings of the Boston Soc. of Nat. Hist.,' with an appendix. After the organization of the Smithsonian Institution, all the natural-history collections belonging to the Federal Government were transferred to its keeping, with liberty to exchange duplicates. The shells remained unopened, and the types not accessible, till, at the request of Professor Henry, I undertook the arrangement of the collections. Fortunately, a considerable part of the shells professing to be the figured types of the new species were found together, with the artist's marks corresponding with the plates and figures. The result of the examination, so far as the general collection is concerned, will shortly be prepared for the press; it is sufficient here to tabulate the observations on the N.W. American species, which were, as it happened, the most satisfactorily preserved in the whole series. The following additional particulars include the "Rectifications" in the 'Otia,' the paging of which is continued from the "Expedition Shells" quoted in Rep. p. 209. The quarto volume quoted in p. 210 is distinguished as "E. E. Mollusca." The folio atlas of plates bears date on title 1856, but was not published till 1861, teste Binn. Bibl. vol. i. p. 504. The comparisons of types were made in 1860, from a proof copy.

Otia, Page.

3. *Chiton lignosus* = [*Mopalia*] *Merckii*, Midd., test. Gld. E. E. Moll. [from worn specimens: = *Ch. Montereyensis*, Cpr., from perfect shells.]

230. *Chiton* (*Chœtopleura*) *vespertinus*. Perhaps = *Ch. lignosus*, var. [A *Mopalia*, differing slightly in the amount of posterior wave. The fig. in E. E. Moll. is made-up from broken specimens.]

6, 242. *Chiton* (*Onithochiton*) *dentiens*. [The shell sent as type of this species, and all the others seen from the coast, agree in belonging to *Ischnochiton*, and are not dentate, as would be presumed from the figures and diagnosis. As Dr. Gould's toothed *Onithochiton* may hereafter be found, the Smithsonian shells have been named *Isch. pseudodentiens*.]

6, 242. *Chiton* (*Chœtopleura*) *muscosus*. [= *Acanthopleura muscosa*, H. & A. Ad. Gen., = *Ch. ornatus*, Nutt. P. Z. S. 1855, p. 232, + *Mopalia consimilis*, Nutt. MS. in B. M. This beautiful species is a true *Mopalia*.]

230. *Chiton* (*Leptochiton*) *interstinctus*. Resembles *C. Sitchensis*, Midd. [= *Callochiton* i., H. & A. Ad., Gen. It is a true *Ischnochiton*. The genera of Chitonidæ cannot always be ascertained by external characters alone, as indicated in Messrs. Adams's genera. All the species in the Smithsonian Museum have been dissected.]

7, 242. *Patella* (*Tectura*) *fimbriata* = *P. cinis*, Rve. [= *Acmæa pelta*, Esch.].

9, 242. *Patella* (*Nacella*) *instabilis*. [Varies greatly in proportions.]

9, 242. *Lottia* (*Tectura*) *pintadina*. [The types represent the normal condition of *Acmæa patina*. One variety is *A. cribraria*, Gld. MS. The specimens of *A. messleuca* intermixed by Dr. G. in the Mexican War collections were, no doubt, affiliated by an oversight.]

10, 243. *Patella* (*Tectura*) *textilis* is a var. of *T. persona*, Esch. [A well-marked form of delicate growth, passing from *A. persona* into *A. pelta*, var.; from the young of which some specimens can hardly be distinguished, except by the fretted pattern.]

10, 243. *Patella* (*Tectura*) *scabra* = *spectrum* (Nutt.), Rve., not *scabra* (Nutt.), Rve. [The type-specimens belong to two species, f. 456, 456a, being *A. spectrum*, Nutt., while 456b represents the flattened variety of *A. persona*, Esch. (approaching the form *digitalis*, Esch.). As the diagnosis best accords with the latter shell, *P. scabra*, Gld., may stand as a synonym of *persona*, var.; the intermixed specimen, accidentally figured as belonging to the species, being removed to *spectrum*, Nutt. Thus the name *scabra*, not being needed as first described, will remain for Nuttall's species, described by Rve., but first named in print by Jay.]

16

Nis. Page.

15.   *Crepidula lingulata.* [Described from a worn specimen. Perfect shells cannot be separated from *C. bilobata*, Rve., = *C. ? dorsata*, var. *bilobata*, Maz. Cat., nor from the supposed *C. dorsata* in Mus. Cum.]

15. . *Crepidula nummaria.* [Described from an aberrant, worn, and rounded specimen. The normal state is *C. navicelloides*, Nutt. When grown in hollow bivalves, it becomes *nummaria*: the contrary extreme, grown in crypts of borers, with another shell or crab over it, is *explanata*, Gld., = *exuviata*, Nutt., =*perforans*, Val. The Lessonoid form is *C. fimbriata*, Rve. The young appears to be *C. minuta*, Midd. But the "*C. nummaria*, Gld.," of Mus. Cum., is quite a distinct species, not known from the American coast.]

50, 244. *Natica (Lunatia) caurina*+ ⎫
50, 244. *Natica (Lunatia) soluta*   ⎬ [= *L. pallida*, Br. & Sby.].

50, 244. *Natica (Lunatia) algida*: " R. Negro," E. E. Shells; "Oregon," E. E. Moll. [verè: = young of *L. Lewisii*, Gld., July 1847, = *L. herculœa*, Midd., 1849].

52.   *Lacuna carinata*, Gld., Nov. 1848 [*L. solidula*, Lov., 1846. Finmark].

52, 245. *Litorina patula*, Gld. [non Jeffr.], Mar. 1849, = *L. planaxis* [Nutt.], Phil., 1847.

52, 53. *Litorina lepida, scutulata,* et *plena* [are shown by large series to be varieties of one species].

99.   *Litorina cincta*, Gld., Aug. 1847, Puget Sd. [= *L. Sitchana*, Phil., 1845. This species appears to have been overlooked in the E. E. Moll.]

61.   *Cerithium irroratum*, Gld. [= *C. obesum*, Sby. sen., teste H. Cuming. The type proves this to be an E. I. species, and not the Panamic *C. stercus-muscarum*, Val., as supposed by Dr. Gld.: v. C. B. Ad. *in loco*].

62.   *Cerithium filosum*, Gld., May 1849 [= *Turritella Eschrichtii*, Midd., 1849, (*Bittium*). Comp. *C. filosum*, Phil., Z. f. M. 1848, p. 84. California].

64, 245. *Fusus (Bela) fidicula.*

64, 245. *Fusus (Trophon) Orpheus* [(non Baird.) = *T. Fabricii*, Moll., in Br. Mus.]

67, 245. *Buccinum (Nassa*, s. g. *Tritia) fossatum. Cœsia* in Ind. p. 253. [= *N. elegans*, Rve., 1842, non Dujardin : = *Zaphon e.*, Add.].

70, 245. *Nassa (Tritia) mendica* = *N. Woodwardi*, Fbs., 1850 [from types : + *N. Gibbesii*, Coop.].

71, 245. *Columbella (Alia) gausapata.* [Belongs to the Nassoid group, *Amycla*.]

75.   *Mya præcisa* [= *M. truncata.* Scarcely even a variety; but approaches the form *Aldrovandi*.]

76, 245. *Lutraria (Tresus) capax.* [Dr. G. revives his excellent name; *L. maxima*, Jonas, 1844, being anterior to Midd. Conrad's name, *Schizothærus Nuttallii*, is, however, very much earlier.]

77, 246. *Osteodesma (Lyonsia) bracteatum* [+ *O. nitidum*, Gld., in different states of preservation, = *L. Californica*, Conr. The "golden nacre" of *O. bracteatum* is due to incipient decay, as generally happens in Anomiads].

83, 246. *Cardita (Actinobolus) ventricosa.* [Appears to be a local variety of the ancient Miocene species, *Venericardia borealis*; + *C. occidentalis*, Conr., + *C. subtenta*, Conr. (fossil) probably.]

83.   *Cardium blandum*, 1850. [A finely grown ?var. of *C. Californiense*, Desh., 1839, Midd. (non *C. Californianum*, Conr., 1837, = *corbis*, var.) = *C. pseudofossile*, Rve., 1844. The name is so like the preoccupied *Californianum* that it may advantageously be dropped.]

85.   *Venus rigida*, 1850 [non Dillw. 1817. It is fortunate that the name is not needed, as the author has joined two very different species, both of which have other names. The original Latin diagnosis applies to the rough northern form of *Tapes staminea*, Conr., which is the *Saxidomus Petitii* of Desh., and includes *V. ruderata*, Desh. But the "specimen, 3¾ in. long," which modified the description in the E. E. Moll., and is figured at f. 538, proves to be the adult form of *Tapes tenerrima*, Cpr., P. Z. S. July 1856, which is a Californian and not a Panamic species, as had been supposed from Col. Jewett's label].

87, 246. *Anodonta cognata* = *A. Oregonensis*, Lea (probably).

87.   *Anodonta feminalis* [= *A. angulata*, var., teste Lea].

2   17

Otia, Page.

93.   *Mytilus (Modiola) flabellatus.* [The northern form of *Modiola recta*, Conr. The "specimens from the Gulf of California" must have been *M. Braziliensis*, intermixed by accident.]

94.   *Mytilus trossulus* [is scarcely a variety of *M. edulis*, which is very abundant along the coast, under its usual modifications of form and colour; but generally of small size].

95.   *Pecten hericeus*, Gld. [= *P. hastatus*, Sby. sen.].

97, 246.   *Terebratula (Waldheimia) pulvinata.*

97, 243.   *Terebratula (Terebratella) caurina.*

E. E. Moll.

Page.

113.   *Planorbis corpulentus* is of Say.

143.   *Melania plicifera* is of Lea.

436.   *Anodonta angulata* is of Lea.

206.   *Scalaria ?australis* [is abundantly confirmed from the Vancouver district. It should be called *Opalia borealis*, Gld.].

244.   *Purpura ostrina*, Gld., 'Otia,' p. 225 [is an aberrant smooth var. of *P. lapillus*, Coop., non Ln.; the normal state being *P. saxicola*, Val.].

The following species, described in the 'Otia' and 'E. E. Moll.' as from 'N. Zealand' and an unknown locality, are really from Puget Sound.

Otia, Page.

56, 245.   *Trochus pupillus*, Gld., March 1849: N. Zealand (*Ziziphinus* in Index): = *Margarita calostoma*, A. Ad., 1851. Comp. *T. modestus*, Midd. [which is, however, = *ligatus*, Gld., = *costatus*, Mart. This species is named in the B. M. Col. " *M. costellata*, Sby.," but is distinct, teste A. Ad. & Mus. Cum.].

64, 245.   *Fusus (Neptunæa) incisus*, Gld., May 1849. Hab.?— [= *Tritonium (Fusus) Sitchense*, Midd., 1849, = *Buccinum dirum*, Rve., 1846.]

B. A. Rep.

Page.

210.   *Venus calcarea* [is correctly described by Dr. G. as from N. Zealand; although quoted by him as the Oregon analogue of *V. mercenaria*].

211.   *Tellina Californica*, Conr. [= *Macoma inconspicua*].

211.   *Triton figrinum* [is from Central America, not] Puget Sd.

211.   *Pecten Fabricii*, Phil. [is the young of *Islandicus*: Dr. G 's shells are the young of *P.* (" *rubidus*, ?var.") *Hindsii*].

211.   *Fusus cancellinus.* [Dr. G.'s shells are *Ocinebra*, var. *aspera*.]

212.   *Purpura lagena*, Gld. [MS., is probably *saxicola*, var.].

213.   *Pecten Townsendi* [has not been identified].

213.   *Venus ampliata* [is believed by Dr. G. to have been first designated by him as a species, afterwards proved = *rigida* (*Petitii*), var.].

44. *Middendorff.*—The synonymy given in Rep. pp. 214–222 is that of the author, not of the writer of the Report, who is by no means prepared to accept the learned doctor's identification of species. The three Chitons quoted with doubt from Tilesius have not been confirmed, as from Kamtschatka, by any other writer. The *Ch. giganteus* has the aspect of the large *Ischnochiton Magdalenis*; the *Ch. muricatus* belongs to the *Lophyrus* group, which is not known so far north; and the *Ch. setosus* has also a S. American aspect. The treatise " De *Chitone Giganteo* Camtschatico additamentum ad Zoographiam Rosso-Asiaticum, auctore Tilesio," was read March 19, 1823, and published in 1824. It contains a very valuable and (for that period) remarkable account of the anatomy of Chitons, but it does not profess to name and describe species in the modern sense. The names, therefore, had better be dropped. Middendorff's new species were first described in the 'Bulletin de la Classe Physico-Mathématique de l'Académie Impériale des Sciences de St. Pétersbourg,' a work of which few complete copies are known in England, under the following dates.

April 20, 1847: vol. vi. No. 8 (total number 128).

Column.
116. *Chiton Stelleri*, n. s.,= *C. amiculatus*, Sby., Rve., non Pallas.
117. *Chiton Pallasii*, n. s.
117. *Chiton Brandtii*, n. s.
118. *Chiton Mertensii*, n. s. [*Ischnochiton*].
118. *Chiton Eschscholtzii*, n. s.
119. *Chiton Wosnessenskii*, n. s.   [A typical *Mopalia*: mantle indented behind.]
120. *Chiton Merckii*, n. s. [= *Ch. lignosus*, Gld., July 1846 : = *Mopalia Montereyensis*, Cpr.].
120. *Chiton liciдus*, n. s.
121. *Chiton scrobiculatus*, n. s., California.
121. *Chiton Sitchensis*, n. s.
        Nov. 1847 (read April 28): vol. vi. No. 20 (total number 140).
317. *Patella* (?*Acmæa*) *ancyloides*, n. s.   [Probably a delicately grown young *patina*: the diagnosis, however, suits *textilis*. Name afterwards altered to *personoides*, to distinguish from *Propilidium ancyloide*, Fbs.]
318. *Patella* (?*Acmæa*) *ærugnosa*, n. s.   [Probably=*textilis*, Gld., 1846; but the figure is more like *scabra*, Nutt.]
318. *Patella* (? *Acmæa*) *pileolus*, n. s.   [Probably the young of *A. pelta*; but assigned in Mus. Cum. to a very different shell,= *A. rosacea*, Cpr.]
318. *Patella* (?*Acmæa*) *Asmi*, n. s.   [A specimen of *A. pelta*, in Dr. Cooper's collection, began life as *A. Asmi*.]
319. *Patella* (?*Acmæu*) *cæca*; genuina, vertice erecto, Atlantic.
319. *Patella* (?*Acmæa*) *cæca*, var *concentrica*; vertice subinflexo; with crowded lamellæ of growth.
        1849; read Oct. 6, 1848   vol. vii. No. 160.   "Vorläufige Anzeige einiger neuer Konchylien aus den Geschlechtern : *Litorina*, &c., von Dr. A. Th. v. Middendorff."
241no. 1. *Litorina grandis*.   [The specimens in B. M. and Mus. Cum. appear to represent a large var. of *L. litorea*.]
242   2. *Litorina Kurila* (like *tenebrosa*).
242   3. *Litorina subtenebrosa*.   [Probably an extreme var. of *L. Sitchana*.]
243   4. *Tritonium* (*Fusus*) *antiquum*, Ln., var. *Behringiana*.
243   5. *Tritonium* (*Fusus*) *Behringii*.
243   6. *Tritonium* (*Fusus*) *Baerii*.
244   7. *Tritonium* (*Fusus*) *Sitchense* [probably = *Chr. dirus*, Rve., var. ; but stated to be " e livido viridescente; columella sæpius umbilicata"].
244   8. *Tritonium* (*Fusus*) *luridum* [= *Vitularia aspera*, Baird, smooth form].
244   9. *Tritonium* (*Buccinum*) *simplex*.
244   10. *Tritonium* (*Buccinum*) *Ochotense*.
245   11. *Tritonium* (*Buccinum*) *undatum*, Linn., var. *Schantarica*.
245   12. *Tritonium* (*Buccinum*) *ooides*.
245   13. *Bullia ampullacea* [is the genus *Volutharpa* of Fischer].
246   15. *Natica herculæa*, North California [= *L. Lewisii*, Gld., July 1847].
246   16. *Margarita arctica*, Leach, var. *major*.

In the text of the 4to volumes, the following corrections are suggested, the numbers referring to the page in the B. A. Report which contains the abstract.

Report, 215. *Acmæa scutum*, D'Orb. [is quite distinct from *A. persona*, Esch.   The latter, as figured by Midd., is a very young shell, not certainly belonging to the species].
        216. *Turritella Eschrichtii*.   [= *Bittium filosum*, Gld., May 1849.   There being no month-date to Midd.'s species, the excellent name of Gld., which may also be of Phil. 1848, should be retained.]
        216. *Trochus ater* and *mostus* [are well-marked South American species. Probably the shells intended are *Chlorostoma funebrale*, A. Ad., and its congeners.]
        216. *Trochus euryomphalus* [= *Phoreus pulligo*, Mart., teste Dohrn].
        216. *Trochus modestus*, Md. [=*filosus*,Wd.,= *Calliostoma costatum*, Martyn].
        216. *Trochus* (*Turbo*) *Fokkesii* [is from the peninsula of Lower Cal.].
        216. *Natica flava*, Gld. ["is entirely different from any of the synonyms under it," teste Gld.].

                        19

Report, 216. *Scalaria Ochotensis* [appears an aberrant *Opalia*; but is the genus *Acirsa* of Mörch, closely allied to *Mesalia*, teste A. Ad.].

216. *Crepidula Sitchana* [is figured like the young of *grandis*; but the specimens in Mus. Cum., when compared with the similar stage of *C. excavata*, display no differences either inside, outside, or in the nuclear whorls].

216. *Crepidula minuta* [appears the young of *C. navicelloides*, Nutt.]

216. *Crepidula grandis* [fossil at Sta. Barbara, = *C. princeps*, Conr. Can hardly be distinguished from very fine specimens of *C. fornicata*, sent from Halifax, Nova Scotia, by Mr. Willes].

217. *Trichotropis cancellata*, Hds. [is quite distinct from *T. borealis*].

217. *Purpura decemcostata*, Midd. [= *P. canaliculata*, Ducl. Var. = *P. attenuata*, Rve. Var. = *P. analoga*, Fbs.]

217. *Tritonium (Trophon) clathratum*, Ln. [is distinct from the shouldered *M. multicostatus*, Esch., = *Gunneri*, Lov.].

217. *Tritonium (Fusus) decemcostatum* [= *Chr. Middendorffii*, Cooper = *Chr. liratus*, Martyn.]

218. *Tritonium (Buccinum) cancellatum* [Midd., non] Lam. [= *Prione Oregonensis*, Redf. *P. cancellata* is the Cape Horn species. Some specimens in alcohol in Sir E. Belcher's collection, however, said to be from Icy Cape, greatly resemble the southern shell].

218. *Tritonium (Pollia) scabrum* [is exclusively a S. American shell. Dr. M.'s shell may have been *Ocinebra*, var. *aspera*].

218. *Pecten rubidus*, Hds. [non Martyn, = *P. Islandicus*, Müll. Midd.'s pl. 13. f. 1–3 are marked in expl. of plates " *Islandicus*, var. *Behringiana*; " they are probably (" *rubidus*, ?var.") *Hindsii*. But the figs. 4–6 are certainly the young of *Hinnites giganteus*].

219. *Venerupis gigantea.* [Decorticated specimens of *Saxidomus squalidus*.]

219. *Petricola gibba.* [Elongated form of *cylindracea*, Desh., = *carditoides*, var.]

219. *Machæra costata.* [The figures represent *M. patula*, Dixon.]

220. *Cingula minuta* [" is quite distinct from *Hydrobia ulvæ*," teste Gld.].

220. *Velutina cryptospira.* [Probably a *Lamellaria*.]

220. *Purpura Freycinettii*, Desh. [is quite distinct from *attenuata*, Rve. It is doubtful whether Midd.'s shells belong to Desh.'s species].

221. *Terebratula frontalis*, Midd. 1851, named in 1849, [may be the young of *Waldheimia Coreanica*, Ad. & Rve., 1850, = *Terebratella miniata*, Gld., 1860, teste A. Ad., Rve.].

221. *Astarte lactea*, Gld. [is distinct from *A. Scotica*, teste Gld.].

221. *Tellina fusca*, Say [is distinct from *T. solidula*, though it may = *T. balthica*; teste Gld. *Macoma inconspicua*, Br. & Sby., is distinct from both].

222. *Lyonsia hyalina* [is distinct from *L. Norvegica*].

222. *Machæra costata*, Say. [Dr. Gould does not believe that any of Midd.'s synonyms belong to this species. *Solen medius*, in Br. Mus., appears = *S. ambiguus*, Lam., as figured by Swains. It is not a *Machæra*.]

45. *Samarang.*—*Litorina castanea*, Ad. & Rve., 1850. " Eastern Seas," p. 49, pl. 11. f. 8 [appears identical with *L. Sitchana*, Phil.].

46. *E. B. Philippi.*—*Columbella tæniata*, Phil., 1846 [is probably identical with *Anachis Gaskoinei*, Cpr. But *C. tæniata*, Ad. & Rve., 1850, is perhaps a *Nitidella*].

47. *The " Mexican War Naturalists.*"—These were Major Rich and Lieut. Green. Col. E. Jewett was not connected with the war, as would be supposed from the introduction to Dr. Gould's pamphlet. The following corrections apply to the new species tabulated in Rep., pp. 226–228. The species of Gould bear date April 1852 (teste Otia, p. 184) and Nov. 1851 (Otia, p. 210); the others, July 1856.

No.
3. *Corbula polychroma* [= *C. biradiata*, var.].
7. *Tellina tersa* [= *Macoma nasuta*, jun. Cal., not Pan.].

No.
8. *Tellina pura* [= *M. Mazatlanica*, jun. Desh., Mus. Cum.].
11. *Donax flexuosus* [= *D. Lamarckii*, Desh., in B. M.].
13. *Gnathodon mendicus* [= *G. trigonum*, Pet., May 1853].
15. *Raëta undulata* [is distinct from *Harvella elegans*].
20. *Cardium luteolabrum* [= *C. quadragenarium*, Conr.].
21. *Cardium cruentatum* [= *Liocardium substriatum*, Conr.].
27 *Modiola nitens* [= *M. subpurpureus*, Mus. Cum., and is not from Cal.].
28. *Adula falcata*. [The locality of Mr. Cuming's specimens has not been confirmed. For "species," in note, read "specimens."]
31. *Lima tetrica*. [The specimens from the Mediterranean, W. Indies, Gulf Cal., and Pacific Islands were all named *L. squamosa* by Mr. Cuming.]
33. *Bulimus vesicalis* (nom. preoc.) = *B. sufflatus*, 'Otia,' p. 184.
40. *Nacella paleacea*. [Col. Jewett's specimens appear distinct from *N. depicta*, Hds.]
41. *Trochus marcidus*. [This shell was called *Omphalius Pfeifferi* by Mr. Cuming, from the resemblance of the figure, in which the umbilicus appears keeled; but the shell marked 'type,' answering to the diagnosis, along with '*Chlorostoma*' *maculosum*, A. Ad., are scarcely varieties of *Phorcus pulligo*, Martyn. The finest series is in the B. M.]
43. *Livona picoides* [has been heard of, but not seen since the explorations of Col. J. Dr. Gld. still considers the species distinct: among the very dissimilar varieties from the W. Indies (*vide* suite in B. M.) it would probably not have been singled out as a species, but for the theory of the author].
45. *Crucibulum Jewettii* [should be *corrugatum*, P. Z. S.].
47. *Modulus dorsuosus*. [Col. J. now thinks that the supposed Acapulco specimens are W. Indian, = *lenticularis*, Chem. When dead, the forms from the two oceans can hardly be distinguished; but the aspect of his shells is Caribbæan.]
54. *Conus ravus* [= *C. Californicus*, Hds.].
56. *Conus pusillus*, Gld. [non Chem. = *nux*, small var., teste Cuming].
57. *Obeliscus achates* [= *O. clavulus*, A. Ad., 1854].
65. *Columbella Sta.-Barbarensis* [so named to correct the statement that California was above the limit of the genus, proves to be a Mexican shell, and was probably obtained at Acapulco. Having been redescribed by Reeve from perfect specimens, it may stand as *C. Reevei*].
66. *Nitidella Gouldii*. [Not to be confounded with *Col. Gouldiana*, Agass., which is probably *Amycla*.]
67. *Fusus ambustus* [is a Californian species. The type stands in Mus. Cum. as *F. fragosus*, Rve., but does not answer to the diagnosis. The typical *fragosus* is marked *fragosus*, var. *F. ambustus* appears absolutely identical with *F. clavatus*, Brocchi, Mediterranean. Some of the diagnostic marks are not constant in the specimens].

Col. Jewett went to Panama, as a private collector, in January 1849, spending ten weeks in that region, including Taboga. This was two years before Prof. Adams's explorations. Thence he sailed to San Francisco, where he spent four months in exploring the shore for about 50 miles from the head of the bay. After labouring for a week at Monterey, he spent ten weeks at Sta. Barbara and the neighbourhood, thoroughly exploring the coast for fifteen miles as far as Sta. Bonadventura. It was here, at the " Rincon," after a violent southern storm, that he obtained the specimens of *Livona picoides*, as well as many other rare species that have not been obtained by any other explorer. "The storm tore up the kelp to such a degree that it formed a bank for many miles on the beach, from 10 to 20 feet broad, and at least 4 feet deep. Many of the plants were more than 60 feet long and 5 inches in diameter, having the appearance of vast cables." Before his return to the east, he also collected at Mazatlan (where he obtained some species not included in the B. M. Catalogue) and at Acapulco. There can be no doubt of the accuracy of the Colonel's observations at the time they were made. Unsurpassed in America as a field-palæontologist, possessed of accurate

21

discrimination, abundant carefulness, and unwearied diligence and patience, no one was better fitted to collect materials for a scientific survey of the coast. But, unfortunately for his (as for the Nuttallian) shells, he did not describe them at the time himself. They were subjected to all the derangements caused by frequent changes of residence, and transmission to various naturalists for identification. As we know what errors creep into the collections of the most learned under such circumstances, it is not surprising that they should now have lost much of their geographical value. After several days spent in a very searching elimination of the west-coast shells from his general collection, I was driven to the conclusion that several labels had become misplaced. This was so clearly the case as to certain N. England and W. Indian species interchanged with Pacific specimens, that it might also affect (e. g.) Sta. Barbara and Panama specimens as compared with each other. The kelp driven up by the great storm may have travelled from remote localities; which will account for tropical shells having been found at Sta. Barbara, as W. Indians occasionally are even on our own shores. It is possible also, as the Californian seas have as yet been but little dredged, that deep-water species live there which as yet are known only in the tropical province. Already some Gulf species have been thus obtained at San Diego and Catalina Island by Dr. Cooper, just as Mr. M'Andrew dredged Mediterranean species on the coast of Norway. But facts of such importance should rest on better evidence than chance shells picked on a beach, and subjected to dangers of altered labels afterwards. What was regarded by Dr. Gould as of authority is catalogued, according to his determinations of species, on pp. 226–231 of the first Report. The following is a list of the species which I found in the collection[a], divided simply into the temperate and the tropical faunas.

Species of the Temperate Fauna, collected by Col. Jewett ‡.

Pholadidea penita, ovoidea.	Tapes staminea, tenerrima *.
Saxicava pholadis.	Saxidomus squalidus.
Schizotheirus Nutta'lii.	Petricola carditoides.
Cryptomya Californica.	Rupellaria lamellifera.
Lyonsia Californica.	Lazaria subquadrata *†.
Solen ?sicarius, var. rosaceus *†.	Chama pellucida.
Machæra patula.	Lucina Californica.
Solecurtus Californianus, subteres.	Diplodonta orbella.
Macoma nasuta, secta.	Mytilus Californianus, edulis.
Lutricola alta.	Modiola modiolus, recta, fornicata *†.
Semele decisa, rubrolineata.	Leda cælata.
Donax Californicus, flexuosus *.	Pecten hastatus, latiauritus, (?ventricosus, var.) æquisulcatus *†, squarrosus *†, paucicostatus *†.
Standella ?Californica.	
Trigona crassatelloides.	
Psephis tantilla *.	Amusium caurinum, jun.
Amiantis callosa.	Hinnites giganteus.
Chione succincta, fluctifraga, simillima.	Bulla nebulosa.

[a] This collection belongs to his daughter, Mrs. Boyce, of Utica, N.Y. The Colonel's invaluable collection of U. S. Palæozoic fossils (probably the largest made by any individual's own hand) may be consulted at the State Museum in Albany, and will probably find its ultimate destination at one of the principal colleges. A large number of the fossils described by Prof. Hall were from this collection, though often without acknowledgment. Only a small proportion of the types of the celebrated 'Palæontology' are to be found in the State Collection, which was subjected to disastrous and very extensive curtailment before Col. J. entered on his present duties as curator.

* These species and marked varieties were first found by Col. J.

† Of these forms, either not seen or not distinguished by Dr. Gould, the diagnoses are written, and will probably be found in one of the scientific periodicals for 1864.

‡ Unless otherwise stated in the list, Report, pp. 228–231, it may be presumed that these species were from the neighbourhood of Sta. Barbara.

Tomatina cerealis*, culcitella*.
Cylichna (?cylindracea, var.) attonsa*†.
Volvula cylindrica*†.
Cryptochiton Stelleri.
Mopalia muscosa.
Nacellà incessa, paleacea*.
Acmæa patina, pelta, persona, scabra, spectrum, Asmi.
Scurria mitra.
Fissurella volcano.
Glyphis densiclathrata.
HaliotisCracherodii,rufescens,splendens.
Phasianella(?compta,vars.)punctulata*†, pulloides*†, elatior*†.
Pomaulax undosus.
Trochiscus Norrisii, convexus*†.
Callostoma canaliculatum, costatum.
Livona picoides*.
Homalopoma sanguineum.
Chlorostoma funebrale, Pfeifferi.
Crucibulum spinosum.
Crepidula adunca, dorsata, rugosa.
Hipponyx tumens*†.
Serpulorbis squamigerus.
Bittium esuriens*†, fastigiatum*†.
Cerithidea sacrata.
Litorina planaxis, scutellata.
Amphithalamus inclusus*†.
Lacuna unifasciata*.
Radius variabilis.
Luponia spadicea   Trivia Californica.
Erato columbella, vitellina.

Drillia inermis, mœsta*†.
Daphnella filosa*†.
Mangelia variegata*†, angulata*†.
Myurella simplex*†.
Conus Californicus.
Odostomia gravida*, inflata*†.
Chemnitzia tenuicula*, torquata* (et ?var. stylina*†), virgo*†, aurantia*†, crebrifilata*†, tridentata*†.
Dunkeria laminata*†.
Eulima Thersites*†.
Opalia bullata*†.
Lunatia Lewisii.
Cerithiopsis ? tuberculata, fortior*†, purpurea*†.
Marginella Jewettii*, ?polita, regularis*†, subtrigona*†.
(Volvarina varia, serrata ; perhaps imported, or label changed.)
Olivella biplicata, bætica† [=petiolita, Gld.,+anazora, Gld., MS. (non Ducl.) =rufifasciata, teste Cum., by error].
Purpura crispata, saxicola.
Nitidella Gouldii*.
Ocinebra Poulsoni.
Pteronotus festivus.
Columbella carinata, Hindsii.
Amycla ? Californiana, gausapata, tuberosa*†.
Nassa perpinguis, mendica.
?Anachis penicillata*†.
Siphonalia fuscotincta*†.

Species of the Tropical Fauna, collected by Col. Jewett.*

Pholas crucigera [=lanceolata].
Dactylina laqueata.
Corbula bicarinata, biradiata, nasuta, tenuis, ovulata§, nuciformis§.
Sanguinolaria miniata*§.
Psammobia casta.
Tellina felix, puella*, punicea, "rubella."
Heterodonax bimaculatus et vars. §.
Strigilla carnaria (white and red vars.)§ pisiformis§, sincera.
Semele pulchra§, venusta§.
Iphigenia altior.
Donax transversus, navicula, gracilis, carinatus, rostratus§. punctatostriatus§, v. cælatus§. assimilis.
Mulinia angulata.
Harvella elegans.
Trigona planulata||, Hindsii§.
Dosinia Dunkeri.

Callista aurantia, chionæa, circinata§, tortuosa, lupinaria||, rosea||, v. puella§.
Chione amathusia, sugillata, neglecta.
Anomalocardia subimbricata, subrugosa.
Tapes grata,+vars. discors, fusculineata.
Petricola pholadiformis, var.
Crassatella gibbosa.
Venericardia laticostata, radiata.
Lazaria affinis.
Chama frondosa, spinosa.
Cardium consors§, senticosum, procerum, obovale.
Hemicardium biangulatum§, graniferum.
Liocardium apicinum§.
Codakia tigerrina||¶
Lucina eburnea§, excavata§, pectinata.
Felania tellinoides§, var.
Modiola Brasiliensis, capax.
Lithophagus aristatus.
Arca grandis, tuberculosa.

* Unless otherwise specified, either by §, ||, or locality-marks in Rep. pp. 228-231, these species may be presumed to have come from the Panama district.
    § These species were probably from Acapulco.
    || Probably from Mazatlan.
    ¶ Another specimen, 3·78 in. across, is marked "Sta. Barbara" on the shell.

Scapharca bifrons *, emarginata, labiata, nux.
Noëtia reversa.
Byssoarca Pacifica, mutabilis.
Barbatia alternata, aviculoides, gradata, illota, solida.
Pectunculus inæqualis, maculatus, parcipictus §, ?pectinoides §.
Leda Elenensis, polita.
Pinna maura, tuberculosa.
Avicula sterna.
Bryophila setosa *.
Isognomon Chemnitzianum.
Pecten ventricosus, subnodosus §.
Lima angulata §.
Spondylus calcifer.
Ostrea palmula.
Anomia lampe.
Bulla Adamsi, Quoyi §.
Siphonaria gigas, lecanium § et vars. maura, palmata §.
Patella Mexicana.
Acmæa mesoleuca, mitella, vernicosa.
Fissurella rugosa, nigropunctata, ?macrotrema §.
Glyphis inæqualis, alta.
Phasianella perforata.
Callopoma saxosum.
Senectus squamigerus §.
Uvanilla inermis.
Calliostoma lima, Leanum §.
Tegula pellis-serpentis.
Omphalius Panamensis, coronulatus *, ligulatus ‖, viridulus.
Nerita Bernhardi, scabricosta.
Neritina picta, Guayaquilensis, intermedia [" =globosa, Brod."].
Crucibulum imbricatum, spinosum, umbrella, radiatum, pectinatum *, corrugatum *.
Galerus conicus, mamillaris.
Crepidula aculeata §, excavata, incurva.
Hipponyx barbatus, Grayanus.
Aletes centiquadrus.
Vermetus eburneus.
Bivonia contorta, albida.
Petaloconchus macrophragma.
Turritella goniostoma.
· Cerithium maculosum, uncinatum, mediolæve, interruptum, alboliratum.
Rhinoclavis gemmata.
Cerithidea Montagnei, varicosa.
Litorina aspera, conspersa, Philippii.
Modulus catenulatus, ?disculus.
Rissoina firmata *, fortis *, expansa *†‖, stricta §, Janus *, Woodwardii ‖.
Planaxis nigritella, planicostata.
Radius avena §, similis.
Carinea emarginata, jun.
Aricia punctulata.
Trivia pustulata, puila, Pacifica §.

Erato scabriuscula §, Mangeriæ.
Strombus galeatus, gracilior, granulatus.
Terebra robusta.
Euryta fulgurata, aciculata §.
Pleurotoma funiculata.
Drillia albovallosa, aterrima, ?exarata §, incrassata, nigerrima, rudis, hexagona, ?gracillima, var.
Mangelia subdiaphana §, hamata *†, cerea *†, ?pulchella.
Cithara stromboides § [? =triticea,Kien.].
Daphnella casta §.
Conus gladiator, mahogani, nux, purpurascens, regularis.
Solarium granulatum.
Torinia variegata.
Obeliscus achates *‖.
Chemnitzia cælata *†.
Scalaria Hindsii *.
Alora Gouldii *.
Cancellaria bulbulus, clavatula, decussata, goniostoma, tessellata, mitriformis.
Natica maroccana et vars., Souleyetiana, zonaria §, catenata §.
Polinices otis, uber.
Neverita patula §.
Ficula ventricosa.
Malea ringens.
Bezoardica abbreviata.
Levenia coarctata.
Persona ridens [? =] constrictus.
Triton lignarius, tigrinus, ?pileare, jun.
Priene nodosa.
Ranella cælata, nitida, triquetra, pyramidalis [like anceps and producta, Rve.].
Fasciolaria granosa, tulipa, jun. [?imported].
Latirus castaneus, ceratus, rudis, tuberculatus.
Leucozonia cingulata.
Mitra lens, tuniculata, nucleola.
Strigatella tristis.
Lyria harpa.
Marginella cærulescens, polita (?§).
Persicula imbricata §.
Volvarina triticea §, varia §, serrata §, fusca § [some of these are assigned to Sta. Barbara. West Indian specimens may have been intermixed: vide Cape St. Lucas list, infra].
Oliva angulata, porphyria.
Olivella azozora, gracilis §, inconspicua, semistriata, tergina, volutella, zonalis, Zanoëti.
Agaronia testacea.
Harpa crenata.
Purpura biserialis, melo, patula, triangularis, triserialis.
Cuma tecta, kiosquiformis.

Rhizocheilus nux.
Vitularia salebrosa.
Ocinebra erinaceoides.
Monoceros brevidentatum.
Sistrum carbonarium §.
Nitidélla cribraria.
Columbella festiva, fuscata, labiosa, major, Reevei *§, uncinata §, ? mille- punctata, *var.*§
Conella coniformis.
Truncaria modesta.
Nassa collaria *, corpulenta, crebristri- ata, luteostoma, pagodus, scabrius- cula, tegula, versicolor, complanata, Stimpsoniana *, nodicincta.
Phos gaudens.

Pyrula patula.
Engina Reeviana, crocostoma.
Anachis Californica *§, coronata, costel- lata, fluctuata, lyrata, nigricans, parva, pygmæa, diminuta *, rugosa, varia.
Strombina bicanalifera, gibberula, re- curva.
Pisania gemmata, insignis, pagodus, ringens, sanguinolenta.
Northia pristis.
Clavella distorta.
Murex recurvirostris, [? =] nigrescens (*Cum.*).
Muricidea alveata§, dubia, vibex, "pin- niger, *Brod.*"

This list, of about 133 species from the northern and 328 from the southern fauna (nearly twice as large as that sent by Dr. Gould and printed in the first Report, and yet not containing several species there quoted), is an instructive instance of what may be accomplished in about three-quarters of a year, simply by picking up shore-shells. It contains about 48 species in the northern and 22 in the southern faunas not previously described.

Besides the recent shells, Col. Jewett brought home a very interesting series of Pliocene fossils from the neighbourhood of Sta. Barbara. Almost all of them are species known to inhabit neighbouring seas, and are chiefly northern forms. Of some no recent specimens have yet been found in such perfect condition. The following is a list of the species, which is of the more value as they have not been intermixed with those of any other locality, and the spot does not seem to have been discovered by any succeeding geological explorer. It was two miles from the coast, and 150 feet high.

Schizotheirus Nuttallii.
Mactra planulata.
Chione succincta *.
Pachydesma crassatelloides.
Psephis tantilla, ?salmonea.
Rupellaria lamellifera.
Cardium graniferum *.
Venericardia *v.* ventricosa †.
Lucina Californica.
Pecten floridus *.
Hinnites giganteus.
Planorbis, sp.
Calliostoma costatum.
Margarita pupilla †.
Omphalius aureotinctus.
Galerus fastigiatus †.
Crepidula grandis † [*Mδld.,*=princeps, *Conr.*, 3·5 inches long].
Crepidula adunca.
,, navicelloides.
Turritella Jewettii, n. s.
Bittium rugatum, n. s.
,, armillatum, n. s.
,, filosum †.
Lacuna solidula †.

Chrysallida, sp.*
Opalia (?crenatoides, var.) insculpta *, n. s.
Lunatia Lewisii.
Natica clausa †.
Priene Oregonensis †.
Olivella biplicata.
Columbella carinata.
Amycla gausapata.
,, tuberosa, n. s.
?Truncaria corrugata.
Nassa fossata.
,, mendica.
Purpura crispata.
Ocinebra lurida.
Trophon tenuisculptus †, ?n. s. [may prove identical with *T. fimbriatula*, A. Ad., Japan].
Trophon Orpheus †.
Fusus ambustus.
Pisania fortis *, n. s.
Chrysodomus carinatus †, Brit. Mus. [probably = *despectus*, var.].
Chrysodomus tabulatus, jun. †, n. s.
,, dirus †.

* These species are of a southern type.
† These forms rank with the northern series. The rest belong to the present Californian fauna.

The following fossils were also collected by Col. Jewett:—

Purpura crispata) San Francisco, 160 ft.
  „   ostrina)   above the Bay.

Tellina congesta, *Conr.* Monterey.
Scalaria: can scarcely be distinguished from *planicostata*, Kien., in Brit. Mus. (?= *Grœlandica*): Panama.

The collections of Major Rich, having been tabulated by Dr. Gould simply as from Upper or Lower California, I had expected to find of but little geographical value. They proved, however, to be of peculiar interest. Major Rich had been one of the naturalists in the U. S. Expl. Exp., and his warlike occupations did not prevent his remaining long enough at particular stations to pay close attention to the Molluscs. His forte lay in procuring shells in the best possible condition; and a study of them was very serviceable in explaining the dead shore-shells usually obtained from other sources. Fortunately, he was quite aware of the importance of geographical accuracy, and arranged those obtained at different places in separate drawers. The "Upper Californian" collections were made at Monterey, San Francisco, San Diego, and San Pedro; the "Lower Californian," in the Gulf, principally at La Paz, partly at San Jose and Mazatlan. At the latter place he met M. Reigen, who had filled his house with decomposing molluscs to such an extent as to induce the neighbours to have recourse to the police. From him he obtained many species not in the Brit. Mus. Cat., and probably sent to Europe in the Havre collection. Major Rich's beautiful series may be consulted at his residence, opposite the British Legation, Washington, D. C.; and are designed ultimately for one of the public museums in the neighbourhood. The following is a list of the species:—

Shells collected by Major Rich, from the Californian Fauna.

Pholadidea ovoidea [1][2].
Parapholas Californica [1]. (The young is very acuminate, with imbricated cups, as in *P. calva*.)
Netastoma Darwinii [1].
Saxicava pholadis [1][3].
Platyodon cancellatus [4].
Schizotheirus Nuttalli [4].
Cryptomya Californica [1].
Thracia curta [1].
Lyonsia Californica [1].
Mytilimeria Nuttalli [1]. (Very fine, with ossicle.)
Solen sicarius [3].
Machæra patula [1].
Solecurtus Californianus [3].
Sanguinolaria Nuttalli [4].
Psammobia rubroradiata [1].
Macoma nasuta [1], secta [1][4].
Scrobicularia alta [4].
Semele decisa [1].
Cumingia Californica [1].
Donax Californicus [1].
Mactra Californica [1].
Pachydesma crassatelloides [1][4].
Amiantis callosa [4].
Chione succincta [4].

Tapes staminea et vars. [1][2][4], laciniata [1][*].
Petricola carditoides [1].
Rupellaria lamellifera [1].
Chama Buddiana [4].
Cardium Nuttalli [4].
Lucina Californica [1].
Diplodonta orbella [4].
Kellia Laperousii [1].
Mytilus Californianus [1], edulis [1], *v.* glomeratus [*][4].
Septifer bifurcatus [1][*].
Modiola modiolus [1].
Lithophagus attenuatus [1].
Adula falcata [1][*].
Pecten *v.* æquisulcatus [4], monotimeris [4].
Hinnites giganteus [1].
Placunanomia macroschisma [1].
Bulla nebulosa [4].
Katherina tunicata [1].
Mopalia muscosa [1], Hindsii [1].
Nacella incessa [2].
Acmæa persona [2], pelta [2], spectrum [2], scabra [2], et var. limatula †[2].
Lottia gigantea [2].
Scurria mitra [2].
Fissurella ornata [4][2].

[1] Monterey. Fresh specimens of seven species from the southern fauna were also obtained at Monterey, probably from commerce.
[2] San Diego.   [3] San Francisco.   [4] Near San Pedro.
[*] These species were first found by Major Rich.

Glyphis densiclathrata[2].
Lucapina crenulata[1] (one spec. Catalina Is.).
Haliotis rufescens[1][4], Cracherodii[1][4], Kamtschatkana[1][4].
Pomaulax undosus[4].
Trochiscus Norrisii[2] (and Catalina Is.).
Calliostoma canaliculatum[1], annulatum[1], cost.tum[1].
Omphalius fuscescens[4].
Chlorostoma funebrale[1], brunneum[1], Pfeifferi[1].
Crucibulum spinosum[2].

Crepidula rugosa[2], adunca[2], explanata[2].
Hipponyx ?antiquatus[2], ?tumens[1].
Serpulorbis squamigerus[2].
Spiroglyphus lituella[2][*].
Litorina planaxis[1].
Trivia Californica[1].
Conus Californicus[4].
Ranella Californica[4].
O.ivella biplicata[1], bætica[1].
Purpura, vars. ostrina[1], emarginata[1].
Cerostoma Nuttalli[4].
Nassa mendica[1], perpingius[1], fossata[4].
Helix, three sp.

Shells collected by Major Rich, near La Paz (west shore of the Gulf of Cal.).

(Thracia) Cyathodonta plicata.
Sanguinolaria miniata.
Tellina Cumingii.
Strigilla carnaria.
Heterodonax bimaculatus.
Iphigenia altior.
Donax navicula, punctato-str., rostratus.
Standella fragilis (common).
Mulinia angulata.
Trigona argentina, radiata, planulata.
Dosinia ponderosa.
Callista concinna, chionæa.
Chione succincta, amathusia, gnidia, pulicaria, var.
Anomalocardia subimbricata.
Tapes grata, histrionica.
Lazaria Californica.
Chama spinosa, producta, corrugata.
Cardium consors, biangulatum.
Liocardium elatum.
Codakia tigerrina (two fine specimens).
Cyrena olivacea, Mexicana.
Anodonta glauca.
Mytilus multiformis.
Modiola capax.
Arca multicostata.
Barbatia Reeviana, solida.
Pectunculus giganteus.
Pinna rugosa.
Margaritophora fimbriata.
Isognomon Chemnitzianum.
Pecten ventricosus, subnodosus.
Lima tetrica[*].
Janira dentata.
Ostrea amara (Maz. Cat. 215. *Is. Crestona*, entrance of Gulf), Virginica (more pearly than the Atlantic shells, teste Rich).
Anomia lampe.
Bulimus sufflatus[*], excelsus[*], pallidior.
Physa elata[*], aurantia.
Patella Mexicana.
Acmæa atrata, mesoleuca.
Fissurella rugosa, virescens.
Glyphis alta, inæqualis.

Haliotis splendens (three fresh specimens from a resident at San Jose).
Callopoma fluctuosum.
Uvanilla olivacea.
Omphalius rugosus, coronulatus.
Nerita scabricosta, Bernhardi.
Neritina picta.
Crucibulum spinosum, imbricatum, pectinatum, umbrella.
Galerus mamillaris, conicus.
Crepidula aculeata, onyx, nivea, unguiformis, arenata.
Hipponyx Grayanus, serratus, antiquatus.
Aletes centiquadrus.
Spiroglyphus lituella (on *Cr. umbrella*).
Turritella goniostoma, tigrina.
Cerithium maculosum, stercus muscarum.
Cerithidea Montagnei.
Litorina fasciata, conspersa.
Modulus catenulatus, disculus.
Cypræa exanthema.
Aricia arabicula.
Luponia Sowerbii, albuginosa.
Trivia sanguinea, radians, Solandri, pustulata, Pacifica.
Strombus granulatus, gracilior.
Euryta fulgurata.
Pleurotoma funiculata, maculosa.
Drillia ?inermis.
Conus puncticulatus, gladiator, purpurascens, regularis, arcuatus, nux.
Solarium granulatum, *v.* quadriceps.
Cancellaria obesa, cassidiformis, solida, goniostoma, ?candida.
Natica maroccana, zonaria.
Polinices Recluziana, bifasciata, otis.
Neverita patula.
Sigaretus debilis.
Oniscia tuberculosa.
Levenia coarctata.
Bezoardica abbreviata.
Priene nodosa.
Turbinella cæstus.
Fasciolaria princeps.

Leucozonia cingulata.
Mitra lens.
Oliva porphyria, Melchersi, Cumingii, subangulata.
Olivella tergina, gracilis, volutella (several taken alive).
Agaronia testacea.
Purpura patula, biserialis, triangularis, muricata, planospira ‡.
Nitidella cribraria.
Columbella fuscata, var.
Conella cedo-nulli.

Nassa luteostoma, scabriuscula, corpulenta.
Pyrula patula.
Fusus Dupetithouarsii.
Siphonalia pallida.
Strombina (? new, deep water, San José).
Pisania sanguinolenta, insignis.
Murex plicatus, recurvirostris.
Phyllonotus nigritus, brassica, princeps, bicolor.
Muricidea dubia.

Lieut. Green having been obliged to pack up his collection and leave home on professional duty, I was not able to make any critical examination of it. Capt. Dupont also, of Delaware, was one of the "Mexican-war naturalists," and made a large collection of La Paz shells during his campaign ; but I had no opportunity of seeing them.

Dr. Gould notes the following corrections in Lieut. Green's list, pp. 231–234 :—

Semele flavicans should be *flavescens.* | *Donax abruptus* should be *obesus.*

50. *Kellett and Wood.*—The locality-marks, on further study, display still greater inaccuracies.

Nassa Woodwardii, Fbs., Sandwich Islands [is the adolescent state of a very abundant Vancouver and Californian shell, = *N. mendica,* Gld.].

Nassa Cooperi, Fbs., Sandwich Islands. [The type is immature and in poor condition ; but it is a rare Californian species, since found by Dr. Cooper.]

Trochita spirata [has not been confirmed from Gulf Cal., but appears in Brit. Mus. from St. Vincent, Cape Verd Is., on the excellent authority of Macgillivray, who did not visit the West Coast. The Cumingian specimens were from K. and W.; but the "*spirata,* var.," from Magellan and Peru, are simply turrited forms of *T. radians*].

Chlorostoma aureotincta [= *C. nigerrima* (Gmel.), Mus. Cum. ; but it is unlikely that Gmelin knew the species. It is not quoted by Desh. (Lam. ix. 157) : but the *Trochus in fauce nigerrimus,* Chemn. f. 1526, = *T. melanostomus,* Gmel., is a *Risella.*]

Margarita purpurata et *Hillii* [are South American shells].

Purpura analoga [is the rough irregular form of *P. canaliculata=decemcostata*].

   ,,   *fuscata,* Fbs. [of which one brown and one whitish specimen (immature) are preserved in the Brit. Mus. as types, is the large, smooth, rather elevated var. of *saxicola.* It belongs to the Vancouver district].

Purpura, like *decem-costatus* and *Freycinetii* [is the normal state of *saxicola.* The banded smooth var. is named in Brit. Mus. "? *Buc. striatum,* Martyn, Un. Conch. no. 7," but does not agree with the figure].

Fusus Kellettii. [This *Siphonalia,* after long remaining unique in the Brit. Mus. Col., has been twice confirmed from the San Diegan district by the Smithsonian collectors. Dr. Cooper's living specimen is 6·25 in. long ; and one specimen was dredged by A. Ad. in the seas of South Japan.]

51. *Reigen.*—The type collection, presented to the Brit. Mus., contains about 8000 specimens. The first duplicate series, containing about 6000 shells, was presented to the State of New York at the urgent request of Dr. Newcomb (well known for his researches in *Achatinella,* made during his professional residence in the Sandwich Islands), and is arranged in the Albany Museum. Three other typical series were prepared for the Museums of Paris, Berlin, and St. Petersburg, and offered on the same terms, viz. that they should be arranged by the author, and preserved intact for the free use

‡ Dead shells at La Paz ; two fresh specimens in deep water from San José ; ditto, Lieut. Green.

of students; but the donations were severally declined by the respective governments. They have since been offered to the Museums of Harvard University, Cambridge, Mass.; M'Gill University, Montreal, C. E.; and the Smithsonian Institution, Washington, D. C.; and accepted on the same conditions *. The writer of the Brit. Mus. Catalogue spared no pains in his endeavours to verify the previously described species of Prof. C. B. Adams; yet a subsequent comparison of types has developed very unexpected coincidences. Those who will take the trouble to compare the two diagnoses in the synonyms now given will add one to the many proofs of the uncertainty of the senses in observation, and the inaccuracy of language in description. The following corrections and additions should be made to the list in the British Association Report, pp. 243-264.

18. *Parapholas acuminata* is united to *P calva* by Tryon, Mon. Phol.
23. The specimens obtained from Madagascar by Sir E. Belcher in the Voy. Samarang appear absolutely identical.
24. *Petricola robusta*. The West Indian form of this species is the *Choristodon typicum* of Jonas; Mus. Cum.
35. *Sphænia fragilis* is perhaps *S. luticola*, **Val.**
38. *Solecurtus politus ? = S. Carpenteri*, Dkr.
40. Should be *Semele flavescens*, Gld.
41. *Semele ?venusta* should be *S. bicolor*, C. B. Ad. Panama. **C. S. Lucas.**
46. Should be *Sanguinolaria miniata*, Gld., as in first Report.
48. Should be *Tellina purpurea*, Brod. & Sby., teste type in Mus. Hanl.
49. *= T. purā*, Gld., nom. prior.
54. Quite distinct from *Tellina alternata*, Say.
56. *Tellina ?eburnea* proves to be the type of a new generic form, probably belonging to *Kelliadæ*, viz. *Cycladella papyracea*. A perfect specimen, since found, is in Mr. Hanley's collection.
65. *Tellidora Burneti* is not *L. cristata*: *v. anteà*, p. 528.
66. *= Strigilla fucata*, Gld. (not *miniata*). Specimens received from different stations on the Pacific Coast vary very greatly in colour and markings.
68. The fragment of " ?? *Psammobia* " is perhaps part of a *Lepas*-valve.
71 and 72. The names of these shells have been altered and re-altered in Mus. Cuming, as will be seen by comparing Brit. Mus. Maz. Cat., p. 43, with the note, p. 548, and with the present arrangement. Mr. Hanley states that no. 72, *D. culminatus*, Cpr., is his true *carinatus*; therefore 71, *D. carinatus*, Cpr., and of most collections, must stand as *D. rostratus*, C. B. Ad., teste typevalve in Mus. Amherst. The two species uniformly retain their distinctive characters.
78. Should be *Mactrella exoleta = Lutraria ventricosa*, **Gld.**, from type.
81. Should be *Gnathodon mendicus*, Gld.
83. *T. Hindsii* is distinct, teste Hanl.
85. *T. argentata*, Sby., 1835, *= T. æquilatera*, **Desh.**, 1839.
92-99. The generic name should be *Callista*.

---

* A few of the duplicate sets having been sent in exchange to one of the principal scientific dealers, he advertises a list of species in which he not merely alters the nomenclature, giving "*Monoceros*" *cingulatum*, "*Pollia*" *insignis* (with "*Pisania*" *gemmata*), "*Trochus*" *olivaceus* (with "*Imperator*" *unguis*), "*Cerithium*" *montagui* (for *Cerithidea Montagnei*), *Cytherea* "*dione*" (for *Dione lupinaria*), "*Astarte*" *Dunkeri*, "*Cytherea*" *Columbiensis*, &c., but inserts Californian species ("*Ziziphinus filosus*," "*Cardium Nutali*") as though from the Gulf, and adds others not known at all in the West Coast faunas, as "*Columbella lævigata*," "*Patella plumbea*," and "*Chiton reticulata*." All these, with such shells as *Oliva Cumingii*, which belong to other regions on the Mexican coast, would be accredited by the reader on the supposed authority of "Carpenter's Catalogue." In these times it appears that naturalists must be content to resemble the dealers in patent medicines, and guard the accuracy of their works! With regard to the Mazatlan collections (now scarce), none can be trusted unless they present an *unbroken* seal, with the initials of the author.

98. *Callista alternata* has a very different aspect from the ordinary *C. circinata*; but several of the Pacific shells affiliate more naturally to the West Indian form.

99. *C. affinis*, *C. tortuosa*, and *C. concinna* appear to be one species.

100. Sir E. Belcher is confident that he dredged *C. petechialis*, in deep water, off S. Blas. He has the same confidence in regard to some of the East Indian Circes. At this distance of time, a written locality-ticket would have had more authority.

105. The hinge proves that this species is distinct from the true *V. crenifera*, Sby. It has been named *V. sugillata* by Rve., Conch. Ic. sp. 43. It was also brought by Kellett and Wood, and is allied to *V. pulicaria*.

110. Among the Panama varieties of this very variable species is *Venus fuscolineata*. *T. grata* takes the place of the Californian *T. staminea*, which is sometimes erroneously given as a synonym, and is not *straminea*, as often quoted.

116. It appears that *Gouldia* (*Thetis*, C. B. Ad., *olim*, non Sby. nec H. & A. Ad.) is congeneric with "*Circe*" *minima*, not with the Astartids. Prof. Adams's fresh specimens of his *G. Pacifica* prove to have the Crassatelloid internal ligament, and represent one of the many remarkable forms of that group.

117. Fresh specimens of *G. varians*, from Cape St. Lucas, have also the internal ligament, and must rank under *Crassatella* until that genus has been naturally divided.

118. *Lazaria Californica*. A well-marked group of species from the West Coast.

121. The purple and orange specimens, here treated as the adolescent state of *Chama Mexicana*, are certainly the *Ch. echinata* of collections, and may possibly prove a distinct species. A large series sent from Socoro Is. by Mr. Xantus confirms this view; but all the specimens seen are decorticated or incrusted.

121*b*. This is the *Chama Buddiana* of C. B. Ad., and probably distinct.

134. The specimens of *Cardium graniferum* in Mus. Cum., from St. Thomas, W. I., appear exactly identical.

136. The specimens from the Pacific coast, some of which are of very large size, have generally a red tinge round the inner margin; as have also the Fiji specimens brought by the U. S. Expl. Exp. In other respects they exactly accord with the W. Indian. The Pacific shells are generally called *C. exasperata*, Rve., a name first given to the rough Caribbean variety from Honduras, &c.

137. *Codakia punctata*. This shell also, brought by the U. S. Expl. Exp. from the Fiji Is., is found sparingly along the American shores, and has the same coloured margin.

142. May possibly prove identical with *L. bella*, Conr., S. Diego.

150. The *Lucina orbella* of Gould, = *Sphærella tumida*, Conr., MS., is the northern form; uniformly larger and smoother than *Diplodonta semiaspera*. This last is fully confirmed from both oceans.

152. "*Felania*" *serricata* appears congeneric with *Miltha*, H. & A. Ad., = *Mittrea*, Gray, the type of which (*M. Childreni*) is a Gulf species.

154. *Lasea rubra*. Mr. J. G. Jeffreys does not consider the Brit. Mus. specimen identical with the British. The Mediterranean specimens are much more unlike. A colony of fresh shells from a burrow at Cape St. Lucas, when examined, under the microscope, side by side with Ilfracombe specimens, did not present even varietal differences. The species also appears on the Californian and Japan coasts. Similar and perhaps conspecific forms are found on most coasts: among them is *Poronia Petitiana*, Chen. Conch. Ill. p. 2, pl. 1. f. 2 ; Callao, not rare, *Petit*.

156. For this species, *corbuloides*, and other angular forms, the name *Bornia* may be revived in a restricted sense. (A. Ad.)

157, 158. Mr. A. Adams, who is about to make the Kelliads a special study, thinks that these intermediate forms would rank better with *Montacuta* or *Tellimya*.

166. This is almost certainly = *Anodonta glauca*, Val.

168. Dr. Dunker renamed this shell *M. Adamsianus*, P. Z. S. Nov. 1856.

177. The subgenus *A lula* may be enlarged to include this and other nestling *?Lithophagi*, which often adhere by byssus, like *Modiola*.

178. *Liosolenus* is quite distinct from *Mytilimeria*, which appears simply an aberrant form of *Lyonsia*. Other "*Lithophagi*" probably rank with it.

180. *Arca semlis* is from W. Africa (not "E. Indies"): one of the many representative species between the two West Coasts.

185. *Noëtia reversa*, Gray.

186. *Argina brevifrons*, Sby.

188. This is the young of *Barbatia alternata.*

191–195 belong to the group *Barbatia.*

193. = *Barbatia Tabogensis*, from type.

203. The young of this shell is *Avicula libella*, Rve. Dr. Gould protests against some of the interpretations here given to his views.

204. The W. American pearl-oyster should stand as *M. fimbriata*, Dkr. It has been redescribed as *M. barbata*, Rve.

212. Dr. Gould protests against the Pacific shells being regarded as *O. Virginica.* Mr. Hanley adheres to his original opinion. Fossils sent from the Sandwich Is. by Mr. Pease (*O. Sandwichensis*, Pse.) appear scarcely to differ.

214*b.* The *O. palmula* appears a distinct species.

215. This species is identical with *O.* no. 384 of C. B. Ad. It may take the name of *O. amara* from its "bitter flavour."

224. *Bulla Adamsi* = *B. punctulata*, C. B. Ad., non A. Ad.

229. *Haminea cymbiformis* is closely allied to *H. virescens*, Sby.

239. *Siphonaria lecanium. S. maura*, Sby., is one of the varieties of this species. The *S. palmata* may prove distinct. *S. ferruginea*, Rve., is probably described from the intermediate form.

242. *Ianthina striulata.* Name given in ignorance of *striolata*, Ad. and Rve.; and not needed, teste Rve.

245. The *Dentalium hyalinum* of Phil. is probably the young of *D. semipolitum* : this species is distinct.

247. The *Dent. pretiosum* of Nutt. is a northern species ; this is most likely *D. lacteum*, Phil.

248-250. This typical group of Chitonids retains the Linnean name in Dr. Gray's arrangement ; and as he first pointed out the generic distinctions in the family, his judgment is to be preferred.

252-254, 256. These species belong to *Ischnochiton*, Gray.

255. *Lepidopleurus*, Risso, has sculptured valves and scaly margin, and is probably synonymous with *Lophyrus*, H. and A. Ad. The name may be retained for the " Lophyroid " *Ischnochiton* here described, the peculiarities of which have been confirmed by adult specimens in Mus. Cuming, and by other species.

257. *Chiton*, H. and A. Ad., = *Acanthopleura* (Guild.), Gray.

262. = *Nacella peltoides*, n. s. (described from Cape St. Lucas specimens).

263. The true *Lottia pintadina* of Gld. (teste figured types) consists entirely of varieties of *A. patina.*

265. The " large flat shell " referred-to is *Tecturella grandis*, Gray, Brit. Assoc. Rep. 1861, p. 137. *Tecturella* is preoccupied by Stimps. Gr. Manan Invert. It being needful to divide the old genus *Acmæa*, *Lottia* may be used for this section. By reviving synonyms as sectional names, when a genus is divided, good names may be retained in a restricted sense, and the burden of a spurious nomenclature lessened. The species is *Lottia gigantea* (Sby. Gen.).

269. *Scutellina navicelloides*, Cpr., = *Crepidula osculans*, C. B. Ad.

280. This should stand as *Gadinia stellata*, Sby., that name having been given to the normal form, Rep. pl. 7. f. 3a, of which *pentegoniostoma*, f. 3*f*, is only an accidental variety.

282. *Callopoma Fokkesii* = *tessellatum*, Rve., is the Lower Californian form, and probably distinct.

283*b.* = *Turbo phasianella*, C. B. Ad., non *Melaraphe phasianella*, Phil.

289. The first name is *T. eximius*, Rve., P. Z. S. 1842, p. 185 ; Mke.'s shell bearing date 1850. It appears identical with "*Javanicus*, Lam.," in Mus. Cum., and is extremely like "*speciosus*, Japan." *Trochus* being now generally retained for the *Niloticus* group, which contains the largest forms, it is best to revive Swainson's excellent name *Calliostoma* for the "*Ziziphinus*" group. A specific name should not be used for a genus, where a distinctive name has already been accurately described.

1863.

290. *Calliostoma McAndreæ* is the normal state, of which *C. Leanum* is the pale variety.

292. Mr. Pease considers that *T. Byronianus* represents a *Polydonta* from the Pacific Islands.

313–316. The non-pearly *Liotiæ* are *Conradia*, A. Ad.

322, 323. Mr. A. Adams thinks that the "*Ethalia*" *amplectans* is probably the young of "*Teinostoma*" *a.*, as suggested in Brit. Mus. Cat. p. 253.

338. *Crepidula adunca*, Cpr. (non Sby., = *solida*, Hds., = *rostriformis*, Gld.). **The** tropical shell is *C. uncata*, Mke., = *C. rostrata*, C. B. Ad., Rve.

341. Should stand as *C. squama*: v. note on C. B. Ad. no. 351.

354. *Vermetus eburneus*, Rve., = *V. ?glomeratus*, C. B. Ad., non Lam.   The note to *Cæcum*, Brit. Mus. Cat. p. 314, should read:—" Of a fourth group, *Meioceras*, three species are known from the Caribbean Sea, one of which is fossil at Grignon.   The earliest Cæcid is the Eocene genus *Strebloceras*." *Vide* Mon. Cæcidæ in P. Z. S. 1858, pp. 413–444.

387. *Cerithium irroratum*. Gld. (teste type sp. in Mus. Smiths.), is a very distinct East Indian species, = *C. obesum*, Sby. sen.

388. This is **not** the *C. interruptum* of C. B. Ad., Sby., and Mus. Cum. (*hodie*), which latter is the roughened form of *C. stercus muscarum*, Val.   *C. Gallapaginis* is the rough form of *C. interruptum*, Mke.

389. *Vertagus* should be changed into *Rhinoclavis*, Swains.; v. note to 289.

391–393. The genus *Triforis* should be removed to *Cerithiopsidæ*.   The true "*Triforis*" *infrequens* of C. B. Ad. is a dextral shell, = *Cerithiopsis tuberculoides*, no. 557.   The shell here doubtfully affiliated is probably a variety of *T. inconspicuus*.

398. *Litorina Philippii* = *L. ?parvula*, C. B. Ad., non Phil., = *L. dubiosa*, C. B. Ad., nom. prov

399. = *Litorina pullata*, Cpr.; described from Cape St. Lucas specimens.

409. Probably = *Rissoina firmata*, C. B. Ad., + *R. scalariformis*, C. B. Ad.

411. " Not a *Barleeia*," teste Jeffr. MS.   It seems, however, too closely allied to *B. rubra* to create a fresh genus for it, unless the animal should display differences.

412, 413. Belong to *Fenella*, A. Ad.*   *F. excurvata* = ? *Rissoa inconspicua*, C. B. Ad., non Alder.

417. Fresh specimens prove this to be not a dead *Hydrobia ulvæ*, but a *Barleeia*. It appears on the Californian coast, as *B. subtenuis*.

418, 421.   Are very similar, and possibly conspecific forms of *Cythna*, A. Ad.

422. Is a *Gemella*, teste A. Ad.

426, 427. Belong to *Styliferina*, A. Ad.

430 *et seq.* Some of these forms **may rank with** *Gottoina*, A. Ad., and thus approach *Fossarus.*

437. *Luponia spurca*.   This shell is quite distinct from *L. albuginosa*, to which it was supposed to belong by Dr. Newcomb.   It is probably a ballast specimen.

438. Quite distinct from the Panamic *A. punctulata.*

445, 446. *Cancellariadæ* should be removed to *Proboscidifera*, teste A. Ad.

450–452. Mr. Reeve unites all these species, with several others, to *M. variegata*; which is certainly the easiest way of meeting the difficulty.

453. *Myurella rufocinerea* = *T. rudis*, Gray, teste Rve.

477. *Conus regalitatis* = *C. purpurascens*, var.   Most Cones vary in the same manner.

484. *Torinia variegata.*   Mr. Hanley restores to this shell the uncomfortable name of Chemn. (*perspectiiuncula*), and unites to it *areola*, Desh.   A careful comparison with shells from the Pacific Islands (teste Pease's specimens) proves them to be completely identical.   The "specific" names of Chemn., when simply the second word of the diagnosis, can hardly claim precedence.

486. The genera in this family have lately been revised by Mr. A. Adams.   A large number of his Japanese groups are here represented.   This species

---

* The generic names here given were assigned by Mr. A. Adams, who kindly examined the figures of the minute Mazatlan shells, all of which have been drawn under the microscope.

ngrees with *Pyramidella*, sp. ind., C. B. Ad., no. 293 (not 294), and may be quoted as *Obeliscus Adamsii*.

487, 488. Belong to *Iralea*, A. Ad.

489. Is a *Syrnola*, A. Ad.

492. The peculiar appearance of the apex is due to decollation, as proved by the discovery of an adolescent and several adult specimens. It probably belongs to *Diala*, A. Ad., and = *Cingula paupercula*, C. B. Ad., no. 253.

498-500. Belong to *Miralda*, A. Ad.   *Parthenia quinquecincta =? Cingula turrita*, C. B. Ad.,+ *Rissoa notabilis*, C. B. Ad.

501, 502. Belong to *Oscilla*, A. Ad.   *Parthenia exarata =? Cingula terebellum*, C. B. Ad.

503-506. The "Odostomoid *Chrysallidæ*" probably rank best with *Mumiola*, A. Ad.

512. *Chrysallida orulum =? Cingula inconspicua*, C. B. Ad. ; non ? *Rissoa inconspicua*, C. B. Ad. nec Alder.

513-515. Are *Pyrgulina*, teste A. Ad.   The Japanese species, however, seem more like *Parthenia*, no. 497.

517. Is a *Styloptygma*, A. Ad.

520. This is not the *Chemnitzia similis* of C. B. Ad.; and is probably a variety of *Ch. Panamensis*.

523. = *Chemnitzia affinis*, C. B. Ad., pars : pars = *Ch. undata*, no. 531.

535. Is perhaps a *Mormula*, A. Ad.

545. The various shells grouped under *Aclis* require revision. Comp. *Onoba*, A. Ad., and *Ebala*, Gray, which is figured as *Aclis* in Add. Gen.

549. Ranks best with *Eulimella*.

550. This is not *Leiostraca recta*, C. B. Ad., and may be called *Mucronalia involuta*.

551. This is not *L. solitaria*, C. B. Ad., and may be called *L. producta*.

552. = *Mucronalia solitaria*, C. B. Ad.

553. Ranks best with *Eulima*, teste A. Ad.

555. *L. retexa* ; distinct from *L. iota*, C. B. Ad.

556. Should be *Eulima*, teste A. Ad.

557. *Vide* note to 393.

563. Belongs to the subgenus *Seila*, A. Ad.

568. *Scalaria raricosta* is perhaps the young of *S. Elenensis*.

569. *S. funiculata* and *S. diadema*, with their congeners, should be removed from *Cirsotrema* to *Opalia*.

570. Dr. Gould dissents from the affiliation of this shell to the West African species on the ground that "he can separate the African from the Pacific shells as fast as we can hand them to him." So easily can any ordinary naturalist separate conspecific British and Mediterranean specimens, or Mazatlan and Panama specimens. It is not found in the West Temperate fauna ; the "var. *Californica*" being the ordinary type from the Pacific Islands, which is much more entitled to be regarded as distinct than are the West American forms.

572. Is shown by perfect Cape St. Lucas specimens to belong to a natural group of species, resembling flattened, perforated *Phasianellæ*, to which the name *Eucosmia* may be given.

580. Appears under genus "*Lagena*, Klein," * in Mus. Cuming; the *Argobuccinu cancellatum*, *Oregonense*, &c., having received a new name, *Priene*, H. & A. Ad.

589. This belongs to *Closia*, Gray, = *Volutella*, Swains., non D'Orb.

* The names of Klein in his 'Tentamen' and 'Lucubratiuncula,' 1773, are not entitled to precedence (according to the Brit. Assoc. rules), because he evidently did not adopt the Linnean mode of binomial nomenclature.   What he calls a "genus" answers more to the modern idea of chapter or section.   By chance, some of his names are allowable; but, if used, the genus must be regarded as that of Adams, Gray, Mörch, or other writer who defines it.   The following will serve as illustrations of Klein's "genera"—"*Sol, Luna, Stella*, &c.; *Auris, Anas, Tigris, Pes-anserinus, Tuba-phonurgica, Cochlea-lunaris, Cochlea-cælata*, &c. ; *Buccinum-lacerum, Buccinum-muricatum, Thema-musicum*, &c.; *Ostreum-imbricatum, Ostreum-muricatum*, &c. ; *Musculus-latus, Musculus-mammarius*, &c. ; *Tellina-arcinata, Tellina-virgata*, &c. ; *Concha-longa-biforis, Concha-longa-uniforis; Concha-τρίλοβος*;" and, in p. 167, "*Musculus-polylepto-ginglymus*," under which remarkable generic name is given as the first species "*Arca-Noæ*."   According to the now fashionable transformation of malacological nomenclature into a branch of archæological research, under pretence of justice to ancient writers, the hitherto universally understood

592. *Oliva intertincta* is very close to the young of *O. subangulata*, but differs in the chestnut stain on the columella. I have not been able to compare it with the young of *O. Cumingii*.

594. Is an abundant species in the Eastern Islands, occasionally seen in West Coast collections.

595. Belongs to *Anazola*, Gray. The remaining Mazatlan species of *Olivella* are now called *Olivina*, Gray.

598. *Olivella aureocincta* = *Oliva pellucida*, C. B. Ad., non Rve.

599. *Olivella inconspicua*, C. B. Ad., is probably the young of the colourless var. of *O. gracilis*, which must be excluded from the synonymy of *O. dama*, no. 600.

606. The figure of *Purpura biserialis*, jun., Brit. Mus. tablet 2232, is stated by Mr. A. Ad. to represent the genus *Sinusigera*, D'Orb., = *Chelitropis*, Fbs. ; just as *Macgillivrayia* is the young of *Dolium*.

611. *Rhizochilus mus* + *R. distans*, Cpr.

612. The young of *Vitularia salebrosa* is named *Fusus lamellosus*, Hds., in Brit. Mus., and is also the "*Ranella triquetra*" of Nuttall's collection.

618. Is probably *C. baccata*, Gask., in Mus. Cum., though Mr. Gaskoin regarded it as new. The var. *obsoleta*, 618b, is probably *C. galaxias*, Rve.

619–622. These shells may perhaps be better studied under *Daphnella*.

631. Certainly = *N. gemmulosa*, C. B. Ad.

633. *Nassa crebristriata* may rank as a var. under *proxima*, C. B. Ad., which is probably itself a var. of *versicolor*.

639. This aberrant group of forms is now transferred to *Cantharus* in Mus. Cuming. Perhaps they rank better with *Siphonalia*, A. Ad.

653. *Anachis rufotincta* ("new," teste Gaskoin) is probably = *Col. diminuta*, C. B. Ad., in Mus. Cum., but scarcely agrees with the diagnosis, nor was the accordance noticed in the Amherst types.

659. = *P. elegans*, Gray, in Griff. Cuv. pl. 25. f. 2. (1834.)

The following species, since found, must be added to the catalogue of the Reigen Collection. The specimens are deposited in the British Museum. The descriptions of nos. 693–695 appear in the appendix to the Brit. Mus. Cat.; the remainder are ready for the press.

704. *Cellepora areolata*, Busk.　On *Omphalius ligulatus*.
705. *Membranipora ? Flemingii*, Busk.　" 　　　"
707. *Dactylina* = C. B. Ad., Pan. no. 516.　Obtained from M. Reigen, at Mazatlan, by Major Rich.
693. *Lyonsia*, sp. ind., 1 sp.
694. *? Montacuta chalcedonica*, 1 sp.
706. *? Montacuta obtusa*, n. s., 2 sp.　Congeneric with 157, 158.
695. *Crenella*, sp. ind., 1 sp.
696. *Pectunculus*, sp. ind., 1 sp.
697. *Cylichna Carpenteri*, Hanl., P. Z. S. 1858, p. 543, 1 sp.　? = *C. luticola*, jun.
698. *Scissurella rimuloides*, n. s., 1 sp.
699. *Vitrinella ornata*, n. s., 1 sp.
700. *Vitrinella tenuisculpta*, n. s., 1 sp.
701. *? Vitrinella*, sp. ind., fragment.
702. *Mangelia sulcata*, n. s., 1 sp.
703. *?? Torinia*, sp. ind., 2 sp.
708. *Malea ringens*.　Obtained from M. Reigen, at Mazatlan, by Major Rich.

53. *Jay's Catalogue.*—Mr. Hanley states that after the return of Prof. Nuttall, his duplicates were bought by the elder Sowerby, who sold part to

designations of Lamarck, &c., must give way to such names as the above; and if some other 'Attempt' or 'Little Lucubration' of a year's earlier date should be disinterred from now-fortunate concealment, the most modern 'Guides' and 'Books of Genera' will have to be re-written. Klein's idea of *Argobuccinum* appears to have been that of a "Spotted Whelk," probably *Ranella argus*. *Argobuccinum*, H. and A. Ad., may stand as defined in their 'Genera' for the thin ventricose Tritons. They have, however, divided the species between *Priene* and *Lagena*.

Dr. Jay, and part to Mr. Stainforth. The specimens in Mus. Cum. were received from Dr. Jay; those in Mus. Hanley from Mr. Stainforth. In the third edition of Dr. Jay's Catalogue, 1839, appear the following species which have not been identified, and localities not confirmed.

14. *Tellina rosea*, Lam. California. [Perhaps *Sanguinolaria miniata*.]
33. *Pecten tumidus*, Brod. Upper California.
37. *Chiton incarnatus*, Nutt. „
„ *Chiton textilis*, Conr. „
38. *Patella plicata*, Nutt. „
40. *Fissurella pica*, Nutt. „
41. *Crepidula squamosa*, Brod. „
„ *Bulla Californica*, Nutt. „
68. *Natica variolaris*. California.
70. *Trochus Californicus*, Nutt. Upper California.
72. *Monodonta fusca*, Nutt. „
73. *Marmorostoma planospira*, Nutt. „
„ *Litorina iostoma*, Nutt. „
„ *Litorina maculata*, Nutt. „
79. *Melongena occidentalis*, Nutt. „
80. *Murex sexcostatus*, Brug. „
86. *Monoceros plumbeum*, Kien. „
87. *Buccinum Boysii*, Nutt. „

54. *C. B. Adams.*—After arranging the duplicate Reigen Collection in the State Museum at Albany, New York, I proceeded to Amherst, Mass., to study the type-collection from which Prof. Adams's book was written. The result is embodied in a " Review of Prof. C. B. Adams's ' Catalogue of the Shells of Panama,' from the Type Specimens," written for the Zool. Soc. in Jan., and published in the Proceedings for July 1863, pp. 339–369. In this paper the synonymy between the Mazatlan and Panama Catalogues is pointed out, and the species assigned to the modern genera. The following are the principal corrections needed in the list, Rep. pp. 267–280. The results in the succeeding paragraphs, pp. 280, 281, should be altered accordingly. (M.=Brit. Mus. Maz. Cat.)

3. *Ovula neglecta*=*arena*, var.
8. *Cyprœa punctulata*; quite distinct from *C. arabicula*.
11. *Cyprœa rubescens*, C. B. Ad.,= *T. sanguinea*, dead.
15. *Marginella sapotilla*, C. B. Ad., is perhaps a large form of *sapotilla*, Hds. It is destitute of the sharp posterior labral angle seen in the West Indian specimens of *cœrulescens*.
33. *Oliva araneosa*, C. B. Ad.,= *O. Melchersi*, M. 591.
35. *Oliva pellucida*, C. B. Ad.,= *O. aureocincta*, M. 598, dead.
40. *Oliva venulata*, C. B. Ad.,= *O. angulata*, jun.
43. *Nassa canescens*=dead sp. of *N. pagodus*.
50. *Nassa pagodus*, C. B. Ad.,=*decussata*, Kien. [? non. Lam.]=*acuta*, M. 625.
51. *Nassa Panamensis* has the operculum of *Phos* and *Northia*,=*exilis*, Pws.
52. *Nassa proxima*+54 *N. striata*, C. B. Ad. [non Mus. Cum.=*N. paupera*, Gld.], +*N. crebristriata*, M. 633, are probably vars. of *N. versicolor*.
53. *Nassa scabriuscula*, C. B. Ad.,+56 *N. Wilsoni*=*N. complanata*, Pws.
70. *Purpura foveolata*, probably=worn sp. of *Cuma costata*, M. 610.
74. *Purpura osculans*+*Rh. Californicus*+*Rh. distans*, are probably vars. of *Rhizocheilus nux*.
81. *Columbella costellata*, C. B. Ad.,=*Anachis scalarina*, Sby.
98. *Columbella parva*, C. B. Ad.,=dead sp. of *Anachis pygmœa*.
103. *Columbella tessellata*, C. B. Ad. (non Gask.),=*A. Guatemalensis*, Rve.
110. *Cassis abbreviata* can scarcely be distinguished, in some of its many varieties from the Texan *Bezoardica inflata*.
154. *Cancellaria affinis* scarcely differs from *C. urceolata*, M. 445.

160. *Cancellaria pygmæa*= *C. goniostoma*, jun., no. 157, = M. 446.
164. *Pleurotoma atrior* = *Drillia* v. *Melchersi*, M. 461.
169. *Pleurotoma discors*, C. B. Ad., is probably a finely developed var. of *D. aterrima*.
182. *Pleurotoma rustica*, C. B. Ad., = worn specimens of *D. Melchersi*, no. 164.
191. *Mangelia neglecta*, probably = *M. aculicostata*, M. 473.
194, 195, 201 belong to *Cerithiopsis*.
196. *Cerithium famelicum* must stand for the West Coast Uncinoids, M. 383; the Cumingian shell, and two out of ten in the type-series, belong to *C. mediolæve*, M. 382.
198, 199, 200 are various forms of *C. stercus muscarum*, Val.; quite distinct from *C. interruptum*, Mke., and *C. irroratum*, Gld.
203. Does not correspond with the diagnosis, and must stand as *Chrysallida paupercula*, a very distinct species.
208. Is scarcely a variety of *Triforis alternatus*, no. 207.
209. Both the specimens are dextral, = *Cerithiopsis tuberculoides*, M. 557.
210. *Turritella Banksii*, C. B. Ad. (non *Rve.*) = *T. goniostoma*, jun., M. 379.
217. A dead, stunted specimen of *Cæcum undatum*, M. 371.
220. *Chemnitzia acuminata* is a very broad but typical species; not *Chrysallida*.
221. *Chemnitzia affinis*, Mus. Cum. and M. 523, has sufficient correspondence with the diagnosis; but the type = *Ch. undata*, M. 531.
222. *Chemnitzia clathratula*. The type-series contains *Chrysallida clathratula*, M. 513 and Mus. Cum., + *Chr. communis* + *Chr. effusa*, M. 510, + *Dunkeria subangulata*, M. 537.
223. *Chemnitzia communis*, the type of *Chrysallida*, M. 507, Cpr. (vix A. Ad.). The type-series also contains *Chr. effusa* + *Chr. telescopium*, M. 508, + *Dunkeria subangulata*, + ?do. var.
225. *Chemnitzia major* ranks with *Dunkeria*.
227. *Chemnitzia Panamensis* contains also *Ch. Adamsii*, M. 519, + *Ch. ? gracillima*, M. 530.
228. *Chemnitzia similis*, like *aculeus*; differs from *Ch. ?similis*, M. 520, which perhaps = *Panamensis*, var.
230. *Chemnitzia turrita* = 251, "*Rissoa*, sp. ind."
231, 235, 237, 238. These species of "? *Litorina*" belong to *Fossarus*.
233. *Litorina atrata* + (adult) 257, ? *Adeorbis abjecta*, are the same (variable) species of *Fossarina*, A. Ad.
239. *Litorina parvula*, C. B. Ad. (non Phil.), = *L. Philippii*, M. 398.
244. *Rissoa firmata* + (jun.) 250, *R. scaliformis* = *Rissoina*, sp. M. 409.
246. ? *Rissoa inconspicua*, C. B. Ad. (non Ald.), does not accord with the diagnosis, but is identical with *Alvania tumida*, M. 414.
249. *Rissoa notabilis* + *Cingula ?turrita* belongs (with 252 and 254) to another suborder, = *Parthenia quinquecincta*, M. 498.
252. ? *Cingula inconspicua* = *Chrysallida ovulum*, M. 512.
253. *Cingula paupercula* = ? *Odostomia mamillata*, M. 492, = *Diala*.
254. *Cingula terebellum* = *Parthenia exarata*, M. 501.
261. *Vitrinella minuta*. The original type accords better with *Ethalia*.
266. *Vitrinella regularis* is also an *Ethalia*.
269. *Vitrinella valvatoides*. Probably an *Ethalia*.
270, 271. Are apparently vars. of *Solarium granulatum*.
272. May be distinguished as *Torinia rotundata*, from its great superficial resemblance to *Helix rotundata*.
275. *Trochus Leanus* is a pale var. of *Calliostoma M'Andreæ*.
276. *Trochus lima* can scarcely be distinguished from *C. Antonii*, Mus. Cum., dredged in the Japan seas by Mr. A. Adams.
277. *Trochus liridus*, C. B. Ad., = *Modulus disculus*, M. 403.
280. *Trochus reticulatus* = *Omphalius viridulus*, M. 292.
281. *Turbo Buschii*, C. B. Ad., = *Uvanilla inermis*, M. 287, = *T. variegatus*, Gray, MS. in Brit. Mus. The true *U. Buschii* is coloured outside like *U. olivacea*, but with a white base like *U. inermis*. St. Elena, Hds. in Brit. Mus.
282. *Turbo phasianella*, C. B. Ad., is probably the perfect form of *Phasianella*, ?var.

striolata, M. 283b.   Its operculum proves it to be a true *Phasianella*, and not *Melaraphe phasianella*, Phil., of Add. Gen.

283. *Turbo rutilus*, the worn remains of what perhaps was once *Pomaulax undosus*, brought in ballast from Lower California.

289. *Scalaria*, sp. *c*, = *Opalia funiculata*, jun., M. 569.

290. *Eulima* [*Leiostraca*] *iota* appears distinct from *L. retexta*, M. 555.

292. *Eulima* [*Mucronalia*] *so ilaria* = *Leiostraca*, sp. *a*, M. 552.

293. *Pyramidella*, sp., = *Obeliscus Adamsii*, M. 486.

296. *Natica lurida*, C. B. Ad., = pale var. of *N. maroccana*.

297. *Natica otis*, C. B. Ad. (non Br. and Sby.), = *Polinices "Salangonensis,"* C. B. Ad., no. 298.

299. *Natica Souleyetiana*, C. B. Ad., closely resembles *N. maroccana*, with larger umbilicus.

300. *Natica virginea*, C. B. Ad., +302, *N.*, sp. ind. *b*, = *Polinices uber*, M. 576.

301. *Natica*, sp. *a*, = *maroccana*, var. *unifasciata*.

318. ?? *Truncatella dubiosa* is probably a *Paludinella*.

321. *Bulla punctulata* = *B. Adamsii*, M. 224.

322. *Bulla*, sp. = *Tornatina carinata*, M. 223.

323. *Vermetus ?glomeratus*, C. B. Ad., = *V. eburneus*, Rve., M. 354.

324. *Vermetus Panamensis*, C. B. Ad., = *Aletes centiquadrus*, M. 352.

325. *Stomatella inflata* is a *Lamellaria*.

326. *Hipponyx ?subrufa*, C. B. Ad., = *H. Grayanus*, jun., M. 350, + ?*barbatus*, jun.

327. *Hipponyx ?barbata*, C. B. Ad.   The type-series contains *H. barbatus*, M. 349, + *H. Grayanus* + *Dicina Cumingii*, M. 14 (valve).

330. *Calyptræa aberrans* is a valve of *Anomia*.

331. *Calyptræa aspersa* = *Galerus conicus*, broken, worn, and young; one sp. may be *mamillaris*.

333. *Calyptræa conica*.   Most of the specimens are *G. mamillaris*, = 340, *G. regularis*; but a few may be the true *G. conicus*, worn, M. 332.

338. *Calyptræa planulata* is a young flat *C. cepacea*.

342. *Calyptræa ??unguis*, C. B. Ad., = *Crucibulum spinosum*, jun.

343. *Crepidula cerithicola* = *C. onyx*, jun., M. 340, + *C. incurva*, jun., M. 339.

349. *Crepidula squama*.   Some of the young shells belong to *C. onyx*; one perhaps to *C. incurva*.

350. *Crepidula unguiformis*.   Some of the specimens belong to this species; others to *C. nivea*.

351. *Crepidula nivea*.   The type-specimens are small, poor, and rough, of the var. *striolata*, passing into *Lessonii*.   Perhaps, therefore, the first name *squama* should be retained for the species (nos. 348, 349, 350, part, and 351), leaving *striolata* and *Lessonii* for the vars.

352. *Crepidula osculans* belongs to another order, = *Scutellina navicelloides*, M. 269.

353. *Crepidula rostrata*, C. B. Ad., Rve., = *C. uncata*, Mke., M. 338 ; and is perhaps distinct from *C. adunca*, Sby., = *solida*, Hds., = *rostriformis*, Gld.

357. *Fissurella microtrema*.   Dead shells, of which part = *V. rugosa*, var. M. 273.

358. *Fissurella mus*.   Intermediate between *Glyphis inæqualis*, M. 279, and var. *pica*.

361. *Fissurella virescens*.   Intermediate between *F. v.*, M. 271, and *F. nigropunctata*, no. 359.

366. *Siphonaria ?pica*, C. B. Ad.   Young dead limpets [?*Acmæa*].

367. *Lottia ?patina*, C. B. Ad. [non Esch.], may stand, until more specimens have been collated, as *Acmæa* (?*floccata*, var.) *filosa*.

368. *Lottia*, sp. ind. *a*, may be quoted as *Acmæa* (?*floccata*, var.) *subrotundata*.

369. *Lottia*, sp. ind. *b*, may rank, for the present, as *Acmæa* (?*vespertina*, var.) *vernicosa*.

371. ?*Patella*, sp. ind., resembles *P. vulgata*, but may be an *Acmæa*.

372-376. There was no opportunity of dissecting the Amherst Chitons ; but among the remaining duplicates of the collection (all of which were obtained and brought to England) were the following :—

373. *Chiton dispar*, C. B. Ad. (? non Sby.), including *Lepidopleurus Adamsii* and var. and *L. tenuisculptus*.

375. *Chiton pulchellus*, along with *Ischnochiton Elenensis*, and ?*var. expressus.*

376. *Chiton Stokesii.* Sent as *C. patulus* by Mr. Cuming.

377–379. Probably vars. of *Anomia tenuis* (non *lampe*).

380, 381. *Ostrea*, sp. ind. *a* and *b*, a peculiar corrugated species, which may stand as *O. Panamensis.*

382. *Ostrea*, sp. ind. *c*, resembles *O. rufa*, Gld., MS. (not Lam. in Deless.), not *Columbiensis.*

383. *Ostrea*, sp. ind. *d*, more like the Gulf Mex. shells than *O. Virginica*, M. 212.

384. *Ostrea*, sp. ind. *e*, may stand as *O. amara.* The "small var." is *O. concha-phila*, M. 214.

386. *Spondylus*, sp., = *Plicatula penicillata*, M. 210.

393, 394. *Perna*, sp. *a, b*, = *I. Chemnitzianum.* The Jamaica conspecific shells are labelled "*bicolor*, Ad."

396. *Pinna tuberculosa*, C. B. Ad., probably = *P. maura*, jun.

398. *Lithodomus*, sp., includes *L. aristatus*, M. 176, *L. attenuatus*, M. 173, and *L.* ?*plumula*, jun., M. 175.

399. *Modiola semifusca*, C. B. Ad., = *M. Braziliensis*, M. 171. More like the Atlantic shells than are those from Gulf Cal. A specimen, undoubtedly from N. Zealand, is pronounced conspecific by Mr. Cuming.

400–404. *Modiola*, sp. ind , contains *M. capax*, M. 170, *Myt. multiformis* [= *Adamsianus*, Dkr.], M. 168, several vars., and *Adula cinnamomea*, var. M. 177.

405. *Chama Buddiana* (in poor condition) = *Ch.* (?*frondosa*, var.) *fornicata*, M. 121 *b.*

406. *Chama* ?*corrugata*, small valve; large one ? = *Ch. Mexicana*, reversed.

407. *Chama echinata*, C. B. Ad., ? = *Mexicana*, jun., + *Buddiana*, jun

414. *Arca* ?*aviculoides*, C. B. Ad., appears a young *Scapharca.*

419. *Arca pholadiformis* = *Barbatia gradata*, var.

422. *Arca similis*, scarcely a variety of *A. tuberculosa*, no. 425.

432. *Cardium planicostatum*, C. B. Ad., may be a worn valve of *Hemicardia biangulata*, but more resembles a ballast specimen of the W. Indian *H. media.*

435. *Venus* ?*amathusia*, C. B. Ad., = *Anomalocardia subimbricata*, M. 113

436. *Venus discors* = *Tapes grata*, M. 110, var., + *T. histrionica*, M. 109.

442. *Venus*, sp. *b*, = *Chione sugillata*, Rve. (= ?*crenifera*, M. 105).

450. *Gouldia Pacifica*, M. 116, does not belong to the Professor's genus, but is a form of *Crassatella.*

451. *Cyrena maritima.* "The discovery of *Cyrenæ* in brackish water is a fact of some importance to geologists, which was duly appreciated by D'Orb." (T. Prime, in Ann. Lyc. N. Y. 1861, p. 314.)

457. *Donax rostratus*, C. B. Ad. (non Gld., MS., and from it Cpr. in M. Appendix, p. 549), teste type-valve = *D. carinatus*, Mus. Cum. *olim*, and from it M. 71; non *D. carinatus*, Mus. Cum. *hodie*, and type, teste Hanl., = *D. culminatus*, M. 72.

459. *Tellina cognata* = *Psammobia casta*, Rve., teste Cuming.

465. *Tellina felix.* The affiliation of this shell to *Strigilla fucata*, Gld., MS., was doubtless due to an accidental error in labelling. No. 476 is the same species, dead.

468. *Tellina puella.* Resembles *T. felix*, not ??*puella*, M. 59.

471. *Tellina simulans.* The type-valve exactly accords with the Professor's W Indian specimens.

473. *Tellina vicina*, C. B. Ad., = *versicolor*, C. B. Ad., MS. on label. Larger than most W. Indian specimens, which exactly accord with the Acapulcans, and are varieties of *Heterodonax bimaculatus.* The Panamic shells resemble the Lower Californian, which are *Psammobia Pacifica*, Conr.

477. *Petricola cognata.* Perfect specimens are *P. pholadiformis*, teste Cum.

478. *Saxicava tenuis*, Sby., C. B. Ad., H. and A. Ad., = *Petricola tenuis*, H. and A. Ad. Gen. pp. 349–441, and better accords with the latter genus.

479, 482. *Cumingia coarctata* = *lamellosa*, var. M. 42.

480, 481. *Cumingia trigonularis*, M. 43.

483. *Cumingia*, sp. *c*. = M. 45, and, if not described, may stand as *C. Adamsii.*

484. *Cumingia*, sp. *d*, = M. tablet 107, p. 31.

485. *Amphidesma bicolor* = *Semele ?renusta*, M. 41 (non A. Ad.).
487. *Amphidesma proximum*, probably = 486, *ellipticum*, var.: not *Semele proxima*, M. 40, = *S. flarescens*, Gld., M. p. 548.
489. *Amphidesma striosum*, resembles *Semele pulchra*, no. 488.
491. *Amphidesma ventricosum*. Scarcely perfect enough to distinguish the genus. The valve outside resembles *Macoma solidula*.
497. *Anatina alta*. A valve of *Periploma*; probably one of the Gulf species.
498. *Pandora cornuta*, named and described from a fractured growth; resembles *Clidiophora clariculata*.
499, 500 are varieties of the same species of *Azara*, of which perhaps no. 501 is an extreme form.
506. *Corbula rubra* = *C. biradiata*, jun., no. 503, M. 31. No. 509 are dead valves of the same, = *C. polychroma*, Cpr.
508. *Corbula*, sp. *a*, resembles *C. pustulosa*, M. 32.
510. *Solecurtus affinis*, probably = *S. Caribbæus* = *Siliquaria gibba*, Spengl., S. I. Check-List, no. 222. The W. African specimens are affiliated to the same species by Mr. Cuming. The Mazatlan shells, M. 37, have a different aspect, but closely resemble the Ariqnibo specimens in Mus. Amherst.
511. *Solen rudis* is named *Solena obliqua*, Spengl., in Mus. Cum. It appears identical with *Ensatella ambigua*, Lam., as figured by Deless.; but *S. ambigua* (Lam.), Swains., is slightly different, and better agrees with the dead valves of "*S. medius*, Alatska," in Brit. Mus. These may, however, be only ballast-valves. As *S. ambigua*, Lam., was described from America, and the form is not known elsewhere, it probably represents the Panamic shell.
515. *Pholas*, sp. *a*, = *laqueata*, teste Cum.
516. *Pholas*, sp. *b*, closely resembles *Dactylina dactylus*; also La Paz, teste Rich.

The following species were collected by Prof. Adams, but do not appear in his Catalogue; they were found either mixed with others in the Amherst Museum or in the shell-washings of his duplicates*.

518. Mumiola ovata.	528. Cæcum clathratum.
519. Chrysallida effusa.	529. Lepidopleurus tenuisculptus.
520. Chrysallida telescopium.	530. Ischnochiton Elenensis.
521. Chrysallida fasciata.	531. Cerithiopsis, n. s.
522. Chrysallida, n. s.	532. Lucina capax.
523. Leiostraca retexta.	533. Kellia suborbicularis.
524. Eulima yod.	534. Sphænia fragilis.
525. Volutella margaritula.	535. Tellina laminata.
526. Cæcum semilæve.	536. Crenella inflata.
527. Cæcum subquadratum.	

55. *British Museum Catalogues.*—To the list of Deshayes, Cat. *Veneridæ*, may be added—

Page.
7. *Dosinia ponderosa*, Gray, = *Cyth. gigantea*, Sby., = *Venus cycloides*, D'Orb. [Gulf] California.
135. *Chione callosa* [Desh. et auct. Brit., = *Ch. fluctifraga*, var., quite distinct from *Callista (Amiantis) callosa*], Conr.
147. *Chione astartoides*, Beck, Greenland. [1849. = *Tapes fluctuosa*, Gld., 1841; teste Gld., Otia, p. 181. Midd.'s figures more resemble *V. Kennerleyi*, jun.]

The authorities are rarely given for localities quoted in this elaborate work. The same species often occur under different names. The *Veneridæ*

---

* With regard to the species which have received different designations in the Reigen and Adamsian catalogues, whether those names be retained of which the specimens exist, and have been widely distributed, in accordance with the diagnoses, or whether the prior ones be adopted of which the unique types do not represent the descriptions, is a matter of little moment to the writer of the Brit. Mus. Cat. He spared no pains in making-out his predecessor's species before describing his own, and has offered the best attainable list of the parallel forms in the review here quoted.

in the Brit. Mus. Coll. have received Deshayes' autograph names, in accordance with this Catalogue, generally on the back of the tablets.

In the Brit. Mus. Catalogue of *Volutidæ* *, 1855, Dr. Gray arranges the
W. Coast species thus :—

Page. No.
1.　7. *Lyria (Enæta) Harpa*, Adams, 167 ; Gray, P. Z. S. 1855, p. 61 ; *Hab.* Peru,
　　　= *Voluta Harpa*, Barnes, Sby., Conch. Thes. [= *Voluta Barnesii*, Gray,
　　　Zool. Journ. vol. i. p. 511, note.]
18　10. *Lyria (Enæta) Cumingii*, Brod. (*loc. cit.*). Central America, S. Salvador,
　　　Gulf Fonseca.

56. *Sailor's Coll.*—*Pecten ?senatorius* may be a form of *sericeus*, Hds.

57. *Gould's Collections.*—" *Planorbis ammon*, = *Traskei*, Lea. *P. graci-*
lentus ?= *Liebmanni*, Dkr., or *Haldemanni*," teste Gld. MS. The collections of Mr. Blake and others will be found under the " Pacific Railway
Explorations," *v. posteà*, par. 98.

58. *Bridges.*—Some of the species described as new on Mr. Cuming's
authority appear, on further comparison, to be identical with those before
known.

?*Scrobicularia producta* = *Lutricola* † *Dombeyi*, Lam.
Strigilla disjuncta appears to the author identical with *S. sincera*, Hanl. [" Quite
distinct." H. Cuming.]
Lyonsia diaphana = *L. inflata*, Conr.
Calliostoma M'Andreæ = normal state of *C. Leanum*, C. B. Ad.
Natica excavata + *N. Haneti*, Recl., appear varieties of *N. Elenæ*, Recl., the
analogue of *lineata*, Chemn.
Add *Alora* (" *Trichotropis*") *Gouldii*, H. and A. Ad., P. Z. S. 1856, p. 369 ; 1861,
p. 272.

59. *Proc. Zool. Soc.*—The following additional synonyms have been observed in the list, Rep. pp. 285–288 :—

Page.
1835　43. *Venus leucodon* + *Californiensis* [= *Chione succincta*, Val. 1833].
　,,　110. *Pecten circularis* [? = *ventricosus*, jun.].
1850　24. Pl. 8. f. 4. (Add) *Cumingia similis*, A. Ad. N.W. coast of America.
　,,　37. *Gena varia*, A. Ad. Mindoro, 9 fms., *Cuming* ; Australia ; Acapulco,
　　　on the sands, *Moffat.* [Clearly imported.]
1851　153. *Infundibulum Californicum* [is a Pacific shell = *I. chloromphalus*, var.].
　,,　168. *Zizyphinus Californicus* [= *Calliostoma eximium*, Rve.].
　,,　190. *Margarita calostoma* [= *M. pupilla*, Gld., = *costellata*, Brit. Mus. Col.,
　　　non Sby.].
1853　185. *Pseudoliva Kellettii*, A. Ad. [= *Macron (Zemira) Kellettii*, Mus. Cum. :
　　　= *Pusio trochlea*, Gray, MS. in Brit. Mus. Cerros Is., *Ayres*].
1854　316. *Chlorostoma funebrale* [= *Tr. marginatus*, Nutt. (non Rve.) ; = *T. mæstus*,
　　　auct. nonnul. ; non Jonas].
　,,　359. *Tellina Mazatlanica* [= *T. pura*, Gld., 1851].
1855　231. *Chiton Montereyensis* [= *Mopalia lignosa*, Gld., 1846 : = *Merckii*, Midd.,
　　　1847].
　,,　231, 232. *Ch. Hartwegii* and *regularis* belong to *Ischnochiton*.

---

* In Donovan's 'Naturalist's Repository,' vol. ii. 1834, p. 61, appears (without
authority) " *Voluta Dufresnii*, Don., California, S. America."
† This belongs to a group of species in which the cartilage is semi-internal, intermediate
between *Scrobicularia* (= *Lutricola*) and *Macoma*. They are arranged under the former
group in Add. Gen. ii. 409, as "subgen. *Capsa*, Bosc." That Lamarckian name being in
common use for *Iphigenia*, Schum., and being also employed for *Asaphis* and *Gastrana*, it
adds to the confusion to use it for a fourth group. The bulk of Blainville's old genus
having migrated to *Lutraria* and *Scrobicularia*, his name may be revived for this group
not otherwise provided-for. The species was redescribed in consequence of *Dombeyi* having
been left among the true *Tellens* in Mus. Cum.

Page.
1855 244. *Callopoma depressum* [= *Senectus funiculatus*, Kien.: not American].

The following species appear in later numbers of the Proceedings :—

1856 360. *Mytilus Adamsianus*, Dkr. [= *M. multiformis*]. Panama, *Cuming.*
„ 365. *Volsella splendida*, Dkr. California.

Dr. Gray, in his elaborate article on the *Olividæ*, 1858, pp. 38 et seq., gives *O. julieta*, Ducl., *O. araneosa*, Lam., and *O. venulata*, Lam., as synonyms of *Strephona reticularis*, Lam. ; and quotes as "species (?) more or less allied to it," *O. polpasta*, Ducl., *O. splendidula*, Ducl., " *O. jaspidea*, Ducl.,= *O. Duclosii*, Rve." [?], *O. kaleontina*, Ducl. (Gallapagos), *O. Cumingii*, Rve., and *Oliva Schumacheriana*, Beck, " California : front of pillar-lip brown" [? = *O. Cumingii*, var.].

For *O. volutella*, Lam. (including *O. razamola*, Ducl.), he constitutes the genus *Ramola*.

For *O. undatella*, Lam. (including *O. ?hieroglyphica*, Rve., *O. nodulina*, Ducl., and *O. ozodina*, Ducl.), and similar species, he forms the genus *Anazola*.

The restricted genus *Olivella* is altered to *Olivina*, and includes (from the West Coast) *O. gracilis*, Sby., *O. anazora*, Ducl., *O. tergina*, Ducl., *O. lineolata* =*dama*, Goodall* ; and, in a section, *O. columellaris*, Sby., *O. semisulcata*, Gray, and *O. zonalis*, Lam.

The Californian species, *O. biplicata*, Sby.,= *O. nux*, Goodall, in Wood, is placed in the genus *Scaphula*. This is constituted for an animal, " *Olivancilla auricularia*," D'Orb., on which, in his work on S. America, he figures the shell of *O. biplicata* (teste Gray). The shell might in some way have become mixed with S. American specimens; but as D'Orb. could not possibly have there observed the living animal, the genus should be restricted to the latter. The shell of *O. biplicata* is very peculiar, and has not been found south of San Diego. D'Orbigny's genus is *Olivancillaria*.

Page.
1859 280. *Terebra strigata*, Sby., Tank. Cat. Panama, Real Lejos. = *Buccinum elongatum*, Gray, Wood,= *Terebra zebra*, Kien.,= *Terebra flammea*, Less.
„ 287. *Terebra Salleana*, Desh. Mexico [?ubi], *Sallé.*
„ 302. *Terebra Petiveriana*, Desh. (Pet. Gaz. pl. 75. f. 5). Panama. Mus. Cum.
„ 303. *Terebra specillata*, Hds. "Probably two species here figured." San Blas, Mexico.
„ 303. *Terebra larviformis*, Hds. "Probably two species here figured." St. Elena, Monte Christi.
„ 307. *Terebra formosa*, Desh. Panama. Mus. Cum.
„ 307. *Terebra incomparabilis*, Desh. [= *T. flammea*, Lam., teste Rve., P. Z. S. 1860, p. 450]. Panama. Mus. Cum.
„ 308. *Terebra insignis*, Desh. Panama. Mus. Cum.
„ 428. *Spondylus Victoriæ*, Sby., pl. 49. fig. 8. Gulf of California. Mus. Cum.
„ 428. *Murex tæniatus*, Sby., pl. 49. fig. 3. Gulf of California. Mus. Cum.
1830 3.0. *Leda Taylori*, Hanl. Guatemala. Mus. Cum., Taylor.
„ 440. *Leda Hindsii*, Hanl. ? Gulf of Nicoya. Mus. Cum., Hanl., Metc.
„ 448–450. } Review of Deshayes' 'Monograph of the *Terebridæ*,' 1859, by Mr. Reeve. His synonyms are quoted under par. 62, 'Conch. Ic.'
1862 239 5 *Bursa fusco-costata*, Dkr. California, Mus. Cum. [No authority.] Like *B. bitubercularis*, Lam.

---

* Many of the names given to the shells in Wood's Suppl. were arbitrarily altered by Dr. Goodall, as the work passed through the press (teste Gray). However, if the first published, they will be allowed the right of precedence.

In the P. Z. S. 1861, pp. 145-181, is the first part of the long-expected "Review of the *Vermetidæ*," by Otto A. L. Mörch. The species of the West Coast are arranged as follows:—

Page.	Sp.	
1.51	4.	*Stephopoma pennatum*, Mörch, pl. 25. f. 3-8. } Realejo, on *Callop:sus*
152	..	*Stephopoma pennatum*, ?var. *bispinosa*, pl. 25.f.9,10. } and *Crucibulum*.
153	5.	*Siphonium (Dendropoma) megamastum*, Mörch, pl. 25. f. 12, 13. "?(California; burrowing in *Haliotis nodosus*, Rve." [Not a Californian species.]
	..	*Siphonium (Dendropoma) megamastum*, var. *centiquadra*, Mörch.
		" = *Aletes centiquadrus*, var. *imbricatus*, Maz. Cat. p. 302," Mörch [non Cpr.]. California, burrowing in *Haliotis splendens* [a strictly Californian species, not found on the Mexican coast].
154	6.	*Siphonium (Dendropoma) lituella*, Mörch. California; deeply imbedded in *Haliotis splendens*; Mus. Cum.
		? = *Stoa ammonitiformis*, M. de Serres.
		= *Spiroglyphus*, sp., Cpr., B. A. Report, p. 324. [Found on shells from Washington Ter. to Cape St. Lucas (also Socoro Is., *Xantus*); but it has not been observed on the Mexican or Central American coast.]
164	20.	*Siphonium margaritarum*, Val. Panama, *Val.*; Mazatlan, *Reigen*.
		" = *Aletes margaritarum*, Maz. Cat. p. 303," [teste Mörch, non Cpr.*].
177	30.	*Vermiculus pellucidus*, Brod. and Sby., pl. 25. f. 17-20.
..	..	Var. *a. planorboides* = *Serpula regularis*, Chenu. *Hab.?*—, on ?.*Margaritifera*. Mus. Cum.
..	..	Var. *aa. laquearis*. W. Columbia, *Cuming*.
178	..	Var. *β. cinnamomina*. W. Columbia, *Cuming*.
..	..	Var. *γ. volubilis*, Mörch, pl. 25. f. 18, 19. = *Vermetus eburneus*, Rve., = *V. lumbricalis*, Knight. *Hab.?*—. Mus. Cum.
..	..	Var. *δ. volubilis (adulta) picta*, Mörch, = *Verm. eburneus*, Maz. Cat. p. 304. W. Columbia, *Cuming*; Puntarenas, *Oersted*, Journ. Conch. viii. p. 30.
..	..	Var. *ε. crassa*, Mörch, = *Serp. Panamensis*, Chen. Ill. pl. 10. fig. 5 = *Vermiculus eburneus*, Mörch, Journ. Conch. viii. 30. Puntarenas, *Oersted*. "Fossil at Newburn, N.C.," *Nuttall* [teste Mörch].
179	..	Var. *ζ. tigrina*, Mörch. W. Columbia, *Cuming*.
..	..	Var. *η. castanea*, Mörch. On *Murex melanoleucus*, Mörch.
..	..	Operculum: W. Columbia, *Cuming*.
..	..	Var. 1, from var. *δ.* = *Vermetus Hindsii*, Gray, Add. Gen. fig. ?8, *a, b*. Puntarenas, *Oersted*.
180	..	Var. 2, *discifer*, from var. *δ*. Puntarenas, *Oersted*.
..	..	Var. 3, from var. *ε*. Pl. 25. f. 17.
		Var. 4, *subgranosa*, from var. *η*. Puntarenas, *Oersted*.
181	38.	*Vermiculus effusus*, Val., = " *Vermetus e.*, Val." Chen. Ill. pl. 5. fig. 4, *a-c.* = *Siphonium e.*, Chen. Man. fig. 2301. "Fig. 4 of Chen. † is from specimen figured in Voy. Ven. as *V. centiquadrus*."

In the second part of Mörch's "Review of the *Vermetidæ*," 1861, pp. 326-365, occur the following. A portion of the genus *Bivonia* is united to *Spiroglyphus*. *Petaloconchus*, *Aletes*, and part of *Bivonia* are united to *Vermetus*, Mörch (non auct.). The name *Aletes* appears to be used in a varietal sense, in no respect according with the subgenus as described by the author.

* I was perhaps wrong in referring the Mazatlan shells to Val.'s species; but if Mr. Mörch is right in his own determination, the Mazatlan synonymy and locality must be expunged. There was no evidence of a typical *Siphonium* when the Reigen Catalogue was published, nor have I seen such from the whole coast, unless th minute operculum *h*, Brit. Mus. Col., tablet 2537, be supposed the young. Mörch says, "the lid is unknown." The operculum of the similar Mazatlan species, on which the subgenus *Aletes* was founded, is described in Maz. Cat. p. 302.

† "Cpr.'s observations respecting Chenu's plates (Maz. Cat. p. 306, lin. 18) are in part erroneous, it being overlooked that Chenu has two plates marked ' V.' ;" note *, p. 337.

Page. Sp.

832 8. *Spiroglyphus albidus*, ?Cpr. Mazatlan, *Reigen.* Operculum *g* et ?*f*, Maz. Cat. p. 311.=*Bivonia albida*, Cpr., Maz. Cat. p. 307. Operc. *g* is without doubt of *Spiroglyphus*, and not of *Bivonia*, var. *indentata.* Operc. *f* is truly congeneric, and perhaps conspecific.

844 4. *Vermetus* (*Thylacodus*) *contortus*, Cpr.* Gulf Calif. Mus. Cum.

.. .. Var. *a. repens* (*Thylacodus*). Gulf Ca if., on *Margaritifera*, Mus. Cum. "This species is perhaps a state of *V.* (*Petaloconchus*) *macrophragma.*" [Mörch: non Cpr.]†

345 .. Var. β. *fuvosa* (*Thylacodus*). Calif., on *Crucibulum.* Mus. Cum.

.. .. Var. γ. *contortula* (*Thylacodus*). Gulf of California.

.. .. Forma 1. ? *Thylacodus contortus*, var. *indentata*, Cpr. "Corresponds to forma 1, *electrina*, of *Vermetus varians*, D'Orb."

.. .. Var. δ. *indentata* (*Vermetus*), [Mörch, non Cpr.]. Sonsonate, on *Spondylus limbatus*, Rve., non Sby. *Oersted.*

346 .. Var. ε. *corrodens* (*Vermetus*). Is. Sibo (?Quibo), *Spengler*, on *Purpura lineata.*

359 20. *Vermetus* (?? *Strebloceras*) *anellum*, Mörch. California, on *Haliotis tuberculatus*, Rve. [Not a Californian *Haliotis.* The diagnosis, however, exactly accords with a Californian shell, which is perhaps the young of *S. squamigerus.* It has no resemblance to *Strebloceras*, Cpr., P. Z. S. 1858, p. 440, which is a genuine Cæcid.]

360 21. *Vermetus* (*Macrophragma*) *macrophragma.* Mazatlan, &c.=*Petaloconchus m.*, Cpr. Realejo, *Oersted.*

362 24. *Vermetus* (*Aletes*) *centiquadrus*, Val. Puntarenas, *Oersted* + *V. effusus*, Val. (the same specimen).

.. .. Var. *a. maxima=V. Panamensis*, Chen. pl. 5. f. 1. Panama, *C. B. Ad.*; Mazatlan, *Melchers.*

.. .. Var. β. *Punctis impressis destituta*,= *V. Péronii*, Val.‡

363 .. Var. γ. *siphonata.* Puntarenas, *Oersted=V. Péronii*, Rouss.

.. .. Var. δ. *tulipa.* Gulf of California, on piece of black *Pinna*, Mus. Cum. [The *Pinna nigrina* is from the E. I.]= *V. tulipa*, Rouss.

.. .. Var. ε. *Bridgesii.* Panama, on *Margaritifera*, Mus. Cum.

The conclusion of the paper is in P. Z. S. 1862, pp. 54-83.

58 4. *Bivonia sutilis*, Mörch. Central America, on *Anomalocardia subimbricata*, Mus. Cum.

.. .. Var. *a. ?major.* On *Pinna*, probably Central America, Mus. Dunker.

.. .. Var. β. *triquetra.* Mazatlan, on valve of *Placunanomia*, Mus. Semper. Like *B. triquetra*, "var. *typica.*"

70 8. *Thylacodes cruciformis*, Mörch. California, on *Crucibulum* ?*umbrella*, Desh., var. Mus. Cum. Analogue of 7, *T. Rüsei*, Mörch, from the east coast.

.. .. Var. *a. lumbricella.* Voy. Ven. pl. 11. f. 2. California, crowded on *Margaritifera.* Mus. Cum.

.. .. Var. β. *erythosclera.* Cal., on young *Margaritifera.* Mus. Cum. Very like *Biv. Quoyi*, var. *variegata.* [This species is on shells from the Mexican, not the "Californian" fauna.]

76 16. *Thylacodes squamigera*, Cpr.,=*Aletes sq.*, Cpr., P.Z.S. 1856, p. 226. Sta. Barbara, *Nutt.* [*Serpulorbis*, not *Aletes*, teste *Cooper*].

* Mr. Mörch has not seen any laminæ inside, but, from the 3–5 spiral line on the columella, believes they will be found. The opercula supposed to belong to this species (Maz. Cat. p. 311) Mr. M. thinks more probably those of *Spiroglyphus albidus.* He states (erroneously) that the shell was not opened by the describer.

† Mörch supposes that *Bivonia contorta*, Cpr., may be the adult of *Petaloconchus macrophragma*, and that both may be forms of *Aletes centiquadrus.* The nuclear portions are, however, quite distinct, and the three shells appear, from beginning to end, as far removed as any ordinary Vermetids can be from each other.

‡ The writer doubts respecting this species, and thinks the shell on which it is parasitical to be a *Melo*, and not *Strombus galea*, simply because named after Péron, who did not visit this district.

Page. Sp.
76 16 Var. *a. pennata,*= *V. margaritacum,* Val. Ven. pl. 11. f. 2. (fig. min.),
        Cal. Mus. Cum. [Affiliated to the Californian species on supposi-
        titious evidence, and probably distinct. These appear to be from the
        tropical fauna.] Analogue of the W. Indian *T. decussatus,* Gmel.
78 21. ?*Thylacodes oryzata,* Mörch. Probably W. Central America, from the
        adhesions; but "China:" Mus. Cum.
.. .. Var. *a. annulata.* Panama. Mus. Cum.*

In P.Z.S. 1861, pp. 229–233, is given a "Catalogue of a Collection of Terrestrial and Fluviatile Molluscs, made by O. Salvin, Esq., M.A., in Guatemala·
by the Rev. H. B. Tristram." But few of the 49 species occur in Mexican
collections; none are identical with W. Indian species, except such as
are of universal occurrence in tropical America; and the 16 new species
show close generic affinities with the shells of the northern regions of S.
America. The shells have been identified from the Cumingian collection.
The new species are described, and some of them figured.

Page.	No.	Pl.	Fig.	
230	1	..	..	*Helix Ghiesbreghti,* Nyst. The largest *Helix* in the New World.
..	2	..	..	*Helix eximia,* Pfr.
..	3	..	..	*Helix Lalliana,* Pfr., var.
..	4	..	..	*Helix euryomphala,* Pfr. Closely allied to the S. American *H. laxata.*
..	5	..	..	*Helix coactiliata,* Fér.
..	6	..	..	*Bulimus Pazianus,* D'Orb.
..	7	..	..	*Bulimus Moricandi,* Pfr.
..	8	..	..	*Bulimus Honduratianus,* Pfr.
..	9	..	..	*Bulimus Dysoni,* Pfr.
..	10	26	8.	*Bulimus semipellucidus,* n. s. Allied to *B. discrepans,* Sby.
..	11	..	..	*Succinea ?putris,* Ln.
..	12	..	..	*Glandina Ghiesbreghti,* Pfr.
..	13	..	..	*Glandina Carminensis,* Morelet. Described from Costa Rica.
..	14	..	..	*Achatina,* sp. ind.
..	15	..	..	*Achatina octona,* Lam.
..	16	..	..	*Spiraxis Lattrei,* Pfr.
..	17	..	..	*Spiraxis Shuttleworthii,* Pfr.
231	18	..	..	*Spiraxis Cobanensis,* n. s.
..	19	..	..	*Spiraxis,* sp. ind.
..	20	..	..	*Leptinaria Emmelinæ,* n. s.
..	21	..	..	*Leptinaria Elisæ,* n. s.
..	22	..	..	*Cylindrella Ghiesbreghti,* Pfr
..	23	..	..	*Cylindrella Salpinx,* n. s.
..	24	..	..	*Physa Sowerbyana,* D'Orb.
..	25	..	..	*Physa purpurostoma,* n. s. Lake of Dueñas.
..	26	..	..	*Planorbis corpulentus,* Say.
232	27	..	..	*Planorbis tumidus,* Pfr. [Comp. *P. tumens,* Maz. Cat. 238.]
..	28	..	..	*Planorbis Wyldi,* n. sp. Lake of Dueñas.
..	29	..	..	*Planorbis Duenasianus,* n. s. Lake of Dueñas.
..	30	..	..	*Planorbis,* sp. nov., in Mus. Cum.
..	31	..	..	*Segmentina Donbilli,* n. s. Lake of Dueñas.
..	32	..	..	*Melampus fasciatus,* Chem. Salt-marshes on coast.
..	33	..	..	*Adamsiella Osberti,* n. s.

* The present posture of binomial nomenclature is well illustrated in this most elaborate paper, which few naturalists have professed to understand. The shell of which the
operculum-spine is figured in plate 25. f. 16, is quoted as "*Siphonium (Stoa) subcre-
natum,* v. *spinosa.*" The shell described in Maz. Cat. p. 307 is quoted as "*Vermetus
(Thylacodus) contortus,* var. γ. *contortula (Thylacodus),* forma 1, *Thylocodus (?) contortus,* var. *indentata,* Cpr." Perhaps the *sentences* of Klein and the early writers are
more easy to understand and remember. The *Chitonidæ* of Middendorff (v. First Report,
p. 214) are simple in comparison.

Page.	No.	Pl.	Fig.	
..	34	..	..	*Cistula trochlearis*, Pfr.
..	35	.,	..	*Chondropoma rubicundum*, Morelet.
..	36	..	..	*Megalomastoma simulacrum*, Morelet. Described from Costa Rica.
..	37	..	..	*Cyclophorus ponderosus*, Pfr.
..	38	..	..	*Cyclophorus translucidus*, Sby.
233	39	26	11.	*Macroceramus polystreptus*, n. s.
..	40	26	9, 10.	*Helicina Salvini*, n. s. Like *H. turbinata*, Wiegm. Mexico.
..	41	..	..	*Helicina amœna*, Pfr.
..	42	..	..	*Helicina Oweniana*, Pfr.
..	43	..	..	*Helicina merdigera*, Sallé. Described from Nicaragua.
..	44	..	..	*Helicina Lindeni*, Pfr.
..	45	..	..	*Helicina chryseis*, n. s. Mountain forests of Vera Paz.
..46,47,48.		..	..	*Paludinella*, 3 species apparently undescribed.
..	49	..	..	*Pachycheilus corvinus*, Morelet. Larger than in previously noted habitats.

The vol. for 1863 contains Dr. Baird's descriptions of new species from the Vancouver collections of Lord and Lyall, which will be tabulated, *infra*, par. 103; and the Review of Prof. Adams's Panama shells, which has already been quoted.

60. *Sowerby,* '*Conchological Illustrations,*' 1841.—The following are additional localities or synonyms:—

No.	Fig.	
2	46.	*Cardium Indicum* [is exotic; closely allied to *C. costatum*].
56	18.	*Cardium maculatum*, Sby. Cal., &c. = *C. maculosum*, Sby. (preoc).
90	..	*Murex imperialis*, Swains. Cal. = *M. pomum*, var. Gmel. [Perhaps distinct; may be the W. I. analogue of *bicolor*.]
91	38.	*Murex erythrostoma*, Swains. Acapulco. [?=*bicolor*, var.]
45	102.	*Cyprea albuginosa*, Gray Mexico, Ceylon. [The Ceylon shell is probably *poraria*, sp. 44.]
1	45.	*Erato scabriuscula*, Gray. Acapulco. = *Marginella cyprœola*, Sby.
62	40.	*Fissurella Lincolni*, Gray, MS. [An extremely fine specimen (supposed "unique ") of *Glyphis aspera*, Esch. Mr. Lincoln is also quoted for the " finest of the four known specimens " of *Lucapina crenulata*, sp. 19, f. 31, 38 : " Monterey."]
54		[Erase this line in the former Report, and substitute as follows :—]
55		*Bulimus unifasciatus*, Sby. Galapagos.

' *Thesaurus Conchyliorum,*' G. B. Sowerby, &c.   To the list in Rep. pp. 288, 289, may be added:—

Page.	Pl.	Fig.	
51	12	23.	*Pecten circularis*, Sby. Cal., St. Vincents. [The name may stand for the W. Indian shell, the Californian being *P. ventricosus*, jun.]
57	12	20, 21.	*Pecten latiauritus*, Conr. Cal. +" *P. mesotimeris*, Conr."
261	59	144.	*Tellina sincera*, Hanl. N.W. Coast America. [=Panama.]
769	165	36–38.	*Venerupis cylindracea*, Desh. Cal., = *Petricola Californica*, Conr., + *P. arcuata*, Desh., + *P. subglobosa*, Sby.
865	179	59–77.	*Cerithium ocellatum*, Brug. Gulf Cal., &c. = *C. irroratum* [C. B. Ad. (Gld. MS.) ; non] Gld. E. E., = *C. interruptum* [C. B. Ad. : non Mke, nec] Gld.

Sp.	Fig.	
47	43, 44.	*Conus** *interruptus*, Mawe, Wood. [Slender, coronated sp.] non Br. and Sby. *Hab.* ?—

---

* Mr. Sowerby remarks, " As the collector's great object is to *know* the shells, I have preferred, in most cases, giving the species as they stand, stating the alleged differences, and leaving the final decision to individual taste."   He further states, with regard to some groups, that " the characters of the shells are very uncertain, and the intentions of the authors still more so."   The names, references, and localities are given on lists to face the plates, and the diagnoses separately, with a copious index.   An attempt also is made to

Sp.   Fig.

64   80. *Conus tiaratus*, Brod. Galapagos.

79 128,120. *Conus puncticulatus*, Brug. Salango, St. Elena, W. Col., *Cuming*.

‥   130. *Conus puncticulatus*, var., = *papillosus*, Kien.

‥   391. *Conus puncticulatus*. [Mazatlan.]

‥   392. *Conus puncticulatus*, var., = *pustulosus*, Kien. : ? + *Mauritianus*, Lam.

.33   190. *Conus virgatus*, Rve., = *zebra*, Sby., non Lam. [Resembles *regularis* var.] Salango, W. Col., *Cuming*.

‥   *Conus virgatus*, var., = *Lorenzianus*, Rve., non Chem.

‥   193. *Conus virgatus*, var., = *Cumingii*.

106   192. *Conus scalaris*, Val., = *gradatus*, Rve. Salango, W. Col., *Cuming*.

127   194. *Conus incurvus*, Brod. [Resembles specimens from La Paz.] Monte Christi, W. Col., *Cuming*.

180 285,402. *Conus Ximenes*, Gray, = *interruptus*, Brod., non Mawe. [Like *puncticulatus*, var.] Mazatlan, W. Columbia, *Cuming*.

157   324. *Conus perplexus*, Sby. Gulf Cal., W. Col., *Cuming*

84   384. *Conus arcuatus*, Br. and Sby. Mazatlan, Pacific [?].

15 26–28. *Fissurella Mexicana*, Sby. Real Llejos, Mexico. } [Both localities

‥   78. *Fissurella Mexicana*, Sby. Porto Praya. } are probably incorrect; it belongs to the Chilian fauna.]

41 46, 47. *Fissurella rugosa*, Sby. W. Indies [= W. Mexico].

32 88, 89. *Fissurella alba*, Cpr. [Gulf of] California.

65 64, 65. *Fissurella nigrocincta*, Cpr. [Gulf of] California.

56   67. *Fissurella tenebrosa*, Sby., jun. [?Gulf of] California. Like the last.

54   80. *Fissurella obscura*, Sby Real Llejos, *Cum*. ["Gal." in P.Z.S. 1834.]

68 154–156. *Fissurella excelsa*, Rve., + *F. alta*, C. B. Ad.

86   123. *Fissurella Panamensis*, Sby. "In Conch. Ill., this very distinct shell is united to that since named *F. excelsa*, Rve."

115 187–189. *Fissurella cancellata*, Soland. St. Vincent's, Honduras Bay, Guadaloup, California. [No authority for the latter.]

7 12, 13. *Harpa Rivoliana*, Less., = *H. crenata*, Swains. Acapulco.

1860.

2   57. *Dentalium pretiosum*, Nutt. " = *striolatum*, Stn. Massachusetts. Less curved and tapering near apex than *D. entale*, more cylindrical throughout, but a doubtful species." [The type-specimens are not striated.] California.

43   10. *Dentalium hexagonum*, Gld. N. America: China, Singapore.

42   34. *Dentalium pseudosexagonum*, Desh. Masbate, Philippines : W. Columbia.

8   41. *Dentalium splendidum*, Sby. Xipixapi, W. Col.

29   32. *Dentalium liratum*, Cpr. "Malgattem." [Maz. Cat. 244.]

48   31. *Dentalium quadrangulare*, Sby. Xipixapi, W. Col. [Like *tetragonum*, but striated, and much smaller.]

49 21, 22. *Dentalium tetragonum*, Sby. W. Col. [Young shell square, adult round.]

In the very elaborate monograph of the *Nuculidæ*, by S. Hanley, Esq., the following species, quoted as from the W. Coast, are minutely described :—

2   33. *Leda Sowerbiana*, D'Orb. Xipixapi.
        = *N. elongata*, Val.
        = *N. lanceolata*, G. Sby., non J. Sby., nec Lam.

7   35. *Leda Taylori*, Hanl., = *N. lanceolata*, Lam., non G. nec J. Sby. Guatemala. (P. Z. S. 1860, p. 370.)

29 70–72. *Leda Elenensis*, Sby. Panama.

33   90. *Leda eburnea*, Sby., = *lyrata*, Hds. Panama : Bay of Caraccas.

classify the forms according to their natural affinities. It is rarely that monographers and artists take such laudable pains to supply the wants of students. In the monograph of *Galeomma* and *Scintilla*, however, the locality-marks have not been observed to a single species, except the "British *G. Turtoni*" and its "Philippine analogue, *G. macroschisma*, Desh." This is the more remarkable, as most of the species were described by Desh., with localities, in P. Z. S. 1855, pp. 167–181.

In the 'Malacological and Conchological Magazine,' by G. B. Sowerby, London, 1838, is a monograph of Leach's genus *Margarita*. The following probably belong to the N. W. Coast, and are figured in the Conch. Ill. :—

Page.
25. *Margarita striata*, Brod. and Sby. Boreal Ocean.
26. *Margarita undu'ata*, Sby. Arctic Ocean.
26. *Margarita costellata*, Sby. [Non Brit. Mus. Col. = *M. pupilla*, Gld.; differs in having the interspaces of the spiral ribs decussated. Arctic Ocean.]
26. *Margarita acuminata*, Sby. Arctic Ocean.
30. *Aphrodite columba*, Lea, = *Cardium Grœnlandicum*.

Several West Coast species were named and figured in the elder Sowerby's 'Genera of Recent and Fossil Shells,' London, 1820–1824; a work of singular merit for its time, but left unfinished*. The stock was purchased by a dealer, with a view to completion; but newer works have occupied its place, and the valuable plates and text remain useless in his hands. As no dates appear in the bound copy of the work, it cannot be stated whether the species here named by Mr. Sowerby had been before published. The loss of the original work has been in some respects supplied by the completion of the extremely similar 'Conchologia Systematica,' by L. Reeve, vol. i. 1841, vol. ii. 1842. It might almost be considered a second edition of the 'Genera,' of which some of the plates occur in the quarto form. References are here given to the species reproduced from Sowerby's unfinished work, which is often quoted by Mr. Reeve according to the "Numbers" in which it appeared:—

Rve. Fig.	Sby. Fig.	Sowerby's Genera.
2.	2.	*Cumingia trigonularis*.
3.	3.	*Cumingia lamellosa*.
4.	4.	*Cumingia coarctata*.
1.	1.	*Tellina opercularis* [" = *T. operculata*, Gmel., = *T. rufescens*, Chem.," Rve.].
1.	1.	*Lucina punctata* [Linn., " = *Lentilaria p.*, Schum." Rve. C. S.].
2.	2,5.	*Venus subrugosa*.
5.	7.	*Venus gnidia*.
2.	2.	*Cytherea planulata*.
3.	3.	*Cytherea aurantiaca*.
4.	4 [non 3].	*Lithodomus caudigerus* [Lam., = *aristatus*, Dillw.].
3.	3.	[Appears to represent *attenuatus*, Desh.]
6.	6.	*Modiola semifusca* [inside view; exactly accords with *Braziliensis*, Maz. Cat., but is not Lamarck's species, teste Hanl.].
2.	2.	*Lima squamosa* [Lam.].
2.	2.	*Ostrea Virginica* [Lam.].
1.	1.	*Placunanomia Cumingii*. "Brought by Mr. Henry Cuming from the Gulf of Dulce, in Costa Rico."
1.	1.	*Lottia gigantea*, Gray. Genus named in Phil. Trans. = *Patelloides*, Quoy and Gaim. ?South America. [The U. S. E. E. specimens were labelled "Valparaiso." It comes to us from many parts of the world, but is only known to live in Middle and Lower California. = *Tecturella grandis*, Cpr., B. A. Rep. 1861, p. 137.
	3.	*Siphonaria Tristensis*. [The figure is singularly like the Vancouver species, *S. thersites*.]
2.	2.	*Crepidula onyx*.
4.	4.	*Crepidula aculeata* : " = *P. auricula*, Gmel."
	3.	*Calyptrœa ?extinctorium*. [Sby., non Lam. The non-pitted form of *imbricata*.]
	4.	*Calyptrœa ?pinosa*.

* The last Part (no. 34) appeared "March 31, 1831," many years after the previous issues; teste Hanl.

Rve.	Shy.
Fig.	Fig. Sowerby's Genera.

5. *Calyptræa imbricata.* [The pitted form. Appears in C. S., f. 1, as "*C. rugosa*, Less."]

7. *Calyptræa ?spinosa*, var. [The flat, smooth form of *spinosa*. Appears in C. S., fig. 4, as "*C. cinerea*, Rve., P. Z. S. 1842," p. 50. On a log of wood floating off Cape Horn.]

2. *Bulla virescens.*

4.   1. *Nerita ornata* [= *scabricosta*, Lam.].
2,3.   2, 3. *Litorina pulchra*, = *Turbo p.*, Swains.
4.   4. *Litorina varia.* Panama.
5.   5. *Cerithium varicosum.*
9.   9. *Cerithium Pacificum.* [Closely resembles *Potamis ebeninus*.]
1.   1. *Fasciolaria aurantiaca* [with operc. (non Lam.) = *F. princeps*, Lam., Rve.].
     5. *Murex phyllopterus* and operc. [Appears = *Cerostoma foliatum.* The operc. seems to have been rubbed outside.]
1.   1. *Columbella strombiformis*, Lam.
2.   2. *Columbella labiosa.* "California" [*i. e.*, Panama, &c.].
1.   1. *Purpura patula* [Linn. "= *Perdicca nodosa*, Petiver, = *Cymbium tuberosum patulum*, Martini." Rve. C. S.].
C.   6. *Purpura planospirata.*
9.*   9. *Purpura callosa* [= *Cuma tectum*].
3.   3. *Monoceros lugubre* [= *cymatum*, Tank. Cat.].
4.   4. *Monoceros cingulatum* [Lam.: *Leucozonia*].
1.   1. *Trichotropis bicarinata*, and [Nassoid] operculum.
1.   1. *Oliva porphyria* [Linn., "= *Cylinder porphyreticus*, D'Arg., = *Castra Turcica*, Martini." Rve. C. S.].
     5. *Cypræa pustulata* [Lam.].

The following additional West Coast species, figured in the 'Conch. Syst.,' may be quoted for their synonymy. The authorities for all the species are given, but no localities :—

Pl.	Fig.	
26	1.	*Solecurtus Dombeyi*, Lam. [appears intermediate between *S. Dombeyi*, Mus. Cum., and *S. ambiguus*, Lam.].
229	7.	*Turbo squamiger*, Rve. P. Z. S. 1842, p. 186 [without locality. 'Galapagos, *Cuming*,' in Conch. Ic. Also Acapulco, *Jewett*, &c.].
229	2.	*Turbinellus acuminatus*, Wood, Kien. [closely resembles *Latirus castaneus*].
263	3.	*Buccinum elegans*, Rve., P. Z. S. 1842, from Hinds's Col. [is the southern, highly developed form of *B. fossatum*, Gld. The name is preoccupied by a Touraine fossil, *B. elegans*, Duj., in Desh. An. s. Vert. x. p. 219, no. 22. As Rve.'s species is a *Nassa*, and there is another *Buc. elegans*, Kien., Coq. Viv. p. 56, pl. 24. f. 97, = *Nassa e.*, Rve. Conch. Ic., it will save confusion to allow Gld.'s later name to stand].
268	5,6.	*Buccinum serratum*, Dufr., = *Nassa Northiæ*, Gray [= *Northia pristis*, Desh.].

62. Reeve, '*Conchologia Iconica.*'—The following corrections should be made in the abstract, Rep. pp. 289-293.

20. [*Semele flavicans* should be *flavescens*, et passim.]
33. *Siphonaria amara* [is a Sandwich Is. species, quite distinct from *C. lecanium*].
38. *Patella clypeaster* [is a S. American species, having no connexion with *A. patina*, or with Monterey].
60. *Patella cinis* [= *A. pelta*, not *patina*, var.].
67. *Patella vespertina.* [*P. stipulata*, sp. 117, is probably a var. of this species.]
69. *Patella torcuma* ["var." in Mus. Cum., "Mazatlan," probably = *hvescens*. No shell of this (N. Zealand) type has been found on the coast by any of the American collectors].

---

* Sowerby's (correct) name appears on Reeve's plate; but in the text of C. S., f. 9 is called "a species of *Turbinellus* inserted inadvertently."

81. *Patella Nuttalliana.* [Mus. Cum.,= *A. pelta*, typical. The figure looks more like *patina.*]

140. *Patella mamillata*, Nutt. [non Esch., is an elevated, stunted form of the black ?var. of *scabra*, Nutt. The name being preoccupied, this distinct form may stand as *limatula*).

64. *Fissurella densiclathrata* [is distinct from *G. aspera.* Sta. Barbara, *Jewett*].

57. *Turbo marginatus* [Rve., non] "Nutt." [is a Pacific species, quoted by Messrs. Adams as the *Collonia marginata* of Gray; but that is a Grignon fossil, olim *Delphinula* (teste type in Brit. Mus.). The Nuttallian shell, published in Jay's Cat., was described by A. Ad. as *Chlorostoma funebrale* = *Chl. mœstum*, auct. (non Jonas, the true *T. mœstus* being S. American, teste A. Ad. and Mus. Cum.)].

39. *Cypræa onyx* [is the E. Indian, *C. spadicea* the similar S. Diegan species].

The following species, either quoted from the W. Coast, or known to inhabit it, or connected with it by synonymy, have been observed in Reeve's 'Conch. Ic.' since the date of the last Report. The number of the species also refers to the figure. For the remarks enclosed in [ ] the writer of this Report, here as elsewhere, is alone responsible.

56. *Fusus turbinelloides*, Rve., Jan. 1848. ?Africa, Mus. Cum. [= *Siphonalia pallida*, Br. and Sby.; spines somewhat angular].

62. *Fusus cancellatus*, Lam. "Unalaska, Kamtschatka, Mus. Cum." [Doubtless the origin of the prevalent locality-error].

70. *Fusus Novæ-Hollandiæ*, Rve., Jan. 1848. N. Hol., *Metcalfe.* [As Mr. Metcalfe gave numerous West Coast shells to Brit. Mus. under locality "N.H.," this shell also was probably from W. Mexico,= *F. Dupetithouarsii*, Kien.]

91. *Fusus Gunneri*, Lov., (*Tritonium*), Ind. Suec. p. 12. Greenland. [= *Trophon multicostatus*, Esch. The fig. should be 90, *b*; f. 91 = *Bamffius.*]

52. *Cardium pseudofossile*, Rve. "P. Z. S. 1844." *Hab.?*— [Not found in P. Z. S.,= *C. Californiense*, Desh., 1839, non *C. Californianum*, Conr., 1837. This is the Eastern form; the Californian ?var.= *C. blandum*, Gld.]

67. *Buccinum modificatum*, Rve., Dec. 1845. *Hab.?*— [Agrees sufficiently well with worn specimens from La Paz, Mus. Smiths.,= *Siphonalia*, closely allied to *pallida.*]

62. *Buccinum dirum*, Rve., Dec. 1846. *Hab.?*— Mus. Cum. [Worn specimen of *Chrysodomus Sitchensis*, Midd., 1849,= *F. incisus*, Gld., May 1849.]

110. *Buccinum corrugatum*, Rve., Feb. 1847. *Hab.?*— [" *Truncaria*," Cuming, MS. " *Pisania*," H. Adams. Vancouver, most abundant.]

2. *Sanguinolaria ovalis*, Rve., March 1857. Cent. Am. [?= *S. miniata*, jun. 3. *S. tellinoides*, A. Ad., is the same, adolescent; 5. *S. purpurea*, Desh., adult.]

4. *Psammobia maxima*, Desh., P. Z. S. 1854, p. 317. Panama. [Closely resembling *Ps. rubroradiata*, Nutt. Puget Sound.]

10. *Mytilus ralliopunctatus*, Dkr. Cal. and Mazatlan. [No authority for Cal.]

41. *Mytilus bifurcatus*, Coar., J. A. N. S. Phil. *Hab.?* [Conr. assigns his Nuttallian species to California; but it is the common Sandw. Is. species, teste Pse. The Californian shell, with the same sculpture, is a *Septifer*, and is the *S. bifurcatus* of Mus. Cum.]

44. *Mytilus Sallei (Dreissina)*, Recl. Central America. [? On which slope.]

52. *Mytilus Cumingianus*, Recl. Panama. [*Septifer.*]

60. *Mytilus glomeratus*, Gld. *Hab.?*—* [Gould's species is from California, but the name is attached to a very different shell in Mus. Cum.]

* Several species occur in the recent monographs without locality, which are well known to inhabit the W. Coast. This is partly due to the writer not thinking it necessary to refer to published books for information, and partly to the changes which have of late years been made in the principal authority, viz. the Cumingian collection. By the redistribution of species into the modern genera, the student is greatly aided in his search for special forms; but, for the sake of uniformity, the autograph labels of collectors or describers of species are generally rejected, the names being either in the handwriting of the clerk or from the printed index in the monograph, and representing only the judgment of the latest worker, which may or may not be correct. Synonyms, whether real

11. *Modiola capax*, Conr. Galapagos, *Cuming*. [Lower] California, *Nuttall*. Mazatlan, *Carpenter*. [*Reigen* is the authority for the shells described in the Maz. Cat., not Cpr.]

17. *Modiola Braziliensis*, Chem. "Brazil." [At f. 31, which appears the true Brazilian shell, we are informed that this specimen is a "variety from Guayaquil."]

.. *Modiola nitens*, "Cpr. Cat. Reigen Col. Brit. Mus. California." [The shell was erroneously described as from "California" in P. Z. S., and does not appear in the Reigen Mazatlan Cat. : = *M. subpurpureus*, Mus. Cum.]

5. *Lithodomus cinnamominus*, Chem. Philippine Is. and St. Thomas, W. I. [= *L. cinnamomeus*, Maz. Cat. 177. Probably an *Adula*.]

8. *Lithodomus Cumingianus*, Dkr., MS. "North Australia and Mazatlan." [The species is *figured* from the Mazatlan specimen, which may probably be the adult form of *L. calyculatus*, Cpr.* The cup is not distinct, but shows a tendency to the peculiar formation described in Maz. Cat. no. 174. Rve.'s diagnosis, however, appears written from Dkr.'s Australian specimens, so labelled in Mus. Cum.—a very distinct species, without incrustations. The name was given by Mr. Cuming to a large Chilian species brought by the U. S. Expl. Exp.]

12. *Lithodomus Gruneri*, Phil. MS. in Mus. Cum. "N. Zealand." [The species = *L. falcatus*, G.d., and is certainly from California, where it is found in the rocks with *Pholadidea penita*.]

13. *Lithodomus teres*, Phil. "Mazatlan." [The specimens in Mus. Cum. are labelled "Cagayan, Phil."]

14. *Lithodomus coarctata*, Dkr. Galapagos, *Cuming*. [= *Crenella c.*, Maz. Cat. 172.]

16. *Lithodomus caudigerus*, Lam. "West Indies" [without authority]. "The calcareous incrustation produced beyond the ant. extremity is no specific characteristic." [*Vide* reasons for contrary opinion, Maz. Cat. no. 176: = *L. aristatus*. Dr. Stimpson has seen *Lithophagus* arranging its peculiar incrustation with its foot.]

24. *Lithodomus pessulatus*, Rve. (Oct. 1857). *Hab.* ?— [The unique sp. figured is labelled "Mazatlan" in Mus. Cum. It resembles *plumula*, with ventral transverse rugæ.]

26. *Lithodomus subula*, Rve. *Hab.* ?— [= *L. plumula*, var.]

6. *Avicula Cumingii*, Rve., March 1857. "Ld. Hood's Is., Pacific Ocean, attached to rocks, 10 fms., *Cuming*." [? = *Margaritiphora fimbriata*, Dkr., var.]

9. *Avicula barbata*, Rve. Panama, under stones at low water, *Cuming*. [= *M. fimbriata*, Dkr., = *M. Mazatlanica*, Hanl.] "Differs from *Cumingii* in regular sequence of scales, developed only at margin, and yellowish tone of colour."

67. *Avicula heteroptera*, Lam. N. Holland. "= *A. sterna*, Gld." [Gould's species is from Gulf Cal.; but in Mus. Cum. it is marked inside "*semisagitta*."]

4. *Placunanomia foliata*, Brod. Is. Muerte, Bay Guayaquil. "May = *echinata*, W. I., but has very much larger orifice."

7. *Placunanomia macroschisma*, Desh. "Onalaska, *Cuming*" [who never was there]. Kamtschatka, *Desh*. [Vancouver district, abundant.]

7. *Thracia plicata*, Desh. "Mr. Cuming has specimens from California and St. Thomas, W. I." [Cape St. Lucas, *Xantus*.]

Melania. [Various species are described from "Central America," &c., which

---

or supposed, are rejected altogether. Thus shells sent to Mr. Cuming, with authentic name and locality attached, may appear soon after without any, or with erroneous, quotation. The error is rendered graver by appearing with the weighty authority of "Mus. Cum."

* The species described in the Brit. Mus. Cat. seldom appear in the monographs, unless there happen to be a specimen in Mus. Cum. Some of the monographers often content themselves with figuring the shells that come most easily to hand; and do not seem to consider it a part of their work to pass judgment on previously described species, or to concern themselves with what are small or difficult.

may or may not belong to the Pacific slope. They should be studied in connexion with U. S. forms, but are not here tabulated.]

50. *Melania Buschiana*, Rve. "California." [No authority. Very like the young of *M. scipio*, Gld.]

367. *Melania nigrina*, Lea, MS. in Mus. Cum. "Shasta, California."

68. *Cancellaria funiculata*, Hds., = *C. lyrata*, Ad. and Rve. Gulf Magdalena.

56. *Litorina irrorata*, Say. "Sitcha." [The "Sitcha" shell is *L. modesta*, Phil. Say's species is the well-known form from the Gulf of Mexico.]

5. *Terebra strigata*, Sby., +*elongata*, Wood., = *flammea*, Less., =*zebra*, Kien. "Panama, Galapagos, and Philippines, *Cuming*; Moluccas, &c." [Painting in stripes.]

10. *Terebra robusta*, Hds. Panama, &c. [= *T. Loroisi*, Guér., teste Rve. P. Z. S. 1860, p. 450. Painting splashed.]

12. *Terebra variegata*, Gray. "Mouth of the Gambia, Senegal, Mazatlan, Columbia. It is well known to those who have studied the geographical distribution of animal life, that the fauna of the West African seas, north of Sierra Leone, is in part identical with the fauna of the seas of California and the W. Indies; and geologists, among whom was the late Prof. E. Forbes, have laboured, not unsuccessfully, to account for this phenomenon." [*Vide* Maz. Cat. p. 157, B. A. Rep. p. 365. In the present instance, however, there will be more than one opinion as to the identity of the species here quoted.]+ *T. africana*, Gray, + *T. Hupei*, Lorois, + *T. intertincta*, Hds., + *T. marginata*, Desh., + *T. albocincta*, Cpr., + *T. Hindsii*, Cpr., + *T. subnodosa*, Cpr.

72. *Terebra armillata*, Hds. "Panama, Galapagos. Somewhat doubtful whether this is not a var. of *T. variegata*." [If the others are, probably this is. Those species of Hinds, which Mr. Reeve has not altered, are not here repeated.]

32. *Terebra dislocata* [as *Cerithium*], Say. "Southern U. S. and California." [No authority given for Cal.]

34. *Terebra rudis*, Gray, " = *M. rufocinerea*, Cpr. S. Carolina, *Jay*. Somewhat doubtful whether this is not a var. of *dislocata*." [The *T. rufocinerea* is one of the difficult Mazatlan shells, and should share the fate of *T. Hindsii* and *T. subnodosa*.]

35. *Terebra cinerea*, Born. "W. Africa, *Hennah*; Japan, *Hds.*; Philippines, *Cuming*; W. I., *C. B. Adams*; Mazatlan, *Cpr.*" [i. e. *Reigen*. The same remarks apply to this group as to *variegata*, &c.]+ *T. castanea*, Kien., non Hds., + *T. laurina*, Hds., + *T. luctuosa*, Hds., + *T. stylata*, Hds., + *T. Jamaicensis*, C. B. Ad.

40. *Terebra aspera*, Hds., + *T. Petiveriana*, Desh. Panama, S. A., *Cuming*, *Bridges*.

2. *Calyptræa tortilis*, Rve. Galapagos, *Cuming*.

8. *Calyptræa alveolata*, A. Ad., MS. Galapagos, *Cuming*.

4. *Crepidula excavata*, Brod. Chili [?], *Cuming*.

6. *Crepidula nautiloides**, Less., MS. in Mus. Cum. "New York." [= *C. dilatata.*]

8. *Crepidula marginalis*, Brod. Panama, *Cuming*. [V. Maz. Cat. p. 292, note.]

10. *Crepidula rugosa*, Nutt. Upper Cal. [An accidentally ribbed specimen, figured from Mus. Taylor.]

11. *Crepidula fimbriata*, Rve. (June 1859). Vancouver's Straits. [This is to *naricelloides*, Nutt., no. 97, as *Lessonii* is to *squama*; simply an accidentally frilled var.]

12. *Crepidula adunca*, Sby. [Not] Panama. = *C. solida*, Hds., =*rostriformis*, Gld. [This is the northern species from Vancouver and Cal., and is not] =*uncata*, Mke.

13. *Crepidula arenata*, Brod. St. Elena (not Helena, *Desh.*), *Cuming*.

22. *Crepidula aculeata*, Gmel. Lobos Is., Peru, *Cuming*; California, *Nutt.*, *Cpr.* [i. e. Mazatlan, *Reigen*]; Honduras, *Dyson*; Sandw. Is., Austr., Kur-

---

* Several S. American forms are here quoted for the synonymy; because in *Calyptraidæ* the species often have a wide range, and should be studied in connexion with their neighbours.

rachee, mouth of Indus. + *C. hystryx*, Brod.,+ *C. echinus*, Brod ,+ *C. Californica*, Nutt.

24. *Crepidula rostrata*, C. B. Ad. Panama. [= *C. uncata*, Mke., nom. prior. This tropical form presents distinctive marks.]

28. *Crepidula exuviata*, Nutt. Monterey. [= *C. explanata*, Gld.,= *C. perforans*, Val. An abnormal form of *C. naricelloides*, Nutt.: *C. nummaria*, Gld., is the opposite extreme.]

29. *Crepidula bilobata*, Gray [i. e. Cpr.], MS. in Mus. Cum. [= *C. dorsata*, Brod. *Vide* Maz. Cat. no. 336, where the origin of the MS. name would have been found explained. It appears to be principally a northern species = *C. lingulata*, Gld.]

30. .*Crepidula lirata*, Rve. [Gulf of] California. [Intermediate form betwe.n *C. incurva* and *C. onyx*, described in Maz. Cat. p. 277.]

2. *Crucibulum scutellatum*, Gray. "= *C. rugosa*, Less.,= *C. imbricata*, Sby., non Brod." Payta, *Less.*; Punta St. Elena, *Cuming.* [*Vide* Maz. Cat. no. 343.]

4. *Crucibulum rugosum*, "Desh., non Less.,= *C. lignaria*, Brod., ?var. = *C. gemmacea*, Val." Island of Chiloë, *Cuming.* [*Vide* Maz. Cat. p. 290.]

5. *Crucibulum ferrugineum*, Rve. Bay of Conception, Chili, *Cuming.* [= *C. quiriquina*, Less., D'Orb., = *C. Byronensis*, Gray, in Brit. Mus. Like a rough degraded form of *C. spinosum.*]

6. *Crucibulum umbrella*, Desh.= *C. rudis*, Brod. Panama and Real Llejos.

8. 　　" 　　*corrugatum*, Cpr. "Cal." [Mazatlan, *Jewett*, P. Z. S. 1856, p. 204.]

9. 　　" 　　*imbricatum*, Brod. Panama. [= *C. imbricatum*, Sby.,= *C. scutellatum*, Gray, no. 2, var.]

10. *Crucibulum spinosum*, Sby. Seas of Central America. [Extends northwards to California; southwards it degenerates into *C. quiriquina.*]= *C. peziza*, Gray,+ *C. hispida*, Brod.,+ *C. maculata*, Brod.,+ *C. tubifera*, Less.,+ *C. cinerea*, Rve.

11. *Crucibulum pectinatum*, Cpr., P. Z. S. 1856, p. 168. Peru. [Panama, *Jewett.*]

17. 　　" 　　*auritum*, Rve.,= *C. striata*, Brod., non Say. Valparaiso, *Cuming.* [Passes into *Galerus.*]

21. *Crucibulum serratum*, Brod. Real Llejos and Muerte, *Cuming.* [Like young of *C. pectinatum*; nearly transparent; white, with purple ray.]

22. *Crucibulum sordidum*, Brod.,+ *C. unguis*, Brod. Valparaiso and Panama, *Cuming.* [= *Galerus*; v. Maz. Cat. p. 292, note. The author distributes the species of this genus between *Trochita* and *Crucibulum.*]

4. *Trochita aspera* [Rve. as of] C. B. Ad. Panama. [The small var. of *Galerus conicus.* Probably = *C. aspersa*, C. B. Ad., no. 331.]

7. *Trochita subreflexa*, Cpr., MS. in Mus. Cum. Gulf of California. [= *Galerus subreflexus*, Cpr. in P. Z. S. 1855, p. 233.]

9. *Trochita corrugata* [?cujus. Comp. *Calyptræa corrugata*, Brod.]. Callao, *Cuming.*

8. *Trochita spirata*, Fbs. "?= *P. trochiformis*, Chem." Gulf California. [*Vide* anteà, p. 542.]

10. *Trochita solida* [?Rve.]. Conchagua, Mus. Cum. [?= *Galerus mamillaris.*]

11. *Perna anomioides*, Rve. March 1858. California, Mus. Cum. [No authority; appears= *P. costellata*, Conr., Sandwich Islands.]

13. *Perna Californica* [Rve., non] Conr. California, *Conr.* [i. e. *Nutt.*] Honduras, *Dyson.* "Distinguished by the *Pedum*-like form and clouded, livid purple colouring. [This is the well-known large flat West Indian species; not known in California.]

3. *Umbrella ovalis*, Cpr. Mouth of Chiriqui River, Bay of Panama, [not] *Cuming* [but *Bridges.* The species was also found at Cape St. Lucas by *Xantus.*]

6. *Ianthina fragilis*, Lam.,= *I. striulata*, Cpr. West Indies, Mazatlan, California. [*Vide* Maz. Cat. no. 242: non *I. striolata*, Ad. and Rve.]

19. *Ianthina decollata*, Cpr. Probably= *I. globosa*, var. [Maz. Cat. no. 243. Of the two Maz. forms, provisionally named, this appears the least entitled to specific rank.]

40. *Columbella Bridgesii*, Rve. April 1858. Panama, *Bridges.* [Appears the small var. of *C. major.*]

43. .*Columbella Boivini* [= *Boivinii*, Kien.]. Gulf Nicoya, *Hinds.*

46. *Columbella acicula*, Rve.   California.   [No authority.]
56. *Columbella encaustica*, Rve.   Gulf California, *Lieut. Shipley*, Mus. **Cum.**
57. *Columbella vexillum*, Rve.   Gulf California.   [No authority.]
62. *Columbella cribraria*, Quoy and Gaim. [i. e. Lam.] = *C. guttata*, Sby. **Panama,**
    common under stones, *Cuming.*   [No other localities given.   V. *Nitidella cribraria*, Maz. Cat. no. 613.]
72. *Columbella electroides*, Rve.   Bay of Guayaquil.
74. *Columbella Pacifica*, Gask.   Galapagos.
109. *Columbella pusilla*, Sby.   Island of St. Vincent, W. I.   "= *Nitidella Gouldii*, Cpr."   [The *Nitidella* is a distinct Upper Californian species.]
120. *Columbella lactea*, Rve.   Gulf Calif., *Mr. Babb, R.N.*   [A *Nitidella*, so transparent that the axis can be seen throughout.]
122. *Columbella Sta-Barbarensis*, Cpr.   Sta. Barbara.   "Not merely faintly striated, teste Cpr., but unusually grooved."   [Described from a worn specimen in Jewett's Col., and named to mark a more northern limit to the genus than had been assigned by Forbes. The label was probably incorrect, as the shell lives in the tropical fauna, C. S. Lucas, *Xantus*: Acapulco, *Newberry*: Guacomayo, Mus. Smiths. The name (as expressing error) should therefore be altered to *C. Reevei*, Cpr.]
123. *Columbella spadicea*, Phil., MS. in Mus. Cum.   Mazatlan.   [Described by Phil. in Zeit. f. Mal. 1846: B. A. Rep. p. 225.]
130. *Columbella venusta*, Rve.   [Mazatlan, *E. Philippi.*] = *C. tæniata*, Phil. [in Zeit. f. Mal. 1846], not Ad. and Rve., [Voy. Samar. 1850; therefore Phil. has precedence. ?= *Anachis Gaskoinei*, Maz. Cat. no. 652. The Samarang shell is probably a *Nitidella*.]
132. *Columbella sulcosa*, Sby   Annaa and Ld. Hood's Islands *.   *Cuming.*
135. *Columbella Gouldii*, Agass., MS. in Mus. Cum., Nov. 1858.   [= *Amycla Gouldiana*, Agass., Atlantic; non *Nitidella Gouldii*, Cpr.]
142. *Columbella uncinata*, Sby.   Is. Muerte, Bay Guayaquil.   [Acapulco, *Jewett.*]
165. *Columbella Californica*, Rve.   April 1859.   California.   [No authority. Like *Anachis lirata*.]
176. *Columbella rorida*, Rve.   Lord Hood's Island *, *Cuming.*   [Transparent, glossy, with necklace of opake white dots.]
Genus *Meta* [= *Conella*, Swains, eliminated by Rve. from *Columbella*; but *Anachis, Strombina, Amycla* (pars), and *Nitidella*, which do not even belong to the same family, if the opercula are to be trusted, are left in the old place. Of the six species, the author only knew the locality for one], *M. Dupontiæ*, Kien.—Ichaboe, South Africa; [but that of] *M. ovuloides*, "C. B. Ad., MS." [is shown by his published works to be Jamaica; and the following are from the West Coast].
3. *Meta cedonulli*, Rve.   [La Paz, Mus. Smiths.; C. S. Lucas, *Xantus*; Panama, *Jewett.*]
4. *Meta coniformis*, Sby.   [? Panama, *Jewett.*]
24. *Ziziphinus luridus*, Nutt., MS. in Mus. Cum.   California.   [Is not known from the American coast; comp. Sandwich Islands.]
25. *Ziziphinus eximius*, Rve., P. Z. S. 1842.   Panama, sandy mud, 10 fms. [= *T. versicolor*, Mke., 1850, = *Z. Californicus*, A. Ad., 1851. Scarcely differs from "*Javanicus*, Lam.," in Mus. Cum. The form was dredged by Mr. A. Adams in the eastern seas.]
31. *Ziziphinus Antonii*, Koch, in Phil. Abbild. pl. 1. f. 4.   Australia.   [Scarcely differs from the shouldered var. of *Calliostoma lima* (Phil.) C. B. Ad., which is called *eximiu*, Rve., in Brit. Mus. Col.]
23. *Trochus Japonicus*, Dkr., [represents *Pomaulax undosus* on the east side].
24. *Trochus digitatus*, Desh.   Distinct from *unguis*, with base like *gibberosus*. Central America. [Mr. Reeve's distinct shell is perhaps not that of Desh., and not from the West Coast.]
26. *Trochus undosus*, Wood. = *T. gigas*, Anton.   California †.

* *Vide* Report, 1856, p. 168, note §§.
† Mr. Reeve states that, although this species is most like *gibberosus*, "Messrs. Gray and Adams contrive to place them in different genera." It is still more remarkable that, while

53

39. *Trochus auripigmentum*, Jonas. Panama. [Probably not from W. America.]
17. *Phasianella perforata*, Phil. Mazatlan, Panama+*Ph. compta*, Gld.* Rather
    out of place †; has neither form nor texture of *Phasianella*. [The aberrant
    form is due to the figured specimen being quite young; the adults in
    Brit. Mus. Col. prove the texture, colouring, and operc. to be normal.]
Genus *Simpulopsis*. This group, intermediate between *Vitrina* and *Succinea*, is
    stated to be peculiar to Brazil and Mexico, where *Vitrina* is not known.

In the Monograph of *Terebratulidæ*, which is prepared with unusual care,
and the general introduction to which is well worth attentive perusal by all
students, occur the following species which bear upon the West Coast fauna
or synonymy :—

2. *Terebratula* (*Waldheimia*) *dilatata*, Lam., = *T. Gaudichaudi*, Blainv. "Str.
    Magellan," teste Gray, in Brit. Mus. Cat., without authority. [The E. E.
    specimens varied considerably in outline ; and according to Darwin, and
    what we know of the var ations of fossil species, it is quite possible to
    believe that this and the next species had a common origin. The great
    development of this most interesting form in the cold regions of South
    America is extraordinary.]
3. *Terebratula* (*Waldheimia*) *globosa* (Val.), Lam., from type. = *T. Californica*,
    Koch. "California, Coquimbo. Californian form well known; small
    specimen in Mus. Taylor, marked 'de Coquimbo.'" [There appears no
    authority for the general belief that this fine species is Californian. It was
    taken in abundance by the naturalists of the U. S. E. E. at Orange Bay,
    Magellan. The Californian shell, which is probably the original *Cali-
    fornica*, Koch. (not of authors) is a distinct species, teste Rve. from Dr.
    Cooper's specimens.]
7. *Terebratula* (*Terebratulina*) *radiata*, Rve., Mus. Cum. ? Straits of Corea,
    Belcher. [Very like the adult of *T. caurina*, Gld.]
11. *Terebratula uva*, Brod. Bay of Tehuantepec, Guatemala ; 10–12 fms. sandy
    mud, on dead bivalve, *Capt. Dare*. Mus. Cum. and De Burgh. [The
    analogue of *T. vitrea*, Med.]
16. *Terebratula* (*Terebratulina*) *Japonica*, Sby., = *T. angusta*, Ad. and Rve. Corea,
    Japan. "Represents *T. caput-serpentis*, and probably the same."
23. *Terebratula physema*, Val., MS. (unique), Coquimbo. *Gaudichaud*, 1833.
    May be a colossal, broadly inflated var. of *globosa*.
6. *Orbicula Cumingii*, Brod. [Besides information in Rep. pp. 183, 244, is given]
    Is. Caña, Guatemala ; sometimes 6–18 fms., *Cuming*. *O. strigata*, Brod.,
    is a less-worn state of this species. [The type-specimens of *Discina stri-
    gata* in Brit. Mus., on *Pecten ventricosus*, appear very distinct, and are
    unusually shelly for the genus.]

---

excluding *Ziziphinus* (= *Calliostoma*), Mr. Reeve "contrives to place" in *Trochus* animals
shown by the opercula to belong to different subfamilies, as though we knew no more than
in Lamarck's days ; his motley group containing *Imperator* (= *Stella*, H. and A. Ad.)+
Lithopoma + *Guildfordia* + *Chrysostoma* + *Bolma* + *Modelia* + *Polydonta* + *Tectus*+
Pomaulax + *Astralium* + *Pachypoma* + *Uvanilla*. Also in a family the genera and species
of which are mainly recognized by the base and mouth, most of the shells are only figured
on the back. Very often the characters of the aperture are not even stated. Remarkable
liberties are, moreover, sometimes taken with geographical facts, to the great astonishment
of Americans, who expect even their schoolboys to avoid such statements as at sp. 57, *Tr.
diminutivus*, Rve., "Oahu Islands ;" and at sp. 1, *Lingula ovalis*, Rve., "from W. H.
Pease, Esq., residing at Honolulu, one of the Sandwich Islands."

  * *P. compta* is a distinct Californian species ; its ?varieties pass into *pulla*. If Mr.
Reeve can be followed in uniting to *pulla*, *pulchella*, Recl. ; + *affinis* + *tessellata* + *pulchella*
+ *concinna*, C. B. Ad. ; + *tennis*, Phil. ; + *intermedia*, Seacchi ; + *Capensis*, Dkr. ; + *elongata*, Krauss, Gould's species should join this goodly company, rather than *perforata*.
The same standard of union followed among the large shells would greatly lessen the size
of this costly work.

  † So is *Phasianella rubra*, Pease MS., sp. 18, which belongs to *Alcyra*, A. Ad.; allied
to *Euchelus*.

7. *Orbicula ostreoides*, Lam.,= *O. Norvegica*, Sby. (non Lam.)+ *O. striata*, Sby.+ *Crania radiosa*, Gld.+ *O.* [*Discina*] *Evansii*, Dav.   ? N.W. Africa. "The locality, ' Bodegas, Cal.,' given by Mr. D. with *O. Evansii*, on Mr. Cuming's authority, must, I think, be a mistake." [The genus has not been found on the Californian coast by any American collector.]

8 *Venus* * *grata*, Sby.,+ *tricolor*, Sby.   Gulf of Mexico, Mus. Cum.   [= *Tapes grata*, Say, Panama. The locality-labels have probably been misplaced. These specimens are undoubtedly from the West Coast, nor has any authority appeared for the species in the Atlantic. The Gulf of Mexican "analogue" is *T. granulata*. The forms are intermediate between *Chione* and *Tapes*.]

9. *Venus multicostata*, Sby. Bay of Panama, in coarse sand at low water, *Cuming*. "Probably = *V. Listeri*,var.,with ribs more tumidly thickened and rounded." [The West Coast shells are distinguished by the very slight crenulation of the ribs at the sides.]

10. *Venus asperrima*, Sby. Guacomayo, Centr. Am., sandy mud, 13 fms., *Cuming*. " A form of *pectorina* ; shell of lighter substance, broader and more depressed ; sculpture more elevately and definitely latticed." [This is the shell named by Mr. Cuming *V. cardioides*, Lam., and should take that name, as prior to Sby.'s, if really distinct from *pectorina*. Also from Panama. Mus. Smiths.]

22. *Venus discors*, Sby., jun. St. Elena and Guacomayo, Centr. Am., sandy mud, 6-9 fms., *Cuming*. " Concentric decussating ridges cease abruptly at the posterior third." [Character very variable, even in the type-specimens ; = *T. grata*, Say, var.]

25. *Venus pectorina*, Lam., p. 344,+ *V. cardioides*, Lam.   Centr. Am., Mus. Cum. [Probably Atlantic : much heavier and stumpy ; sculpture coarser ; teeth more like *casina*, whereas *cardioides*, no. 10, has a long anterior tooth like *sugillata* †.]

26. *Venus cingulata*, Lam.,= *pulicaria*, Brod. W. Columbia, *Cuming*. [= *V. Pinacatensis*, Sloat, MS. in Mus. Smiths. Guaymas.   The peculiar smoothing-off of the central sculpture in the adult may be varietal. It is improbable that Lam. was acquainted with the species.]

33. *Venus crenulata*, Chem.,= *crenata*, Gmel. W. I. = *V. eximia*, Phil.,+ *V. crenifera*, Sby.,+ *V. Portesiana*, D'Orb. [Not to be confounded with the *V. crenifera*, Maz. Cat.: has a small Cyprinoid lateral tooth, but no radiating ribs near lunule, nor long anterior tooth†.]

35. *Venus Californiensis*, Brod.,= *V. leucodon*, Sby. Guaymas, Gulf Cal., sandy mud, low water, [teste] *Cuming*. Mus. Cum. [= *V. crassa*, Sloat, MS. in Mus. Smiths. Not *V. Californiana*, Conr.,= *V. simillima*, Sby. This species, with *V. neglecta, compta*, &c., having the mantle-bend nearly obsolete, approach *Anomalocardia subimbricata*, and with that species form a natural group, differing from the typical *Venus* as *Lioconcha* does from *Callista* := *V. succincta*, Val.]

41. *Venus Kennerleyi*, Cpr., MS. ‡ in Mus. Cum. *Hab.*—? [Puget Sound, *Kennerley*.]

43. *Venus sugillata*, Rve. California, Mus. Cum. Characterized by the shining purple umbos, finely latticed sculpture, dark-stained lunule and ligamentary area. [="*V. crenifera*, Sby., teste Rve.," Maz. Cat. no. 105, in all essential characters. Differs in the long anterior tooth being still

---

* Through the kindness of Mr. Reeve, with a view to the completion of this Report, I was enabled to compare the figured specimens in this genus with the text, and with the shells of the Smithsonian collection, before they were distributed. The bracketed notes in the text are based on this examination. They are given with unusual detail, because of the unique opportunity of throwing some light on a confessedly difficult family.

† The characters of the teeth and pallial line frequently afford satisfactory diagnostic marks between critical species, which are often overlooked by monographers.

‡ The descriptions of Dr. Kennerley's shells had long been written, and would have been published but for the American war. The localities of all the West Coast shells sent from the Smiths. Col. to Mr. Cuming were duly marked in the accompanying catalogues,

longer, and in the purple colour. This, however, in the figured specimen, has been brought-out by the free use of acid, and the markings have
been considerably obliterated by the "beautifying" process.]

44. *Venus simillima*, Sby. San Diego, Cal. "Resembles *V. compta* in detail of
sculpture" [but perfectly distinct, belonging to the *amathusia* group.
It shows the evil of the very brief diagnoses of the earlier conchologists
that so discriminating an author as Mr. Conrad should have taken this
shell for the *V. Californiensis*, Brod.; and, quoting it *(lapsu)* as *V. Cali-
formiana*, redescribed the true *V. Californiensis* as *V. Nuttallii*. It is
known by the great closeness of the fine sharp ribs.]

46. *Venus = crenulata*, no. 33, very distinct var. Gulf Cal.; more globose, interior
purple rose. [This was sent as "Cape St. Lucas, *Xantus*." It appears
truly distinct from the W. I. *crenulata*, and to be the normal form
of which *pulicaria*, no. 26, is an extreme var. Inside, and outside in
the adolescent state, they agree exactly; differing outside, in the adult,
in smoothed-off ribs and more distinct V-markings. Mr. Reeve, however,
still thinks it more like *cremifera*. It may stand as "? var. *lilacina*."]

47. *Venus gibbosula*, Desh., MS. in Mus. Cum. *Hab.* ?— [Guaymas := *V. Cortezi*,
Sloat. This is the more rounded and porcellanous form of *V. fluctifraga*,
= *V. Nuttalli* of Brit. Assoc. Report, and Nuttallian paper in P. Z. S.
1856, p. 21; but not the true *V. Nuttalli*, Conr., v. *infrà*, no. 49. Interior
margin very finely crenated on both sides of the hinge.]

48. *Venus compta*, Brod. Bay of Sechura, Peru, coarse sand and mud, 7 fms.,
Cuming. [This rare species seems to represent *V. Californiensis* in the
South American fauna. It is well distinguished by its shouldered form,
produced ventrally, and by the Circoid pallial line, far removed from the
margin. Guacomayo, Mus. Smiths.]

49. *Venus Nuttalli*, Conr. California. [Named from type, teste Conr. ips., v.
antcà, p. 526. This is the dull northern form of *V. succincta*, as *fluctifraga* is of *gibbosula*, the species appearing nearly in the same parallels in
the Gulf and on the Pacific coast, but not found in the Liverpool Reigen
Co'.; nor at Cape St. Lucas. In all essential characters, *Nuttalli* (though
pointed) and *Californiensis* (though rounded) appear the same; but Mr.
Reeve still thinks otherwise. The figured specimen has been altered with
acid. The *V. excavata* is not noticed by Mr. R.]

51. *Venus mundulus*, Rve. *Hab.* ?— [This shell was obtained by Dr. Stimpson
in the N. P. Expl. Exp., and bears the Smiths. Cat. number "1845. San
Francisco, very common at low water," = *Tapes diversa*, Sby. jun. This
is the highly painted, finely sculptured state of *T. staminea*, Conr. (not
" *T. straminea*, Conr." Sby., = *T. grata*, var.) The abnormally ridged form
is *V. ruderata*, Desh. Conch. Ic. sp. 130. By its large pallial sinus and
bifid teeth it is a true *Tapes*.]

52. *Venus intersecta*, Sby. Puerto Puero [? Portrero], Centr. Am., *Cuming*.
[The shell is exactly identical with no. 19, *asperrima = cardioides*; but the
figure might mislead, the colour-lines appearing as ribs.]

54. *Venus subrostrata*, Lam.[*] vi. p. 343, = *V. neglecta*, [Gray] Sby. *Hab.* Mazatlan
and West Indies. "Lam. having cited a figure of the China species, *V. Lamarckii*, the species was lost sight of till Sby. renamed it." [The *Lamarckian* species was probably West Indian. *V. neglecta* closely resembles
the young of *V. Californiensis*, but has the ligamental area smooth only
on one valve, instead of both.]

56. *Venus Stutchburyi* (Gray), Wood, Sandwich Is. Comes very near to the
Californian *V. callosa*, [Sby., non] Conr., of which specimens have been
found also at the Sandwich Is. [*V. Stutchburyi* is the New Zealand
species, which may easily be confounded with the Californian. Although
both may be *obtained* at the Sandwich Is., there is no evidence that either

---

[*] In critical species, when it is impossible to be positive which of two or more was
intended by an old author, it appears best to retain the name of the first *discriminator*.
The old name belongs to the general form: the discriminator ought to retain it for a
part; but if that has not been done, it avoids confusion to drop it.

lives there. The shell here figured is beaked like *Nuttalli*, no. 49; lunule very faint; concentric ridges very faint, but sharp; radiating ribs very coarse. Inside deeply stained; margin not created on the sharp anterior edge, though faintly on the lunule; hinge-teeth stumpy.]

60. *Venus muscaria*, Rve. *Hab.?*— [Has the aspect of a West Coast species, between *cardioides* and fine var. of *staminea*; sinus large; teeth strong, not bifid; lunule with radiating ribs.]

68. *Venus undatella*, Sby. Gulf Calif. [Not a satisfactory species, the type having the aspect of a poor specimen altered for cabinet. The "sculpture much changing in its development towards the margin" is an accident often seen in the cancellated species. Similar specimens of *V. neglecta*, no. 54, collected at Cape St. Lucas by Mr. Xantus, agree with *undatella* in all respects, except that this is violet within, *neglecta* being white. Ligament-area (as in *neglecta*) smooth in one valve only.]

77. *Venus Adamsii*, Rve. Japan. [Closely related to *Tapes laciniata*, San Diego, in size, aspect, hinge, &c. Differs in mantle-bend being not so long or pointed, and the radiating sculpture much finer:= *V. rigida*, Gld., MS., in Stimpson's list; non Gld. in 'Otia.']

80. *Venus ornatissima*, Brod. Panama, sandy mud, 10 fms., *Cuming*. Still unique. [Like *V. gnidia*, jun., but radiating ribs coarser and more distant; concentric frills not palmated; lunule pale, laminated.]

87. *Venus callosa* [Sby., non] Conr. Sandwich Is. and Calif. [*Vide* note to no. 50. This is the *V. Nuttallii* of the Brit. Assoc. Report. Those who regard it as distinct from *fluctifraga*, of which *gibbosula*, no. 47, is the extreme form, may retain the name *callosa* of Sby., but not of Conr. Conrad's species = *C. nobilis*, Rve.; differing from the true *Callistæ*, as *Mercenaria* does from *Venus*, in having the ligament-plate rugose.] = *V. fluctifraga*, Sby., teste Rve. *in errata.*

105. *Venus bilineata*, Rve. Gulf Calif. Partakes of the characters of *compta* and *subimbricata*: all three may indeed be different states of one and the same species. [The shell figured at 105*b* has all the peculiar features of *compta*, which are clearly marked within; only the concentric waves are closer than usual. The shell figured at 105*a* appears to be the true *undatella*, only in fine condition, the type being rubbed. It has exactly the same internal characters, including colour; only the colour-lines outside are arranged in rays instead of ⋁s. Mr. Reeve, however, retains his different opinion.]

116. *Venus Cypria*, Sby., P. Z. S. 1852. Is. Plata, West Columbia. [From same district, teste Schott in Mus. Smiths.] Has all the appearance of being an attenuately produced form of the West Indian *V. paphia* [which is also from Cape Verd Is., teste Macgillivray in Brit. Mus.].

11. *Dione* * *maculata*, List. West Indies; Brazil; Pacific Ocean. Widely distributed in both hemispheres. [No authority for the Old World; the Pacific shells are *Callista chionæa*, var]

15. *Dione nobilis*, Rve., 1849. Cal. [= *C. callosa*, Conr., 1837. The original name, from type, had been communicated to Mr. R., but is not quoted.]

20. *Dione semilamellosa* †, Gaud., = *C. lupanaria*, Less. Centr. Am. [= *lupinaria*, Maz. Cat., no. 95. *Vide* Deless. Rec. Coq. pl. 19. f. 2: "China Seas," no authority.]

21. *Dione brevispinata*, Rve., = *brevispina*, Sby. [Gulf of] California. [Scarcely differs from *C. rosea*, jun.]

22. *Dione multispinosa*, Sby. Peru. Concentric ridges thinly laminated; spines slender and numerous. [An extreme form of the Pacific *C. Dione* (teste Hanl.); distinct from *semilamellosa*.]

23. *Dione Veneris*, D'Arg. Conch. pl. 21. f. 1, = *V. Dione*, Ln. West Ind. and

---

* The figured types of this genus had been accidentally mislaid; and might alter the judgments given in the text.

† "For obvious reasons, I think it best to abandon the foul name given to this lovely species by Lesson," Rve. (*Vide* Maz. Cat. p. 70, note.) ?Would not the same reasons lead to the alteration of *meretrix*, *impudica*, &c.

Centr. Am. [The Pacific shells should rank with species 22, if supposed distinct. The fig. is 24, not 23.]

24. *Dione exspinata*, Rve. Centr. Am. Distinct, if the others are; like *semilamellosa*, without spines. [Appears to be *C. rosea*, jun. The fig. is 23, not 24.]

25. } *Dione circinata*, Born. Mazatlan, Mus. Cum. [without authority.] = *V.*
28, *a, b.* } *rubra*, Gmel., + *V. Guineensis*, Gmel., + *C. alternata*, Brod. [f. 28 represents *alternata*; the other figures appear to be from West Indian specimens, though that ancient locality is not mentioned. Several of the reputed West Coast shells are, however, of the typical form and colour.]

33. *Dione unicolor*, Sby., = *Chione badia*, Gray, = *Cyth. ligula*, Anton. W. Columbia.

38. *Dione prora*, Conr. "Cape St. Lucas, Xantus, California; Carpenter." [A very distinct form among the thin inflated species; only yet found at the Sandwich Is., v. no. 45.]

45. "(Mus. Smithsonian Institute of N. America.) This shell, from Cape St. Lucas, Xantus, California, proves to be the *Dione prora* (*Cytherea prora*, Conr.) of our preceding plate." [Mr. Sowerby's figure well represents the unique specimen from Cape St. Lucas, which was taken alive by Mr. Xantus. The quotations in Conch. Ic. would lead to the inference that "Xantus" was regarded as that part of "California" in which Cape St. Lucas is situated. Both the external and internal characters require that a separate name be given to the shell, which stands as *Callista pollicaris*, Annals Nat. Hist. vol. xiii. p. 312.]

46. *Cytherea consanguinea*, C. B. Ad. Mus. Cum. Apparently a small specimen of a variety of *C. læta*. [Panama. Differs from *C. læta* in internal characters.]

62. *Dione pannosa*, Sby., = *Cytherea lutea*, Koch, + *Callista puella*, Cpr. Chili, Peru, Mazatlan. [No authority for Mazatlan. The name *puella* given to the Cape St. Lucas specimens was intended as varietal; although Mr. Cuming regards the Peruvian and Peninsular forms as distinct. It is not known along the Central American coast.]

25. *Circe nummulina*, Lam. "Central America." [Probably not from the American seas. Admiral Sir E. Belcher is, however, confident that he dredged many well-known E. Indian forms in deep water, off San Blas.]

27. *Cytherea*. In this genus are grouped the *Trigonæ*; besides the typical species, = *Meretrix*, Gray.

3. *Cytherea crassatelloides*, Conr. "Bay of California." [Not known geographically. The shell is not found in the Gulf, being a most characteristic Californian species. San Francisco, S. Diego, &c.]

27. *Cytherea radiata*, Sby., + *C. gracilior*, Sby., = *V. Salangensis*, D'Orb. = *T. Byronensis*, Gray. Salango and Xipixapi, 9 fms. sandy mud, *Cuming*.

45. *Cytherea nitidula*, Lam. Mediterranean. [The figures and descriptions of Sby. and Rve. well represent specimens from Cape St. Lucas, *Xantus*. Perhaps not identical with Lam.'s species.]

9. *Tapes grata*, Desh. Philippines. [May stand as *T. Deshayesii*, if it be conceded that Say's *V. grata* ranks best with *Tapes*.]

7. *Solarium granulatum*, Lam. Mexico.

8. *Solarium verrucosum*, Phil. W. Indies. ? = *S. granulatum*, var.

13. *Solarium placentula*, [Rve. = *placentale*,] Hds. Bay Magdalena, 7 fms., *Belcher*.

19. *Solarium quadriceps*, Hds. Panama. Young state of same type as sp. 7 and 8, "from same locality (Pan., Mex., W. I.)," but grows much larger. [The Texan shells in Mus. Smiths. are as large as those from Cape St. Lucas: the variations on each coast are coordinate.]

63. *Kiener.*—The following species may be added to the list quoted from "Coquilles Vivantes," in Rep. pp. 293, 294:—

Page.	Pl.	Fig.	
15.	{ 3.	2. }	*Conus regius*, Chem., = *C. princeps*, Ln., W. Mexico.
	{ 11.	4. }	
212.	{ 98.	3. }	*Conus Largillierti*, Kien. Mexico. [Coast not stated.]
	{ 100.	1,1*. }	

Page.	Pl.	Fig.		
213.	98.	2.	*Conus Philippii*, Kien. Mexico.	[Coast not s'ated.]
65.	27.	3.	*Pleurotoma triticea*, Kien. Indian Ocean. [Probably *Cithara stromboides*, Val.; Cape St. Lucas.]	
45.	9.	2.	*Columbella suturalis*, Gray (Griff. pl. 41. f. 2)= *C. costata*, Ducl. Mon. pl. 12. f. 1, 2. Pacific, Coasts of Peru [=*Anachis fluctuata*, Sby.].	
46.	16.	4.	*Columbella bicolor*, Kien. *Hab.* ?— [=*A. rugosa.*]	

64, 65. (*German Authors.*) *Pfeiffer.*—Everything relating to the land-shells of North America will be found so thoroughly collated in the works of Mr. Binney (v. *infrà*), that it is only judged needful to present here the most important references to the writings of the great authority on the *Pulmonata*. The student must necessarily consult the ' Symbolæ ad Historiam Heliceorum, Cassel, 1841 ' *et seq.*, which contains the following original authorities :—

1846. p. 89. *Achatina Californica*, Pfr. Monterey, Cal.
       91. *Achatina (Glandina) turris*, Pfr. *Hab.*?— [Genus altered to *Oleacina*, Mon. Hel. iv. p. 640. Maz. Cat. 231.]

In the same author's great work, 'Monographia Heliceorum Viventium,' Lipsiæ, 1847-8, occur—

		Page.	
Vol. I.	1847.	324.	*Helix Sagraiana*, D'Orb. Cuba, California. [Sowerby's error, copied by succeeding writers. The species is exclusively Cuban.]
		338.	*Helix fidelis*, Gray. Oregon.= *H. Nuttalliana*, Lea.
		339.	*Helix Califo niensis*, Lea. California. + *H. Nickliniana*, Lea. [Quoted as a distinct species in Vol. IV. p. 269.]
(Vol. 3.		229.	= *H. arboretorum*, Val.)
		341.	*Helix Townsendiana*, Lea. California.
(Vol. 3.		229.	= *H. pedestris*, Gld.,+*ruida*, Gld.)
		428.	*Helix Oregonensis*, Lea. Oregon.
(Vol. 4.		227.	= *H. Dupetithouarsii*, teste Pfr)
Vol. II.	1848.	101.	*Bulimus Mexicanus*, Lam. Tabasco, Mexico.= *H. (Cochlogena) vittata*, Fér.
(Vol. 4.		402.	= *Orthalicus M.*, Cpr.)
		143.	*Bulimus zebra*, Müll.* Mexico. &c =*Zebra Mülleri*, Chem. =*Bulimus undatus*, Brug.* = *Orthalicus livens*, Beck *, + *B. princeps*, Brod.+ *B. melanocheilus*, Val.
		231.	*Bulimus (Cochlogena) melania*, Fér. California.= *Melania striata*, Perry= *B. borinus*, Brug.
Vol. III.	1853.	127.	*Helix Pandoræ*, Fbs. St. Juan del Fuaco.
(Vol. 4.		347.	= *H. Damascenus*, Gld.)
		415.	*Bulimus Humboldti*, Rve.= *B. Mexicanus*, Val. [? non Lam.] Mexico.
		422.	*Bulimus Californicus*, Rve. California.
Vol. IV.	1859.	89.	*Helix Mazatlanica*, Pfr., n. s. (Mal. Blätt., Apr. 1856, p. 43.) Mazatlan.
		268.	*Helix exarata*, Pfr., n. s. California.
		270.	*Helix reticulata*, Pfr. (Mal. Blätt. May 1857, p. 87). Cal.
		276.	*Helix Mormonum*, Pfr. Mormon Island, California.
		347.	*Helix cultellata*, Thomson. Contra Costa Co., California.
		350.	*Helix arrosa*, Gld. *Hab.* ?— [California.]+*æruginosa*,Gld.
		420.	*Bulimus chordatus*, Pfr. (Mal. Blätt., April 1856, p. 46.) Mazatlan.
		472.	*Bulimus Ziegleri*, Pfr. (Mal. Blätt., Dec. 1856, p. 232.) Mexico. = *Orthalicus Z.*, Cpr.

* These appear as three distinct species in Vol. IV. p. 588-9, with the addition of *B. longus*, Pfr. (= *Orthalicus L.*, Mal. Blätt., Oct. 1856, p. 187.)

In the 'Monographia Pneumonopomorum Viventium, &c., Cassellis, 1852,' by the same learned author, the following is the only species which occurs :— Suppl. 1858, Vol. II. p. 7. *Truncatella Californica*, Pfr.   San Diego.

In Wiegmann's 'Archives für Nat.,' 1837, vol. i. p. 285, occurs the following species, also without authority :—

Perna quadrata, Anton.   California.

In Troschel's ' Archives für Natur' are quoted the following :—

1843. Vol. II. p. 140. *Fasciolaria sulcata*, Less.   Acapulco.
1840.   „   p. 99. *Terebratula Californica*, Linsley.

In the 'Abbildungen und Beschreibungen neuer oder wenig gekannter Conchylien, herausgegeben von Dr. R. A. Philippi,' Cassel, 1845-51, are figured the following, which must be quoted as being original descriptions, or for the synonymy:—

	Page.	Pl.	Fig.			
Feb.	1846.	4.	1.	9.	*Cyrena solida*, Phil. California, &c.	
Aug.	1846.	24.	4.	7.	*Tellina pisiformis*, Ln. Mazatlan, &c. = *L. pulchella*, Ad. ? = *Cardium discors*, Mont.	
Oct.	1844.	4.	..	..	*Cytherea Dunkeri*, Phil. W. C. Mexico. = *C. Pacifica*, Mus. Berol., non Dillw.	
Apr.	1847.	33.	7.	1.	*Cytherea (Artemis) gigantea*, Sby. California. ? = *Artemis ponderosa*, Gray.	
Jan.	1845.	1.	1.	1.	*Murex nigritus*, Phil. ? W. C. Mexico.	
April	1847.	11.	7,8.	1.	*Haliotis fulgens*, Phil. ? California. = *H. splendens*, Rve.	
Oct.	1846.	5.	2.	1,10.	*Turbo Fokkesii*, Jonas. Gulf of California.	
		8.	2.	9.	*Trochus strigilatus*, Ant. California. = *T. pellis-serpentis*, Wood.	
July	1844.	7.	2.	5.	*Patella (Acmæa) discors*, Phil. Mexico.	
April	1850.	9.	2.	8.	*Lucina obliqua*, Phil. ? W. C. America.	
		9.	2.	9.	*Lucina pisum*, Phil. Mazatlan.	
		2.	1.	3.	*Pecten tunica*, Phil. "Sandwich Islands *. E. B. Philippi." Jan. 1844. [= *P. latiauritus*, Conr., teste Hanl. S. Diego, &c.]	
		5.	1.	5.	*Pecten Fabricii*, Phil. Greenland. [= *P. Islandicus*, jun. Non *P. Fabricii*, Gld., = *P. Hindsii*, jun.]	
		11.	6.	9.	*Litorina aberrans*, Phil., P. Z. S. 1845. p. 142. Panama, on rocks. [= Tall var. of *L. conspersa*.]	

In Dr. L. Pfeiffer's ' Novitates Conchologicæ,' Series II., Marine Shells, by Dr. W. Dunker, Cassel, 1858, occur the following species from Sitka:—

Page.	Pl.	Fig.		
1.	1.	3, 4.	*Tritonium carinatum*, Dkr. Sitka. [Should be pl. 2. f. 3, 4.] [= *T. angulosum*, Mörch, on plate.]	
2.	1.	1, 2.	*Tritonium Mörchianum*, Dkr. Sitka. [Should be pl. 2. f. 1, 2.]	
3.	2.	5, 6.	*Tritonium rutilum*, Mörch. „ [Should be pl. 1. f. 5, 6.]	
4.	1.	5, 6.	*Tritonium Rombergi*, Dkr. „ [Should be pl. 2. f. 5, 6.]	
2.	2.	3, 4.	*Neptunea harpa*, Mörch. „ [Should be pl. 1. f. 3, 4.]	
7.	2.	1, 2.	*Neptunea castanea*, Mörch. „ [Should be pl. 1. f. 1, 2.] [= *N. badia*, on plate.]	
35.	10.	6, 7.	*Murex (Hemifusus) Belcheri*, Hds., var. ?— [= *Chorus B.*, L. Cal.]	
30.	12.	7-9.	*Cytherea (Tivela) arguta*, Röm. Isthmus of Panama. Resembles *C. (Trigona) mactroides*, Born. [Probably Caribbean.]	

66. *British Museum Collection.*—" *Lunatia ravida*, Souleyet, Panama,"

* A large number of Californian shells have been assigned to the Sandwich Is., in consequence of the abundant trade between the two localities. They may often have been obtained at Honolulu by naturalists, who had no reason to doubt their having lived there. All that is known of the genuine Hawaian fauna will shortly be published by Mr. Sowerby, for W. H. Pease, Esq., of Honolulu.

is given without authority; and the locality is probably erroneous. Various other shells are scattered in the national collection, assigned either generally to the West Coast or to special localities, which it has not been considered needful to tabulate without confirmation.

68. *Various sources.*—Under this head may be arranged gleanings from European authors not consulted in preparing the first Report.

In the ' Histoire Naturelle des Coquilles,' by L. A. G. Bosc, Paris, 1830, the following species, not previously quoted, are assigned to the West Coast, but without authority :—

Vol.	Page.			
III.	44.	*Venus paphia.*	W. America.	
	280.	*Nerita fulgurans*, Bosc.	W. C. America.	
	290.	*Natica rugosa*, Chem.	„	
IV.	60.	*Helix peregrina.*	Island on „	
	152.	*Trochus solaris.*	„	&c.
	156.	*Trochus radiatus.*	„	&c.
	219.	*Murex lima.*	W. C. N. America.	

In Lesson's ' Illustrations de Zoologie,' Paris, 1831-2, appear—

Plate.		
2.	*Calypæopsis tubifera*, Less. [= *Crucibulum spinosum*].	
41. (1832.)	*Trichotropus Sowerbiensis*, Lesson. Seas of New World. = *Trichotropis bicarinata*, Br. & Sby. = *Turbo bicarinatus*, Sby.	
48.	*Terebra flammea*, Less. [? = *T. strigosa*], Antilles ; Isth. Panama.	
51.	*Tegula elegans*, Less. [= *T. pellis-serpentis*]. Isth. Panama.	

The following West Coast shells are named and figured by Dr. Gray in ' Griffith's Edition of Cuvier's Animal Kingdom,' London, 1834. In some instances there are also a few words of description :—

Plate. Fig.		
1. 3.	*Litorina pulchra.*	
41. 5.	*Turbenella ceratus* [? *Turbinellus*].	
41. 6.	*Columbella suturalis* [Kiener figures this shell for *Anachis fluctuata*, Sby., 1832. The original might stand for many species].	
36. 2.	*Nassa Northiæ* [= *Northia serrata*, Kien.].	
36. 3.	*Turbinella tubercularis* [= *Latirus tuberculatus* (= *ceratus*, C. B. Ad.)].	
23. 5.	*Terebra Africana.* [The Gulf Cal. shell, = *variegata.*]	
25. 2.	*Triton (Pusio) elegans* [= *Pisania insignis*, Rve., 1846].	
37. 2.	*Columbella harpaformis* [= *harpiformis*, Sby.].	
37. 6.	*Clavatula Griffithii.* [Probably = *Pl. funiculata.* The shells in this plate are reversed, but are repeated correctly in pl. 37 *.]	
19. 1.	*Cytherea Dronea*, var. [= *C. semilamellosa*, Gaud. ; perhaps intended for *C. dione*, var.].	

In Woodward's most valuable ' Manual of the Mollusca,' London, 1851-6, the following species are quoted as from " California " :—

Page.	Pl.	Fig.	
108.	5.	5.	*Cancellaria reticulata*, Dillw. [? W. Indies.]
171.			*Physa Maugeræ.* [? Ecuador.]
329.	23.	22.	*Parapholas bisulcata*, Conr. [v. Rep. p. 265. Not known from the Californian or W. Mexican coasts. Resembles *P. calva*].

In the very valuable handbook of bivalves, ' Recent Shells, by S. Hanley, London, 1842-56,' will be found either quoted or original diagnoses of all West Coast species known to the learned, patient, and minutely exact compiler. As the locality-marks are simply transcripts, they are not here repeated, especially as " California " is used for both the temperate and the tropical faunas. The following synonyms will be serviceable to the student :—

Page.		
13.	*Solen subteres*, Conr., ? = *S. Dombei*, ? + *Californianus.* Upper Cal.	
28.	*Lutraria lineata*, Say, = (*Cryptodon*) *Nuttallii* [teste Hanl., non] Conr.	

Page.
72. *Tellina inconspicua*, Br. and Sby., ? = *Sanguinolaria* [*Californiana*, Conr., non]
     fusca, Conr. [= the Eastern species].

In the Appendix are the following species, of which small figures are given
to correspond with those in Wood's Ind. Test :—

Page.   Pl.   Fig.
339.   13.   50. *Periploma obtusa*, Hanl.   W. America.
341.   12.   5. *Amphidesma proximum*, C. B. Ad., = *A. corrugatum*, Ad.   Mexico.
373.   18.   51. *Arca Reeveana*, D'Orb.   W. America. = *A. squamosa*, var., D'Orb.
                = *A. Helbingii*, Rve.
388.   24.   40. *Meleagrina Mazatlanica*, Hanl.   Mazatlan [= *M. fimbriata*, Dkr.].

The following are extracted from the 'Journal de Conchyliologie,' Paris,
1850 :—

                Page.   Pl.   Fig.
No. 1. Feb. 1850. 57.   3.   4.   *Columbella Haneti*, Petit.   ? Mazatlan.
    4. Dec. 1850. 410.   Observations on *Nerita scabricosta*, Lam., by
                          Petit.   West Coast of N. America.
Vol. 3.   1852. 57.   2.   11.   *Mitra Haneti*, Petit.   Mazatlan.
   4.   1853. 53.   2.   11,12. *Natica Taslei*, Recl.   Mazatlan.
   4.   1853. 84,166. 6.   13–15. *Gnathodon trigonum*, Petit.   Mazatlan [= *M.*
                          mendica, Gld., 1851].
   4.   1853. 119.   5.   12.   *Recluzia Rollandiana*, Recl.   [Genus de-
                          scribed.]   Mazatlan.
   4.   1853. 154.   5.   9,10. *Natica Moquiniana*, Recl.   ? West Coast of
                          America.

Series II.
Vol. 2. Oct. 1857. 171.   *Adeorbis Verrauxii*, Fischer. } California.
            285.   6.   *Skenea Verrauxii*, Fischer. }
            292.   Review of the Brit. Assoc. Report and Brit.
                          Mus. Reigen Catalogue, by Fischer.
Vol. 9.   200.   Review of the Smithsonian Check Lists, by
                          Fischer.

The following species are figured in Chénu's ' Illustrations Conchyliologiques'; but no authority is given for the localities, nor etymology for the
remarkable names :—

Page.   Pl.   Fig.
8.   2.   19, 20.   *Oliva selasia*, Ducl.   Acapulco.
13.   7.   3, 4, 21, 22.   *Oliva caldania*, Ducl.   California.
13.   7.   5, 6, 23, 24.   *Oliva razamola*, Ducl.   California.
17.   {14.   7.   } *Oliva azemula*, Ducl.   California.
     {15.   1, 2, 10, 11. }
19.   16.   7, 8.   *Oliva mantichora*, Ducl.   California.
19.   {12.   10, 11. }   *Oliva pindarina*, Ducl.   California.
     {17.   7, 8.   }
28.   27.   9, 10.   *Oliva todosina*, Ducl.   California.

An excellent commentary on the above species, and on the difficult genus
to which they belong, is supplied in the ' Revue Critique du genre Oliva,' by
M. Ducros de St. Germain, Clermont, 1857. It was written, not from the
well-known London collections, but from a very large series containing all
the types figured by Duclos. The following is the author's arrangement of
the West Coast forms, excluding citations of well-known species.

No.   Page.
25.   49. *Oliva angulata* does not include *azemula*, Ducl., as Rve. says; that being
       a var. of *ponderosa + erythrostoma*.
26.   50. *Oliva Maria*, n.s., pl. 2. f. 26, *a, b*; intermediate between *Julietta* and *an-*
       gulata. California, teste Duclos. [Appears to be one of the vars. of
       Cumingii.]
28.   52. *Oliva reticularis*. To the typical W. Indian shells are united those from
       California, Panama, Madagascar, Japan, N. Holland, N. Zealand, &c.

No. Page.
    The synonymy includes *venulata*+*araneosa*+*Cumingii*+*oriola* (Ducl. non Lam.) + *pindarina* + *fusiformis* + *timoria* + *obesina* + *tisiphona* + *memnonia*+*aldinia*+*oniska*+*caldania*+*harpularia*+*candida*+*ustulata*.
63. 83. *Oliva Steerie*, Rve. Mazatlan, *Ed. Verreaux.* = [*testacea*, var.]
67. 86. *Oliva Deshayesiana*, n. s. Atlas, pl. 3. f. 67, *a*, *b* : intermediate between *Braziliensis* and *auricularia.* California, teste Duclos. [Certainly not from the West Coast.]
68. 87. *Oliva volutella*, Lam.+*razamola*, Ducl.
71. 89. *Oliva undatella*, Lam.+*nedalina*, Ducl. ; but not *ozodona*, Ducl., as Rve. says.
73. 89. *Oliva lineolata*, Gray in Wood's Ind. Test. = *purpurata*, Swains.=*dama*, Ducl. [i. e. *dama*, Goodall in Wood, = *lineolata*, Gray MS. in B. M., Zool. Beech. Voy.]
75. 91. *Oliva selasia*, Ducl. Acapulco ; teste Ducl. " We know nothing of this remarkable shell but the specimen figured by the author."
85. 96. *Oliva mutica*, Say+*rufifasciata*, Rve. [assigned by error to the Californian *O. bætica*, var.]+*fimbriata*, Rve.

In the most recent and among the most valuable of the contributions to our knowledge of local faunas, ' Mollusques de l'île de la Réunion, par M. G. P. Deshayes,' Paris, 1863, occur very unexpectedly the following species connected with the West Coast, either by name or by identity. The list of 560 species from this little island, which the researches of M. Maillard has brought to light, contains several West Indian forms and a large number known in the Central Pacific and even the Sandwich Islands.

No. Page.
38. 16. *Chama imbricata*, Brod.
47. 19. *Lucina tigerina*, Ln. " Common on sands, with *Capsa deflorata*, as at the Antilles."
65. 23. *Modiola cinnamomea*, Chem. [*Botula*, Mörch, teste A. Ad.]
110. 40. *Chiton sanguineus*, Desh. pl. 6. f. 4–7. [Non *Ch. sanguineus*, Rve. As the West Coast shell = *Ischnochiton limaciformis*, Sby., the Bourbon species may retain its name, especially if, as is probable, it belongs to another genus.]
197. 68. *Solarium* [*Torinia*] *variegatum*, Lam.
216. 74. *Turbo phasianellus*, Desh. Minute edition of *T. petholatus* ; nacreous. [Not congeneric with *T. phasianella* (Phil.), C. B. Ad., Panama shells, no. 282.]
233. 79. *Natica Marocchiensis*, Lam., Q. and G. Astr. pl. 66. f. 16–19. [? = *maroccana*, Chem.]
307. 95. *Cerithium uncinatum*, Gmel. Thes. Conch. pl. 180. f. 78, 79. [? = *C. uncinatum* (Gmel.), Sby]
393. 114. *Purpura patula*, Lam. [Linn.].
403. 115. *Purpura ?ochrostoma* (BL), Rve. [*Sistrum*].
405. 115. *Purpura* (*Coralliophila*) *madreporarum*, Sby. [? *Rhizocheilus.* = *Leptoconchus monodonta*, Quoy, teste Gld. Otia, p. 215.]
446. 132. *Terebra luctuosa*, Hds.
560. 140. *Cerithium Gallapaginis* (A. Ad.), Sby. Thes. [Sby.'s species = *interruptum*, Mke., non C. B. Ad., no. 198, rough var.] *

93. *Smithsonian Institution.*—At the time of the first Report, the temperate fauna of the West Coast was only known through sources liable to error, the collectors having visited other regions besides Oregon and California, and the species described by American authors being but imperfectly understood in this country. The large accession to the number of authentic species, the important elimination of synonyms, and the assignment of ascertained loca-

---

* The review of the remainder of the first Report, nos. 69–92, will be postponed till after the production of the new materials, which are almost entirely from American sources.

1863.

lities, which are placed on record in this Report, are due almost entirely to the stimulus afforded to science in general, and to this branch especially, by the Smithsonian Institution at Washington, D.C. The fund bequeathed by Mr. Smithson, "for the increase and diffusion of knowledge among men," having been declined by the Universities to which it was offered in the Old World, is held (in trust only) by the U. S. Government *. It is administered by a permanent body of Regents, according to a constitution drawn-out at their instance by the Secretary, Prof. J. Henry, LL.D. It may be safely stated that to his unswerving consistency, cautious judgment, and catholic impartiality it is mainly owing that, during various political and social changes, the Institution has not only steered clear of all party bias in the United States, but has distributed its advantages with equal hand on both sides of the Atlantic. The Natural History department is under the special superintendence of the Assistant-Secretary, Prof. Spencer Baird, M.D., whose indefatigable zeal, fertility of resource, and thorough knowledge of the requirements of the science have enabled the Institution, by a comparatively small outlay, not only to amass in a few years an enormous store of accurate materials, but also to eliminate from them a series of publications on various important branches of American zoology. The contributions of the Smithsonian Institution to our knowledge of the West Coast fauna may be considered under [A] its collections and [B] its publications.

[A] *Smithsonian Collections.*—According to the present law, all collections made in expeditions fitted out by the Government become the property of the Smiths. Inst., with liberty to exchange duplicates. Its museum, therefore, is rich in types; and its liberal policy allows of all duplicates being transmitted to public collections, to schools of science, or to individuals engaged in special departments of study. Not being forced into an unalterable plan of operations, like many leading museums of the Old World, permission was given to send nearly the whole of the molluscs to this country, that they might be compared with the Cumingian, the Brit. Mus., and other leading collections†. The importance of thus establishing a harmony of nomenclature for species on both sides of the Atlantic can scarcely be over-estimated. The previous want of it can be abundantly seen by comparing paragraphs 39, 43, 54, &c., in the first and in this Report. The West Coast collections belonging to the Smiths. Inst. are mainly from the following sources:

a. The United States Exploring Expedition, under Capt. (afterwards Admiral) Wilkes, 1837–1840, v. par. 43.

b. The North Pacific Exploring Expedition, under Capt. Rogers, 1853–1855. Collector, Dr. Stimpson.

c. The Pacific Railroad Expedition, 49th parallel, under Governor J. J. Stevens, 1853–54. Collections made in Puget Sound by Dr. Suckley, and at Columbia River by Dr. J. G. Cooper. Dr. Suckley also collected at Panama.

* The war has but to a limited extent curtailed the funds and interfered with the operations of the Institution.

† The Cunard Steamship Company have most liberally conveyed these stores across the Atlantic, free of cost. The British and American Governments have allowed special facilities for passing the Custom Houses without derangement. Similar acts of liberality and courtesy are continually afforded to the Smiths. Inst.—The materials for this Report have been placed unreservedly in the hands of the writer, although he went to Washington as a complete stranger, and with no other introduction than his published writings.

d. The Pacific Railroad Survey, under Lieutenant R. S. Williamson, 1853.
   Collector, Dr. A. L. Heermann.
e. The Pacific Railroad Survey, under Lieutenant R. S. Williamson, 1855.
   Collector, Dr. J. S. Newberry.
f. United States and Mexican Boundary Survey, under Major W. H. Emory,
   1852. Collector, Arthur Schott.
g. Colorado Expedition, under Lieutenant J. C. Ives. Collector, Dr. J. S.
   Newberry.
h. The United States North-West Boundary Survey, under Com. A. Campbell. Collectors, Dr. Kennerley and Mr. George Gibbs.

Besides the above official explorations on the American side, during a
period in which the British Government only fitted out a single expedition
coordinate with *h*, the Smiths. Inst. has received a large number of private collections from their correspondents, of which the following are the
principal:—
i. Mr. Jas. G. Swan, from Port Townsend, Cape Flattery, Neeah Bay, and the
   neighbouring shores of Vancouver; at intervals, during many years.
j. Dr. J. G. Cooper, early private collections from Shoalwater Bay and various
   stations in California and from Panama; and lately the dredged collections
   of the California State Geological Survey, of which a portion were sent
   in advance by Dr. Palmer.
k. California Academy of Natural Sciences, duplicates of their collection,
   with the privilege of inspecting unique specimens.
l. Dr. E. Vollum, U.S.A., from Fort Umpqua.
m. Lieutenant W. P. Trowbridge, from coast of Oregon and California.
n. Dr. J. A. Veatch, from the peninsula of Lower California, and especially
   from Cerros Island.
o. Mr. A. S. Taylor, from Monterey.
p. Mr. Andrew Cassidy, from S. Diego.
q. Rev. J. Rowell, now of San Francisco, from various stations in both faunas,
   and especially from Sta. Crux, and the Farallones Is.
r. Mr. John Xantus, of the U. S. Coast Survey, from Cape St. Lucas. Specimens were received through him from Socorro Island (one of the Revilla-
   gigedo group), Tres Marias and Margarita Island.
s. Captain C. P. Stone, from Guaymas and the northern part of the Gulf of
   California.
t. Captain C. M. Dow, from the coast of Central America.
u. Dr. J. H. Sternberg, from Panama.
v. Dr. J. H. Frick, Mr. James Hepburn, and others, from San Francisco.
v. Mr. C. N. Riotte, U. S. Minister to Costa Rica, from Puntas Arenas.
x. Mr. W. H. Pease, of Honolulu, collections made by his agents at various
   stations on the coast, particularly at Margarita Bay.

Collections have also been received from various expeditions already tabulated in the first Report; and from stray quarters not here included because
their accuracy may admit of doubt. The species received from the most important of these sources will be enumerated in their order; of the remainder,
exact lists may be consulted by the student in the Smithsonian Catalogues,
and the combined results will be found tabulated as ' Pacific Railroad Expeditions' or 'Smithsonian Collections.'

[B] *Smithsonian Publications.*—These may be classed under three heads.
(1.) Works published by the U. S. Government, with more or less of assistance derived from and through the Smiths. Inst. (2.) The 'Smithsonian
Contributions to Knowledge,' printed in 4to, and answering to the 'Trans-

actions' of English learned societies; and (3.) The 'Miscellaneous Collections,' in 8vo, answering to the 'Proceedings' of the societies:—

(1.) The series of ten 4to volumes, called 'Pacific Railroad Reports,' contains a complete *résumé* of the natural history of the western slope of North America. The Recent and Tertiary Fossil Mollusca will be analyzed in the following pages. Accounts have also been published of the natural history of other expeditions.—The annual volumes of 'Reports of the Regents of the Smithsonian Institution,' published by the U. S. Government, contain exact accounts of the assistance rendered to the expeditions by the Smiths. Inst., as well as lectures and articles on special subjects. In these will be found full particulars of the principles which regulate the natural-history workings of the Institution*.

(2.) The only paper bearing on our present inquiry as yet published in the 'Contributions' is on the "Invertebrata of the Grand Manan," by Dr. W. Stimpson, which should be consulted by all who desire to institute a comparison between the sub-boreal faunas on the two sides of the Atlantic.

(3.) The 'Miscellaneous Collections' are all stereotyped, and very freely circulated. Among them will be found "Directions" for collecting specimens of natural history, with special instructions concerning the desiderata on the Pacific coasts. These have been widely distributed among the various government officials, the *employés* of the U. S. Coast Survey, and the variously ramified circulating media at the command of the Smiths. Inst.; and have already borne a fair share of important results, although the war has greatly impeded the expected prosecution of natural-history labours. "Check Lists" have been published "of the Shells of North America, by I. Lea, P. P. Carpenter, W. Stimpson, W. G. Binney, and T. Prime," June 1860. No. 1 contains the Marine Shells of the "Oregonian and Californian Province," and No. 2 of the "Mexican and Panamic Province." They are chiefly compiled from the first British Association Report, with such elimination of synonyms and doubtful species, and addition of fresh materials, as had become available up to the date of publication. They were not intended to be quoted as authorities; and so rapid has been the accumulation of fresh information that no. 1 is already out of date. In the "Terrestrial Gasteropoda," by W. G. Binney, list no. 1 contains the "species of the Pacific coast, from the extreme north to Mazatlan," to which many additions have since been made. In the list of "Fluviatile Gasteropoda," also by W. G. Binney, "the letter W distinguishes those confined to the Pacific coast, WE is affixed to those found in both sections of the continent, and M designates the Mexican species. From the starting-point of this list considerable progress has already been made. In the brief list of "Cyclades, by Temple Prime," the Mexican and Central American species are similarly designated; but the western species and those common to the Pacific and Atlantic United States are not distinguished. In the list of "Unionidæ," by Dr. I. Lea, whose lifelong devotion to the elucidation of that family is everywhere gratefully acknowledged, the Pacific species are designated by a P. The large series

* The 'Lectures on Mollusca,' in the Vol. for 1860, pp. 151–283, will perhaps be found useful as a digest of classical forms. It was to have been illustrated with copies of woodcuts, kindly promised by Dr. Gray, and since placed at the disposal of the Smiths. Inst. by the courtesy of the Trustees of the British Museum; but, unfortunately, the blocks were not to be found at the time. They will appear, however, in forthcoming Smithsonian publications. The 'Lecture on the Shells of the Gulf of California,' in the Vol. for 1859, pp. 195–219, contains in a popular form much of the information distributed through the Brit. Mus. Maz. Cat.

of specimens, representing varieties and ages, in Dr. Lea's private collection are well deserving of close study. Their owner shares the liberality of Mr. Cuming in making them available for all purposes of scientific inquiry.

The Smiths. Inst. has just issued from the press the first part of the 'Bibliography of North American Conchology, previous to the year 1860,' by W G. Binney, containing references to all printed information on North American shells by native writers. It is divided into " § A. American descriptions of North American molluscs; § B. American descriptions of foreign molluscs; § C. Descriptions of foreign species by American authors in foreign works." The work is prepared with unusual care and completeness, and with the accurate judgment which characterizes all Mr. Binney's writings. It contains, under every separate work or paper, " a list of species therein described or in any important manner referred-to, together with their synonymy, locality, and the volume, page, plate, and figure relating to them." The second part, containing similar references to American species described by European writers, is now passing through the press. Mr. Binney has most kindly sent the proofs to the writer (as far as p. 287), which have been freely used in preparing this Report, and have supplied various important sources of information. It undertakes to provide for the whole North American continent what has been here attempted for the West Coast; and in much greater detail, as not only the first description, but all subsequent quotations are duly catalogued. It may be regarded as a complete index of references to all works on North American malacology. The student, in making use of it, will remember that it is only with the Pulmonates that Mr. Binney professes an intimate acquaintance. For these the work may be regarded as complete. But, in other departments of the science, only those shells which are *assigned by the authors* to North America are quoted; consequently a large number of species are passed-over which are truly American, but are assigned to other places, or described without locality. Also, species really belonging to other faunas, but falsely attributed to North America, duly appear as though genuine ; and the additional localities frequently assigned by the authors (which are often the real habitats) are seldom quoted. Moreover the citations stop at Mazatlan; consequently, the tropical fauna of the West Coast is but imperfectly represented. Lastly, the authors are not presented in chronological or indeed in any other ostensible order; but it is promised that the necessary information will be given in the index on the completion of the work. The student will further bear in mind that for many reasons no second-hand reference can serve the same purpose as a consultation of the original book. With these cautions the work will be found invaluable by all who are engaged in working-out American species; and great thanks are due to Mr. Binney for undertaking the extreme labour of its compilation, and to the Smiths. Inst. for supplying the expense of its publication. Probably no such work has yet been printed on the malacology of any other country.

Lastly, there is now in preparation a complete series of hand-books on North American malacology, copiously illustrated with wood engravings, and containing a digest of all that is known in each department. The marine shells of the Atlantic are being described by Dr. Stimpson, who is now also engaged in the dissection of the Freshwater Rostrifers; the marine shells of the Pacific are placed in the hands of the writer; the Pulmonates will be thoroughly worked-out by Mr. Binney, the Melaniaæ by Mr. Tryon, and the Cycladidæ by Mr. Prime. Thus it appears that the malacologists have been unusually zealous in advancing their before somewhat slumbering study; and that the Smiths. Inst. has displayed unexpected liberality in preparing and issuing from the press works of a comprehensive character, for the " increase and diffusion of" what will hereafter be regarded as an important branch of "knowledge among men."

94. *North Pacific Exploring Expedition.*—In the year 1853, Dr. W. Stimpson, well known in very early life for his dredging-researches and observations on the marine animals of the Atlantic coast, accompanied Captain Ringold as naturalist to the U. S. " North Pacific Exploring Expedition." Its principal object was to obtain more correct information with regard to the Japan seas and the extreme north of the Pacific, and it was only incidentally that it visited the Californian province. However, Dr. Stimpson's extensive dredgings in the fiords of Japan developed the interesting fact, that while the southern shores presented a fauna essentially Indo-Pacific in its character, and abounding in the usual Cones, Cowries, Olives, &c., the northern slopes of the same islands presented an assemblage of forms far more analogous to the fauna of the Sitka and Vancouver region, and containing many species common to the American coast. During the course of the voyage dredging-collections† were made by Dr. Stimpson at Madeira, Cape of Good Hope, Sydney Harbour, Coral Seas, Port Jackson, Hong Kong (also by Mr. Wright; New Ireland, Lieut. Van Wycke; Gasper Straits, Squires; vicinity of Canton, presented by Mr. Bowring; interior of Hong Kong, Wright); China Sea; Whampoa; Bonin Island; Loo Choo Island; Ousima; Katonasima Straits; Kikaia; Kikaisima; Kagosima [alas!]; Hakodadi; Taniogesima (also Wright, Kent, Kern, Boggs, Carter); Simoda; Niphon (also Brook); Arvatska Bay, Kamtschatka; Amincheche Island, Avikamcheche Island, Behring Straits; Seniavine Straits, Arctic Ocean (also Captain Rogers); San Francisco; (Puget Sound and Shoalwater Bay, Dr. Cooper, Cat. no. 1849–1856); Tahiti (also Captain Stephens, Kern), Hawaii (also Garrett; Sea of Ochotsk, Captain Stevens). All these were duly catalogued, with stations, depths, and other particulars, and living animals preserved in spirits after being drawn. The expedition appears to have returned in 1856. Although Dr. Stimpson devoted his chief attention to articulate animals, and molluscs occupied but a subordinate share of his attention, it is safe to say that in this short period he collected more trustworthy species of shells, with localities, than were received at the Smiths. Inst. from the united labours of the naturalists of Captain Wilkes's celebrated expedition. Through some unaccountable cause, certain of the most valuable boxes were " lost" between New York and Washington; the remainder were placed in the hands of Dr. Gould for description, with the MS. catalogue, a copy of which forms the " Mollusca, Vol. I.," nos. 1–2003, of the Smiths. Mus. Fortunately, Dr. Gould embraced the opportunity to bring the uncertain shells to London, and compare them with the Cumingian Collection.

† A fuller account of this expedition is here given than is justified from its contributions to the W. American fauna, because no other information respecting it is as yet available to the malacological student.

Thus a large body of species, *named from types*, was prepared for the New World; but, unfortunately, through imperfect packing and the practice of marking by numbers only, much of the value of this identification was lost. The new species were described by Dr. Gould in the 'Boston Proc. Soc. Nat. Hist.,' 1859–1861; and on completion of the series, the author collected the papers embodying the new species of the two great scientific expeditions, as well as his other scattered publications, and issued them in a most valuable book, entitled 'Otia Conchologica: Descriptions of Shells and Molluscs, from 1839–1862,' Boston, 1862; with "Rectifications," embodying such changes of nomenclature and synonyms as he desired to represent his matured views. In quoting Dr. Gould's writings, therefore, this table should always be consulted. A considerable portion of the specimens have been returned to the Smiths. Inst., of which the larger species are mounted in the collection, and the smaller ones have been sent to the writer to compare with those collected by Mr. A. Adams, which were unfortunately being described in the London journals almost simultaneously. The war has unhappily postponed the intention of publishing the complete lists of species collected and identified with so much accurate care. The following, however, have already been determined by Dr. Gould from the region in which American species occur. The list is given entire (so far as identified), because species as yet known only on one coast of the North Pacific may hereafter be found on the other. It contains (as in the comparison of the Caribbean and West Mexican fauna) (*a*) species certainly identical, (*b*) probably identical, (*c*) "interesting anagues," and (*d*) representative forms.

S.I.Cat. no.

1263. *Crepidula hystryx*, var. Kagosima Bay, Japan. Dead on shore. [=*aculeata*, Maz. Cat. no. 334.]

1319. *Poronia rubra*, Mont. Kagosima Bay, Japan. [*Vide* Maz. Cat. no. 154.] Among sea-weeds and barnacles in 2nd and 3rd leve's; rocky shore.

1339. *Natica marochiensis* [?*maroccana*; *v.* Maz. Cat. no. 570]. Kagosima Bay, Japan. Dead on shore.

1344. *Acmæa ?Sieboldi*; very near *patina*. Kagosima Bay, Japan. Rocks at l. w.

1351. *Torinia variegata*, Lam. Kagosima Bay, Japan. [*Vide* Maz. Cat. no. 484.] Dead on shore.

1414. *Nassa gemmulata*, Lam. [non C. B. Ad.] Kagosima Bay, Japan. 5 fm. sd.

1476. *Acar* [*Barbatia*] *gradata*, Brod. and Sby. Taniogesima, Kagosima Bay, Japan. [*Vide* Maz. Cat. no. 194.] Dead in ten fm.; sand and shells.

407,476. *Acar* [*Barbatia*] *gradata*, Brod. and Sby. Port Jackson.

1502. *Lima squamosa*, Lam. Taniogesima, Japan. [= *L. tetrica*, Gld., teste *Cum.*]

The remaining species from these localities are either local or belong to the Philippine and Polynesian fauna. At Simoda and Hakodadi we enter on a mixed fauna.

1574. *Haliotis discus*, Rve. Simoda and Hakodadi. Rocks at low water, four fm. "*Kamtschatkana* seems to be the small growth of the same." [It is locally abundant, however, on the West Coast; while *discus* has never been found there, and is much flatter.]

1577. *Lutraria* [*Schizothærus Nuttallii*, Conr.] Hakodadi Bay. Eight fm. sand.

1579. *Cytherea petechialis*, Lam. Hakodadi Bay. Sand, 4th level.

1582. *Tritonium* [*Chrysodomus*] *antiquum*, Ln. Hakodadi Bay (also Okhotsk and Arctic Oc., 1779). Low-water mark and laminarian zone, on weedy rocks.

1585. *Tritonium* [*Priene*] *Oregonense*, Redf. Hakodadi Bay. Dead on shore, and in twenty fm. Also no. 1955.

1588. *Tellina Bodegensis*, Hds. Hakodadi Bay. Dead on shore.

1589. *Mya arenaria*, Ln. Hakodadi Bay.

1592. *Mercenaria orientalis*, Gld. [A West Atlantic type, probably = *M. Stimpsoni*, Otia, p. 109.] Hakodadi Bay. Six fm. sand.

S.I.Cat. no.
1596. *Venus rigida*, Gld. [MS. non Gld., Otia, p. 85,= *Tapes*, var. *Petitii*. The Japanese shell is *Adamsii*, Rve., from type]. Hakodadi Bay. Four to ten fm. sand.

The above occur in connexion with local and with diffused tropical species.

1601. *Euthria ferrea*, Rve. Simoda. Among stones and pebbles, 3rd level. [Almost identical with the Cape Horn species, *E. plumbea*, Phil.]
1630. *Tritonium* [*Chrysodomus*] *cassidariæformis*, Rve. East Coast of Japan, lat. 37°, and Hakodadi. Twenty fm., black coarse sand.
1632. *Chiton* "largest" [? *Cryptochiton Stelleri*]. Hakodadi. On large stones and under shelving rocks, low-water mark.
1634. *Pecten*, like [=] *Islandicus*. Hakodadi. Ten fm. shell-sand.
1635. *Sanguinolaria Nuttallii*, Conr.,= *decora*, Hds. Hakodadi. "Possibly= *Soletellina obscurata*, Desh." Sand, low-water mark.
1637. *Macoma lata*, "Gmel. in Mus. Cum.,= *calcarea*, Chem.,= *proxima*, Brown,= *sordida*, Couth.,= *Suensoni*, Mörch." Hakodadi. 4th level, sandy mud.
1639. *Litorina Grænlandica*, Chem. Hakodadi. Rocks, 1st level.
1648. *Cardium pseudofossile*, Rve.,= *blandum*, Gld., perhaps= *Californiensi*, Desh. Hakodadi. Twenty fm. sand.
1651. *Terebratula* [*Waldheimia*] *Grayi*, Desh. Hakodadi. Shelly gravel, 8–15 fm.
1665. *Leda arctica*, Brod. [= *Y. lanceolata*, J. Sby.]. Hakodadi. Sandy mud, 4–12 fm. Seniavine Str., 10–30 fm.
1674. *Drillia inermis*, Hds. Hakodadi. Shelly sand, 4–10 fm.
1700. *Pecten Yessoensis*, Jay. [Probably a var. of *Amusium caurinum*.] Hakodadi. Weedy mud, 4 fm.
1702. *Cardium* (*Serripes*) *Grænlandicum*. Awatska Bay, Kamtschatka. Mud, 12 fm. Also Avikamcheche Is., Behring Str., and Arctic Ocean.
1703. *Yoldia thraciæformis*, Storer. Hakodadi. Mud, 12 fm.
1704. *Mytilus edulis*. Hakodadi. Also Avikamcheche Is., Behring Str., and Arctic Ocean. Low-water mark, and in 3rd and 4th level.
1705. *Cardium Californiense*, Desh. Hakodadi. Mud, 12 fm. [= no. 1648.]
1706. *Mya truncata*. Hakodadi; also Avikamcheche Is. Mud, 6–15 fm. Also Arctic Ocean, in mud, 30 fm.
1708. *Buccinum glaciale*. Hakodadi, and Straits of Seniavine, at Amincheche Is., Behring Str.
1710. *Tritonium* [*Chrysodomus*] *antiquum*+*deformis*, Rve., and vars. Hakodadi and Avikamcheche Is. Gravel, 4 fm.
1711. *Buccinum tortuosum*, Rve.,= *scalariforme*+vars. Straits of Seniavine.
1714. *Mya ? arenaria*. Hakodadi and Avikamcheche Is.
1715. *Bullia* [*Volutharpa*] *ampullacea*, Midd. Hakodadi. Gravel, 5–6 fm.
1716. *Lanistes lævigata*, Gray (= *discors*, Ln., teste Dkr. in Mus. Cum.). Mud, 20 fm. Hakodadi and Arctic Ocean ; common, in nests, 30 fm. ; no. 1739.
1717. *Trichotropis multicaudata* [? = *Tr. coronata*, Otia, p. 121 : related to *insignis*, Midd., teste A. Ad.]. Hakodadi. Gravelly mud, 15 fm.
1718. [*Lepeta*] *cæca*, var. *concentrica*, Midd. Hakodadi and Arctic Ocean.
1719. *Trichotropis bicarinata*, Sby. Hakodadi. Not uncommon in laminarian zone. Arctic Ocean ; common.
1720. *Macoma proxima*, Brown. Hakodadi; mud, 5–25 fm. Awatska Bay. Arctic Ocean ; common, no. 1727.
1721. *Macoma edentula*, Brod. and Sby. Hakodadi. Avikamcheche Is.
1722. *Crepidula grandis*, Midd. Hakodadi. Okhotsk, 15 fm. : no. 2002.
1723. *Venus flucuosa*, Gld., 1841. ? = *astartoides*, Beck, 1849. Hakodadi and Arctic Ocean ; not uncommon. Mud, 5–10 fm.
1725. *Cardita* (*Actinobolus*) *borealis*, Conr. Avikamcheche Is., Behring Straits ; mud, 5–30 fm. Awatska Bay ; 10 fm. mud. Arctic Ocean ; common.
1726. *Saxicava pholadis*, L.,= *rugosa*+*distorta*. Avikamcheche Is., Arctic Ocean. Awatska Bay ; on shells, &c. Lam. zone ; no. 1729.
1728. *Margarita obscura*, Couth. Awatska Bay, Kamtschatka. Mud, 10 fm.
1732. *Bela turricula*., Mont. Awatska Bay ; mud, 6–15 fm. Also Seniavine Str.; no. 1782.

S.I.Cat. no.
1733. *Yoldia limatula*, Say. Awatska Bay and Arctic Oc. Mud, common, 5–20 fm.
1734. *Natica clausa*, Brod. Awatska Bay. Mud, 5–15 fm.
1735. *Yoldia myalis* (or *hyperborea*). Awatska Bay. Mud, 10 fm.
1736. *Leda minuta*. Seniavine Str.; Arctic Oc., near Behr. Str. Mud and pebbly sand, 15–30 fm., coarse striæ.
1737. *Leda minuta*, var. Ditto. Mud and pebbly sand, 5–20 fm., fine striæ.
1740. *Modiolaria corrugata*. Ditto. Mud, in nests, 30 fm.
1741. *Rhynchonella psittacea*. Ditto. Gravel and sponges, 20–30 fm.
1742. *Margarita striata*, Leach. Ditto. Shelly gravel, common, 15–30 fm.
1744. *Admete arctica*, Midd. Ditto. Mud, 30 fm.
1745. *Admete viridula*, Couth. Ditto. Gravel, 4 fm.; mud, 10–30 fm.
1747. *Velutina haliotoidea*. Ditto. Gravel, 10–25 fm.
1748. *Margarita argentata* [Gld. Inv. Mass.]. Ditto. Mud, 30 fm.; shelly, 15–25 fm.
1749. *Turritella* (sp.), Migh. Ditto. Mud, 30 fm.; clean gravel, 4–20 fm.
1750. *Trichotropis bicarinata*. Ditto. Pebbly mud, 5–6 fm.
1751. *Lunatia pallida*, Brod. Ditto. Mud, 10–30 fm.
1752. *Cylichna triticea*, Couth. Ditto. Mud, 15–30 fm.
1753. *Velutina* [*Morvilia*] *zonata* [Gld. Inv. Mass.]. Ditto. On stones, 5 fm.
1754. *Nucula tenuis*, Mont. Ditto. Mud, common, 20–30 fm.; pebbly mud, 5–20 fm. Also Hakodadi; sandy mud, 10 fm.; no. 1687.
1756. *Trophon clathratus*, Linn. Ditto. Mud, 20–30 fm.; gravel, 4 fm.
1757. *Lunatia septentrionalis*, Beck. Ditto. Gravelly mud, common, 20 fm.; gravel, 4 fm.
1758. *Amicula vestita*, Sby. Ditto. Gravel, common, 10–40 fm.
1750. *Scalaria Grœnlandica*, Chemn. Ditto. Mud, 30 fm.
1760. *Lunatia pallidoides*. Ditto. Mud, 30 fm.
1761. *Chrysodomus Islandicus*, Chemn. Ditto. Mud, 30 fm.
1762. *Patella* [*Lepeta*] *candida*, Couth. Ditto. Mud, 30 fm.
1763. *Chiton albus*, Linn. Ditto. On shells in mud, 30 fm.
1765. *Chrysodomus Schantaricus*, Midd. Ditto. Mud, 20–30 fm.
1770. *Astarte lactea*, Br. and Sby. Arctic Oc. Mud, 30 fm.
1771. *Pecten Islandicus*, Chemn., var. Arctic Oc. Mud, 30 fm.
1773. *Buccinum ?undatum* (probably bicarinate var. of *glaciale*). Arctic Ocean.
1774. *Buccinum ?undatum*, var. *pelagica*. Arctic Ocean.
1775. *Buccinum ?Ochotense*, Midd. Arctic Ocean.
1776. *Buccinum angulosum*, Gray (= *glaciale*, var.). Arctic Ocean.
1777. *Buccinum ? tenue*, Gray. Arctic Ocean.
1778. *Mangelia*, like *simplex*, Midd. Arctic Ocean.
1781. *Bela rufa*, Mont. Seniavine Str. Pebbly mud, common, 5 fm.
1783. *Turritella erosa*. Seniavine Str. Mud, 10–20 fm.
1784. *Lyonsia Norvegica*, Chem. Seniavine Str. Pebbly mud, 5 fm.
1785. *Trichotropis insignis*, Midd. Seniavine Str. Gravel, 10 fm.
1789. *Bela decussata*, Couth. Seniavine Str. Sandy mud, 10–20 fm. Also Awatska Bay; no. 1790.
1790. *Yoldia myalis*, Couth. Seniavine Str. Mud, 10–20 fm.; pebbly mud, 5 fm.
1791. *Bela harpularia*, Couth. Pebbly mud, 5 fm.
1793. *Margarita helicina*, Fabr. Behring Str. Clean gravel and algæ, 5 fm.
1796. *Turtonia* [? *minuta*, Fabr.]. Behring Str. Common on sponges, 20–40 fm.
1798. *Lunatia* [*Acrybia*] *aperta*, Lov. Kamtschatka.
1799. *Modiolaria nigra*, Gray. Arctic Ocean.
1821. *Chama lobata* [= *exogyra*, Jay, non Conr.]. China Sea, west of Formosa. Shell-gravel, 30 fm.
1836. *Purpura emarginata*, Desh. San Francisco. On rocks in 4th level.
1837. *Litorina plena*, Gld. San Francisco. On rocks in 3rd and 4th levels.
1838. *Acmœa textilis*, Gld. San Francisco. On piles and rocks between tides.
1838*b*. *Acmœa patina*, Esch. San Francisco. On piles and rocks between tides.
1839. *Cryptomya Californica*, Conr. San Francisco. On sandy beaches.
1840. *Macoma nasuta*, Conr. San Francisco. Common in sandy mud, l. w. 10 fm.
1841. *Cardium Nuttallii*, Conr. San Francisco. Common in sandy mud, l. w. 10 fm.

71

S.I.Cat. no.

1843. *Mytilus edulis*, var. San Francisco. On rocks and gravel, 4th level.

1844. *Mytilus Californianus*, Conr. Near entrance to San Francisco. On rocks and gravel, 4th level.

1845. *Tapes diversa*, Sby. San Francisco Bay. Very common, low-water mark [= *V. staminea*, Conr., var.,= *V. mundulus*, Rve. ; *v. antea*, p. 570].

1846. *Chiton [Mopalia] muscosus*, Gld. Entrance of San Francisco Bay. Not uncommon on rocks at low-water mark.

1847. *Cryptodon [Schizothærus] Nuttallii*, Conr., jun. San Francisco. One sp.

1848. *Machæra lucida*, Conr. San Francisco. Common. [= *M. patula*, Portl.]

The shells brought back by the Expedition from Puget Sound and Shoal-water Bay were collected by Dr. Cooper, whom Dr. Stimpson met at San Francisco, and are not here catalogued, as they appear again in his own collections, *v. infra*, par. 101.

1800. *Lithophagus cinnamomeus*. China coast, lat. 23½°. Dead, 25 fm., sand.

1924. *Helix tudiculata*, Bin. Petaluma, Cal.; under stems in open grove of scrub oak.

1956. *Mytilus splendens*, Gld. Hakodadi Bay. Rocks below tide-marks, com.

1957. *Anomia olivacea*, Gld. Hakodadi Bay. On shells or gravelly sand, 10 fm.

1958. *Cerastoma foliatum*, var. *Burnettii*, Ad. and Rve. Hakodadi Bay and N. E. part of Niphon. Low-water mark, on rocks and boulders.

1959. *Haliotis Kamtschatkana*, Jonas. N. E. shore of Niphon. See no. 1574.

1860. *Purpura Freycinettii*, Desh. N. E. shore of Niphon. Common on rocks.

1861. *Purpura Freycinettii*, var. with muriciform lamellæ. N. E. shore of Niphon.

1863. *Placunanomia macroschisma*, Desh. West Coast of Jesso. Gravel, 30 fm.

1968. *Terebratula pulvinata*, Gld. Arctic Ocean. Gravel, 30 fm.

2090. *Puncturella noachina*, Linn. Sea of Okhotsk. Gravel, 20 fm.

2091. *Astarte luctea*, Brod. and Sbv. Sea of Okhotsk. Gravel, 20 fm.

2033. *Terebratula globosa*, Lam. Sea of Okhotsk. Gravel, 36 fm. [Perhaps *Californica*, Koch.]

The following, from among the new species described by Dr. Gould in his ' Otia Conch.,' belong to the same province, and to forms which may be expected to appear on the northern shores of West America. They were first published in the Proc. Bost. Soc. Nat. Hist., under the dates quoted :—

Otia.p. Bost. Proc.S.N.H.

109. 1859. June. *Natica severa*, Gld., like *heros*, but with umbilicus resembling *unifasciata*. Hakodadi, W. S.

109. „ „ *Natica russa*, Gld., like *clausa*. Arctic Ocean, W. S.

115. „ Dec. *Patella pallida*, Gld. Hakodadi. On stones and gravel, 10 fm.

115. „ „ *Patella grata*, Gld. N. E. shore of Niphon.

115. „ „ *Acmæa dorsuosa*, Gld., like *patina*, var. *monticula [monticola]*, Nutt. Hakodadi, on rocks of 2nd and 3rd lamin. zone. W. S.

117. „ „ *Chiton (Leptochiton) concinnus*, Gld., like *albus*, but with lines of punctures. Hakodadi, W. S.

118. „ „ *Chiton (Acanthochætes) achates*, Gld. Kikaia, Hakodadi, W. S.

118. 1859. Dec. *Chiton (Mopalia) Stimpsoni*, Gld., like *Blainvillei*, without anterior radiating lines. ["On stones, clean bottom, 25 fm., and under stones and rocks, low-water mark."—Smiths. Cat. no. 1646. Not to be confounded with *M. Simpsoni*, Gray.] Hakodadi, W. S.

120. 1860. Sept. *Terebratula [? Waldheimia] transversa*, Gld., like *Grayi*, with shorter internal supports : [= *Grayi*, teste A. Ad.] Hakodadi, W. S.

120. „ „ *Terebratella miniata*, Gld., like *Zelandica*. Apophyses united to central crest. [= *Waldheimia Koreanica*, Ad. and Rve., teste Rve. from type. "On pebbles, clean bottom, 30 fm." Smiths. Cat. 1597.] Hakodadi, W. S.

120. „ „ *Rhynchonella lucida*, Gld.; in aspect like *T. vitrea*, jur.

121. „ „ *Trichotropis (Iphinoö) coronata*, Gld.; like *T. cihata*, Kruger. Straits of Semiavine, Arctic Ocean, 20 fm. mud. W. S.

Otia, p. Bost. Proc. S.N.H.

122. 1860. Sept. *Buccinum Stimpsoni*, Gld.; like *undatum*, but quite distinct. Avikamcheche Is., Behring Str., W. S. Arctic Ocean, *Rodgers*. [Not *B. Stimpsonianum*, C. B. Ad.]

123. . ,,   ,,   *Neptunea (Sipho) terebralis*, Gld.; like *Icelandica*. Arctic Oc.

125.   ,,   ,,   *Trophon incomptus*, Gld.; like *crassus*. Hakodadi, W. S.

134.   ,,   Oct.   *Bela turgida*, Gld. Kamtschatka, W. S.

153. 1861. Mar. *Margarita ianthina*, Gld.; like *Schantarica*. Arctic Ocean.

154.   ,,   ,,   *Margarita albula*, Gld.; like an overgrown *arctica*. Arctic Ocean., W. S.

154.   ,,   ,,   *Margarita mustelina*, Gld. Hakodadi; low water, W. S.

159.   ,,   ,,   *Gibbula redimita*, Gld.; like *nivosa*, A. Ad. Hakodadi, W. S.

162.   ,,   ,,   *Lyonsia ventricosa*, Gld.: shorter than *Norvegica*. Hakodadi, 2–6 fm., sandy mud, W. S. ["? = *navicula*, jun." A. Ad.]

162.   ,,   ,,   *Lyonsia (Pandorina) flabellata*, Gld.; like *arenosa*. Arctic Ocean, W. S.

162.   ,,   ,,   *Theora lubrica*, Gld. Hakodadi; common in mud, 6 fm., W. S.

163.   ,,   ,,   *Panopæa fragilis*, Gld. Hakodadi, W. S.

163.   ,,   ,,   *Panopæa ? generosa*, var. *sagrinata*. Awatska Bay, Kamtschatka, W. S. ["Epidermis projects ¼ in., as in *Glycimeris*. Mud, 12 fm." Smiths. Cat. 1701.]

164.   ,,   ,,   *Corbula venusta*, Gld. Hakodadi, 5–8 fm., shelly sand, W. S.

165.   ,,   ,,   *Solen strictus*, Gld.; like *corneus*. Hakodadi, W. S.

165.   ,,   ,,   *Solen gracilis*, Gld. [non Phil.] Hakodadi, sandy beaches, W. S.

165.   ,,   ,,   *Machæra sodalis*, Gld.; like *costata*. Hakodadi, W. S.

165.   ,,   ,,   *Solemya pusilla*, Gld.; like *velum*. Hakodadi, 5 fm., mud, W.S.

167.   ,,   ,,   *Tellina lubrica*, Gld.; like *felix* and *fabagella*. Hakodadi, 6 fm., sandy mud, W. S.

168.   ,,   ,,   *Saxidomus aratus*, Gld.; like *V. maxima*, Phil. San Francisco. [Described as 4·5 in. long, yet] smaller than *Nuttallii*. ["Open bays at Sir F. Drake's; l. w., sand." Smiths. Cat. 1842.]

169.   ,,   ,,   *Venus (Mercenaria) Stimpsoni*, Gld.; like the Atlantic forms. Hakodadi, 6 fm., W. S.

170.   ,,   ,,   *Mysia (Felania) usta*, Gld.; like an *Astarte*. Hakodadi, 8 fm., sandy mud, W. S.

173.   ,,   Apr.   *Montacuta divaricata*, Gld. Hakodadi, on *Spatangus*-spines,W.S.

175.   ,,   ,,   *Nucula (Acila) insignis*, Gld.; like *mirabilis*: [identical, teste A. Ad.] E. Japan, lat. 37°, and Hakodadi, W. S. ["20 fm. black coarse sand."—Smiths. Cat. 1628.]

177.   ,,   ,,   *Mytilus coruscus*, Gld.* Hakodadi; common on rocks between tide-marks, W. S. [? = *M. splendens.*, no. 1956.]

177.   ,,   ,,   *Pecten lætus*, Gld.; resembles generally *P. senatorius*, is still more like *P.* [*Amusium*] *caurinus*. Hakodadi, shelly mud, 10 fm., W. S. [Non *P. lætus*, Gld., in U. S. Expl. Exped. Shells, Otia, p. 95, = *P. Dieffenbachii*, Gray, teste Cuming.]

95. The United States Expedition to Japan, under Commodore M. C. Perry, 1852–4, was not undertaken for scientific purposes; and no special provision was made either for collecting or describing objects of natural history. A large number of shells, however, were obtained, and identified by Dr. Jay of New York. In Vol. II. of the 'Narrative of the Expedition, &c.' (Washington, 1856, pp. 289–297) is given a list of Japanese shells, with descriptions and figures of the (supposed) new species. The following are related to the molluscs of the West Coast †. Specimens of the most important may be seen in the Cumingian Collection.

* The *M. mutabilis*, described on the same page from Kagosima, is a *Septifer*; it is presumed that the learned author did not open a specimen.

† The student should also consult, for related forms, the 'Mollusca Japonica' by Dr. W. Dunker, Stuttgart, 1861;—like all the other works of the same author, most valuable for the patient care, accurate judgment, and enlarged experience displayed; but relating chiefly to the subtropical portion of the fauna.

Page.	Pl.	Fig.		
292.	1.	7,10.	*Mya Japonica*, n. s. Volcano Bay, Is. Yedo. Closely related to *M. arenaria* : [identical, teste A. Ad.].	
292.	1.	8,9.	*Psammobia olivacea*, n. s. Bay of Yedo. [Nearly allied to *Hiatula Nuttalli*.]	
293.	{4.	1,2. }	*Pecten Yessoensis*, n. s. Hakodadi. [Resembles *Amussium*	
	{3.	3,4. }	*caurinum*, Gld.]	
295.	5.	16,17.	*Purpura septentrionalis*, Rve. [=*P. crispata*, var.] ?Japan.	
295.	5.	13,15.	?*Bullia Perryi*, n. s. Bay of Yedo, one sp. dredged. [= *Volutharpa ampullacea*, Midd.]	
296.			*Venerupis Nuttalli*, Conr. [*Saxidomus*]. Japan.	
296.			*Tellina secta*, Conr. Japan.	
296.			*Tapes decussata*, Ln. [Probably *T. Petitii*, var. or *Adamsii*. Japan.]	
296.			*Ostrea borealis*, Ln. Japan.	
296.			*Ianthina communis*, Lam. Japan.	
296.			*Ianthina prolongata*, Blainv. Japan.	

96. At the time that Dr. Gould was describing Dr. Stimpson's Japanese shells in the Boston Proc. Ac. N. S., Mr. A. Adams, R.N., one of the learned authors of the 'Genera of Recent Mollusca,' was making extensive and accurate dredgings in the same seas. The new genera and species have been and are being published, in a series of papers, in the Ann. & Mag. Nat. Hist. and in the Proc. Zool. Soc., preparatory to an intended complete work on the mollusc-fauna of the Eastern North Pacific. The collections of Mr. Adams have already displayed the Japanese existence of several species, as *Siphonalia Kellettii*, *Solen sicarius*, *Homalopoma sanguineum*, &c., before supposed to be peculiar to the West coast. Unfortunately for our present purpose, while the comparison of specimens was going on, Mr. Adams was unexpectedly called to service on board H.M.S. 'Majestic,' and was obliged to pack up his collections. Enough has been ascertained, however, to prove that it will be unsafe henceforth to describe species from either coast without comparison with those of the opposite shores.

97. *Pacific Railroad Reports.*—As it is necessary, in studying any fauna, to make comparisons far round in space, so it is essential to travel far back in time. The fullest account of the fossils of the West Coast of America is to be found in the 'Explorations and Surveys for a Railroad Route from the Mississippi River to the Pacific Ocean,' which form ten thick quarto volumes, copiously illustrated with plates, and published by the U.S. Senate, Washington, 1856 *. The natural-history department was conducted under the superintendence and with the aid of the Smithsonian Institution; and science is under special obligations to Prof. Spencer S. Baird, the Assistant Secretary, for his Reports on the Vertebrate Animals. It would hardly be expected in Europe that the best *résumé* of the zoology, the botany, and the geology of the vast region between the Great American desert and the Pacific should be found in a railroad survey. Unfortunately, it has not been the custom to advertize and sell the valuable documents printed at the expense of the U. S. Government, in the ordinary channels of trade. They often become the perquisites of the members of Congress, and through them of the various *employés*, by whom they are transferred to the booksellers' shelves. The fifth volume of the series is devoted to the explorations of Lieut. Williamson; the second Part contains the Report by W. P. Blake, geologist and mineralogist of the expedition. In the Appendix, Art. II., are found " Descriptions of the Fossil Shells," by T. A. Conrad. They were first published in the

* This extremely costly and valuable assemblage of documents was selling in Washington, in 1860, at £5 sterling the set.

'Appendix to the Preliminary Geological Report,' 8vo, Washington, 1855. They are divided into, I. " Eocene," and II. " Miocene and Recent Formations."

I. *Eocene* (all from Cañada de las Uvãs *).

Plate.	Fig.	No.	
II.	1.	1.	*Cardium linteum*, Conr., n.s. Allied to *C. Nicolleti*, Conr.
„	2.	2.	*Dosinia alta*, Conr., n.s.
„	3.	3.	*Meretrix Uvasana*, Conr., n.s.
„	4.	4.	*Meretrix Californiana*, Conr., n.s. Allied to *M. Poulsoni*, Conr.
„	5.	5.	*Crassatella Uvasana*, Conr., n.s.
		6.	*Crassatella alta*, Conr., n.s. In small fragments, but abundant, as at Claiborne. Al.
„	10.	7.	*Mytilus humerus*, Conr., n.s.
„	6.	8.	*Cardita planicosta*, Lam., = *Venericardia ascia*, Rogers. First discovered in Maryland in 1829, by Conr.; occurs abundantly in Md., Va., Al., and is quite as characteristic of the American as of the European Eocene period.
„	7.	9.	*Natica ? otites*, Conr., 1833.
„	7.	10.	*Natica ? gibbosa*, Lea, 1833, or *N. semilunata*, Lea ; also found at Claiborne, Al.
„	8.	11.	*Natica alveata*, Conr., n.s.
„	12.	12.	*Turritella Uvasana*, Conr., n. s. Allied to *T. obruta*, Conr., = *T. lineata*, Lea, from Claiborne, Al.
„	9.	13.	*Volutatithes* [? *Volutilithes*] *Californiana*, Conr., n.s. Resembles *V. Sayana*, Conr.
„	13.	14.	*? Busycon Blakei*, Conr., n.s.
„	11.	15.	*Clavatula Californica*, Conr., n.s. Allied to *C. proruta*, Conr., of Claiborne Eocene.

II. *Miocene and Recent Formations* (from various localities).

III.	15.	16.	*Cardium molestum*, Conr., n.s. San Diego. [May be *Hemicardium biangulatum*, jun.]
„	19.	17.	*Nucula decisa*, Conr., n.s. Resembles *N. divaricata* of the Oregon Miocene. [Closely allied to *N. castrensis*, &c., but too imperfect to determine.] San Diego.
III.	16.	18.	*Corbula Diegoana*, Conr., n.s. San Diego.
„	20.	19.	*Meretrix uniomeris*, Conr., n.s. Monterey Co.
„	27.	20.	*Meretrix decisa*, Conr., n.s. Ocoya Creek.
„	22.	21.	*Meretrix Tularena*, Conr., n.s., [in list, "*Tularana*" in text]. From a boulder in Tulare Valley. [Comp. *Tapes gracilis*, Gld.]
„	28.	22.	*Tellina Diegoana*, Conr., n.s., San Diego.
„	14, 18 & 21	23.	*Tellina congesta*. Conr., n.s. [Appears a *Heterodonax*, allied to *bimaculata*, Lam.] Abundant at Monterey, Carmello, and San Diego.
„	17.	24.	*Tellina Pedroana*, Conr., n.s. [? = *T. gemma*, Gld.] Recent formation. San Pedro.
„	29.	25.	*Arca microdonta*, Conr., n.s. Resembles *A. arata*, Say, of the Maryland Miocene. Miocene, ? Tulare Valley.

* The existence of Eocene strata on the Pacific slope is ascertained by a single boulder of very hard sandstone, which, though very small, furnished fifteen species. Of these, three correspond with forms from Claiborne, Alabama ; and the "finger-post of the Eocene" appears in its usual abundance. Mr. Conrad characterizes the specimens as " beautifully perfect ;" which would not have been supposed from his descriptions and figures. They " seem to indicate a connexion of the Atlantic and Pacific Oceans during the Eocene period ;" and the author expects that " when the rock shall have been discovered and investigated *in situ*, fresh forms will be obtained, with which we are already familiar in eastern localities."

Plate	Fig.	No.	
IV.	31.	26.	*Tapes diversum*, Sby. [= *Tapes staminea*, Conr., var. *Petitii*,
(III. in text).			Desh.] Recent formation. San Pedro.
III.	25.	27.	*Saxicava abrupta*, Conr., n.s. [Probably the shortened form of
			Petricola carditoides, Conr.] Recent formation. San Pedro.
„	24.	28.	*Petricola Pedroana*, Conr., n.s. [Allied to *P. ventricosa*, Desh.]
			Recent formation San Pedro.
IV.	33.	29.	*Schizothærus Nuttalli*, Conr., "n.s."= *Tresus capax*, Gld. Recent
			formation. San Pedro.
III.	23.	30.	*?Lutraria Traskei*, Conr., n.s. [Not improbably = *Saxidomus*
			Nuttallii, Conr., jun.] ?Miocene. Carmello.
V.	45.	31.	*Mactra Diegoana*, Conr., n.s. Like *M. albaria*, of the Oregon
			Miocene. [Resembles *Mulinia angulata*, Gray.] ?Miocene.
			San Diego.
„	35.	32.	*Modiola contracta*, Conr., n.s. [Very like *M. recta*, Conr.] ?Mio-
			cene. Monterey Co. Recent formation.
„	40.	33.	*Mytilus Pedroanus*, Conr., n.s. [Probably= *M. edulis*, jun.]
			Recent formation. San Pedro.
„	41.	34.	*Pecten Deserti*, Conr., n.s. [Resembles *P. circularis*.] Mio-
			cene. Carrizo Creek, Colorado Desert.
„	34.	35.	*Anomia subcostata*, Conr., n.s. [?= *Placunanomia macroschisma*.]
			Miocene. Colorado Desert. Allied to *A. Ruffini*.
„	36–38.	36.	*Ostrea vespertina*, Conr., n.s. [Resembles *O. lurida*, var.] Mio-
			cene. Colorado Desert. Like *O. subfalcata*, Conr.
		37.	*Ostrea Heermanni*, Conr., n.s. Colorado Desert.
„	43.	38.	*Penitella spelæa*, Conr., n.s.* Recent formation. San Pedro.
„	44.	39.	*Fissurella crenulata*, Sby. [= *Lucapina c.*] Recent formation.
			San Pedro.
VI.	52.	40.	*Crepidula princeps*, Conr., n.s. [= *C. grandis*, Midd.] Recent
			formation. Santa Barbara.
V.	39.	41.	*Narica Diegoana*, Conr., n.s. ?Miocene. San Diego.
„	42.	42.	*Trochita Diegoana*, Conr., n.s. [Like *T. ventricosa*; but may be
			Galerus contortus.] ?Miocene. San Diego.
„	46.	43.	*Crucibulum spinosum*, Conr., n.s.† Recent formation. San Diego.
VI.	49.	44.	*Nassa interstriata*, Conr., n.s. [= *N. mendica*, Gld.]. Recent
			formation. San Pedro.
„	48.	45.	*Nassa Pedroana*, Conr., n.s. [Comp. *Amycla gausapata* and its
			congeners.]‡ Recent formation. San Pedro.
„	51.	46.	*Strephona Pedroana*, Conr., n.s. [Comp. *Olivella bætica*.] Recent
			formation. San Pedro.
• „	50.	47.	*Litorina Pedroana*, Conr., n.s. [= *L. plena*, Gld.] Recent forma-
			tion. San Pedro.
„	47.	48.	*Stramonita petrosa*, Conr., n.s. [Is perhaps *Monoceros lugubre*.]
			?—. Tulare Valley.

* Mr. Conrad regards the "coriaceous cup as characteristic of the genus." It appears a subgenus of *Pholadidea*, differing in the form of the plate. Mr. Tryon, "Mon. Pholad.," p. 66, restricts it to the *Penitella penita*, which (according to his diagnosis) has one central and two anterior dorsal plates. The closely related *P. ovoidea* he leaves in the original genus, as having "two dorsal accessory valves," although he allows that "its position cannot be accurately determined on account of the loss of its dorsal valves." Conrad's fossil has the shape of *P. ovoidea*; but although he says that it is "widely distinct" from *P. penita*, I am unable to separate it from the ovoid form of that species, which will be found in the Smithsonian series.

† This is certainly Sowerby's species, to which Conrad gives a doubting reference. In the text he gives it as "*spinosum*, Conr.," in his table marking it as "nov. sp."

‡ Conrad compares *N. interstriata* to *N. trivittata*, Say, and *N. Pedroana* to *N. lunata*, Say, and states that the two Atlantic species are "associated with each other both in the sea and in the Miocene deposits of Virginia and Maryland." As the two correlative species are found together, living and fossil, on the Pacific side, there is presumptive evidence for their having descended from a common stock.

ON MOLLUSCA OF THE WEST COAST OF NORTH AMERICA. 591

Plate	Fig.	No.	
VI.	54.	49.	?*Gratelupia mactropsis*, Conr., n.s. [?=*Donax punctatostriatus*.] ?Miocene. Isthmus of Darien. Resembles *G. Hydeana*, Conr. Eocene.
„	55.	50.	*Meretrix Dariena*, Conr., n.s. [Comp. *Cyclina subquadrata*.] ?Miocene. Isthmus of Darien.
„	53.	51.	*Tellina Dariena*, Conr., n.s. ?Miocene. Isthmus of Darien.
VII	57.	52.	*Natica Ocoyana*, Conr., n.s. [Marked 51 on plate: err.] Ocoya or Posé Creek.
„	67.	53.	*Natica geniculata*, Conr., n.s. Ocoya Creek. Resembles *N. alveata*.
„	62.	54.	*Bulla jugularis*, Conr., n.s. Ocoya Creek.
„	69.	55.	*Pleurotoma transmontana*, Conr., n.s. [Marked 60 on plate: err. Closely resembles *Chrysodomus dirus*, Rve.] Ocoya Creek.
		56.	*Pleurotoma Ocoyana*, Conr., n.s. [Omitted in the text.] Ocoya Cr.
„	72.	57.	*Syctopus* [Ficula.] *Ocoyanus*, Conr., n.s. Ocoya Creek.
VIII.	73.	58.	*Turritella Ocoyana*, Conr., n.s. Ocoya Creek.
„	76.	59.	*Colus arctatus*, Conr., n.s. Ocoya Creek.
„	75.	60.	*Tellina Ocoyana*, Conr., n.s. Ocoya Creek.
„	77.	61.	*Pecten Nevadanus*, Conr., n.s. Very like *N. Humphreysii*, Maryland, Miocene. Ocoya Creek.
IX.	83.	62.	*Pecten calilliformis*, Conr., n.s. Very like *P. Madisonius*, Say, Virginia, Miocene. Ocoya Creek.

The following species are not described in the text, but quoted in the list. *Vide* p. 320:—

Plate	Fig.	No.	
VIII.	?78.	63.	*Cardium*, sp. ind. Ocoya Creek.
		64.	*Arca*, sp. ind. Ocoya Creek.
„	?80.	65.	*Solen*, sp. ind. Ocoya Creek.
„	?81.	66.	*Dosinia*, sp. ind. Ocoya Creek.
„	?79.	67.	*Venus*, sp. ind. Ocoya Creek.
		68.	*Cytherea ? decisa*, Conr. Ocoya Creek.
		69.	*Ostrea*, sp. ind. San Fernando.
		70.	*Pecten*, sp. ind. San Fernando.
		71.	*Turritella biseriata*, Conr., ?n.s. San Fernando.
VII.	?58.	72.	*Trochus*, sp. ind. Benicia.
„	?59.	73.	*Turritella*, sp. ind. Benicia.
„	?71.	74.	*Buccinum ?interstriatum*. San Pedro.
*		75.	*Anodonta Californiensis*, Lea. Colorado Desert.

Mr. Conrad, than whom there is no higher authority for American Tertiary fossils, considers the age of the Eocene boulder ascertained; and that " the deposits of Santa Barbara and San Pedro represent a recent formation, in which (*teste* Blake) the remains of the Mammoth occur: and the shells indicate little, if any, change of temperature since their deposition." But he acknowledges that the intermediate beds are of uncertain age. Those on Carrizo Creek he refers to the Miocene, some characteristic species being either identical with the Eastern Miocene or of closely related forms. In addition to the species tabulated in this Report, he quotes, as having been collected in California by Dr. Heermann, " *Mercenaria perlaminosa*, Conr., scarcely differing from *M. Ducatelii*, Conr.; and a *Cemoria, Pandora*, and *Cardita* of extinct species, closely analogous to Miocene forms." The casts from Ocoya Creek were too friable to be preserved, and are figured and described from Mr. Blake's drawings; these also are regarded as Miocene. The San Diegan specimens are too imperfect for identification; they are referred to the Miocene by Conrad, but may perhaps be found to belong to a later

---

* Several fossils are figured in plates vii. and viii., to which no reference is made in the text. It is unsafe to conjecture the genus to which many of them belong, but it is presumed that they relate to the indeterminate species here quoted.

age. The types of these species in the Smithsonian Museum a᷄, ᷄ea᷄ too imperfect to determine specifically with any confidence ; and by no means iɪ. a suitable condition to allow of important conclusions being drawn from them.

98. The third article in the Appendix to the same volume of Reports contains a "Catalogue of the Recent Shells, with Descriptions of the New Species," by Dr. A. A. Gould. The specimens were (apparently) in the hands of Dr. Gould for examination when he prepared the MS. for the first Report; and some of them were included in the "Mexican War Collections," B. A. Report, pp. 227, 228. "The freshwater shells were collected in the Colorado desert and other localities ; the land and marine shells between San Francisco and San Diego." The following is the list of species as determined by Dr. Gould, pp. 330–336. The specimens belong to the Smithsonian Institution, where a large portion of them were fortunately discovered and verified. They were collected by W. P. Blake, Esq., and Dr. T. H. Webb.

Plate.	Fig.	No.	
		1.	*Ostrea*, sp. ind. Parasitic on twigs; thin, radiately lineated with brown. [= *O. conchaphila*, Cpr.] Another species, elongated, solid, allied to *Virginica* [var. *rufoides*]. San Diego.
		2.	*Pecten monotimeris*, Conr. San Diego.
		3.	*Pecten ventricosus*, Sby., +*tumidus*, Sby. [Dead valves, of the form *æquisulcatus*.] San Diego.
		4.	*Mytilus ?edulis* [= *M. trossulus*, Gld., *antea*]. San Francisco.
		5.	*Modiola capax*, Conr. San Diego.
		6.	*Venus Nuttallii*, Conr. [= *V. succincta*, Val.] San Pedro.
		7.	*Venus fluctifraga*, Sby. San Diego.
		8.	*Tapes grata*, Say,= *T. discors*, Sby., "=*straminea*, Conr."* San Pedro.
XI.	19,20.	9.	*Tapes gracilis*, Gld., n.s. Prel. Rep. 1855. [Quite distinct from every other *Tapes* known from the coast. It is supposed by Dr. Cooper to be the young of *Saxidomus aratus*, which in shape and pattern exactly accord with the figure and diagnosis. But the "*Tapes*" is figured without sculpture. The shell was not found at the Smiths. Inst.] San Pedro, *Blake.*
		10.	*Cyclas*, sp. ind. Colorado Desert.
XI	21.22.	11.	*Cardium cruentatum*, Gld., n.s. Prel. Rep. 1855. [P. Z. S. 1856, p. 201, = *C. substriatum*, Conr.] San Diego. [San Pedro, *Blake*, in text.]
		12.	*Lucina orbella*, Gld. [= "*Mysia (Sphærella) tumida*," Conr.] San Pedro.
		13.	*Lucina Nuttallii*, Conr. San Pedro.
		14.	*Mesodesma ?rubrotincta*, Sby.† San Pedro.
		15.	*Tellina vicina*, C. B. Ad. [Dead specimens of = *Heterodonax* ("*Psammobia*," var.) *Pacifica*, Conr.] San Diego.
		16.	*Tellina secta*, Conr. San Pedro.
		17.	*Sphænia* [*Cryptomya*] *Californica*, Conr. San Diego.
		18.	*Petricola carditoides*, Conr.,= *cylindracea*, Desh. Monterey ; San Pedro.
		19.	*Solecurtus Californiensis*, Conr. San Diego.
		20.	*Gnathodon Lecontii*, Conr.,= *G. trigonum*, Petit. Colorado Desert. [*Lecontei* is probably the large Texan species. *trigonus* = *mendicus* is a very distinct shell from Mazatlan.]

* Neither Dr. Gould, nor Conrad himself, in his later geological writings, appears to have called to mind the true *T. staminea*, to which the Smithsonian shells belong. It is the northern representative of *T. grata*, but quite distinct : v. synonymy under *Venus Petitii* = *rigida*, pars.

† No "*Mesodesma*" was found among the shells returned to the Smithsonian Institution, nor has any been heard-of from the coast. Dr. Gould's shell may have been *Semele pulchra*, which was in the collection.

78

Plate.	Fig.	No.

21. *Lottia scabra*, Gld. [non Nutt., Rve.:= *spectrum*, Nutt., Rve.] San Francisco.
22. *Lottia patina*, Esch.   San Pedro.
23. *Scurria pallida*, Gray,= *Lottia mitra*, Brod. [= *Scurria mitra*, Esch.,= *L. conica*, Gld., *anteà.*]   San Pedro.
24. *Calyptræa hispida*, Brod. [= *Crucibulum spinosum*, Sby.]   San Pedro ; San Diego.
25. *Crepidula incurva*, Brod.*   San Pedro.
26. *Bulla nebulosa*, Gld.   San Diego.
27. *Bulla (Haminea) virescens*, Sby.   San Diego.

XI.   29. 28. *Bulla (Haminea) vesicula*, Gld., n.s.   Prel. Rep. 1855. [P. Z. S. 1856, p. 203.]   San Diego, *Blake.*

XI.   27, 28. 29. *Bulla (Tornatina) inculta*, Gld., n.s.   Prel. Rep. 1855.   S. Diego. [P. Z. S. 1856, p. 203.   Appears to be a *Utriculus.*]

30. *Trochus mœstus*, Jonas [= *Chlorostoma funebrale*, A. Ad.,= *marginatum*, Nutt.   Jonas's species is S. American.]   San Diego.

XI.   25, 26. 31. *Phasianella compta*, Gld., n.s.   Prel. Rep. 1855.   [P. Z. S. 1856, p. 204.]   San Diego, *Webb, Blake.*

32. *Litorina*, sp. ind. [var. *plena*, Gld.]   San Diego.
33. *Melampus*, sp. ind. [*oliraceus*, Cpr.]   San Diego.
34. *Olira biplicata*, Sby.   San Pedro.

XI.   23, 24. 35. *Potamis pullatus*, Gld., n.s.   Prel. Rep. 1855.   [= *Cerithidea fuscata*, Gld., n.s.   P. Z. S. 1856, p. 206. = *C. sacrata*, var., teste Nuttall, Cooper.]   San Diego, *Webb, Blake.*

XI.   6–9. 36. *Amnicola protea*, Gld., n.s.   Proc. Bost. Soc. N. H., March 1855. Colorado Desert (Gran Jornada), *Webb, Blake.*

XI.   10, 11. 37. *Amnicola longinqua*, Gld., n.s.   Proc. Bost. Soc. N. H., March 1855.   Colorado Desert (Cienaga Grande), *Blake.*

XI.   12–18. 38. *Planorbis ammon*, Gld., n.s.   Proc. Bost. Soc. N. H., Feb. [Otia, Mar. in text] 1855.   A very variable species.   Colorado Desert and Ocoya Creek, *Webb, Blake.*

XI.   1–5. 39. *Physa humerosa*, Gld., n.s.   Proc. Bost. Soc. N. H., Feb. 1855. Colorado Desert, *Blake* ; Pecos River, *Webb.*

40. *Succinea*, sp. ind.   Ocoya Creek.
41. *Helix Vancouverensis*, Lea.   San Francisco.
42. *Helix San-Diegoensis*, Lea.   Point Reyes.   [No such species, teste Binney.]
43. *Helix infumata*, Gld. [Otia, p. 215.]   Point Reyes.
44. *Helix Oregonensis*, Lea.   Cypress Point.

99. The fossils of the various Western expeditions were being arranged in 1860 in the Smithsonian Museum by Prof. J. S. Newberry, M.D., a naturalist of rare experience and accomplishments, and author of " Reports on the Geology, Botany, and Zoology of Northern California and Oregon." Washington, 1857.   They are embodied in vol. vi. of the ' Pacific Railroad Reports.'   The following is a list of the fossils, which were described by Mr. Conrad in pp. 69–73, having first appeared in the Proceedings of the Academy of Natural Sciences, Philadelphia, Dec. 1856, to which page-references are added.

Dr. Newberry's Californian Fossils.

Page.	Plate.	Fig.
69.	II.	1.

1. *Schizopyga Californiana*, Conr., Phil. Proc. Dec. 1856, p. 315. [Partaking of the characters of *Cancellaria* and *Pyramidella.*] Santa Clara, Cal.

„   „   2. *Cryptomya ovalis*, Conr., p. 314. [Closely approaching the recent species, *C. Californica.*]   Monterey Co.

„   „   3. *Thracia mactropsis*, Conr., p. 313.   Monterey Co.

---

* The *Crepidulæ* returned in this collection were *adunca* and ? *rugosa*, var.

1863.

P.ge.	Plate.	Fig.	
70.	II.	4.	*Mya Montereyana*, Conr., p. 313. [Figure resembles *Periploma argentaria*.] Monterey Co.
"	"	5.	? *Mya subsinuata*, Conr. [Comp. *Macoma inquinata*.] Monterey Co.
"	"	6.	*Arcopagia medialis*, Conr., p. 314. Like *A. biplicata*, Conr., of the Maryland Miocene. [Closely resembles *Lutricola alta*, Conr.] Monterey Co.
"	"	7.	*Tapes linteatum*, Conr., p. 314. California.
"	"	8.	*Arca canalis*, Conr., p. 314. Santa Barbara.
"	"	9.	*Arca trilineata*, Conr., p. 314. Santa Barbara.
"	"	10.	*Arca congesta*, Conr., p. 314. California.
71.	III.	11.	*Axinœa Barbarensis*, Conr. [Closely resembles *Pect. intermedius*.]
"	"	12.	*Mulinia densata*, Conr., p. 313. ? Santa Barbara and shores of Pablo Bay.
"			*Dosinia longula*, Conr., p. 315. Monterey.
"	"	13.	*Dosinia alta*, Conr., p. 315. Monterey.
"	"	14.	*Pecten Pabloensis*, Conr. San Pablo Bay.
"	"	15.	*Pallium Estrellanum*, Conr., p. 313. Estrella Valley.
"	"	16.	*Janira bella*, Conr., p. 312. Santa Barbara.
72.	IV. V.	17. 17a.	} *Ostrea Titan*, Conr., Phil. Proc. 1855. San Luis Obispo.
73.	V.	25.	*Pandora bilirata*, Conr., p. 267. [Closely resembles *Kennerlia bicarinata*.] Santa Barbara.
"	"	24.	*Cardita occidentalis*, Conr., 1855, p. 267. [? = *C. ventricosa*, Gld.] Santa Barbara.
"	"	23.	*Diadora crucibuliformis*, Conr., 1855, p. 267. [? = *Punctureila cucullata*, Gld.] Santa Barbara.

Fossils of Gatun, Isthmus of Darien.

72.	V.	22.	*Malea ringens*, Swains. Gatun.
"	"	19.	*Turritella altilira*, Conr. Gatun.
"	"	20.	*Turritella Gatunensis*, Conr. Gatun.
"	"	20.	*Triton*, sp. ind. Gatun.
"	"	21.	? *Cytherea Dariena*, Conr. [The figure does not appear conspecific with that in the Blake collection, no. 50.] Gatun.

The northern fossils are supposed by Mr. Conrad to be of the Miocene period, and not to be referable to existing species. Those from Sta. Barbara, however, are clearly of a very recent age, and probably belong to the beds searched by Col. Jewett. But by far the most interesting result of Dr. Newberry's explorations was the discovery of the very typical Pacific shell, *Malea ringens*, in the Tertiary strata on the Atlantic slope of the Isthmus of Darien, not many miles from the Caribbean Sea. The characters of this shell being such as to be easily recognized, and not even the genus appearing in the Atlantic, it is fair to conclude that it had migrated from its head waters in the Pacific during a period when the oceans were connected. We have a right, therefore, to infer that during the lifetime of existing species there was a period when the present separation between the two oceans did not exist. We may conclude that species as old in creation as *Malea ringens* may be found still living in each ocean; and there is, therefore, no necessity for creating " representative species," simply because, according to the present configuration of our oceans, we do not see how the molluscs could have travelled to unexpected grounds.

100. In vol. vii. of the Pacific Railroad Reports, part 2, is the Geological Report, presented to the Hon. Jefferson Davis, then Secretary of War, by Thos. Antisell, M.D. He states reasons for believing that during the Eocene period the Sierra Nevada only existed as a group of islands; that its final uplifting was *after the Miocene period*; and that during the whole of that

period the coast-range was entirely under water. The Miocene beds are above 2000 feet in thickness, and abound in fossils generally distinct from those of the eastern strata. There is nothing in California answering to the Northern Drift of the countries bordering on the Atlantic. The molluscs of Dr. Antisell's Survey were described by Mr. Conrad, pp. 189–196. He remarks that "the fossils of the Estrella Valley and Sta. Iñez Mountains are quite distinct from those of the Sta. Barbara beds, and bear a strong resemblance to the existing Pacific fauna. The Miocene period is noted, both in the eastern and western beds, for the extraordinary development of *Pectinidæ*, both in number, in size, and in the exemplification of typical ideas." It also appears to be peculiarly rich in *Arcadæ*, which are now almost banished from that region, while they flourish further south. The large *Amusium caurinum* and the delicate *Pecten hastatus* of the Vancouver district, as well as the remarkable *Janira dentata* of the Gulf, may be regarded as a legacy to existing seas from the Miocene idea; otherwise the very few Pectinids which occur in collections along the whole West Coast of North America is a fact worthy of note. Mr. Conrad has "no doubt but that the Atlantic and Pacific oceans were connected at the Eocene period;" and the fossils here described afford strong evidence that the connexion existed during the Miocene epoch. All the species here enumerated (except *Pecten deserti* and "*Anomia subcostata*") were believed to be distinct from those collected by the preceding naturalists.

Dr. Antisell's Californian Fossils.

Page.	Plate.	Fig.	
190.	II. [L. err. typ.]	1, 2.	*Hinnites crassa*, Conr. [?= *H. gigantea*, Gray.] Sta. Margarita.
"	I.	1.	*Pecten Meekii*, Conr. San Raphael Hills.
"			*Pecten deserti*, Conr. Blake's Col., p. 15. Corrizo Creek.
"	III.	1.	*Pecten discus*, Conr. Near Sta. Iñez.
191.	I.	2.	*Pecten magnolia*, Conr. [Probably= *P. Jeffersonius*, Say, Virginia.] Near Sta. Iñez.
"	III.	2.	*Pecten altiplicatus*, Conr. San Raphael Hills.
"	III.	3, 4.	*Pallium Estrellanum*, Conr. [*Janira*.] Estrella.
"	I.	3.	*Spondylus Estrellanus*, Conr. [?*Janira*.] Estrella.
192.	V.	3, 5.	*Tapes montana*, Conr. San Buenaventura.
"	VII.	1.	*Tapes Inezensis*, Conr. Sta. Iñez.
"	IV.	1, 2.	*Venus Pajaroana*, Conr. Pajaro River.
"	IV.	3, 4.	*Arcopagia unda*, Conr. Shore of Sta. Barbara and Estrella. [Closely resembles *A. biplicata*; ?= *Lutricola alta*.]
"	VII.	4.	*Cyclas permacra*, Conr. Sierra Monica. Resembles *C. panduta*, Conr.,= *Lucina compressa*, Lea.
"	VI.	6.	*Cyclas Estrellana*, Conr. Estrella.
"	V.	1.	*Arca Obispoana*, Conr. San Luis Obispo.
193.	V.	2, 4.	*Pachydesma Inezana*, Conr. [Like *P. crassatelloides*.] Sta. Iñez Mts.
"	VI.	1, 2.	*Crassatella collina*, Conr. Sta. Iñez Mts.
"	II.	3.	*Ostrea subjecta*, Conr. "May be the young of *O. Panzana*." Sierra Monica.
"	II.	4.	*Ostrea Panzana*, Conr. Panza, Estrella, and Gaviote Pass.
"			*Dosinia alta*, Conr. Salinas River.
"	VII.	2.	*Dosinia longula*, Conr. Salinas River.
194.	VI.	4.	*Dosinia montana*, Conr. Salinas River.
"	VI.	5.	*Dosinia subobliqua*, Conr. Salinas River. Also a small *Venus*, a *Natica*, and a *Pecten*.
"	VIII.	2, 3.	*Mytilus Inezensis*, Conr. Sta. Iñez.
"	V.	6.	*Lutraria transmontana*, Conr. Allied to *L. papyria*, Conr. Los Angeles; also San Luis.

Page.	Plate.	Fig.	
192.	VI.	3.	*Axinea Barbarensis*, Conr. Los Angeles. [?= *intermedius.*]
„	VII.	3.	? *Mactra Gabiotensis*, Conr. Gaviote Pass. May be a *Sch. zodesma.* Associated with *Mytilus* sp. and *Infundibulum Gabiotensis.*
„	VII.	5.	*Glycimeris Estrellanus*, Conr. Panza and Estrella Valleys. Allied to *Panopæa reflexa*, Say. [?= *P. generosa*, Gld.]
195.			*Perna montana*, Conr. S. Buenaventura. Allied to *P. maxillata*
„	VII.	3.	*Trochita costellata*, Conr. Gaviote Pass.
„	VIII.	4.	*Turritella Inezana*, Conr. Sta. Iñez Mts.
„	VIII.	5.	*Turritella variata*, Conr. Sta. Iñez Mts.
„	X.	5, 6.	*Natica Inezana*, Conr. [?*Lunatia Lewisii.*] Sta. Iñez Mts.

As before, the fossils appear to be in very bad condition. The succeeding palæontologists who have to identify from them are not to be envied. Their principal value is to show what remains in store for future explorers. The extreme beauty of preservation in the fossils collected by Col. Jewett, rivalling those of the Paris Basin, and sometimes surpassing the conspecific living shells, makes us astonished that so large a staff of eminent men, employed by the Government, made such poor instalments of contribution to malacological science. The plan, too often followed, of remunerating naturalists, not according to the skilled labour they bestow, but according to the number of " new species" they describe, is greatly to be deprecated. Further knowledge concerning the old species may be more important in scientific inquiries than the mere naming of new forms. It is generally a much harder task to perform, and, therefore, more deserving of substantial as well as of honourable acknowledgment.

101. The shells collected on the North Pacific Railroad Survey were intrusted to W. Cooper, Esq., of Hoboken, New Jersey, for description: Dr. Gould being occupied with preparing the diagnoses of the N. Pacific E. E. species. Judge Cooper was at that time the only naturalist in America known to be actively engaged in studying the marine shells of the West Coast, of which he has a remarkably valuable collection. He had rendered very valuable service to the Smithsonian Institution by naming their specimens. Unfortunately, there is such great difficulty even in New York city (of which Hoboken is a suburb) in obtaining access to typically named shells, as well as to many necessary books *, that, notwithstanding the greatest care, errors of determination are almost sure to arise.

The " Report upon the Mollusca collected on the Survey, by Wm. Cooper," forms No. 6 of the Appendix, pp. 369–386, and *errata.* (Unfortunately the

* Both Judge Cooper and Dr. Lea informed me (1860) that they had not been able even to see a copy of the plates to the U. S. Expl. Exped. Mollusca. Through special favour, I was enabled to obtain a series of the proofs to work by. The Smithsonian Institution, though intrusted with the keeping of the collections, was not favoured with a copy until after the war began, when the whole series was granted by Congress. Judge Cooper had derived great assistance from the British Association Report, and has communicated many corrections in it. In the alterations of synonymy, and in defining the limits of specific variation, I have had the benefit of his counsel and experience; and have rarely felt compelled to differ from him. Having himself collected extensively in the West Indies, he had excellent opportunities of comparing fresh specimens from the now separated oceans. I was fortunate enough to meet his son, Dr. J. G. Cooper, at the Smithsonian Institution, and to examine the types of the species he collected (which are here enumerated) with the advantage of his memory and knowledge. His later contributions to the malacology of W. America will be afterwards enumerated: his valuable Treatise on the Forests and Trees of North America will be found in the Smithsonian Reports, 1858, pp. 246–280.

work had been carelessly printed.) It contains the following species, the localities quoted in the text from other sources being here omitted :—

Page.

369. *Murex foliatus*, Gmel., = *M. monodon*, Esch. (*Cerostoma*). San Diego, ?foss:l, Cassidy.

„ *Murex festivus*, Hds. Dead. San Diego, *Cassidy*.

„ *Triton Oregonensis*, Redfield (non Jay, nec Say) = *T. cancellatum*, Midd., Rve., non Lam. Straits of De Fuca, *Suckley, Gibbs, J. G. Cooper.*

370. *Chrysodomus antiquus*, var. *Behringiana*, Midd., one specimen. Straits of De Fuca, *Suckley.* [Comp. *Chr. tabulatus.*]

„ *Chrysodomus Middendorffii*, Coop., n. s., = *Tritonium decemcostatum*, Midd. One specimen on the shore of Whidby's Island. Straits of De Fuca, *J. G. Cooper.* [= *Buc. liratum*, Mart. This being a remarkable instance of a "representative species," it requires to be minutely criticized. Judge Cooper compared his specimen with 130 eastern shells, and noted the differences with great fulness and accuracy. A series of Middendorff's Pacific shells having been brought to England by Mr. Damon, and sold at high prices, I made a searching comparison of one of them with the eastern specimens furnished me by Judge Cooper and other most trusty naturalists. According to the diagnosis of *Middendorffii*, it should be referred to *C. decemcostatus*, Say, and *not* to the De Fuca species, as it agrees in all respects with the eastern peculiarities quoted, except that the riblets near the canal are rather more numerous and defined. As it might be suspected that Mr. Damon's shells were mixed, I have made a similar comparison with a shell from the N. W. coast, sent to the Smiths. Inst. by Mr. Pease, and with the same result. On examining the specimens in the Cumingian Collection, in company with A. Adams, Esq., we were both convinced that the eastern and western forms could not be separated. In the similar shells collected by Mr. Adams in the Japan seas there are remarkable variations in the details of sculpture.]

371. *Chrysodomus Sitchensis*, Midd. [= *incisus*, Gld., = *dirus*, Rve.]. Str. De Fuca, *Suckley, Gibbs.*

„ *Nassa mendica*, Gld. Puget Sound, *Suckley.*

„ *Nassa Gibbsii*, Coop., n. s. "Resembles *N. trivittata* more than *N. mendica*." Port Townsend, Puget Sound. [In a large series, neither Dr. Stimpson nor I were able to separate this species from *N. mendica*. Similar variations are common in British *Nassæ*. Picked individuals from the Neeah Bay series would probably be named *trivittata*, if mixed with eastern shells.]

„ *Purpura lactuca*, Esch., + *M. ferrugineus*, Esch., = *P. septentrionalis*, Rve. Puget Sound, *Suckley, Gibbs*; Shoalwater Bay, Str. de Fuca, *J. G. Cooper.* "Abounds on rocks and oyster-beds in Shoalwater Bay, the form and amount of rugosity depending on station. The oyster-eaters are smooth even when young."—*J. G. C.*

372. *Purpura ostrina*, Gld., = *P. Freycinetii*, Midd., non Desh. + *P. decemcostata* [Coop., non] Midd. Rocks above low-water mark ; from mouth of Hood's Canal to Str. Fuca ; Puget Sound, common, *J. G. Cooper.*

„ *Purpura lapillus* [Coop., non] Linn. [= *P. saxicola*, Val.] Str. De Fuca, Puget Sound, *J. G. Cooper.* "Found with *P. ostrina*, and equally common." [Some varieties run into the New England form of *P. lapillus*, sufficiently nearly to justify the identification ; but the bulk of the specimens are easily distinguished by the excavated columella. They pass by insensible gradations to *P. ostrina*, Gld., which is a rare and extreme variety. Many of the shells called *P. Freycinetii* by Midd. are certainly referable to this species. Some forms pass towards the true *P. Freycinetii*, Desh., while others are equally close to the very different *P. emarginata*, Desh.]

„ *Purpura emarginata*, Desh., = *P. Conradi*, Nutt. MS. "Upper California," *Trask* ; San Diego, *Trowbridge*. [This appears to be exclusively a southern form = *saxicola*, var.]

„ *Monoceros engonatum*, Conr., = *M. unicarinatum*, Sby. San Pedro, *Dr. Trask.*

373. *Monoceros lapilloides*, Conr., = *M. punctatum*, Gray. San Pedro, *Dr. Trask.*

83

Page.
373. *Columbella gausapata*, Gld. Str. de Fuca, *Suckley*.
  „ *Columbella valga* [Cooper, non] Gld. [=*Buccinum corrugatum*, Rve.] Str.
    de Fuca, *Suckley*.
  „ *Natica Lewisii*, Gld.,=*N. herculea*, Midd. Puget Sound, *J. G. Cooper, Suck-
    ley*. "Shell sometimes remarkably globose, sometimes with spire much
    produced." *W. C.* "Abundant throughout the N.W. sounds, and col-
    lected in great numbers by the Indians for food. In summer it craw ls
    above high-water mark to deposit its eggs" in the well-known sand-coils,
    which are "beautifully symmetrical, smooth, and perfect on both sides."—
    J. G. C.
  „ *Potamis pullatus*, Gld. A variable species. U. Cal., *Trask*.
374. *Melania plicifera*, Lea. Very common in rivers, W. T., *J. G. Cooper*.
  „ *Melania silicula*, Gld. [=one of the many vars. of *M. plicifera*, teste Lea].
    In rivers, W. T., Nisqually and Oregon, *J. G. Cooper*.
  „ *Melania Shortaënsis*, Lea, MS. [=*Shastaënsis*, Lea]. Willopah River, *J. G.
    Cooper*.
  „ *Amnicola Nuttalliana*, Lea, Phil. Trans. pl. 26. f. 80. Columbia River, *J. G.
    Cooper*.
  „ *Amnicola seminalis*, Hds. U. Cal., *Trask*. [Belongs to Dr. Stimpson's new
    genus, *Flummicola*.]
  „ *Turritella Eschrichtii*, Midd. [=*Bittium filosum*, Gld.]. Puget Sound, *Suck-
    ley, Gibbs*.
  „ "*Litorina rudis*, Gld., Stn." [Cooper, non Mont.]. Shoalwater Bay, De
    Fuca, *J. G. Cooper, Suckley, Gibbs*. "Very abundant on the N.W. coast,
    where it presents the same varied appearances as our eastern shell."—*W. C.*
    [To an English eye, it appears quite distinct. *L. rudis*, Coop., with *sub-
    tenebrosa*, Midd., and *modesta*, Phil., are probably vars. of *L. Sitkana*, Phil.,
    =*L. sulcata*, Gld.]
  „ *Litorina scutulata*, Gld. On rocks, from the head of Puget Sound to De Fuca,
    J. G. Cooper.
  „ *Litorina planaxis*, Nutt. [=*L. patula*, Gld.]. San Luis Obispo, *Dr. Antisell*.
375. *Trochus filosus*, Wood,=*T. ligatus*, Gld.,=*T. modestus*, Midd. Str. de Fuca,
    J. G. Cooper; U. Cal., *Trask*. [=*T. costatus*, Mart.]
  „ *Trochus Schantaricus* [Coop., non] Midd. [=*Marg. pupilla*, Gld.,=*M. calo-
    stoma*, A. Ad.] Str. de Fuca, *J. G. Cooper*, abundant.
  „ *Haliotis Kamtschatkana*, Jonas. Nootka Sound, *Capt. Russell*, teste Trask.
  „ *Haliotis corrugata*. San Diego, *Cassidy*.
  „ *Haliotis splendens*. San Diego, *Cassidy*.
  „ *Haliotis rufescens*. San Diego, *Cassidy*.
  „ *Haliotis Cracherodii*. (None of the rare var. *Californiensis*.) S. Diego, *Cassidy*.
  „ *Fissurella nigropunctata*, Sby. Two specimens sent by Dr. Trask as coming
    from Catalina Is., U. Cal. [?imported].
  „ *Fissurella aspera*, Esch.,? =*eratitia*, Gld., ? =*densiclathrata*, Rve. [=*Lincolni*,
    Gray. This is certainly Gould's species from type; but Reeve's shell is
    southern, and appears distinct.] U. Cal., *Lieut. Trowbridge*.
376. *Nacella instabilis*.
  „ *Acmæa pelta*.
  „ *Acmæa persona*.   ⎫   The few shells collected of this family are mostly imper-
  „ *Acmæa spectrum*.   ⎪   fect, but appear to belong to the species quoted: for
  „ *Acmæa scabra*.   ⎬   the synonymy of which, reference is made to the Bri-
  „ *Acmæa æruginosa*.   ⎪   tish Association Report.
  „ *Scurria mitra*.   ⎭
  „ *Chiton muscosus*.   ⎫   Still fewer materials, among which the quoted species
  „ *Chiton submarmoreus*.⎪ were identified. [The "*submarmoreus*," both of
  „ *Chiton tunicatus*. ⎬   Midd. and Coop., may prove to be *Tonicia lineata*,
  „ *Chiton lignosus*.   ⎭   var.] Chiefly from Oregon.
  „ *Helix fidelis*, Gray,=*Nuttalliana*, Lea. Forests W. of Cascade Mountain,
    W. T., *J. G. Cooper*.
  „ *Helix Townsendiana*, Lea. "Common in open prairies near the sea, but not
    near Puget Sound," W. T., *J. G. Cooper*.

Page.

376. *Helix Columbiana*, Lea,=*labiosa*, Gld. "In wet meadows from Vancouver to the coast, not near Puget Sound," W. T., *J. G. Cooper.*

377. *Helix Vancouverensis*, Lea [+*sportella*, Gld., teste Bland]. "West of Cascade Mountain; most abundant under alder-groves; also on Whidby's Island," W. T., *J. G. Cooper.*

   „ *Helix devia*, Gld.,=*Baskervillei*, Pfr. Two sp. in damp woods, near Vancouver, W. T., *J. G. Cooper.*

   „ *Helix tudiculata*, Binn. Rare, with the last, Vancouver; also Washington Territory, *J. G. Cooper.*

   „ *Succinea Nuttalliana*, Lea. Rare and dead, at Vancouver, *J. G. Cooper.*

   „ *Limax Columbianus*, Gld. "Abundant in dense, damp spruce-forests, near Pacific coast; grows to 6 inches, and is smooth, not rugose, when living," *J. G. Cooper.*

378. *Limnæa umbrosa*, Gld. Lake Oyosa, Okanagan River, *J. G. Cooper.*

   „ *Limnæa emarginata*, Say. Lake Oyosa, Okanagan River, *J. G. Cooper.*

   „ *Limnæa jugularis*, Say. Lake Oyosa, Okanagan River, *J. G. Cooper.*

   „ *Physa elongata*, Say. Near Puget Sound, *J. G. Cooper.*

   „ *Physa heterostropha*, Say. Ponds in W. T., *J. G. Cooper.*

   „ *Physa bullata*, Gld. MS. Lake Oyosa, W. T., *J. G. Cooper.*

   „ *Ancylus caurinus*, Coop., ?n. s. ["?=*A. Nuttalli*, Hald.," Coop. MS.] Black River, near Puget Sound, *J. G. Cooper.*

   „ *Planorbis corpulentus*, Say. Lake Oyosa, W. T., *J. G. Cooper.*

   „ *Planorbis trivolvis*, Say. Exceedingly abundant in shallow lakes near Vancouver, W. T., *J. G. Cooper.*

   „ *Planorbis planulatus*, Coop., n. s. "A small carinated species, found only in lakes on Whidby's Island," *J. G. Cooper.* [Comp. *P. opercularis*, Gld.]

379. *Bulla nebulosa*, Gld. Bay of S. Pedro, *Trask.*

   „ *Bulla tenella*, A. Ad., in Sby. Thes. pl. 134. f. 104 [?]. Puget Sound, one sp., *Suckley.* [?=*Haminea hydatis.*]

   „ *Ostrea edulis*, Coop. [non Linn.:=*O. lurida*, Cpr.]. De Fuca and Puget Sound, *Gibbs*; Shoalwater Bay, *Cooper.* "Small in Puget Sound; finer in Shoalwater Bay, which supplies S. Francisco market; large at Vancouver's Island; very large near mouth of Hood's Canal."

   „ [*Placun*]*anomia macroschisma*, Desh. De Fuca, *Gibbs*; Nootka Sound, *Capt. Russell.*

   „ *Pecten caurinus*, Gld. De Fuca, *Suckley.* One of the specimens measures 2½ inches in circumference and 8 in. across.

380. *Pecten ventricosus*, Sby.,+*tumidus*, Sby. [= ?var. *æquisulcatus*, Cpr.]. Upper Cal., *Trask*; San Diego, *Cassidy.*

   „ *Mytilus edulis*, Ln. Shoalwater Bay, *Cooper.* "As abundant as in Europe and N England, with the same variations, and when eaten occasionally causing urticaria."—*J. G. Cooper.*

   „ *Mytilus Californianus*, Conr. Puget Sound, Port Townsend, *Suckley, Gibbs*; Upper Cal., *Trask.* One specimen is 9¼ inches long.

   „ *Modiola capax* [Cooper, non] Conr. [=*M. modiolus*, Ln.]. Not common. Str. de Fuca, *Gibbs, Cooper.*

   „ *Modiola flabellata*, Gld. Puget S. and Str. de Fuca, *Gibbs.* [=*M. recta*, var.]

   „ *Lithophagus*, sp. ind., like *falcatus.* [Probably *Adula stylina*, Cpr.] Rocks near mouth of Umpqua River, Oregon, *Dr. Vollum.*

381. *Arca grandis*, Coop. [non Brod. and Sby.,=*A. multicostata*, Sby.]. One sp. living. San Diego, *Cassidy.*

   „ *Margaritana margaritifera*, Lea,=*Alasmodonta falcata*, Gld. River Chehalis, &c., W. T., *Cooper*; Shasta River, Or., *Trask.* After careful comparison with eastern U. S. specimens, and those from Newfoundland and Europe, Judge Cooper agrees with Dr. Lea that the N.W. shells are at most a slight variety. "The most abundant of the freshwater bivalves, and the only one yet found in the Chehalis, the streams running into Puget Sound, and most branches of the Columbia. No species is found in the streams running into Shoalwater Bay. Eaten by the Indians E. of the Cascade Mountains," *J. G. C.*

Page.
381. *Anodonta angulata*, Lea,+*A. feminalis*, Gld. Plentiful in Yakima River,
     W. T., *Cooper*. A series of specimens of var'ous ages leads Judge Cooper
     to endorse Dr. Lea's opinion of the identity of the two species.
  „ *Anodonta Oregonensis*, Lea. Rivers of W T., *Cooper*.
  „ *Anodonta Wahlamatensis*, Lea. Lagoons in Sacramento River, *Dr. Trask*.
382. *Cardium Nuttalli*, Conr. Shoalwater Bay and Puget Sound, *Cooper*; San
     Franc., *Dr. Bigelow, Trask*. "The most abundant clam of Shoalwater Bay,
     inhabiting sandy mud, a few inches below the surface. The Indians feel
     for them with a knife or sharp stick with great expertness. In July many
     come to the surface and die, ? from the sun's heat."
  „ *Cardium quadragenarium*, Conr. One valve. San Luis Obispo, *Dr. Antisell.*
  „ *Lucina Californica*. Conr. San Diego, *Cassidy*.
  „ *Cyclas*, sp. ind. Whidby's Island; pools near Steilacoom, *Cooper*.
  „ *Venus staminea*, Conr.,+ *Venerupis Petitii*, Desh.,+ *Venus rigida*, Gld. [pars],
     + *Tapes diversa*, Sby. Shoalwater Bay and Puget Sound, *Cooper, Suck-
     ley*; San Francisco, *Trask*; San Diego, *Lieut. Trowbridge*. [To the
     above synonymy, by Judge Cooper, the large series of specimens in the
     Smithsonian Mus. compels an assent. He considers *Tapes staminea*, of
     Sby. Thes., to be a variety of *V. histrionica*, but it more probably = *T.
     grata*, as Dr. Gould appears to have considered it, having copied Sowerby's
     error. Conrad named it, not from the colour, as was supposed when quoting
     it as "*staminea*," but from the thread-like sculpture (teste Conr. ips.).
     Whatever be the form, colour, or sculpture of the shell, Judge Cooper
     remarks in all the same characters of teeth and h'nge, we may add also, of
     the pallial sinus.]
383. *Saxidomus Nuttallii* [Coop., non] Conr.,+ *Venerupis gigantea*, Desh.,+ *Venus
     maxima*, Phil. [?]. Near Copalux River, south of Shoalwater Bay, com-
     mon at Puget Sound, *Cooper*; Bodegas, Cal., *Trask*. "Much superior to
     the Atlantic *quahog* as food, but called by the same name. Its station is in
     somewhat hard sand, near l.-w. mark," *J. G C*. [Judge Cooper regards all
     the *Saxidomi* of the coast, except *S. aratus*, as one species. The southern
     form, "with rough concentric striæ and brown disc," is Conrad's species;
     "others from Oregon are much smoother, without regular striæ." These are
     S. squalidus, Desh. Dr. Cooper found "a fossil variety, in coast-banks 10
     feet above sea-level, which is well figured in Midd. and (less distinctly) by
     Desh. A Californian specimen measures 4·8 in. across." The fossils, through
     disintegration, often assume the aspect of *Venus Kennerleyi*, the former
     margins remaining as varical ridges, while the softer interstices have
     perished.]
  „ *Venus lamellifera*, Conr.,= *Venerupis Cordieri*, Desh. San Diego, *Cassidy*.
384. *Lutraria maxima*, Midd., = *L. capax*, Gld. [= *Schizothærus Nuttalli*, Conr.]
     Shoalwater Bay, *Cooper*. San Francisco, *Trask*. "Lives buried nearly 2 feet
     in hard sand, near l. w. mark, its long siphons reaching the surface; also in
     many parts of Puget Sound up to near Olympia. It is excellent food, and
     a chief article of winter stores to the Indians, who string and smoke them
     in their lodges. Length, 7½ in. The burrows are found in the cliffs, 10 feet
     above high water, with all the other Mollusca now living; and two, not
     now found, were then common [viz. ?...]. The Indians have no tradition
     as to the elevation, and the ancient trees show no signs of the irregular
     upheavings which raised the former levels of low water, by successive
     stages, to a height now nearly 100 feet," *J. G. C.*
  „ *Tellina nasuta*, Conr. Common, from L. Cal. to the Arctic Seas. Shoal-
     water Bay, *Cooper*; Puget Sound, *Suckley*; San Francisco, *Trask*.
  „ *Tellina edentula* [Cpr., Coop., not Brod. and Sby.,= *Macoma secta*, var. *edulis*,
     Nutt.]. Puget Sound, *Gibbs*.
  „ *Tellina Bodegensis*, Hds. Shoalwater Bay, rare, *Cooper*; mouth of Umpqua
     River, *Vollum*.
385. *Sanguinolaria Californiana*, Conr. "Common at the mouth of the Columbia
     and other rivers, and high up salt-water creeks," *Cooper*. [= *Macoma
     inconspicua*, Brod. and Sby.]

Page.
385. *Solen sicarius*, Gld.   One dead shell, neai Steilacoom, Puget Sound, *Cooper.*
"Probably abundant on the mud-flats near the mouth of the Nisqually River," *J. G. C.*

" *Machæra patula*, Portl. and Dix. (Coop. errata: *Nuttalli* in text), = *Solen maximus*, Wood, non Chemn., = *Solecurtus Nuttallii*, Conr., = *Machæra costata*, Midd., non Say.   Washington Ter., *Cooper.* "Burrows a few inches from the surface, at the edge of the usual low tide; is justly considered (except the oyster) the best of the many fine eatable molluscs of the coast. It is the only truly marine mollusc found near the Columbia River; extends northwards wherever the beach is sandy, but not known in the Straits of de Fuca," *J. G. C.*

" *Mya cancellata*, (*Platyodon*), Conr.   Dead valves, St. Luis Obispo, *Dr, Antisell.*

" *Sphænia Californica*, (*Cryptomya*), Conr.   San Francisco, *Trask.*
386. *Mytilimeria Nuttalli*, Conr.   A group, nestling in a white, friable, arenaceous substance, was obtained at San Diego by *Lieut. Trowbridge.*

" *Pholas* [*Pholadidea*] *penita*, Conr., = *P. concamerata*, Desh.   From worn rock which drifted into Shoalwater Bay, attached to the roots of *Macrocystis*, the giant seaweed, *Cooper*; De Fuca, *Suckley*; mouth of Umpqua River, Oregon, *Dr. Vollum.*

The above list must be considered as a *résumé*, not merely of the shells of the N. P. Railroad Survey, but also of all those examined by Judge Cooper, from the Smithsonian Museum and from his own private collection.   It is peculiarly valuable as preserving the notes concerning station, &c., of the original explorers, and has therefore required a more lengthened analysis.

The land-shells collected by Dr. Newberry in the Pacific Railroad Survey were described by W. G. Binney, Esq., with his accustomed accuracy.   His paper will be found in the Reports, vol. vi. pp. 111–114.   The following are the only species enumerated:—

1. *Helix fidelis*, Gray, Chem., Pfr., Rve., = *H. Nuttalliana*, Lea, Binney, sen., De Kay.   Portland, Oregon, *Newberry.*   Local.
2. *Helix infumata*, Gld., Proc. Bost. N. H. S., Feb. 1855, p. 127.   Hills near San Francisco, *Newberry.*   Extremely rare.
3. *Helix æruginosa*, Gld., var. β. loc. cit.   North of San Francisco, *Newberry.* Rare.
4. *Helix Dupetithouarsi*, jun., Desh., Chem., Pfr., Rve., = *H. Oregonensis*, Lea, Pfr.   San Francisco, Benicia, Cal.; Klamath Lake, Oregon; *Newberry.* "One of the commonest and most widely distributed species of the Pacific region."

102. The U. S. Government also sent out a "North-west Boundary Commission," in charge of Archibald Campbell, Esq.   The natural-history arrangements were superintended by the Smithsonian Inst., and Dr. C. B. R. Kennerly was appointed naturalist to the Expedition.   At his request, I undertook to prepare a Report of the Mollusca, to be published and illustrated in a form corresponding to the Pacific Railroad Reports; Dr. Alcock kindly undertaking to dissect the animals, and Mr. Busk to examine the Polyzoa. Dr. Kennerly died on his return from a three years' exploration; and the civil war has thus far delayed any further publication.   The materials have, however, been thoroughly investigated.   They consist principally of dredgings in Puget Sound.   On reference to the maps published by the U. S. Coast Survey, it will be seen that this inland sea consists of a remarkable labyrinth of waters, fiord within fiord, and only indirectly connected with the currents of the Pacific Ocean.   It might therefore be expected to furnish us with the species of quiet migration, and perhaps with those still living from a period of previous altered conditions.   No doubt it will furnish new materials to reward the labours of many successsive naturalists.   The pre-

maturely closed investigations of Dr. Kennerley are only the beginning of a rich harvest. Dr. George Suckley, late assistant-surgeon of the U. S. army, was appointed to complete the natural-history work, after his lamented death. A complete list of the species collected will be found in the fifth column of the Vancouver and Californian table, *v. infrà*, par. 112. The particulars of station, &c., and all the knowledge which the laborious explorer had collected, are lost to science. It is quite possible that some of the species here accredited to Puget Sound were obtained in neighbouring localities in the Straits of De Fuca. The specimens are in beautifully fresh condition, and of most of them the animals were preserved in alcohol. The following are the shells first brought from the Vancouver district by the American N. W. Boundary Commission, the diagnoses of new species being (according to custom) first published in the Proceedings of the Ac. Nat. Sc. Philadelphia.

No.
1. *Zirphœa crispata.* Two living specimens of this very characteristic Atlantic sp.
2. *Saxicava pholadis.* Several living specimens.
3. *Sphænia ovoidea*, n. s. One sp. living.
4. *Cryptomya Californica.* Several living sp.
5. *Thracia curta.* One specimen.
6. *Mytilimeria Nuttallii.* Three sp. living at base of test of Ascidian. [The animal appeared too peculiar to venture on a dissection. It has been entrusted to Dr. Alcock, of the Manchester Museum.]
7. *Neœra pectinata*, n. s. One sp. living.
8. *Kennerlia filosa*, n. s. and n. subg. Several living specimens.
9. *Psammobia rubroradiata.* One fresh specimen of uniform tint.
10. *Macoma (? v.) expansa.* Adult broken; young living. Belongs to a group of forms classed together by some writers under *lata* or *proxima*, but the characters of the hinge and mantle-bend have not yet been sufficiently studied.
11. *Macoma yoldiformis*, n. s. One valve.
12. *Angulus modestus*, n. s., but closely allied to the eastern *A. tener*, Say. Two sp. living.
12b. *Angulus (? modestus*, var.) *obtusus.* Several fresh specimens.
13. *Clementia subdiaphana*, n. s. Very rare, living. Intermediate between *Clementia* proper and the *prora* group of thin *Callistæ*.
14. *Psephis Lordi*, Baird. Several living sp. from which the subg. was eliminated.
15. *Venus Kennerlyi*, Rve. Very rare. One sp. living. Some of the shells called *V. astartoides* by Midd. may be the young of this.
16. *Petricola carditoides.* Several fresh specimens.
17. *Astarte (? var.) compacta.* One sp. living; may hereafter be connected with *A. compressa.*
18. *Serripes Granlandicus.* Several young living specimens.
19. *Lucina tenuisculpta*, n. s. Two living specimens, of which one had the surface disintegrated.
20. *Cryptodon serricatus*, n. s. One living sp.
21. *Kellia Laperousii.* A few living specimens.
22. *Kellia suborbicularis.* A few living specimens.
23. *Lasea rubra.* One sp. living.
24. *Pythina rugifera*, n. s. Two living sp. Intermediate between *Pythina* and *Kellia.*
25. *Tellimya tumida*, n. s. One sp. living.
26. *Modiolaria lævigata.* Two living sp.
27. *Modiolaria marmorata.* One sp. living. (A shell in the U. S. E. E. Col., though marked "Fiji" in Dr. Gould's MS. list, probably came from Puget Sound, being thus confirmed.)
28. *Nucula tenuis.* Two sp. living*.
29. *Acila castrensis.* One sp. living.
30. *Leda fossa*, Baird. One normal sp. living.

* These species were kindly determined by Mr. Hanley.

No.
31. *Leda minuta*, Linn.   One sp. living*.
32. *Yoldia lanceolata*, J. Sby.   Two sp. living*.
33. *Yoldia amygdala*.   One sp. living*.
34. *Haminea hydatis*.   Two sp. living.
35, 36. Two species of Tectibranchiates, not yet worked-out by Dr. Alcock.
37. *Tornatina eximia*, Baird.   Abundant, living.
38. *Cylichna* (?var.) *attonsa*.   One living sp.   Probably a variety of *cylindracea*.
39. *Dentalium rectius*, n. s.   Very rare, dead.
40. *Acanthopleura scabra*.   One young living sp.
41. *Mopalia Grayii*, n. s.   One living sp.
42. *Mopalia Hindsii*.   One living sp.
43. *Mopalia sinuata*, n. s.   Two sp. living. ⎱ A well-marked group in the genus.
44. *Mopalia imporcata*, n. s.   Two sp. living. ⎰
45. *Ischnochiton* (*Trachydermon*) *trifidus*, n. s.   One living sp.
46. *Ischnochiton* (*Trachydermon*) *flectens*, n. s.   One living sp.
47. *Ischnochiton* (*Trachydermon*) *retiporosus*, n. s.   One living sp.
48. *Ischnochiton* (*Lepidopleurus*) *Mertensii*.   Rare, living.
49. *Lepeta cæcoides*, n. s.   Three sp. living.
50. *Calliostoma variegatum*, n. s.   One living sp.
51. *Margarita ? Vahlii*.   Three sp. living, = *M. pusilla*, Jeffr., teste A. Ad.
51*b. Margarita* (? v.) *tenuisculpta*.   Perhaps a var. of *Vahlii*, but sculptured.   Several
     living specimens.
52. *Margarita lirulata*, n. s.   Several living specimens, forming a Darwinian group,
     of which var. *α. subelevata*, var. *β. obsoleta*, and ?var. *γ. conica* might pass
     for species from single specimens.
53. *Margarita inflata*, n. s.   Two sp. living.
54. *Mesalia lacteola*, ?n. s.   Two sp. living, but eroded.   May prove a var. of
     lactea, but with different sculpture.
54*b. Mesalia* (?*lacteola*, var.) *subplanata*.   Two sp. living, but eroded.
55. *Lacuna vincta*.   One fresh specimen.
56. *Rissoa compacta*, n. s.   Not uncommon, living.
57. *Drillia incisa*, n. s.   Two fresh specimens.
58. *Drillia cancellata*, n. s.   One adolescent specimen.
59. *Mangelia levidensis*, n. s.   One fresh specimen.
60. *Mangelia angulata*†.   One fresh specimen.
61. *Bela excurvata*, n. s.   (Like *Trevelyana*.)   One fresh specimen.
62. *Chemnitzia* (? v.) *aurantia*†.   One fresh specimen.
63. *Chemnitzia torquata*†.   Two fresh specimens.
64. *Chemnitzia tridentata*†.   Two fresh specimens.
65. *Eulima micans*, n. s.   One fresh specimen.
66. *Velutina lævigata*.   Several fine living specimens.
67. *Ocinebra interfossa*.   Rare, dead.
68. *Nitidella Gouldii*†.   Two living specimens, proving the genus.
69. *Trophon multicostatus*.   Two fresh specimens.
70. *Chrysodomus* ?*tabulatus*, jun.   One young sp.
71. *Chrysodomus rectirostris*, n. s.   One living sp.
72, 73. Two species of Cephalopods, not yet affiliated.

Besides adding more than 70 marine species to the Vancouver branch of the
Californian fauna, from specimens in good condition, without a single ballast or exotic admixture, the confirmation of many species, which before
rested only on the uncertain testimony of the U. S. E. E. labels, and the
affiliation of others which, on the same testimony, had been wrongly assigned
to distant and erroneous localities, was no slight benefit to science.   The
land and freshwater species of the Expedition will be found tabulated, with
others, in the separate lists; par. 115.

103. While the American naturalists were thus actively engaged in ex-

† These species were first found by Col. Jewett at Sta. Barbara.   *Vide* p. 537.

ploring the regions south of the political boundary, similar explorations, on a less extensive scale, were being made under the direction of the British Government. The naturalist to the British North American Boundary Commission, during the years 1858–1862, was J. K. Lord, Esq., F.Z.S. He made a very valuable collection of shells in Vancouver Island and British Columbia, the first series of which was presented to the British Museum. The new species were described by W. Baird*, Esq., M.D., F.L.S., in a paper communicated to the Zool. Soc., and published in its 'Proceedings,' Feb. 10th, 1863, pp. 66–70.—Another series of shells, from the same district, was presented to the Brit. Mus. by the Lords of the Admiralty, collected by Dr. Lyall, of H. M. Ship 'Plumper.' Two new species from this collection were described by Dr. Baird, in a separate paper, P. Z. S., Feb. 10th, 1863, p. 71. The new species from Mr. Lord's collections have been drawn on stone by Sowerby. The figure-numbers here quoted correspond with the proof-copy kindly furnished by Dr. Baird.—A third series was collected by Dr. Forbes, R.N., in the same Expedition. After Mr. Cuming had made his own selections, this passed into the ordinary London market. It contained several species of peculiar interest. The following are the (supposed) new species of the Survey:—

P.Z.S. Page.	Plate I. No.	Fig.	
66	1	1.	*Chrysodomus tabulatus*, Baird. One broken specimen, Esquimalt Harb., Vancouver Island, *Lord*. [One perfect shell, Neeah Bay, *Swan*.]
..	2	2.	*Vitularia aspera*, Bd. Several living specimens, Esquimalt Harb., Vanc. Island, *Lord*. [Belongs to a group of grooved muricoid Purpurids, intermediate between *Rhizocheilus* and *Cerostoma*, for which the subgenus *Ocinebra* may be reconstituted. These shells are the rough form of *Ocinebra lurida*, Midd.]
67	3	3.	*Chemnitzia Vancouverensis*, Bd. [= *torquata*, Gld.]. Esquimalt Harb., Vanc. Island, *Lord*. From the crop of a pintail Duck. [The artist has failed to represent the peculiar character of the species, which is, that the ribs end above the periphery, so that a smooth belt appears round the spire above the sutures.]
..	4	4.	*Amnicola Hindsii*, Bd. Seven sp., River Kootanie East; nine sp., Wigwam River, west slope of Rocky Mts., 4626 ft. high, Br. Col., *Lord*. Resembles *Paludina* [*Fluminicola*] *seminalis*, Hds.
..	5	5.	*Bullina (Tornatina) eximia*, Bd. Esquimalt Harb., V. I., *Lord*. Alive in 12 fm.; dead in Duck's stomach. [Not *Bullina*, Add. Gen.]
68	6	6.	*Succinea Hawkinsii*, Bd. Six sp. Lake Osoyoos, Brit. Col., *Lord*.
..	7	7.	*Limnæa Sumassii*†, Bd. Like *L. elodes*, Say. Plentiful. Sumass Prairie, Fraser R., Brit. Col., *Lord*. [Extremely like *L. palustris*.]
..	8	8.	*Physa Lordi*, Bd. Plentiful. Lake Osoyoos, British Columbia, *Lord*. [Larger than *Ph. humerosa*, Gld., and with strong columellar fold.]
69	9	9.	*Ancylus Kootaniensis*, Bd. Six sp., River Kootanie East; five sp., River Spokane, British Columbia, *Lord*.

* It is due to the memory of Dr. Kennerley, as well as to the other naturalists connected with the various American surveys, and the officers of the Smiths. Inst., who so generously entrusted to the writer their unique specimens for comparison with the London museums, to state, that (with two exceptions) the new marine species of the British Survey would have been published long before the appearance of Dr. Baird's paper, but for the derangement of the U. S. natural-history publications, consequent on the secession movement. Although the Smithsonian Inst. had offered to present to the Brit. Mus. their first series of duplicate specimens from these expeditions, which was exhibited at the Manchester Meeting of the Brit. Assoc., where this Report was called for, no notice was given to the writer of the valuable results of the British survey; and it was only through the private kindness of Drs. Sclater and Baird that he was prevented from adding to the list of synonyms, already, alas! so numerous and perplexing.

† These species are named after places, not after persons, as would be supposed by the terminations.

P.Z.S. Plate II.
Page. No. Fig.

69 10 10. *Chione Lordi*, Bd. From a Duck's stomach. Plentiful. Esquimalt Harb., V. I., *Lord*.

.. 11 11. *Sphærium (Cyclas) tumidum*, Bd. Plentiful. Sumass Prairie, Fraser River, British Columbia, *Lord*.

.. 12 12, 13. *Sphærium (Cyclas) Spokani*†, Bd. Two sp., River Spokane; two young sp., Kootanie River, British Columbia, *Lord*. [Closely related to *tumidum*, but more delicate.]

70 13 14. *Lyonsia saxicola*, Bd. Holes in rocks in Esquimalt Harb., V. I., *Lord*. Japan, teste *A. Ad.* Closely resembles *L. navicula*, Ad. and Rve. [Abundant, and very variable in outline, sometimes like *Saxicava pholadis*, sometimes like *Mytilimeria*. Neeah Bay, *Swan*.]

.. 14 15. *Crassatella Esquimalti*†, Bd. One sp. Esquimalt Harb., V. I., *Lord*. [A true *Astarte*, with external ligament, with one ant. lat. tooth in one valve, and one post. lat. tooth in the opposite, well developed. This character was noticed by J. Sby. in constituting the genus, but becomes obsolete in the typical species. The same peculiarity of margin is seen in *Crassatella*. The external rugæ are singularly irregular, and not always continuous.]

71 15 *Leda fossa*, Bd. 10–15 fm.; one sp. Esquimalt Harb., V. I., *Lyall*. [= *L. foveata*, Baird, MS., on tablet.]

71 16 *Nucula Lyallii*, Bd. 8–10 fm.; one sp. Esquimalt Harb., V. I., *Lyall*. Resembles *N. divaricata*, Hds., *N. castrensis*, Hds., *N. mirabilis*, Ad. and Rve., and especially *N. Cobboldiæ* from the Crag. [In the early stage, the sculpture has several angles, afterwards only one. Both Dr. Kennerley's and Dr. Lyall's specimens appear to be = *Acila castrensis*, Hds.]

The Vancouver Collections having been deposited in separate drawers, except the series mounted for the table-cases, permission has been given (with the kind assistance of Dr. Baird) to examine them minutely, and prepare a revised list of the species. The marine shells will be found in the sixth column of the general Vancouver and Californian Table. The following require special mention.

No.

17. " *Teredo fimbriata*," teste Jeffr.; out of block of wood from Nai-ni-mo Harb., V. I., *Lord*.
    Teredo. Shelly tube of large sp. Esquimalt Harb., *Lord*.

18. *Netastoma Darwinii*. Esquimalt Harb., *Lord*. One adult but injured specimen. [For this singular Pholad, with duck-bill prolongations of the valves, a subgenus of *Pholadidea* is proposed, as its characters do not accord with *Jouanettia*, under which it is placed in the Cumingian Collection.]

19. " *Saxicava rugosa*." Several typical specimens; Esquimalt Harb., *Lord*, taken out of interior of hard stone, into which they appear to have bored.

20. " *Callista ? pannosa*." Esquimalt Harb., *Lord*. One young sp. [= *Saxidomus squalidus*, jun.]

21. " *Tapes rigida*." Esquimalt Harb., *Lord*, common. [An instructive series, some with very close and fine, others with distant, strong ribs. Some have ribs large and rounded, approaching the sculpture of *Cardia*. Some change suddenly from one form to another. = *T. staminea*, var. *Petitii*.]

22. " *Cardium Californiense*, Desh." 8–15 fm. Vancouver Is., *Lyall*. [= var *blandum*. Tablet contains also young sp. of *C. corbis*.]

23. " *Cardita ventricosa*, Gld." 8–15 fm. Vanc. Is., *Lyall*. [Not ventricose, exactly resembles the East Coast specimens of *Ven. borealis* dredged by Dr. Stimpson.]

24. " *Anodonta cognata*, Gld." [= *A. Oregonensis*, Lea.] Lake Osoyoos, Br. Col. *Lord*. Two sp. Also Freshwater Lake, Nootka Sound, *Lyall*.
    Anodonta ? Oregonensis, jun. Freshwater Lake, Nootka, V. I., *Lord*; one sp.

25. *Anodonta ? Nuttalliana*. Freshwater Lake, Nootka, Vanc. Is., *Lord*; one sp.

26. *Anodonta Wahlamatensis*. Freshwater Lake, Nootka, Vanc. Is., *L rd*; four sp,

No
26. *Anodonta ? Wahlamatensis*, jun.　Sumass Prairie, Fraser River, Brit. Col., *Lord*; one specimen.
27. *Anodonta angulata.*　Fort Colville, Columbia R., *Lord*; one specimen [irregular and much eroded.　The hinge-line is waved and a false "tooth" produced, in consequence of which it has been named] "*Alasmodon.*"
28. "*Pecten rubidus*, Hds." Vanc. Is., *Lyall.* [Hinds's type in Br. Mus. appears the ordinary form, of which *P. hastatus* = *hericeus* is the highly sculptured var. This shell, which is more allied to *Islandicus*, may stand as *P. Hindsii.*]
29. *Hinnites giganteus.*　Island 3 miles above Cape Mudge, *Lyall.*
30. *Ostrea lurida.*　Esquimalt Harb., *Lord.*　Dredged-up by Indians in small hand-nets with long handles, in 2–3 fm., on mud-flats.
31. "*Placunanomia cepio*, Gray."　Esquimalt Harb., *Lord.*　On island rock, between tide-marks.　[= *P. macroschisma*, smooth, hollow form.]
32. "*Chiton (Platysemus) Wossnessenskii*, Midd., = *C. Hindsii*, Rve." Esquimalt Harb., *Lord.*　One very fine specimen.　[Quite distinct from *Mopalia Hindsii* (Gray); differs but slightly from *M. muscosa*, Gld.]
33. "*Chiton ? lævigatus.*"　Esquimalt Harb., *Lord.*　One specimen.　[= *Ischnochiton flectens.*]
34. "*Chiton dentiens*, Gld., ? = *marginatus.*"　Esquimalt Harb., *Lord.*　Two specimens.　[= *Ischnochiton pseudodentiens.* Not congeneric with the British *Leptochiton cinereus* = *marginatus.*]
35. *Acmæa* "*mitella*, Mke."　Esquimalt Harb., *Lord.*　[Probably *A. pelta*, jun. Not sculptured, as is the tropical species.]
36. "*Acmæa ? testudinalis*, jun."　Esquimalt Harb., *Lord.*　One young sp. [with extremely close fine striæ; colour in festoons of orange-brown pencilling on white ground.　Might stand well for *A. testudinalis*, but probably = *A. patina*, var. *pintadina.*]
37. *Margarita* "*costellata*, Sby."　Esquimalt Harb., *Lord.*　[= *M. pupilla*, Gld.]
38. *Crepidula lingulata*, Gld.　Esquimalt Harb., *Lord.*　Three young sp.　[Apex smooth, imbedded, passing into the *aculeata* type.　The species probably = *C. dorsata*, Brod.]
39. "*Melania silicula*, Gld., ? = *rudens*, Rve."　Attached to weeds and float'ng sticks in swift stream on prairie, at Nisqually, W. T., *Lord.*　[= *plicifera*, small var.]
40. *Priene Oregonensis.*　Port Neville, 6 fm., *Lyall.*　[Very fine; but opercula probably misplaced.]
41. "*Nitidella*" *gausapata*, Gld.　Esquimalt Harb., *Lord.*　[A beautiful series of highly painted specimens.　Operculum Nassoid, not Purpuroid; therefore ranks under *Amycla.*]
42. "*Vitularia lactuca.*"　Vancouver's Island, *Lyall.*　[A fine series of *Purpura crispata* and vars., among which is a lilac-tinted specimen.]
43. *Purpura decemcostata*, Vanc. Is., *Lyall.*　[= *canaliculata.*　Operc. as in *Ocinebra lurida.*]
44. "*Fusus Orpheus*" [Bd., not] Gld.　Esquimalt Harb., *Lord.*　Five sp., with crabs.　[= *Ocinebra interfossa*, very fine.]
45. *Trophon Orpheus*, Gld.　Esquimalt Harb., *Lord.*　One fresh specimen.
46. *Helix Townsendiana*, very fine.　Sumass Prairie, Fraser River, *Lord.*
46*b.* "*Helix Townsendiana*, small var."　Fort Colville, Columbia R.; also summit of Rocky Mts., *Lord.*
47. *Helix fidelis*, typical, jun. and adult.　Vanc. Is., *Lord.*
47*b. Helix fidelis.*　Large but very pale var.　Sumass Prairie, Fraser R., *Lord.*
48. "*Helix Thouarsii*, jun."　Sumass Prairie, Fraser R., *Lord.*
49. "*Helix labiata* = *Columbiana*, var."　Vancouver Is., *Lord*, [closely resembling *H. rufescens*].
50. "*Helix vellicata*, Fbs."　Sumass Prairie, Fraser R., *Lord.*　[= *Vancouverensis.*]
51. *Helix* [like *rotundata*].　Fort Colville, Columbia R., *Lord.*　Two specimens.
52. *Zonites* [like *excavata*].　Fort Colville, Columbia R., *Lord.*　One specimen.
53. *Zonites* [like *electrina*].　Fort Colville, Columbia R., *Lord.*　Seven specimens.
54. *Pupa*, sp. ind. jun.　Lake Osoyoos, British Columbia, *Lord.*　One specimen. [Genus not found before, north of California.]

No.
55. " *Succinea rusticana*, Gld." Sumass Prairie, Fraser R., *Lord*. [Scarcely to be distinguished from the European *S. putris*.]
56. " *Planorbis corpulentus*, Say." Lake Osoyoos; Syniakwateen; Marsh, Kootanie East, Brit. Col., *Lord*.
57. *Planorbis ? subcrenatus*, var. Sumass Prairie, Brit. Col., *Lord*.
58. " *Limnæa stagnalis*," typical, fine, and abundant. Lake Osoyoos, Fraser R., *Lord*.
58. *Limnæa stagnalis*, long narrow spire, mouth swollen, closely fenestrated. Marshy stream, Syniakwateen, *Lord*.
58. " *Limnæa ? desidiosa*, Say." Lake Osoyoos; three sp., *Lord*. [Exactly resembles a var. of the widely distributed *L. cataracta*, which was found in profusion in the Madison Lakes, Wisc.]
60. " *Limnæa ? desidiosa*, Say." Syniakwateen, Brit. Col., *Lord*. One sp. [Very turrited, whirls swollen; epidermis finely striated. The same species occurs as " *L. megasoma*, Say. Lake Osoyoos."]
61. " *Physa heterostropha*, Say." Sumass Prairie, Fraser R. A variety from Lake Osoyoos, *Lord*.
62. *Physa* [probably young of *Lordi*, but with orange band inside labrum.] Kootanie R. East, Brit. Col., *Lord*. One sp.

Besides the shells preserved in the National Collection, the following species were also brought by the Expedition:—

63. *Terebratula unguiculus*, n. s. Vanc. Is., *Forbes*. One adult specimen, Mus. Cum. [Extremely interesting as being the only sculptured species known recent. The young shells from California were naturally affiliated to *Terebratella caput-serpentis* by Messrs. Reeve and Hanley; but the adult has the loop similarly incomplete.]
64. *Rhynconella psittacea*. Vanc. Is., *Forbes*. One specimen, Mus. Cum.
65. *Darina declivis*, n. s. Vanc. Is., *Forbes*. One specimen. [The only other species of *Darina* is from the West Coast of S. America.]
66. *Clementia subdiaphana*. Vanc. Is., *Forbes*. One broken sp.
67. *Saxidomus brevisiphonatus*, n. s. This unique shell is marked "Vancouver Island" in Mr. Cuming's Collection, and is believed by him to have formed a part of Dr. Forbes's series. The shape resembles *Callista*, without lunule. The mantle-bend is remarkably small for the genus.
68. *Melania*, n. s., teste Cuming. Vanc. Is., *Forbes*. [Two specimens, with very fine spiral striæ, sent to Philadelphia for identification.]
69. *Mesalia lacteola*. Vanc. Is., *Forbes*. One sp., Mus. Cum.
70. *Pteropoda*, several species, of which two are new, teste Cuming; but they may have been collected on the voyage. *Forbes*.

The collections made on the British Survey are peculiarly valuable to the student in consequence of the great perfection of the specimens. They have generally been obtained alive, and are often the finest known of their kinds. The occurrence, however, of a specimen of the tropical *Orthalicus zebra*, marked " Vancouver's Island," in Mr. Lord's collection*, is a useful lesson. When such reliable data are thus found possessed of adventitious materials, it will not be regarded as a slight on the collections of the most careful naturalists when specimens are regarded as of doubtful geographical accuracy. In Dr. Lyall's collections there also occur specimens of the well-known *Patella Magellanica* and *Trophon Magellanicus*, duly marked " Vancouver's Island," though no doubt collected in the passage round Cape Horn. The naturalists of the American Expl. Expeditions generally travelled across the continent.

104. The latest exploration undertaken for State purposes is also for our present object by far the most important, both as relates to the number of

* Mr. Lord writes, "The fact of my having found this shell, *alive*, on Vancouver Island is beyond question. How it got there I do not pretend to say; it was very possibly brought by some ship."

species authentically collected and the thoroughly competent and accurate manner in which the necessary information is being recorded. It is no longer left to the great nations bordering on the Atlantic to send exploring expeditions to the Pacific. The State of California, only born in 1850, has so rapidly attained maturity that when she was barely ten years old she considered science a necessary part of her political constitution, and organized a "State Geological Survey," under the direction of Prof. Whitney. To this survey Dr. J. G. Cooper (whose collections for the Pacific Railway Explorations have already been reported, *vide* pp. 597–601) was appointed zoologist, and Mr. W. M. Gabb (formerly of Philadelphia) palæontologist. The friendly relations established with both these gentlemen at the Smithsonian Institution not only put them in possession of the special desiderata on the present branch of inquiry, but have resulted in unreserved interchange of facts and opinions, by means of which a large instalment of the malacological results of the Survey can be embodied in this Report. Dr. Cooper has not only explored the whole coast and the neighbouring islands from Monterey to San Diego, but has dredged extensively from shoal-water to 120 fathoms, keeping accurate lists of all acquisitions from each locality. Having an artist's pencil as well as a naturalist's eye, he has drawn the animals from life, and already subjected many of them to dissection. The war has to some extent suspended the operations of the survey; but it is confidently expected that the State will do justice to herself by issuing, with suitable illustrations, the full results of her officers' labours. The first public notice of the molluscs appears in the Proc. Cal. Ac. N. S., Nov. 3rd, 1862, pp. 202–207. Here Dr. Cooper, speaking of the new species, writes with a modesty which is not always credited to American naturalists by Europeans,—"As they may have been collected either by the N.W. Boundary Survey or at Cape St. Lucas, it has been considered safest, in order to avoid confusion, to send specimens or drawings of them to [the writer], that he may compare them with the above collections, and decide whether they are really new." He gives valid reasons, however, for describing the following soft Mollusca. Unfortunately for French and German naturalists, the diagnoses are in English only.

Page.

202. *Strategus* (n. g.) *inermis*, n. s. More highly organized than any other genus of *Opisthobranchiata* ; creeps slowly among the grasses in the muddy parts of San Diego Bay, looking like a large caterpillar. Not uncommon.

203. *Pleurophyllidia Californica*, n. s. Closely resembles *P. lineata* of S. Europe. "From the distance of locality there can, however, be no identity of species." [?] Numerous in Dec., crawling and burrowing on sandy flats in San Diego Bay; none in Jan., after the floods. [Dr. Cooper writes that the body of fresh water was so great in some places as to kill the marine molluscs for a considerable distance beyond the estuaries, and thus materially alter the pre-existent fauna.]

204. *Doris Montereyensis*, n. s., 6–10 fm., adhering to sandstone. Monterey Bay, very rare. Small specimens in San Francisco Bay, *Frick*.

204. *Doris* (*Asteronotus*) *sanguinea*, n. s. Under stones in San Diego Bay ; rare.

204. *Doris* (? *Asteronotus*) *alabastrina*, n. s. Under stones in S. Diego Bay. One sp.

204. *Doris* (? *Actinocyclus*) *Sandiegensis*, n. s. Very active among grass on mudflats near low-water mark, San Diego Bay; common before the flood.

205. *Æolis* (? *Flabellina*) *opalescens*, n. s. Common among grass in San Diego Bay.

205. *Æolis* (? *Phidiana*) *iodinea*, n. s. Among algæ on rocks outside San Diego Bay.

207. *Tritonia Palmeri*, n. s. San Diego, common "in same localities as the *Diphyllidia*. Named after Mr. Edward Palmer, a zealous naturalist, who assisted me while at San Diego."

Dr. Cooper's second paper "On New or Rare Mollusca inhabiting the Coast of California," in the Proc. Cal. Ac. N. S., Aug. 17, 1863, contains (English) descriptions of the following species. He observes that "*Santa Barbara* and *Santa Barbara Island* are very different in the groups of animals inhabiting them, although the island is only thirty-five miles from the mainland. *Catalina Island* is twenty-four miles from the mainland, and the molluscs are very different from both the mainland and the other islands, being the richest locality on our shores."

Page.

57. *Aplysia Californica*, Cp.; for which is constituted a subgenus, *Neaplysia*; 15 inches by 5*. Three specimens; San Pedro beach, after storm; stomach full of algæ. Fig. 14.

58. *Navarchus*, Cp.   Pr. Cal. Ac., Apr. 1863.

"   *Navarchus inermis*, Cp.,= *Strategus i.*, Cp., *anteà*.   Catalina Island, 10 fms., in seaweed.   1 specimen.

"   *Doris albopunctata*, Cp.   Santa Barbara, 20 fm., rocky bottom.   Catalina Island, rocks, l. w.

"   *Doris Montereyensis*, Cp.   Santa Barbara Island, rocks, l. w.

"   *Doris sanguinea*, Cp.   4 sp. with the last. "Stellate structure not discovered."

"   *Doris Sandiegensis*, Cp.   2 sp., with the last. "All these species belong to *Doris*, typical."

60. *Triopa Catalinæ*†, Cp.   4 sp., on algæ among rocks, l. w.   Catalina Island.

"   *Dendronotus iris*, Cp.   Several sp. thrown on beach by storm, Santa Barbara; 1 sp. dredged on seaweed, 28 fm.   Very variable in colour.   ?="*Dendronotus*, sp.," Gld., E. E. Moll.

"   *Æolis Barbarensis*, Cp.   1 sp., 16 fm., rocky bottom, Santa Barbara.

60. *Flabellina opalescens*, Cp.,= *Æolis o.*, Cp., *anteà*.   With the last: also shore of Santa Barbara Island, rare.

"   *Phidania iodinea*, Cp.,= *Æolis i.*, Cp., *anteà*.   Santa Barbara, beach, 1 sp.

"   *Chioræra leonina*, Gld.   1 sp., in 20 fm.   Santa Barbara.

Sept. 7th, 1863.   Dr. Cooper described a very interesting new genus of Pulmonates, only found at the head of one ravine in Santa Barbara Island, with "myriads of *Helix Kellettii* [=*H. Tryoni*, v. note *, p. 116], and two other species, probably new." Full particulars of its habits are given. It has the mantle of *Limax*, dentition of *Helicidæ*, and shell resembling *Daudebardia* and *Homalonyx* [=*Omalonyx*, D'Orb.].

62, 63. *Binneya notabilis*, Cp.   3 living and 18 dead shells.   Fig. 15 (five views).

Jan. 18th, 1864.   The remaining land-shells of the Survey were described (with Latin diagnoses) by Dr. Newcomb, in a paper communicated to the Academy by Dr. Cooper.   Specimens of many of them will be found in the Cumingian Collection.

116. *Helix Tryoni*, Newc.   Santa Barbara and S. Nicholas Islands, abundant; living. "= *H. Kellettii*, Cp., p. 63."

"   *Helix crebristriata*, Newc.   San Clemente Island; abundant. "Closely allied to *H. intercisa*, and very variable."

117. *Helix rufocincta*, Newc.   Catalina Island, æstivating under stones; rare. S. Diego; 1 dead sp.   Outline like *H. Pytyonesica*: umbilicus open or nearly closed.

"   *Helix Gabbii*, Newc.   San Clemente Isl.   1 sp., like *H. facta*.

118. *Helix facta*, Newc.   Santa Barbara Isl., very common; San Nicholas Isl., rare.   Somewhat like *H. Rothi*.

"   *Helix Whitneyi*, Newc.   Near Lake Taho, Sierra Nevada, 6100 feet high. 3 sp. under bark, near stream, with *H. Breweri* and *H. chersina*.   Resembles *H. striatella*.

* Molluscs, as well as trees, assume giant proportions in California: e. g. *Schizothærus* (with siphons) 16 in., *Amusium* 8 in., *Lunatia* (crawling) 16 in., *Mytilus* 9 in., &c.

† *Vide* note †, p. 604.

1863.

118. *Helix Breweri*, Newc.   Near Lake Taho ; 8 sp.   (Also 1 sp. from mountains in Northern California, *Prof. Brewer.*)   Like *H. arborea.*
,,   *Helix Duranti*, Newc.   Santa Barbara Isl.   "Like *Planorbis albus=hirsutus*, Gld."

Dr. Newcomb also identified the following species in the State Collection :—

119. *Helix arrosa*, Gld.   Common near mouth of S. Francisco Bay.
,,   *Helix arrosa*, yellow var.   Santa Cruz, *Rowell.*
,,   *Helix ?Californiensis*, Lea, or *?Nickliniana*, Lea ; var., *Cooper.*
,,   *Helix Carpenteri*, Newc.   Broken dead shell, head of S. Joaquin Valley, *Gabb.*
,,   *Helix Columbiana*, Lea.   Near S. Francisco.
,,   *Helix chersina*, Say.   Very large, near Lake Taho, *Cooper.*
,,   *Helix Thouarsii*, Desh.   Pt. Cypress, Monterey, *Cooper.*
,,   *Helix exarata*, Pfr.   Mt. Diablo, *Brewer* ; Santa Cruz, *Rowell.*
,,   *Helix fidelis*, Gray.   Humboldt Bay and mountains, lat. 42°, *Brewer.*   Black var., *Frick.*
,,   *Helix infumata*, Gld.   Near Ballenas Bay, *Rowell.*
,,   *Helix Kellettii*, Fbs.   S. Diego, Catalina Isl., fine var., *Cooper.*
,,   *Helix loricata*, Gld.   Near Oakland, *Newcomb.*
,,   *Helix Newberryana*, Bin.   Temescal Mountains, near Los Angeles, *Brewer.*
,,   *Helix Nickliniana*, Lea.   Common near S. Francisco Bay, *Cooper.*
,,   *Helix sportella*, Gld.   Near S. Francisco Bay, *Cooper.*
,,   *Helix Mormonum*, Pfr.   San Joaquin Valley, *Gabb* ; north to Mt. Shasta, *Brewer.*
,,   *Helix Traskii*, Newc.   Mountains near Santa Barbara, *Brewer.*   May be = *Il. Thouarsii*, var.
,,   *Helix tudiculata*, Bin.   Near S. Diego and S. Pedro, *Cooper.*
,,   *Helix Vancouverensis*, Lea.   De Fuca, *Gabb* : perhaps extends south to Humboldt Bay.

Dr. Palmer sent a valuable consignment of shells collected by him between San Diego and S. Pedro to the Smithsonian Institution. Dr. Cooper obtained permission to send the first series of duplicates, duly numbered, for identification, to the Smithsonian Institution. This invaluable series was lost in the "Golden Gate." The gold was recovered, and much of it stolen ; the far more precious shells remain, unnaturally located, in their native element— a puzzle, perhaps, to palæontologists in some coming age. Other series, though not so complete, have since been received in safety; and through the liberality of the Californian Survey and of the Smithsonian Institution, as well as through the energy and kindness of Dr. Cooper, they are already being distributed to the Cumingian Collection, the British Museum, the museums at Cambridge, Mass., Philadelphia, Albany, Montreal, &c., as well as to the collections of working naturalists. The stations being now discovered, it is to be hoped that in a few years Californian shells will cease to be objects of great rarity in this country. At the request of Dr. Cooper, in order that he might proceed with other departments of his labours, all the new species which have been seen in England have been described in conjunction with those from other sources. On those which are only known here by the beautiful drawings sent by the collector, it would be unsafe and premature to impose a name. The diagnoses are being published in the Proc. Cal. Ac. N. S., and should be accredited to the zealous zoologist of the Survey, rather than to the mere artist-in-words who endeavours to represent their forms to the reader. It will be understood that the lists now to be presented, though corrected to the date of going to press, are still incomplete; and that the information has been compiled from Dr. Cooper's letters received at different times, without opportunity for his revision. Should errors, however, have escaped detection, they will, no doubt, be corrected, and omissions supplied, in the forthcoming Reports of the Survey. The species either new to science, or now first found in the Californian branch of the fauna, are as follows :—

No.
1. *Defrancia intricata.* S. Diego, on *Phasianella compta*, &c. Maz. Cat., no. 13.
2. *Terebratula unguiculus.* Monterey to S. Diego: young shells in 6-20 fm.: not rare.
3. *Terebratella ? caurina.* Catalina Is., 80 fm.; living; rare.
4. *Waldheimia Grayi.* Catalina Is., 120 fm.
5. *Zirphœa crispata.* Fragments from S. Diego appear (very unexpectedly) to belong to this northern species.
6. *Corbula luteola*, n.s. S. Pedro—S. Diego; common near shore.
7. *Neæra pectinata.* Santa Barb., Cat. Is., 40-60 fm. (Puget Sd., *Kennerley*).
8. *Kennerlia bicarinata*, n.s. Cat. Is., 40-60 fm.; rare.
9. *Entodesma inflata*, Conr., = *diaphana*, Cpr. Near S. Diego; 1 valve (*Palmer*).
10. *Plectodon scaber*, n.g. and n.s. Cat. Is.; 2 similar valves, 40-60 fm.
11. *Macoma inquinata.* S. Francisco; rare.
12. *Macoma yoldiformis.* S. Diego. (Puget Sound, *Kennerley.*)
13. *Macoma indentata*, n.s. S. Diego.
14. *Angulus variegatus*, n.s. Mont., Cat. Is., 20-60 fm.; rare. (Neeah Bay, *Swan.*)
15. *Arcopagia lamellata.* S. Diego. = Maz. Cat., no. 58.
16. *Œdalia (Cooperella) scintillæformis*, n. subg., n.s. S. Diego. Santa Barbara Is.
17. *Semele rupium.* Catalina Is.; not rare. (Also Galapagos.)
18. *Semele pulchra.* S. Diego. (Also Cape St. Lucas, Acapulco.)
19. *Semele incongrua*, n.s. Catalina Is., 40-60 fm.; common.
20. *Psephis salmonea*, n.s. S. Diego, Cat. Is., 30-40 fm.; rare.
21. *Psephis Lordi.* Cat. Is., 20-40 fm.; common. (Puget Sound, *Kennerley.*)
22. *? Astarte fluctuata*, n.s. Cat. Is.; 2 similar valves; 40 fm. (Very like the Crag fossil, *A. omaria*, jun.; but Dr. Cooper considers it a *Crassatella.*)
23. *Venericardia borealis.* Cat. Is., 120 fm. The typical, flat New England form. The small swollen var., = *V. ventricosa*, Gld., is also found at Cat. Is., in 30-40 fm.
24. *Miodon prolongatus.* (Neeah Bay, *Swan.*) Identified from tracing only.
25. *Trapezium.* One extremely young sp. = Maz. Cat., no. 120 (not like *T. Duperryi*). S. Diego.
26. *Chama ? spinosa.* S. Diego. (One young valve sent.)
27. *Cardium (? modestum*, var.) *centifilosum.* Cat. Is., 30-40 fm. [The differences between this and the Eastern Pacific shell are probably only varietal.]
28. *Hemicardium biangulatum.* Cat. Is., living in 10-20 fm. (Also Acapulco, Panama.)
29. *Liocardium elatum.* S. Diego; very large (Maz. Cat., no. 124).
30. *Lucina tenuisculpta.* S. Diego, living in 4 fm. (Also Puget Sound, *Kennerley.*) Var., dead in 120 fm., Cat. Is. (approaching *L. Mazatlanica*, Maz. Cat., no. 144.)
31. *Lucina borealis.* Cat. Island, 120 fm. " = *L. aculelirata*, Conr., foss. E. E." [Exactly agrees with British examples.]
32. *Cryptodon flexuosus.* Cat. Is., 120 fm. Ditto.
33. *Kellia suborbicularis.* S. Diego; Cat. Is., 30-40 fm. Ditto.
34. *Kellia* (var.) *Chironii.* S. Diego. (Also Neeah Bay, *Swan.*)
35. *Lasea rubra.* Cat. Is., shore (typical).
36. *Lepton meroëum*, n.s. S. Diego.
37. *Tellimya tumida.* S. Diego. (Also Puget Sound, *Kennerley.*)
38. *Pristes oblongus*, n.g., n.s. S. Diego.
39. *Crenella decussata.* Cat. Is., 10-40 fm.; not rare. (The ordinary British, not the New England form.)
40. *Barbatia gradata.* S. Diego; Maz. Cat., no. 194.
41. *Axinæa intermedia.* Monterey—S. Diego, Cat. Is., 40-60 fm. [Scarcely differs from the South American shell. It is the *A. Barbarensis*, Conr., of Pac. R. R. fossils, teste Cooper.]

No.

42. *Acila castrensis.* Cat. Is., 40–60 fm. (Also Puget Sound, *Kennerley.*)
43. *Leda cuneata,* teste Hanl. Mont.—S. Diego ; Cat. Is., 10–60 fm.
44. *Leda hamata,* n.s. Santa Barbara ; Cat. Is., 20–60 fm. ; common.
45. *Verticordia ornata,* D'Orb. Santa Barbara ; Cat. Is., 20–40 fm. [Exactly accords with the Japanese species, *novemcostata,* teste A. Adams.]
46. *Bryophila setosa.* (Cape St. Lucas, *Xantus.*) Identified from tracing, no. 980.
47. *Lima orientalis* (in Mus. Cum.,= *dehiscens,* Conr., teste Cooper). Mont.—San Diego ; Cat. Is., beach to 20 fm. ; common.
48. *Limatula subauriculata.* 40–120 fm., Cat. Is. : not rare : 1 valve in 4 fm., San Diego. [Exactly agrees with British specimens.]
49. *Janira dentata.* Monterey, S. Diego, beach to 20 fm. (Also Cape St. Lucas, *Xantus.*)
50. *Cavolina telemus.* Cat. Is. ; dead in 30–60 fm. (Also Vancouver, *Lyall.*)
51. *Tornatina carinata.* S. Diego. (Also Mazatlan, *Reigen.*)
52. *Pedipes liratus.* S. Diego. (Also Cape St. Lucas, *Xantus.*)
53. *Dentalium* (var.) *Indianorum.* Mont.—Cat. Is., 20 fm. ; common. [Probably a striated var. of *pretiosum,* which Sowerby doubtfully, and Dr. Baird confidently, affiliate to *D. entale.*]
54. *Dentalium semipolitum.* S. Diego. (Also La Paz.)
55. *Dentalium hexagonum.* S. Diego. (Also W. Mexico.)
56. *Acanthochites avicula,* n.s. Cat. Is., 8–20 fm. ; rare.
57. *Acanthopleura fluxa,* n.s. Cat. Is.
58. *Ischnochiton veredentiens,* n.s. Cat. Is., 10–20 fm.
59. *Ischnochiton* (*Lepidopleurus*) *pectinatus,* n.s. Cat. Is., beach.
60. *Ischnochiton* (*Lepidopleurus*) *scabricostatus,* n.s. Cat. Is., 8–20 fm.
61. *Ischnochiton* (*Trachydermon*) *pseudodentiens.* S. Diego. (Also Puget Sound, *Kennerley.*)
62. *Ischnochiton* (*Trachydermon*) *gothicus,* n.s. Cat. Is., 8–20 fm.
63. *Leptochiton nexus,* n.s. Cat. Is., 20–80 fm.
64. *Nacella* (?*paleacea,* var.) *triangularis.* Monterey.
65. ?*Nacella subspiralis.* Cat. Is., 10–20 fm. [May be the young of the long-lost *Patella calyptra,* Mart. ; unless that be a broken *Crepidula adunca.*]
66. *Scurria* (? var.) *funiculata.* Monterey ; rare.
67. *Puncturella cucullata.* Monterey. (Also Puget Sound, U. S. E. E.)
68. *Puncturella Cooperi,* n.s. Cat. Is., 30–120 fm. ; not rare.
69. ?*Imperator serratus,* ??n.s. Monterey ; Cat. Is., 10–20 fm. [Dr. Cooper thinks this shell probably the young of *Pomaulax.*]
70. ?*Leptonyx bacula,* n.s. Cat. Is., beach, dead.
71. *Gibbula optabilis,* n.s. S. Diego.
72. *Calliostoma supragranosum,* n.s. S. Diego.
73. *Calliostoma gemmulatum,* n.s. S. Diego.
74. *Calliostoma splendens,* n.s. Mont. ; Cat. Is., 6–40 fm.
75. *Margarita* (?var.) *sulmonea.* Mont. ; Cat. Is., 6–40 fm. [Intermediate between *undulata* and *pupilla.*]
76. *Margarita acuticostata.* Mont. ; Cat. Is., 8–20 fm. [Fossil, Santa Barbara, *Jewett.*]
77. *Solariella peramabilis,* ?n.s. Cat. Is., 40–120 fm. ; living. [Differs but slightly from *S. aspecta,* Japan, *A. Ad.*]
78. *Ethalia supravallata,* n.s., and ?var. *invallata.* S. Diego.
79. *Liotia fenestrata,* n.s. Cat. Is., beach to 40 fm. ; dead.
80. *Liotia acuticostata,* n.s. Mont. ; Cat. Is., 10–20 fm.
81. *Crepidula excavata,* var. jun. Santa Barbara Island.
82. *Galerus contortus,* n.s. Mont.—S. Diego, 20–40 fm.
83. *Hipponyx serratus.* Santa Barbara Island ; 1 sp. Maz. Cat., no. 346.
84. *Cæcum crebricinctum,* n.s. Mont.—S. Diego ; Cat. Is., 8–20 fm.
85. *Cæcum Cooperi,* n.s. S. Diego. [Two fine species of the *Anellum* group.]
86. *Turritella Cooperi,* ?n.s. S. Diego ; Cat. Is. ; common. [May prove identical with one of Conrad's imperfectly described fossils in P. R. E. E.]
87. *Mesalia tenuisculpta,* n.s. S. Diego ; shoal water.

No.
88. *Bittium armillatum.* S. Diego. [Fossil, Santa Barbara, *Jewett.*]
89. *Bittium asperum.* S. Diego ; Cat. Is., beach to 40 fm. [Fossil, Santa Barbara, *Jewett.*]
90. *Isapis fenestrata,* n.s. S. Diego. (Also Neeah Bay, *Swan.*)
91. *Isapis obtusa,* n.s. Mont.—S. Diego; Cat. Is., 10–20 fm.
92. *Rissoina interfossa,* n.s. Mont.; Cat. Is., 8–10 fm.
93. *Rissoa acutelirata,* n.s. S. Diego *.
94. *Fenella pupoidea,* n.s. Mont., 20 fm.; rare.
95. *?Amphithalamus lacunatus,* n.s. S. Diego. 1 immature specimen.
96. *Diala acuta,* n.s. Mont.; Cat. Is., beach to 10 fm.
97. *Diala marmorea,* n.s. Monterey, S. Diego; very rare.
98. *Styliferina turrita,* n.s. S. Diego.
99. *Jeffreysia translucens,* n.s. S. Diego.
100. *Cythna albida,* n.s. S. Diego.
101. *Trivia Solandri.* Santa Barbara and St. Nicholas Is.; common.
102. *Obeliscus ?variegatus.* S. Diego. (Also La Paz, Cape St. Lucas.)
103. *Chrysallida pumila,* n.s. S. Diego; Cat. Is.
104. *Chrysallida cincta,* n.s. Sta. Barbara Is.; very rare.
105. *Chemnitzia chocolata,* n.s. S. Diego.
106. *Chemnitzia (?tenuicula, var.) subcuspidata.* S. Diego.
107. *Eulima micans,* n.s. S. Diego. Cat. Is., 30–40 fm. (Also Puget Sound, *Kennerley.*)
108. *Eulima compacta,* ?n.s. S. Diego. ⎫ ⎰Dr. Cooper has not decided whether
100. *Eulima rutila,* ?n.s. Monterey. ⎭ ⎱ these be distinct species.
110. *Scalaria bellastriata,* n.s. Monterey.
111. *Scalaria subcoronata,* n.s. Monterey.
112. *Scalaria crebricostata,* n.s. Monterey, S. Diego.
113. *Scalaria ?Cumingii.* S. Diego.
114. *Scalaria ?Indianorum,* var. S. Diego. [Probably conspecific with the Vancouver shells.]
115. *Opalia borealis.* Farallones Is. (Also Neeah Bay, *Swan.*)
116. *Opalia spongiosa,* n.s. Monterey.
117. *Opalia retiporosa,* n.s. Cat. Is., rare and dead in 40 fm.
118. *Cerithiopsis columna,* n.s. Monterey.
119. *Cerithiopsis assimilata.* Cat. Is. = Maz. Cat., no. 563.
120. *Triforis ?adversa.* Cat. Is., 10–40 fm., very rare. [The specimens sent cannot be distinguished from the Herm shells.]
121. *Priene Oregonensis.* "Comes south to Monterey."
122. *Nassa insculpta,* n.s. Cat. Is., living in 40 fm., rare.
123. *Amycla undata,* n.s. Cat. Is., not rare in 40 fm.
124. *Amycla chrysalloidea,* n.s. S. Diego, shoal water.
125. *Anachis subturrita,* n.s. S. Diego.
126. *Trophon triangulatus,* ? n.s. Cat. Is., 60 fm. [Resembles the young of *Murex centrifugus.*]
127. *Argonauta argo.* "Hundreds on beach at Sta. Cruz Is."
128. *Octopus punctatus,* Gabb. San Clemente Is.
129. *Onychoteuthis fusiformis,* Gabb. San Clemente Is.
130. *Ommastrephes giganteus,* D'Orb. San Clemente Is.
131. *Ommastrephes Ayresii,* Gabb. San Clemente Is. "Hundreds on the beach."

Besides the above, several species are now satisfactorily assigned to the fauna, the evidence for which was before considered doubtful. Such are—

132. *Waldheimia Californica,* Koch [non auct., =*globosa,* Patagonia]. 120 fm. Catalina Is.
133. *Clidiophora punctata.* S. Diego to Sta. Cruz; valves common, but rare living.
134, 135. *Standella Californica, planulata,* et *?nasuta.* Conrad's types being lost, and his species imperfectly described from very young specimens, a difficulty

* Most of the minute shells from S. Diego, quoted without station, were found in the shell-washings of the consignments from Dr. Cooper and Dr. Palmer.

No.

attends their identification. Dr. Cooper found very large valves (resembling *Schizotherus*) in abundance, but much deformed by the entrance of sand, and apparently killed by the fresh waters of the great flood. The large shells belong to two very distinct species, which are probably those of Conrad; among the small shells is perhaps a third, which may be Dr. Gould's suppressed *nasuta*.

136. *Raëta undulata.* This remarkable reverse of the Atlantic *R. canaliculata* is also confirmed by rare valves from the S. Diegan district. It is not congeneric with *Harvella elegans*, to which it bears but a slight external resemblance.

137. *Tapes tenerrima.* Large dead valves of this very distinct species were found with the *Standellæ*, and confirm Col. Jewett's young shells described as from Panama.

138. *Pecten paucicostatus.* Sta. Barbara Is. [Described from Col. Jewett's valves.]

139. *Bulla Quoyii.* S. Diego. Maz. Cat. no. 226.

140. *Truncatella Californica.* S. Diego.

141. *Acmæa rosacea.* Monterey to S. Diego. This shell is named *pileolus*, Midd., in Mus. Cuming, but does not agree with the diagnosis. It can hardly be distinguished from Herm specimens of *A. virginea*. It was first brought by Col. Jewett, but referred to Panama.

142. *Amphithalamus inclusus.* S. Diego. [Several specimens of this minute but remarkable new genus confirm a solitary shell in Col. Jewett's mixed collections.]

143. *Myurella simplex.* Very variable in sculpture, as befits the species which forms the northern limit of a group common between the tropics. Col. Jewett's shell was in poor condition, and supposed to be the young of a Gulf species.

144. *Volvarina varia.* S. Diego, Cat. Is. [Sta. Barbara, *Jewett*; also C. S. Lucas.]

145. *Nassa Cooperi*, Fbs. S. Diego, Cat. Is. [This Kellettian shell has a double right to its name, now that Dr. Cooper has ascertained its habitat.]

The information on station, &c., which Dr. Cooper has sent with regard to previously known species, will be found incorporated in the general table of the fauna. The following notes, extracted from his letters, are too valuable to be omitted:—

Haliotis Californiensis. "This form is so rare that I think it only a var. of *Cracherodii.*"

Haliotis. Several specimens from the Farallones present characters intermediate between *corrugata*, *rufescens*, and *Kamtschatkana*. It is not yet ascertained whether they are hybrids or a distinct species.

" *Livona picoides* I have not found, though I have seen fresh ones from Pt. Conception."

" *? Serpulorbis squamigerus.* Common south of Pt. Conception; has no operculum." [The young begins like *V. anellum*, Mörch.]

Macron lividus. Point Loma, S. Pedro, common; extends northwards to the Farallones. [= *Planaxis nigritella*, Newcomb, MS.; non auct.]

" *Olivella semistriata*, Gray, fide Newc., is a species found N. of Monterey only." [As Dr. Gray's species is from Panama, that of Newcomb is probably *O. batica.*]

" *Nassa interstriata*, Conr., foss. (?= *N. paupera*, Gld.); resembles *N. fossata*, Gld. (= *B. elegans*, Rve.*), but distinct. Common south from Sta. Barbara." [Probably = *N. perpinguis*, Hds. *N. paupera* is quite distinct, = *N. striata*, C. B. Ad., teste Cuming.]

" *Fissurella violacea* I have seen from Catalina Is." [Esch.'s shell is generally considered S. American. ? May Dr. Cooper's be a form of *volcano.*]

Acmæa. With regard to limpets and other variable shells, Dr. C. writes:— " From my examination of large numbers of specimens, I am more and more compelled to believe that hybrids are very frequent between allied

---

* *Nassa elegans* was first published, by J. Sowerby, in the Min. Conch. 1824.

species, and that the comparatively few links that are met-with in large series of two forms should not be allowed to unite them, but be considered as hybrids."

Lunatia Lewisii. Abundant on beach. [One sp. measures 5¾ in., and the animal of a much smaller one (4 in.) is 11 inches long.]

Ostrea. "The same species throughout to S. Franc.: S. Diego," *Cooper.* [Besides the typical northern shell, *O. lurida*, are well-marked ?vars. *laticaudata, rufoides,* and *expansa.*]

There are also several species which are quoted in Dr. Cooper's letters, or appear from his sketches to be quite distinct, or at least new to the fauna: but they have not yet been sent for identification. Among these the following are the most important. The MS. numbers refer to the tracings which Dr. Cooper kindly copied from his original drawings. Where a " — " appears, the information is derived from his letters only.

MS. No.

402. Allied to ? *Thracia.*

— *Cyathodonta,* probably *plicata,* Desh. (Cape St. Lucas, *Xantus*).

620a. Figure accords exactly with *Venus toreuma,* Gld. Catalina Is., beach.

1058. Figure accords with *Lioconcha hieroglyphica.* Catalina Is., 120 fm.

1060. Resembles *Sunapta.* Catalina Is., 40 fm.

676. Resembles *Crassatella Pacifica.*

874. *Lucina.*

983. *Nucula,* with concentric sculpture. Sta. Barbara, 15 fm.

— *Yoldia.* One fresh valve of a large and remarkable species, 2·6 by 1·2 in., with fine concentric sculpture, very inequilateral. Sta. Cruz; on beach.

751a. ? *Ianthina.*

1077, 1078. *Chitonidæ.* Two highly sculptured species. Sta. Barbara, 12 fm.

— ? *Gadinia.* Cat. Is., *Cooper;* Farallone, Is., *Rowell.* "The animal differs in having pectinated flattened tentacles. It may be the type of a new genus *Rowellia.*"

466. *Emarginula.* [The first appearance of the genus on the W. American coast.]

415a. *Glyphis.*

354a. Like *Haplocochlea.* Sta. Barbara, 15 fm.

564. Like *Pyrgola.* 40 fm.

— *Trivia sanguinea.* Dredged dead in Cat. Is.

— *Trivia.* "Thinner and larger than *sanguinea.* Common in Lower Cal." [? = *Pacifica.*]

— "*Terebra specillata.*" One sp. near S. Pedro.

— *Pleurotomidæ.* Several species are represented only by single specimens. Among them are

588. *Drillia.*

1021. *Drillia,* 2 in. long, shaped like *Mitra.* One worn sp. Catalina Is., 120 fm.

1020. *Drillia,* reversed. Catalina Is., 60 fm., living.

479a. *Clathurella* (large). Sta. Barb., 20 fm.

663. *Clathurella,* 15 fm., Sta. Barb.

1852. ? *Clathurella,* 40 fm.

1053. ? *Daphnella,* 60 fm.

419, 426. Two species of shells resembling *Daphnella.*

1055. ? *Bela,* 80 fm.

423a. *Mangelia,* 15 fm., Sta. Barb.

397b. Shape of *Cithara,* without ribs. Catalina Is., beach.

1028. "? *Aclis,*" reversed. One sp., Cat. Is., 120 fm. [The figure more resembles a young Vermetid.]

463. "*Cancellaria ? Tritoniæ,*" Sby. Agrees with Dr. Newcomb's specimen." S. Diego, one dead on beach, 2¼ in. long.

817. *Cancellaria.* Fragment of a second species equally large.

1038. *Sigaretus.* 40 fm., dead, Cat. Is.

1050. *Lamellaria.* 10 fm., Sta. Barbara.

(385a, 464, 818.) *Naticidæ.* 3 sp.

MS. No.
576. Possibly a scaly var. of *Monoceros engonatum*; like the *Purpura*, var. *imbri-
     cata*, of Europe, but of different colour and texture; ?= *spiratum*, Blainv.
1001. Figure resembles *Vexilla fuscolineata*, Pse.   Sandwich Is.
—   " *Nassa*, smooth, with thick lip."   Cat. Is., 30 fm.   [Comp. *insculpta*.]
—   ? *Macron Kellettii*.   Cat. Is., dead, in 60 fm.
—   *Chrysodomus* ? *tabulatus*.   Cat. Is., 120 fm., young, dead.
—   *Fusus*, " like *geniculus*, Conr."   Farallones Is.
411. *Trophon*, like *multicostatus*.
515b. *Muricidea*.   Cat. Is., 40 fm.   [The young shells called *Trophon, Typhis*,
     &c., by Dr. Cooper can scarcely be identified without a series, and from
     tracings only.]
515d. ? *Typhis*.   Sta. Barb., 15 fm.
520. *Pteronotus centrifugus*, jun.   S. Pedro; rare on beach.
384b. *Muricidea*, like *alveata*.   Mont.—S. Diego.
956. ? *Siphonalia*.   Monterey, Sta. Barb., beach.

In Prof. Whitney's Preliminary Report on the Survey, Proc. Cal. Ac. p. 27,
May 4th, 1863, he states approximately as the result of Dr. Cooper's malacological labours, up to the close of 1862:—

No. of species in the collection 335
Of which are new to California, and believed to be undescribed 123
Other supposed Californian species not yet collected 65

In a Survey conducted with such care, even negative evidence is of some
importance, though not conclusive.   Dr. Cooper has not been able to obtain
the following species:—

Discina Evansii.
Strigilla carnaria.   [Mr. Nuttall's specimens were probably Atlantic.]
Venus dispar.
Trapezium Californicum.   [= *Duperryi*, = *Guiniacum*.]
Lucina bella.   [Perhaps = *pectinata*, Cpr.; but the type seems lost.]
Modiola nitens.   [Probably an error in the Cumingian label.]
Mytilus glomeratus, " = *edulis*, var."   [Perhaps an accidental var. from being
     crowded on a floating stick.]
Barbatia pernoides.   [Very probably an error in Dr. Gould's label.]
Arca multicostata.   "Must have been brought to S. Diego."
Pecten purpuratus.   [Ascribed to the fauna from abundant valves marked
     " Cal." in the U. S. E. E. collections, but certainly from S. America.   Dr.
     Cooper has unfortunately not been able to discover any of the species
     described by Hds.]
Radius variabilis.   "Doubtless exotic."
Polinices perspicua.   "Probably Mexican."
Ranella triquetra.   "Probably Mexican."   [Guaymas.]

105. Having now presented to the student an analysis of all that is yet
known of the results of public surveys, it remains that we tabulate what has
been accomplished by private enterprise.   Mr. J. Xantus, a Hungarian gentleman in the employ of the United States Coast Survey under the able
direction of Professor Bache, was stationed for eighteen months, ending July
1861, at Cape St. Lucas, the southern point of the peninsula of California.
It is a source of great benefit to natural science that the Secretary of the
Smithsonian Institution is also one of the acting members of the Coast Survey
Board; and that a harmony of operations has always existed between the
directors of these two scientific agencies in Washington.   The publications
of the Coast Survey have earned for themselves a reputation not surpassed by
those of the oldest and wealthiest maritime nations.   For obtaining data on
geographical distribution, Cape St. Lucas was a peculiarly valuable station,
being situated near the supposed meeting-point of the two faunas (v. B.A.

Rep. p. 350); and also, not being a place of trade, or even an inhabited district, likely to be free from human importations, although we should be prepared to find dead exotics thrown on its shores both by northern and by tropical currents. In his solitary and what would otherwise have been monotonous life, Mr. Xantus found full employment in assiduously collecting specimens in all available departments of natural history; having received ample instructions, and the needful apparatus, from the Smithsonian Institution. The bulk of the shells at first received from him were worn beach specimens; but afterwards several species were preserved, with the animals, in alcohol. Mr. Xantus generously presented the first series of the molluscs to the Smithsonian Museum, reserving the second for his native land. The first available duplicates of the shells not occurring in the Reigen collection will be found in the British Museum or in the Cumingian cabinets*. Although the whole series would have found little favour in the eyes of a London dealer or a drawing-room collector, it proved a very interesting commentary on the Reigen and Adams Catalogues: it added about sixty new forms to the accurately located species of the marine fauna, besides confirming many others, which rested previously on doubtful evidence; and disproved the intermixture of northern species, which, from the map alone, had before been considered probable.

The collection is not only essentially tropical, but contains a larger proportion of Central American and Panama species than are found in the Reigen Catalogue. This may partly be due to the accidents of station, and partly to this projecting southern peninsula striking the equatorial currents. It must also be remembered that the Reigen Catalogue embraces only the Liverpool division of his collection; and that many more species may have existed in that portion of the Havre series which did not find its way to the London markets. Mr. Xantus also obtained individuals of identical species from Margarita Island, and a series containing living specimens of *Purpura planospira* (only thrown up dead on the promontory), from Socorro Island, one of the Revilla-gigedo group. A very few specimens of *Haliotis* and of Pacific shells may have been given to him by sailors or residents: they were not distinguished from his own series in opening the packages. The collection is not yet complete. In consequence of the French occupation of Mexico, it was with difficulty that Mr. Xantus himself "ran the blockade" at Manzanello; and he was compelled to leave there thirty-one boxes of shells, alcoholics, &c., subject to the risks of war.

The Polyzoa were placed in the hands of Mr. G. Busk for examination, and the alcoholics were intrusted to Dr. Alcock, the Curator of the Manchester Natural History Society. Neither of these gentlemen have as yet been

* During the period that Mr. Xantus was out of employment, owing to the derangements of the war, a portion of the duplicates were offered for sale, and will be found in some of the principal collections.

able to report concerning them. The first notice of the shells appears in the Proc. Ac. Nat. Sc. Philadelphia, Dec. 1859, pp. 331, 332. The new species are described in the 'Annals and Magazine of Nat. Hist.,' 1864, vols. xiii. and xiv., as follows:—

A. N. H. Vol. XIII.

Sp. Page.

1.   311.   *Asthenothærus villosior*, n.g. 1 living sp. and fragm.
2.   „   *Solemya valvulus.* 1 living sp.
3.   „   *Tellina (Peronæoderma) ochracea.* 1 sp.
4.   312.   *Psammobia (?Amphichæna) regularis.* Valves.
5.   „   *Callista pollicaris.* 1 sp., living (= *C. prora*, var., teste Rve., C. I. f. 45).
6.   „   *Callista (?pannosa*, var.) *puella.* Extremely abundant, living. Also Acapulco, *Jewett.* (Very variable, yet always differing from the typical South American shells.)
7.   313.   *Liocardium apicinum.* Extremely abundant, living. Also La Paz; Acapulco, *Jewett.*
8.   „   *Lucina lingualis.* Extremely abundant, valves.
9.   „   *?Crenella inflata.* Valves; very rare. (An aberrant form.) Also Panama, *C. B. Ad.*
10.   314.   *Bryophila setosa*, n.g. Abundant; living among sea-weed, on *Purpura planospira.* Also California, *Cooper.*
11.   „   *?Atys casta.* Rare: allied to *Cylichna.*
12.   „   *Ischnochiton parallelus.* Rare; living.
13.   „   *Ischnochiton (?var.) prasinatus.* 1 living sp. Possibly a form of *parallelus.*
14.   315.   *Ischnochiton serratus.* 1 living sp., like *Elenensis.*
15.   474.   *Nacella peltoides*, = *Nacella*, sp. ind., Maz. Cat., no. 262.
16.   „   *Acmæa (?var.) atrata.* Intermediate between *P. discors*, Phil., and *P. floccata*, Rve. Also La Paz, Margarita Bay.
17.   „   *Acmæa strigillata.* Intermediate in characters and station between *A. patina* and *A. mesoleuca.* Also Margarita Bay.
18.   475.   *Glyphis saturnalis.* Not uncommon: living.
19.   „   *Eucosmia variegata.* (Probably a subgenus of *Phasianella.*) Rare, dead.
20.   „   *Eucosmia (?variegata*, var.) *substriata.* Very rare.
21.   „   *Eucosmia punctata.* 1 sp.
22.   476.   *Eucosmia cyclostoma.* 1 sp.
23.   „   *Haplocochlias cyclophoreus*, n. g. (?Related to *Ethalia.*) Very rare, dead.
24.   „   *Narica aperta.* 1 sp.
25.   „   *Fossarus parcipictus.* 3 sp.
26.   477.   *Fossarus purus.* 1 sp.
27.   „   *Litorina pullata*, = *Litorina*, sp. ind., Maz. Cat., no. 390. Abundant.
28.   „   *Litorina (Philippii*, var.) *penicillata.* Like the W. Indian *L.* (*ziczac*, var.) *lineata.* Abundant.
29.   „   *Rissoa albolirata.* 1 sp.
30.   „   *Fenella crystallina.* 1 sp.
31.   478.   *?Hydrobia compacta.* May be a *Barleeia.* 1 sp.
32.   „   *Hyala rotundata.* 1 sp.
33.   „   *?Diala electrina.* 1 sp.
34.   „   *Acirsa* [teste A. Ad.] *menesthoides.* 1 sp.
35.   „   *Cythna asteriaphila.* Imbedded in a star-fish, like *Stylina.* 1 living sp.
36.   „   *Bittium nitens.* 1 sp.

Vol. XIV.

37.   45   *Mangelia subdiaphana.* 1 sp.
38.   46   *Drillia appressa.* 1 sp.
39.   „   *Cithara fusconotata.* Very rare.
40.   „   *Obeliscus variegatus.* 2 worn sp. Described from a fresh Guaymas shell, Mus. Cal. Ac.
41.   „   *(Odostomia) Evalea æquisculpta.* 1 sp.
42.   47.   *(Odostomia) Evalea delicatula.* 1 sp.
43.   „   *Chrysallida angusta.* 1 sp.

A. N. H. Vol. XIV.

Sp. Page.

44. 47. *Eulima fuscostrigata.* 1 sp.
45. „ *Opalia crenatoides.* 1 perfect and a few rubbed specimens. This, and
        the Santa Barbara fossil, *O. ?var. insculpta,* are so close to the Por-
        tuguese *O. crenata,* that additional specimens may connect them.
46. „ *Truncaria eurytoides.* Common; rubbed. Also Guacomayo, in the
        Smithsonian Museum.
47. 48. *Sistrum (?ochrostoma,* var.) *rufonotatum;* connected with type by a few
        intermediate specimens. Rare ; dead.
48. „ *?Nitidella millepunctata.* Also Guacomayo, Mus. Smiths. Very rare, dead.
49. „ *Nitidella densilineata.* Very rare ; dead.
50. „ *?Anachis tincta.* 1 sp.
51. 49. *Anachis fuscostrigata,* 1 sp.
52. „ *Pisania elata.* A few worn specimens; like *Peristernia,* without plait.

The following table contains the species previously described, with the addition of the other localities in which they are known to occur. The numbers
in the first column are those in Prof. C. B. Adams's Panama Catalogue : a
P in the same column signifies that the species has been found at Panama
by other collectors. The second column contains the shells of La Paz, collected by Major Rich and others, and are marked by an italic *P.* In the
third column, A shows that the shell has been found at Acapulco, on good
authority; and C, that it is known at other stations on the Central American
coast. The fourth column exhibits the corresponding numbers of the species
in the B. M. Reigen Catalogue; and G shows that the shell has been found
in the Gulf district by other collectors. In the fifth column, Cal. stands
for Upper, and L for Lower California ; Marg. for Margarita Bay, Gal. for
the Galapagos, E for Ecuador and the tropical shores of S. America, and WI
for the West Indies. The sixth column continues the numbering of the
species from the list in the 'Annals.'

Pan. Cat.	La Paz.	Aca-pul.	Maz. Cat.	Other habitats.	No.	List of Cape St. Lucas Shells.
517		A	14	E	53	*Discina Cumingii.* On *Margaritiphora.*
P			22	E	54	*Gastrochæna ovata.* In *Spondylus.*
		A	23	Marg.	55	*Saxicava pholadis.* In *Spondylus.*
					56	*Eucharis,* sp. ind. 1 dead valve, resembling W. Indian species.
P			35		57	*Sphænia fragilis.* In *Spondylus.*
			G		58	*Thracia squamosa.* 1 broken pair.
	P			L	59	*Thracia (Cyathodonta) plicata* ("?=truncata. Migh."). 1 sp., jun.
P			G		60	*Lyonsia inflata.* 1 sp.
			36	E	61	*Lyonsia picta.* 1 valve.
463	P	C	55		62	*Tellina Cumingii.* 1 pair.
469		A		E	63	*Tellina rubescens* [= *Hanleyi*]. Smashed valve.
472					64	*Strigilla sincera.* 1 valve.
		A	67		65	*Strigilla lenticula.* Valves.
P					66	*Lutricola viridotincta.* 2 valves.
485			41		67	*Semele bicolor.* Valves.
			G	Marg.	68	*Semele Californica,* var. Valves.
			40	L	69	*Semele flavescens.* Rare.
480		A	43	E	70	*Cumingia trigonularis,* jun. In *Spondylus.*
473	P	A		WI	71	*Heterodonax bimaculatus.* Abundant ; normal, and numerous vars.

Paz. Cat.	La Paz.	Aca-pul.	Maz. Cat.	Other habitats.	No.	List of Cape St. Lucas Shells.
		A	75b	(Mar.)	72	*Donax*, var. *cœlatus*. Valves.
			76		73	*Donax ? Conradi*, jun.
456		C	77	L	74	*Donax ? navicula*, jun.
493	P	C	80		75	*Mulinia angulata*. Valves.
	P		79	WI	76	*Standella fragilis*. 1 sp. living, and numerous adult valves.
446	P	C	83	E	77	*Trigona radiata*, jun.
					78	*Trigona nitidula*, Sby. Several living sp. agree exactly with Sby.'s figure. [Perhaps Lam.'s Mediterranean shell is different.]
448		C	90	E	79	*Dosinia Dunkeri*. Rare.
	P		88	E.Mar.	80	*Dosinia ponderosa*. Several pairs [jun. = *distans*].
444		A	92		81	*Callista aurantia*.
447	P	A	93	E.Mar.	82	*Callista chionæa*.
		C	96	Marg.	83	*Callista vulnerata*. Living, and dead valves.
			98	E	84	*Callista (?var.) alternata*. 1 living.
				L	85	*Amiantis callosa*. Rare, living [= *C. nobilis*, Rve.].
	P		G	L.Mar.	86	*Chione succincta*. Very rare.
	P	C		E	87	*Chione pulicaria*, var. *lilacina*. Valves, abundant.
	P	A		E	88	*Chione neglecta*. Living and valves.
			106		88b	*Chione undatella*+var. *bilineata*, Rve. (pars). Very rare. [Probably = *neglecta*, var.]
435	P	C	113	E	89	*Aæmalocardia subimbricata*. Valves.
			111		90	*Tapes squamosa*. 1 sp.
P		A	24	E	91	*Petricola robusta*. In *Spondylus*.
			27		92	*Rupellaria linguafelis*.
			117	E	93	*Crassatella varians*. Living. Large and abundant.
492		C		E	94	*Crassatella gibbosa*. Valves.
	P		118		95	*Lazaria Californica*. Very rare.
		C			96	*Venericardia crassa*. 1 valve.
405		C	121b		97	*Chama Buddiana*, jun. On syenitic rock.
407		A	121	E	98	*Chama echinata*, Brod. Living, from Socorro Is.
P		C	121	Marg.	98b	*Chama frondosa*, var.
			123	L	99	*Chama ? exogyra*. Worn valves.
	P	A	122	Gal.	100	*Chama spinosa*. 1 sp.
	P	A		E	101	*Cardium consors*. Valves. (Very fine at Acapulco.)
433		C	125	E.Mar.	102	*Cardium procerum*. Valves.
434			126	E	103	*Cardium senticosum*. Valves.
P	P	A		L	104	*Hemicardium biangulatum*. Valves.
	P	C	136	WI	105	*Codakia tigerrina*. Living, very large, and young valves. [Of the Pacific Is. type.]
			137	Pac.Is.	106	*Codakia ? punctata*, jun.
P	P	A	147	E	107	*Lucina eburnea*. Living, rare.
P		A	140		108	*Lucina excavata*. 1 valve.
			145		109	*Lucina prolongata*. Valves.
			143		110	*Lucina cancellaris*. Valve.
			G		111	*Diplodonta subquadrata*. 1 sp.
		C			112	*Diplodonta calculus*. Several living sp.
					113	*Miltha Childreni*. [A few fresh specimens correct the habitat "Brazil," previously assigned to this extremely rare and remarkable shell, which appears to be a gigantic *Felania*.]
P		A	153		114	*Kellia suborbicularis*. In *Spondylus*.
		A	154		115	*Lasea rubra*. 6 sp. living.
?		C	167		116	*Mytilus palliopunctatus*. Fragment.
P	P	A	168		117	*Mytilus multiformis*. Abundant.
P			169		118	*Septifer Cumingianus*. Common.

Pan. Cat.	La Par.	Aca-pul.	Maz. Cat.	Other habitats.	No.	List of Cape St. Lucas Shells.
	P	A	170	L.Mar.	119	*Modiola capax.* A few living sp. "Gal." [?].
		A	172	Gal.	120	*Crenella coarctata.* In *Spondylus.*
P		A	176		121	*Lithophagus aristatus.* In *Spondylus.*
P		A	175		122	*Lithophagus plumula.* In *Spondylus.*
	P	C	181		123	*Arca multicostata.* Adult valves, and jun. living.
P		C	189	E	124	*Byssoarca Pacifica.* Rare.
418		A	190	E	125	*Byssoarca mutabilis.* Valve.
420	P			E	126	*Barbatia Reeviana.* Valves.
			192		127	*Barbatia vespertilio.* Valves.
424		C	193		128	*Barbatia illota.* Valve.
423	P		195	E	129	*Barbatia solida.* Rare.
416		A	194	E.Mar.	130	*Barbatia gradata.* Valve.
	P		G		131	*Axinæa gigantea.* Large valves, and jun. living.
			606		132	*Axinæa,* sp. ind.
			201	E	133	*Pinna lanceolata.* Fragment.
395			200		134	*Pinna maura.* 1 sp., jun.
P	P	A	202		135	*Pinna rugosa.* 1 sp., jun.
391	P	C	204		136	*Margaritiphora fimbriata.* Living.
				E	137	*Avicula Peruviana.* Valves.
393	P	A	205		138	*Isognomon Chemnitzianus.* Common, living.
			206		139	*Isognomon Janus.* 4 sp. living. [One has close ligament-pits, passing into *costellatus*, just as no. 138, var. passes into *incisus.*]
	P	A	G	E	140	*Pecten subnodosus.* Several valves, and 1 living. [*P. intermedia* is only a var. of this species.]
387	P	A	207	E.Mar.	141	*Pecten ventricosus.* Valves. [The young is *P. circularis,* Sby., pars.]
	P		G		142	*Janira dentata.* Very plentiful.
	P				143	*Lima tetrica.* 1 living, and valves [= *L. squamosa,* teste *Cuming.* W. I., Mediter., Pac. Is.].
390				Gal.	144	*Lima arcuata.* 1 fresh pair. [Can hardly be separated from *L. fragilis,* Gal., Pac. Is., in Mus. Cum.]
385			208		145	*Spondylus calcifer.* Valves. Red var., and specimen changing into purple.
386		C	210		146	*Plicatula penicillata.* 1 sp. on *Fasciolaria.*
381		A	211		147	*Ostrea iridescens.* A few living.
383	P		212	Marg.	148	*Ostrea ? Virginica,* jun.
			213	E	149	*Ostrea Columbiensis.* Valves.
384	P		215	Marg.	150	*Ostrea amara.* On *Pomaulax.*
				Cal.	151	*Cavolina ?telemus.* Fragment. (Pelagic.)
					152–156	[Nudibranchs and *Aplysia.* Not yet determined.]
321	P	A	224	E	157	*Bulla Adamsi,* and var. Common.
			225	L	158	*Bulla nebulosa.* Rare.
		A	226	L.Gal.	159	*Bulla Quoyi.* Very rare.
				L	160	*Haminea vesicula.* Plentiful, living.
			229	?L	161	*Haminea cymbiformis.* 1 sp. [Closely related to *H. virescens.*]
			240	Marg.	162	*Siphonaria æquilirata.* Dead. [ful.
P		A	239		163	*Siphonaria lecanium,* with var. *palmata,* &c. Plenti-
					164	*Onchidium Carpenteri.* Very rare.
			235	L.Cal.	165	*Melampus olivaceus.* Rare.
					166–172	[The rest of the Pulmonates will be tabulated afterwards, *vide* p. 630.]
			243		173	*Ianthina decollata.* Very rare.
				L	174	*Ischnochiton Magdalensis.* Large and highly sculptured. Very rare.

Pan. Cat.	La Paz.	Aca-pul.	Maz. Cat.	Other habitats.	No.	List of Cape St. Lucas Shells.
		C	252	E	175	*Ischnochiton limaciformis.* 2 specimens.
			256		176	*Ischnochiton Beanii.* 1 sp.
			258		177	*Acanthochites arragonites.* A few living sp.
		C	261		178	*Patella discors.* Dead.
		A	260		179	*Patella pediculus.* Dead.
			264	Marg.	180	*Acmæa fascicularis.* Abundant, living.
			268		181	*Acmæa mitella,* jun.
	P	A	273	Gal.	182	*Fissurella rugosa,* jun. [A var. is first black, with two white rays : afterwards changes to whitish.]
357		C			183	*Fissurella microtrema.* Common. [Passes into *rugosa.*]
			274		184	*Fissurella nigrocincta.* 1 young sp.
	P	A	279	E	185	*Glyphis inæqualis.* Rare.
			281		186	*Rimula Mazatlanica.* 2 sp.
				L. Cal.	187	*Haliotis Cracherodii.* (Turtle Bay.)
				L. Cal.	188	*Haliotis splendens.* (Margarita Island, with 4, 5, and 6 holes.)
				L	189	*Callopoma Fokkesii.* Dead.
				L. Cal.	190	*Pomaulax undosus.* Fresh, with Gulf Polyzoa.
	P	C	286		191	*Uvanilla olivacea.* Dead.
		A	288		192	*Uvanilla unguis.* Dead.
			289	Marg.	193	*Calliostoma eximium.* Dead.
274	P				194	*Omphalius coronulatus.* Dead ; not uncommon.
263			295		195	*Vitrinella Panamensis.* 1 sp. off *Spondylus.*
304	P	A	326	Marg.	196	*Nerita scabricosta.* Abundant.
305	P	C	327	E.Mar.	197	*Nerita Bernhardi.* Abundant.
336	P	A	343	E.Mar.	198	*Crucibulum imbricatum.* Dead.
337	P	A	344	E.Mar.	199	*Crucibulum spinosum.* Dead.
344	P	A	334	E. Cal.	200	*Crepidula aculeata.* Dead. West and East Indies.
	P	A		E.Mar.	201	*Crepidula ? arenata,* jun. *
345		A	337	C.Mar.	202	*Crepidula excavata,* jun. et var.*
346	P		340	E.Mar.	203	*Crepidula onyx.* Dead.
328	P	A	347	E	204	*Hipponyx antiquatus.* Dead.
327		A	349		205	*Hipponyx barbatus.* Pacific Is. Fresh sp.
329	P	A	350	Gal.	206	*Hipponyx Grayanus.* Rare.
323	P	A	352		207	*Aletes centiquadrus.* On *Margaritiphora,* &c.
			355		208	*Bivonia contorta.* Frequent, on shells.
		A	359		209	*Petaloconchus macrophragma.* Frequent, on shells.
	P			L	210	*Spiroglyphus lituella.* On *Purpura planospira* and *muricata,* from Socorro Is.
			367		211	*Cæcum subimpressum.* Very rare.
	P	A	380		212	*Turritella tigrina* et var. *Cumingii.*
	P				213	*Turritella sanguinea.* (Whirls not shouldered.)
193	P	A	381	Gal.	214	*Cerithium maculosum* and dwarf var., like *medio-læve.* Abundant.
196	P	A	383		215	*Cerithium uncinatum.* Common ; dead.
200	P	A	387	G.Mar.	216	*Cerithium stercus muscarum.* Rare ; dead.
	P	A	388	Gal.	217	*Cerithium interruptum,* Mke. Common.
197	P	A	389	Marg.	218	*Rhinoclavis gemmata.* Rare.
				Marg.	219	*Pyrazus incisus.* Rare.
?206			395	?E.Mr.	220	*Cerithidea Mazatlanica.* Dead.

* A difficulty attends the identification of young specimens of these rare species, no series having yet been obtained. "*C. excavata,* var.," in Mus. Cum. is exactly intermediate between the two. The young of *excavata* has a large swelling umbo projecting beyond the margin ; the umbo in "? var." has the margin spreading round it, as in *onyx,* jun., and in consequence appears turned in the contrary direction. The umbilicus above the deck exists in both forms ; but it is not an absolutely constant character, even in *adunca.*

Pan. Cat.	La Paz	Aca-pul.	Maz. Cat.	Other habitats.	No.	List of Cape St. Lucas Shells.
232		C	397	Marg.	221	*Litorina aspera.* Very rare.
234	P	C	396		222	*Litorina conspersa.* Common. A distorted specimen has a Lacunoid chink; another a Nassoid shape.
P			398		286	*Litorina Philippii.* Rare: *v. anteà,* var. *penicillata.*
273	P		401	E	223	*Modulus catenulatus,* jun.
244					224	*Rissoina firmata.* Rare.
245					225	*Rissoina fortis.* Very rare.
		A	408		226	*Rissoina stricta.* Rare.
243					227	*Rissoina clandestina.* Dead.
247					228	*Rissoina infrequens.* Dead, worn.
246			414		229	*Alvania tumida.* 1 sp., off *Spondylus.*
		C	417	L	230	*Barleeia subtenuis.* 1 sp.
			411		231	*Barleeia lirata.* 1 sp.
			422		232	*Gemella,* sp. 1 sp.
			420	L	233	*Jeffreysia Alderi.* 1 sp.
			419		234	*Jeffreysia bifasciata.* Very rare.
			425		235	*Alaba supralirata.* Not uncommon.
			427		236	*Alaba terebralis.* 1 dead, broken specimen.
		A	424		237	*Planaxis nigritella.* Dead; some of the specimens may be a dwarf form of
42					237b	*Planaxis ? planicostata.*
4			435	?L	238	*Radius variabilis.* 1 sp.
6	P	A	438	E	239	*Aricia arabicula.* Very rare.
8	P	C		E	240	*Aricia punctulata.* Very rare.
	P				241	*Luponia Sowerbyi.* 1 living and several worn.
	P				242	*Luponia albuginosa.* Dead; plentiful.
						[*Cyprœa tigris* and *Pteroceras lambis*; doubtless received through traders.]
9	P	A	439		243	*Trivia pustulata.* Dead.
10	P	A	440	Gal. E.	244	*Trivia radians*; intermediate specimens towards
?	P	A	441		245	*Trivia Solandri.* Dead.
	P	A		Gal.	246	*Trivia Pacifica.* 1 sp.
12	P	A	442	E	247	*Trivia sanguinea.* Dead.
		A			248	*Erato Maugeriæ.* [Exactly like the W. Indian specimens: also Crag fossil, teste S. Wood.]
13		A		Gulf E	249	*Erato scabriuscula.* Rare.
122		C	447		250	*Strombus galeatus,* jun. 1 sp.
124	P	A	448	Gal. E	251	*Strombus granulatus.* Abundant; dead.
123	P		449	E	252	*Strombus gracilior.* 1 dead specimen.
P		C			253	*Subula strigata.* 2 dead specimens.
		C	454	E	254	*Subula ? luctuosa,* jun.
	P	A	455		255	*Euryta fulgurata.* Dead.
		A	456	E	256	*Euryta aciculata.* Dead.
		C			257	*Terebra lingualis.* 1 sp.
	P		G		258	*Myurella variegata.* Very rare.
			450		259	*Myurella albocincta.* 1 dead specimen.
			452		260	*Myurella submodosa.* 1 dead specimen.
	P	C	457		261	*Pleurotoma funiculata.* Rare; dead.
163			461	E	262	*Drillia aterrima.* Rare; and var. *Melchersi.*
			465		263	*Drillia albovallosa.* 1 sp., dead.
			467	E	264	*Drillia luctuosa.* 1 sp., dead.
	P				265	*Drillia maura,* Val. Fragment.
		A			266	*Daphnella casta.* 1 sp. [Coarser striæ than W. I. species, but scarcely differs from *crebriplicata,* Rve., "Philippines."]
		A			267	*Cithara stromboides* 1 sp. [Probably=*triticea,* Kien.]

109

Pan. Cat.	La Paz.	Aca-pul.	Maz. Cat.	Other habitats.	No.	List of Cape St. Lucas Shells.
117	P	A		E	268	*Conus princeps.* Dead.
113	P	A		Gal. E	269	*Conus brunneus.* Dead.
118	P	A	476		270	*Conus purpurascens* and var. *regalitalis.* Dead.
114	P	A	480		271	*Conus gladiator.* Dead.
116	P	A	481	Gal.	272	*Conus nux* et var. *pusillus* [Gld. non Chem.]. Living; plentiful.
118		C	G		273	*Conus scalaris.* 1 sp., dead.
P	P			E	274	*Conus tornatus.* Rare, dead.
270	P	A			275	*Solarium granulatum,* and ? var. *quadriceps.* Common.
				L	276	*Odostomia ?straminea.* 1 sp.
			489		277	*Syrnola lamellata.* 1 sp., off *Spondylus.*
254			501		278	*Oscilla exarata=terebellum.* 1 sp.
223			507		279	*Chrysallida communis.* 1 sp., off *Spondylus.*
227			518		280	*Chemnitzia Panamensis.* Very rare.
			519		281	*Chemnitzia Adamsi.* 1 sp., off *Spondylus.*
			524		282	*Chemnitzia prolongata.* 1 sp., off *Spondylus.*
			532		283	*Chemnitzia flavescens.* 1 sp., off *Spondylus.*
194		A	563	L	284	*Cerithiopsis assimilata.* 1 sp.,off *Spondylus.*
207			557	L	285	*Cerithiopsis tuberculoides.* 1 sp.
208		C	391		286	*Triforis alternatus.* 1 sp., off *Spondylus.*
P					287	*Scalaria ?tiara.* 1 sp.
295	P	A	570	Gal.	288	*Natica maroccana.* Com. W. Afr.; ?Pacific Is.
P	P	A			289	*Natica zonaria.* Common. Operc. grooved as in *canrena* [=*alapapilionis,* var., teste Rve.: non Chem.].
		A			290	*Natica catenata.* Common.
302	P	A	576	E	291	*Polinices uber.* Common. [The young shells go through all shapes, from globose to pointed. Operc. thin, light green, horny.]
P		A	G	Gal.	292	*Polinices otis* et var. *fusca.* Rare; dead.
	P		G	Marg.	293	*Polinices bifasciata.* Living; rare.
	P	A	G	E	294	*Neverita glauca.* 1 sp.
			577		295	*Lamellaria,* sp. ind. 1 sp.
146		A	579		296	*Ficula ventricosa.* Not uncommon. Animal preserved of both sexes, and of surpassing beauty.
66		C	G	E.Mar.	297	*Malea ringens.* 1 dead sp. [Fossil, Atlantic shores, Newberry.]
112	P	A	G	Gal.	298	*Oniscia tuberculosa.* Very rare.
111	P	A	G	Gal.	299	*Levenia coarctata.* Very rare.
110	P	C			300	*Bezoardica abbreviata.* 1 living, with very small normal operculum. Common; dead. [Varies greatly in form and sculpture, like the Texan "analogue," which may be conspecific.]
131		C			301	*Triton vestitus.* 1 sp. [Scarcely differs from *pilearis.*]
132					302	*Ranella caelata.* 1 sp., dead.
				L	303	*Ranella Californica.* Very rare. Grows 4 inches long.
151		A	582	Gal.	304	*Latirus ceratus.* 2 dead sp.
P			584	E	305	*Fasciolaria princeps.* 2 dead sp.
18		A			306	*Mitra crenata,* Rve., teste Dohrn. 1 sp. [?=*nucleola.*]
19					307	*Mitra solitaria,* C. B. Ad. 1 sp.
20			586	Gal. E	308	*Strigatella tristis.* Rare.
		A	G	E	309	*Æneta harpa.* 1 sp.
P			589		310	*Volutella margaritula.* Off *Spondylus*; common.
14			587		311	*Marginella minor.* Off *Spondylus*; rare.

Pan. Cat.	La Paz.	Aca-pul.	Maz. Cat.	Other habitats.	No.	List of Cape St. Lucas Shells.
		A			312	*Volvarina varia.* Rare. [Cannot be distinguished from some W. I. specimens.]
		A		?WI	313	*Persicula imbricata.* 1 sp. [Can scarcely be separated from *interrupta*, jun. Also Guacomayo.]
					314	*Persicula phrygia.* Rare. [Closely allied to *frumentum*. Differs from the W. I. *sagittata* by having the painting in loops instead of zigzag, and an orange callosity over the sunken spire, bordered by a spotted sutural line.]
36	P		G	Marg.	315	*Oliva porphyria.* 1 sp.
?33	P	A	591		316	*Oliva Melchersi,* var. Rare.
	P		?592	Marg.	317	*Oliva subangulata.* Very common, dead. [This species, very rare elsewhere, is known by the shouldered shape, toothed paries, and violet-stained mouth and columella.]
	P		600		318	*Olivella dama.* Rare; dead.
	P	C	596		319	*Olivella tergina.* Rare; dead.
39		A	595		320	*Olivella undatella.* 3 sp.; dead.
		C	601		321	*Olivella zonalis.* Rare; dead.
			598	?WI	322	*Olivella v. aureocincta.* 3 sp.; dead.
		A	597	E	323	*Olivella anazora.* Very rare; dead. Perhaps a var. of
34	P	A			324	*Olivella gracilis.* Extremely abundant. [With many varieties: among which is one with dark median and sutural bands and light spire; another with dark spire; another pure white, of which the young is *inconspicua*, C. B. Ad. The Acapulcan varieties are somewhat different.]
		A	G		325	*Harpa crenata.* Dead.
76	P	A	606	E.Mar.	326	*Purpura biserialis.* Abundant.
	P	A	607		327	*Purpura triserialis.* Common.
69	P	A	608	Gal.	328	*Purpura triangularis.* Not uncommon.
	P	A	603	G.Mar.	329	*Purpura patula.* Common. Also West Indies.
P	P	C	605	E	330	*Purpura muricata.* Rare; dead at C. S. L.; living at Socorro Island.
	P			Gal.	331	*Purpura planospira.* Dead shells at C. S. L. and La Paz; abundant and fine at Socorro Island.
74			611		332	*Rhizocheilus nux*+tall var. [= *Californicus.*]
107		A		Gal.	333	*Sistrum carbonarium.* Living; plentiful.
89	P	A	613	WI	334	*Nitidella cribraria.* Abundant.
94		A	615	E	335	*Columbella major.* Rare.
86	P	A	617	E	336	*Columbella fuscata.* Abundant.
		A			337	*Columbella festiva.* Not rare.
90	P			Gal.	338	*Columbella hæmastoma.* Not rare.
				E	339	*Columbella solidula.* Abundant *.
		A		E	340	*Columella Reevei* [= *Sta. Barbarensis,* Cpr. (error)].
				E	341	*Columella baccata.* Rare.
	P				342	*Conella cedonulli.* 1 sp.
	P		624	L.Mar.	343	*Nassa tegula.* Rare; pale var.
55		C	632		344	*Nassa versicolor.* Rare; dead.
45	P	A			345	*Nassa corpulenta.* Very rare.

* The young shell is thin, semitransparent, with Alaboid tuberous vertex. The nuclear part is rather more tumid than the next whirl, and set slanting as in some *Chrysodomi*. Adolescent, whirls smooth, except a sutural line. Sculpture of adult gradually developed, with spiral lines, sometimes all over, sometimes only anteriorly and posteriorly. Last whirl sometimes with blunt radiating riblets, but generally smooth. Siphonal notch deeply cut back, as in *Strombina*, to which the species may belong.

Pan. Cat.	La Paz.	Aca-pul.	Maz. Cat.	Other habitats.	No.	List of Cape St. Lucas Shells.
P				Gal.	346	*Fusus Thouarsii* [+*Novæ-Hollandiæ*, Rve.]. Rare; dead.
P			639	E	347	*Siphonalia pallida.* Very rare.
109				Gal.	348	*Engina Reeviana.* 1 sp.
P		A		Gal.	349	*Engina crocostoma.* 1 sp.
P		C	647		350	*Anachis coronata.* Very rare.
			652	E	351	*Anachis tæniata* [= *Gaskoinei*]. Very rare.
99					352	*Anachis pulchrior.* Very rare.
			G		353	*Anachis ?pallida*, Phil. Very rare.
98				E	354	*Anachis ?parva*, var. Dead shells : may be *pygmæa*, var.
			650		355	*Anachis serrata.* A few perfect specimens.
(100)		A	(651)	) (E)	356	*Anachis pygmæa* (var. *auriflua*). Rare.
	P	C	657		357	*Strombina maculosa.* Very rare.
87				E	358	*Strombina gibberula.* Very rare.
64	P	A	662		359	*Pisania sanguinolenta.* Dwarf var.; common.
60		A			360	*Pisania lugubris.* Rare; dead.
	P	C	664		361	*Murex plicatus.* Rare; dead.
140	P	A	665		362	*Murex recurvirostris.* 1 sp., dead.
	P	A	669		363	*Phyllonotus bicolor.* Rare.
	P	A	671		364	*Phyllonotus princeps.* Rare; dead.
136	P	A	673		365	*Muricidea dubia.* Rare; dead.
					366	*Argonauta argo.* 1 large sp. of the ?var. *papyracea.* Pelagic.
					367	*Octopus*, sp. Pelagic.

As would be expected, the bulk of these species (203 out of 367) are the same as have been already enumerated in the Reigen Catalogue. Of those which do not appear in the Mazatlan lists, no fewer than 37 appear in the Panama collections (beside 10 others, known to inhabit the equatorial region). Of those not quoted from Mazatlan, 34 are also found in the Acapulco region, and 30 at La Paz. Of the whole number, 79 have also been found in South America, and 28 in the Galapagos. 38 have also been found in Margarita Bay, of which *Pyrazus incisus* and *Siphonaria æquilirata* are Lower Californian rather than Gulf species; but only 13 belong to that portion of the Lower Californian fauna which is known to reach S. Diego, exclusive of the same number of Gulf species, which also stray into the S. Diegan district. There are also 10 species, which (with more or less distinctness) represent West Indian forms. Of these, five, viz. *Heterodonax bimaculatus, Erato Maugeriæ, Volvarina varia, Persicula imbricata* and *phrygia*, are new to the Gulf fauna: the other five appear in the Reigen Catalogue.

106. The most extensive collections in the Vancouver district, both as far as the number of species and of specimens is concerned, have been made for the Smithsonian Institution by Mr. J. G. Swan, teacher at the Indian Reserve, Neeah Bay, W. T. For several years * valuable consignments have been received from him of shells collected at Cape Flattery, Port Townsend, and other stations. Latterly he has trained the native children to pick up shore-shells in large quantities. The labour of sorting and arranging these has been enormous; it has, however, been repaid not only by observing the

* In consequence of boxes having been received at different times, through the accidents of transit, it has not always been possible to ascertain with certainty to whom, among simultaneous collectors, should be allowed priority in the discovery of new species.

variations of form in large numbers of individuals, but by the discovery of several new species and the addition to the district-fauna of many others. The duplicates are made-up in series for distribution by the Smithsonian Institution; and, though of the worst quality from a "collector's" point of view, they will be found very serviceable by real students, being carefully named in accordance with this Report. He has now received a dredge, constructed for him by Dr. Stimpson; and if he succeeds in training the young Indians to use it, there is little doubt that a rich harvest of fresh materials will shortly be obtained. Some of the collections were made on the neighbouring shores of Vancouver's Island, among which was a large series of *Pachypoma gibberosum*, Chem., with attached *Bivonia*, both of an essentially Eastern Pacific type, the former having been brought from Japan by Mr. A. Adams. The Indians have taken a fancy to the opercula of this shell for the purpose of ornamenting their canoes. As it is an article of trade among themselves, it is remarkable that so large a shell should have so long escaped the notice of collectors. Dead specimens have been washed-up in California; but it is not known even to enter the Straits of De Fuca alive. The shore-pickings of the Indian children, which have already added 25 species to science, are singularly free from ballast-importations, although they present a few (supposed) extra-limital shells, probably washed-up by the ocean currents. The following are the species new to the Vancouver fauna; the remainder will be found tabulated in the 7th column of the general Table, par. 112, *infrà*.

No.
1. *Waldheimia Coreanica*, valves.
2. *Xylotrya pennatifera*, teste Jeffr.
3. *Clidiophora punctata*, one worn valve.
4. *Macoma ? edentula*. Two living shells may be the young of this species, or an extreme var. of *inquinata*.
5. *Mæra salmonea*. Plentiful.
6. *Angulus variegatus*. Rare.
7. *Semele rubrolineata*. One large valve may belong to this species, or (more probably) be distinct and new.
8. *Standella ? Californica*. One young valve.
9. *Miodon prolongatus*, n. subg., n. s. Several valves of this curious shell, intermediate between *Lucina* and *Venericardia*, accord with forms not before eliminated, from the Coralline Crag and Inferior Oolite.
10. *Lazaria subquadrata*. One valve.
11. *Diplodonta orbella*. Very large valves.
12. *Kellia* (var.) *Chironii*. A few valves.
13. *Adula stylina*. Plentiful.
14. *Axinæa* (? *septentrionalis*, var.) *subobsoleta*. Numerous valves.
15. *Siphonaria Thersites*, n. s. Rare, dead. Like *tristensis* and other Cape Horn and N. Zealand types. The genus was not known north of Margarita Bay.
16. *Mopalia* (*Kennerleyi*, var.) *Swanii*. One sp. and valves.
17. *Ischnochiton* (*Trachydermon*) *Nuttalli*. One sp.
18. *Haliotis Kamtschatkana*. Rare.
19. *Pachypoma gibberosum*, Chem. Living; plentiful.
20. *Leptonyx sanguineus*, Linn. Very plentiful. (Japan, *A. Ad.*; = *Homalopoma sanguineum*, anteà p. 588 (nom. preoc.); Mediterranean, *Philippi*.)
21. *Chlorostoma funebrale* (et var. *subapertum*. One sp.).
22. *Calliostoma canaliculatum*. Living; abundant.
23. *Margarita cidaris*, n. s. One fresh specimen, with aspect of *Turcica*.
24. *Margarita helicina*. Very rare.
25. *Gibbula parcipicta*. One sp.
26. *Gibbula succincta*, n. s. Rare.
27. *Gibbula lacunata*, n. s. One sp.

8   113

No.
28. *Gibbula funiculata*, n. s. Very rare.
29. *Hipponyx cranioides*, n. s. Plentiful.
30. *Biconia compacta*, n. s. Frequent on *Pachypoma*; externally resembles *Petaloconchus macrophragma*.
31. *Bittium* (? var.) *esuriens*. Common, dead.
32. *Lacuna porrecta*, n. s. Plentiful, with intermediate ? vars. *exæquata* and *effusa*.
33. *Lacuna* (? *solidula*, var.) *compacta*. Rare.
34. *Lacuna variegata*, n. s. Not common; resembles the Japanese *L. decorata*.
35. *Isapis fenestrata*, n. s. Very rare.
36. *Alvania reticulata*, n. s. Very rare.
37. *Alvania filosa*, n. s. One specimen.
38. *? Assiminea subrotundata*, n. s. One specimen.
39. *? Paludinella*, sp. One specimen.
40. *Mangelia crebricostata*, n. s. Very rare.
41. *Mangelia interfossa*, n. s. Several dead specimens.
42. *Mangelia tabulata*, n. s. Several dead specimens.
43. *Daphnella effusa*, n. s. One broken specimen.
44. *Odostomia satura*, n. s. and ? var. *Gouldii*. Very rare.
45. *Odostomia nuciformis*, n. s. and ? var. *avellana*. Very rare.
46. *Odostomia inflata*. Very rare.
47. *Odostomia tenuisculpta*, n. s. Very rare.
48. *Scalaria Indianorum*, n. s. Rare.
49. *Opalia borealis*. Very common. This fine species, indicated by Dr. Gld. (E.
      E. Mol., p. 307) under *Scalaria australis*, closely resembles *O. Ochotensis*,
      Midd. It is not referred to in the 'Otia,' and the locality was naturally
      suspected.
50. *Cerithiopsis munita*, n. s. Rare.
51. *Cerithiopsis columna*. Very rare.
52. *Cerithiopsis tuberculata.* } Rare. No differences have been detected on comparing
53. *Triforis adversa.*   } the Herm and Neeah Bay specimens.
54. *Trichotropis inermis*. A few specimens differ from the decorticated *T. cancellata*, and agree with Hinds's diagnosis.
55. *Cancellaria modesta*, n. s. One sp. and fragment.
56. *Velutina prolongata*, n. s. Very rare.
57. *Olivella biplicata*. Very fine and abundant.
58. *Purpura* (var.) *fuscata*. Forbes's species, the locality of which was before uncertain, is here connected by easy transitions with the normal *saxicola*.
59. *Columbella* (var.) *? Hindsii*. May be a stunted form of *A. gausapata*.
60. *Amycla tuberosa*. Rare.
61. *Chrysodomus tabulatus*. One beautifully perfect specimen; described and figured from Mr. Lord's broken shell, sent simultaneously.

The following appear to be due to currents:—

62. *Pachydesma crassatelloides*. Fragment.
63. *Fissurella volcano*. One broken specimen.

107. A collection of shells received from the Farallones Islands by Mr. R.
D. Darbishire, of Manchester, soon after the publication of the first Report,
contained several species at that time new to science, but in too imperfect a
condition for description. Among them were—

Martesia intercalata, Maz. Cat., no. 19. Burrowing in *Haliotis rufescens*.
Odostomia inflata, n. s. Young shells, abundant, in *Haliotis rufescens*.
Ocinebra lurida.
Ocinebra interfossa, n. s.

Collections from the same locality were afterwards sent by the Rev. J.
Rowell, and are tabulated with the rest of the Smithsonian series in the 4th
column of the general Table, par. 112.

108. In 1860, previously to the commencement of the Californian Geological Survey, Dr. J. G. Cooper joined a military expedition across the Rocky Mountains, under the command of Major Blake, U.S.A. Having forwarded his notes and specimens to Judge Cooper, they were placed in the hands of Mr. Thomas Bland, of New York. He prepared a "Notice of Land and Freshwater Shells, collected by Dr. J. G. Cooper in the Rocky Mountains, &c.," which appears in the 'Ann. Lyc. N. H. of N. York,' 1861, pp. 362 *et seq.* We have here the judgment of one of the most distinguished students of American land-shells, whose labours on the tropical forms have accumulated facts so important in their bearing on the Darwinian controversy [*]. The following is an outline of the Report, which is peculiarly valuable for the copious notes on the station and distribution of species :—

No.
1. *Helix Townsendiana*, Lea. "Both slopes of the Bitter Root Mountains, from 2200–5600 ft. high. Large var. at the base of the range to 4800 ft. Small var. in dry prairie at junction of Hell-Gate and Bitter Root Rivers ; also in Wash. Ter., west of the Coast Mountains. The most wide-spread of the species," *J. G. C.* ; Puget Sound, Cape Disappointment, teste *Bland.*

2. *Helix Mullani*, n.s., Bland. "Under logs and in dry pine-woods : dead, Cœur d'Alêne Mission : living, west side of Bitter Root Mountains," *J. G. C.* ; St. Joseph's River, 1st Camp, Oregon, teste *Binney.* Closely allied to *H. Columbiana*, Lea, = *labiosa*, Gld. A beautiful hyaline var. was found under a stone, by the Bitter Root River, 4000 ft. high.

3. *Helix polygyrella*, n.s., Bland. "Moss and dead wood in dampest parts of spruce-forests ; common on the Cœur d'Alêne Mountains, especially eastern slope," *J. G. C.* Entirely unlike any other N. A. species, and having affinity with *H. polygyrata* from Brazil.

4. *Helix Vancouverensis*, Lea, = *H. concava*, Bin. sen. olim, non postea, nec Say ; = *H. vellicata*, Fbs., certainly ; = *H. sportella*, Gld., probably. "West side of Cœur d'Alêne Mountains, W. T., in forests of Coniferæ, such as it inhabits west of the Cascade Range. Between these two ranges, for 200 miles, is a wide plain, quite uninhabitable for snails, on account of drought. This sp. and *H. Townsendiana* probably travel round it through the northern forests in lat. 49°," *J. G. C.* Also Crescent City, Cal., *Newcomb* ; Oregon City, Whidby's Is., W. T. ; Mus. Bland. Found on the Pacific slope, from Puget Sound to San Diego.

5. *Helix strigosa*, Gld. "Æstivating under pine-logs, on steep slope of shale, containing veins of lime, 4000 ft. high, near Bitter Root River, Rocky Mountains," *J. G. C.* ; Big Horn Mountains, Nebraska ; Rio Piedra, W. New Mexico ; teste *Bland.* One sp. reached N. York alive, and deposited six young shells. [?May not these have been abnormally hatched in the body of the parent, from the unnatural confinement.]

6. *Helix Cooperi*, Binn., jun. "East side of Mullan's Pass, Rocky Mountains, W. T., at an elevation of 5500 ft.," *J. G. C.* ; Black Hills of Nebraska, *Dr. V. Hayden* ; Big Horn Mountains, Nebraska ; west side of Wind River Mountains ; Rio Piedra, W. N. Mexico, teste *Bland.* Passes by varieties towards *H. strigosa*, Gld. Hayden's shell from Bridger's Pass, Nebr., referred to by Binn., jun., Journ. A. N. S. Phil. 1858, p. 115, as *H. solitaria*, var., is the young of this species.

7. *Helix solitaria*, Say. Both slopes of Cœur d'Alêne Mts., 2500 feet high, *J. G. C.* Also Prairie States, teste Bland.

8. *Helix arborea*, Say. "Damp bottom lands, along the lower valley of Hell-Gate River, 4500 ft. high," *J. G. C.* Found from Labrador to Texas, and from Florida to Nebraska ; also on the River Chama, N. Mex. ; also Guadaloupe, teste *Beau* and *Férussac*, letter to Say, 1820 ; teste *Bland.*

[*] *Vide* "Geographical Distribution of the Genera and Species of Land Shells of the West Indies, &c.," by Thomas Bland. Reprinted from Ann. Lyc. Nat. Hist., vol. vii. New York 1861.

No.
9. *Helix striatella*, Anth.   With *H. arborea, J. G. C.*   From Canada E. to Kansas, and from Pembina (Red River N.) to Virginia; teste *Bland.*
10. *Succinea rusticana*, Gld.   "Rocky Mountains of Bitter Root Valley, 2500–4500 ft.," *J. G. C.*

The freshwater shells collected on the Rocky Mountains by Dr. Cooper were determined, with the assistance of Dr. Lea and of Messrs. Binney and Prime, as follows :—

11. *Limnæa fragilis* [as of] Linn. [Binney].   Hell-Gate River; Missouri River, above the Falls.   [=*L. palustris*, auct.]
12. *Limnæa humilis*, Say.   Hell-Gate River.
13. *Limnæa bulimoides*, Linn. [Binney].   Missouri River, above the Falls.
14. *Limnæa desidiosa*, Say.   Missouri River, above the Falls.
15. *Physa hypnorum*, Linn.   Hell-Gate River.
16. *Physa heterostropha*, Say.   Hell-Gate River; Missouri River, above the Falls.
17. *Planorbis trivolvis*, Say.   Hell-Gate River.
18. *Planorbis ?parvus*, Say.   Hell-Gate River.
19. *Ancylus*, sp. ind.
20. *Melania plicifera*, Lea.   Hell-Gate River.
21. *Leptoxis*, sp. ind.
22. *Amnicola*, sp. ind.
23. *Sphærium* [*Cyclas*] *occidentale*, Prime.   Hell-Gate River.
24. *Sphærium* [*Cyclas*] *striatinum*, Lam.   Missouri River, above the Falls.
25. *Unio luteolus*, Lam.
26. *Margaritana margaritifera*, Linn.   Missouri River, above the Falls; also Spokan River, below Lake Cœur d'Alêne, = *A. falcatus*, Gld.; the purple var. hitherto only found on the Pacific slope.

109. The land-shells of the peninsula of California present points of great interest to the student of geographical distribution. While those of the eastern shore of the Gulf belong exclusively to the Mexican or Central American fauna, those of the western present in their general features that form of the South American type which belongs to the region of the Andes. The contrast between the Glandinæ and painted Bulimids of Mazatlan, and the small dull forms, or solid white shells of the peninsula, is evident even to the superficial observer. They are catalogued by Mr. Binney in the 'Proc. Ac. Nat. Sc. Philadelphia,' 1861, pp. 331–333, and are as follows, outline-figures being given of the new species :—

No.
1. *Helix areolata*, Sby.   Cerros Is., *Dr. Veatch.*
2. *Helix Pandoræ*, Fbs.   Margarita Is. (*Binney*).
3. *Bulimus excelsus*, Gld.   La Paz. (Mus. Cal. Acad. N. S.)
4. *Bulimus vesicalis*, Gld.   Lower California.   [Altered in 'Otia,' p. 184, to *B. sufflatus*; nom. preoc.]
5. *Bulimus pallidior*, Sby., = *vegetus*, Gld.   With *B. incendens*, v. infrà.   (S. America, *Cuming.*)   [Cape St. Lucas List, no. 166.]
6. *Bulimus proteus*, Brod.   One large and many young specimens; Cape St. Lucas, *Xantus.*   (Mountains of Peru, teste *Pfeiffer.*)   [C. S. L., no. 167.]
7. *Bulimus Xantusi*, n.s.   Promontory of St. Lucas.   4 sp.   *Xantus.*   [No. 168.]
8. *Bulimus artemisia*, n.s.   Promontory of St. Lucas.   1 sp., on small species of *Artemisia*; *Xantus.*   [C. S. L., no. 169.]
9. *Bulimus pilula*, n.s.   Todos Santos Mission and Margarita Is., in rocky spots under mosses, not uncommon, *Xantus.*   Resembles *B. sufflatus*, jun. [No. 170.]
10. *Bulimus incendens*, n.s.   In great numbers with *B. pallidior*, Sby., climbing high "copal" or copaiva trees, on dry hills 800–1000 ft. high; Cape St. Lucas, Margarita Bay, *Xantus.*   Resembles *B. excelsus*, Gld.   [No. 171.]
11. *Pedipes lirata*, Binn.   Cape St. Lucas, *Xantus.*   [C. S. L., no. 172.]

110. At the time of the preparation of the first Report, not a single naturalist was known in Europe to be resident on the western slope of North America, to whom communications could be addressed on the subject of it. There was, however, even at that time, a "Californian Academy of Natural Sciences," which met at S. Francisco, and published its 'Proceedings.' This Academy is now in a flourishing condition, under the presidency of Col. L. Ransom. The general zoological department is under the care of Dr. J. G. Cooper; the shells under that of Dr. J. B. Trask, Vice-President of the Academy, whose name has already appeared in Judge Cooper's Report, *antea*, p. 597; and the fossils under that of Mr. W. M. Gabb. The corresponding secretary is Dr. W. O. Ayres; and the librarian Prof. J. D. Whitney, the director of the State Geological Survey. Already the nucleus has been formed of a very valuable collection, many of the critical species in which have been sent to England for identification. The coasting-trade between S. Francisco and many stations in L. California, the Gulf, and the Mexican coast, offers peculiar facilities for obtaining valuable information. Two of the contributors to the Californian Academy require special and grateful mention. Dr. Wesley Newcomb (whose labours had greatly enriched the State Collection at his native city, Albany, New York, and whose researches among the *Achatinellæ* in the Sandwich Islands are well known) is stationed at Oakland, near Francisco, and has already furnished valuable papers, an abstract of which is here given, as well as emendations and additions to the British Association Report, which are included in their appropriate places*. The Rev. J. Rowell has long been a regular correspondent of the Smithsonian Institution, and has submitted the whole of his West-coast collections for analysis. He has displayed peculiar industry in searching for small species on the backs of the larger shells, especially the Haliotids of the Californian coast, and the *Ostrea iridescens*, which is imported in large quantities from Acapulco for the San Francisco market †.

In the 'Proc. California Ac. Nat. Sc.,' vol. i. pp. 28–30, Feb. 1855, Dr. J. B. Trask published descriptions of *Anodonta Randalli*, Trask, Upper San Joaquin; *Anodonta triangularis*, Trask, Sacramento River; *Anodonta rotundovata*, Trask, Sacramento Valley; *Alasmodonta Yubaënsis*, Trask, Yuba River.

In the 'Ann. Lyc. N. H. New York,' vol. vii. 1860, p. 146, Dr. Newcomb describes the first *Pupa* found on the Pacific slope, viz. *Pupa Rowellii*, Newc. Near Oakland, Cal. "Approaches nearest to *P. ovata*, Say."

* The "*Chiton amiculatus*," Newc., MS., = *Cryptochiton Stelleri*. "Rare near S. Francisco; somewhat more abundant in the Bay of Monterey." His "*Panopæa generosa*," in the Albany Museum, was found to be *Schizothærus Nuttallii*.

† As an instance of the way in which mistakes arise, may be placed on record a series of shells sent to Mr. Rousseau, of Troy, New York, by Mr. Hilman, formerly of that city, now a resident at San Francisco. They were sent as Californian; yet, of the thirty-four species which it contained, only one could be called a native of that province. All the rest were tropical, and of that peculiar character which belongs to Acapulco. No doubt, the gentleman had obtained them from a trader to that city. If only a few species had been sent, mixed with Californian shells, they might have puzzled the learned; for they were obtained, on the spot, by a gentleman of known integrity. As it was, the magnitude of the error led to its discovery: but in how many similar cases such error is thought impossible!—*Strigilla carnaria*; *Donax carinatus, puncto-striatus*; *Heterod. bimaculatus*; *Callista aurantia, chionæa*; *Petr. robusta*; *Card. consors, biangulatum*; *Liocard. apicinum*; *Trigona radiata, Hindsii*; *Anom. subimbricata*; *Lima tetrica*; *Siphonaria gigas, lecanium*; *Patella discors, pediculus*; *Fiss. rugosa*; *Cruc. imbricatum, spinosum, umbrella*; *Crep. aculeata*; *Hipp. antiquatus, barbatus*; *Cerith. uncinatum*; *Modulus disculus*; *Nat. ca maroccana, catenata*; *Polinices uber*; *Leuc. cingulata*; *Æneta harpa*; *Purp. triangularis*. The single shell from the temperate fauna is *Glyphis aspera*.

In the 'Ann. Lyc. N. H. New York,' 1861, p. 287, the Rev. J. Rowell, of San Francisco, describes the second species of *Pupa* * discovered on the western slope, viz. " *P. Californica*, Row., San Francisco : plentiful."

On February 4th, 1861, Dr. Wesley Newcomb published (Latin) diagnoses of the following Californian Pulmonates in the ' Proceedings of the Cal. Ac. Nat. Sc.,' vol. ii. pp. 91-94. A second Part bears date March 18th, pp. 103, 104.

Page.
91. *Helix Bridgesii*, Newc. San Pablo, Cal. 1 sp. Distinct from all described forms.
  " *Helix Traskii*, Newc. Los Angelos, Cal. " Distinguished from *H. Thouarsii* at a glance."
92. *Vitrina Pfeifferi*, Newc. Carson Valley. More rounded than *diaphana*, Drap.
94. *Pisidium occidentale*, Newc. Ocean House, S. Francisco, *Rowell*.
103. *Helix Carpenteri*, Newc. Tulare Valley, Mus. Cal. Ac. Belongs to the Cyclostomoid group, and has the aspect of a desert species. [Quite distinct from *H. Carpenteriana*, Bland, Florida.]
  " *Helix Ayresiana*, Newc. Northern Oregon ; Mus. Cal. Ac. Resembles *H. reticulata*, Pfr., a Californian species not identified by the author.
104. *Physa costata*, Newcomb. Clear Lake, Cal., *Veatch*, Mus. Cal. Ac.

In the ' Proc. Ac. Nat. Sc. Philadelphia, 1861,' pp. 367-372, Mr. W. M. Gabb published " Descriptions of New Species of American Tertiary Fossils," in which occur several Californian shells. The authorities for the localities are not given, and the diagnoses are in English only. Considerable confusion often arises from the study of tertiary fossils without knowledge of recent shells, and *vice versâ*. Mr. Gabb's writings on the Cretaceous fossils of America display an ability with which this paper is perhaps not commensurate. Some errors which had been found very difficult to understand are here corrected by the author himself, who regrets the incompleteness of his earlier work.

368. *Turbonilla aspera*, Gabb. Sta. Barbara, Miocene. [=*Bittium*, sp., teste *Gabb*, MS.]
  " *Modelia striata*, Gabb. Sta. Barbara, ?Miocene. [=*Lacuna carinata*, Gld. teste *Gabb* MS. and specimens. Mr. Gabb considers that *Litorina Pedroana* Conr., is the same species, which is probably not correct.]
369. *Sphenia lilirata*, Gabb. Sta. Barbara. [Description accords with *Saxicava arctica*, jun., var. ; but Mr. Gabb considers it a good species.]
  " *Venus rhysomia*, Gabb. ? Miocene, Sta. Barbara. [= *Psephis tantilla*, Gld., teste *Gabb* MS. and specimens.]
371. *Cardita monilicosta*. ?Miocene, Sta. Barbara. [Description accords with *Venericardia ventricosa*, Gld. jun.; but Mr. Gabb considers it a good species.]
  " *Morrisia Hornii*. ?Miocene. Sta. Barbara. " First pointed out by Dr. Horn in a rich fossiliferous marl, and not uncommon."

In the ' Proceedings of the Calif. Ac. Nat. Sc.' for April 7th, 1862, pp. 170-172, Mr. W. M. Gabb published detailed English " Descriptions of two Species of Cephalopoda in the Museum of the Academy," of which one, *Onychoteuthis fusiformis*, is said to be from Cape Horn, the other from California.

170. *Octopus punctatus*, Gabb. Common near San Francisco. Also abundant in Scammon's Lagoon, Lower California, *Capt. C. M. Scammon*. Arms more than seven feet long, *Dr. W. O. Ayres*. " Differs from *O. megalocyathus*,

---

* That the race of small *Pupæ* is very ancient on the North American continent, as in Europe, is evident from the very interesting discovery, by Prof. Dawson, of a fossil *Pupa*, *in situ*, nestling in an upright tree, fossilized in the Nova Scotian coal-beds ; which can scarcely be distinguished, even specifically, from some living forms.

Page.
Couth., E. E. Moll. p. 471, in absence of lateral membrane, size of mouth and cupules, and general coloration."

171. *Onychoteuthis fusiformis*, Gabb. "Cape Horn," Mus. Ac. [San Clemente Is., Cal., *Cooper*, MS.]

From the ' Proc. Cal. Ac. N. S.,' 1863, p. 11, it appears that at least one mollusc, a *Teredo* or *Xylotrya*, has already established for itself an economic celebrity. Piles have been entirely destroyed in six months from the time they were placed in the water.

On March 2, 1863, Mr. Auguste Remond published, in the same Journal, English " Descriptions of two new Species of Bivalves from the Tertiaries of · Contra Costa County:"—

13. *Cardium Gabbii*, Rem. Late tert. deposit near Kirker's Pass, in shelly sand, with *Tapes regularis*, Gabb, and *Murex ponderosus*, Gabb, both extinct. " Easily recognized by heavy hinge and enormous laterals ; lunule carinated." [? *Liocardium*.]

„ *Ostrea Bourgeoisii*, Rem. Same locality.

On April 20, 1863, Dr. Cooper described (in English) the following mollusc, of which the only species previously known is from Cuba :—

21. *Gundlachia Californica*, Rowell. Fig. 5 (three views). Fifty specimens on water-plants in clear, stagnant ponds, at Marysville, Feather River, *Rowell*.

On January 8, 1864, Dr. Newcomb described (in Latin) the following, with other Pulmonates from the State Survey, already tabulated in p. 609 :—

115. *Helix Hillebrandi*, Newc. Tuolumne Co., Cal. One recent and several fossi shells, *M. Voy*. Like *H. Thouarsii*, but depressed and hirsute.

The latest contribution to the malacology of California is one of the most interesting. It is described (in Latin) by Dr. Newcomb, Feb. 1, 1864 :—

121. *Pedicularia Californica*, Newc. One specimen from coral growing on a monster *Echidnocerus*, very deep water, Farallones Is., *D. N. Robinson*. " As beautiful as *P. elegantissima*, Desh., from Is. Bourbon." [Mr. Pease also obtained a deep-water *Pedicularia* from coral in the Pacific Is., which Mr. Cuming affiliated to the Mediterranean *P. Sicula*. Dr. Gould (Otia, p. 215) also describes *P. decussata*, coast of Georgia, 400 fm., U. S. Coast Survey.]

111. The following descriptions of species, and notes on habitats and synonymy, have been collated from various American scientific periodicals, chiefly by the assistance of Mr. Binney's ' Bibliography.'

In the 'American Journal of Science and Art,' O. S., vol. xxxviii. p. 396, April 1840, Dr. A. A. Gould records the following species, said to be from " California." His *Trochus vittatus* is not known :—

Murex tricolor et bicolor.	Trochus vittatus.
Cardium Californianum.	Bulimus undatus.

In the 'Annals of the New York Lyceum of Natural History,' vol. iv 1846, No. 5, p. 165, Mr. John H. Redfield first described *Triton Oregonense*, Straits of San Juan de Fuca : plate 11. fig. 2.

In the 'Proceedings of the Academy of Natural Sciences of Philadelphia,' 1848, vol. iv. p. 121, Mr. T. A. Conrad described new genera, and gave notes on *Parapholas Californica*, *Cryptomya Californica*, and *Psammobia Californica*, altering *Osteodesma hyalina* (nom. preoc.) into *Lyonsia Floridana*. In the same work, March 1854, vol. vii., Mr. Conrad described *Cyathodonta undulata*. He also states that *Gnathodon trigonum*, Petit, is probably identical with *G Lecontei*, Conr. [?] (nom. prior), and alters genus *Trigonella* to *Pachydesma*.

In the 'Proc. Boston Ac. Nat. Hist.,' July 1851, vol. iv. p. 27, Dr. A. A. Gould published "Notes on Californian Shells," and, in vol. vi. p. 11, described *Helix ramentosa*, California, and *Helix damascenus*, from the desert east of California.

In the 'Proceedings Ac. Nat. Sc. Phil.,' April 1856, vol. viii. pp. 80, 81, Dr. Isaac Lea described the following species of new freshwater shells from California:—

> *Pompholyx effusa.*   Sacramento River.
> *Melania Shastaënsis.*   Shasta and Scott Rivers.
> *Melania nigrina.*   Clear Creek, Shasta Co.
> *Physa triticea.*   Shasta Co.
> *Planorbis Traskii.*   Kern Lake, Tulan Co.
> *Lymnæa proxima.*   Arroya, St. Antonio.
> *Ancylus patelloides.*   Sacramento River.

and offered notes on

> *Margaritana margaritifera*, Lea,=*Alasmodonta falcata*, Gld.,=*Alasmodonta Yubaënsis*, Trask. Klamath and Yuba.
> *Anodonta Wahlamatensis*, Lea,=*A. triangulata*, Trask,+*A. rotundovata*, Trask. Sacramento River.
> *Anodonta angulata*, Lea,+*A. feminalis*, Gld.,+*A. Randalli*, Trask. Upper San Joaquin.
> *Helix Oregonensis*, Lea.   Point Cypress, Monterey Co.
> *Helix Nickliniana*, Lea.   Tomales Bay and Dead Man's Island.
> *Helix Californiensis*, Lea.   Point Cypress.
> *Lymnæa exigua*, Lea.   San Antonio Arroya.
> *Lymnæa pallida*, Ad.   San Antonio Arroya.
> *Physa heterostropha*, Say.   Los Angeles.
> *Melania occata*, Hds.   Sacramento River.
> *Melania (Paludina) seminalis*, Hds.   Sacramento River.
> *Planorbis trivolvis*, Say.   Horn Lake.
> *Planorbis ammon*, Gld.   Lagoons, Sacramento Valley.

In the New Series of the 'Proc. Ac. Nat. Sc. Philadelphia' occur descriptions and notes on species, as under :—

		Page.	
1857.	Feb.	18.	*Helix intercisa*, W. G. Bin.,=*H. Nickliniana*, Bin. sen., var. Oregon.
1857.	„	19.	*Succinea lineata*, W. G. Bin. Nebraska.
1857.	June.	165.	Mr. T. A. Conrad described the genus *Gonidea* for *A. angulata*, Lea; and for *Gonidea Randalii*, Trask, and *Gonidea feminalis*, Gld.; regarding the three species as probably distinct. [Dr. Lea, however, considers them varietal.]
1858.	March.	41.	Dr. I. Lea described *Planorbis Newberryi*. Klamath Lake and Canoe Creek, California.
1860.	March.	23.	*Melania Newberryi*, Lea. Upper Des Chutes River, Oregon, Newberry.

In the "Notes on Shells, with Descriptions of New Genera and Species," by T. A. Conrad, reprinted from the 'Journ. Ac. Nat. Sc. Phil.,' Aug. 1849, are given the following synonyms, pp. 213, 214:—

> *Petricola Californica*, Conr.,=*Saxicava C.*, Conr.,=*P. arcuata*, Desh.
> *Petricola carditoides*, Conr.,=*Saxicava c.*, Conr.,=*P. cylindracea*, Desh.
> *Siliqua Nuttallii*, Conr.,=*Solecurtus N.*, Conr.,=*Solecurtus maximus*, Gld., non Wood, =*Solen splendens*, Chenu.
> *Siliqua lucida*, Conr.,=*Solecurtus l.* Conr.,=*Solecurtus radiatus*, Gld., non Linn.

In his "Synopsis of the Genera *Parapholas* and *Penitella*," from the same source, p. 335, are given as synonyms—

Parapholas Californica, Conr., =*Pholas C.*, Conr., =*Pholas Janelli*, Desh.
Penitella Conradi, Val., = *Pholas penita*, Conr., =*Pholas concamerata*, Desh.
Penitella melanura, Sby., =*Penitella Wilsoni*, Conr. (not *Parapholas bisulcata*).

In the elaborate but somewhat intricate "Monograph of the Order *Pholadacea*," &c., by G. W. Tryon, jun., Philadelphia, 1862, the following species are quoted from the West Coast, and form the conclusion of the marine shells hitherto described, so far as known to the writer:—

Page.
49. *Rocellaria [Gastrochæna] ovata*, Sby.   Panama, W. I., and Charleston, *Stimpson.*   "Not the slightest difference between the Pacific and Atlantic specimens."
74. *Pholas (Cyrtopleura) truncata,* Say.   Massachusetts ; S. Carolina ; Payta, Peru, *Ruschenberger* ; Chili.
77. *Dactylina (Gitocentrum) Chiloënsis*, King, 1832, = *Ph. laqueata*, Sby., 1849. Peru, Chili [Panama, *Jewett*].   Scarcely differs from *D. Campechensis,* = *Ph. oblongata*, Say, = *Ph. Candeana*, D'Orb. ; Southern U. S., W. I.
82. *Navea subglobosa*, Gray, Ann. N. H. 1851, vol. viii. p. 385.   California.   ["In a hole in a shell.   Cabinet Gray."   Neither shell nor authority stated.]
85. *Pholadidea (Hatasia) melanura*, Sby.   Lower California,= *Penitella Wilsoni*, Conr., J. A. N. Sc. Ph., fig. 4 (non 5).   "This error in figuring led Dr. Gray to misunderstand both the species and Conrad's idea of the genus *Penitella.*"   [*Vide* Brit. Assoc. Rep. 1856, p. 265.]
87. *Penitella penita.*   [Mr. Tryon erroneously quotes (*Netastoma*) *Darwinii*, as well as *Ph. cornea*, as synonyms.]
88. *Jouannetia (Pholadopsis) pectinata*, Conr.,= *Triomphalia pulcherrima*, Sby. "California" [no authority], W. Columbia.
127. "*Pholas retifer*, Mörch, Mal. Blätt. vii. 177, Dec. 1860.   One broken right valve.   *Hab.* Real Llejos."   = *Dactylina (Gitocentrum) Chiloënsis*, King [teste Tryon].

112. The following Table contains a complete list of all the Molluscs which have been identified, from Vancouver Island to S. Diego, arranged so as to show at the same time their habitat, and the principal collectors who have obtained them.   The species in the first column were obtained by Prof. Nuttall; in the second, by Col. Jewett.   The third column (marked B.A.) contains the species tabulated from other sources in the First Report.   Those to the right of the double column are the fresh explorations recorded in this Supplementary Report.   The fourth column contains the shells brought by the Pacific Railroad Expeditions, as well as the species sent to the officers of the Smithsonian Institution by the Rev. J. Rowell and their various correspondents.   The fifth column ('Ken.') contains the species of the American, and the sixth ('Lord') of the British North Pacific Boundary Survey.   The seventh records the collections of Mr. Swan and his Indian children ; the last, those of Dr. Cooper in the Californian Geological Survey.   As a large proportion of the species are as yet unknown, and the diagnoses will be found scattered in various periodicals, some of which are rarely accessible in this country, it has been judged needful to add a few words of description, with references to well-known books.   By this means the student will have before him a compact handbook of the fauna, and will distinguish at a glance the range of localities, and the amount of authority for each.   For the full synonymy, the previous pages of the two Reports must be consulted.

Results of the Explorations in the Vancouver and Californian Province. 1864.
(Omitting the doubtfully located and undetermined species.)

The letters stand for the localities in which the shells were collected, as follows:—

V. Vancouver Island, Straits of S. Juan de Fuca, and adjoining shores of Washington Territory, formerly known as 'Oregon.'
P. Puget's Sound and the neighbourhood.
O. Oregon; and the region on each side of the Columbia River.
C. California; or the district north of the peninsula, generally.
L. Peninsula of Lower California.
F. Neighbourhood of S. Francisco.

M. Neighbourhood of Monterey.
B.   „   Sta. Barbara.
D. The region between S. Diego and S. Pedro.
I. The islands: in the 4th column, generally the Farallones; in the last, the Sta. Barbara group.
H. Species obtained from the backs of Haliotids: locality unknown; probably Lower California.
fr. Fragments only.
fos. Only found fossil.

	Nutt.	Jew.	B. A.	Smiths. Ins.	Ken.	Lord.	Swan.	Cooper.
Defrancia intricata	—	—	—	—	—	—	—	D
1. Lingula albida	—	—	D	—	—	—	—	BD
2. Rhynconella psittacea	—	—	—	—	—	V	—	—
3. Terebratula unguiculus	—	—	—	—	—	V	V	MD
4. Waldheimia pulvinata	—	—	P	—	P	—	—	—
5. —— Californica	—	—	C	—	—	—	—	I
6. —— Grayi	—	—	—	—	—	—	—	I
7. Terebratella Coreanica	—	—	—	—	—	—	V	—
8. —— caurina	—	—	P	—	P	V	V	? I
9. Xylotrya pennatifera	—	—	—	F	—	—	V	—
10. —— fimbriata	—	—	—	—	—	V	—	—

Guide to the Diagnosis of the Vancouver and Californian Shells.

Class POLYZOA. Family *Discoporidæ.*

Defrancia intricata, Busk. Maz. Cat. no. 13. From Southern fauna. The remaining species in this class have not yet been determined.

Class PALLIOBRANCHIATA. Family *Lingulidæ.*

1. *Lingula albida,* Hds. Voy. Sulph.; Rve., Hanl., Davidson et auct. 20 fm. c. *Cp.*

Family *Rhynconellidæ.*

2. *Rhynconella psittacea,* Linn. auct. E. & W. Atlantic: circumpolar.

Family *Terebratulidæ.*

3. *Terebratula unguiculus,* n. s. Like *Terebratella caput serpentis* in size, shape, and sculpture; but loop incomplete in adult, as in *T. vitrea.* 6–20 fm. not r. *Cp.*
4. *Waldheimia pulvinata,* Gld. E.E. Smooth, subglobular, ashy. 80 fm., living, *Cp.,* CI.
5. ? *Waldheimia Californica,* Koch, non auct. Colour ashy. Intermediate between *Coreanica* and *globosa,* Lam., Rve. (which is *Californica,* auct. non Koch).
6. *Waldheimia Grayi,* Davidson. Very transverse, reddish, deeply ribbed.
7. *Terebratella Coreanica,* Ad. & Rve. Voy. Samarang. Size of *globosa;* reddish. *= miniata,* Gld. Jun. ?=*frontalis,* Midd., Asia.
8. *Terebratella caurina,* Gld. E.E. Like *dorsata;* subtriangular, ashy, with strong or faint ribs.

Class LAMELLIBRANCHIATA. Family *Teredidæ.*

9. *Xylotrya pennatifera,* Blainv. Ann. Nat. Hist. 1860, p. 126.
10. *Xylotrya fimbriata,* Jeffr. in Ann. Nat. Hist. 1860, p. 126; =*palmulata,* Fbs. & Hanl., non Lam. Phil.

	Nutt.	Jew.	B. A.	Smiths. Ins.	Ken.	Lord.	Swan.	Cooper.
11. Zirphæa crispata	—	—	—		P	—	?V	D fr.
12. Pholadidea penita	B	B	C	VOFMB	P	—	V	MD
13. —— ovoidea	—	D	D	H	—	—	—	M
14. Netastoma Darwinii	—	—	M	—	—	V	—	C
15. Martesia intercalata	—	—	—	I	—	—	—	—
16. Parapholas Californica....	B	—	C	—	—	—	—	D
17. Saxicava pholadis	—	M	CL	MCH	P	V	V	D
18. Glycimeris generosa	—	—	P	PF	—	—	—	D
19. Mya truncata..........	—	—	P	—	P	—	—	—
20. Platyodon cancellatus	B	—	C	FD	—	—	—	FDI
21. Cryptomya Californica ..	B	B	C	F	P	—	V	D
22. Schizothærus Nuttalli	—	B	C	OFM	P	—	V	D
23. Darina declivis	—	—	—	—	—	V	—	D
24. Corbula luteola	—	—	—	—	—	—	—	D
25. Sphænia ovoidea	—	—	—	—	P	—	—	—
26. Neæra pectinata	—	—	—	—	P	—	—	BI

Family *Pholadidæ*.

11. *Zirphæa crispata*, Linn. auct.   E. & W. Atlantic and circumpolar.
12. *Pholadidea penita*, Conr. Hanl. auct. = *concamerata*, Desh.   Shape from elongate to ovoid ; umbonal reflexion closely adherent.
13. *Pholadidea ovoidea*, Gld. Otia.   Umbonal reflexion with anterior opening.
14. *Netastoma Darwinii*, Sby.   New subgenus · valves prolonged, like duck's bill instead of cups.   Surface with concentric frills.   Quoted from " S. A."
15. *Martesia intercalata*, Cpr. Maz. Cat. no. 19.   From Southern fauna.
16. *Parapholas Californica*, Conr. Hanl. auct. = *P. Janellii*, Desh.   Very large ; with layers of thin, short cups.

Family *Saxicavidæ*.

17. *Saxicava pholadis*, Linn. auct.+var. *arctica*, Linn. auct. Maz. Cat. no. 23+var. *gastrochænoidea*, ovoid and gaping like Maz. Cat. no. 21+var. *legumen*, Desh., elongate, cylindrical, scarcely gaping.
18. *Glycimeris generosa*, Gld. E.E.   Perhaps = *Panopæa Faujasii*, S. Wood, Crag Moll. : pipes like *Saxicava*.

Family *Myadæ*.

19. *Mya truncata*, Linn. auct. = *M. præcisa*, Gld.   Atlantic : circumpolar.
20. *Platyodon cancellatus*, Conr. Hanl.   Pipe-ends 4-valved.   Low water : common. Sold in S. Francisco market, *Cp.*
21. *Cryptomya Californica*, Conr.   Outside like young *Mya*; mantle-bend nearly obsolete.

Subfamily *Lutrarinæ*.

22. *Schizothærus Nuttalli*, Conr.+*Tresus maximus*, Midd. Gray = *L. capax*, Gld. Shape from ovoid to elongate ; very large and tumid ; beaks swollen ; hinge-sides channeled ; mantle-bend joined to ventral line.
23. *Darina declivis*, n. s.   Outside like *Machæra*.   Cartilage-pits produced, gaping.

Family *Corbulidæ*.

24. *Corbula luteola*, n. s.   Shape of young *biradiata*; small, ashy yellow   Com. *Cp.*
25. *Sphænia ovoidea*, n. s.   Siphonal area small ; front excurved ; mantle-bend large.
26. *Neæra pectinata*, n. s.   Principal ribs about 12 ; beak smooth.   Like *sulcata*. 40–60 fm. *Cp.*

123

	Nutt.	Jew.	B. A.	Smiths. Ins.	Ken.	Lord.	Swan.	Cooper.
27. Clidiophora punctata	B	—	—	—	—	—	V	D
28. Kennerlia filosa	—	—	—	—	P	—	—	—
29. —— bicarinata	—	—	—	—	—	—	—	I
30. Periploma argentaria	D	—	—	—	—	—	—	D
31. Thracia curta	B	—	—	—	P	—	V	—
32. Lyonsia Californica	B	B	PC	—	P	—	V	MD
33. —— Entodesma saxicola..	—	—	—	I	—	V	V	—
34. —— inflata	—	—	L	—	—	—	—	D
35. Mytilimeria Nuttalli	C	—	—	D	P	—	V	—
36. Plectodon scaber	—	—	—	—	—	—	—	I
37. Solen sicarius	—	—	P	P	P	—	V	—
37 b.—— v. rosaceus	—	B	—	—	—	—	—	D
38. Solecurtus Californianus ..	B	B	C	—	—	—	—	D
39. —— subteres	B	B	C	—	—	—	—	D
40. Machæra patula	OB	F	OC	VOF	—	—	V	D
41. Sanguinolaria Nuttalli	D	—	C	L	—	—	—	DI
42. Psammobia rubroradiata ..	C	—	—	—	P	—	V	D

Family *Pandoridæ*.

27. *Clidiophora punctata*, n. g.   (Type of genus = *Pandora claviculata*, P. Z. S. 1855, p. 228.)   Teeth ½, posterior long, with ossicle.   Conr. sp.; like *Cl. trilineata*, but teeth more divergent; inside strongly punctate.

28. *Kennerlia filosa*, n. s.   New subgenus of *Pandora* with ossicle: outer layer radiately grooved.   Shell beaked.

29. *Kennerlia bicarinata*, n. s.   Not beaked; 2 post. keels in convex valve. 40–60 fm. r. *Cp.*   May prove = *P. bilirata*, Conr.

Family *Anatinidæ*.

30. *Periploma argentaria*, Conr. Hanl.   Large, subquadrate.

31. *Thracia curta*, Conr. Hanl.   Strong, subovate.

32. *Lyonsia Californica*, Conr. Hanl. + *bracteata* + *nitida*, Gld.   Outline variable : often close to Atlantic *L. Floridana* : striated external layer fugacious.

33. *Entodesma saxicola*, Baird.   Subgenus of *Lyonsia*: animal nestling, irregular. Close to *E. cuneata*, Ad. & Rve.   Form protean : brittle, thick, lurid, with enormous ossicle.   Var. *cylindracea* has the form of *Saxicava pholadis*.

34. *Entodesma inflata*, Conr. = *diaphana*, Cpr. P. Z. S. 1855, p. 228.   From Southern fauna.   Like *picta*, but pale, without pinch.

35. *Mytilimeria Nuttalli*, Conr. Hanl.   ? Subgenus of *Lyonsia* : rounded, with spiral umbos.

36. *Plectodon scaber*, n. g., n. s.   Shape of *Theora* : dorsal margins twisted-in spirally inside umbos.   Lateral teeth laminated, with internal cartilage hidden, appressed.   2 r. valves, 40–60 fm. *Cp.*

Family *Solenidæ*.

37. *Solen sicarius*, Gld. Otia.   Nearly straight, rather short, truncated.

37 b. *Solen* ? var. *rosaceus*.   Straight, narrower, longer, smaller ; glossy, rosy.

Family *Solecurtidæ*.

38. *Solecurtus Californianus*, Conr. Hanl.   May be a var. of the Peruvian ? *Dombeyi*. Yellowish ash, with ventral parallel grooves.   A ? var. without grooves closely resembles *gibbus*.

39. *Solecurtus subteres*, Conr. Hanl.   Small, compact, with violet rays.

40. *Machæra patula*, Dixon = *S. maximus*, Wood = *grandis*, Gmel. = *Siliqua Nuttalli* ? + *lucida*, Conr. (var. jun.) Asia.

Family *Tellinidæ*.

41. *Sanguinolaria Nuttalli*, Conr. Hanl. = *Psammobia decora*, Hds.   Flat, rounded.

42. *Psammobia rubro-radiata*, Nutt.   Large : shape of *vespertina* : rayed with lilac.

	Nutt.	Jew.	B. A.	Smiths. Ins.	Ken.	Lord.	Swan.	Cooper.
43. Macoma secta	D	D	C	MIL	—	—	—	D
43 b.—— v. edulis	O	—	—	PO	P	—	—	—
44. —— indentata	—	—	—	—	—	—	—	D
45. —— yoldiformis	—	—	—	—	P	—	V	D
46. —— nasuta	OD	D	OC	VPOF	P	V	V	MD
47. —— inquinata	—	—	O	O	P	—	V	F
47 b.—— ? edentula..........	—	—	—	—	—	—	V	—
48. —— v. expansa..........	—	—	—	—	P	—	—	—
49. —— inconspicua	O	—	—	OF	P	V	V	FM
50. Angulus modestus	—	—	—	—	P	—	—	—
50 b.—— —— obtusus	—	—	—	D	P	—	V	D
51. —— variegatus..........	—	—	—	—	—	—	V	MI
52. —— Gouldii	—	—	—	DL	—	—	—	D
53. —— Mæra salmonea	—	—	—	F	—	—	V	M
54. Tellina Bodegensis	—	—	OF	O	—	—	V	D
55. —— Arcopagia lamellata..	—	—	—	—	—	—	—	D
56. Œdalia subdiaphana......	—	—	—	D	—	—	—	—
57. Cooperella scintillæformis .	—	—	—	—	—	—	—	DI
58. Lutricola alba	B	B	C	—	—	—	—	DI

43. *Macoma secta*, Conr. Hanl. Large, flat, rounded, glossy; winged behind ligament.

43 b. *Macoma* var. *edulis*, Nutt. Northern form, less transverse; texture dull.

44. *Macoma indentata*, n. s. Like *secta*, jun., but beaked, indented, and ventrally produced.

45. *Macoma yoldiformis*, n. s. Small, white, glossy, very transverse; ligament-area scooped-out.

46. *Macoma nasuta*, Conr. auct.+*tersa*, Gld. Large, beaked, twisted; mantle-bend touching opposite scar in one valve. From Kamtschatka to S. Diego. Cape Lady Franklin, 76°, *Belcher*, 1826. 3 ft., mud, between tide-marks, *Lord.*

47. *Macoma inquinata*, Desh. P. Z. S. 1854, p. 357. Like degraded *nasuta*; mantle-bend a little separated from scar in both valves.

47 b. *Macoma ?edentula*, Brod. & Sby. jun.; or an abnormal var. of *inquinata*.

48. *Macoma ?*var. *expansa*. Scars like *lata* and *calcarea* in Mus. Cum., but teeth not bifid, very thin, glossy. Scarcely differs from *lata*, Desh. in B. M. Greenland.

49. *Macoma inconspicua*, Br. & Sby.= *Sang. Californiana*, Conr. Probably = "*Fabricii*=*fragilis*, Fabr." in Mus. Cum. Like thin, flat *solidula*: pink; var. large, white. 8–15 fm. *Lyall.*

50. *Angulus modestus*, n. s. (Subg. of *Tellina*.) Like *tener*, Say; but with callus between mantle-bend and scar. White.

50 b. *Angulus ?*var. *obtusus*. Inside like *modestus*; but beaks obtuse.

51. *Angulus variegatus*, n. s. Shape of *obtusus*: no callus; rayed with pink and yellow. 20–60 fm. r. *Cp.*

52. *Angulus Gouldii*, Hanl. MS. in Mus. Cum. Small, white; ant. ventr. side swollen.

53. *Mæra salmonea*, n. s. (Scarcely differs from *Angulus*.) Small, subquadrate, glossy, salmon-tinted. Beach–20 fm. *Cp.*

54. *Tellina Bodegensis*, Hinds, Voy. Sulph. Large, strong, transverse, with concentric grooves.

55. *Arcopagia lamellata*, Maz. Cat. no. 58. One fine pair in shell washings.

56. *Œdalia subdiaphana*, n. g., n. s. Thin, swollen, shape of *Kellia*, ligament surrounding beaks: hinge with 5 bifid teeth (3-2); no laterals; large mantle-bend.

57. *Cooperella scintillæformis*, n. s. New subgenus of *Œdalia*. Cartilage semi-internal: only 1 tooth bifid.

58. *Lutricola alta*, Conr. (*Tellina*). For this group (= *Capsa*, "Bosc," Add. non Lam.), scarcely agreeing with either *Macoma* or *Scrobicularia*, Blainville's

	Nutt.	Jew.	B. A.	Smith's Ins.	Ken.	Lord.	Swan.	Cooper.
59. Semele decisa	D	D	C	—	—	—	—	D
60. —— rupium	—	—	—	—	—	—	—	I
61. —— rubrolineata	D	D	—	—	—	—	V	—
62. —— pulchra	—	—	—	D	—	—	—	D
63. —— incongrua	—	—	—	—	—	—	—	I
64. Cumingia Californica	B	—	—	—	—	—	—	DI
65. Donax Californicus	B	D	C	DL	—	—	—	D
66. —— flexuosus	—	B	—	—	—	—	—	—
67. —— navicula	—	—	—	D	—	—	—	D
68. Heterodonax bimaculatus	D	—	—	L	—	—	—	D
69. Standella Californica	B	B	—	F	—	—	V fr.	D
69b.—— nasuta	—	—	C	—	—	—	—	? D
70. —— planulata	B	—	—	—	—	—	—	D
71. —— falcata	—	—	P	—	P	—	V	—
72. Raëta undulata.........	—	—	L	—	—	—	—	D
73. Clementia subdiaphana ..	—	—	—	—	P	V	—	—
74. Amiantis callosa	B	B	C	L	—	—	—	D
75. Pachydesma crassatelloides	BD	B	C	FM	—	—	V fr.	D
76. Psephis tantilla..........	—	B	—	O	P	V	V	I

synonymic name may be revived in restricted sense. Species = *biangulata*, P. Z. S. 1855, p. 230.

59. *Semele decisa*, Conr. auct. Large, rough, like Peruvian *corrugata*, but truncated.
60. *Semele rupium*, Sby. Smaller, rough, swollen; with smaller mantle-bend. Galapagos. Not r. *Cp.*
61. *Semele rubrolineata*, (? Conr.). Flattened, same shape, with faint sculpture each way, and pink rays. [Conrad's lost shell may be young *decisa.*]
62. *Semele pulchra*, Sby. Transverse, crowded concentric sculpture, with radiating lines at sides. Southern fauna.
63. *Semele incongrua*, n. s. Like *pulchra*, with concentric sculpture differing in r. and l. valves: fine radiating striæ all over. 40–60 fm. c. *Cp.*
64. *Cumingia Californica*, Conr. auct. Maz. Cat. no. 44.
65. *Donax Californicus*, Conr. (non Desh.) = *obesus*, Gld. (non Desh.). Smooth, stumpy: outline and colour variable.
66. *Donax flexuosus*, Gld. Like *punctostriata* jun. with stronger keel, and no punctures.
67. *Donax navicula*, Sby. Maz. Cat. no. 77. From Southern fauna.
68. *Heterodonax bimaculatus*. Broad var., generally violet, = *Psammobia Pacifica*, Conr. = *Tellina vicina*, C. B. Ad. Cape St. Lucas, Acapulco, W. Indies.

Family Mactridæ.

69. *Standella Californica*, Conr. (non Desh.). Large, shaped like *Schiz. Nuttalli*, but beaks narrow. Mantle-bend separate from ventral line.
69 b. *Standella* ? var. *nasuta*, Gld. (suppressed). Revived for young shells between *Californica* and *planulata*, till more is known.
70. *Standella planulata*, Conr. Nearly as large ; shape approaching *Mactrella exoleta.*
71. *Standella falcata*, Gld. Otia. Shape like *planulata*, but flatter.
72. *Raëta undulata*, Gld. Otia. Like the Atlantic *R. canaliculata*, but reversed. Rare at S. Pedro, *Cp.*

Family Veneridæ.

73. ? *Clementia subdiaphana*, n. s. Hinge normal, very thin, ashy.
74. *Amiantis callosa*, Conr. (not auct.). Subgenus of *Callista*: hinge-plate roughened as in *Mercenaria* : mantle-bend as in *Dosinia.* L. w. com. *Cp.*
75. *Pachydesma crassatelloides*, Conr. auct. Subgenus of *Trigona*, with fewer teeth: jun. = *stultorum*, Gray.
76. *Psephis tantilla*, Gld. Otia. Subgenus of *Venus* : animal ovoviviparous. Teeth elongate, approaching *Pachydesma*. Small, with purple spot. 12–20 fm. c. *Cp.*

	Nutt.	Jew.	B. A.	Smiths. Ins.	Ken.	Lord.	Swan.	Cooper.
77. Psephis Lordi	—	—	—	—	P	V	V	I
78. —— salmonea	—	—	—	—	—	—	—	DI
79. —— tellimyalis	—	—	—	II	—	—	—	—
80. Venus Kennerleyi	—	—	—	—	P	—	V	—
81. Chione succincta	BD	D	C	—	—	—	—	D
82. —— excavata	D	—	—	—	—	—	—	—
83. —— simillima	D	D	C	L	—	—	—	—
84. —— fluctifraga	D	D	C	D	—	—	—	D
85. Tapes tenerrima	—	B	F	F	—	—	V	D
86. —— laciniata	—	—	M	D	—	—	—	D
87. —— staminea	DC	F	F	FD	—	—	—	FD
87 b. —— var. Petitii	—	—	C	VPOM	P	V	V	FM
87 c. —— var. ruderata	—	—	—	—	—	—	V	—
88. Saxidomus aratus	—	—	—	F	—	—	—	FD
89. —— Nuttallii	D	D	C	—	—	—	—	FD
90. —— squalidus	—	F	O	VPOF	P	V	V	—
91. —— brevisiphonatus	—	—	—	—	—	V	—	—
92. Rupellaria lamellifera	D	M	C	D	—	—	—	M
93. Petricola carditoides	BD	MB	C	F	P	—	V	M
94. Chama exogyra	BD	—	C	LII	—	—	—	D
95. —— pellucida	B	B	C	MD	—	—	—	FMD

77. *Psephis Lordi*, Baird, P. Z. S. 1863. Teeth normal: pure white. 20–40 fm. c. *Cp.*

78. *Psephis salmonea*, n. s. Very small, rounded, teeth elongate: salmon-coloured. 30–40 fm. r. *Cp.*

79. *Psephis tellimyalis*, n. s. Shape of *Tellimya*: central tooth minute; outside teeth long.

80. *Venus Kennerleyi*, Rve. Large, transverse, flattened, ashy: strong conc. ribs. Young like *astartea*, Midd. (not *fluctuata*, Gld.).

81. *Chione succincta*, Val.= *Californiensis*, Brod.= *Nuttalli*, Conr. Conc. ribs smooth.

82. *Chione excavata*, Cpr. P. Z. S. 1856, p. 216. Scarcely differs from *cancellata*. Possibly exotic.

83. *Chione simillima*, Sby. Finely sculptured each way.

84. *Chione fluctifraga*, Sby.+*callosa*, Sby. Like *Stutchburyi*: swollen, irregular.

85. *Tapes tenerrima*, Cpr. P. Z. S. 1856, p. 200, (jun.)= *V. rigida*, Gld. pars, f. 538. Very large, thin, flat; long pointed sinus.

86. *Tapes laciniata*, n. s. Large, swollen, brittle, ashen; sculpture pectinated.

87. *Tapes staminea*, Conr. Strong, shape of *decussata*; sculpture close; yellowish. Var. *diversa*, Sby.=*mundulus*, Rve. More swollen, clouded with chocolate. Var. *Petitii*, Desh.=*rigida*, Gld. pars. Dead white, sculpture strong or faint, open or close. 2 ft. deep in mud, between tides, *Lord.* Var. *tumida*, Sby. Very swollen. Var. *orbella*, rounded, globose. Var. *ruderata*, Desh. Concentric sculpture laminated.

88. *Saxidomus aratus*, Gld. Otia. Very large, oval, with regular concentric ridges.

89. *Saxidomus Nuttallii*, Conr. auct. Transverse, subquadrate, irregularly grooved.

90. *Saxidomus squalidus*, Desh. Large, variable outline, broader, scarcely sculptured.

91. *Saxidomus brevisiphonatus*, n. s. Smaller, *Callista*-shaped; close, faint concentric lines over distant waves; mantle-bend very small.

Family *Petricolidæ.*

92. *Rupellaria lamellifera*, Conr.= *Cordieri*, Desh. With large concentric laminæ. No radiations.

93. *Petricola carditoides*, Conr.+*Californica*, Conr.+*cylindracea*, Desh.+*arcuata*, Desh.+*gibba*, Midd. Of various aspects, like *Saxicava*. Normally shaped like *Cypricardia*, with fine sculpture like *Naranio*.

Family *Chamidæ.*

94. *Chama exogyra*, Conr. Reversed; texture opaque; rudely frilled.

95. *Chama pellucida*, Sby. Dextral, texture porcellanous, rosy; closely frilled. S.A.

	Nutt.	Jew.	B.A.	Smiths. Ins.	Ken.	Lord.	Swan.	Cooper
96. Chama spinosa	—	—	OC	—	—	—	—	?D
97. Cardium corbis	OB	—	OC	VPOF	P	V	V	F
98. —— quadragenarium	B	—	—	D	—	—	—	D
99. —— var. blandum	—	—	P	—	P	V	V	—
100. —— var. centifilosum	—	—	—	—	—	—	—	I
101. Hemicardium biangulatum	—	—	—	—	—	—	—	I
102. Serripes Grœnlandicus....	—	—	—	—	P	—	—	—
103. Liocardium elatum	—	—	—	—	—	—	—	D
104. —— substriatum	D	—	C	—	—	—	—	D
105. Astarte compacta	—	—	—	—	P	—	—	—
106. —— Esquimalti	—	—	—	—	—	V	—	—
107. —— fluctuata	—	—	—	—	—	—	—	I
108. Miodon prolongatus......	—	—	—	—	—	—	V	?C
109. Venericardia borealis	—	—	—	—	—	V	—	I
109 b. —— var. ventricosa	—	B fs.	P	—	P	—	—	I
110. Lazaria subquadrata......	—	B	—	II	—	—	V	MDI
111. Lucina Nuttallii	D	—	—	—	—	—	—	I
112. —— Californica	D	B	—	D	—	—	—	I
113. —— bella	D	—	—	—	—	—	—	—
114. —— tenuisculpta........	—	—	—	—	P	—	—	DI

96. *Chama spinosa*, Sby. Ridges broken into close short spines. Maz. Cat. no. 122.

Family *Cardiadæ.*

97. *Cardium corbis*, Mart. = *Nuttalli* + *Californianum*, Conr. Large, earthen, rather nodulous; posterior margin strongly indented by 2 first ribs. Asia. 8–15 fm. *Lyall.* Jun. in stomach of starfish, 12 fm. *Lord.*

98. *Cardium quadragenarium*, Conr. = *luteolabrum* (= *xanthocheilum*), Gld. Very large; 40 ribs, with aculeate spines.

99. *Cardium* var. *blandum*, Gld. Otia. Delicate form of the Asiatic *pseudofossile*, Rve. = *Californiense*, Desh. Transverse; close, flat ribs; margin regular. 8–15 fm. *Lyall.*

100. *Cardium* var. *centifilosum*. Probably = *modestum*, Ad. & Rve.; but rounder, ribs sharper and more distant. Belongs to subg. *Fulvia*, Gray. 30–40 fm. *Cp.*

101. *Hemicardium biangulatum*, Sby. Southern fauna. 10–20 fm. living. *Cp.*

102. *Serripes Grœnlandicus*, Chem. auct. Boreal. Rounder than *S. Laperousii.*

103. *Liocardium elatum*, Sby. Maz. Cat. no. 124. Gulf fauna. Very large, *Cp.*

104. *Liocardium substriatum*, Conr. = *cruentatum*, Gld. Almost identical with the Peruvian *Elenense.*

Family *Astartidæ.*

105. *Astarte compacta*, n. s. Like *compressa*, but closer; dorsal margins straight, at right angles.

106. *Astarte Esquimalti*, Baird, P. Z. S. 1863, p. 70. Subtrigonal; ribs irregular.

107. ?*Astarte fluctuata*, n. s. Very close to *Omalii*, jun. of Coralline Crag. 2 right v. 30–40 fm. *Cp.*

108. *Miodon prolongatus*, n. g., n. s. Outside Lucinoid; hinge and scars nearer to *Venericardia*. Congeneric with *A. tarte orbicularis*, J. Sby. Min. Conch. pl. 444. f. 2, 3 (non ejusdem, pl. 520. f 2). G. Oolite; and with the Crag *Cardita corbis*.

109. *Venericardia borealis*, Conr. N. Atlantic, from Miocene. 120 fm. Cat. Is. *Cp.*

109 b. *Venericardia* var. *ventricosa*, Gld. Small, swollen. 30–40 fm. *Cp.*

110. *Lazaria subquadrata*, n. s. Hinge of *Lazaria*: outside like *Cardita variegata*, jun.

Family *Lucinidæ.*

111. *Lucina Nuttallii*, Conr. Hanl. Like *muricata*, with more delicate sculpture.

112. *Lucina Californica*, Conr. Dosinoid, with waved lunule. Jun. ? = *L. Artemidis*, P. Z. S. 1856, p. 201.

113. *Lucina bella*, Conr. Shell not known; may be = *pectinata*, Maz. Cat. no. 142.

114. *Lucina tenuisculpta*, n. s. Like *Mazatlanica*, Cat. no. 144, more convex, with finer sculpture. 4 fm. living, *Cp.* The island var. is intermediate. 120 fm. dead, *Cp.*

	Nutt.	Jew.	B. A.	Smiths. Ins.	Ken.	Lord.	Swan.	Cooper.
115. Lucina borealis	—	—	—	—	—	—	—	I
116. Cryptodon flexuosus	—	—	—	—	—	—	—	I
117. —— serricatus	—	—	—	—	P	V	—	I ?
118. Diplodonta orbella	B	B	C	D	—	—	V	D
119. Kellia Laperousii	—	—	C	M	P	—	V	—
119 b. —— var. Chironii	—	—	—	—	—	—	V	D
120. —— rotundata	—	—	—	M	—	—	—	—
121. —— suborbicularis......	—	—	—	H	P	—	—	DI
122. Lasea rubra............	—	—	—	—	P	—	—	I
123. Pythina rugifera........	—	—	—	—	P	—	—	—
124. Lepton meroëum	—	—	—	—	—	—	—	D
125. Tellimya tumida........	—	—	—	—	P	—	V	D
126. Pristes oblongus	—	—	—	—	—	—	—	D
127. Mytilus Californianus....	MD	C	C	PFC	P	V	V	FDI
128. —— edulis	C	C	C	PC	P	V	V	F
128 b. —— var. glomeratus ..	—	—	F	—	—	—	—	—
129. Septifer bifurcatus	?C	—	F	FH	—	—	—	DI
130. Modiola capax	B	C	C	—	—	—	—	D
131. —— modiolus..........	—	M	P	VH	P	V	V	M
132. —— fornicata..........	—	B	—	M	—	—	—	—
133. —— recta	B	B	C	—	—	—	—	D

115. *Lucina borealis*, Linn. auct.+*acutilineata*, Conr. Widely diffused, from Coralline Crag. Philippines, teste Cuming. 30–120 fm. *Cp.*
116. *Cryptodon flexuosus*, Mont. auct. Atlantic, circumpolar. Cat. Is. 120 fm. *Cp.*
117. *Cryptodon serricatus*, n. s. Small, circular, flat; epidermis silken. ? Cat. Is. *Cp.* 120 fm.

Family *Diplodontidæ.*

118. *Diplodonta orbella*, Gld. Otia.＝(*Mysia*) *Sphærella tumida*, Conr.

Family *Kelliadæ.*

119. *Kellia Laperousii*, Desh. Woodw. Typically large, strong, transverse.
119 b. *Kellia* var. *Chironii.* Thinner, less transverse, margins rounded.
120. *Kellia rotundata*, n. s. Larger, flatter, and less pearly than *suborbicularis.* Margin circular.
121. *Kellia suborbicularis*, Mont. auct. Maz. Cat. no. 153. N. Atlantic : W. Mexico. Exactly accords with British sp. 30–40 fm. *Cp.*
122. *Lasea rubra*, Mont. auct. Maz. Cat. no. 154. N. Atlantic: W. Mexico. Exactly accords with British sp.
123. *Pythina rugifera*, n. s. Large, thin, slightly indented; teeth minute; epidermis shaggy.
124. *Lepton meroëum*, n. s. Small, shaped like *Sunapta.*
125. *Tellimya tumida*, n. s. Between *bidentata* and *substriata*: ossicle minute.
126. *Pristes oblongus*, n. g., n. s. Like *Tellimya*, with long marginal teeth, serrated near hinge.

Family *Mytilidæ.*

127. *Mytilus Californianus*, Conr. 9 in. long : stained with sienna : obsoletely ribbed.
128. *Mytilus edulis*, Linn. auct.＝*trossulus*, Gld. Abundant on whole coast, with the usual Atlantic vars. Between tide-marks, *Lord* : also brown var. on floating stick.
128 b. *Mytilus* ? var. *glomeratus*, Gld. Otia. Short, stumpy, solid, crowded.
129. *Septifer bifurcatus*, Rve. Outside like *Mytilus b.* Conr. from Sandw. Is.
130. *Modiola capax*, Conr. Maz. Cat. no. 170. From Southern fauna.
131. *Modiola modiolus*, Linn. auct. Circumboreal. 8–15 fm. jun. *Lyall.*
132. *Modiola fornicata*, n. s. Short, swollen, like large *M. marmorata*; but smooth, not crenated.
133. *Modiola recta*, Conr. 6 in. long, thin, narrow, rhomboidal. Chaff-like hairs over glossy epidermis.

9 129

	Nutt.	Jew.	B. A.	Smiths. In.	Ken.	Lord. Swan.	Cooper.
133 b. Modiola var. flabellata..	—	—	V	VP	P	— V	—
134. Adula falcata	—	M	M	FM	—	— —	D
135. —— stylina..........	—	—	—	OFM	—	— V	—
136. Lithophagus plumula....	—	—	—	M	—	— —	D
137. —— attenuatus	—	—	L	H	—	— —	—
138. Modiolaria lævigata	—	—	—	—	P	V V	—
139. —— marmorata	—	—	P	—	P	— —	—
140. Crenella decussata	—	—	—	—	—	— —	I
141. Arca multicostata	—	—	—	D	—	— —	—
142. Barbatia gradata	—	—	—	—	—	— —	D
143. Axinæa intermedia	—	—	—	—	—	— —	MDI
144. —— var. subobsoleta	—	—	—	ODI	—	— V	—
145. Nucula tenuis	—	—	—	—	P	— —	—
146. —— Acila castrensis	—	—	—	—	P	V —	I
147. Leda cælata............	—	B	F	—	—	— —	MD
148. —— cuneata	—	—	—	—	—	— —	MDI
149. —— minuta............	—	—	—	—	P	— —	—
150. —— fossa	—	—	—	—	P	V —	—
151. —— hamata	—	—	—	—	—	— —	BI

133 b. *Modiola* var. *flabellata*, Gld. Northern form, somewhat broader.

134. *Adula falcata*, Gld. Otia. Subgenus enlarged to include species intermediate between *Modiola* and *Lithophagus*: shape of latter, byssiferous like former, nestling in crypts. Sp.=*Gruneri*, Phil. MS. Shape not always falcate: chestnut, rugose.

135. *Adula stylina*, n. s. Shorter, broader; epidermis brown, glossy.

136. *Lithophagus plumula*, Hanl. Maz. Cat. no. 175. From Southern fauna.

137. *Lithophagus attenuatus*, Desh. Maz. Cat. no. 173. From Southern fauna.

138. *Modiolaria lævigata*, Gray. Exactly accords with Atlantic specimens. Circumboreal.

139. *Modiolaria marmorata*, Fbs. & Hanl. Exactly accords with Atlantic specimens. Circumboreal.

140. *Crenella decussata*, Mont. Exactly accords with Atlantic specimens. Circumboreal. 10–40 fm. not r. *Cp.*

Family *Arcadæ.*

141. *Arca multicostata*, Sby. Maz. Cat. no. 181. }
142. *Barbatia gradata*, Sby. Maz. Cat. no. 194. } From Southern fauna.

143. *Axinæa intermedia*, Brod. = *Barbarensis*, Conr. fossil. Closely accords with the Peruvian specimens. 40–60 fm. *Cp.*

144. *Axinæa* (? *septentrionalis*, Midd. var.) *subobsoleta*. Sculpture much fainter than in Midd.'s fig.

Family *Nuculidæ.*

145. *Nucula tenuis*, Mont. auct. Agrees with var. *lucida*, Gld. Circumboreal.

146. *Acila castrensis*, Hds. Sulph.+*Lyalli*, Baird. Subg. of *Nucula* with divaricate sculpture; only known in Crag and N. Pacific. 40–60 fm. *Cp.*

147. *Leda cælata*, Hds. Sulph. Swollen, strongly sculptured: teeth very numerous. 10–60 fm. *Cp.*

148. *Leda cuneata*, Sby. D'Orb. teste Hanl. (Scarcely differs from *commutata*, Phil. in Mus. Cum.) =*inornata*, A. Ad. Chili. 0–60 fm. *Cp.*

149. *Leda minuta*, O. Fabr. teste Hanl. Circumboreal. Agrees with Norwegian specimens of "*caudata*, Don." teste M'Andr.

150. *Leda fossa*, Baird, P. Z. S. 1863, p. 71. Between *minuta* and *pernula*. Sculpture nearly obsolete.

151. *Leda hamata*, n. s. Like *Steenstrupi* and *pernuloides*, but very hooked, sculpture strong. 20–60 fm. c. *Cp.*

	Nutt.	Jew.	B. A.	Smiths. Ins.	Ken.	Lord.	Swan.	Cooper.
152. Yoldia lanceolata	—	—	—	—	P	—	—	—
153. —— amygdala	—	—	—	—	P	—	—	—
154. Verticordia ornata	—	—	—	—	—	—	—	BI
155. Bryophila setosa........	—	—	—	H	—	—	—	?C
156. Lima orientalis	—	—	—	—	—	—	—	MDI
157. Limatula subauriculata ..	—	—	—	—	—	—	—	DI
158. Pecten hastatus	—	B	P	—	P	V	V	M
159. —— ?var. Hindsii	—	—	P	—	P	V	V	—
160. —— var. æquisulcatus ..	—	B	—	D	—	—	—	BD
161. —— paucicostatus	—	B	—	—	—	—	—	I
162. —— ?var. latiauritus	BD	D	C	D	—	—	—	D
162b.—— monotimeris	BD	D	C	DL	—	—	—	D
163. Amusium caurinum	—	Cjn.	O	VO	P	—	V	—
164. Janira dentata..........	—	—	—	—	—	—	—	MD
165. Hinnites giganteus	C	C	C	PM	P	V	V	D
166. Ostrea lurida	—	—	—	VPO	P	V	V	F

152. *Yoldia lanceolata*, J. Sby. Hanl.=*arctica*, Brod. & Sby. (Not *Adrana l.*, Lam. G. Sby.) With ant. diagonal lines.

153. *Yoldia amygdala*, var. teste Hanl. Like *lanceolata*, without posterior wing, and anterior sculpture.

Family ? *Trigoniadæ.*

154. *Verticordia ornata*, D'Orb.=*novemcostata*, Ad. & Rve. Samarang. Exactly accords with Chinese types. S. A. 20–40 fm. Cp.

Family *Aviculidæ.*

155. *Bryophila setosa*, n. g., n. s., Ann. N. H. 1864, p. 10. Like minute, broad *Pinna*. Animal ovoviviparous. Sta Barbara, 20 fm. Cp.

Family *Pectinidæ.*

156. *Lima orientalis*, Ad. & Rve., Samarang, in Mus. Cum.= *dehiscens*, Conr. fossil, teste Cp. Very close to young of *L. hians*, var. *tenera*. Beach to 20 fm. c. Cp.

157. *Limatula subauriculata*, Mont. Fbs. & Hanl. Circumboreal. Fossil in Crag. Islands, 40–120 fm. not r.; S. Diego, 1 valve, 4 fm. Cp.

158. *Pecten hastatus*, Sby.=*hericeus*, Gld. Elongated ; a few principal ribs serrated : ears unequal. In var. *rubidus*, Hds. (non Mart.), the ribs are equal, not serrated.

159. *Pecten* (? var.) *Hindsii.* Broader ; ribs close, small, smooth, bifurcating. Passes from *hastatus* towards *Islandicus.*

160. *Pecten æquisulcatus,* ? n. s. Thinner and flatter than *ventricosus*, with narrower ribs.

161. *Pecten paucicostatus,* ? n. s. Somewhat resembling very young *caurinus*; but ribs fewer, stronger.

162. *Pecten latiauritus*, Conr. (pars). Ribs sharply defined, with sharp concentric laminæ. Possibly an extreme form of

162b.*Pecten monotimeris*, Conr.=*tunica*, Phil.+*latiauritus*, Conr. pars. Passes into *Amusium.* Very slanting, thin, with faint ribs.

163. *Amusium caurinum*, Gld. E. E. Large, flat, thin, very inequivalve. Var.= *Yessoensis*, Jay. Japan.

164. *Janira dentata*, Sby.=*excavata*, Val. Ven. Like *media.* From the Gulf fauna. Beach–20 fm. Cp.

Family *Spondylidæ.*

165. *Hinnites giganteus*, Gray, Analyst.=*Poulsoni*, Conr. Very large, Spondyloid : ligament as in *Pedum*, strongly adherent along the ears.

Family *Ostreidæ.*

166. *Ostrea lurida*, n. s. Shape of *edulis*: texture dull, lurid, olivaceous, with purple stains. 2–3 fm. on mud flats, Lord.

	Nutt.	Jew.	B.A.	Smiths. Ins.	Ken.	Lord.	Swan.	Cooper.
166b. Ostrea var. laticaudata ..	—	—	—	—	—	—	—	F
166c.—— var. rufoides	—	—	—	D	—	—	—	D
166d.—— var. expansa	—	—	—	—	—	—	—	D
167. —— conchaphila .. [ma	D	—	C	L	—	—	—	D
168. Placunanomia macroschis-	—	—	OC	VF	P	V	V	F
169. Anomia lampe..........	—	—	C	L	—	—	—	D
170. Cavolina telemus	—	—	—	—	—	V	—	I
171. Bulla nebulosa	B	D	C	DL	—	—	—	DI
172. —— Quoyi	—	?B	—	L	—	—	—	D
173. Haminea hydatis.......	—	—	—	?P	P	V	—	—
174. —— vesicula	—	—	C	—	—	—	—	D
175. —— virescens	—	—	C	D	—	—	—	BD
— Philinid	—	—	—	—	P	—	—	—
— ?	—	—	—	—	P	—	—	—
176. Tornatella punctocœlata..	—	—	—	I	—	—	—	D
177. Tornatina culcitella	—	B	C	—	—	—	—	MI

166b. *Ostrea* var. *laticaudata*, Nutt. MS. Purple, winged, waved: denticles near hinge. Passes towards *palmula*, Maz. Cat. no. 214, *b*.

166c. *Ostrea* ? var. *rufoides*=*rufa*, Gld. (non Lam.). Passing towards *Virginica*, jun. Thin, with umbos hollowed; reddish in scar-region. Also fossil.

166d. *Ostrea* ? var. *expansa*. Flat, affixed to whole surface, like *Columbiensis*. Round, or winged to left, or right, or both, like *Malleus*. Also passes into

167. *Ostrea conchaphila*, Cpr. Maz. Cat. no. 214. From Southern fauna.

Family *Anomiadæ.*

168. *Placunanomia macroschisma*, Desh. Kamtschatka. Vars. =*alope*+*cepio*, Gray. Shape most variable, according to station. Sculpture often obsolete. On rock, between tides, *Lord.*

169. *Anomia lampe*, Gray, Maz. Cat. no. 219. From Southern fauna.

Class PTEROPODA.　　Family *Hyalæidæ.*

170. *Cavolina telemus*, Linn.= *Hyalæa tridentata*, Forsk. non Lam. Pelagic. 30–60 fm. dead, *Cp.*
　　[Other Pteropods were brought by the Brit. N. P. Boundary Survey, but may have been collected on the voyage *v.* p. 607.]

Class GASTEROPODA.

Subclass OPISTHOBRANCHIATA.　　Order TECTIBRANCHIATA.

Family *Bullidæ.*

171. *Bulla nebulosa*, Gld. Otia. Large, globular, thin. Maz. Cat. no. 225+var. *fulminosa*, Cp.

172. *Bula Quoyi*, Gray. Small: angular at umbilicus. Maz. Cat. no. 226. Pacific.

173. *Haminea hydatis*, Linn. auct. Exactly accords with European specimens.

174. *Haminea vesicula*, Gld. Otia. Smaller, paler, and thinner.

175. *Haminea virescens*, Sby. Gen. Var.=*cymbiformis*, Maz. Cat. no. 220.

Family ? *Philinidæ.*

Two species not yet dissected: one with internal shell like *Phanerophthalmus*.

Family *Tornatellidæ.*

176. *Tornatella punctocœlata*, n. s. Small: grooved with rows of dots: pillar twisted as in *Bullina*, Add. non Gray.

Family *Cylichnidæ.*

177. *Tornatina culcitella*, Gld. Otia. Large, brownish, with faint striæ. Fold close to paries.

	Nutt.	Jew.	B. A.	Smitha. Ins.	Ken.	Lord.	Swan.	Cooper.
177b. Tornatina cerealis	—	B	—	—	—	....	—	M
178. —— eximia	—	—	—	—	P	V	...	—
179. —— carinata	—	—	—	—	—	—	...	D
180. Cylichna ? cylindracea	—	B	—	—	—	—	—	MDI
180b. —— var. attonsa	—	—	—	—	P	—	—	—
181. —— planata	—	—	—	D	—	—	—	—
182. —— inculta	—	—	D	D	—	—	—	—
183. Volvula cylindrica	—	B	—	—	—	—	—	—
184. Neaplysia Californica	—	—	—	—	—	...	—	D
185. Navarchus inermis	—	—	—	—	—	—	—	DI
186. Pleurophyllidea Californic.	—	—	—	—	—	—	—	D
187. Doris sanguinea	—	—	—	—	—	—	—	DI
188. —— alabastrina	—	—	—	—	—	—	—	D
189. —— albopunctata	—	—	—	—	—	—	—	BI
190. —— Sandiegensis	—	—	—	—	—	—	—	DI
191. —— Montereyensis	—	—	—	—	—	—	—	FMI
192. Triopa Catalinæ	—	—	—	—	—	—	—	I
193. Tritonia Palmeri	—	—	—	—	—	—	—	D
194. Dendronotus iris	—	—	—	—	—	—	—	B
195. Æolis Barbarensis	—	—	—	—	—	—	—	B
196. Phidiana iodinea	—	—	—	—	—	—	—	BD
197. Flabellina opalescens	—	—	—	—	—	—	—	BDI
198. Chioræra leonina	—	—	P	—	—	—	—	B
199. Melampus olivaceus	—	—	C	DL	—	—	—	DI
200. Pedipes liratus	—	—	—	L	—	—	—	D
201. Siphonaria Thersites	—	—	—	—	—	—	V	—

177b. *Tornatina cerealis*, Gld. Otia. Small, white, smooth: but probably = worn young *culcitella*.
178. *Tornatina eximia*, Baird, P. Z. S. 1863, p. 67. Size moderate: fold appressed: subrectangular.
179. *Tornatina carinata*, Maz. Cat. no. 223.
180. *Cylichna ? cylindracea*, Linn. auct. Intermediate specimens, passing into
180b. *Cylichna* var. *attonsa*, rounded off at apex.
181. *Cylichna planata*, n. s. Like *mamillata*, with apex flattened-off, and fold distinct.
182. *Cylichna inculta*, Gld. Otia.
183. *Volvula cylindrica*, n. s. Like grain of rice, pointed at one end.

Family *Aplysiadæ*.
184. *Neaplysia Californica*, Cp. Proc. Cal. Ac. 15 inches long.
185. *Navarchus inermis*, Cp. Proc. Cal. Ac. Grasses, on shore, *Cp.*

Family *Pleurophyllidiadæ*.
186. *Pleurophyllidea Californica*, Cp. Proc. Cal. Ac. Sandy flats, *Cp.*

Order NUDIBRANCHIATA.
137–198. All the new Nudibranchs are described in the Proc. Cal. Ac. *Vide antea*, p. 609. *Vide* also Gld.'s Otia, and Esch. Zool. Atlas.

Subclass PULMONATA.
For land and freshwater species, both of Pulmonates, Rostrifers, and Bivalves, *vide posteà*, paragraphs 115–119.

Family *Auriculidæ*.
199. *Melampus olivaceus*, Cpr. Maz. Cat. no. 235.
200. *Pedipes liratus*, Binn. Proc. Ac. N. S. Phil. 1861, p. 333.

Family *Siphonariadæ*.
201. *Siphonaria Thersites*, n. s. Like *lateralis*: with strong lung-rib and obsolete sculpture.

	Nutt.	Jew.	B.A.	Smiths. Ins.	Ken.	Lord.	Swan.	Cooper.
2 2. Dentalium v. Indianorum	—	—	P	—	P	—	V	MI
203. —— rectius	—	—	—	—	P	—	—	—
204. —— semipolitum	—	—	—	—	—	—	—	D
205. —— hexagonum	—	—	—	—	—	—	—	D
206. Cryptochiton Stelleri	—	C	OC	FMI	P	V	V	I
207. Katherina tunicata	—	—	O	OF	P	V	V	I
208. Tonicia lineata	—	—	C	PFM	P	V	V	—
209. —— submarmorea	—	—	—	O	—	—	V	—
210. Mopalia muscosa	M	F	P	OFMI	—	V	V	I
211. —— Wosnessenskii	—	—	C	—	—	V	—	—
212. —— Kennerleyi	—	—	—	—	P	—	V	—
212b.—— var. Swanii	—	—	—	—	—	—	V	—
213. —— Hindsii	—	—	—	F	P	—	—	—
214. —— Simpsonii	—	—	C	—	—	—	—	—
215. —— vespertina	—	—	P	F	P	—	V	—
216. —— lignosa	—	—	PM	O	P	—	—	—
217. —— acuta	M	—	—	—	—	—	—	—
218. —— sinuata	—	—	—	—	P	—	—	—
219. —— imporcata	—	—	P	—	P	—	—	—

Subclass PROSOBRANCHIATA.   Order LATERIBRANCHIATA.

Family *Dentaliadæ.*

202. *Dentalium* (? *pretiosum,* Nutt. Sby. var.) *Indianorum.* Like *entalis,* with very fine posterior striæ. 20 fm. c. *Cp.*
203. *Dentalium rectius,* n. s. Long, thin, slightly curved : like *eburneum,* Singapore.
204. *Dentalium semipolitum,* Br. & Sby. ? = *hyalinum,* Phil. not Maz. Cat. no. 245. From Southern fauna.
205. *Dentalium hexagonum,* Sby. From Southern fauna.

Order SCUTIBRANCHIATA.   Family *Chitonidæ.*

206. *Cryptochiton Stelleri,* Midd. Very large : valves hidden. Reaches Sta Cruz, *Cp.*
207. *Katherina tunicata,* Sby. = *Douglasiæ,* Gray. Mantle smooth, black : valves partly concealed. Between tide-marks, *Lord.* Reaches Farallone Is. *Cp.*
208. *Tonicia lineata,* Wood. Closely resembling *lineolata,* Peru. Painting variable.
209. *Tonicia submarmorea,* Midd. Perhaps= *lineata,* var. without lines.
210. *Mopalia muscosa,* Gld. E. E. = *C. ornatus,* Nutt. (= *armatus,* Jay)+*consimilis,* Nutt. Highly sculptured : mantle crowded with strong hairs. Between tide-marks, *Lord.*
211. *Mopalia Wosnessenskii,* Midd. Mantle slit behind, with few hairs. Sculpture like *muscosa.*
212. *Mopalia Kennerleyi,* n. s. = *Grayi,* anteà, p. 603, nom. preoc. Sculpture fainter : olive with red : ridge angular ; post. valve waved.
212b.*Mopalia Kennerleyi,* var. *Swanii* : red, ridge arched ; less sculptured.
213. *Mopalia Hindsii,* Gray. Olive : distinctly shagreened : flat : post. valve waved.
214. *Mopalia Simpsonii,* Gray, in B.M. Col. Like *Hindsii,* with valves beaked.
215. *Mopalia vespertina,* Gld. E. E. Shape of *Hindsii,* with very faint sculpture and slight wave. Olive clouded with brown.
216. *Mopalia lignosa,* Gld. E. E. = *Merckii,* Midd. = *Montereyensis,* Cpr. P. Z. S. 1855, p. 231. Like *vespertina,* without wave : brown in streaks.
217. *Mopalia acuta,* Cpr. P. Z. S. 1855, p. 232. Subgeneric, aberrant form ; with small blunt plate, instead of post. sinus, between the two principal lobes.
218. ? *Mopalia sinuata,* n. s. Small, raised sharp back, red and blue, engine-turned ; post. valve deeply notched.
219. ? *Mopalia imporcata,* n. s. Pale : central areas ribbed : post. valve slightly notched. Indications of sutural pores in these two species, if confirmed, will require a new genus.

	Nutt.	Jew.	B. A.	Smiths. Ins.	Ken.	Lord.	Swan.	Cooper.
220. Acanthopleura scabra	M	—	C	FI	P	—	—	I
221. —— fluxa	—	—	—	—	—	—	—	I
222. Ischnochiton Magdalensis	—	—	L	LM	—	—	—	DI
223. —— veredentiens	—	—	—	—	—	—	—	I
224. Lepidopleurus regularis ..	—	—	C	—	—	—	—	—
225. —— scabricostatus	—	—	—	—	—	—	—	I
226. —— pectinatus	—	—	—	—	—	—	—	I
227. —— Mertensii	—	—	C	M	P	—	V	—
228. Trachydermon retiporosus	—	—	—	—	P	—	—	—
229. —— interstinctus	—	--	P	—	—	—	—	—
230. —— trifidus	—	—	—	—	P	—	—	—
231. —— dentiens	—	—	P	—	—	—	—	—
231 b. —— pseudodentiens ..	—	—	—	—	P	V	—	D
232. —— Gothicus	—	—	—	—	—	—	—	I
233. —— Hartwegii	—	—	C	F	—	—	—	—
234. —— Nuttallii	M	—	C	M	—	—	V	I
235. —— flectens	—	—	—	M	P	V	—	D

220. *Acanthopleura scabra*, Rve. = *Californicus*, Nutt. Insertion-plates resemble *Katherina*. Valves with coarse V-shaped ribs, and projecting beaks.

221. *Acanthopleura fluxa*, n. s. Green, mottled with orange-red; not beaked; with only marginal and diagonal ribs.

222. *Ischnochiton Magdalensis*, Hds. Large, strong-valved, typical. Sculpture much fainter than in southern shells. Mantle-margin with striated scales like flattened bristles. Side plates 2- or 3-lobed. Beach-20 fm. *Cp.*

223. *Ischnochiton veredentiens*, n. s. Margin similar. Small, arched, sculptured like *Mertensii*, but with 2 rows of bosses, one of which dentates the sutures. 10-20 fm. *Cp.*

224. *Lepidopleurus regularis*, Cpr. P. Z. S. 1855, p. 232. Subgenus of *Ischnochiton*: mantle-scales Lophyroid, generally striated. Sp. arched, green, shagreened. Side lobes 2-4: eaves spongy, not projecting.

225. *Lepidopleurus scabricostatus*, n. s. Small, arched, orange: rows of prominent granules over shagreened surface. Lobes blunt, slightly rugulose, close to eaves. 8-20 fm. *Cp.*

226. *Lepidopleurus pectinatus*, n. s. Olive: strong sculpture over shagreened surface: side areas ribbed: outer margin and inner sutures pectinated. Bch. *Cp.*

227. *Lepidopleurus Mertensii*, Midd. Red: highly sculptured over smooth surface: side areas with rows of bosses. Mantle-scales smooth, rounded.

228. *Trachydermon retiporosus*, n. s. Subgenus of *Ischnochiton*: mantle-scales very small, close, smooth. Sp. like *scrobiculatus*, central pattern in network, 3-6 side ribs.

229. *Trachydermon interstinctus*, Gld. E.E. Centre minutely punctured: 6-8 blunt side ribs.

230. *Trachydermon trifidus*, n. s. Centre-punctures few, deep: 2-4 blunt ribs: side plates with 2 slits.

231. [*Trachydermon dentiens*, Gld. E.E. No shell known answering to diagnosis and figure.] The 4 following species have incisors blunt, eaves not projecting.

231 b. *Trachydermon pseudodentiens* = type specimen of *dentiens*. False appearance of teeth due to colour or ridges of growth. Closely granular: areas indistinct. Sinus broad, squared: eaves spongy.

232. *Trachydermon Gothicus*, n. s. Blunt parallel riblets along very arched back. Sutural lobes united at sinus: eaves not spongy. 8-20 fm. *Cp.*

233. *Trachydermon Hartwegii*, Cpr. P. Z. S. 1855, p. 231. Large, arched. Inside callous, without rows of punctures to slits: eaves spongy.

234. *Trachydermon Nuttallii*, Cpr. P. Z. S. 1855, p. 231. Large, plain, flat. Incisors slightly rugulose: eaves spongy.

235. *Trachydermon flectens*, n. s. Mantle-margin scarcely granular. Rosy, very small, scarcely sculptured: valves beaked and waved as in *M. Simpsonii*: eaves and incisors normal.

135

	Nutt.	Jew.	B.A.	Smiths. Ins.	Ken.	Lord.	Swan.	Cooper.
236. Leptochiton nexus	—	—	—	—	—	—	—	I
237. Acanthochites avicula ..	—	—	—	—	—	—	—	I
238. Nacella instabilis........	—	—	P	—	—	V	V	—
239. —— incessa...........	—	B	D	D	—	—	—	MD
240. —— subspiralis	—	—	—	—	—	—	—	I
241. —— depicta...........	—	—	D	—	—	—	—	D
242. —— paleacea	—	B	—	—	—	—	—	—
242 b. —— var. triangularis ..	—	—	—	—	—	—	—	M
243. Acmæa patina..........	C	C	C	VFM	P	V	V	FMBI
244. —— pelta	C	C	C	VFM	P	V	V	FMBI
244 b. —— var. Asmi.......	—	B	—	I	—	—	—	M
245. —— persona	O	C	C	VF	P	V	V	FBDI
246. —— scabra	D	C	C	DHI	—	—	—	MDI
247. —— spectrum	D	C	C	FDH	—	—	—	MBD
248. —— rosacea	—	B	—	—	—	—	—	MD
249. Lottia gigantea	—	—	C	FMIL	—	—	—	MBDI
250. Scurria mitra	M	C	PC	VPF	P	V	V	MI
250 b. —— ? var. funiculata ..	—	—	—	—	—	—	—	M

236. *Leptochiton nexus*, n. s. Like *asellus*: scarcely sculptured: mantle-margin with striated chaffy scales, like *Magdalensis*, interspersed with transparent needles. 20–80 fm. *Cp.*

237. *Acanthochites avicula*, n. s. Like *arragonites*, but valves sculptured in large snake-skin pattern. 8–20 fm. r. *Cp.*

Family *Patellidæ*.

238. *Nacella instabilis*, Gld. E E. Large: shape of *compressa*.

239. *Nacella incessa*, Hds. Sulphur. Small: Ancyloid.

240. ? *Nacella subspiralis*, n. s. Shaped like *Emarginula rosea*, and may be a *Scutellina*. 10–20 fm. *Cp.*

241. *Nacella depicta*, Hds. Sulphur. Small, long, flat, smooth: colour in rays.

242. *Nacella paleacea*, Gld. Otia. Narrower, brown, striated at each end.

242 b. *Nacella* ? var. *triangularis*. Shorter: apex raised: scarcely striated: whitish, with brown spots.

Family *Acmæidæ*. (For synonyms, *v.* Reports *in locis.*)

243. *Acmæa patina*, Esch. Large, blackish or tessellated: with very fine distant striæ. Between tides, *Lord.*

244. *Acmæa pelta*, Esch. More conical; border narrow; smooth, with blunt ribs often obsolete. Between tides, *Lord.*

244 b. *Acmæa* ? var. *Asmi*, Midd. Stout, small, black, conical. Probably an abnormal growth of *pelta*, jun. (1 sp. beginning on *pelta*) *Cp.*

245. *Acmæa persona*, Esch. Smaller: apex posterior: colour blotched or freckled: sculpture in irregular ribs. Maz. Cat. no. 266. Var. *umbonata*, arched, with narrow distant ribs. Var. *digitalis*, apex near margin. Var. *textilis*, apex far from margin, approaching *pelta*.

246. *Acmæa scabra*, Nutt. Rve. Outside with close rows of fine granules: orange-red tint, glossy. Var. *limatula*, sculpture stronger, border black: perhaps = Maz. Cat. no. 265.

247. *Acmæa spectrum*, Nutt. Rve. Flattened, with very strong ribs, irregular.

248. *Acmæa* (? *pileolus*, Midd. var.) *rosacea*. Pink, small: like Herm specimens of *virginea*.

249. *Lottia gigantea*, Gray. (Genus reconstituted: mantle with papillæ interrupted in front. Shell large, flat, dark, lustrous (= *Tecturella grandis*, Smiths. Inst. Check List).

250. *Scurria mitra*, Esch. Papillæ all round the mantle. White, conical: young sometimes faintly sculptured. In dead clam, 12 fm. *Lord.*

250 b. *Scurria* ? var. *funiculata*. With rounded riblets, somewhat nodulous.

	Nutt.	Jew.	B. A.	Smiths. In&.	Ken.	Lord.	Swan.	Cooper.
251. Lepeta cæcoides	—	—	—	—	P	—	.—	—
252. Gadinia (Rowellia)	—	—	—	I	—	—	—	I
253. Fissurella volcano	M	B	C	I	—	—	?V	DI
254. Glyphis aspera..........	—	—	OC	P	—	V	V	—
255. —— densiclathrata	?B	B	C	—	—	—	—	M
256. Lucapina crenulata......	D	—	C	C	—	—	—	D
257. Puncturella cucullata	—	—	P	—	P	—	V	M
258. —— galeata............	—	—	P	—	P	—	V	—
259. —— Cooperi	—	—	—	—	—	—	—	I
260. Haliotis Cracherodii	D	C	C	FDIL	—	—	—	MI
261. —— splendens..........	D	C	C	DIL	—	—	—	MDI
262. —— corrugata..........	—	—	C	D	—	—	—	I
263. —— rufescens	—	C	C	D	—	—	—	M
264. —— Kamtschatkana	—	—	C	FI	—	—	V	DI
265. Phasianella compta......	—	BD	C	D	—	—	—	MDI
266. Pomaulax undosus	M	C	C	L	—	—	—	DI
267. Pachypoma gibberosum ..	—	—	—	M	—	—	V	MB

251. *Lepeta cæcoïdes,* ?n. s. Like *cæca,* but apex turned back. Farallone I.:, teste R. D. Darbishire.

Family *Gadiniadæ.*

252. *Rowellia,* sp. Genus proposed by Cooper: tentacles flattened, pectinated. Cat. Is. *Cp.* Far. Is. *Row.*

Family *Fissurellidæ.*

253. *Fissurella volcano,* Rve. = *ornata,* Nutt. Approaches *Peruviana:* hole variable.
254. *Glyphis aspera,* Esch. = *Lincolni,* Gray = *cratitia,* Gld. Large, coarsely sculptured, with colour-rays.
255. *Glyphis densiclathrata,* Rve. Smaller: with closer, finer sculpture.
256. *Lucapina crenulata,* Sby. Tank. Very large: internal.
257. *Puncturella cucullata,* Gld. E.E. Large, with strong, variable ribs, 15–40. Hole simple.
258. *Puncturella galeata,* Gld. E.E. Scarcely differs from *noachina,* but tripartite process more strongly marked.
259. *Puncturella Cooperi,* n. s. Outside like *galeata,* but without props to the lamina. 30–120 fm. not r. *Cp.*

Family *Haliotidæ.*

260. *Haliotis Cracherodii,* Leach, auct. The trade species, smooth, dark olive: holes 5–9. Var. *Californiensis,* holes 9, 10, 11.
261. *Haliotis splendens,* Rve. Flatter, grooved, lustrous. Holes 4–7. Below tide: on rocks, *Cp.*
262. *Haliotis corrugata,* Gray. Large, arched, very rough. Holes 3–5. Below tide: on rocks, *Cp.*
263. *Haliotis rufescens,* Swains. Large, flatter, waved, rich orange-red. Holes 3–5. Below tide: on rocks, *Cp.*
264. *Haliotis Kamtschatkana,* Jonas. Small, thin, arched, waved. Holes 4, 5. Below tide: on rocks, Far. Is. *Cp.*

Family *Trochidæ.*

265. *Phasianella compta,* Gld. Otia. Maz. Cat. no. 284. Like *pullus,* a little longer and flatter; but operc. bevelled and striated. ? Var. *pulloides,* exactly like Herm shells: ? var. *elatior,* dwarfed, longer and flatter: var. *punctulata,* with close rows of dots; pillar chinked. 8–20 fm. *Cp.*
266. *Pomaulax undosus,* Wood. Very large: operculum with 2 ridges.
267. *Pachypoma gibberosum,* Chem. ? = *inæquale,* Mart. Large, rough: operc. swollen, simple. (Dead.)

137

	Nutt.	Jew.	B. A.	Smiths. Ins.	Ken.	Lord.	Swan.	Cooper.
268. ? Imperator serratus	—	—	—		—	—	—	MI
269. Leptonyx sanguineus	—	M	—	OFMI	—	—	V	MI
270. —— bacula	—	—	—	—	—	—	—	I
271. Liotia fenestrata	—	—	—	—	—	—	—	I
272. —— acuticostata	—	—	—	—	—	—	—	MI
273. Ethalia supravallata	—	—	—	—	—	—	—	D
273 b. —— var. invallata	—	—	—	—	—	—	—	D
274. Livona picoides	—	B	—	—	—	—	—	—
275. Trochiscus Norrisii	M	B	C	—	—	—	—	DI
276. —— convexus..........	—	M	—	—	—	—	—	—
277. Chlorostoma funebrale ..	M	C	C	FI	—	—	V	MD
277 b.—— var. subapertum	—	—	—	—	—	—	V	—
278. —— gallina............	—	—	D	L	—	—	—	DI
279. —— brunneum	—	—	C	FMDI	—	—	—	M
280. —— Pfeifferi	—	M	C	—	—	—	—	D
281. —— aureotinctum	C	—	C	L	—	—	—	I
282. Omphalius fuscescens	B	M	C	D	—	—	—	DI
283. Calliostoma canaliculatum	M	C	C	M	—	—	V	M
284. —— costatum	M	C	C	VFMI	P	V	V	—
285. —— annulatum	M	—	C	M	—	V	V	—
286. —— variegatum	—	—	—	—	P	—	—	—

268. ? *Imperator serratus*, n. s. Small, finely sculptured, base stellate, nucleus Plauorboid : operc. flat, with more whirls. 10–20 fm.=266 or 267 jun. teste *Cp.*

269. *Leptonyx sanguineus*, Linn. n. g. Like *Collonia*, not umbilicate. Operc. with horny and shelly layers, many whirls, outside flattish, not ribbed, margin broad. Species red or purple, lirate. Bch.–20 fm. *Cp.*

270. *Leptonyx bacula*, n. s. Small, ashy, Helicina-shaped, nearly smooth. Bch. d. *Cp.* Genus=*Homalopoma*, p. 537 : nom. preoc.

271. *Liotia fenestrata*, n. s. Small. Strongly ribbed each way. Bch.–40 fm. d. *Cp.*

272. *Liotia acuticostata*, n. s. Small. Sharply keeled, without radiating sculpture. 10–20 fm. *Cp.*

273. *Ethalia supravallata*, n. s. Minute : with keel and furrow near suture.

273 b. *Ethalia* ? var. *invallata*. Without keel.

274. *Livona picoides*, Gld. Otia. Probably the remnant of an ancient colony of *pica*.

275. *Trochiscus Norrisii*, Sby. Tank. Nucleus as in *Solarium* : perhaps a Proboscidifer, though pearly.

276. *Trochiscus convexus*, n. s. Small, subturrited, whirls swollen : umbilicus with 2 ribs, the outer crenated.

277. *Chlorostoma funebrale*, A. Ad. P. Z. S. 1854, p. 316=*marginatum*, Nutt. non Rve. Blackish, often puckered near suture.

277 b. *Chlorostoma funebrale*, var. *subapertum*, with umbilical pit.

278. *Chlorostoma gallina*, Fbs. P. Z. S. 1850, p. 271. Olive, dashed with purple. Var. *pyriformis*, Gld., umbilicus partly or wholly open.

279. *Chlorostoma brunneum*, Phil. Auburn : finely striate : Gibbuloid aspect. The young (teste *Cp.*) has a basal rib.

280. *Chlorostoma Pfeifferi*, Phil. Like *brunneum* : outside Ziziphinoid : umbilicus keeled.

281. *Chlorostoma aureotinctum*, Fbs. P. Z. S. 1850, p. 271=*nigerrimum*, Gmel. ? Mus. Cum. Gibbuloid : with distant grooves and fine sculpture ; mouth orange-spotted.

282. *Omphalius fuscescens*, Phil. Almost identical with *ligulatus*, Maz. Cat. no. 293.

283. *Calliostoma canaliculatum*, Mart.=*doliarium*. Large, with strong grooves.

284. *Calliostoma costatum*, Mart.=*filosum*, &c. Smaller, swollen, reddish ; finely ribbed. 8–15 fm. *Lyall.*

285. *Calliostoma annulatum*, Mart.=*virgineum*. Large, granular, stained with violet.

286. *Calliostoma variegatum*, n. s. Small, more conical, nodules more distant, white on rosy ground.

	Nutt.	Jew.	B. A.	Smiths. Ins.	Ken.	Lord.	Swan.	Cooper.
287. Calliostoma supragranosum	—	—	—	—	—	—	—	D
288. —— gemmulatum	—	—	—	—	—	—	—	D
289. —— splendens	—	—	—	—	—	—	—	MI
290. Phorcus pulligo	—	—	M	—	—	V	V	M
291. Gibbula parcipicta	—	—	—	FI	—	—	V	I
292. —— optabilis	—	—	—	—	—	—	—	D
293. —— funiculata	—	—	—	—	—	—	V	—
294. —— succincta	—	—	—	FIII	—	—	V	I
295. —— lacunata	—	—	—	—	—	—	V	—
296. Solariella peramabilis	—	—	—	—	—	—	—	I
297. Margarita cidaris	—	—	—	—	—	—	V	—
298. —— pupilla	—	—	P	VOI	P	V	V	—
298 b. —— var. salmonea	—	—	—	—	—	—	—	MI
299. —— acuticostata	—	B fs.	—	—	—	—	—	MI
300. —— inflata	—	—-	—	—	P	V	V	—
301. —— lirulata	—	—	—	—	P	V	V	—
302. —— ? Vahlii	—	—	—	—	P	—	—	—
303. —— tenuisculpta	—	—	—	.	P	—	V	—
304. —— helicina	—	—	—	—	—	—	V	—

287. *Calliostoma supragranosum*, n. s. Swollen, with sharp ribs; posterior 1–4 granular.

288. *Calliostoma gemmulatum*, n. s. Very swollen: painted like *eximium*: with 2 principal and 2 smaller rows of granules.

289. *Calliostoma splendens*, n. s. Orange-chestnut, with fleshy nacre; small, rather flattened, base glossy. 6–40 fm. *Cp.*

290. *Phorcus pulligo*, Mart.+*maculosus*, A. Ad.=*euryomphalus*, Jonas+*marcidus*, Gld. Subgenus of *Gibbula*, with expanded, rounded umbilicus, and flat whirls; sometimes obsoletely ribbed.

291. *Gibbula parcipicta*, n. s. Like strong growth of *Marg. lirulata*, var.

292. *Gibbula optabilis*, n. s. Wider: decussated between ribs: 2 spiral lines inside umbilicus.

293. *Gibbula funiculata*, n. s. Shaped like *Montagui*: with rounded spiral riblets.

294. *Gibbula succincta*, n. s. Small, scarcely sculptured, with spiral brown pencillings.

295. *Gibbula lacunata*, n. s. Very small, nearly smooth; umbilicus hemmed-in by swelling of columella.

296. *Solariella peramabilis*, n. s. Subgenus of *Margarita*, with open, crenated umbilicus. Species most ornate, with delicate sculpture. Umbilicus with 3 internal spiral lines, crossed by lirulæ: operculum sculptured. Like *Minolia aspecta*, A. Ad. 40–120 fm. living, *Cp.*

297. *Margarita cidaris*, A. Ad. n. s. Large, knobby, like thin *Turcica*, with simple pillar and small umbilicus.

298. *Margarita pupilla*, Gld. E.E.=*calostoma*, A. Ad. Strong, with sharp ribs, decussated between, and fleshy nacre. 8–15 fm. *Lyall.*

298 b. *Margarita?* var. *salmonea.* Between *pupilla* and *undulata*: salmon-tinted, sculpture fine, not decussated: sutures not waved. 6–40 fm. *Cp.*

299. *Margarita acuticostata*, n. s. Small, painting clouded: 3 sharp ribs on spire. 8–20 fm. *Cp.*

300. *Margarita inflata*, n. s. Thin, whirls very swollen; sculpture very fine; spiral hollow inside keeled umbilicus.

301. *Margarita lirulata*, n. s. Small: operc. smooth: 2 sharp principal riblets on spire: outline variable. Var. *subelevata*, raised, livid: var. *obsoleta*, sculpture evanescent: ? var. *conica*, very tall, with intercalary ribs, like *G. parcipicta.*

302. *Margarita Vahlii*, Möll. Raised, smooth: operc. with spiral rib.

303. *Margarita tenuisculpta*, ? n. s. Like *obsoleta*, but operc. ribbed.

304. *Margarita helicina*, Mont. Like the Finmark shells. Circumboreal.

	Nutt.	Jew.	B. A.	Smiths. Ins.	Ken.	Lord.	Swan.	Cooper.
305. Crucibulum spinosum....	M	B	C	DIL	—	—	—	DI
306. Crepidula aculeata......	B	—	—	—	—	—	—	—
307. —— dorsata..........	C	B	P	—	P	V	V	MD l
308. —— excavata, *var*......	—	—	—	—	—	—	—	—
309. —— adunca...........	—	B	OC	P	P	V	V	MDr
310. —— rugosa...........	B	B	C	C	—	—	—	DI
311. —— navicelloides......	M	—	C	OI	—	V	V	I
311 b. —— *var*. nummaria....	—	—	P	—	—	—	V	—
311 c. —— *var*. explanata....	C	—	M	—	—	V	V	—
312. Galerus fastigiatus......	—	—	P	—	P	V	V	—
313. —— contortus.........	—	—	—	—	—	—	—	MDI
314. Hipponyx cranioides....	—	—	—	—	—	—	V	—
315. —— antiquatus........	—	?B	—	—	—	—	—	PMI
316. —— serratus..........	—	—	—	—	—	—	—	l
317. —— tumens..........	—	B	—	—	—	—	—	MDI
318. Serpulorbis squamigerus..	B	B	C	D	—	—	—	D
319. Bivonia compacta ..[gma	—	—	—	—	—	—	V	—
320. Petaloconchus macrophra-	D	—	—	—	—	—	—	—
321. Spiroglyphus lituella....	B	—	—	C	—	—	—	—

Order PECTINIBRANCHIATA.   Suborder ROSTRIFERA.

Family *Calyptræidæ*.

305. *Crucibulum spinosum*, Sby.   Maz. Cat. no. 344.   From Southern fauna.
306. *Crepidula aculeata*, Gmel.   Maz. Cat. no. 334.   From Southern fauna.   Round the world.
307. *Crepidula ?dorsata*, Brod., var. *lingulata*, Gld. E.E.=var. *bilobata*, Maz. Cat. no. 336=*C. bilobata*, Rve.   Appears identical with the S. American shells.
308. *Crepidula excavata*, Brod.   Maz. Cat. no. 337.   S. American.
309. *Crepidula adunca*, Sby. Tank.=*solida*, Hds.=*rostriformis*, Gld. E.E.   Dark liver, rough epidermis, solid deck with produced sides. [Not *uncata*, Mke.=*rostrata*, C. B. Ad., Rve.=*adunca*, Maz. Cat. no. 338.]   Between tides, *Lord*; 10 fm. *Cp*.
310. *Crepidula rugosa*, Nutt. P. Z. S. 1856, p. 224.   Probably northern var. of *onyx*, Sby. Maz. Cat. 340, with epidermis less shaggy.
311. *Crepidula navicelloides*, Nutt.   Shape of *squama*, with nucleus of *unguiformis* (Maz. Cat. no. 342).   Rounded var. in hollow bivalves=*nummaria*, Gld.   Var. drawn out in layers like *Lessonii*=*fimbriata*, Rve.   Var. elongated in crypts, scooped by crab or bivalve=*explanata*, Gld.=*exuriata*, Nutt.=*perforans*, Val.
312. *Galerus fastigiatus*, Gld. E.E.   Like *mamillaris*, nucleus large, immersed.   Large, in 8–15 fm. *Lyall*.
313. *Galerus contortus*, n. s.   Whirls twisted: nucleus minute, prominent.   20–40 fm. *Cp*.

Family *Capulidæ*.

314. *Hipponyx cranioides*, n. s.   Large, rough, flat, intermediate between *planatus* and
315. *Hipponyx antiquatus*, Linn. Maz. Cat. no. 347.   From Southern fauna.
316. *Hipponyx serratus*, Cpr. Maz. Cat. no. 346.   From Southern fauna.
317. *Hipponyx tumens*, n. s.   Growth like *Helcion*: sculpture more open than *barbatus*.

Family *Vermetidæ*.

318. *Serpulorbis squamigerus*, Cpr. P. Z. S. 1856, p. 226 (not *Aletes*).   Large, scaly.   *Verm. anellum*, Mörch, P. Z. S. 1861, p. 359, is perhaps the young.
319. *Bivonia compacta*, n. s.   Entirely open within: but colour and growth like
320. *Petaloconchus macrophragma*, Cpr. Maz. Cat. no. 359.   From Southern fauna.
321. *Spiroglyphus lituella*, Mörch, P. Z. S. 1861, p. 154.

	Nutt.	Jew.	B.A.	Smiths. Ins.	Ken.	Lord.	Swan.	Cooper.
322. Cæcum crebricinctum....	—	—	—	—	—	—	—	MDI
323. —— Cooperi	—	—	—	—	—	—	—	DI
324. Turritella Cooperi	—	—	—	—	—	—	—	DI
325. —— Jewettii	—	B fs.	—	D ?fos.	—	—	—	—
326. Mesalia lacteola	—	—	—	—	P	V	—	—
326 b. —— var. subplanata ..	—	—	—	—	P	—	V	—
327. —— tenuisculpta	—	—	—	—	—	—	—	D
328. Cerithidea sacrata	MB	C	C	CF	—	—	—	FD
329. Bittium filosum	—	—	P	P	P	V	V	—
329 b. —— ?var. esuriens	—	B	—	—	—	—	V	MD
330. —— attenuatum........	—	—	—	M	—	—	—	—
331. —— quadrifilatum	—	—	—	D	—	—	—	D
332. —— asperum	—	B fs.	—	—	—	—	—	DI
333. —— armillatum	—	B fs.	—	—	—	—	—	D
334. —— fastigiatum	—	B	—	—	—	—	—	—
335. Litorina planaxis........	C	C	C	FDI	—	—	—	MDI
336. —— Sitchana	—	—	O	PO	P	V	V	—-

Family *Cæcidæ.*

322. *Cæcum crebricinctum*, n. s. Large, with aspect of *Elephantulum*, but very fine close annular sculpture; plug subungulate. 8–20 fm. *Cp.*
323. *Cæcum Cooperi*, n. s. Small, with 30–40 sharp narrow rings.

Family *Turritellidæ.*

324. *Turritella Cooperi*, n. s. Extremely slender, with many narrow whirls. c. *Cp.*
325. *Turritella Jewettii*, n. s. Like *sanguinea*, with very faint sculpture.
326. *Mesalia lacteola*, ? n. s. May be a local var. of the circumpolar *lactea*, with altered sculpture: distinct, *teste* Cuming.
326 b. *Mesalia* ?var. *subplanata.* Sculpture fainter: whirls flattened.
327. *Mesalia tenuisculpta*, n. s. Very small, slender, whirls rounded, lip waved. Shoal-water, *Cp.*

Family *Cerithiadæ.*

328. *Cerithidea sacrata*, Gld. E.E.= *Californica*, Nutt.+*pullata*, Gld. Variable in shape and sculpture: passes into *Mazatlanica*, Maz. Cat. no. 395.
329. *Bittium filosum*, Gld. E.E.= *Eschrichtii*, Midd. Strong, broad, grooved.
329 b. *Bittium* ? var. *esuriens.* Like starved *filosum*, very narrow, adult scarcely sculptured.
330. *Bittium attenuatum*, n. s. Like *plicatum*, A. Ad., or drawn-out *esuriens*, with threads instead of grooves.
331. *Bittium quadrifilatum*, n. s. Broad: 4 threads, equal from beginning, coiling over strong radiating ribs.
332. *Bittium asperum*, n. s. Same aspect: upper whirls with 2 strong and 2 faint keels over less prominent ribs. Bch.–40 fm. *Cp.*
333. *Bittium armillatum*, n. s. Same aspect: 3 nearly equal rows of knobs.
334. *Bittium fastigiatum*, n. s. Small, slender: apex normal: sutures indented, anterior rib strong.

Family *Litorinidæ.*

335. *Litorina planaxis*, Nutt. Phil.=*patula*, Gld. E.E. Outside plain; columella scooped.
336. *Litorina Sitchana*, Phil.=*sulcata*, Gld.=*rudis*, Coop. Rounded, flat, with spiral ribs. Var. *modesta*, Phil. (pars) has sculpture faint: *subtenebrosa*, Midd., is perhaps a degraded var. Rocks between tides, *Lord*; 8–10 fm. *Lyall* [?].

---

* These species have so peculiar a nucleus that they can scarcely rank near *Cerithium* or *Rissoa*: perhaps they are related to *Alaba.* The nucleus of *esuriens* and *attenuatum* has not been seen.

	Nutt.	Jew.	B. A.	Smiths. Ins.	Ken.	Lord.	Swan.	Cooper.
337. Litorina scutulata	—	B	PF	POFMI	P	V	V	MDI
338. ? Assiminea subrotundata	—	—	—	—	—	—	V	—
339. ? Paludinella	—	—	—	—	—	—	V	—
340. Lacuna vincta	—	—	—	—	P	—	V	—
341. —— porrecta	—	—	—	—	—	—	V	—
342. —— solidula	—	—	P	IO	P	V	V	—
342 b. —— var. compacta	—	—	—	—	—	—	V	—
343. —— variegata..........	—	—	—	—	—	—	V	—
344. —— unifasciata	—	B	B	I	—	—	—	DI
345. Isapis fenestrata	—	—	—	—	—	—	V	DI
346. —— obtusa	—	—	—	—	—	—	—	MBDI
347. Rissoina interfossa	—	—	—	—	—	—	—	MI
348. Rissoa compacta	—	—	—	—	P	—	V	. —
349. —— acutelirata	—	—	—	—	—	—	—	D
350. Alvania reticulata	—	—	—	—	—	—	V	—
351. —— filosa	—	—	—	—	—	—	V	—
352. Fenella pupoidea	—	—	—	—	—	—	—	M
353. Barleeia subtenuis	—	—	—	DI	—	—	—	DI
353 b. —— ? var. rimata	—	—	—	D	—	—	—	D
354. —— haliotiphila	—	—	—	H	—	—	—	—
355. Amphithalamus inclusus	—	B	—	—	—	—	—	D

337. *Litorina scutulata*, Gld. E.E.+*lepida*, Gld. Var.=*plena*, Gld. Small, solid, pointed, flattened, smoothish. Rocks between tides, *Lord*.

338. ? *Assiminea subrotundata*, n. s. Like a very thin *Litorina* : ashen, plain.

339. ? *Paludinella*, sp. May be an aberrant *Assiminea*.

340. *Lacuna vincta*, Mont. auct. Circumboreal.

341. *Lacuna porrecta*, n. s. Upper whirls flattened, effuse anteriorly; chink large.

341 b. *Lacuna* ? var. *effusa*. Larger, taller, more swollen.

341 c. *Lacuna* ? var. *exæquata*, same shape but flattened.

342. *Lacuna solidula*, Lov.=*sexangula*, Gld., not A. Ad.= *Modelia striata*, Gabb. Solid, variable, chink small; sometimes keeled or angular.

342 b. *Lacuna* ? var. *compacta*. Very small, narrow, orange, scarcely chinked.

343. *Lacuna variegata*, n. s. Very tall, effuse, irregular with wide chink : clouded or with zigzag stripes: like *decorata*, A. Ad.

344. *Lacuna unifasciata*, Cpr. P. Z. S. 1856, p. 205. Small, glossy, generally with a coloured keel, sometimes broken into dots. Var. *aurantiaca*, keel obsolete, resembling the chinked *Phasianellæ*. 8–10 fm. *Cp.*

345. *Isapis fenestrata*, n. s. Like *oroidea*, with sharp distant ribs.

346. *Isapis obtusa*, n. s. Whirls flattened behind : ribs swollen, uneven. 10–20 fm. *Cp.*

Family *Rissoidæ*.

347. *Rissoina interfossa*, n. s. With 5 sharp keels crossing 14 strong ribs. 8–10 fm.

348. *Rissoa compacta*, n. s. Sculptured like *Beanii*, with short broad whirls.

349. *Rissoa acutelirata*, n. s. Alvanoid : 15 sharp, distant, spiral riblets, travelling over 18 sharp distant ribs, obsolete in front.

350. *Alvania reticulata*, n. s. Open network : radiating threads travelling over 12 stronger distant spiral threads.

351. *Alvania filosa*, n. s. Turrited : pillar purple-stained : 18 close spiral striæ, passing over very faint waved riblets.

352. *Fenella pupoidea*, n. s. Variegated, truncatelloid shape. 20 fm. rare, *Cp.*

353. *Barleeia subtenuis*, n. s.= *Hydrobia* ? *ulvæ*, Maz. Cat. no. 417 ; but with normal Barleeoid operculum. On grass, *Cp.*

353 b. *Barleeia* ? var. *rimata*. Whirls more swollen : base chinked.

354. *Barleeia haliotiphila*, n. s. Longer, narrower, much smaller. On *H. splendens*.

355. *Amphithalamus inclusus*, n. g., n. s. Habit of minute *Nematura* ; labrum not contracted, but labium in adult travels forward to meet it, leaving a chamber behind. Nucleus cancellated : base bluntly ribbed.

	Nutt.	Jew.	B. A.	Smiths.	Ins.	Ken.	Lord.	Swan.	Cooper.
356. ?Amphithalamus lacunatus	—	—	—	—	—	—	—		D
357. Truncatella Californica ..	—	—	—	—	—	—	—		D
358. Jeffreysia Alderi	—	—	—	D	—	—	—		—
359. —— translucens	—	—	—	—	—	—	—		D
360. Cithna albida	—	—	—	—	—	—	—		D
361. Diala marmorea	—	—	—	II	—	—	—		MD
362. —— acuta	—	—	—	—	—	—	—		MI
363. Styliferina turrita	—	—	—	—	—	—	—		D
364. Radius variabilis........	—	?B	—	—	—	—	—		—
365. Luponia spadicea	—	C	C	—	—	—	—		DI
366. Trivia Californica	—	B	C	L	—	—	—		DI
367. —— Solandri	—	—	—	L	—	—	—		I
368. Erato vitellina..........	—	B	C	—	—	—	—		DI
369. —— columbella	—	B	C	L	—	—	—		MDI
370. Myurella simplex	—	B	—	—	—	—	—		D
371. Drillia inermis..........	—	B	C	—	—	—	—		BDI
372. —— incisa	—	—	—	—		P	—	V	—
373. —— moesta	—	B	—	—	—	—	—		D
374. —— torosa	—	—	—	M	—	—	—		M
374 b. —— ?var. aurantia	—	—	—	D	—	—	—		D

356. ? *Amphithalamus lacunatus*, n. s. Same nucleus; base chinked, not keeled. (Adult not found.)

Family *Truncatellidæ*.
357. *Truncatella Californica*, Pfr. Pneum. Viv. Suppl. vol. ii. p. 7.

Family *Jeffreysiadæ*.
358. *Jeffreysia Alderi*, Cpr. Maz. Cat. no. 420.
359. *Jeffreysia translucens*, n. s. Possibly a *Barleeia*: pillar thickened, base rounded.
360. *Cithna albida*, n. s. Very close to *C. tumens*, Maz. Cat. no. 421, but umbilicus angled, not keeled.

Family *Planaxidæ*.
361. *Diala marmorea*, n. s. Solid, glossy, clouded with red: base faintly angled.
362. *Diala acuta*, n. s. Base flattened, sharply angled: turrited. Bch.-10 fm. *Cp*.
363. *Styliferina turrita*, n. s. Minute, slender, base rounded.

Family *Oculidæ*.
364. *Radius variabilis*, C. B. Ad. Maz. Cat. no. 435. Probably exotic.

Family *Cypræidæ*.
365. *Luponia spadicea*, Gray. Like *onyx*, but light-coloured.
366. *Trivia Californica*, Gray. Small: ribs sharp, distant.
367. *Trivia Solandri*, Gray Maz. Cat. no. 441. From Southern fauna. Sta. Barb. and St. Nich. Is. common, *Cp*.
368. *Erato vitellina*, Hds. Sulph. Large, wide-mouthed: paries callous.
369. *Erato columbella*, Mke.=*leucophæa*, Gld. Maz. Cat. p. 537. Perhaps a var. of *Maugeræ*, from the tropics. 20–40 fm. c. *Cp*.

Suborder TOXIFERA. Family *Terebridæ*.
370 *Myurella simplex*, n. s. Sculpture very faint and variable: shape of *albocincta*. c. *Cp*.

Family *Pleurotomidæ*.
371. *Drillia inermis*, Hds. Sulph. Early whirls close sculptured. Beach-16 fm. living. *Cp*.
372. *Drillia incisa*, n. s. Like *inermis*: spiral sculpture grooved, not raised.
373. *Drillia mæsta*, n. s. Like large *luctuosa*: middle whirls with long transverse ribs and posterior knobs; adult obsolete.
374. *Drillia torosa*, n. s. Whirls rounder, olivaceous: with one row of strong bosses throughout: no posterior knobs.
374 b. *Drillia* ?var. *aurantia*. Orange, with sutural riblet and faint spiral sculpture.

1863.

	Nutt	Jew.	B. A.	Smiths. Ins.	Ken.	Lord.	Swan.	Cooper.
375. Drillia penicillata	—	—	—	L	—	—	—	—
376. —— cancellata	—	—	—	—	P	—	—	—
377. Mangelia levidensis	—	—	—	—	P	—	V	—
378. —— tabulata	—	—	—	—	—	—	V	—
379. —— interfossa	—	—	—	—	—	—	V	—
380. —— crebricostata	—	—	—	—	—	—	V	—
381. —— variegata..........	—	B	—	—	—	—	—	—
381 b. —— ?var. nitens	—	B	—	—	—	—	—	—
382. —— angulata	—	B	—	—	P	—	—	M
383. Bela fidicula	—	—	P	—	P	V	—	—
384. —— excurvata	—	—	—	—	P	—	—	—
385. ? Daphnella aspera	—	—	—	M	—	—	—	—
386. ? —— filosa............	—	B	—	—	—	—	—	—
387. ? —— effusa	—	—	—	—	—	—	V	—
388. Conus Californicus	—	B	C	D	—	—	—	DI
389. Obeliscus ?variegatus	—	—	—	L	—	—	—	D
390. Odostomia nuciformis....	—	—	—	—	—	—	V	—
390 b. —— ?var. avellana	—	—	—	—	—	—	V	—
391. —— satura	—	—	—	—	—	—	V	—
391 b. —— ?var. Gouldii	—	—	—	—	—	—	V	—
392. —— gravida	—	B	—	—	—	—	—	D
393. —— inflata	—	—	—	—	—	—	V	—

375. *Drillia penicillata*, n. s. Like *inermis*, with delicate brownish pencillings.

376. *Drillia* cancellata, ? n. s. Like the young of *incisa*, but nodosely cancellated.

377. *Mangelia levidensis*, n. s. Stumpy, purplish brown, with rough sculpture.

378. *Mangelia tabulata*, n. s. Stout, strongly shouldered, coarsely cancellated. Pillar abnormally twisted.

379. *Mangelia interfossa*, n. s. Like *attenuata*, delicately cancellated.

380. *Mangelia crebricostata*, n. s. Like *septangularis*, with closely set ribs.

381. *Mangelia variegata*, n. s. Small, slender, thin, zoned with brown : 9 narrow ribs, and strong spiral striæ.

381 b. *Mangelia* ?var. *nitens*. Glossy : spiral lines almost obsolete.

382. *Mangelia angulata*, n. s. Shape of *variegata*, but brown, whirls broad, angular.

383. *Bela fidicula*, Gld. E.E. Very close to *turricula*, var. 8–10 fm. *Lyall*.

384. *Bela excurvata*, n. s. Like *Trevelliana* : stumpy, Chrysalloid.

385. ?*Daphnella* aspera, n. s. Elongated, with coarse fenestration.

386. ?*Daphnella* filosa, n. s. Small, diamond-shaped, but rounded periphery ; spirally threaded.

387. ?*Daphnella* effusa, nom. prov. Thin, extremely drawn-out, sculpture faint.

Family *Conidæ*.

388. *Conus Californicus*, Hds. Sulph.=*rarus*, Gld. Chestnut, plain.

Suborder PROBOSCIDIFERA.   Family *Pyramidellidæ*.

389. *Obeliscus* ?*variegatus*, n. s. From Gulf fauna. Periphery with spiral groove. Colour-pattern clouded.

390. *Odostomia nuciformis*, n. s. Very large, solid, Tornatelloid.

390 b. *Odostomia* ?var. *avellana*. Shape of *conoidalis*.

391. *Odostomia satura*, n. s. Large, with swollen whirls like *Bithinia similis*.

391 b. *Odostomia* ?var. *Gouldii*. Taller, base gently rounded.

392. *Odostomia gravida*, Gld. Otia. Like *conoidalis*, but nucleus minute.

393. *Odostomia inflata*, n. s. Like large *dolioliformis* : with most minute spiral striulation. Farallone Is. On *Hal. rufescens*, teste Darbishire.

---

* A peculiar group of species, resembling *Clionella* (marine, teste *Stimpson*.)

† Generic position of all these doubtful : perhaps they belong to genera not yet eliminated : *filosa* resembling the Eocene forms between *Conus* and *Pleurotoma*.

	Nutt.	Jew.	B. A.	Smiths. Ins.	Ken.	Lord.	Swan.	Cooper.
394. Odostomia straminea	—	—	—	H	—	—	—	C
295. —— tenuisculpta	—	—	—	—	—	—	V	—
396. Chrysallida cincta	—	—	—	—	—	—	—	I
397. —— pumila......	—	—	—	—	—	—	—	DI
398. Dunkeria laminata	—	B	—	—	—	—	—	D
399. Chemnitzia tridentata ..	—	B	—	—	P	—	—	MD
400. —— chocolata.........	—	—	—	—	—	—	—	D
400 b.—— var. aurantia	—	B	—	—	P	—	—	—
401. —— tenuicula.........	—	B	B	—	—	—	—	D
401 b.—— ?var. subcuspidata ..	—	—	—	—	—	—	—	D
402. —— crebrifilata	—	B	—	—	—	—	—	—
403. —— torquata	—	B	—	—	P	V	—	—
403 b.—— ?var. stylina	—	B	—	—	—	—	—	M
404. —— virgo	—	B	—	—	—	—	—	—
405. Eulima micans	—	—	—	—	P	—	V	DI
406. —— compacta.........	—	—	—	—	—	—	—	D
407. —— rutila	—	—	—	—	—	—	—	M
408. —— thersites	—	B	—	—	—	—	—	—

394. *Odostomia straminea*, n. s. Like tall var. of *inflata*, with straw-coloured epidermis, not striulate.

395. *Odostomia tenuisculpta*, n. s. Like *sublirulata*, Maz. Cat. no. 487, with obsolete sculpture throughout.

396. *Chrysallida cincta*, n. s. Passing towards *Mumiola*. Radiating sculpture very faint.

397. *Chrysallida pumila*, n. s. Like *ovulum*, Maz. Cat. no. 512, but slender; spiral lines delicate.

398. *Dunkeria laminata*, n. s. Subgenus of *Chemnitzia*, with rounded whirls: typical species. Aspect of *Fenella*, finely cancellated.

399. *Chemnitzia tridentata*, n. s. Large, chestnut: 19–24 ribs, evanescent at periphery: waved interspaces with 8–10 spiral grooves: labrum with 3 teeth, hidden as in *Obeliscus*: base round.

400. *Chemnitzia chocolata*, n. s. Same size and colour: not toothed: base prolonged: crowded ribs minutely striulate between.

400 b. *Chemnitzia* ?var. *aurantia*. Intermediate between the above: orange, base round: 26 ribs, striulate between.

401. *Chemnitzia tenuicula*, Gld. Otia. Shape of *tridentata* dwarfed: whirls flatter, base prolonged, spiral grooving strong.

401 b. *Chemnitzia* ?var. *subcuspidata*. Ribs more distant, muricated at sutures.

402. *Chemnitzia crebrifilata*, n. s. Slender, whitish: with 8 spiral threads passing over 24 ribs, evanescent round base.

403. *Chemnitzia torquata*, Gld. Otia = *Vancouverensis*, Gld. Ribs truncated before periphery, leaving plain band above sutures.

403 b. *Chemnitzia* ?var. *stylina*. Like *torquata*, tapering, less swollen in front, with more ribs, band less marked.

404. *Chemnitzia virgo*, n. s. Very slender, with short, smooth base: 18 ribs, evanescent at periphery, and 8 spiral grooves.

Family *Eulimidæ*.

405. *Eulima micans*, ? n. s. Perhaps a small var. of the European *polita*. 30–40 fm. living. *Cp.*

406. *Eulima compacta*, ? n. s. Small, with blunt spire and elongated base.

407. *Eulima rutila*, ? n. s. Leiostracoid, rosy, base lengthened. Like *producta*, Maz. Cat. no. 551.

408. *Eulima thersites*, n. s. Very broad, short, twisted.

	Nutt.	Jew.	B. A.	Smiths. Ins.	Ken.	Lord.	Swan.	Cooper.
409. Scalaria Indianorum	—	—	—	—	—	—	V	—
409b. —— ?var. tincta	—	—	—	L	—	—	—	D
410. —— ?Cumingii	—	—	—	—	—	—	—	D
410b. —— ?gracilis	—	—	—	D	—	—	—	—
411. —— subcoronata	—	—	—	—	—	—	—	M
412. —— crebricostata	—	—	—	—	—	—	—	MD
413. —— bellastriata	—	—	—	—	—	—	—	M
414. Opalia borealis	—	—	P	—	—	—	V	—
415. —— ?var. insculpta	—	Bfs.	—	—	—	—	—	—
416. —— spongiosa	—	—	—	—	—	—	—	M
417. —— retiporosa	—	—	—	—	—	—	—	I
418. —— bullata............	—	B	—	—	—	—	V	—
419. Cerithiopsis tuberculata..	—	B	—	—	—	—	V	MD
420. —— columna	—	—	—	—	—	—	V	M
421. —— munita	—	—	—	—	—	—	V	—
422. —— purpurea..........	—	B	—	—	—	—	—	MD
423. —— fortior	—	B	—	—	—	—	—	—
424. —— assimilata	—	—	—	—	—	—	—	I
425. Triforis ?adversa	—	—	—	—	—	—	V	I
426. Cancellaria modesta	—	—	—	—	—	—	V	—

Family *Scalariadæ*.

409. *Scalaria Indianorum*, ? n. s. Between *Turtonis* and *communis*: like " *Georgettina*, Kien. Mus. Cum. no. 34, Brazil."

409b. *Scalaria* ?var. *tincta*. Purple-brown behind: like *regularis*, without spiral sculpture.

410. *Scalaria* ? *Cumingii*, Cpr. P. Z. S. 1856, p. 165.

410b. *Scalaria* ?*gracilis*, Sby. in Mus. Cum.

411. *Scalaria subcoronata*, n. s. Like young *communis*, with more and sharper ribs, faintly coronated when adolescent.

412. *Scalaria crebricostata*, n. s. = Mus. Cum. no. 32: 15 sharp reflexed ribs, coronated against the sutures.

413. *Scalaria bellastriata*, n. s. Shape like *pretiosa*, jun.: ribs very close, spinous at shoulder, crossed by spiral riblets.

414. *Opalia borealis*, Gld. E. E. Very close to *australis*: obsolete forms like *Ochotensis*, Midd.

415. *Opalia* (?*crenatoides*, var.) *insculpta*. Like the C. S. L. form and *crenata*, but ribs closer, without spiral sculpture, sutural holes behind the basal rib.

416. *Opalia spongiosa*, n. s. Like small, very slender *granulata*: surface riddled with deep punctures in spiral rows.

417. *Opalia retiporosa*, n. s. Sculpture in network, with deep holes. 40 fm. d. r. *Cp.*

418. *Opalia bullata*, n. s. Shape of *Rissoina*: with sutural bosses: no basal rib.

Family *Cerithiopsidæ*.

419. *Cerithiopsis tuberculata*, Mont. Fbs. & Hanl. Agrees with the British rather than with the Mazatlan form, Cat. no. 557.

420. *Cerithiopsis columna*, n. s. Very tall: nodules close, like strung figs.

421. *Cerithiopsis munita*, n. s. Stout: strongly sculptured: base evenly ribbed.

422. *Cerithiopsis purpurea*, n. s. Stained with purple: nodules fine: base finely lirate.

423. *Cerithiopsis fortior*, n. s. Sculpture open: strong basal rib.

424. *Cerithiopsis assimilata*, C. B. Ad. Maz. Cat. no. 563. With spiral keels. From Southern fauna.

425. *Triforis* ?*adversa*, Mont. Fbs. & Hanl. Agrees with British specimens. 10-40 fm. v. r. *Cp.*

Family *Cancellariadæ*.

426. *Cancellaria modesta*, n. s. Like *Trichotropis borealis*, with two slanting pits and spiral ribs travelling up the paries. See also p. 615, nos. 463, 817.

	Nutt.	Jew.	B. A.	Smiths. Ins.	Ken.	Lord.	Swan.	Cooper.
427. Trichotropis cancellata ..	—	—	P	—	P	—	V	—
428. —— inermis	—	—	—	—	—	—	V	—
429. Velutina lævigata	—	—	—	—	P	—	V	—
430. —— prolongata	—	—	—	—	—	—	V	—
431. Natica clausa	—	—	P	—	P	—	V	—
432. Lunatia Lewisii	—	C	P	P	P	—	V	D
433. —— pallida............	—	—	P	—	P	V	V	—
434. Neverita Recluziana	—	—	—	D	—	—	—	D
435. Priene Oregonensis......	—	—	P	VP	P	V	V	M
436. Ranella Californica......	—	—	—	L	—	—	—	BD
437. Mitra maura	C	—	—	I	—	—	—	DI
438. Marginella Jewettii	—	B	—	—	—	—	—	MI
439. —— subtrigona	—	B	—	—	—	—	—	—
440. —— regularis	—	B	—	—	—	—	—	MDI
441. Volutella pyriformis	—	—	—	F	—	—	—	D
442. Volvarina varia	—	B	—	—	—	—	—	DI
443. Olivella biplicata........	C	C	C	D	—	—	V	MDI
444. —— bætica............	—	B	OC	M	P	—	V	D

427. *Trichotropis cancellata*, Hds. Sulph. Sculpture strong, open. Epidermis bristly.
428. *Trichotropis inermis*, Hds. Sulph. Sculpture faint: not bristly.

Family *Velutinidæ*.

429. *Velutina lævigata*, Linn. Fbs. & Hanl. Exactly accords with British specimens. ?=*Kamtschatkana*, Desh.
430. *Velutina prolongata*, n. s. Spire very small. Labrum produced in front.

Family *Naticidæ*.

431. *Natica clausa*, Brod. & Sby. Umbilicus closed. Operc. shelly. Circumboreal.
432. *Lunatia Lewisii*, Gld. E. E. = *herculæa*, Midd. Whirls flattened behind. Abundant on beach, *Cp.*
433. *Lunatia pallida*, Br. & Sby. = *caurina*+*soluta*, Gld. Globular, compact, whitish. Boreal.
434. *Neverita Recluziana*, Petit, Rve. Large, solid, raised, with brown grooved lump on pillar. Also Guaymas.

Family *Tritonidæ*.

435. *Priene Oregonensis*, Redf. Like *cancellata*, but coarser sculpture. 6 fm. *Lyall*.
436. *Ranella Californica*, Hds. Sulph. Scarcely differs from fine specimens of *R. ventricosa*, in Mus. Cum.

Family *Fasciolaridæ*.

437. *Mitra maura*, Swains. Nutt.=*orientalis*, Gray='*Chilensis*, Gray,' Kien. Very dark and plain. Peru. Sand between rocks, l. w. *Cum.* Peru.

Family *Marginellidæ*.

438. *Marginella Jewettii*, Cpr. P. Z. S. 1856, p. 207. Like the Mogador species, somewhat shorter and broader. 10–20 fm. *Cp.*
439. *Marginella subtrigona*, n. s. Shape of *Erato columbella*.
440. *Marginella regularis*, n. s. Between *Jewettii* and *minor*, C. B. Ad. Maz. Cat. no. 587. Beach–20 fm. *Cp.*
441. *Volutella pyriformis*, n. s. Genus of Swainson (not D'Orb.) = *Closia*, Gray. Like *V. margaritula*, Maz. Cat. no. 589, but produced in front.
442. *Volvarina varia*, Sby. C. S. Lucas, W. Indies.

Family *Olividæ*.

443. *Olivella biplicata*, Sby. Tank. = *glandinaria*, Nutt. Nut-shaped.
444. *Olivella bætica*, n. s. Narrow, dull, thin: has been erroneously called *anazora*, *terginа*, *petiolita*, and *rufifasciata*.

147

	Nutt.	Jew.	B.A.	Smiths. Ins.	Ken.	Lord.	Swan.	Cooper.
445. Nassa fossata	—	—	PC	—	P	—	V	D
446. —— perpinguis	—	B	C	(?P)L	—	—	—	BDI
447. —— insculpta..........	—	—	—	—	—	—	—	I
448. —— mendica	—	C	P	POF	P	V	V	MD
449. —— Cooperi	—	—	?	—	—	—	—	DI
450. —— tegula	—	—	LC	L	—	—	—	D
451. Amycla gausapata	—	B	P	VD	P	V	V	M
452. —— ? Californiana	—	B	C	—	—	—	—	—
453. —— tuberosa	—	B fs.	—	—	—	—	V	MDI
454. ? —— chrysalloidea	—	—	—	—	—	—	—	D
455. ? —— undata	—	—	—	—	—	—	—	I
456. ? Truncaria corrugata	—	—	O	VPFMI	P	—	V	DI
457. Columbella carinata	—	B	C	—	—	—	—	MDI
457 b. —— ?var. Hindsii......	—	B	D	—	—	—	V	MJ
458. Purpura crispata	C	F	C	VPOF	P	V	V	F
459. —— canaliculata	—	—	—	VF	—	V	V	—
460. —— saxicola	—	C	C	VPF	P	V	V	FI
460 b. —— var. fuscata	—	—	?	—	—	—	V	—
460 c. —— var. emarginata ..	B	B	C	D	—	—	—	D
460 d. —— var. ostrina	—	F	C	POC	P	V	V	FD

Family *Buccinidæ.*

445. *Nassa fossata*, Gld. E. E. = *elegans*, Rve. non Desh. Large, broad, flattened spire.
446. *Nassa perpinguis*, Hds. Sulph. Same type, smaller, rounder, narrower.
447. *Nassa insculpta*, n. s. *Zeuxis*, with varix and non-reflexed callus. Spirally grooved. 40 fm. living, r. *Cp.*
448. *Nassa mendica*, Gld. E. E. + *Gibbesii*, Coop. = *Woodwardii*, Fbs. Very variable : some forms approach *trivittata.*
449. *Nassa Cooperi*, Fbs. P. Z. S. 1850, p. 273. Like *mendica*, with 7 distant ribs, and fine spiral sculpture.
450. *Nassa tegula*, Rve. Maz. Cat. no. 624. From Southern fauna.
451. *Amycla gausapata*, Gld. E. E. (Genus rearranged for Columbellids with Nassoid opercula, probably including *Alia* and *Astyris*.) Strong, solid, variegated, smooth.
452. *Amycla ? Californiana*, Gask. P. Z. S. 1851, p. 12. Whirls more swollen.
453. *Amycla tuberosa*, n. s. Very close to *minor*, Scacchi, but with different nucleus. 8–10 fm. c. *Cp.*
454. ? *Amycla chrysalloidea*, n. s. Shape of *Truncaria eurytoides*, but mouth not effuse : spirally furrowed. Shoal-water, *Cp.*
455. ? *Amycla undata*, n. s. Like stumpy, small *corrugata*, with waved sculpture. 40 fm. not r. *Cp.*
456. ? *Truncaria corrugata*, Rve. Conch. Ic. (" *Buccinum :*" " *Pisania,*" Add. May be an *Amycla.*) Large, with waved ribs and spiral striæ. Dwarfed at 40 fm. *Cp.*
457. " *Columbella*" *carinata*, Hds. Sulph. Small, turrited, smooth, with stout posterior keel. (Perhaps *Amycla.*) Beach, *Cp.*
457 b. *Columbella ?*var. *Hindsii*, Rve. Keel shorter, till it ceases, as in *gausapata.*

Family *Purpuridæ.*

458. *Purpura crispata*, Chem. = *plicata*, Mart. = *lactuca*, Esch. = *septentrionalis*, Rve. + &c. Large, strong, canal distinct, smooth or foliated.
459. *Purpura canaliculata*, Ducl. = *decemcostata*, Midd. + *attenuata*, Rve. + *analoga*, Fbs. With elegant spiral grooves. Chrysodomoid.
460. *Purpura saxicola*, Val. = *lapillus*, Coop. Like the Atlantic species, rough, pillar scooped, with brown spiral lines.
460 b. *Purpura* var. *fuscata*, Fbs. Raised thin form, dull, with faint sculpture.
460 c. *Purpura* var. *emarginata*, Desh. Short, swollen, with scaly sculpture.
460 d. *Purpura* var. *ostrina*, Gld. E. E. Short, swollen, nearly smooth.

	Nutt.	Jew.	B. A.	Smiths. Ins.	Ken.	Lord.	Swan.	Cooper.
461. Monoceros engonatum ..	B	—	C	D	—	—	—	DI
461b.—— ?var. spiratum	—	—	—	—	—	—	—	I
462. —— lapilloides	B	—	C	D	—	—	—	I
463. Ocinebra lurida and vars.	—	B fs.	—	FI	—	V	V	M jun. I
464. —— interfossa..........	—	—	—	MI	P	V	V	M jun.
465. ? —— Poulsoni	C	? B	—	L	—	—	—	—
466. Cerostoma foliatum	—	—	O	PODI fs.	P	V	V	—
467. —— Nuttallii	B	B	C	—	—	—	—	DI
468. —— monoceros	—	—	C	L	—	—	—	? D
469. Chorus Belcheri	—	—	D	I	—	—	—	D
470. Nitidella Gouldii........	—	B	—	M	P	—	V	MD
471. Pedicularia Californica ..	—	—	—	(I)	—	—	—	—
472. Pteronotus festivus......	—	C	L	D	—	—	—	D
473. Muricidea Californica....	—	—	LC	—	—	—	—	MBDI
474. Trophon multicostatus ..	—	—	—	—	P	V	V	—
475. —— Orpheus	—	—	P	—	P	V	—	—
476. —— triangulatus	—	—	—	—	—	—	—	I
477. Siphonalia Kellettii	—	—	?	D	—	—	—	BD
478. —— fuscotincta	—	B	—	—	—	—	—	—
479. Chrysodomus tabulatus ..	—	B fs.	—	—	?Pjn	V	V	? I
480. —— liratus	—	—	A	V	—	—	—	—

461. *Monoceros engonatum*, Conr.=*unicarinatum*, Sby. Brown-dotted, with sharp posterior keel, smoothish. Beach, *Cp.*

461b. *Monoceros* ?var. *spiratum* (Blainv.). Light colour; scaly; horn not developed.

462. *Monoceros lapilloides*, Conr.=*punctatum*, Gray+*brevidens*, Conr. Not shouldered: shape of *lapillus*.

463. *Ocinebra lurida*, Midd. (Genus reconstituted for Muricoid Purpurids with irregular varices.) Like *canaliculata*, brown, with swelling ribs. Beach on Cat. Is. living. *Cp.*

463b. *Ocinebra* var. *aspera*, Baird. Sculpture rough.

463c. *Ocinebra* var. *munda*. Tall, with faint sculpture.

464. *Ocinebra interfossa*, n. s. Purple-brown, with latticed sculpture.

465. ? *Ocinebra Poulsoni*, Nutt. Shape like *M. monoceros*, with brown spiral lines.

466. *Cerostoma foliatum*, Gmel.=*monodon*, Esch. Large, with winged varices.

467. *Cerostoma Nuttallii*, Conr. Smaller, pear-shaped: interstices scarcely sculptured.

468. *Cerostoma monoceros*, Sby. Spire raised : whirls rough, rounded.

469. *Chorus Belcheri*, Hds. Sulph. Very large, with irregular varices like *Trophon*. L. w. com. *Cp.*

470. *Nitidella Gouldii*, Cpr. P. Z. S. 1856, p. 208. Slender : like thin *A. gausapata*, with Purpuroid operc.

471. *Pedicularia Californica*, Newc. Small, purple, highly sculptured.

Family *Muricidæ*.

472. *Pteronotus festivus*, Hds. Sulph. Form irregular; frills reflexed.

473. *Muricidea Californica*, Hds. Sulph. Varices faintly developed. L.w.–20 fm. *Cp.*

474. *Trophon multicostatus*, Esch.=*Gunneri*, Lov. Rve. Frills spiny behind : not sculptured spirally. Circumpolar.

475. *Trophon Orpheus*, Gld. E. E. Like the last, with distant spiral riblets.

476. *Trophon triangulatus*, n. s. Typhoid shape : frills triangular, white. 60 fm. *Cp.*

477. *Siphonalia Kellettii*, Fbs. P. Z. S. 1850, p. 274. Very large, turrited, with swollen whirls. Also Japan. 1 living 6½ in. long.

478. *Siphonalia fuscotincta*, n. s. Like the same in extreme miniature.

479. *Chrysodomus tabulatus*, Baird, P. Z. S. 1863, p. 66. Large, with posterior keel, and delicate sculpture. 120 fm. dead, Cat. Is. *Cp.*

480. *Chrysodomus liratus*, Mart.=*decemcostatus*, Midd. (? Say)=*Middendorffii*, Coop. Swollen, with distant keels. Whidby's Is.

	Nutt.	Jew.	B.A.	Smiths. Ins.	Ken.	Lord.	Swan.	Cooper.
481. Chrysodomus dirus	—	—	P	VI	P	V	V	—
482. —— rectirostris	—	—	—	—	P	—	—	—
483. Fusus ambustus	—	B fs.	C	FMI	—	—	—	BDI
484. Macron Kellettii	—	—	L	L	—	—	—	?I
485. —— lividus	—	—	—	L	—	—	—	D
486. Anachis subturrita	—	—	—	—	—	—	—	D
487. ? —— penicillata........	—	B	—	—	—	—	—	DI
488. Argonauta Argo	—	—	—	—	—	—	—	I
489. Octopus punctatus	—	—	—	(FL)	?P	—	?V	I
490. Ommastrephes giganteus .	—	—	—	—	—	—	—	I
491. —— Ayresii	—	—	—	—	—	—	—	I
492. Onychoteuthis fusiformis .	—	—	—	?M	?P	—	—	I

481. *Chrysodomus dirus*, Rve.=*incisus*, Gld.=*Sitchensis*, Midd. Dark liver, with spiral grooves.
482. *Chrysodomus rectirostris*, n. s. Small, white, smooth, with straight canal.
483. *Fusus ambustus*, Gld. Otia. Close to *clavata*, Brocchi, from Mediterranean. Farallone Is. teste Darbishire; 16 fm. c. *Cp.*
484. *Macron Kellettii*, A. Ad. P. Z. S. 1853, p. 185. Large, with blunt keels. Dead, 60 fm. Cat. Is. *Cp.*
485. *Macron lividus*, A. Ad. Small, smooth.
486. *Anachis subturrita*, n. s. Aspect of small *Rissoina*. 20 faint ribs: no spiral sculpture.
487. ? *Anachis penicillata*, n. s. Small, with Metuloid sculpture. Beach–10 fm. *Cp.*

Class CEPHALOPODA.   Family *Argonautidæ.*

488. *Argonauta Argo*, Linn. auct. Like the Mediterranean form. Hundreds on Sta Cruz Is. *Cp.*

Family *Octopidæ.*

489. *Octopus punctatus*, Gabb, Proc. Cal. Ac. 1862, p. 170. S. Clemente Is. *Cp.*

Family *Loligidæ.*

490. *Ommastrephes giganteus*, D'Orb. Peru. Common at S. Clemente Is. *Cp.*
491. *Ommastrephes Ayresii*, Gabb, Proc. Cal. Ac. Hundreds on S. Clemente Is. *Cp.*
492. *Onychoteuthis fusiformis*, Gabb, Proc. Cal. Ac. 1862, p. 171. "Cape Horn, Mus. Ac." S. Clemente Is. *Cp.*

113. It remains to tabulate the shells which have been received from special localities, south of the State of California, either by the writer or by the Smithsonian Institution; *vide* Br. Assoc. Rep., par. 77.
   The promontory of Lower California has been so little explored, that the existence of a large inland fiord, in lat. 28°, was not known to the authorities. It appears that the whales have long delighted in its quiet waters; and those whalers who were in the secret carefully preserved the exclusive knowledge of so profitable a hunting-ground. All that we know at present of the molluscs of that region is from collections made at Cerros Island, by Dr. Ayres and Dr. Veitsch. They are mostly shore shells, and are sadly intermixed with an abundance of cowries, cones, strombs, and other clearly Pacific species, which throw great doubt upon those which may be truly from the coast. As it is manifestly a "hotbed of spurious species," nothing can safely be built upon the data, which present a singular intermixture of northern and southern forms. Excluding the Central Pacific importations, the lists stand as follows, the temperate species being distinguished (as in the first Report) by a *, the tropical by a †:—

*Sanguinolaria Nuttalli.
*Macoma secta.
Angulus Gouldii.
*†Heterodonax bimaculatus.
*Donax Californicus.
†Donax punctatostriatus.
*Standella ?Californica.
*Pachydesma crassatelloides.
*†Amiantis callosa.
*Chione simillima.
†Chione neglecta.
*Tapes staminea, Conr.
†Tapes grata and vars.
*Lucina Californica.
Lucina bella.
*Mytilus edulis. (One young specimen,
    perhaps from San Francisco.)
*Septifer bifurcatus.
†Pecten subnodosus, ventricosus.
*Pecten monotimeris and vars.
*Hinnites giganteus.
*†Ostrea conchaphila.
*†Anomia ?lampe.
Siphonaria æquilirata.
*†Melampus olivaceus.
Helix arrosa.
*†Bulla nebulosa.
*†Ischnochiton Magdalensis.
*Acmæa persona, var. textilis.
*Acmæa scabra, var. limatula.
*Acmæa ?spectrum, jun.
*Lottia gigantea.
*Lucapina crenulata.
*Fissurella volcano.
*Haliotis splendens.
*Haliotis Cracherodii.
*Pomaulax undosus.
Callopoma tessellatum = Fokkesii.

*Trochiscus Norrisii.
*Omphalius ?fuscescens.
*Omphalius aureotinctus.
†Crucibulum imbricatum.
*†Crucibulum spinosum.
†Crepidula arenata and var.
†Cerithium uncinatum.
*Cerithidea pullata.
†Cerithidea Montagnei.
*Litorina planaxis.
Luponia sp. ind., jun.
†Trivia Solandri.
*Trivia Californica.
Drillia penicillata.
Myurella, sp.
*†Neverita Recluziana.
†Natica Maroccana.
*Scalaria (Ind. var.) tincta.
*Bezoardica abbreviata.
†Leucozonia cingulata.
†Strigatella tristis.
*Olivella biplicata.
*Purpura ostrina, vars.
†Purpura biserialis.
Monoceros lugubre.
†Vitularia salebrosa.
Cerostoma monoceros.
Ocinebra Poulsoni.
Chorus Belcheri.
†Columbella fuscata.
*Columbella carinata.
†Strombina gibberula.
†Anachis coronata.
*†Nassa tegula.
†Nassa complanata.
Macron Kellettii.
*Macron lividus.

The shells of Margarita Bay, on the Pacific coast of Lower California, in lat. 24°, have become known through W. Harper Pease, Esq., of Honolulu, Sandwich Islands. Through his labours we are likely soon to be favoured with accurate accounts of the distribution of species in the various parts of the Pacific Ocean. Already his researches have greatly enriched our knowledge of the quaint fauna of the Sandwich Islands, from which he has eliminated the spurious species, and added those erroneously ascribed to California by previous naturalists. The principal trade from these islands is with San Francisco; and "the coast," in Mr. Pease's writings, signifies the coast of California or (generally) of Western America. Many of our best specimens of rare West-coast shells have been received from him, and in remarkably fresh preservation. The Margarita Bay species were obtained by one of his trained collectors, and are as follows :—

Martesia intercalata.
Saxicava pholadis.
Solecurtus violascens.
Hiatula compacta.
*Tellina secta.
Strigilla carnaria (pink).
Semele Californica.

Donax punctatostriatus.
Dosinia ponderosa.
Callista chionæa.
Callista vulnerata (?=tricolor, Pse.).
Chione succincta
Chione gnidia.
Tapes grata.

*Tapes staminea.
Chama frondosa.
Cardium procerum.
Liocardium elatum.
Modiola capax.
Modiola Brasiliensis.
Lithophagus attenuatus.
Barbatia gradata.
Pecten ventricosus.
Ostrea Virginica (Maz. Cat.).
*Ostrea lurida, var.
Ostrea conchaphila.
Ostrea amara.
Siphonaria æquilirata (=leviuscula,
    Sby., teste Cuming).
Siphonaria gigas.
*Helix areolata, Fbs. (The only land-
    shell received from the Bay.)
Dentalium tetragonum, Sby.
Dentalium semipolitum.
Dentalium lacteum, Phil.
Acmæa strigatella.
Acmæa atrata.
Gadinia reticulata.
Calliostoma versicolor.
*Chlorostoma gallina.
*Chlorostoma aureotinctum.
Nerita scabricosta.
Nerita Bernhardi.
Crucibulum spinosum.
Crucibulum imbricatum.

Crepidula onyx.
Crepidula excavata.
Galerus conicus.
Cerithium stercus muscarum.
Pyrazus incisus and var.
Rhinoclavis gemmata.
Cerithidea Mazatlanica.
Litorina fasciata.
Litorina aspera, var.
Conus "reticulatus" (Pease). Dead.
Conus "emarginatus" (Pease). Dead
Conus interruptus.
Neverita Recluziana.
Polinices bifasciata.
Cancellaria urceolata.
Cancellaria goniostoma.
"Cypræcassis testiculus" [perhaps
    tenuis].
Malea ringens.
Priene nodosa.
Oliva subangulata.
Oliva porphyria.
Purpura patula.
Purpura biserialis.
*Purpura ostrina. [Normal, living.]
Vitularia salebrosa.
Monoceros lugubre, var.
Cerostoma monoceros.
Nassa tegula.
Siphonalia anomala.
Phyllonotus nigritus.

In the above list, the only strictly Californian species are those marked with a *.

The following species have been received from La Paz, besides those tabulated in Major Rich's list, p. 541, in the C. S. L. list, p. 619, and the B. A. Rep. p. 352. It is clear that the fauna of the district is essentially tropical, and remarkably free from Californian species.

Dentalium semipolitum.
Turritella punctata.
Modulus cerodes.
Olivella fulgida, Lieut. Trowbridge [teste W. Cooper; but probably added by
    him accidentally from his W. African collections. It has not been received
    from any other West-coast source].
Siphonalia modificata. Dead.

A very interesting series of shells were collected at Guaymas and Pinacati Bay, by Capt. Stone and Mr. Sloat. The latter gentleman affixed MS. names to those which he regarded as new. They were in remarkably beautiful condition, the bivalves having an unusually porcellanous aspect, and many of the species presenting local peculiarities.

Mulinia carinulata, Desh.,= Mactra modesta, Sloat MS.
Dosinia ponderosa. Very large.
Chione fluctifraga, Sby.,= V. Cortezi, Sloat MS. [=gibbosula (Desh.), Rve.,=
    callosa, Sby., non Conr.].
Chione succincta, Val.,= Californiensis, Brod.,= V. crassa, Sloat MS. [Very
    variable in sculpture; also, with the last, varies greatly in shape, some of the
    specimens being much produced, others rounded.]
Chione gnidia, Brod. Passing into amathusia.

Chione pulicaria, Sby., var.,= *V. Pinacatensis*, Sloat MS. Sculpture pressed
smooth in the middle.
Cardium elatum. Fine.
Cardium procerum. Fine.
Modiola capax. "Choros." Also Sta. Iñez Bay.
Modiola Brasiliensis. (Typical.)
Byssoarca Pacifica.
Ostrea conchaphila et *amara*, Maz. Cat. 215.
Chiton (Lophyrus) Stokesii. Also San Salvador, *Capt. Dow.*
Callopoma fluctuatum.
Bivonia contorta.
Turritella goniostoma.
Turritella tigrina (light var.),= *leucostoma*, Val.
Cerithidea albonodosa. Common. [Probably a var. of *Mazatlanica.*]
Strombus gracilior. Also Mulege Bay.
Neverita Recluziana. [Operc. strong, horny.]
Ranella triquetra. [Operc. sub-Buccinoid, oval; nucleus internal, near middle
of labrum; scar with few ridges, as in *Purpura.*]
Oliva angulata. Not rare.
Oliva Cumingii, very callous var.
Agaronia testacea.
Monoceros lugubre. Very tall var.
Phyllonotus nigritus. Very large, of form described by Philippi, with Pholads
in situ. Agiobampo Bay.
Phyllonotus bicolor. [Operc. thin, without frills or raised layers; of uniform
colour.] Also Angeles Bay.

To these may be added, from a second voyage by Capt. Stone to the
northern part of the Gulf of California, and in equally good condition—

Arca grandis. Agiobampo Bay.
Callista semilamellosa. Agiobampo Bay.
Lozaria pectunculus (teste Cuming). St. Luis Bay.
Cardium consors. St. Luis Bay.
Avicula Peruviana. Mulege Bay.
Lucina tigerrina. Very fine. San Marcos Island.
Margaritiphora fimbriata. "Topo."
Janira dentata [= *excavata*, Val.]. "Caballito del mar," St. Luis Bay.
Bulla nebulosa. "Huevitos."
Glyphis inæqualis. St. Luis Bay.
Crucibulum imbricatum. St. Luis Bay.
Cypræa exanthema. (Large.) Cape de Haro.
Myurella variegata. Mulege Bay.
Solarium granulatum et var. *quadriceps.* Agiobampo Bay.
Polinices bifasciata. Angeles Bay.
Cypræcassis tenuis [= *Marsenæ*, Kien.]. Carmen Island.
Harpa crenata. Very fine. Mulege Bay.
Bezoardica abbreviata. Mulege Bay.
Ficula decussata. Angeles Bay.
Pyrula patula. Agiobampo Bay.
Malea ringens. Lobos Island.
Argonauta hians. 1 fine sp. Upper part of Gulf of California.

To the **Guaymas** fauna must be added, from Dr. Gould's portion of the
same collection, "*Pecten pyxidatus*" [?=*subcrenatus*, jun.). Also from the
collection of the Calif. Ac. Nat. Sc., *Nassa nodocincta*, A. Ad. [Galapagos,
Cuming]. On comparing these lists with the shells given in B. A. Rep.
p. 352 (in which the *Venus* quoted is not "*staminea*, Conr.," but a southern
species), it will be seen that the fauna of the upper part of the Gulf, as far
north as it has been explored, is essentially tropical. The *Chione fluctifraga*

and *C. succincta*, however, and the *Polinices Recluziana* indicate a connexion
with California which may have been, at a previous age, more direct than at
present.

114. (See first Report, pars. 79–83.) Acapulco being notorious for the
exotic species quoted in its fauna, it is desirable to examine all authentic
collections from that prolific locality. The Smithsonian series were obtained by Dr. Newberry * (*N.*), after his Pacific R. R. Explorations (*vide*
p. 593); by Mr. Belcher (*B.*); and by the Rev. J. Rowell (*R.*), who obtained
them principally from the valves of the large oysters. The private collections of Judge Cooper, Col. Jewett (*J.*), and other American naturalists have
also afforded valuable information. The species from these various sources,
which were also found by Mr. Xantus, are tabulated with his Cape St. Lucas
series, *anteâ*, pp. 619–626. The following have not been obtained from the
northern localities :—

Corbula nuciformis, *J.*
Corbula ovulata, and smooth var., *B., J.*
Machæra patula, var., *N.* [Surely im-
    ported.]
Sanguinolaria miniata, *J., N., B.*
Tellina princeps, *B.*; punicea, *N., B.*;
    opercularis, *N.*
Strigilla carnaria, pale and crimson vars.,
    N., B.
Semele proxima, *J.*; pulchra, *J., N.*;
    venusta, *J.*
Donax carinatus, *J., N.*; rostratus, *J.*;
    transversus, *N.*
Trigona Hindsii, *J.*
Mactrella carinata, *Lam.*, = alata, *Spengl.*,
    N. [Perhaps imported.]
Dosinia Annæ, *N.*
Callista circinata, *J.*; semilamellosa, *N.,
    B.*; spinosissima, *B.*
Chione amathusia, *N.*
Rupellaria foliacea, *R.*
Petricola ventricosa, *R.*
Chama corrugata, *R.*
Cardium ?aculeatum, jun., *N.* [proba-
    bly from ballast]; graniferum, *N.*
Lucina ?pectinata, var., *J.* [More like
    imbricatula, W. I.; perhaps Jamaican.]
Diplodonta semiaspera, *R.*
Felania tellinoides, var., *J.* [More like
    subglobosa, W. I.; perhaps Jamaican.]
Corbicula ?convexa, 1 worn valve, *N.*
Scapharca bifrons, *N.*; labiata, *B.*
Noëtia reversa, *J., B.*
Argina brevifrons, *N.*
Axinæa parcipicta [=multicostata],
    J., N.; pectenoides, *J.*; inæqualis, *J.*
Lima angulata, *J.*
Ostrea megodon [P.Z.S.1845,p.106], *N.*
Anomia lampe, *J.*

Tornatina infrequens, *B.*
Dentalium ?hexagonum, var., *B.*
Fissurella nigropunctata, *J.*; ?macro-
    trema, *J.*; alba, jun., *B.* (1 worn sp.)
Calliostoma lima, *var.* æquisculpta, *N.*;
    Leanum, *J.*
Senectus squamigerus, *J.*
Galerus conicus, *N.*; mamillaris, *N.*
Crepidula nivea, *R.*; incurva, *N.*
Turritella Banksii, *N.*; leucostoma, *B.*
Ampullaria Columbiensis, *R.* [West
    Mexico; locality uncertain.]
Truncatella Bairdiana, *B.*
Radius avena, *J.*
Cypræa exanthema, *N.*
Luponia timbriolata, *Beck*, *N.* [Pro-
    bably imported, and perhaps an im-
    perfectly developed form of *semipo-
    lita*, Migh.]
Terebra tuberculosa, *N.*
Drillia incrassata, *B.*; eburnea, n. s.,
    R. [W. Mexico; locality uncertain.]
Mangelia subdiaphana, *J.*
Conus interruptus, *Br. & Sby., B.*; ma-
    hogani, *N.*; puncticulatus, *N.*
Eulima hastata, *R.*
Eulima, *like* yod, *R.*
Eulimella, sp. (worn), *B.*
Chemnitzia tenuilirata, *B.*
Fasciolaria, sp. [size of *tulipa*, but with
    row of knobs and serrated lip], *N.*
Latirus castaneus, *N.*
Volvarina ?fusca, *J.* [More regularly
    cylindrical than the W. I. specimens,
    broader in proportion near suture
    and at base, spire much shorter; but
    locality uncertain.]
Oliva Julietta, *B.* 1 worn sp. [proba-
    bly imported]; ?kaleontina, dead, *N.*

* The collections of Dr. Newberry passed principally into the hands of Dr. E. Fore-
man, late of Washington, who kindly presented a series to the Mus. Smiths.

Agaronia testacea, *N.*
Rhizocheilus madreporarum. 2 living sp. on coral, *J.*
Columbella uncinata,*J.*; humerosa, n. s., *R.*; varians, var., *N.* [?Imported from Sandw. Is.]

Nassa collaria, *N.*; ambigua, *Mont.*, teste *Hanl., N.* [Probably imported from W. I.]
Anachis coronata, *N.*; Californica, *J.*
Muricidea alveata, *J.*
Phyllonotus brassica, *N.*

The following species are part of a collection received at the Smithsonian Inst. from Real Llejos, and fill up gaps which existed in the Central American fauna at the time of the first Report :—

Discina Cumingii.
Trigona Hindsii.
Hemicardium obovale.
Crassatella gibbosa.
Kellia suborbicularis.
Barbatia mutabilis.
Noëtia reversa.
Axinæa ?multicostata.
Fissurella rugosa.
Phasianella perforata.
Omphalius viridulus.
Hipponyx barbatus.

Cæcum liratocinctum.
Cæcum læve.
Cerithium interruptum, var.
Barleeia subtenuis.
Aricia punctulata.
Terebra strigata.
Cerithiopsis assimilata.
Triforis alternata.
Olivella gracilis.
?Nitidella millepunctata.
Northia pristis.
Pisania sanguinolenta.

The collections received at the Smithsonian Inst. from Panama consist, in the main, of species already tabulated from that region. The following, however, are new to that well-searched portion of the fauna :—

Tellina striata (teste Cuming), Rowell, Pease.
Tellina (Angulus) amplectans, n. s., Rowell, Pease.
Adula stylina. { Californian species: either ballast or error in num-
Pecten æquisulcatus, jun. { bering: Rowell.
Litorina. Small spotted species, n. s., teste Cuming, but appears identical with the W. Indian: probably imported: Rowell.
Fluminicola, sp., Rowell.
Drillia albolaqueata, n. s., Rowell.
Natica catenata, Rowell.
Cuma costata, Rowell.

115. The Pulmonates of the Pacific slope have not formed a special study with the writer of this Report, as they were already in the abler hands of Messrs. Binney, Bland, and other eminent Transatlantic naturalists. The opinions of Mr. Binney as to synonymy, &c., with descriptions of new species and details of those previously known, were given in papers published in the 'Proc. Ac. Nat. Sc. Phil.' as follows:—" Descriptions of American Land Shells," Feb. 1857; "Notes on American Land Shells," Oct. 1857, May 1858, Nov. 1858, July 1859 : and also in the 'Proc. Bost. N. H. S.,' " Description of two supposed new species of American Land Shells," Apr. 1857. These are embodied in ' The Terrestrial Air-Breathing Molluscs of the United States and the adjacent Territories of North America,' vol. iv., by W. G. Binney, Boston, 1859. It was first printed in the 'Boston Journal of Natural History,' vol. vii., and is intended as a Supplement to the great treatise by his father, vols. i.-iii., on the same subject. It is impossible to speak in too high terms of commendation of the manner in which this work has been prepared and executed, and of the beautiful figures drawn by Otto Köhler. The more matured views of the author were embodied in the ' Check-List of the Terrestrial Gasteropoda of North America,' published by the Smithsonian Inst., June 1860, of which a second edition was soon issued. The species were divided into three series,—(1) those of the Pacific coast,

155

from the extreme north to Mazatlan; (2) those of eastern **N. A.**, from the boreal regions to the Rio Grande; (3) those found in Mexico, to which sixteen from the first series are added. The freshwater Pulmonates are catalogued by the same most industrious author, in the 'Check-List of the Fluviatile Gasteropoda of N. America,' which contains the *Melaniadæ, Paludinidæ, Ampullariadæ, Valvatidæ,* and *Limnæidæ;* the West Coast species being distinguished by the letter **W**, and the Mexican by **M**. Mr. Binney next undertook a monograph of the *Paludinidæ*, &c., the proofs of which were widely distributed in 1862. Afterwards, assisted by the extensive series of specimens received from the Smithsonian Museum, and with access to those of the principal public and private collections in the U. S., and with the benefit of Say's types preserved in the Acad. Nat. Sc. Phil., he prepared a preliminary synopsis of the *Limnæidæ*, with full synonymy, proofs of which were issued by the Smithsonian Inst., May 4th, 1863. Last of all, under date Dec. 9, 1863, the Smithsonian Inst. has distributed proof copies of a complete 'Synopsis of the Species of Air-Breathing Molluses of N. A., as eliminated from their synonyms by Mr. Binney'*. Of all these works the author not only sent the earliest slip-proofs to assist in the preparation of this Report, but in several instances took the pains to write separately what related to the W. coast, and even sent the manifold-duplicate of part of the printer's copy. It is not considered necessary to tabulate each of these publications separately, as they can easily be obtained by post, on application to Professor Henry, Washington, D.C. The following list embodies—(1) the classification and nomenclature of Dec. 9th, 1863; (2) the synonymy as given in previous synopses; and (3) the localities and authorities supplied by Mr. Binney in MS. The following reservation requires attention:—" As a mere proof, which will undoubtedly receive many corrections, this list should not be quoted as authority, or referred-to as a published work."

Mr. Binney's Arrangement of the West Coast Pulmonates.

† The species thus marked have not been seen by Mr. Binney.

PHANEROPNEUMONA.

ECTOPHTHALMA. (None known in the region.)

OPISTHOPHTHALMA. Fam. *Truncatellidæ.*

1. *Truncatella Californica,* Pfr., + *T. gracilenta,* Gld. S. Diego, *Cooper.* [Comp. Maz. Cat. no. 423.]

PULMONATA.

GEOPHILA. § 1. *Vermivora.* Fam. *Oleacinidæ.*

†2. *Glandina (Glandina) turris,* Pfr. (= *Achatina* = *Oleacina,* Pfr.) W. Mexico. Maz. Cat. no. 231.

3. *Glandina (Glandina) Albersi,* Pfr. (= *Achatina,* Pfr.)., + *G. Albersi,* var. *turrita,* Cpr. W. Mexico. Maz. Cat. no. 230.

* The first Transatlantic attempt to revise the genera of N. A. *Helicidæ* was made by Mr. Bland, in his " Remarks on Classifications of N. A. *Helices* by European authors, and especially H. and A. Adams and Albers," printed in the 'Annals of the Lyceum of Nat. Hist. N. York,' Oct. 1863. In an addendum, he gives a list of the Pacific species, with an account of two "genera" not represented in the eastern division. Mr. Binney, continuing Mr. Bland's labours, issues the species for the most part in the trinomial nomenclature, which now appears to be taking the place of the Linnean binomial system. No attempt is here made to review the work, as the writer felt justified in doing with reference to marine shells; the only alterations made consisting of corrections in some of the citations with which he happened to be more familiar.

§ 2. *Phyllovora.* Fam. *Helicidæ.*

Subfam. *Vitrininæ.*

+4. *Vitrina Pfeifferi*, Newc. Carson Valley, Cal., *Newcomb.*
5. *Binneya notabilis*, Cp. Catalina Island, Cal., *Cooper.*
6. *Macrocyclis Newberryana*, Bin. S. Diego, common, *Newberry.*
7. *Macrocyclis Vancouverensis*, Lea, *Helix V.*, Lea, Trosch., Pfr., Gld., Rve.,= *H. vellicata*, Fbs., Rve., Pfr.,+*H. concava*, Binn. VANCOUVER TO CALIFORNIA :—Columbia R., *Nuttall, U. S. E. E.*; Puget Sound, *U. S. E. E.*; Vancouver, *B. N. P. B. S.*; Oregon City, *Newberry*; California, *Trowbridge*; St. Joseph's R., 2nd Camp.
7b. *Macrocyclis* [?var.] *sportella**, Gld. PUGET SD. TO S. DIEGO :—Puget Sd., *U. S. E. E.*; Fort Umpqua, Oregon ; S. Diego, *Ives, Newberry* ; S. Francisco, Mus. Cal. Ac. ; Contra Costa Co., *Thomson.* "Animal solitary."

Subfam. *Helicinæ.*

8. *Helix (Patula) strigosa*, Gld. INTERIOR BASIN ; N. MEXICO TO BRIT. AM. : —Int. of Oregon, *U. S. E. E.*; Cañon Largo, Rio Pedro, N. M., *Newberry.*
9. *Helix (Patula) Cooperi*, Bin. California.
10. *Helix (Patula) Mazatlanica*, Pfr. Mazatlan.
11. *Helix (Polygyra) acutedentata*, Bin.,+*H. Loisa*, Bin. Guaymas. Mazatlan, *Gambel.*
12. *Helix (Polygyra) ventrosula*, Pfr. [No locality given : not " w." in Check-Lists.]
13. *Helix (Polygyra) polygyrella*, Bland. " w." [teste Check-List, not in MS.]
14. *Helix (Stenotrema) germana*, Gld. Oregon, *U. S. E. E.*
15. *Helix (Triodopsis) Mullani*, Bland. WASHINGTON TERRITORY AND OREGON : —St. Joseph's River, 1st Camp.
16. *Helix (Triodopsis) loricata*, Gld., Pfr.,=*H. Lecontei*, Lea. Sacramento River, *U. S. E. E.*
17. *Helix (Mesodon) Columbiana*, Lea, Trosch., Rve., Pfr.,+*H. labiosa*, Gld., Pfr. VANCOUVER TO OREGON :—Ft. Vancouver, *Nuttall* ; Ft. George, *U.S.E.E.*; Nootka Sound, *Hinds* ; Astoria, *Drayton* ; Oregon City, *Newberry.*
18. *Helix (Mesodon) devia*, Gld., Pfr.,=*H. Baskervillei*, Pfr., Rve. Puget Sound, *U. S. E. E.*; Oregon.
19. *Helix (Aglaia) fidelis*, Gray, Müll., Rve., Pfr.,=*H. Nuttalliana*, Rve., Trosch., Gld. VANCOUVER TO OREGON :—Puget Sound, Columbia River, *U. S. E. E.*; Esquimault Harb., *Lord* ; Umpqua Valley, Or., and San Francisco, *Newberry* ; De Fuca, *Gibbs* ; Oregon City, *Shimard* ; Ft. Steilacoom, *Suckley.*
20. *Helix (Aglaia) infumata*, Gld. San Francisco, *Bigelow.*
21. *Helix (Arianta) arrosa*, Gld., =*H. æruginosa*, Gld. (nom. preoc.). OREGON, CALIFORNIA :—San Francisco, *Bigelow, Samuels*; Petaluma and Columbia River, *Newberry.*
22. *Helix (Arianta) Townsendiana*, Lea, Trosch., Rve., Pfr., Gld.,+*H. pedestris* +*ruida*, Gld. OREGON AND CALIFORNIA :—Wahlamat River, *Nuttall, Townsend, U. S. E. E.*; Nisqually, *Dyes.*; Puget Sound, *Kennerley.*
23. *Helix (Arianta) tudiculata*, Binn. WASHINGTON TERRITORY TO CALIFORNIA: —San Diego, *Newberry.*
24. *Helix (Arianta) Nickliniana*, Lea,=*H. Californiensis*, Rve., Pfr. (non Lea), =*H. arboretorum*+*nemorivaga*, Val.—Var. =*H. anachoreta*, Binn. "Widely distributed, but solitary," *Thompson.* CALIFORNIA :—Sacramento River, *U. S. E. E.* ; San Francisco, *Bigelow* ; Tomales, *Newberry.*
25. *Helix (Arianta) redimita*, Binn. (jun.),=*H. Nickliniana*, var. Binn. (sen.). California.

* In the Check-List of Dec. 9th, *sportella* does not appear. It is generally treated by Mr. Binney as a small variety of *Vancouverensis*, with stronger radiating and spiral lines ; but in the MSS. sent for publication in this Report it takes rank as a species. Mr. Bland considers the two identical ; yet in Add. Gen. the form is thus divided :—" *Iberus (Campylæa) sportella*, in fam. *Helicidæ*," and " *Discus Vancouverensis*, in fam. *Stenopidæ*." In Albers it is divided as " *Macrocyclis vellicata*," " *M. Vancouverensis*," and " *Helix (Patula) sportella*."

26. *Helix (Arianta) intercisa*, Binn. (jun.),= *H. Nicklinana*, var. Binn. (sen.), Oregon.

†27. *Helix (Arianta) exarata*, Pfr.   California.

†28. *Helix (Arianta) reticulata*, Pfr.   California.

†29. *Helix (Arianta) ramentosa*, Gld.   California, *Newcomb*.

†30. *Helix (Arianta) Ayresiana*, Newc.   Northern Oregon.

†31. *Helix (Arianta) Bridgesii*, Newc.   San Pablo, California, *Newcomb*.

†32. *Helix (Arianta) Carpenteri*, Newc.   Tulare Valley, California.   [Not *Carpenteriana*, Bland; Florida.]

¶ 33. *Helix (Arianta) Californiensis*, Lea, Trosch., Dekay (non auct.),= *H. vincta*, Val., Rve., Pfr.   CALIFORNIA :—Interior of Cal, *U. S. E. E.*; Monterey, *Ives*.

†34. *Helix (Arianta) Mormonum*, Pfr.   Mormon Is., California.

35. *Helix (Arianta) Dupetithouarsi*, Desh., Rve., Pfr., + *H. Oregonensis*, Trosch., Dekay, Pfr.   WASHINGTON TERRITORY TO CALIFORNIA.   Interior of Cal., *U. S. E. E.* ; Puget Sound, *Dyes*. ; Klamath Lake and Benicia, *Newberry* ; Tulan Lake, Cal. ; Monterey, *Trowbridge* ; San Diego, *Ives*.

†36. *Helix (Arianta) Traskii*, Newc.   Los Angelos, California, *Newcomb*.

37. *Helix (Arianta) Kellettii*, Fbs., Rve., Pfr.   Sta. Barbara, *Kellett* and *Wood* ; San Diego, teste Gould.

38. *Helix (Arianta) Pandoræ*, Fbs., Rve., Pfr.,= *H. damascenus*, Gld.   Sta. Barbara, *Kellett* and *Wood* ; Desert East of California, Mus. Newcomb.

39. *Helix (Arianta) levis*, Pfr.,+var. β.   Columbia River.

40. *Helix (Euparypha) areolata*, Sby., Pfr., Phil., Rve.,+vars. β. γ.   PENINSULA OF LOWER CALIFORNIA.   [Margarita Bay, *Pease.*]

†41. *Columna (Rhodea) Californica*, Pfr.   [*Achatina*, Pfr., Rve.]

Subfam. *Orthalicinæ*.

42. *Bulimulus (Liostracus* [not *Leiostraca*, Add.]) *Ziegleri*, Pfr.   Mazatlan, *Reigen*.

[†43. *Bulimulus Mexicanus* ‡, Lam., Deless., Pfr., Rve. (non Val.),= *Cochlogena vittata*, Fér.   Mazatlan, *Reigen*.]

44. *Bulimulus (Mesembrinus) pallidior*, Sby.,= *B. vegetus*, Gld., teste Cum., Binn.   SAN DIEGO TO CAPE ST. LUCAS :—C. S. Lucas, *Xantus*.

45. *Bulimulus (Mesembrinus) excelsus*, Gld. (text),= *B. elatus*, Gld. (fig.).   SAN DIEGO TO CAPE ST. LUCAS :—C. S. Lucas, *Xantus*.

46. *Bulimulus (Mesembrinus) inscendens*, Binn.   LOWER CALIFORNIA :—Margarita Bay, and C. S. Lucas, *Xantus*.

†47. *Bulimulus (Thaumastus) Californicus*, Rve.

†48. *Bulimulus (? Mormus) sufflatus*, Gld.,= *B. vesicalis*, Gld. (nom. preoc.).   LOWER CALIFORNIA.

49. *Bulimulus (? Mormus) pilula*, Binn.   LOWER CALIFORNIA :—Todos Santos Mission, Margarita Is., *Xantus*.

50. *Bulimulus (Scutalus) proteus*, Brod.   Cape St. Lucas, *Xantus*.

51. *Bulimulus (Scutalus) Xantusi*, Binn.   Cape St. Lucas, *Xantus*.

52. *Bulimulus (Peronæus* [non *Peronæa*, Poli]) *artemisia*, Binn.   Cape St. Lucas, *Xantus*.

53. *Orthalicus (Orthalicus) zebra*, Müll., Pfr.   Mazatlan, *Reigen*. }   Also Eastern

53b. *Orthalicus (Orthalicus) undatus*, Fér., Pfr. §   " Mazatlan." }   slope.

Subfam. *Pupinæ*.

†54. *Pupa (Pupilla) Rowellii*, Newc.   San Francisco, *Rowell*.

†55. *Pupa (Pupilla) Californica*, Row.   San Francisco, *Rowell*.

56. *Pupa (Leucochila) chordata*, Pfr.   Cinaloa, Mexico.

---

* See also Dr. Newcomb's new species, tabulated in pp. 609, 633.

‡ Included among the doubtful species by Mr. Binney ; but the shell so named in the Maz. Cat., no. 234 (perhaps erroneously), was certainly found on opening the Mazatlan boxes by Mr. Archer.

§ Mr. Binney follows Pfr., in his later works, in separating these ? varieties.   The shells in the Reigen Collection were clearly conspecific.   *Vide* Maz. Cat., no. 232.

Subfam. *Succininæ*.

†57. *Succi.ua* * (*Succinea*) *Hawkinsi*, Baird. British Columbia, *Lord*.

†58. *Succinea* (*Succinea*) *cingulata*, Fbs. Mazatlan, *Kellett* and *Wood*.

59. *Succinea* (*Succinea*) *rusticana*, Gld. OREGON AND CALIFORNIA:—Oregon, U. S. E. E.; Ocogo Creek, California, *Williamson*.

60. *Succinea* (*Succinea*) *Nuttalliana*, Lea. "Scarcely differs from *S. ovalis*, Hudson River," *Gld*. OREGON AND CALIFORNIA:—Lewis's River, Or., *Nuttall*; Interior of Oreg., *U. S. E. E.*; Wright's Lake, Rhell's Lake, Cal., *Newberry*.

61. *Succinea* (*Succinea*) *Oregonensis*, Lea. " Resembles *S. aurea*," Gld. OREGON AND CALIFORNIA:—Oregon, *Nuttall*. San Francisco, *Rowell*.

Subfam. *Limacinæ*.

62. *Limax* ‡ (*Amalia*) *Columbianus*, Gld. PUGET SOUND TO SAN FRANCISCO:— Puget Sound, *U. S. E. E.*, *Dyes*: Oregon City and Cape Flattery, *Williamson*; San Francisco and Port Oxford, *Trowbridge*: Nisqually, *Case*.

Fam. *Arionidæ*.

Subfam. *Arioninæ*.

63. *Arion* (*Lochea*) *foliolatus*, Gld. Puget Sound, *U. S. E. E., Pickering*.

Subfam. *Zonitiæ*.

64. *Zonites* § (*Ægopis*) *cultellata*, Thoms. " Closely resembles the Dalmatian *H. albanica* and *acies*." Contra Costa Co., Cal., common, *Thomson*.

Fam. *Onchidiadæ*.

65. *Onchidium Carpenteri*, Binn. Cape St. Lucas, *Xantus*.

LIMNOPHILA. Fam. *Auriculidæ*.

Subfam. *Melampinæ*.

66. *Melampus olivaceus*, Cpr. SAN DIEGO TO MAZATLAN:—Mazatlan, *Reigen*; San Diego, *Blake, Cooper*.

67. *Pedipes lirata*, Binn. LOWER CALIFORNIA:—C. S. Lucas, *Xantus*; San Diego, *Cooper*.

Fam. *Limnæidæ*.

Subfam. *Limnæinæ*.

68. *Limnæa* (*Limnæa*) *stagnalis*, Linn.,+*L. jugularis*, Say, Hald., De Kay, Küst., Binn. (1st list),+*L. appressa*, Say, Hald., De Kay, Küst., C. B. Ad.,+*L. speciosa*, Ziegl. EUROPE, ASIA, AMERICA:—Rhett Lake, California, *Newberry*; Ruby Valley and S. Utah, *Captain Simpson*. Fort Simpson and Hudson's Bay, common; throughout British America and northern tier of U. S., from Vermont to Pacific, teste Binn. [Var.=*H. fragilis*, Linn., teste Hanl., Ips. Linn. Conch. p. 385; non Rve., Binn. (1st list).]

69. *Limnæa* (*Limnæa*) *lepida*, Gld. Lake Vancouver, *U. S. E. E.*

70. *Limnæa* (*Limnophysa*) *reflexa*, Say, Hald., De Kay, Küst.,+*L. elongata*, Say, *L. umbrosa*, Say, Hald., De Kay, Küst.,+*L. exilis*+*L. Haydeni*, Lea. San Francisco, *Rowell*. Also through British America and northern tier of States from New York to Pacific; teste Binn.

†71. *Limnæa* (*Limnophysa*) *Sumassii*, Baird ‖.

* So great is the difficulty of ascertaining (even approximately) the specific relations of *Succineæ* without a comparison at least of single specimens, that Mr. Binney considers it safest, until series have been examined, simply to quote the species which have been described by other authors. He has followed the same course with *Ancylus*, and for the same reason.

‡ " Has a pore. Why not *Arion*? "—*Binney*, in MS. list.

§ This appears among "doubtful species" in the MS., but is printed in the text of the Check-List.

‖ Probably a variety of *palustris*=*Nuttalliana*, Lea. British authors have as yet had but poor opportunities of studying typically-named American freshwater Pulmonates, 1863.

72. *Limnæa (Limnophysa) palustris*, Müll. et auct.,=*L. fragilis* (as of Linn.), Hald., De Kay, Binn. (1st list), Rve. (hodie). [Non Linn., teste Hanl. in Ips. Linn. Conch., p. 385]. +*L. elodes*, Say, Gld., C. B. Ad., Küst.,+*L. Nuttalliana*, Lea, Küst., ?+*L. plebeia*, Gld.,+*L. expansa*, Hald., De Kay, Küst. NORTHERN EUROPE, ASIA, AND AMERICA:—Columbia River, *Nuttall*; Puget Sound, *Kennerley*; Klamath Lake and Summer Lake, Or.; Rhett Lake and Wright's Lake, Cal., *Newberry*: Clear Lake, Cal., *Veatch*; San Francisco, *Rowell*; Monterey, *Canfield*; Porcupine and Yuckron Rivers, Rus. America, *Kennicott*. Also from Pennsylvania westward to Pacific, and from this line northwards, wherever searched, even to interior of Russian America; teste Binn.

73. *Limnæa (Limnophysa) proxima*, Lea. San Francisco, *Cooper*. Arroya San Antonio, *Trask*.

74. *Limnæa (Limnophysa) emarginata*, Say, Hald., De Kay, Küst.,=*L. Ontariensis*, Muhlf., Küst.,+*L. serrata*, Hald. NEW ENGLAND TO WASHINGTON TERRITORY.

75. *Limnæa (Limnophysa) catascopium*, Say, Hald., Gld., De Kay, Mrs. Gray. Pot. & Mich., Küst.,+*L. pinguis*, Say (non Dohrn), =*L. Virginiana*, Lam., Desh., Deless., = *L. cornea*, Val., = *L. sericata*, Ziegl. NEW ENGLAND TO LEWIS RIVER, AND THROUGH BRITISH AMERICA; teste Binn.

76. *Limnæa (Limnophysa) Adelinæ*, Tryon. San Francisco.

77. *Limnæa (Limnophysa) Traskii*, Tryon. Mountain Lake, California.

78. *Limnæa (Limnophysa) pallida*, C. B. Ad., Hald., De Kay. San Francisco, *Rowell*; San Antonio Arroya, teste Lea.

79. *Limnæa (Limnophysa) bulimoides*, Lea, Hald., De Kay. Fort Vancouver. San Francisco, *Rowell*. Also Eastern States. (Check-List.)

80. *Limnæa (Limnophysa) solida*, Lea, Hald., De Kay,+*L. apicina*, Lea, Küst. Oregon. Also Eastern States. (Check-List.)

81. *Limnæa (Limnophysa) ferruginea*, Hald., De Kay. Oregon.

82. *Pompholyx effusa*, Lea, Add. Pitt River, *Newberry*; Sacramento River, teste Lea.

83. *Physa (Physa) Lordi*, Baird. British Columbia, *Lord*; east of Fort Colville, W. T., *Am. N. P. B. Surv.*

84. *Physa (Physa) gyrina*, Say, De Kay, Küst., C. B. Ad., Hald.,=*Ph. elliptica*, Lea, De Kay,+*Ph. cylindrica*, De Kay,+*Ph. Hildrethiana*, Lea. Washington Territory, *Captain Simpson*; San Francisco, *Rowell*.

85. *Physa (Physa) ampullacea*, Gld.,=*Ph. bullata*, Gld. (non Pot. & Mich.). Oregon, *Cooper*; Lakes Rhett and Upper Klamath, *Newberry*.

86. *Physa (Physa) Gabbii*, Tryon. Sta. Aña Riv., Angelos Co. Also Mountain Lake, California.

87. *Physa (Physa) heterostropha*, Say, Gould, C. B. Ad., Desh., Küst., De Kay, Mrs. Gray, Pot. & Mich., Eaton,+*Ph. fontana*, Hald.,+*Ph. cylindrica*, Newc.,+*Ph. aurea*, Lea, De Kay,+*Ph. plicata*, +*Ph. glabra*, De Kay, +*Ph. osculans*, Hald. (part),+*Ph. striata*,+*Ph. subarata*, Mke.,+*Ph. Charpentieri*, +*Ph. Phillipi*, Küst., + *Ph. elliptica*, + *Ph. inflata*, Lea,=*Bulla crassula*, Dillw., =*B. fontinalis*, Chemn., Schröter,=*Cochlea neritoides*, List. NORTH AMERICA, *passim*:—Chiloncynck, *Kennerley*; Hell Gate River, *Newberry*; San Francisco and Washington Territory, *Cooper*; Los Angeles, teste Lea. Also from Texas to British America and Arctic regions, and from Atlantic to Pacific, teste Binn.

+88. *Physa (Physa) costata*, Newc. Clear Lake, Cal., *Veatch*.

89. *Physa (Physa) virginea*, Gld. San Francisco, *Rowell*.

90. *Physa (Physa) humerosa*, Gld. Rio Colorado, *Willamson*; San Diego, *P. R. R. E.*

91. *Physa (Physa) virgata*, Gld. San Diego, *Webb*; Los Angelos; Cal. Ac. N. S.

several of which are perhaps but modifications of circumboreal species which have been already traced to Eastern Asia. Even the series in Mus. Cum. are far from being accurate or complete. The inflexible rules of the British Museum have not yet allowed a single specimen of Dr. Baird's species to be transmitted to America, even for comparison.

92. *Physa (Physa) triticea,* Lea, Binn. MSS.* California, *Cooper.*
†93. *Physa (Physa) concolor,* Hald. Oregon.
94. *Bulinus ‡ (Bulinus) aurantius,* Cpr. [=*Aplexa,* auct.: *v.* Maz. Cat. p. 179],=
    Ph. Peruviana, Mke. [non D'Orb.]. Mazatlan, *Reigen.*
95. *Bulinus (Bulinus) elatus,* Gld. Mazatlan, *Reigen.*
96. *Bulinus (Bulinus) hypnorum,* Linn., Hald., C. B. Ad., Chen. et auct.,=*Ph.
    elongata,* Say, Gld., De Kay,=*Ph. elongatina,* Lewis. NORTHERN EUROPE,
    ASIA, AMERICA. Puget Sound, *Cooper*; common at junction of Yukron
    and Porcupine Rivers, Russ. Amer., *Kennicott.* Through Brit. and Russ.
    America, and from Kansas to Washington, D. C.; teste Binn.

Subfam. *Planorbinæ.*

97. *Planorbis (Planorbis) subcrenatus §,* Cpr. Oregon, *Nuttall.* [?Puget Sound,
    Kennerley.]
98. *Planorbis (Planorbis) tumens,* Cpr.,=*P. tenagophila,* Mke. (non D'Orb.),=*P.
    affinis,* Cpr. [Cat. Prov., non C. B. Ad.] Mazatlan, *Melchers, Reigen.* San
    Francisco, *Cooper*; Petaluma, teste Gld.
99. *Planorbis (Planorbis) vermicularis,* Gld.
100. *Planorbis (Helisoma) ammon,* Gld., =*P. Traskei,* Lea. Klamath Lake, Or.
    and Rhett Lake, Cal., *Newberry.* Ocogo Creek, Cal., *Williamson*; Kern
    Lake, Cal., *Cooper*; Monterey Co., *Trask*; Lagoons, Sacramento Valley,
    teste Lea.
101. *Planorbis (Helisoma) corpulentus,* Say, Hald., De Kay, Gld., Chenu, =*P. tri-
    volvis* (pars), C. B. Ad. Columbia River, abundant, *U. S. E. E.* Also
    Eastern States.
102. *Planorbis (Helisoma) trivolvis,* Say, De Kay, Gld., Hald., C. B. Ad., Küst., Pot.
    & Mich., Eaton=*Bulla fluviatilis,* Say,+*Pl. regularis,* Lea,+*Pl. megastoma*
    +*Physa planorbula,* De Kay,+*Pl. macrostomus*+*Pl. corpulentus,* Whiteaves,
    +*Pl. lentus,* Gld.,+*Pl. trivolvis,* var. *fallax,* Hald.,= *Cochleat rinm-orbinm,*
    Lister, Petiver. Puget Sd., *Campbell*; Wright's Lake, Cal., *Newberry*; Ft.
    Vancouver, *Cooper*]; San Francisco, *Rowell*; S. Diego; Mus. Smiths.; Horn
    Lake, teste Lea. Probably extends over whole continent, teste Binn.
103. *Planorbis (Menetus) opercularis,* Gld.,= *P. planulatus,* Coop. S. Francisco, *U. S.
    Expl. Exp.*; Whidby's Is., Cal., *Cooper.*
104. *Carinifex ‖ Newberryi,* Lea. Klamath Lake and Canoe Creek, Cal., *Newberry*;
    Clear Lake, Cal., *Veatch.*

Subfam. *Ancylinæ.*

105. *Ancylus Newberryi,* Lea. Klamath Lake, *Newberry.*
†106. *Ancylus crassus,* Hald. "W." [Check-List.]
107. *Ancylus caurinus,* Coop. California, *Cooper.*
108. *Ancylus patelloides,* Lea. S. Francisco, *Cooper*; Arroya, San Antonio, Cal.,
    Mus. Smith.
†109. *Ancylus Kootaniensis,* Baird. Brit. Columbia, *Lord.*
110. *Ancylus fragilis,* Tryon. "W." [Check-List.]
111. *Acroloxus Nuttalli,* Hald. [*Velletia N.,* Binn. in list, May 4th.] Oregon, *Nutt.*
112. *Gundlachia Californica,* Rowell.

* So in first printed list and in two MSS.; but in Check-List of Dec. 9, *Ph. Troos-
tiana,* Lea, is assigned to the West, instead of this species. The MSS. are probably
correct.

‡ Non *Bulinus,* Sby., *olim,*=*Bulimus,* auct. However clearly *Bulinus,* Binn., may be
right according to the antiquaries, it is far too like *Bulimus,* which has taken complete
possession of the entire malacological world, to be allowed a resurrection in the same
order. Surely burial for a given number of years ought to be allowed as evidence of
death, especially if the infant-name scarcely even breathed the air of use, and its resurrection would breed malaria among terms thriving in the vigorous manhood of universal
acceptance.

§ It is quite possible that this may prove a very finely grown specimen of *P. lentus.* Dr.
Kennerley's shells are intermediate.

‖ Thus in Check-List, Dec. 9th. In that of May 4th, it appears as *Planorbis N.*; in the
MS. list as *Carinifera.*

Suborder THALASSOPHILA.

Fam. *Siphonariadæ.*

†113. *Siphonaria lecanium,* Phil.: [Var.= *S. maura,* Sby. Var. *palmata,* Cpr., is possibly distinct. Mazatlan, *E. B. Philippi, Reigen* ; Acapulco, *Jewett* ; Cape St. Lucas, *Xantus.*]

†114. *Siphonaria æquilirata,* Cpr.,[= *S. æquilorata,* Rve. Mazatlan, *Reigen* ; C. S. Lucas, *Xantus* ; Margarita Bay, very fine, teste *Pease.*]

†115. [*Siphonaria thersites,* Cpr. Neeah Bay, *Swan.*]

Doubtful, spurious, and extralimital species :—

Helix aspersa, Müll. "Sta. Barbara," *Kellett* and *Wood.* [Imported.]
Helix arbustorum, Linn.
Helix Sagraiana, D'Orb. [Certainly Cuban.]
Helix " *Sandiegoënsis,* Lea." Gld., P. R. R., vol. v. p. 331. "No such sp. de-scribed," teste *Binney.*
Helix peregrina, Bosc.
Bulimus Humboldti, Rve. ?" Mazatlan."
Bulimus Laurentii, Sby. "Sitka:" probably Sitcha in San Salvador, teste *Binney.*
Melania [*Bulimus*] *striata,* Perry. [*Vide anteà,* p. 520.]
Succinea aperta, Lea,= *S. rotundata,* Gld. Sandwich Is., *U. S. Expl. Exp.*
†*Physa Maugeriæ,* Gray, teste Woodward, Manual, p. 171 ; but probably equi-torial S. America.
†*Siphonaria amara,* [Nutt. Admitted into the list by Mr. Binney, on the autho-rity of Rve., as of Nutt. ; but it lives on the Sandwich Is. ; teste *Pease, New-comb, U. S. E. E.*].

116. The Smithsonian Institution has lately issued a " Descriptive Cata-logue of the species of *Amnicola, Vivipara, Bithynia, Valvata,* and *Ampul-laria,*" by Mr. W. G. Binney. It is abundantly illustrated with outline-woodcuts, and contains the synonymy corrected from all the accessible types. Dr. Stimpson is at present engaged in dissecting the molluscs ; but none of his investigations have yet been published. The following is a *résumé* of the West Coast species, from a proof kindly furnished by the author

Page. Fig.
  4.   *Amnicola longinqua,* Gld., Bost. Proc. v. 130.   Colorado Desert, *Blake.*
  5.   6. *Amnicola protea,* Gld., Bost. Proc. v. 129.   Colorado Desert, *Blake, Webb.*
 12. 45. *Vivipara,* Lam.,= *Paludina,* Lam. [This genus, so fine and plentiful east of the Rocky Mountains, does not appear on the west.]
 44.   „   *Paludina Nuttalliana,* Lea, Trans. Am. Phil. Soc. vi. p. 101, pl. 23. f. 109. [In text. In later manuscript list, this name appears as a synonym of] *Fluminicola* (Stimps., MS.) *Nuttallii,* Lea, = *Amnicola Nuttalliana,* Cp., Minn. Rep. p. 374, = *Leptoxis Nuttallii,* Hald., = *Anculosus Nuttallii,* Rve. ? + *Paludina seminalis,* Hds. (p. 46, f. 81). [? + *P. Hindsii,* Baird.]   Co-lumbia River, *Nuttall, Cooper* ; Upper des Chutes Riv. and Klamath Lake, Or., *Newberry* ; Roques R., Or. ; Sacramento R., *Hinds* ; Brit. Columbia, *Lord* ; Canoe Creek and Pitt River, Cal., *Newberry.*
 46. 80. *Bithinia nuclea,* Lea, = *Paludina n.,* Trans. Am. Phil. Soc. vi. p. 91, pl. 23. f. 103 [in text. In later MS. list, appears as synonym of] *Fluminicola virens,* Lea (*Paludina v.,* Lea; *Leptoxis v.,* Hald.),+ *Paludina nuclea,* Lea. Wahlamat River, Oregon, *Nuttall* [Willamette, MS. list].

The following are added by Mr. Binney in his later MS. list :—

Valvata virens, Tryon. Clear Lake, Calif. [The Smithsonian duplicates have been unfortunately distributed under the name " *V. sincera,* Say," which had been previously given to the specimens, and under which they are quoted in the Check-List of 1860, no. 456. According to Mr. B., *V. sincera* is " like

ecarinate forms of *V. tricarinata*, Say," to which the Clear Lake specimens bear but slight resemblance.]
Pomatiopsis Binneyi, Tryon.
Fluminicola fusca, Hald. (*Leptoxis f.*).   Shores of Lake Utah, *Capt. Burton.*

117. Of the West Coast species of Melaniadæ we are unable to offer any list embracing the synonymy, as the materials are at present in the hands of Mr. Tryon for elimination, and his labours are not yet sufficiently advanced to furnish a report. His Manual of the North American Melaniadæ will be published by the Smithsonian Institution. The animals of many species have already been dissected by Dr. Stimpson[*]. It is unfortunate that in the two most important branches of North American freshwater molluscs, the Melaniadæ and the Unionidæ, there exists a radical difference of opinion between the leading writers, which has sometimes assumed the appearance of personal animosity. Malacologists east of the Atlantic, unwilling to become partisans when the leading nomenclators of the rival schools are equally honoured, have to a great extent declined to pay attention to the unexhausted riches of the American waters, regarding any settlement of the disputed points as hopeless. Dr. Isaac Lea, who has spared no expense in illustrating his publications of the results of a life-long study, follows the restrictions on the priority-rule allowed by the British Association Committee. Other writers, however, claim a certainty in identifying the supposed species of Rafinesque and other similarly inaccurate authors, which would be considered by most English naturalists as not warranted by the few loose words of description given. It would be well if the student were permitted to start from the first carefully ascertained landmark, rather than from the defaced tracks of the first hunter.

In the Check-List of North-American Fluviatile Gasteropods, published by the Smithsonian Institution, June 1860, which contains the names of 405 (supposed) species of *Melania, Lithasia, Gyrotoma, Leptoxis*, and *Io*, Mr. Binney assigns the following eleven to the West Coast. None of them are accredited to the eastern division.

43. *Melania bulbosa*, Gld.	242. *Melania Shastaënsis*, Lea. Shasta
104. *Melania exigua*, Conr.	and Scott Rivers.
166. *Melania Menkeana*, Lea.	243. *Melania silicula*, Gld. [= *M. plicifera*, small var., teste *Lea.*]
174. *Melania Newberryi*, Lea.	
177. *Melania nigrina*, Lea. Clear Creek,	296. *Melania Wahlamatensis*, Lea.
Shasta Co.	297. *Melania Warderiana*, Lea.
211. *Melania plicifera*, Lea.	360. *Melania fusca*, Hald.

118. Dr. Lea's Check-List of the Unionidæ (June 1860), after eliminating synonyms, assigns to America, north of Mexico, no fewer than 552 species of *Unio, Margaritana*, and *Anodonta*. The type-specimens of the species described by Dr. Gould from the United States Exploring Expedition were submitted to Dr. Lea's inspection, and confirmed his previous opinion that they were varieties of those before known. The *U. famelicus*, Gld., he pronounced to be a South-American shell ; but it appears, without note, in the Check List, no. 133, probably by oversight. The only widely diffused species is the long-famed "pearl-mussel" of the Conway and other British streams. The following seven are accredited to the Pacific coast :—

* See his very interesting and important paper "On the structural Characters of the so-called Melanians of North America," in the 'American Journal of Science,' vol. xxxviii., July 1864, pp. 41–53. It appears that the sexual system is quite distinct from that of the ordinary Ctenobranchiate Gasteropods, and approaches the Cyclobranchiates.

281. *Unio Oregonensis,* Lea [Comp. 534.]
484. *Margaritana margaritifera,* Lea.
  [Linn.]
494. *Anodonta angulata,* Lea.

499. *Anodonta Californiensis,* Lea.
531. *Anodonta Nuttalliana,* Lea.
534. *Anodonta Oregonensis,* Lea.
551. *Anodonta Wahlamatensis,* Lea.

Besides these, 36 species of *Unio* and *Anodonta* are assigned to Mexico and Central America in a separate list; but no distinction is indicated between the Pacific and the Atlantic slope of the mountain-range.

119. At the request of the Smithsonian Institution, Mr. Temple Prime, of New York, well known for his special devotion to this department, has consented to prepare a Manual of the Cyrenidæ inhabiting American waters. All the accessible materials from the West Coast are in his hands for examination. The first part of his "Monograph of the Species of *Sphærium* of North and South America" is printed in the ' Proc. Ac. N. Sc. Phil.' 1861, pp. 402 *et seq.*, and contains quotations of five species, nos. 4, 7, 9, 10, 11, with synonymy, from Washington Ter., Oregon, and California. He has kindly (in advance of his intended publications) furnished to Mr. W. G. Binney the following MS. "Synopsis of the Corbiculidæ of the West Coast of North America," with liberty to publish in this Report. It is here condensed, with synonyms and references, in the nomenclature of the writer.

Mr. Prime's List of West North-American Corbiculidæ* [Cyrenidæ].

1. *Corbicula convexa,* Desh., P. Z. S. 1854, p. 342, = *C. ventricosa,* Pr. MS. Mazatlan.
2. *Cyrena radiata,* Hanl., P. Z. S. 1844, p. 159. Realejo.
3. *Cyrena solida,* Phil., Abbild. 1846, p. 78, pl. 15. f. 9. Nicaragua; Belize.
4. *Cyrena triangula,* V. de Busch, P. Z. S. 1849, p. 78, pl. 2. f. 3, = *C. altilis,* Gld., Bost. Pr. 1852, p. 400, pl. 16. f. 5 *bis,* = *C. Mexicana,* pars, Maz. Cat., no. 165 (= *C. varians,* cat. prov.). Mazatlan.
5. *Cyrena insignis,* Desh., P. Z. S. 1854, p. 20; Il. Conch. 1861, p. 39, pl. 2. f. 2. California.
6. *Cyrena olivacea,* Cpr., Maz. Cat., no. 164, = *C. Fontainei,* Desh., MS. (non D'Orb., B. M. Cat. no. 253). Mazatlan.
7. *Cyrena acuta,* Pr., Ill. Conch. 1862, p. 387, pl. 14. f. 1. Centr. America.
8. *Cyrena Mexicana,* Sby., Zool. Il. 1829, p. 364 [Maz. Cat., no. 165 =] *C. varians,* cat. prov. pars, + *C. fragilis,* Desh. MS. + *C. æquilateralis,* Desh., P. Z. S. 1854, p. 20. Mazatlan.
9. *Cyrena Californica,* Pr., Proc. A. N. S. Phil. 1860, p. 276, = *C. subquadrata,* Desh., P. Z. S. 1854, p. 21 (nom. preoc.). California.
10. *Cyrena Panamensis,* Pr., Proc. A. N. S. Phil. 1860, p. 283, = *C. inflata,* Desh., P. Z. S. 1854, p. 23 (nom. preoc.). Panama.
11. *Cyrena Recluzii,* Pr., = *C. cordiformis,* Recl., Il. Conch. 1853, p. 251, pl. 7. f. 9 (nom. preoc.). Centr. America.
12. *Cyrena Cumingii,* Desh., P. Z. S. 1854, p. 22. Centr. America.
13. *Cyrena tumida,* Pr., = *C. angulata,* Desh., P. Z. S. 1854, p. 22 (nom. preoc.). Centr. America.
14. *Cyrena pullastra,* Mörch, Mal. Bl. 1860, p. 194. Realejo.
15. *Cyrena maritima,* C. B. Ad., Pan. Sh., no. 451. Panama.
16. *Cyrena sordida,* Hanl., P. Z. S. 1844, p. 159. Central America.
17. *Sphærium triangulare,* Say (*Cyclas t.*), New Harm. Dissem. 1829, p. 356. Mexico.
18. *Sphærium striatinum,* Lam. (*Cyclas s.*), An. s. Vert. vol. v. p. 560, 1818, = *C. edentula,* Say, *loc. cit.* p. 2, = *C. cornea* (Lam.), C. B. Ad., Cat., 1847, + *C. albula,* Pr., Bost. Proc. 1851, p. 155, + *C. tenuistriata,* Pr., p. 156, + *C. acuminata,* Pr., p. 158, + *C. inornata,* Pr., + *C. simplex,* Pr., + *C. modesta,* Pr., p. 159. *Hab.* N. York to Alabama, Connecticut to Illinois ; Hell-gate River, W. T.
19. *Sphærium dentatum,* Hald. (*Cyclas d.*), Proc. A. N. S. Phil. 1841, p. 100. Oregon.

---

* The name *Corbicula,* having been first given to a species, and being itself a diminutive, is scarcely fitted to displace long-used generic appellations in marking the family-group.

20. *Sphærium occidentale*, Pr., Proc. A. N. S. Phil. 1860, p. 295, = *C. ovalis*, Pr., Bost. Proc. 1852, p. 276 (nom. preoc.), = *Sph. ovale*, Stn.,' Add. Gen. vol. ii. p. 450. *Hab.* New York to Georgia; Vermont to Wisconsin; Hell-gate River, W. T.

21. *Sphærium nobile*, Gld. (*Cyclas n.*), Bost. Proc. 1855, p. 229 [Otia, p. 218]. San Pedro, *Webb.*

22. *Sphærium patella*, Gld. (*Cyclas p.*), Bost. Proc. 1850, p. 292 [Otia, p. 86; E. E. Moll. f. 527, type not returned to S. I.] Oregon.

23. *Sphærium Spokani*, Baird [P. Z. S. 1863, p. 69, f. 12, 13: *anteà*, p. 605]. B. Col.

' 24. *Sphærium tumidum*, Baird [P. Z. S. 1863, p. 69, f. 11: *anteà*, p. 605]. B. Col.

25. *Sphærium meridionale*, Pr., Proc. Ac. N. S. Phil. 1861, p. 414. Panama; Mus. Prime.

26. *Sphærium lenticula*, Gld. (*Lucina* * *l.*), Bost. Proc. 1850, p. 256. California.

27. *Sphærium subtransversum*, Pr., P. Z. S. 1860, p. 322. Mexico.

28. *Pisidium abditum*, Hald. [?ubi] = *Cyclas minor*, C. B. Ad. Bost. Proc. 1841, p. 48, = *P. obscurum*, Pr., Bost. Proc. 1851, p. 161, + *P. Kurtzii*, Pr., p. 162, + *P. zonatum*, Pr., p. 162, + *P. regulare*, Pr., Bost. Il. vi. 363, pl. 12. f. 11–13, 1852, + *P. notatum*, Pr., Bost. Il. vi. 365, pl. 12. f. 20–22, 1852, + *P. amplum* + *P. resartum*, Ingalls, MS., + *P. rubrum* + *P. plenum*, Lewis, MS., + *P. retusum*, Pr., P. Z. S. 1859, p. 322.

29. *Pisidium occidentale*, Newc. [Proc. Cal. Ac. Nat. Sc. 1861, p. 94]. San Francisco, *Rowell.*

120. Of the tertiary fossils throwing light on existing species no additional information has yet been published. We cannot but hope that the researches of Mr. Gabb, on the fossils collected by the Californian Geological Survey, will develope relations of great interest between the existing and former conditions of the continent. The Astorian fossils described by Mr. Conrad from the U. S. Exploring Expedition (vol. x., Geology, Philadelphia, 1849), and tabulated in the first Report, p. 367, belong to the Smithsonian Institution, but were not discovered there in 1860. All of them, however (including the indeterminate species), are figured in the atlas of plates. They resemble the fossils of the Pacific Railroad Expeditions in being very imperfect, for which reason the following criticisms may prove erroneous. The general aspect of the collection betokens the Miocene period.

Mya abrupta, Conr., may be the young of *Glycimeris generosa*, **Gld.**
Thracia trapezoides, Conr., may be *curta*, Conr.
Solemya ventricosa, Conr., has the aspect of a large *Lazaria.*
Tellina aretata, Conr., closely resembles *Macoma*, var. *expansa.*
Tellina emacerata, Conr., is perhaps *Bodegensis*, Hds.
Lucina acutilineata, Conr., appears to be *borealis*, Linn.
Cardita subtenta, Conr., = *Venericardia borealis*, Conr.
Nucula divaricata, Conr., = *Acila castrensis*, Hds.
Pectunculus patulus, Conr., may be *septentrionalis*, Midd.
Pectunculus nitens, Conr., resembles *Psephis tantilla*, Gld.
Pecten propatulus, Conr. A very fine specimen, enclosed in a large nodule from Oregon, was presented to the Brit. Mus. by Mr. C. Pace. If not identical with *Amusium caurinum*, Gld., it is most closely allied, especially to the Japanese form.

---

* Mr. Prime assigns no reason for changing Dr. Gould's *Lucina* into a *Cyclas*, nor any authority for "California." He was, perhaps, misled by the artist's engraved references to the figures 528, *a, b*, where he has drawn a rule, referring to the Cyclades above, instead of writing *Lucina.* It is assigned to "?Coast of Patagonia" in 'Otia,' p. 63, and to "?R. Janeiro" in ' E. E. Moll.,' p. 414. In each place the shell is compared to an *Astarte* or *Cyprina*, with lateral teeth. The type was not returned to the Smithsonian Institution; but the diagnosis states that it is "chalky, thickened within the deep and jagged pallial line, sculpture faint but decussated, and margin finely crenulated,"—characters more consistent with *Lucina*, s. g. *Myrtæa*, than with *Cyclas.* If the type cannot be recovered, perhaps the species may be dropped, as it is not the *Lucina (Myrtæa) lenticula*, Rve.

Terebratula nitens, Conr., is very probably *Waldheimia pulvinata*, Gld.
Bulla petrosa, Conr., has the shape of *Tornatina eximia*, Bd.
Crepidula prorupta, Conr., is certainly *princeps*, Midd.
Turritella, sp. ind., resembles *Mesalia lacteola*.
?*Dolium petrosum*, Conr., resembles the young of *Priene nodosa*, Chemn.
Fusus geniculus, Conr. A similar shell has just been taken at the Farallones
   by Dr. Cooper.

121. To correct the general table of "Mollusca of the West Coast of N.
America" (First Report, pp. 298–345), and the deductions founded upon it
(pp. 346–367), would involve the necessity of reprinting a considerable portion. The student, being now in possession of all the known sources of
fresh information, can with his own pen strike out the spurious species, alter
the synonyms, insert the newly discovered forms, and make the requisite
corrections in the classified results.

122. With regard to the tropical fauna, the researches at Cape St. Lucas
and in the interior of the Gulf of California, though leaving much to be
desired, bear-out the general conclusions arrived-at in paragraphs 78–87.
The evidence for the identity of specific forms on the Atlantic and Pacific sides
of Central America has been greatly confirmed. Dr. Gould writes, "The
doctrine of local limitations meets with so few apparent exceptions that we
admit it as an axiom in zoology that species strongly resembling each other,
derived from widely diverse localities, especially if a continent intervenes,
and if no known or plausible means of communication can be assigned,
should be assumed as different until their identity can be proved (*vide* E. E.
Moll. Intr. p. xi). Much study of living specimens must be made before
the apparent exceptions can be brought under the rule." It has, however,
to be borne in mind that the researches of modern geology clearly point to
considerable alterations in the existing configuration of continents, and in
the consequent direction of ocean-currents, during the ascertained period of
many species now living. Nor are we warranted in the belief that the
existing fauna in any locality has been created at any one time, or has
radiated from any single spot. To study the relations of living shells simply
in connexion with the existing map of the world must lead but to partial
results. The facts accumulating with regard to the British species, by
tracing them through the northern drift (now found even on the Snowdonian
range), to the oldest crag deposits when Europe was contained in far different
boundaries, show how altered may have been the configuration of the new
world when the oldest of its molluscs were first created. Coordinately with
the glacial period, Central America may have been a group of islands; coordinately with the creation of *Saxicava pholadis* and *Chrysodomus antiquus*,
the gulf-weed may have floated between the Rocky Mountains in the
archipelago of West America, and Japanese molluscs may have known how
to migrate to the Mediterranean shores. Dr. Gould's position may therefore be accepted in theory; yet, in practice, the "imperfection of the geological
record"[*], and even of our knowledge of existing species and their variations,
demands that the greatest caution be exercised in building results on deductions from our ignorance. Already the fossil *Malea ringens* of the Atlantic
has proved a "Rosetta Stone" to interpret the *Cypraea exanthema*, *Purpura
patula*, and other Caribbean shells of the Pacific; and as the geology of the
West Coast advances, so may we expect to find traces of previous denizens of

---

* No student of geographical distribution should omit to weigh carefully the chapter
on this subject in Darwin's 'Origin of Species,' and the information given in Lyell's
'Antiquity of Man.'

American waters, which have bequeathed some species now flourishing, and others dying-out, to the existing seas. The present faunas of West America are perhaps the most isolated on the surface of the globe; yet, if we knew the ancestry of each specific form, we might find some first appearing with man on this planet, others first living even in historic times, others tracing their descent from remote periods, and it may be very distant localities, in the ages of the Miocene, possibly even of the Eocene oceans. These suppositions are not set forth as theories, but simply to guard against interpretations of facts based on conclusions which may be only the results of our necessarily imperfect information.

123. With regard to forms offering local peculiarities sufficient to distinguish them from correlative forms offering equal peculiarities in some other fauna, we are by no means warranted in assuming that these have sprung from different creations. If a race of men, migrating to a new continent, in a very few generations, or even in the next, develope an essentially different *physique*, it is fair to conclude that molluscs, borne by a change of currents to a distant region, or steadily migrating to the extreme limit of their conditions of life, will also change their appearance. If the publication of the " Darwinian Theory " has had no other effect, it has at least checked the propensity to announce "new species" for differences which may fairly be regarded as varietal. It must also be borne in mind, that if the views of Mr. Darwin be only a theory, such also is the name required for the prevalent opinion of separate creations for all diverse forms. What indeed can we possibly know of the mode of original creation of a single species? We can only prove that one or the other supposition best explains a certain class of facts. It is not necessary for a working naturalist to commit himself to an exclusive belief in either of these theories. He may perhaps best explain some facts by the doctrine of separate creation, others by that of natural selection. In either case it is his duty to trace-out, as far as possible, the limits as well as the powers of variation in every living form, and to guard against seeing that only which accords with his prevailing belief.

124. The study of European shells, as they exist in Norway, in Britain, in the Mediterranean, at the Canaries, or as they appear at different depths and stations in our own seas, still more as they occur in the widely separated periods of the later and middle tertiary ages, is an excellent preparation for the examination of either recent or fossil faunas in districts where our knowledge is fragmentary and unconfirmed. It may be safely stated that there are, in the American waters, many tropical forms from the West Indies and the Pacific shores, some temperate forms from California and the Atlantic, and many sub-boreal species in the Vancouver district and the European seas, not differing from each other more or even so much as forms universally allowed by malacologists to have had a common origin from Britain and the Mediterranean, from the Red and the Coralline Crag.

125. It is interesting to observe that, notwithstanding the probable connexion of the oceans through the Rocky Mountains during the Miocene age, there is extremely little similarity between the special temperate faunas of East and West America. Not a single species has yet been proved identical, and the allied forms are but few in number. They appear as follows:—

Californian species.	*U. S. Atlantic species.*
Clidiophora punctata.	C. trilineata (? =nasuta).
Lyonsia Californica.	L. (hyalina=)Floridana.
Macoma inconspicua.	M. fusca.
Angulus modestus.	A. tener.
Raëta undulata.	R. canaliculata.

Californian species.	*U. S. Atlantic species.*
Liocardium substriatum.	L. Mortoni.
Lunatia Lewisii.	L. heros.
Nassa mendica.	N. trivittata.
Amycla (species).	Amycla (species).

126. When, however, we approach the region in which boreal and sub-boreal forms occur, many species are found in common, and between others there is but slight difference. Yet even here there are more British than New England species in the West-coast fauna. As might be expected, the British species are for the most part those which are also found fossil, and therefore have had time to diffuse themselves widely over the hemisphere. It is, however, remarkable that many Crag species have reached Eastern Asia and West America which are not found in Grand Manan and New England. It is also extraordinary that certain special generic forms of the Crag, as *Acila, Miodon, Verticordia,* and *Solariella,* reappear in the North Pacific*. When seeking for an explanation of so remarkable a connexion between faunas widely removed in space and time, the correlative fact must be borne in mind, that the northern drift†, so widely diffused over Europe and Eastern America, has not yet been traced in the western region. The following Table exhibits, not only the identical but the similar species belonging to the northern faunas of the Atlantic and Pacific. In the Asiatic column, K denotes that the species occurs in the Kamtschatka region, J in Japan. In the second column, V signifies the Vancouver district, C the Californian, and I the Sta. Barbara group of islands. The species marked F are also fossil. In the third column, C denotes the Coralline, R the Red, and M the Mammaliferous Crag. The fourth contains the species living in the British seas; the fifth, on the American side of the Atlantic, *Gr.* standing for Greenland.

East Asia.	West America.	Crag.	British.	E. America.
K	V Rhynconella psittacea ..	(Pleistocene)	psittacea	psittacea
—	V C Xylotrya pennatifera	—	pennatifera	—
—	V Xylotrya fimbriata......	—	fimbriata	—
—.	V C Zirphæa crispata	C R M	crispata	crispata
K	V C Saxicava pholadis	C R M	pholadis	pholadis
J	V C Glycimeris generosa	Faujasii, C R	—	—
—	V Sphænia ovalis	'?Binghami '‡	Binghami	—
J K	V Mya truncata	C R M	truncata	truncata
J K, lata	V Macoma inquinata......	lata, R M	proxima	proxima,&c
K	V Serripes Groenlandicus ..	R M	—	Groenland.
K	V I Venericardia borealis....	—	—	borealis
—	V Astarte (compacta)	compressa, R M	compressa	compressa
—	V Miodon prolongatus	corbis, C R	—	—
—	I F Lucina borealis	C R M	borealis	—
—	I Cryptodon flexuosus	C	flexuosus	—
China	I Verticordia 9-costata....	cardiiformis, C	—	—
—	V C Kellia suborbicularis	C R	suborbicul.	—

* Whether there be any similar correspondence in the Polyzoa is not yet known, Mr. Busk not having had time to complete his examination.

† See, in this connexion, a very accurate Table of the species which travel round Cape Cod, with their distribution in existing seas and over different provinces of the various drift-formations in the Old and New World, by Sanderson Smith, in Ann. Lyc. Nat. Hist. N. York, vol. vii. 1860, p. 166.

‡ From the Coralline Crag. Looks more like *ovalis.*

East Asia.	West America.	Crag.	British.	E. America.
J	V C Lasea rubra	C	rubra	—
J K	V C Mytilus edulis	R M	edulis	edulis
—.	V C Modiola modiolus	?C R M	modiolus	modiolus
—	V Modiolaria marmorata ..	C R	marmorata	marmorata
J K	V Modiolaria lævigata	—	nigra	lævigata
—	I Crenella decussata	—	decussata	glandula
J K	V Nucula tenuis..........	C R M	tenuis	tenuis
insignis,&c.	V C I F Acila eastrensis	Cobboldiæ,RM	—	—
J K	V Yoldia lanceolata	R M	—	lanceolata
—	V Leda minuta	R M	caudata	minuta
—	I Limæa subauriculata....	C	subauricul.	—
—	V C Hinnites giganteus	Cortesyi, C	—	—
(Asia)	V Limnæa palustris	M	palustris	palustris
—	V C Cylichna attonsa	cylindracea,CR	attonsa	—
—	V Haminea hydatis	M	hydatis	—
—	V C Dentalium Indianorum..	entale, M	entale	striolatum
J K, cæca	V Lepeta cæcoides	—	(cæca,Nor.)	cæca, Gr.
—	V Margarita helicina......	—	helicina	helicina
—	V Margarita ?Vahlii	—	—	Vahlii, Gr.
—	V Mesalia lacteola........	—	—	lactea, Gr.
—	V Lacuna vincta	M	vincta	vincta
K (turricula)	V Bela fidicula	turricula, R	turricula	turricula
—	V Bela excurvata	Trevelliana, R	Trevelliana	—
—	V C Scalaria Indianorum	—	communis	—
K	V Velutina lævigata	M	lævigata	lævigata
K	V Natica clausa	R	(Norway)	clausa
—	V C I Eulima micans........	polita, C R	micans	—
—	V Cerithiopsis tubercularis	C	tubercularis	—
—	V I Triforis adversus	C	adversus	—
—	C I Erato columbella	Maugeriæ, C R	—	(W. I.)
—	V C Purpura saxicola	—	lapillus	lapillus
—	V Chrysodomus liratus....	—	—	10-costatus
—	V Trophon multicostatus ..	—	(Norway)	Gunneri

127. The following species (besides others dredged by Mr. A. Adams, but not yet determined) have been found on both the Asiatic and American shores of the N. Pacific, in addition to those recorded by Middendorff, v. Brit. Assoc. Report, p. 223.

Terebratella Coreanica.
Waldheimia Californica.
Waldheimia pulvinata.
Waldheimia Grayi.
Glycimeris generosa.
Schizothærus Nuttallii.
Solen sicarius.
Sanguinolaria Nuttallii.
Tellina Bodegensis.

Cardium modestum.
Amusium caurinum.
Placunanomia macroschisma.
Crepidula grandis.
Drillia inermis.
Lunatia pallida.
Priene Oregonensis.
Cerostoma foliatum.
Siphonalia Kellettii.

128. The Vancouver and Californian districts have so many characteristic species in common (111 out of 492), that they must be regarded as constituting one fauna, differing as do the British and Mediterranean regions. Full particulars as to the range of the different species may be expected in Dr. Cooper's Report to the Californian Geological Survey. One fact must, however, be here specially noted, viz. the great peculiarity of the island-fauna. Although the Sta. Barbara group are so near the mainland, the dredge has not only produced many species not known on the continent, but also many

before considered as essentially tropical. Along with these are not only some species of types hitherto regarded as almost exclusively Asiatic, as *Verticordia, Solariella,* and *Fulvia modesta,* but also some which belong to the sub-boreal district, as *Lucina borealis, Venericardia borealis,* and *Crenella decussata.* The latter belongs to the British, and not to the N. England form.

129. Of the blending of the temperate and tropical faunas on the peninsula of L. California we are still in ignorance. All we know is, that at Margarita Bay the shells are still tropical, and that at Cerros Island they are strangely intermixed. There is peculiar evidence of connexion between the faunas of the peninsula and of S. America, not only in the land-shells (*v. anteâ,* p. 630), but in some of the marine forms. Beside identical species with wide range, as many Calyptræids, the following are coordinate between the North and South Pacific:—

Upper and Lower California.	South America.
Netastoma Darwinii.	N. Darwinii.
Solecurtus Californianus.	S. Dombeyi.
Semele rupium.	(Ditto, Galapagos.)
Callista *var.* puella.	C. pannosa.
Chama pellucida.	C. pellucida.
Liocardium substriatum.	L. Elenense.
Axinæa (Barbarensis.)	A. intermedia.
Verticordia novemcostata.	V. ornata.
Pecten æquisulcatus.	P. ventricosus.
Siphonaria thersites.	S. lateralis, &c.
Tonicia lineata.	T. lineolata.
Acmæa patina.	A. scutum, *D'Orb.*
Acmæa persona.	A. "Oregona," *H. C.*
Scurria mitra.	S. scurra.
Chlorostoma funebrale.	C. mœstum.
Mitra maura.	M. maura.
Ranella Californica.	R. ventricosa.
Priene Oregonensis.	P. cancellata.
Trophon multicostatus.	T. Magellanicus.

Time and space do not avail for pointing out further relations with exotic faunas; which indeed will be performed with greater correctness after Dr. Cooper shall have published his complete lists.

130. For the sake of avoiding the inconvenience of trinomial nomenclature, the subgeneric and varietal names have often been cited in this Report instead of the generic and specific, in order that the exact form of the shell quoted might be more quickly determined. The diagnoses of all the new species here tabulated are written for the press, and will shortly appear in the different scientific journals. Additional specimens will probably prove several forms to be conspecific which are here treated as distinct. In the present state of the science, absolute certainty is not to be attained. The object of the writer* has been principally to bring together the works of his predecessors, and so to arrange and describe the new materials that those who continue his labours may be able to draw their own conclusions from existing data. In order to facilitate reference, a brief index is here given of the subject-matter of the former and of the present Reports.

* The best thanks of the writer are due to Hugh Cuming, Esq., for the free use of his collection; to Messrs. H. & A. Adams, Hanley, Reeve, and Sowerby, for aid in identifying specimens; to the officers and naturalists connected with the Smithsonian Institution; to Dr. A. A. Gould, for very valuable corrections; and generally to authors and friends, who have kindly rendered him all the assistance in their power. He earnestly invites criticisms on the subject-matter of the two Reports; in order that they may be embodied, and errors corrected, in the Manuals of the West-Coast Mollusca which he has undertaken to prepare for the Smithsonian Institution.

Warrington, Aug. 22nd, 1864.

TABLE OF CONTENTS.

172

B.

REVIEW

OF

PROF. C. B. ADAMS'S CATALOGUE

OF THE

SHELLS OF PANAMA, FROM THE TYPE SPECIMENS.

BY

PHILIP P. CARPENTER, B. A., Ph. D.

From the Proceedings of the Zoölogical Society of London, pp. 339–369,
June 23, 1863.

(173)

REVIEW OF PROF. C. B. ADAMS'S 'CATALOGUE OF THE SHELLS
OF PANAMA'*, FROM THE TYPE SPECIMENS. BY PHILIP P.
CARPENTER, B.A., PH.D.

A résumé of this important contribution to our knowledge of local
faunas, and a comparison with the British Museum 'Descriptive
Catalogue of the Reigen Collection of Mazatlan Mollusca,' is given
in the 'Report of the British Association' for 1856, pp. 265–281.
Full series of the old species, and the first specimens of the new,
were deposited by Prof. Adams in the Museum of Amherst College,
which also contains similar series of the Professor's Caribbean collections. The second specimens of new species were sent to Mr.
Cuming, and through his kindness were freely used in preparing
the Mazatlan Catalogue, thus avoiding the necessity of many synonyms. An instructive lesson in candour and forbearance may be
learnt by comparing together the works of any two naturalists of
equal celebrity, or by comparing either of them with the types.
With the best desires for accuracy, and the greatest care, it is hardly
possible for an author to describe so that his readers shall see shells
as he sees them. If this be true of such full and precise diagnoses
as those of Adams and Gould, how much greater must be the difficulty to foreigners of recognizing shells from the brief descriptions
of Broderip, Lamarck, and the older writers generally. The careful

* Catalogue of Shells collected at Panama; with Notes on their Synonymy,
Station, and Geographical Distribution · by C. B. Adams, Professor of Zoology,
&c., in Amherst College, Mass. Reprinted from the 'Annals of Lyceum of Nat.
Hist. N. Y.,' vol. v. New York, 1852.

preservation of types therefore, and the interchange of specimens named from types, is of the first importance to save the time and ensure the accuracy of succeeding writers. The Smithsonian Institution has fully recognized this principle by directing that the first available duplicate of all type species described from its collections shall be deposited in some museum open to students on the other side of the Atlantic.

As the authorities of Amherst College had not taken any steps to figure their unique specimens, and as Prof. Adams's determinations of old species had not been verified, I made it my business (when visiting America to deposit the first duplicate series of the Mazatlan Shells in the New York State Museum at Albany) to compare Prof. Adams's collection, on the spot, with his published book, in my copy of which I made my notes and sketches at the time. Every facility was afforded me by the Curator. I was allowed freely to handle the specimens in the presence of his assistant, and to draw the minute species under my microscope. I took with me for comparison the drawings of the minute Mazatlan shells in the British Museum. The species being numbered in both the Panama and the Mazatlan lists, it is easy now to institute a comparison between them. They are here distinguished by the initials P. and M.

P. 1. *Ovula avena.* May be distinct from *Radius variabilis*, M. 435, being much more stumpy, with a thicker lip; but the few specimens are in poor condition, and the differences may be accidents of station.

2. *Ovula emarginata* = *Carinea e.* Quite distinct from its Caribbean analogue *C. gibbosa.*

3. *Ovula neglecta*, C. B. Ad., is probably a small variety of *Radius variabilis.*

4. *Ovula variabilis*, C. B. Ad. = *Radius v.*, M. 435.

5. *Ovula*, sp. ind., probably = *variabilis*, jun.

6. *Cypræa arabicula* = *Aricia a.*, M. 438.

7. *Cypræa cervinetta* = *C. exanthema*, M. 436. Having now examined a multitude of specimens from different stations on the west coast, which differ from each other quite as much as they do from the typical Caribbean forms, I am confirmed in the belief of their identity.

8. *Cypræa punctulata* = *Aricia p.* Erroneously given, in M. p. 374, as a probable synonym of *A. arabicula*. It is less thickened at the sides, with smaller spots. Although specimens of *arabicula* graduate into it at the back, it may always be known by the mouth, which has its teeth much further apart.

9. *Cypræa pustulata* = *Trivia p.*, M. 439.

10. *Cyprœa radians=Trivia r.*, M. 440.

11. *Cyprœa rubescens=*dead sp. of *Trivia sanguinea*, M. 442.

12. *Cyprœa sanguinea=Trivia s.*, M. 442.

13. *Erato scabriuscula.* Stet.

14. *Marginella minor.* Stet, M. 587.

15. *Marginella sapotilla.* The Panama specimens collected by Prof. Adams, and abundantly by others, more closely resemble *M. prunum* than the type *M. sapotilla* of Hinds, which is a much smaller shell. The Caribbean shells (which are found across the Isthmus at Aspinwall) differ only in having a sharper angle in the labrum at the posterior notch. Adanson's habitat, doubted by Prof. Adams (note, p. 41), is confirmed by specimens in the Bristol Institution brought from Sierra Leone by Chief Justice Rankine. The Pacific shells are probably conspecific, sufficient evidence being now in our possession that the two oceans were united at least as late as the Miocene epoch*.

16. *Mitra funiculata.* Stet.

17. *Mitra lens*, M. 585.

18. *Mitra nucleola.* Closely resembling young specimens of the Caribbean *M. granulosa.*

19. *Mitra solitaria*, C. B. Ad.*=Zierliana s.* Other specimens have since been found of this characteristic species. The "transverse ribs" can scarcely be said to be "obsolete anteriorly."

20. *Mitra tristis=Strigatella t.*, M. 586.

21. *Terebra elata=Myurella e.*

22. *Terebra larvæformis=Myurella l.*

23, 24. Stent.

25. *Terebra tuberculosa=Myurella t.*

26. *Terebra varicosa.* This may possibly be a very young specimen of *Subula v.*; but I think it distinct.

27–31. Sp. ind. A specimen of *Euryta fulgurata*, M. 455, is in the museum, as from Panama, but not of Prof. Adams's collecting.

32. *Oliva angulata*, M. 590.

* The specimens in the Cumingian Museum, named *M. cœrulescens* at the time of the British Association Report, are now labelled "*sapotilla*, Hds., 5–13 fathoms sandy mud, Panama, H. C." Another set of Pacific shells (notch-angle rounded) are given as "*Marginella* n. s., Panama," "San Domingo" having been erased. The large West Indian form (notch-angle sharp) is given as "*cœrulescens*, var., Lam., 10 fathoms sandy mud, Panama." Another set of large shells, with sharp angle, and labrum tinted behind, is given as "*cœrulescens*, Lam., Panama," but without authority. The small West-Indian form (like the typical *sapotilla*) is given as "*glans*, Mke." Either in this, as in other instances, error has crept into the locality-marks, or else even the distinction pointed out by Mr. Redfield (who has given peculiar study to this genus) cannot be relied on for separating the species geographically.

33. *Oliva araneosa* = *O. meichersi*, M. 591. Prof. Adams's shanty specimen can scarcely be distinguished from that which he marked "*O. literata*, Alabama." But the ordinary aspect of the shells *O. reticularis* from the Caribbean Islands, *O. literata* from the coast of the Southern States, and *O. melchersi* from the Pacific, is sufficiently distinct (for the genus).

34. *Oliva inconspicua*, C. B. Ad. = *Olivella i.*, M. 599. Some of the shells referred to this species from Panama, Mazatlan, and Cape St. Lucas graduate into the Caribbean *O. oryza*; others into dwarf forms of *O. gracilis*. The species either needs revision from fresh specimens, or should be merged into *O. gracilis*.

35. *Oliva pellucida*, C. B. Ad. Dead specimen; differs from *Olivella p.*, Rve.

36. *Oliva porphyria*. Stet.

37. *Oliva semistriata* = *Olivella s.* Closely resembles *O. columellaris*.

38. *Oliva testacea* = *Agaronia t.*, M. 602.

39. *Oliva undatella* = *Olivella u.*, M. 595.

40. *Oliva venulata*. This shanty specimen is *O. angulata*, jun. The *O. venulata*, M. 593, is named by Prof. Adams *O julietta*, as also by Mke. (non Ducl.). The true *O. julietta* (Guacomayo, Mus. Smiths.) is the Pacific "analogue" of *O. fusiformis*.

41. *Oliva volutella* = *Olivella r.* It is surprising that this species, so immensely common at Panama and up the coast, should not reach the Gulf, and that the equally common *O. tergina* of Mazatlan and *O. gracilis* of Cape St. Lucas and Acapulco should be rare elsewhere, while the larger Olives are found from Guaymas to the equator. *O. dama* (= *lineolata*, Gray, C. B. Ad.), abundant at Mazatlan, was bought, not collected, by the Professor at Panama.

42 *Planaxis planicostata*. Stet. Also immensely common at Panama, though absent from Mazatlan.

43. *Nassa canescens*, C. B. Ad. Having compared this unique specimen with P. 50, q. v., I can speak to their complete identity. The "pale grey" of the "interspaces" is due to the shell being dead.

44, 45. Stent.

46. *Nassa gemmulosa* = M. 631, exactly.

47. Stet.

48. *Nassa luteostoma* = M. 623.

49. *Nassa nodifera*. Also found at Guaymas.

50. *Nassa pagodus*, C. B. Ad. (+ *N. canescens*, P. 43) = *N.* (? *pagodus*, var.) *acuta*, M. 625. It is certainly the *N. decussata* of Kien., but probably not of Lam. Whether it is the *Triton pagodus* of Rve. I am still unable to say, the type being apparently lost. We are bound to suppose that Mr. Reeve could not mistake so de-

cided a *Nassa* for a *Triton* ; so that if Lamarck's is a similar Eastern species, the West American may stand as *N. acuta.*

51. *Nassa panamensis,* C. B. Ad. The Professor rightly marked his duplicates "*exilis,* Pws." This abundant shell, having a Pisanoid, not a Nassoid operculum, probably belongs to *Phos, Northia,* or some genus not yet eliminated. *N. obsoleta,* Say, has a similar operculum, and appears nearly related.

52. *Nassa proxima.* The unique specimen appears to be an extreme form of *N. versicolor,* P. 55.

53. *Nassa ? scabriuscula,* C. B. Ad. (non Pws.)=*N. complanata,* Pws.: v. P. 56.

54. *Nassa striata,* C. B. Ad. The two type specimens, one young, the other adult, both belong to a variety of *versicolor.* The phrase, "last whorl spirally canaliculate on the left side," simply expresses the ordinary character of *Nassa.* The specimens in Mus. Cuming., however, from another source, differ somewhat in the nucleus from the small form of *N. versicolor.* These = *N. paupera,* Gld., teste Cuming, and should take that name.

55. *Nassa versicolor,* C. B. Ad., M. 632. The revolving striæ vary so greatly in this species, as well as the size, obesity, and colour, that it is hard to assign its limits. The specimens marked *versicolor* by the Professor vary much more among themselves than the extreme ones do from his *proxima* and *striata.* The apex and early whorls of each are exactly the same under the microscope. It is possible that the unique *crebristriata,* M. 633, is also an extreme variety.

56. *Nassa wilsoni* appears to be only a dwarf form of P. 53, *N. complanata.*

57. *Buccinum crassum* = *Phos c.*

58. *Buccinum distortum* = *Clavella d.*

59. *Buccinum insigne* = *Pisania i.,* M. 659.

60. *Buccinum lugubre,* C. B. Ad. The Professor marked this shell on his card "*Murex ? ?* " ; then "*Fusus?* "; then "*Fusus nodulosus,* Ad., n. s."; then "*Buccinum* (?) *lugubre,* Ad., n. s."; so that the old genera were sometimes as badly defined as the new ones. It may rank with *Pisania.*

61. *Buccinum pagodus* = *Pisania p.*

62. *Buccinum pristis* = *Northia serrata.*

63. *Buccinum ringens* = *Pisania r.,* M. 663.

64. *Buccinum sanguinolentum* = *Pisania s.,* M. 662.

65. *Buccinum stimpsonianum* = *Nassa st.*

66. *Dolium ringens* = *Malea r.*

67. *Monoceros brevidentatum.* This species, very common at Panama, has been transported over (not through) the Pacific, to San Francisco and Monterey . v. P page 75.

68. *Monoceros cingulatum* = *Leucozonia c.*, M. 583.

69. *Purpura carolensis* = *P. triangularis*, M. 608.

70. *Purpura foveolata* = *Cuma costata*, M. 610, probably; but the markings have been too much obliterated to decide with confidence.

71. *Purpura kiosquiformis* = *Cuma k.*, M. 609. There are in the collection three shells, labelled by the Professor "*P. purpuroides* (*Fusus*), Orb., Panama" = *Pisania d'orbignyi*, Rve. No authority is given, and they probably came from Peru.

72. *Purpura*, sp. ind. This shell is not to be found. It has probably been put with the last, of which it is no doubt a variety : v. M. p. 482.

73. *Purpura melo.* Stet.

74. *Purpura osculans* appears to be the young of *Rhizocheilus nux*, M. 611; of which *R. distans*, Cpr., and probably *R. californicus*, A. Ad., are only varieties.

75. *Purpura tecta* = *Cuma t.*

76. *Purpura undata* = *P. bixerialis*, M. 606.

77. *Columbella atramentaria* = *Anachis a.*

78. *Columbella bicanalifera* = *Strombina b.*

79. *Columbella boivinii.* This species must rank with (*Anachis* or) *Engina*[*], the operculum being Pisanoid.

80. *Columbella conspicua* = *Anachis c.*

81. *Columbella costellata*, C. B. Ad. = *Anachis scalarina*, Sby., M. 645; not *A. costellata*, Sby., M. 646.

82. *Columbella diminuta* = *Anachis d.*

83. *Columbella dorsata* = *Strombina d.*

84. *Columbella fluctuata* = *Anachis fl.*

85. *Columbella fulva* = *Anachis f.*, M. 648.

86. *Columbella fuscata*, M. 617. The small var. is *C. festiva*, Kien.

87. *Columbella gibberula* = *Strombina g.*

88. *Columbella gracilis* = *Anachis g.*

89. *Columbella guttata* = *Nitidella cribraria*, M. 613.

90, 91, 92. Stent.

93. *Columbella lyrata* = *Anachis l*

94. *Columbella major*, M. 615.

95. *Columbella modesta* = *Truncaria m.* It might be convenient to leave this genus as arranged by Messrs. H. and A. Ad. Mr. Henry Adams desires to restrict it to the type species, in which

---

[*] Of the shells called by French authors *Semi-Ricinula*, those with a Purpuroid operculum may be retained as *Sistrum*, while those with Pisanoid operculum should be removed as *Engina*, with *Anachis*, to the *Muricidæ*.

case this and similar species must be moved to *Nitidella*, if the operculum be (as is presumed) Purpuroid; or to *Amycla*, if Nassoid.

96. *Columbella mœsta = Anachis m.*

97 *Columbella nigricans = Anachis n.*

98. *Columbella parva.* This appears to be only a dead specimen of *C. pygmœa*, P. 100.

99. *Columbella pulchrior* is probably a *Nitidella.*

100. *Columbella pygmœa = Anachis p.*, M 651.

101. *Columbella rugosa = Anachis r.* This appears to be the commonest and most variable species of the genus. The typical specimens are somewhat stumpy, with stout knobs. Then the knobs pass into long, compressed ridges, and finally change into narrow bars. These are wide apart, or close, or nearly evanescent on the back. The shape passes from the stumpy to an acuminate form like *costellata*. Some adults are more than twice the size of others; but the same variations are found in both extremes. The colours are generally laid on in patches on the knobby specimens; in fine flames, on the smoother ones. In all varieties, it is known from *fluctuata* by the spiral striæ over the whole surface; and from *varia* by the shoulder, more or less developed into a keel, on the whorls of the spire.

102. *Columbella strombiformis*, M. 616.

103. *Columbella tessellata*, C. B. Ad. (non Gask.) = *Anachis guatemalensis*, Rve.

104. *Columbella turrita = Strombina t.*

105. *Columbella varia = Anachis v.*

106. *Columbella* sp. ind. is the young of a species in Mus. Cuming., resembling *harpæformis.*

107 *Ricinula carbonaria = Engina c.*

108. *Ricinula jugosa* may be an *Engina*, but has more the aspect of the Pacific group *Peristernia.*

109. *Ricinula reeviana = Engina pulchra*, Rve.

110. *Cassis abbreviata = Bezoardica a.* On comparing a large series of specimens from Cape St. Lucas with a similar series of *C. inflata* from Texas, I was unable to discover any specific differences. It varies greatly, from each ocean, in painting, sculpture, height of spire, &c.

111. *Cassis coarctata = Levenia c*

112, 113, 114(=M. 480), 115, 116 (=M. 481), 117, 118* (=M. 476), 119* (=M. 477), 120 (=M. 475), 121, 122 (=M. 381, *galeatus*), 123 (=M. 449), 124 (=M. 448), 125. Stent.

* Having now examined a large number of specimens of these two forms, I have no hesitation whatever in regarding *Conus regalitatis* as simply a variety of *C. purpurascens.* Similar differences may be observed in comparing large series of almost all Cones.

181

126. *Triton chemnitzii = Argobuccinum nodosum*, M. 580. These shells are small and turreted. Those Prof. Adams marked "*T. cingulatum*, Lam., E. Indies," are much more like the Mazatlan shells.

127. *Triton constrictus = Distortio c.* The specimens of this group from the Pacific Coast, from the Gulf of Mexico, and from the China Seas are very difficult to discriminate.

128. *Triton fusoides.* This unique and very elegant shell can scarcely be called a *Triton*, even of the *Epidromus* type. It may perhaps rank with *Euthria*, but is peculiar in possessing a distinct anterior sinus, near the canal, like *Rostellaria*.

129, 130, 131, 132*, 133, 134*, 135. Stent.

136. *Murex dubius = Muricidea dubia*, M. 673.

137. *Murex erosus = Muricidea e.*

138. *Murex radix = Phyllonotus r.* The Professor's specimens of this species are remarkably fine, more nearly resembling the Gulf *nigritus* than the heavy stumpy shells usually seen. His young specimens are heavier, but more turreted, than the young *nigritus*. The opercula appear to have fewer frills; but such differences may be due only to station. The specimens he marked *ambiguus* (without locality) belong to the typical *nigritus*. *Phyllonotus radix* and *nigritus* graduate into each other almost as freely as the latter does into *ambiguus*: v. M. 666.

139. *Murex rectirostris.* This and kindred species run into each other too closely, when adult, to speak with any confidence on so young a specimen in bad condition.

140. *Murex recurvirostris.* This specimen is also far too imperfect to affiliate: v. M. 665.

141. *Murex regius = Phyllonotus r.*, M. 670.

142. *Murex salebrosus = Vitularia s.*, M. 612. The curious group of Muricoid Purpurids culminates on the West American shores. It is represented in the north temperate regions by *Cerastoma*, on the warmer shores by *Chorus*, and in the tropical regions by *Vitularia*. The Lower Californian *Murex belcheri*, Hds., belongs to the group. Dr. Alcock (who has succeeded the late Capt. Brown as Curator of the Manchester Natural History Museum) has pointed out very well-marked physiological distinctions between the two families, which are coordinate with the differences in the opercula.

---

* Dr. Gray (Guide to Mollusca, pp. 39, 42) leaves the round-variced Ranellids, as *Apollon*, in the *Tritonidæ*, "operc. annular, nucleus subapical, within the apex;" but removes the sharp-variced species, as *Ranella*, to the *Cassididæ*, and figures the operculum like *Bezoardica*, "half-ovate, nucleus central, lateral, internal." The operculum of *R. cælata*, No. 132, is almost identical with *Murex*, and the shell accords with *Apollon*; but *R. nitida*, No. 134, which has very sharp varices, has its operculum widely removed from *Bezoardica*. It is closely related to that of *Cerastoma*, *Rhizocheilus*, and some of the *Ocinebræ*; nucleus near the anterior end of the labrum: labral portions of the annular layers eroded; scar as in Purpurids, with about three roughly angular ridges of growth.

143. *Murex vibex.* This Peruvian species also probably belongs to the Purpurid group.

144. *Murex vittatus*=*Muricidea v.*

145. (=M. 638), 146 (=M. 579). Stent.

147. *Fusus bellus,* C. B. Ad. This is a pretty little shell, resembling a young *Metula,* and is probably one of the species assigned with doubt to that genus, M. 619–622, or to *Fusus*, M. 642. I should erase the words, "some of which are varicoid" (referring to the radiating ribs), as my glass did not enable me to detect a single one.

148. *Fasciolaria granosa.* A minute specimen is of the size and general appearance of the fry of *Chrysodomus antiquus,* with one and a half irregular nuclear whorls. An adult has its operculum broken and mended from a subcentral nucleus—a mode of proceeding which I have now observed in such a multitude of species belonging to different families of Proboscidifers and Toxifers that I venture to assign it as the original type of their opercula, from which the special family forms are modifications of high development. Of the spiral Rostrifers there is not yet sufficient evidence to speak *.

149. *Turbinella cæstus,* M. 581.

150. *Turbinella castanea*=*Latirus c.*

151. *Turbinella cerata*=*Latirus c.,* M. 582.

152. *Turbinella rudis*=*Latirus r.*

153. *Turbinella spadicea*=*Latirus s.*

154. *Cancellaria affinis.* Very closely allied to *C. urceolata,* M. 445.

155, 156, 157 (=M. 446), 158, 159. Stent.

160. *Cancellaria pygmæa* is simply a young specimen of *C. gcniostoma,* no. 157.

161, 162. Stent.

163. *Pleurotoma aterrima*=*Drillia a.*

164. *Pleurotoma atrior.* This is a fine specimen, not quite mature in the lip, of *Drillia aterrima,* var. *melchersi,* M. 461.

165. *Pleurotoma bicanalifera*=*Clathurella b.*

166. *Pleurotoma collaris*=*Drillia c.*

167. *Pleurotoma concinna*=*Cithara c.*

168. *Pleurotoma corrugata*=*Drillia c.*

169. *Pleurotoma discors*=*Drillia d.* Probably a finely developed variety of *aterrima.*

---

* When at Charleston, S. C., I had an opportunity of examining many very fine specimens of the giant *Fasciolaria,* so seldom seen in this country, of which a broken specimen in my collection measures 20 in. In sculpture, colour, and general appearance some were so very like *F. princeps,* M. 584, that I was tempted to consider the latter a degraded local variety, till I found the operculum, which is destitute of the singular grooving of the Gulf species.

170. *Pleurotoma duplicata*= *Drillia d.*

171. *Pleurotoma excentrica*= *Drillia e.* I cannot endorse this
and some other determinations of critical species of Pleurotomids,
not being able to remove the specimens for comparison with types.
Even the types in Mus. Cuming. do not always present satisfactory
diagnostic characters.

172. *Pleurotoma exigua*= *Mangelia e.* I could not discover "the
rest in pairs."

173. *Pleurotoma gemmulosa*= *Mangelia g.*

174. *Pleurotoma grandimaculata*= *Drillia g.*

175. *Pleurotoma incrassata*= *Drillia i.*, M. 459. The collection
contains *D. luctuosa*, M. 467, as from Panama, but not of the Professor's collecting.

176. *Pleurotoma nigerrima*= *Drillia n.*

177. *Pleurotoma obeliscus*= *Drillia o.* Very worn and doubtful.

178. *Pleurotoma olivacea.* Closely resembles *P. funiculata*,
M. 457.

179. *Pleurotoma pallida*= *Drillia p.*

180. *Pleurotoma rigida*= *Clathurella r.*

181. *Pleurotoma rudis.* It is probable that this is not the true
Drillia rudis, being distinguished by white spots on the knobs :
v. M. 460.

182. *Pleurotoma rustica*= *Drillia aterrima*, var. *melchersi*, M.
461. These specimens being very worn, their specific identity with
P. 164 was not recognized by the Professor. One shell, marked
"*rustica*, var.," may be the true *rustica*—a species by no means
satisfactorily distinguished.

183. *Pleurotoma striosa*= *Drillia s.*

184. *Pleurotoma zonulata*= *Drillia z.*, M. 463.

185. *Pleurotoma*, sp. *a.* A small, dark, purple-brown *Mangelia*,
of the *leufroyi* type.

186. *Pleurotoma*, sp. *b.* A slender, pure-white, ribbed shell;
probably a *Cithara*.

187. *Mangelia*, sp. *c.* A young *Daphnella*.

188. *Mangelia*, sp. *d.* A very worn, black shell; with white,
knobby ribs.

189. *Mangelia*, sp. *e.* A very small, white shell; resembling a
young *Bela turricula*.

190. *Mangelia*, sp. *f.* A very small, white *Drillia*, with distinct
posterior notch; spirally striated, with rather sharp ribs.

191. *Mangelia neglecta.* Of the "elevated spiral line on the
middle of the whorls" I could discover no trace, except of colour.
It is therefore probable that it= *M. acuticostata*, M. 473.

192. *Mangelia sulcosa* is the true *Columbella s* of Sby.

193. *Cerithium adustum = C. maculosum*, M. 381.

194. *Cerithium assimilatum = Cerithiopsis a.*, M. 563.

195. *Cerithium bimarginatum = Cerithiopsis b.* A good species; but I could not detect the "intermediate raised line." The apical whorls are almost smooth. The "prominent spiral fold" on the columella is simply that which bounds the recurved canal.

196. *Cerithium famelicum.* Confusion has arisen from the Professor having sent to Mr. Cuming as his type a shell which does not answer to the diagnosis, and which is described as (? var.) *mediolæve*, M. 382. Ten specimens are retained in the Amherst Museum, of which eight are of the *uncinatum* type, = M. 383, and two of the Cumingian. *C. uncinatum*, being an old species, is probably from the Atlantic or E. Indies: if this should prove identical, the name *famelicum* must be dropped; if distinct, retained for the west coast uncinoids, according to the diagnosis. After an examination of a large series of specimens collected by Mr. Xantus at Cape St. Lucas, I am confirmed in the belief that the Cumingian shell is a distinct species, which must stand as *C. mediolæve*.

197. *Cerithium gemmatum = Rhinoclavis gemmatus*, M. 389. So much confusion has arisen from raising specific names to the generic peerage, that whenever a good distinct name has been given, it appears best to retain it—the unbending rule of mere priority for work which is sometimes slovenly, and therefore best forgotten, notwithstanding.

198. *Cerithium ? interruptum*, C. B. Ad. (non Mke. = M. 383). Great confusion has arisen from this erroneous determination, as may be seen by comparing the Maz. Cat. *in loco* with the monograph of Sowerby, jun., who has redescribed the southern, highly sculptured forms of the true *interruptum* as *C. galapaginis*.

198 and 199 are regarded by Messrs. Cuming and Sowerby as varieties of

200. *Cerithium irroratum*, C. B. Ad. (Gld. ipse et MSS., non Gld. in Expl. Exp.) = *C. stercusmuscarum*, M. 387. The aspect of the Panama shells is so different from that of the Mazatlan specimens that I did not wonder at Dr. Gould's opinion that they were distinct. He was, however, misled in affiliating the former to his *C. irroratum*, of which I fortunately discovered the figured type in the Smithsonian Institution, and which proves to be (according to Mr. Cuming) the *C. obesum* of Sby. sen., from the Philippines. It is fortunate therefore that the name may be entirely dropped. Some of the specimens of no. 198 graduate sufficiently closely to the Mazatlan form; those of no. 199 are intermediate; while those of no. 200 present a stronger but smaller shell, well armed with small nodules, which are not to be seen in the fine Gulf specimens.

201. *Cerithium neglectum = Cerithiopsis n.*

202. *Cerithium pacificum.* Stet.

203. *Cerithium pauperculum* is a good, new species of *Chrysallida.* The Professor probably did not recognize the Chemnitzoid apex and the Odostomoid plait. The following alterations may be made in the diagnosis:—Shell pale orange [not horn], with six [not five] keels on the spire; spiral ridges anteriorly fainter [not obsolete]; apex sinistral [not acute], of three Paludinoid whorls, the last large in proportion; columella effuse [not canaliculated], with a long, slender, slanting plait.

204. *Cerithium pulchrum* = *Cerithidea p.* A distinct and truly beautiful species, seldom obtained by collectors.

205. *Cerithium reevianum* = *Cerithidea montagnei*, M. 394.

206. *Cerithium validum* = *Cerithidea raricosa*, M. 395. The Southern shells, in all their changes, present such a different aspect from the Gulf specimens, that I am inclined to regard the form *Mazatlanica* as distinct, of which *C. albonodosa* may prove a variety.

207. *Triphoris alternatus*, M. 391.

208. *Triphoris inconspicuus* is scarcely even a variety of the last; and does not differ so much as the specimens described under the same name, M. 392.

209. *Triphoris infrequens* is not the shell described, under the same name, M. 393, but is the *Cerithiopsis tuberculoides*, M. 557. It would have been strange if I had recognized the shell from the diagnosis; for *both of the specimens are dextral.* The apex is nearly smooth. I forbear to redescribe nos. 392, 393 of the Maz. Cat., as they were separated principally in deference to Prof. Adams's authority, until more numerous specimens should have been examined.

210. *Turritella banksii* = *T. goniostoma*, jun., M. 379.

211. *Cæcum diminutum* = *Cæcum firmatum*, jun., with numerous close rings. All the Professor's specimens of this genus were dead; most of them pierced by Proboscidifers. They fully confirmed the judgments I ventured to form of them in the Maz. Cat. and in the "Monograph of the Cæcidæ," P. Z. S. 1858, p. 413 *et seq.*

212. *Cæcum eburneum* = *C. firmatum.* The rings vary from twenty-six to thirty-three.

213. *Cæcum firmatum*, M. 368. Add to the diagnosis in Maz. Cat. p. 320, last line, "*operculo vix concavo, suturis minus definitis.*"

214. *Cæcum læve.* The two specimens are too worn for identification, but will pass sufficiently for the species described under the same name, M. 372.

215. *Cæcum laqueatum.* A good species of the *Elephantulum* group: v. Maz. Cat. p. 315, and P. Z. S. *loc. cit.* p. 420.

216. *Cæcum monstrosum* = *C. firmatum* in the adolescent stage.

217. *Cæcum parvum* turns out, as was expected, to be = *C. undatum*, M. 371. The unique specimen is stunted and dead.

218. *Cæcum pygmæum* is a small but nearly adult *C. firmatum.*

219. *Chemnitzia aculeus*, M. 521.

220. *Chemnitzia acuminata* is a true *Chemnitzia*, and not a *Chrysallida*, as supposed in the Br. Assoc. Report, p. 334. The name misleads, as it is a peculiarly broad species. The vertex consists of three Paludinoid whorls, of which the apex is visible, projecting a little beyond the spire. The ribs, instead of "terminating abruptly on the periphery of the last whorl," become gradually evanescent round the base *.

221. *Chemnitzia affinis*. Comp. M. 523, which was identified from Mr. Cuming's specimen. The diagnosis needs the following corrections from the type. The "ribs terminate" not very "abruptly at the periphery." Anteriorly very finely striated [not "smooth"]. "Last whorl" not "angular at the periphery." Base prolonged. It is probably the adult form of my *Chemnitzia undata*, M. 531, the characteristic fine, waved, spiral striæ having escaped the Professor's notice. The only difference is that the ribs evanesce more suddenly in the Panama than in the Mazatlan shell, which may be due simply to age.

222. *Chemnitzia clathratula*, part. = *Chrysallida clathratula*, M. 513, which was identified from the Cumingian specimen. The specimens preserved as types contain, along with this species, one of *Chrysallida communis*, one (almost certainly) of *Chrysallida effusa*, M. 510, and one of *Dunkeria subangulata*, M. 537. Some parts of the description appear taken from the latter species: *e. g.* the "five or six" spiral lines, of which there are only four in the *Chrysallida*; and the angle on the "upper part" of the whorls, which in the latter are well rounded.

223. *Chemnitzia communis*, M. 507. This is the type of the genus *Chrysallida*: v. M. pp. 416, 420. Prof. Adams's tray contains also one specimen of *Chrysallida effusa*, M. 510 ; one of *Chrys. telescopium*, M. 508 ; one of *Dunkeria subangulata*, M. 537 ; and one which may be a variety of the latter, or a distinct species.

224. *Chemnitzia gracilior*. The "well-impressed spiral line" is only seen in some of the whorls.

225 *Chemnitzia major* belongs to the section *Dunkeria*. I counted eighteen (not twenty-four) ribs.

226. *Chemnitzia marginata* is a good species of *Chrysallida* ; but I could not find the "spiral, compressed ridge."

227 *Chemnitzia panamensis*, M. 518. I counted twenty-four (not twenty-seven) ribs. The tray also contains one specimen of

---

* As several errors are here pointed out in the diagnoses of small shells, it is right to state that Prof. Adams had not the advantage of a microscope during a considerable portion of the work ; nor was the instrument a good one when obtained. Moreover the incessant demands on his attention as Professor of Astronomy and Mathematics, as well as of Natural History, and his duties as State Geologist of Vermont, did not leave him much time for original research. What he accomplished during his short life is marvellous. Had that life been spared to revise his works, the necessity for this friendly criticism would not have arisen.

Ch. C-B-Adamsii, M. 519, with straight ribs; and one with spiral sculpture, which may belong to *Ch. gracillima*, M. 530, but wants the produced apex.

228. *Chemnitzia similis.* This species most nearly resembles *aculeus*, but is broader, larger, and with more ribs, of which I counted from twenty to twenty-two (not twenty-six). I should not call the whorls "convex." They are, however, more rounded, and the base is more produced, than in the shell called "? *similis*," M. 520, which is perhaps a variety of *panamensis*.

229. *Chemnitzia striosa.* The early whorls, are very slender. The spiral striæ are on the tops of the ribs, of which I counted from twenty-four to thirty-two (instead of "about forty").

230. *Chemnitzia turrita.* This species includes the "*Rissoa*, sp. ind." no. 251.

231. ? *Littorina angiostoma* is a *Fossarus.*

232. *Littorina aspera*, M. 397. The Mazatlan periwinkles, being in good condition, divide themselves very naturally into three species. The Panama specimens, being generally eroded, are not so easily dealt with. Of Prof. Adams's specimens here retained, the majority belong to *aspera*, although several of the smaller ones are *philippii*, M. 398. The young appear to be of both species mixed. The "variety" consists of the abnormal tall specimens of *conspersa*, M. 396, with a few very large *philippii* intermixed.

233. *Littorina atrata.* This abundant little shell is a *Fossarus*, of which the Professor's ?*Adeorbis abjecta*, no. 257, is a more advanced form. It is possible that one of the *Fossari* described in Maz. Cat., nos. 404, 405, may be conspecific; but among the multitude of specimens I could not find one with the nuclear whorls sufficiently perfect to decide. The shells vary extremely in shape and sculpture.

234. *Littorina conspersa*, M. 396. Smaller and generally more stumpy than the Mazatlan shells, but containing a few specimens of the same extreme forms.

235. ? *Littorina excavata* = *Fossarus e.*

236. *Littorina fasciata*, M. 400. The specimens of this species and of *L. varia* graduate rather closely towards each other.

237. ? *Littorina foveata.* A good species of *Fossarus.* Read, "Last whorl angular" at the umbilicus [not "below the middle"].

238. ? *Littorina megasoma.* This is also a good species of *Fossarus.* The Professor was doubtful whether to refer these forms to *Littorina* or to *Narica.*

239. *Littorina* ? *parvula*, C. B. Ad. This is not Philippi's *L. parvula*, but is a dwarf form of the *L. philippii*, M. 398. The Professor suggests the name *L. dubiosa* for this sufficiently well-marked species; but as he catalogued and distributed his specimens under ? *parvula*, and kept others under *aspera*, it may be best to retain

the name *philippii* under which it has been very extensively circulated.

240. *Littorina pulchra.* A very rare species, belonging (with *fasciata* and *varia*) to the *Melaraphe* group.

241. *Littorina puncticulata.* This is the normal state of *L. conspersa* : v. M. 396.

242. *Littorina varia* : v. note on P. 236.

243. *Rissoa clandestina.* Three specimens appear of this species of *Rissoina*, closely resembling *R. woodwardii*, M. 410, but with more ribs, and not displaying the intercostal striulæ.

244. *Rissoa firmata.* Another species of *Rissoina*, resembling *R. stricta*, M. 408, but smaller. The Professor did not observe the fine spiral sculpture, as described in no. 250 ; q. v.

245. *Rissoa fortis.* A good species of *Rissoina*, differing from *R. janus* in the absence of spiral punctures.

246. ? *Rissoa inconspicua*, C. B. Ad., non Alder. The name being preoccupied, it is fortunate that the unique shell proves identical with *Alvania tumida*, M. 414. I found twenty (not "twelve or fourteen") ridges, which are not "obsolete," but become fainter anteriorly. The two upper whorls are very finely cancellated.

247. *Rissoa infrequens.* The unique specimen of this *Rissoina* is too much worn for description. It has more than the sixteen ribs ; and the diagnostic marks must be received with caution.

248. *Rissoa janus.* The description of this *Rissoina* is drawn from a very small, dead, broken specimen, from which the sculpture is almost entirely worn away. The "var. *a*" should be considered as the type, being in perfect condition, and the diagnosis be altered as follows :—The "fine crowded spiral striæ" are seen all over, as are also the "ribs," which on each whorl "appear as striæ," and are not "obsolete near the periphery." The diagnostic character is that the spiral striæ are composed of rows of minute dots.

249. *Rissoa notabilis.* After drawing this unique shell carefully under the microscope, and making copious notes on the diagnosis from the specimen, an untoward cough lodged it among the meshes of the Curator's carpet, whence I endeavoured in vain to extricate it. This unfortunate accident is, however, the less to be regretted, as I can state with perfect confidence that it was exactly identical with another shell in the collection, P. 255, q. v. ; and with M. 498, *Parthenia quinquecincta.* The "concave summits" of the ribs imply that the ribs are sharp, with concave interstices ; and the "upper keel" is simply due to the angulation of the whorls. Though the lip was broken, the columellar plait, as well as the sinistral apex, escaped the Professor's notice.

250. *Rissoa scalariformis.* This unique specimen is simply the young of *Rissoina firmata*, P. 244; and probably = *Rissoina* sp. ind. M. 409.

189

251. *Rissoa*, sp. ind.   This is a broken specimen of *Chemnitzia turrita*, P. 230.

252. ? *Cingula inconspicua.*   This unfortunate name, liable to be confounded with *Rissoa inconspicua*, Alder, and ? *Rissoa inconspicua*, C. B. Ad., will not be needed, as the type belongs to another sub-order, and = *Chrysallida ovulum*, M. 512.   The Professor did not observe its close relationship with his *Chemnitzia communis.*

253. *Cingula paupercula*, C. B. Ad.   A good species.

254. ? *Cingula terebellum* = *Parthenia exarata*, M. 501. Although I took every pains, in preparing the Maz. Cat., to identify Prof. Adams's species, I was not prepared, in the writings of so careful a naturalist who had devoted special attention to the minute species, to find a Pyramidellid under Trochidæ, especially with the mark "apex subacute." The finding of a more perfect Mazatlan specimen enables me to add to the diagnosis:—"*vertice nucleoso parvo, satis extante, decliviter sito; interstitiis carinarum transversim rugulosis; labro solidiore.* Long. ·087, long. spir. ·057, lat. ·038."

255. ? *Cingula turrita* (+ P. 249, *Rissoa notabilis*) = *Parthenia quinquecincta*, M. 498.   When a shell is described under two genera in the same sheet, the advocates of unbending priority will find it difficult to decide.   As each name belongs to a widely removed family, that last given is at least the most correct and distinctive.

256. ? *Litiopa saxicola.*   The Professor states that this "shell has the appearance of a *Litiopa*;" but it wants both the peculiar nucleus and the semitruncated columella ; also that the "labium has a distinct deposit," of which I could not see any trace in either of the specimens.   It is probably a *Cingula.*

257. ? *Adeorbis abjecta.*   This is the adult form of the shell, of which P. 233, *Littorina atrata*, is the young.   The striæ are seen on the lower as well as the "upper part of the whorls."   The umbilicus, though "small" for an *Adeorbis*, is rather large for a *Fossarus*, to which genus the species undoubtedly belongs.

258. *Vitrinella concinna.*   I could not find the "more or less distinct ridge between the first two keels."

259. *Vitrinella exigua* = M. 305.   The omissions in the Professor's diagnoses of this and other species, being supplied in the Maz. Cat., need not be repeated here : v. M. pp. 236–247.

260. *Vitrinella janus.*   The Professor does not mention the fifth keel, which bounds the umbilicus, and within which are the "minute spiral striæ."   The "transverse striæ" are strong between keels 2, 3, and 4 ; faint between 4 and 5, and between 1 and 2 ; and evanescent near the suture.

261. *Vitrinella minuta.*   The original type of this species accords better with *Ethalia* than with *Teinostoma*, to which I had referred the Cumingian type.

262. *Vitrinella modesta.*   The "modesty" of this unique shell is

coordinate with considerable attrition, and an umbilicus filled with dirt. It appeared to me regularly rounded, without any keel. The "few spiral striæ" are probably the remains of what once covered the whole surface.

263. *Vitrinella panamensis*=M. 295.

264. *Vitrinella parva*=M. 296.

265. *Vitrinella perparva*=M. 304. The coronation of the upper keel is seen (though not described) in the type specimen.

266. *Vitrinella regularis.* The unique shell can hardly be called "subdiscoidal," since the "spire is convex, moderately elevated." I could not find the "impressed spiral line." It belongs to *Ethalia*.

267. *Vitrinella seminuda.* The unique type of this species also is much worn. I could not discover the "minute striæ of growth." Beneath, there are five spiral liræ, and a few spiral striæ near the mouth. The umbilical region and the base have fine radiating distant striæ. It comes nearest to *V. carinulata*, M. 309, but is distinct.

268. *Vitrinella tricarinata.* This unique type is also worn. The spiral keels are scarcely "prominent," that on the periphery being decidedly faint. The "transverse striæ" are between the suture and the nearest rib. The umbilical striæ are very faint.

269. *Vitrinella vulvatoides.* This species probably belongs to *Ethalia*. Beside the keels, there are three obsolete spiral liræ—two on the base, and one above the periphery. The umbilicus is bounded by a long, thin callosity, which gives a character to the shell intermediate between the two genera.

270. *Solarium*, sp. ind. *a.* Of the form represented by this species and the next I have been able to examine a large number of specimens collected at Cape St. Lucas by Mr. Xantus, and in the Gulf of Mexico. I know of no mark by which to distinguish the shells from the two oceans. From each locality they vary greatly in the size of the umbilicus, and in the strength of sculpture, number of knobs, &c. I should consider them all as varieties of *S. granulatum*, Lam. *S. quadriceps*, Hds., appears distinct, though it may only be an extreme variety.

271. *Solarium*, sp. ind. *b.* This contains the specimens with coarser sculpture than the last.

272. *Solarium*, sp. ind. *c.* This is a distinct species of *Torinia*, having the size and general aspect of *Helix rotundata.*

273. *Trochus catenulatus*=*Modulus c.*, M. 401.

274. *Trochus coronulatus*=*Omphalius c.* This species reappears at Cape St. Lucas, and is closely allied to *O. ligulatus*, M. 293.

275. *Trochus leanus*=*Calliostoma l.* This distinctive generic name is strongly to be preferred to the specific *Ziziphinus.*

276. *Trochus lima.* This shell exactly accords with *Calliostoma antonii*, Koch, in Mus. Cuming.

277. *Trochus liridus*=*Modulus disculus*, M. 403.

278. *Trochus panamensis*=*Omphalius p.* A good species, though apparently very rare ; for I had the pleasure of adding it to the Cumingian collection.

279. *Trochus pellis-serpentis*=*Tegula p.*

280. *Trochus reticulatus*=*Omphalius viridulus*, M. 292. This is the common Trochid of the Panama region, as is *ligulatus* of the Mazatlan.

281. *Turbo buschii*=*Uvanilla inermis*, M. 287. This shell appears to replace *U. olivacea* in the southern fauna. Besides the differences indicated in Maz. Cat. p. 229, the operculum is quite distinct.

282. ? *Turbo phasianella*=*Collonia ph.*: not (*Melaraphe*) *phasianella*, Phil.

283. *Turbo rutilus.* The unique type is in miserable condition, to which the "bright red with pale streaks" is owing. The shell may possibly have been originally a *Pomaulax undosus*, which is truly a Lower Californian species. It appears, however, to be a favourite with sailors, as specimens are continually appearing, not only high and low on the West Coast, but also from the Pacific Islands. The specimens brought by Comm. Wilkes's U.S. Expl. Exp. were obtained in N. S. Wales ! Prof. Adams's fragments were probably due to ballast.

284. *Turbo saxosus*=*Callopoma saxosum.* This replaces the *C. fluctuosum* of the Gulf, M. 282, and the *C. tessellatum* of Lower California. The "var. *depressum*" of P. Z. S., 1855, I believe to be really a *Senectus* from the Pacific Islands.

285. *Scalaria hexagona*, C. B. Ad.: non Sbv., M. 564. The Professor's shell is (I think) one of the species I described in P. Z. S. from Mr. Bridges's collection ; but the distinctions in this genus are too critical to decide without comparison of types. This shell is broad ; whorls very separate ; varices long and sharp ; spirally finely striated.

286. *Scalaria obtusa*, C. B. Ad.; ? non Sby. This also appeared to me one of Mr. Bridges's species. It is a very pretty shell, with close, sharp, coronated varices.

287. *Scalaria*, sp. ind. *a.* Like the next, but larger, and with spiral striæ between the extremely crowded, sharp varices.

288. *Scalaria*, sp. ind. *b.* Of the *Clathratula* type, without spiral sculpture.

289. *Scalaria*, sp. ind. *c*, is probably the young of *Cirsotrema funiculatum*, M. 569, which, with its congeners, may be removed to *Opalia*.

290. *Eulima iota.* This shell, which is a *Leiostraca* (not "? *Stylifer*"), is probably distinct from the Mazatlan form, M. 555, which should stand as *L. retexta.*

192

291. *Eulima recta.* The type is a very good species of *Leiostraca*; but I doubt its identity with the Cumingian specimen, with which the Mazatlan shell, M. 550, was compared. It most resembles the *L. linearis*, M. 554, with which it agrees in divergence and general shape; but that is very much smaller, with the upper whorls more tumid. In the Professor's type of *L. recta*, I searched in vain for traces of the "two brown spots." They were probably thrown by defective light. The "two opaque spiral bands" are simply the effect of the suture, and the previous whorl showing through. For the Mazatlan shell, M. 550, I propose the name of *L. involuta*.

292. *Eulima solitaria.* This also is a *Leiostraca*, not "? *Stylifer*," and accords exactly with the *Leiostraca*, sp. ind. *a*, M. 552, but not with the supposed *L. solitaria*, M. 551. The latter agrees in shape with the unique Panama shell, whorl for whorl; but its base and labrum are much more produced anteriorly. For this reason, it may be known as *L. producta*.

293. *Pyramidella*, sp. ind. This is probably the *Obeliscus* described in Maz. Cat. no. 486.

294. *Pyramidella conica* = *Obeliscus conicus*, C. B. Ad., not M. 486.

295. *Natica chemnitzii*=*N. maroccana*, M. 570. The Professor first labelled these shells " *N.* ? *maroccana*, Chem.," but crossed it off in pencil. Another tray appeared (without number) labelled "? *unifasciata*, Lam." They all belong to the large West Coast form of *maroccana*. [N.B. The shells described in P. Z. S. as "var. *californica*," on the authority of the late Mr. Nuttall, are (with others from the same source) undoubtedly from the Sandwich Islands. The Pacific specimens (of which I have examined many thousands, brought by Comm. Wilkes's E. E.) present a very different type from those of the west coasts of Africa and America; but are regarded by Mr. Cuming as only a local variety.]

296. *Natica* ? *lurida.* These shells are simply a pale variety of *N. maroccana.*

297. *Natica otis*, C. B. Ad. (not Brod. & Sby.). These shells appear to be the young of *Polinices* "*salangonensis*," P. 298.

298. *Natica* ? *salangonensis.* I had no opportunity of comparing this *Polinices* with the species of Récluz.

299. *Natica souleyetiana.* The shells closely resemble *N. maroccana*, but with a larger umbilicus.

300. *Natica* ? *virginea*, C. B. Ad. (not Récl.) = *Polinices uber*, M. 576.

301. *Natica*, sp. ind. *a*. There is no ticket answering to this number, which was probably intended for the *N. maroccana*, var. "*unifasciata*."

302. *Natica*, sp. ind. *b*. The shells are marked *e*, and are the young of *Polinices uber*, P. 300, M. 576.

303. *Natica*, sp. ind. c.   The shell is marked *f*, and is probably
=*N. haneti*

304. *Nerita scabricosta*=M. 326.   After examining a multitude
of specimens from different parts of the coast, I have not the slightest
doubt of the identity of the forms called *ornata* and *deshayesii*.

305. *Nerita*, sp. ind. *a*=*N. bernhardi*, M. 327.

306. *Neritina guayaquilensis*. Stet.+*N. intermedia*, Sby.

307. *Neritina picta*=M. 329.

308–316. Stent.   The shells described as "*Auricula*" belong to
Melampus.

317. *Truncatella bairdiana*.   A good species.

318. ?! *Truncatella dubiosa*.   This belongs to *Hydrobia* or some
similar Rissoid.

319. *Bulla (Tornatina) infrequens*=*Tornatina i.*, M. 222.

320. *Bulla (Cylichna) luticola*=*Cylichna l.*, M. 221.   The Mazatlan shell is much more constricted than most of Prof. Adams's
specimens.

321. *Bulla punctulata*=*B. adamsi*, M. 224.   The *B. punctata*,
A. Ad.=*B. punctulata*, A. Ad., but is not the *B. punctulata*,
C. B. Ad.=*B. puncticulata*, C. B. Ad., MS. on ticket.

322. *Bulla*, sp. ind.=*Tornatina carinata*, M. 223.

323. *Vermetus ? glomeratus*, C. B. Ad. (not *Bivonia glomerata*,
Lam.)=*V. eburneus*, M. 354.   The shells sometimes assume a ru-
fous tint in the later whorls, in which state (if the Turritelloid apex
be concealed) it is liable to be confounded with *Aletes centiquadrus*.
Some of the Professor's shells belong to the latter species.

324. *Vermetus panamensis*, C. B. Ad. (? Rouss.)=*Aletes centiquadrus*, M. 352.

325. *Stomatella inflata* is a *Lamellaria* with broken lip and very
much curved columella: v. M. 577.   [A *Sigaretus*, with somewhat
sharper columella than the ordinary W. Indian form, was found
among the Professor's duplicate Panama shells; but as it does not
occur either in the catalogue or the collection, it was probably dropped
in from the Jamaica series.]

326. *Hipponyx*, sp. ind.   Of the Professor's "two small specimens" marked "*subrufa*, jun.," one is *H. grayanus*, jun., M. 350.
The other may be the same, but is probably the young of *H. barbatus*.   Neither are sufficiently perfect to determine with confidence.

327. *Hipponyx ? barbata*.   Part of these specimens belong to *H.
barbatus*, M. 349; part to *H. grayanus*; part are too much worn
to determine; and one is a valve of *Discina cumingii*.

328. *Hipponyx panamensis*=*H. antiquatus*, M. 347.   The species
is very widely diffused, and varies greatly in each locality.

329. *Hipponyx radiata*=*H. grayanus*, M. 350.   The collection

also contains a tray labelled " Panama : C. B. Ad. don.," in which are *Hipponyx serratus*, M. 346, *H. barbatus*, and *Gadinia pentagoniostoma*, M. 270. This last name should be dropped, except as a variety of *G. stellata*, Sby., which is the normal state : v. B. A. Rep. 1857, pl. 7. f. 3, *a–g*.

330. *Calyptræa aberrans*. The Professor candidly allows that "in texture this shell much resembles a valve of an *Anomia*," which it undoubtedly is, the supposed "probably imperfect cup" being the ligamental pit. The large muscular scar is very clearly developed ; but the others are faint, as is customary in young shells, and might stand for either *Anomia* or *Placunanomia*. The valve is thin and glossy inside. The outside is smooth, excepting the lines of growth, and is encrusted with beautiful zoophytes. A tiny *Serpula*, which has coiled itself close to the umbo, carries out the idea of a Calyptræid spiral apex ; but a careful microscopic examination displayed the true Anomoid nucleus, at a little distance from the margin, as is common in the Mazatlan specimens of *A. lampe*, M. 219.

331. *Calyptræa (Syphopatella) aspersa*=*Galerus conicus*, very worn and young, with the lamina broken away. One of the specimens may perhaps be *mamillaris*.

332. *Calyptræa cepacea*=M. 345.

333. *Calyptræa conica*. These are dead specimens, of which a few may be the true *Galerus conicus*, M. 332. But most of them belong to the brown-tinted variety of (the Professor's *G. regularis*=) *mamillaris* : v. no. 340.

334. *Calyptræa dentata*=*Crucibulum imbricatum*, M. 343.

335. *Calyptræa hispida*=*Crucibulum spinosum*, M. 344.

336. *Calyptræa imbricata*. The two specimens are too much worn to affiliate with confidence, the cups being broken out. The outside is ribbed, with arrow-headed striæ between the ribs. They probably =*Crucibulum i.*, var.

337. *Calyptræa maculata*=*Crucibulum spinosum*, M. 344. See the attempt to unravel the confusion in the synonymy of this family in Maz. Cat. pp. 264–295. Three specimens marked by the Professor " *C. maculata*, var.," are young, dead *radiata*, no. 339.

338. *Calyptræa planulata*. This unique shell is simply a young, flat *C. cepacea*, with the cup prominent, and the outside sculpture faintly developed, from living in a hollow place. The striæ are not "obsolete around the apex."

339. *Calyptræa radiata*=*Crucibulum r.* This rare and beautiful species is quite distinct, even in the early stages, from all varieties of *C. spinosum*.

340. *Calyptræa (Syphopatella) regularis*=*Galerus mamillaris*, M. 333.

341. *Calyptræa umbrella*=*Crucibulum u.* (=*C. rudis*, Brod.).

342. *Calyptræa ?!unguis*, C. B. Ad.= *Crucibulum spinosum*, jun. (not *Galerus unguis*, Brod.).

343. *Crepidula cerithiicola*. Most of the specimens are the young of *C. onyx*, M. 340; but a few are of *C. incurva*, M. 339.

344. *Crepidula echinus* = *C. aculeata*, M. 334.

345. *Crepidula excavata*, M. 337.

346. *Crepidula ? hepatica* = *C. onyx*, M. 340.

347. *Crepidula incurva*, M. 339. A very interesting series of specimens; of which two or three are probably the twisted form of *C. onyx*. One tray contains specimens adhering to other shells. One, fixed diagonally on a *Calliostoma*, takes exactly the arrow-headed sculpture of the var. *Cal. imbricata*, Brod. Another, grown diagonally on *Pisania gemmata*, has the general aspect of a *Chiton*. One, fixed on the back of its neighbour which has grown on a *Calliostoma*, has the granular interruptions of the ribs transmitted *through* the first specimen. The same is true of one which has grown on another which was planted on a *Pisania*. One specimen, which had established itself on a *Calliostoma*, and began with normal ribs, is losing these at the margin, adopting the sculpture of the Trochid. An extremely twisted specimen in the tray of separate shells has a bifid deck. A young one had edged itself into the apical part of the deck, as into a maternal pouch; so the old one made a fresh deck over it.

348. *Crepidula lessonii*. Most of the specimens are of *C. nivea*, var., M. 341. Two shells, which have the apex perfect, display the characteristic nuclear riblets. One dark-coloured specimen may be a hybrid, and another (though too much worn for confident affiliation) appears to be *C. unguiformis*. Among the duplicates, all the specimens which were perfect at the apex presented the niveoid nucleus, though white; but generally the riblets were more or less worn off.

349. *Crepidula squama*. These are the flat form (mostly dead and worn) of *C. nivea*, M. 341. Some of them pass into *lessonii*. Some are highly coloured, and may be the young of *C. onyx*; one even of *C. incurva*. One of the young shells in phial appears to be *C. onyx*; but whenever the apex is perfect, it presents the typical riblets: v. Maz. Cat. *in loco*.

350. *Crepidula unguiformis*. The apex being hidden in dead shells, which I was not at liberty to break away, I could only examine one specimen, which appeared to be a *C. nivea*, var., as supposed in Maz. Cat. p. 285. Of the loose specimens, scarcely any are sufficiently perfect at the apex to speak with confidence. Most of them, however, have the characteristic painting of the variety *squama*; and all may belong to the common species (*C. nivea*), except one which is a true *C. unguiformis*, M. 342, on the back of another shell, and a few which are probably *C. onyx*, var. Of the duplicates, which I was at liberty to extract from the dead shells,

some are undoubtedly *C. nivea*; others truly *C. unguiformis*; and others probably *C. nivea*, but with the riblets worn away by the crabs.

351. *Crepidula nivea*, M. 341. The specimens are small and poor; mostly rough, of the variety *striolata* passing into *lessonii*. Wherever the apex is perfect, it presents the characteristic riblets, but is generally white, not brown as in most of the finely grown Mazatlan shells.

352. *Crepidula osculans.* This is a perfect and extremely beautiful specimen of *Scutellina navicelloides*, M. 269. The Professor did not observe the non-spiral patelloid apex, and regarded the "navicelloid" columella as an extremely narrow deck. To the diagnosis in the Maz. Cat. may now be added "*apice obtuso, sublævi; vertice haud spirali, vix conspicuo.*"

353. *Crepidula rostrata=C. adunca*, M. 338, ?non Sby. The examination of a large series of specimens from the temperate fauna has led me unexpectedly to confirm Mr. Reeve's opinion that they are distinct. The northern shell is *C. adunca*, Sby. (=*Garnotia* [Gray] *solida*, Hds.=*C. rostriformis*, Gld.); and the tropical shell must take the prior name, *C. uncata*, Mke. (=*C. rostrata*, C. B. Ad., Rve.=*C. adunca*, Maz. Cat., non Sby.).

354. *Fissurella æqualis=Fissurellidæa æ.*

355. *Fissurella alta=Glyphis alta*, M. 280.

356. *Fissurella macrotrema.* Stet.

357. *Fissurella microtrema.* These are dead specimens, of which some are *F. rugosa*, var., M. 273.

358. *Fissurella mus=Glyphis inæqualis*, var., M. 279. These shells are intermediate between the typical form and *pica*.

359, 360. Stent.

361. *Fissurella virescens.* It is doubtful whether any of the specimens are of the true *virescens*, M. 271, as they run into *nigropunctata* by insensible gradations. Perhaps both species may prove identical.

362. *Siphonaria characteristica=S. gigas*, var.

363, 364, 365. Stent.

366. *Siphonaria ?pica.* These are young dead limpets (not *Siphonariæ*).

367. *Lottia ?patina*, C. B. Ad. (non Esch.). These shells differ from *Acmæa mesoleuca*, M. 263, in being black instead of green, and are prettily striped.

368, 369, 370. *Lottia*, sp. ind. There may be two or even more species of *Acmæa*, but it is not impossible that there is only one among the professor's *Lottiæ*, some of the specimens being the young of ? *Patella*, no. 371.

371. ? *Patella*, sp. ind.   This has the general appearance of *P. vulgata*, but may be an *Acmæa*.

372. *Chiton clathratus*.   (Genus indet.)

373. *Chiton dispar*, C. B. Ad.; not *Lophyrus dispar*, Sby.   I doubt whether any of the Professor's specimens belong to Sowerby's species, which is black mixed with grey; area-sculpture very faint; and sides imbricated, not rugulose.   Among the duplicates were two (if not three) species:—the principal one with side-sculpture in lobated knobs, which may be named *Lophyrus adamsii*; a ?variety with simple knobs; and a well-marked species without distinct side areas, which may be called *Lophyrus tenuisculptus*.

374. *Chiton ?luridus*.   Probably correct.

375. *Chiton pulchellus*= *Callochiton p.* + *C. elenensis*.

376. *Chiton stokesii*= *Lophyrus s.*

377. *Anomia lampe*, C. B. Ad.   It is doubtful whether this is identical with the northern species, M. 219.

378. *Anomia tenuis*.   This is probably the young of the last species, and may give it a name, if new.   It is doubtful how the diagnosis of the scars was made out; as they were not visible in either of the specimens retained, being encrusted with dead animal matter.   They were not distinct even after its removal.

379. *Anomia*, sp. ind. *a*.   Probably the same species as the two last, although far too dead, worn, and young to decide.   See notes on the variations of *A. lampe*, Maz. Cat. p. 168.

380. *Ostrea*, sp. ind. *a*.   The hinge notches of the upper valve fit between corresponding teeth in the lower.   Inside rather flesh-coloured; white, round margin.   Scar kidney-shaped, dark in one valve, light in the other.   A young valve is white, and as pearly as *O. iridescens*, M. 211.   The species is best known by its tendency to make a very broad limb in the exterior coloured part, spreading out into palmations.   A very young specimen, though covered above with *Membraniporæ*, shows the characteristic corrugations through.   It may stand provisionally as *O. panamensis*.

381. *Ostrea*, sp. ind. *b*.   This is probably a variety of *O. panamensis*, but more coarsely grown, so that there is a smaller limb, without palmations.   Wherever the sculpture appears, there are evident traces of the peculiar corrugations.   The inside has the same characters, both of hinge, colour, iridescence, and scar.

382. *Ostrea*, sp. ind. *c*.   Rather square hinge, without plications; one shell with an umbonal cavity.   Pearly white.   One specimen is tinted on the scar, which may become coloured in the adult.   It is by no means "pentangular," and is more probably = *O. rufa*, Gld., than *O. columbiensis*, M. 213.

383. *Ostrea*, sp. ind. *d*.   The shells are broader than the Mazatlan specimens of *O. virginica*, M. 212, probably from not growing on twigs.   The younger shells are very like *O. edulis*; the older ones

have hollow umbos. One long shell, first marked *e*, but altered to *d*, is the adult form ; several of the younger shells are doubtful.

384. *Ostrea*, sp. ind. *e.*=*Ostrea*, M. 215. Being a good species, I propose the name of *O. amara*. The Professor's "small var." is not plicated, and appears to belong to *O. conchaphila*, M. 214. [N.B. Additional specimens confirm me in the belief that *O. palmula*, M. 214 *b*, is a distinct species.]

385. *Spondylus lamarckii*, C. B. Ad.=*S. calcifer*, M. 208.

386. *Spondylus*, sp. ind. *a*=*Plicatula penicillata*, M. 210.

387. *Pecten inca*=*P. ventricosus*, Sby., as in errata.

388. *Pecten tumbezensis*=*P. aspersus*, Sby., Hanl. (? Lam.).

389. *Lima angulata*. Shells inflated, not gaping.

390. *Lima pacifica* (=*L. arcuata*, Sby., Hanl.). Young shells, species uncertain.

391. *Avicula ?margaritifera*=*Margaritiphora fimbriata*, Dkr., M. 204=*M. mazatlanica*, Hanl.=*M. barbata*, Rve.

392. *Avicula sterna*, M. 203. *A. libella*, Rve., appears to me the young of this species.

393. *Perna*, sp. ind. *a*=*Isognomon chemnitziana*, M. 205.

394. *Perna*, sp. ind. *b*=*I. chemnitziana*, var. Rather more finely grown, and with less colour, but certainly the same species. The Professor's Jamaica specimens are labelled "*bicolor*, Ad."

395. *Pinna maura*, M. 200.

396. *Pinna tuberculosa*. Three of the specimens appear to me =*P. maura*, jun. The other may be the same, but is worn nearly smooth.

397. *Mytilus*, sp. ind. *a*. Resembles the young of *Modiola brasiliensis*, but with a few hinge-teeth, as in *M. edulis*.

398. *Lithodomus*, sp. ind. *a*. Most of these specimens are of *Lithophagus aristatus*, M. 176 ; one (perhaps two) are *L. attenuatus*, M. 173 (which is found from Lower California to Chili) ; and one appears to be *L. plumula*, M. 175 ; but they are too young to decide with confidence.

399. *Modiola ? semifusca*. These specimens all belong to the *M. brasiliensis*, M. 171, but are much more like the ordinary Brazilian specimens than are those from Mazatlan. As compared with the latter, the Panama shells are more rounded, with stronger posterior grooving, and with the angular ridge less marked. A similar shell, undoubtedly from New Zealand, is considered by Mr. Cuming conspecific.

400–404. *Modiola*, sp. ind. *a, b, c, d, e*. I could find no *a* or *e* in the collection ; but there were two trays marked *f*. Tray *b*=*M. capax*, M. 170. *c* contains several specimens of *Mytilus multiformis*, M. 168, strongly ribbed variety, perhaps intended for *b*, no. 401.

d contains parts of six specimens, and perhaps should be *a*, no. 400. They appear to be a variety of *Lithophagus cinnamomeus*, M. 177, but with broken shells, &c., agglutinized on the posterior side. *f* (1) contains four specimens of *M. multiformis*, the semigreenish variety (Maz. Cat. p. 119), and are probably intended for *c*. *f* (2) contains two specimens of the same variety of *M. multiformis*, in the burrow of a *Lithophagus*, and may stand for *d* or *e*.

405. *Chama buddiana* = *C.* (? *frondosa*, var.) *fornicata*, M. 121, *b*. Additional specimens confirm me in regarding this species as distinct from all varieties of *frondosa*. The Professor's shells not being very characteristic, the diagnoses do not exactly accord. The shell stands as *C. buddiana*.

406. *Chama ? corrugata.* The large valve appears a dead reversed *C.* (*frondosa*) *mexicana*, M. 121, with the teeth perforated by *Lithophagi*. The other may be *corrugata*, very dead, of sienna-tint, very pointed dorsally.

407. *Chama echinata.* These appear to me to be the young, partly of *C. buddiana*, but principally of *C. mexicana*.

408. *Nucula elenensis* = *Leda e.*, M. 199.

409. *Nucula exigua*, M. 198.

410. *Nucula polita* = *Leda p.* With semidiagonal lines.

411. *Pectunculus assimilis* + *P. inæqualis*, M. 196.

412. *Pectunculus ? maculatus.* Stet.

413. *Arca alternata* = *Barbatia a.*, M. 188.

414. *Arca ? aviculoides* appears a young *Scapharca*.

415. *Arca emarginata* = *Scapharca e.*, M. 187.

416. *Arca gradata* = *Barbatia g.*, M. 194.

417. *Arca grandis*, M. 180.

418. *Arca mutabilis* = *Byssoarca m.*, M. 190.

419. *Arca* (*Byssoarca*) *pholadiformis.* This is simply an elongated form of *Barbatia gradata*, probably from growing in the hole of a *Lithophagus*. The umbos are "flattened" by erosion; teeth not "obsolete" under the glass; "ligament concealed" simply by the compressed and elongated growth.

420. *Arca reeviana* = *Barbatia r.*

421. *Arca reversa* = *Noetia r.*, M. 185.

422. *Arca similis.* This is scarcely a variety of *A. tuberculosa*, M. 184. The specimens are dead and oiled, with most of the epidermis abraded.

423. *Arca solida* = *Barbatia s.*, M. 195.

424. *Arca* (*Byssoarca*) *tobayensis* = *Barbatia illota*, M. 193.

425. *Arca tuberculosa*, M. 184.

426. *Arca*, sp. ind. *a.* These little shells approach the *Noetia*

type. Ribs fine, tuberculous, coarse on the angular side. Ligament very narrow, truncated.

427. *Cardita affinis.* (*Lazaria.*)

428. *Cardita laticostata* = *Venericardia l.*

429. *Cardita radiata.* (*Lazaria.*)

430. *Cardium graniferum*, M. 134.

431. *Cardium obovale* = *Hemicardia o.*

432. *Cardium planicostatum*, C. B. Ad., not Sby. This looks like a dead ballast-valve of *Hemicardia media*; but it may be *H. biangulata*.

433. *Cardium procerum*, M. 125.

434. *Cardium senticosum*, M. 126.

435. *Venus ?amathusia* = *Anomalocardia subimbricata*, M. 113.

436. *Venus discors* = *Tapes gratus*, Say, M. 110. The Professor's specimens of this species and *T. histrionicus* are somewhat intermixed.

437. *Venus gnidia*, M. 101. Dead specimens; of which one may possibly be *Chione amathusia*, M. 102.

438. *Venus multicostata.* Closely resembling the West Indian form.

439. *Venus pectunculoides* = *Tapes histrionicus*, M. 109.

440. *Venus subrugosa* = *Anomalocardia s.*, M. 112.

441. *Venus*, sp. ind. *a.* A small species with concentric laminæ, armed with one posterior row of blunt spines. Interstices with minute concentric striæ.

442. *Venus*, sp. ind. *b* = *Chione crenifera*, M. 105 = *V. sugillata*, Rve. C. I. no. 43.

443. *Cytherea affinis.* Probably = *Callista concinna*, var., M. 99.

444. *Cytherea aurantiaca* = *Callista aurantia*, M. 92.

445. *Cytherea consanguinea* = *Callista c.* Messrs. H. and A. Adams have not made a subgenus to include this group of thin, inflated, almost colourless species.

446. *Cytherea radiata* = *Trigona r.*, M. 83.

447. *Cytherea squalida* = *Callista chionæa*, M. 93.

448. *Artemis dunkeri* = *Dosinia d.*, M. 90.

449. *Artemis saccata* = *Cyclina subquadrata*, M. 91.

450. *Gouldia pacifica*, M. 116.

451. *Cyrena maritima.* Stet. The collection also contains two tubes, containing a very young "? *Cyclas*" and another "*Cyrena*, jun.," marked "Panama, C. B. Ad."

452. *Lucina tellinoides* = *Felania t.* Differs from *F. sericata*,

M. 152, in having a yellow, not silky, epidermis. The specimens vary considerably in thickness. The genus scarcely differs from *Miltha*.

453. *Capsa altior*=*Iphigenia a.*, M. 69.

454. *Donax assimilis*, M. 74.

455. *Donax gracilis*. Stet.

456. *Donax naricula*, M. 77.

457. *Donax rostratus.* This single valve proves to be the true *D. carinatus*, M. 71, and not the shell which I called *D. culminatus*, M. 72 (= *carinatus*, var., Hanl. in Mus. Cum.), which I subsequently affiliated to the supposed *rostratus*, Maz. Cat. p. 548, on the authority of Dr. Gould's specimen. We were probably both misled by the "*very sharp* angle," which (as compared with the other form) I should call *rounded*, and the "concave" surface, which I should translate into flat. The names have been altered in the Cumingian collection since the Mazatlan shells were identified; but Mr. Hanley informs me that they are now correct; that the *D. culminatus*, M. 72, is his own original *carinatus*; and that the *D. carinatus*, M. 71 (olim Mus. Cum.), which is certainly *D. rostratus*, P. 457, must stand under Prof. Adams's name.

458. *Tellina aurora*. Stet.

459. *Tellina cognata*, C. B. Ad.=*Psammobia casta*, Rve., *teste* Cuming. The sculpture consists of semidiagonal striæ passing over the lines of growth. In other specimens examined from Panama these are sometimes crowded, sometimes distant, occasionally flexuous, sometimes almost evanescent.

460. *Tellina columbiensis*. (*Peronæa.*)

461. *Tellina concinna*=*Macoma c.* The "slight tinge of pink" I could not discover.

462. *Tellina crystallina*=*Tellidora c.*

463. *Tellina cumingii*, M. 55.

464. *Tellina dombeyi*=*Macoma d.*, M. 50.

465. *Tellina felix*, M. 51. (*Angulus.*)

466. *Tellina laceridens*. (*Peronæoderma.*)

467. *Tellina prora*. (*Peronæoderma.*)

468. *Tellina puella.* Not unlike *T. felix*, and distinct from M. 59.

469. *Tellina rubescens*. (*Peronæoderma.*)

470. *Tellina siliqua.* The two odd valves belong probably to a *Macoma*, in shape resembling *Thracia phaseolina*.

471. *Tellina simulans*=*T.* (*Peronæoderma*) *punicea*, M. 54. The species was described, for geographical reasons, from a young, pale, and undeveloped valve. On comparing it with the Professor's own West Indian specimens, I could detect no difference.

202

472. *Tellina sincera* = *Strigilla s.*

473. *Tellina vicina* = *Heterodonax vicinus.* The shells are labelled *T. versicolor* by the Professor. They are larger than the general run of West Indian specimens; but the form is probably a local variety of the old *Heterodonax bimaculatus.*

474. *Tellina,* sp. ind. *a.* The doubt concerning "concave" and "convex" probably arises from an error in description.

475. *Tellina,* sp. ind. *b.* Looks exactly like the young of No. 474, but with lateral teeth.

476. *Tellina,* sp. ind. *c.* Dead valves of *T. felix,* No. 465.

477. *Petricola cognata.* More characteristic specimens from the same coast are affiliated by Mr. Cuming to *P. pholadiformis,* from which this would probably not have been separated had it appeared on the Atlantic coast.

478. *Saxicava ? tenuis.* The Panama shell is more like *Petricola* than *Saxicava,* having two teeth in each valve, one of which is bifid. Sowerby's species is called by Messrs. H. & A. Adams "*Saxicava tenuis*" (ii. p. 349) and "*Petricola tenuis*" (ii. p. 441). Shell with very fine radiating striæ, crossed by irregular striæ of growth.

479. *Cumingia coarctata* = *C. lamellosa,* var., M. 42.

480. *Cumingia trigonularis,* M. 43.

481. *Cumingia,* sp. ind. *a* = *C. trigonularis,* No. 480.

482. *Cumingia,* sp. ind. *b* = *C.* var. *coarctata,* No. 479.

483. *Cumingia,* sp. ind. *c* = M. 45. This appears a distinct species, and may be quoted as *C. adamsii,* in remembrance of the labours of Messrs. H., A. and C. B. Adams.

484. *Cumingia,* sp. ind. *d* = Maz. Cat. tablet 107, p. 31; well rounded, with close striæ. Probably distinct.

485. *Amphidesma bicolor* = *Semele ? venusta,* M. 41 (non A. Ad.). The "species" in this genus are often separated by very variable characters.

486. *Amphidesma ? ellipticum* = *Semele e.*

487. *Amphidesma proximum.* The type is not quite so elliptical as the last species; but as this is a very variable character (v. Maz. Cat. p. 28), I should regard it as the same. It is not the *Semele proxima,* M. 40 (= *S. flavescens,* v. Maz. Cat. p. 548).

488. *Amphidesma pulchrum* = *Semele p.*

489. *Amphidesma striosum* = *Semele s.* I should describe the shell as smooth, with very fine diagonal striæ crossing the lines of growth. It has the general aspect of *S. pulchra.* The teeth in one valve are long and sharp.

490. *Amphidesma tortuosum* = *Semele t.* Teeth short and faint.

491. *Amphidesma ventricosum* = *Semele v.* The "zones" are very

"ill-defined." Teeth scarcely visible. It looks outside like a dead valve of *Macoma solidula*.

492. *Crassatella gibbosa*. Also found at Cape St. Lucas.

493. *Mulinia donaciformis* = *M. angulata*, M. 80.

494. *Mulinia ventricosa* = *Mactrella exoleta*, M. 78.

495. *Lutraria elegans* = *Harvella elegans*; ascribed by Messrs. H. & A. Adams to Florida (ii. p. 378), from which I have never 'seen it. It is a rare, but (under different names) somewhat widely diffused west-tropical shell. Its "analogue" from Florida and Carolina is *Raëta canaliculata*.

496. *Mactra velata* = *Standella v. Vide* M. 79. The "small variety" is conspecific.

497. *Anatina alta*. This valve of *Periploma* may prove identical with one of the four Gulf species. The spoon is supported underneath by a linear plate.

498. *Pandora cornuta*. It is singular that neither Prof. Adams nor Dr. Gould observed that the peculiar characters of this species are due to a fracture, producing a beak and sinus which are not seen on the lines of growth. The sentences about the "rostriform projection," the "sinus," and the "prominent angle," should therefore be erased from the diagnosis. The hinge-teeth consist of a long sharp tooth, very pointed, in one valve, fitting against a less prominent one in the other; a slight ligamental tooth in the first valve only; and a very long, sharp, clavicular tooth in each valve, running near the posterior margin, against the inside umbonal portion of which the ligament is attached. Should it prove identical with *P. claviculata*, the earliest name (as being given in error) may advantageously be dropped. It is surprising that Messrs. H. & A. Adams have not divided the old Lamarckian genus even into subgenera.

499. *Potamomya æqualis*. 500. *P. inflata*. 501. *P. trigonalis*. These three forms of *Azara* differ in outline, but not more than do some other species of Corbulids and such shells as *Trigona radiata*. The teeth, pallial lines, and general characters are the same in each. The first two I should consider certainly identical; and a large series of specimens would probably graduate to the third.

502. *Corbula bicarinata*, M. 30.

503. *Corbula biradiata*, M. 31.

504. *Corbula obesa*. Stet.

505. *Corbula ovulata*, M. 33.

506. *Corbula rubra*. A young orange-tinted specimen of *C. biradiata*, No. 503. The "broad flexure" is an accidental growth, not shown in the lines of growth of an earlier stage.

507. *Corbula tenuis*. Stet.

508. *Corbula*, sp. ind. *a*. A very small angular valve, with sharp concentric ridges. It may belong to *C. pustulosa*, M. 32.

509. *Corbula*, sp. ind. *b.*   Dead valves of *C. biradiata*, No. 503. To the same species may be referred *C. polychroma.* We were misled by the different appearance of the dead shell, and by the locality-mark in Col. Jewett's collection. His specimens were probably from Panama or Acapulco.

510. *Solecurtus affinis*, M. 37.   It is probable that this species is identical with *S.* (? *Novaculina*) *caribbæus.* The Ariquibo specimens of the latter in Mus. Amherst are more like the Mazatlan shells than those are to the Panama type.   Shells from Cape Palmas were affiliated to the Caribbæan species by Mr. Cuming.

511. *Solen rudis=Ensatella r.*   This interesting form passes towards *Pharella.*   It is called " *Solena obliqua*, Spengl., var." in Mus. Cuming.

512. *Pholas crucigera.* With the general aspect of *Barnea candida.*

513. *Pholas tubifera=Pholadidea t.* Of the *melanura* type, with a solid tube fitting on to the ends of the cups.

514. *Pholas xylophaga.* Of the *Martesia* type, without cups. Dorsal and ventral plates long; umbonal plates moderate; wave of the adolescent gape rather suddenly arched.

515. *Pholas* ——, sp. ind. *a.*   Col. Jewett's specimens of the same shell are named *laqueata* by Mr. Cuming.   It is of the non-waved, concameroid type; without radiating sculpture; concentric lamellæ beautifully frilled.

516. *Pholas*, sp. ind. *b.*   So like *P. dactylus* that it might be taken for a worn valve from ballast.   The sculpture-ridges are, however, further apart; hinge-chambers larger and more numerous, with a little twisted lamina beyond; gape less conspicuous.

517. *Orbicula cumingii=Discina c.*, M. 14.

The shells unfortunately are all loose, in trays, with the autograph names on tickets.   Prof. Adams's West Indian collections are in the same condition; and both series are arranged together, in zoological order, in the midst of the general collection.   There is no evidence, however, that they have been handled since the Professor left them, none of the leading conchological writers in the New World having thought it needful to go out of their way to complete a review of the Professor's work.   Amherst is situated on a branch railway, and is within an easy walk of Northampton, Mount Holyoak, and the delicious scenery of the Connecticut River.   In the College buildings are also deposited the most complete series of the Fossil Footprints of the Connecticut River, and the mineralogical collection (including the meteorolites) belonging to Prof. Shepnerd.

C.

DIAGNOSES

OF

NEW FORMS OF MOLLUSKS COLLECTED AT CAPE ST. LUCAS BY MR. J. XANTUS.

BY

PHILIP P. CARPENTER, B. A., Pʜ. D.

From the Annals and Magazine of Natural History. Third Series, Vol. XIII., pp. 311–315, April, 1864. Ibid. (Nos. 15–36) pp. 474–479, June, 1864. Ibid. Vol. XIV. (Nos. 37–52), pp. 45–49, July, 1864.

(207)

DIAGNOSES

OF

NEW FORMS OF MOLLUSKS

COLLECTED AT CAPE St. LUCAS BY Mr. J. XANTUS.

BY

PHILIP P. CARPENTER, B.A., Ph.D.

THE specimens here described belong to the Museum of the
Smithsonian Institution, Washington, D. C. The first available
duplicates will be found in the British Museum or in the
Cumingian Collection. An account of the labours of Mr. Xantus
will appear in the forthcoming volume of British Association
Reports; and detailed notes on the species may be consulted in
the American scientific periodicals for the current year.

Genus ASTHENOTHÆRUS*.

Testa extus "*Thraciæ*" similis: intus cardine edentulo, haud
spathulato; cartilagine infra umbones sita.

1. *Asthenothærus villosior.*

A. testa inæquivalvi, inæquilaterali, umbonibus ad trientem longitudinis sitis; tenuissima, alba, (sub lente) omnino minutissime
et creberrime pustulosa; rugis incrementi obtusissimis, irregularibus, maxime t. juniore, ornata; epidermide tenui, pallide olivacea
induta; parte postica truncata, parum hiante; antica valde rotundata; marginibus dorsalibus et ventrali parum excurvatis; umbonibus angustissimis; regionibus lunulari et nymphali subcari-
natis: intus, margine cardinali utriusque valvæ acuto; ligamento
inconspicuo; cartilagine subspongiosa, satis elongata, postice de-
flecta; fovea haud indentata; cicatricibus adductorum parvis,
subrotundatis; sinu pallii majore, ovali, ad dimidium interspatii
porrecto. Long. ·38, lat. ·26, alt. ·14 poll.†

* Ἀσθενής, weak; θαιρός, hinge.
† The measures of length are taken from the anterior to the posterior
margins. The "detailed notes" are still in MSS.

14   209

2. *Solemya valvulus.*

S. testa minore, tenuissima, diaphana, vix testacea, cornea, pallidiore, lineis tenuibus, distantibus, fuscis, radiatim ornata ; postice tenuiter radiatim striata ; tumente, satis elongata, marginibus antico et postico regulariter excurvatis ; umbonibus vix conspicuis ; linea anticis divaricantibus, extus parentibus, intus lacunam cartilagineam definientibus ; cardine edentulo ; ligamento postice elongato, antice curto, latiore, bifurcato ; cicatricibus adductorum subrotundatis.   Long. ·85, lat. ·25, alt. ·14 poll.

3. *Tellina (Peronæoderma) ochracea.*

T. testa majore, parum inæquilaterali, tenui, satis planata ; carneoochracea, intus intensiore ; lævi, nitida, marginem versus striis incrementi ; postice vix radiatim striatula ; ventraliter antice valde excurvata, postice vix angulata ; marginibus dorsalibus obtuse angulatis, umbonibus conspicuis ; ligamento tenui et cartilagine subinternis ; nymphis intortis : dent. card. utriusque valvæ ii., quarum i. bifidus ; dent. lat. valvæ dextræ ii. ; sinu pallii irregulariter ovali, per duos trientes interstitii porrecto ; cicatr. adduct. subovatis, nitidissimis.   Long. 1·9, lat. 1·4, alt. ·44 poll.

4. *Psammobia (?Amphichæna) regularis.*

P. testa minore, regulariter ovali, subæquilaterali ; violacea, plus minusve radiata seu maculata ; lævi, striolis incrementi ornata ; epidermide tenui, flavido-olivacea induta, postice rugulosa ; marginibus undique regulariter excurvatis ; umbonibus vix projectis ; ligamento conspicuo : intus dent. card. ii.–i., haud bifidis ; cicatr. adduct. postica rotundata, antica ovali ; sinu pallii elongato, haud incurvato, per duos trientes interstitii porrecto.   Long. 1·05, lat. ·5, alt. ·26 poll.

5. *Callista pollicaris.*

C. testa magna, ventricosa, solidiore ; epidermide tenuissima induta ; sordide albida, umbonibus rufo-fuscis ; (t. adolescente) punctulis crebris rufo-fuscis, et tæniis paucis circa nymphas ornata ; lævi, striis incrementi exceptis ; postice, et paululum antice, quasi pollice impresso notata ; latiore, antice producta, sed haud angulata ; postice unda depressa, supra nymphas radiante, inter costas duas obsoletas sinuante, margine subtruncato ; marginibus ventrali regulariter excurvato, dorsali rectiore ; lunula elongata, linea impressa definita, medio tumente, postice flaccida : intus candida ; dent. card. normalibus ; dente laterali valvæ dextræ postico, valvæ sinistræ antico, usque ad extremitatem lunulæ porrecto ; cicatr. adduct. subrotundatis ; sinu pallii magno, rotundato, usque ad medium interstitii porrecto.   Long. 2·58, lat. 2·25, alt. 1·43 poll.

Figured by Mr. Reeve (Conch. f. 45) as " *Dione prora,* var." The above diagnosis proves it to be a distinct and (considering the general similarity of the thin, colourless, inflated group) a well-marked species.

6. *Callista* (? *pannosa*, var.) *puella.*

C..testa "*C. pannosæ*"-simili, sed multo minore, tenuiore, plerumque latiore ; sinu pallii majore, eleganter incurvato ; dent. card multo tenuioribus, lat. ant. magis elongato ; lamina cardinali umbones versus sinuata : colore maxime variante ; nonnunquam ut in *C. pannosa* triangulariter maculata ; plerumque ut in *Tapete virginea* notata ; interdum albida, seu aurantia, seu fusca, haud maculata ; rarius ut in *Tapete fuscolineata* penicillata ; rarissime paucistrigata, seu maculis paucissimis. Long. ·66. lat. ·5, alt. ·32 poll.

Variat t. transversa. Variat quoque t. subtrigona, et formis intermediis.

Quoted by Mr. Reeve, under *Dione pannosa*, as " *D. puella*, Cpr."; but the name was only given in MS. in accordance with Mr. Cuming's assertion that it was distinct. The colourless subtrigonal shells were regarded by Mr. Reeve as a separate species ; but he did not allude to them in his monograph.

7. *Levicardium apicinum.*

L. testa subtrigona, parva, tenuissima, nitidissima, subcompressa, epidermide tenui induta ; radiis seu striis radiantibus nullis ; striis concentricis satis regularibus, subobsoletis, t. jun. magis extantibus ; umbonibus angustis, parum incurvatis ; margine ventrali satis excurvato, antico parum producto, postico subtruncato, dorsalibus obtuse angulatis : colore valde variante ; plerumque pallide viridi-cinereo, rufo-fusco seu angulatim tæniato seu maculato seu punctato ; regione umbonali plerumque pallida, interdum rufo-fusca seu aurantiaca ; parte postica haud intensiore : intus plerumque citrina, hepatico varie penicillata : dent. card. et lat. acutis, tenuibus ; margine minutissime subobsoletim crenulato. Long. ·55, lat. ·5, alt. ·3 poll.

Variat t. latiore. Variat quoque colore fere omnino hepatico, seu carneo, seu pallide aurantiaco, seu pallide cinereo, seu albido : rarissime ut in *Tapete fuscolineata* ornata.

8. *Lucina lingualis.*

L. testa solida, linguiformi, valde prolongata ; plerumque aurantiaco-carnea, intus intensiore ; lirulis concentricis obtusis crebre ornata ; marginibus undique excurvatis ; lunula minima, altissime excavata ; parte postica obscure biangulata, seu subrotundata ; umbonibus anticis incurvatis ; ligamento subinterno, lamina valida ; dent. card. et lat. normalibus, validis ; cicatr. adduct. posticis subovalibus, anticis satis elongatis ; linea pallii lata, rugosa ; margine interno crenulato. Long. ·88, lat. ·92, alt. ·4 poll.

Variat t. minus prolongata. Variat quoque t. pallide viridi, seu pallide carnea, seu alba.

9. *?Crenella inflata.*

?C. testa valde inflata, minuta, albida, subrhomboideo-orbiculari ;

diagonaliter parum producta; marginibus subquadrangulatim rotundatis; umbonibus prominentibus, valde antice intortis; tota
superficie ut in *C. decussata* sculpta, costulis crebris radiantibus
æquidistantibus, hic et illic aliis intercalatis; lirulis concentricis decussantibus : intus margine dorsali brevissimo, arcuato,
dentato ; ligamento curtissimo, in fossa omnino interna, celata, lamina definiente, sito; lamina cardinali sub umbonibus intus porrecta, dentibus validis instructa ; marginibus internis omnino cre-
natis ; cicatr. adduct. subæqualibus, ventraliter sitis.   Long. ·1,
lat. ·12, alt. ·09 poll.

Located provisionally in *Crenella* from its likeness to *C. decussata*, but with peculiarities of hinge and adductors which
approach *Nuculina* on one side and *Cardilia* on another.

Genus BRYOPHILA*.

Animal Aviculidæum, viviparum : inter algas, etc., habitans.
Testa Pinnæformis, extus prismatica, intus subnacrea : ligamentum
solidum : umbones extantes, terminales, intus concavi.

10. *Bryophila setosa.*

B. testa parva, regulari ; cinerea, salmoneo seu chocolateo, intus sub-
nacreo, exquisite tincta : t. juniore planata, semirotundata, dorsaliter recta, æquilaterali, conspicue punctata : t. adolescente subdiaphana : t. adulta solidiore; umbonibus rectis, terminalibus,
intus alte excavatis ; marg. dorsali breviore, recto ; antico recto ;
ventrali et postico late rotundatis : extus epidermide subspongiosa
vestita, radiis setarum subdistantibus, marginibus eleganter pectinatis : intus ligamento solido dorsaliter producto ; limbo pallii
æqualiter prope marginem decurrente ; cicatr. adduct. submediana,
inconspicua ; postice hiante ; antice propter byssum tenuem sinuata.   Long. ·13, lat. ·2, alt. ·1 poll.

Like a minute *Pinna*, or a transverse *Margaritiphora* without
ears, or an *Isognomon* without pits.   Differs from the other
Aviculids in being viviparous, like some other minute bivalves.

11. ?*Atys casta.*

?*A.* testa elongata, tenui, subdiaphana, albida ; antrorsum paulum
tumidiore ; spira celata, lacunata, (t. adultæ) haud umbilicata ;
columella paulum intorta, effusa ; umbilico antico minimo ; labro
postice producto, obtuse angulato ; tota superficie subtiliter spiraliter striatula.   Long. ·4, lat. ·18 poll.

On the confines of the genus, related to *Cylichna.*

12. *Ischnochiton parallelus.*

I. testa ovata, subelevata (ad angulum 120°) : rufo-fusca, olivaceo
tincta ; valvis latis, marginibus parum rotundatis, interstitiis par-

* Βρύον, sea-moss; φίλος, loving.

vis; valvis intermediis valde insculptis; areis lateralibus seriebus granulorum a jugo radiantibus circiter vi.; interdum irregularibus, granis rotundatis, separatis, extantibus; areis centralibus clathris creberrimis, jugo parallelis, horridis, extantibus, interdum granulosis, ornatis; valvis terminalibus seriebus granulorum, circ. xx., interdum bifurcantibus, ut in areis lateralibus, ornatis; mucrone vix conspicuo; limbo pallii angusto, pilulis furvicaceis creberrimis minutis conferto; lobis valvarum bifidis, terminalibus fis?·is circ. xi. a parte externa simplici disjunctis. Long. ·7, lat. ·48, alt. ·16 poll.

Belongs to the group with minute setose scales.

13. *Ischnochiton* (? var.) *prasinatus.*

I. testa *I. parallelo* forma et indole simili, sed vivide viridi; ar. diag. seriebus bullularum irregulariter ornatis; ar. centr. clathris valde extantibus, acutis, jugo obtuso parallelis, utroque latere circ. xvi.; valv. term. seriebus bullularum circ. xviii.; mucrone submediano, inconspicuo; umbonibus haud prominentibus; tota superficie minutissime granulosa: intus valvarum lobis mediarum i.- term. circiter x.-fissis; sinu lato, planato; suturis planatis; limbo pallii angusto, minutissime squamulis furvicaceis creberrime instructo; interdum pilulis intercalatis. Long. ·8, lat. ·4 poll., div. 125°.

14. *Ischnochiton serratus.*

I. testa parva, cinerea, olivaceo hic et illic, præcipue ad suturas, punctata, interdum sanguineo maculata; ovali, subdepressa, suturis indistinctis; tota superficie minutissime granulata; ar. diag. valde distinctis, costis latissimis obtusis ii.-v. munitis, interstitiis nullis; marginibus posticis eleganter serratis; ar. centr. costis acutis, parallelis, utroque latere circ. xii.; jugo obtuso, haud umbonato: costis transversis, subradiantibus, fenestrantibus, interstitiis impressis: mucrone mediano, obtuso; valv. term. costis obtusis, ut in ar. diag., circ. xx.: intus valvarum mediarum lobis bifissis, terminalium circ. ix.-fissis; lobis suturalibus magnis: l'mbo pallii squamis majoribus, imbricatis, vix striatulis. Long. ·34, lat. ·2 poll., div. 115°.

Differs from *Elenensis* in the sculpture of the terminal valves.

15. *Nacella peltoides.*

N. testa parva, lævi, cornea, subdiaphana, ancyliformi, apice elevato, valde inæquilaterali, strigis pallide castaneis radiata; intus nitidissima, subaurantia. Long. ·14, lat. ·11, alt. ·05 poll.

= *Nacella,* sp. ind., Maz. Cat. no. 262, p. 202.

16. *Acmæa* (? var.) *atrata.*

A. testa solida, rugosa, conica, apice paulum antrorsum sito; extus costis crebris rotundatis irregularibus, hic et illic majoribus sculpta, haud apicem versus discordanter corrugatis; interstitiis

minimis; intus alba, castaneo et nigro varie maculata; margine latiore, nigro tessellato.   Long. 1·3, lat. 1·0, alt. ·5 poll.
Variat margine nigro-punctato, punctis plerumque bifidis.   Variat quoque costis parvis, creberrimis ; margine nigro.

Intermediate between " *P. discors*," Phil., and " *P. floccata*," Reeve.

17. *Acmæa strigatella.*

A. testa *A. mesoleucæ* simili, sed minore, haud viridi; striolis minimis, confertissimis, plerumque erosis tenuissime sculpta ; albida, strigis olivaceo-fuscis, plerumque radiantibus, interdum confluentibus picta ; apice sæpius nigro; intus albida, margine satis lato, strigis tessellato.   Long. ·9, lat. ·74, alt. ·3 poll.
Variat colore hic et illic aurantiaco tincto : strigis omnino tessellatis.

According to Darwin, this might be regarded as a cross between the northern forms *A. pelta* and *A. patina*, about to change into the Gulf species, *A. mesoleuca.*   The dark variety resembles *A. cantharus*, but the very delicate crowded striæ well distinguish it when not abraded.

18. *Glyphis saturnalis.*

G. testa *G. inæquali* simili, sed minore, latiore, altiore, tenuissime cancellata ; striis radiantibus plus minusve propinquis, plus minusve nodulosis ; fissura prope trientem longitudinis sita, minima, lineari, medio lobata ; intus callositate albida, truncata.   Long. ·38, lat. ·24, alt. ·18 poll.

The minute hole resembles the telescopic appearance of Saturn when the rings are reduced to a line.

Subgenus Eucosmia*.

Testa solida, nitida, variegata, haud nacrea : apertura et anfractus rotundati : conspicue umbilicata : peritrema vix continuum, haud callosum.

The shells here grouped are like small, round-mouthed, perforated *Phasianellæ*.   The animal and operculum of the Cape St. Lucas species are unknown.   The *Phasianella striulata*, Maz. Cat. no. 283 *b* (= *Turbo phasianella*, C. B. Ad. Pan. Sh. no. 282), and even the *Lunatia tenuilirata*, Maz. Cat. no. 572, are perhaps congeneric.

19. *Eucosmia variegata.*

E. testa parva, lævi, turbinoidea, nitente, marginibus spiræ valde excurvatis ; rosaceo et rufo-fusco varie maculata ; anfr. nucleosis regularibus, vertice mamillato ; normalibus iv., valde tumentibus, rapide augentibus, suturis impressis ; anfr. ultimo antice producto ; basi rotundata ; umbilico carinato ; apertura vix a pariete inden-

* Th. εὖ, well ; κοσμία, adorned.

tata; peritremate pene continuo, acuto. Long. ·1, long. spir. ·05, lat. ·07 poll., div. 70°.
Variat interdum rugulis incrementi ornata.

20. *Eucosmia* (? *variegata*, var.) *substriata.*

E. testa *E. variegatæ* simillima, sed anfr. circa basin et supra spiram (nisi in anfr. nucl. lævibus), interdum tota superficie tenuiter et crebre striatis; striis anfr. penult. circ. x.

21. *Eucosmia punctata.*

E. testa *E. variegatæ* simili, sed multo majore, multo magis elongata, angustiore, Phasianelloidea; plerumque fusco creberrime punctata; umbilico parvo. Long. ·22, long. spir. ·11, lat. ·15 poll., div. 50°.

22. *Eucosmia cyclostoma.*

E. testa parva, valde obtusa, lata, regulari, valvatoidea; marginibus spiræ vix excurvatis; pallide cinerea, fusco-olivaceo dense punctata seu maculata; anfr. nucleosis pallidis, mamillatis; normalibus iii., valde tumentibus, suturis valde impressis; apertura vix a pariete indentata; umbilico magno, subspirali. Long. ·05, long. spir. ·025, lat. ·05 poll., div. 90°.

Curiously like a small depressed *Valvata obtusa*, but with the texture of *Phasianella*.

Genus HAPLOCOCHLIAS*.

Testa *Colloniam* simulans, sed haud margaritacea: apertura circularis, varicosa: columella haud callosa.

The animal and operculum are unknown. Its affinities may be with *Ethalia*.

23. *Haplocochlias cyclophoreus.*

H. testa compacta, parva, solidiore; albida, seu pallide aurantiaca; anfr. v., rapide augentibus, suturis impressis; tota superficie minutissime spiraliter striolata, nitida; apertura rotundata; peritremate continuo, incrassato, extus varicoso; labio distincto; axi t. jun. umbilicata, adultæ lacunata. Long. ·19, long. spir. ·06, lat. ·2 poll., div. 100°.

When laid on its base, this shell resembles *Helicina*; but the mouth is more like *Cyclophorus*. The young shell is semitransparent, and resembles a *Vitrinella* with thickened lip.

24. *Narica aperta.*

N. testa parva, inflata, tenui, alba; anfr. nucl. ?....; norm. rapide augentibus, lirulis crebris spiralibus, in spira hic et illic majoribus, a striolis creberrimis radiantibus minutissime decussatis; suturis valde impressis; apertura subcirculari; umbilico maximo,

---

* *Th.* ἁπλοῦς, unadorned; κοχλίας, snail.

carinato, anfractus intus monstrante.   Long. ·28, long. spir. ·08,
lat. ·3 poll., div. 110°.

25. *Fossarus parcipictus.*

F. testa parva, solidiore, spira plus minusve elevata ; albida, rufo-
fusco varie maculata ; carinulis spiralibus acutioribus, quarum
circ. vi. majores, striolisque crebris cincta ; anfr. ultimo tumidiore ;
labro acuto, haud intus incrassato ; umbilico satis magno, ad marginem carinato : operculo normali.   Long. ·24, long. spir. ·06,
lat. ·2 poll., div. 90°.

The few specimens found are very variable in outline.

26. *Fossarus purus.*

F. testa F. *angulato* simili, sed alba, subdiaphana ; anfr. nucl. ii.,
fuscis, ut in F. *tuberoso* cancellatis ; norm. ii. et dimidio, altis,
valde tumentibus, carinatis ; carinis iv., validissimis, acutissimis,
quarum ii. in spira monstrantur ; carinulis aliis antice et postice
plus minusve expressis ; tota superficie minute spiraliter striata ;
carinularum basalium interstitiis subobsolete decussatis ; apertura
late semilunata ; labro a carinis valde indentato ; labio recto, angusto ; umbilico magno, carinato ; operculo fusco, valde pauci-
spirali, minutissime ruguloso, nucleo antico.   Long. ·08, long.
spir. ·03, lat. ·08 poll., div. 90°.

27. *Litorina pullata.*

L. testa parva, solidiore, luctuosa ; spira satis exserta ; nigrescente,
seu livido-fusco tincta, lineis spiralibus exilissimis pallidioribus ornata ; interdum obscure tessellata ; anfr. v., subplanatis, suturis
parum impressis ; sublævi, striolis spiralibus tenuiter insculpta ; columella intus incrassata ; pariete haud excavato.   Long. ·4, long.
spir. ·18, lat. ·29 poll., div. 60°.

= *Litorina,* sp. ind., Maz. Cat. no. 399, p. 350.

28. *Litorina (Philippii,* var.) *penicillata.*

L. Ph. testa parva, lineis radiantibus, variantibus, delicatulis, rarius
ziczacformibus, et cingulis duobus spiralibus, quorum unum in
spira monstratur, elegantissime penicillata.   Long. ·33, long.
spir. ·14, lat. ·2 poll., div. 50°.

Closely resembling the West-Indian L. *ziczac,* var. *lineata,*
D'Orb.   Intermediate specimens, however, clearly connect it
with the common Mazatlan form.

29. *Rissoa albolirata.*

R. testa parva, alba, crystallina, normali ; marginibus spiræ undatis;
anfr. nucl. iii., lævibus, mamillatis ; norm. iv., medio subconvexis,
postice supra suturas planatis ; basi subplanata, effusa, haud umbilicata ; lirulis spiralibus crebris, obtusis, quarum circ. x. in spira
monstrantur ; apertura subovata, peritremate continuo ; labro

arcuato, vix antice et postice sinuato, calloso; labio valido.
Long. ·1, long. spir. ·08, lat. ·04 poll., div. 25°.

30. *Fenella crystallina.*

F. testa alba, subdiaphana, turrita, rudiore; marginibus spiræ rectis,
parum divergentibus; anfr. nucl. ?... (decollatis); norm. v., valde
rotundatis, suturis impressis; costis radiantibus circ. xvi.. valde
rotundatis, haud extantibus, interstitiis latis; striis spiralibus
regularibus, in anfr. penult. xvi.; apertura rotundata; basi rotundata; peritremate continuo; labro extus varicoso; labio calloso. Long. ·14, long. spir. ·11, lat. ·05 poll., div. 20°.

31. ? *Hydrobia compacta.*

?*H.* testa lævi, curta, compacta, latiore; marginibus spiræ vix excurvatis; anfr. nucl. normalibus, apice mamillato; norm. iv., tumidis, suturis distinctis; spira curtiore; basi rotundata; apertura
subovata; peritremate continuo; labio definito. Long. ·04, long.
spir. ·02, lat. ·03 poll., div. 70°.

This unique shell may be a *Barleeia.*

32. *Hyala rotundata.*

H. testa (quoad genus) magna, tenui, alba, diaphana; anfr. nucl.
normalibus, apice mamillato; norm. iv., globosis, rapide augentibus, suturis valde impressis; basi rotundata; apertura subrotundata, ad suturam subangulata; peritremate continuo; labio a
pariete separato, rimulam umbilicalem formante; columella valde
arcuata. Long. ·18, long. spir. ·09, lat. ·1 poll., div. 40°.

A unique shell, resembling a marine *Bithinia.*

33. ? *Diala electrina.*

?*D.* testa subdiaphana, rufo-cornea, nitida; marginibus spiræ parum
excurvatis; vertice nucleoso, helicoideo; anfr. iii., tumidis, suturis
haud impressis, apice magno mamillato; anfr. norm. iii., subplanátis,
suturis distinctis; sculptura haud expressa; tota superficie costulis obscuris, latis, spiralibus, quarum vi.–viii. in spira monstrantur, et iii.–v. circa basim rotundatam, interdum obsoletis, cincta;
costulis radiantibus circ. xviii., subobsoletis; apertura regulariter
ovata, ad suturam angulata, peritremate continuo; basi haud umbilicata; columella regulariter arcuata. Long. ·09, long. spir. ·07,
lat. ·03 poll., div. 30°.

34. *Acirsa Menesthoides.*

A. testa nitida, turrita, majore, solidiore, pallide fusca; anfr. nucl.
lævibus; norm. vi., subplanatis, suturis distinctis; lineis crebris
spiralibus insculpta, quarum circ. viii. in spira monstrantur; testa
adolescente lirulis radiantibus obsoletis decussata; apertura subovali; columella solida, imperforata. Long. ·42, long. spir. ·3,
lat. ·16 poll., div. 25°.

35. *Cythnia asteriaphila.*

C. testa *C. tumenti* simillima, sed umbilico minore, haud carinato, tenuissima, diaphana ; anfr. iv., tumidis ; vert. nucl. normali, haud stylineo, apice mamillato : operculo tenuissimo, elementis concentricis, nucleo submediano sinistrorsum sito. Long. ·03, long. spir. ·015, lat. ·025 poll., div. 60°.

A solitary specimen was found by Dr. Stimpson, imbedded in a star-fish, like *Stylina* ; from which genus the vertex and operculum distinguish it.

36. *Bittium nitens.*

B. testa regulari, rufo-fusca, hic et illic pallida, maxime nitente ; anfr. nucl. iii., lævibus, tumidis, apice submamillato, subdeclivi ; norm. vi., tumidis, suturis impressis ; costis radiantibus circ. xiv., haud contiguis, angustis, interstitiis undatis ; costulis rotundatis, spiralibus, in spira iv., quarum postica multo minor, supercurrentibus, ad intersectiones subnodosis ; costulis circa basim subrotundatam iv., haud decussatis ; apertura subquadrata ; columella haud truncata, obtuse angulata ; labro acuto, a costulis indentato ; labio inconspicuo. Long. ·21, long. spir. ·16, lat. ·06 poll., div. 20°.

37. *Mangelia subdiaphana.*

M. testa parva, subdiaphana, albida, interdum rufo-fusco pallide tincta ; satis turrita, marginibus spiræ parum excurvatis ; anfr. nucleosis iii., lævibus, diaphanis, apice mamillato ; norm. iv., satis excurvatis, haud angulatis, suturis impressis ; fascia super spiram pallide fusca, alteraque candida contigua ; costulis radiantibus xiv.–xviii., acutis, subrectis, distantibus, interstitiis undatis ; tota superficie minute et creberrime spiraliter striata ; basi producta, striis magis expressis ; apertura subelongata ; labro ad dorsum incrassato, postice distincte emarginato, intus haud dentato ; labio tenuissimo ; columella recta, antice late canaliculata. Long. ·19, long. spir. ·1, lat. ·06 poll., div. 30°.

38. *Drillia appressa.*

D. testa parva, compacta ; rufo-fusca, interdum supra costas pallidiore ; marginibus spiræ excurvatis ; anfr. norm. vi., planatis, suturis indistinctis ; costis tuberculosis radiantibus circ. xiv., antice et postice obsoletis ; striolis spiralibus creberrimis ; costa spirali irregulari postica, tuberculosa, super suturas appressa ; area sinus parvi vix definita ; basi satis prolongata ; apertura subquadrata ; labio distincto. Long. ·3, long. spir. ·17, lat. ·12 poll., div. 40°.

39. *Cithara fusconotata.*

C. testa parva, satis turrita, tenui, albida ; postice linea, seu serie macularum, rufo-fusca, interdum altera peripheriali ornata ; marginibus spiræ rectioribus ; anfr. nucl. ii., rotundatis, apice mamillato ; norm. vi., in spira rotundatis, suturis impressis ; basi satis rotundata ; costis radiantibus circ. ix., acutis, distantibus, antice

et postice subobsoletis ; tota superficie spiraliter sulcata, sulculis
subdistantibus, undatis, costas superantibus ; apertura subovali,
satis elongata, postice valde sinuata ; labro acuto, dorsaliter costu-
láto, intus haud dentato ; labio tenui. Long. ·36, long. spir. ·18,
lat. ·16 poll., div. 40°.

40. *Obeliscus variegatus.*

O. testa *O. hastato* simili ; nitidissima, striolis incrementi exilissimis ;
livido et castaneo varie nebulosa ; prope suturam canaliculatam
lineis albidis picta ; hic et illic callositate alba interna ; peripheria
circa basin insculpta, unicolore ; columella truncata, triplicata ;
plica superiore acuta, exstante, circa basim continua ; plicis anticis
parvis, spiralibus. Long. ·44, long. spir. ·3, lat. ·15 poll., div. 23°.

41. *Odostomia (Evalea) æquisculpta.*

O. testa parva, ovoidea, alba, subdiaphana; marginibus spiræ subrectis ; vert. nucl. ?. . . ., normaliter truncato ; anfr. norm. iv.,
parum arcuatis, suturis impressis ; tota superficie costulis spiralibus circ. xiv., quarum vi. in spira monstrantur, latis, planatis,
æquidistantibus ; interstitiis parvis ; basi rotundata ; apertura
ovata ; peritremate haud continuo ; labro acuto ; labio subobsoleto ;
plica juxta parietem conspicua, acuta, transversa ; columella arcuata,
rimulam umbilicalem formante. Long. ·07, long. spir. ·04, lat,
·03 poll., div. 40°.

42. *Odostomia (Evalea) delicatula.*

O. testa tenuissima, alba, diaphana, nitente, elongata ; marginibus spiræ eleganter excurvatis ; vert. nucl. lævi, globoso, decliviter immerso ; anfr. norm. iii., subplanatis, suturis impressis ;
liris subacutis, spiralibus, quarum v. in spira monstrantur ; interstitiis latis, undatis, creberrime decussatis ; basi elongata ; apertura oblonga, peritremate haud continuo ; labro tenui ; labio vix
conspicuo ; plica juxta parietem exstante, declivi. Long. ·075,
long. spir. ·04, lat. ·03 poll., div. 30°.

43. *Chrysallida angusta.*

C. testa parva, satis elongata, nitida, alba, sculptura minus expressa;
marginibus spiræ parum excurvatis ; vert. nucl. parvo, subito
immerso, dimidium truncationis tegente ; anfr. norm. v., planatis,
elongatis, suturis minus impressis ; costis radiantibus circ. xiii.,
plerumque lineis continuis marginibus utrinque parallelis, circa
basim productam obsoletis ; lirulis spiralibus angustis, in spira
circ. v., interstitiis decussantibus, supra costas haud nodulosis ;
apertura ovali ; peritremate parum continuo ; labro tenui, trans-
lucido ; labio tenui ; plica juxta parietem parva, obtusa. Long.
·095, long. spir. ·065, lat. ·028 poll., div. 20°.

44. *Eulima fuscostrigata.*

E. testa minore, gracillima, albida, striga latiore rufo-fusca supra peripheriam ornata; basi quoque rufo-fusca, valde prolongata, regulariter excurvata; anfr. nucl. ii., tumidioribus; norm. viii., planatis, suturis haud conspicuis; varicibus nullis; apertura valde elongata; labro vix sinuato; labio vix calloso. Long. ·17, long. spir. ·12, lat. ·05 poll., div. 20°.

45. *Opalia crenatoides.*

Ø. testa turrita, alba, marginibus spiræ rectis; anfr. nucl.?....; norm. vi., compactis, attingentibus; costis radiantibus circ. x., in spira plerumque obsoletis, ultimo anfractu validioribus, latis, haud exstantibus, attingentibus, spiram lineis fere rectis ascendentibus; suturis inter costas altissime indentatis; carina obtusa basali, suturæ continua; inter costas radiantes undique, ut in suturis, indentata; costis interdum, propter lirulas spirales subobsoletas, subnodosis; columella haud umbilicata; basi antice lævi. Long. ·54, long. spir. ·38, lat. ·23 poll., div. 30°.

Additional specimens may connect this with the Portuguese *O. crenata.*

46. *Truncaria eurytoides.*

T. testa parva, turrita, gracili; albida, sæpius fascia circa peripheriam maculis fusco-aurantiacis picta; anfr. nucl. mamillatis, lævibus; norm. v., effusis, subplanatis, ultimo paulum constricto; costulis radiantibus circ. xx., aperturam versus evanidis; apertura subquadrata; labro haud incrassato, interdum intus subtiliter striato, haud dentato; labio appresso; columella abrupte truncata. Long. ·3, long. spir. ·2, lat. ·11 poll., div. 23°.

Variat basi fusco tincta, seu tota superficie ut in *Nitidella cribraria* picta.

47. *Sistrum* (? *ochrostoma*, var.) *rufonotatum.*

S. testa *S. ochrostomati* simili, sed minore, angustiore, vix tabulata; alba, linea punctorum rufo-fuscorum subperipheriali, interdum lineis spiralibus, interdum ejusdem coloris maculis, ornata; vert. nucl. mamillato, anfr. iii., lævibus, vix tumidis; norm. v., plus minusve elongatis, in medio nodoso-angulatis, postice planatis, suturis ad angulum valde obtusum conspicuis; seriebus nodulorum spiralibus iii., quarum postica major, secundum costas radiantes obsoletas circ. vi.–viii. ordinatis; seriebus anticis inconspicuis ii.; interdum costulis spiralibus intercalatis; canali brevi, rectiore, aperto, angusto; apertura subovali, vix subquadrata, intus pallide aurantiaca; labro acutiore, dorsaliter subvaricoso, postice sæpe sinuato, intus obscure vi.-dentato; labio conspicuo, interdum exstante. Long. ·5, long. spir. ·23, lat. ·32 poll., div. 60°.

Variat testa obesa, nodulis validis. Variat quoque testa acuminata, nodulis subobsoletis. Long. ·52, long. spir. ·23, lat. ·25 poll., div. 42°.

48. *?Nitidella millepunctata.*

?N. testa parva, nitida, livida; spira exstante, anfractibus subplanatis, suturis distinctis; anfr. nucl. lævibus, adolescentibus obsolete radiatim lirulatis, adultis lævibus; zona alba postica, suturam attingente, aurantiaco maculata; tota præter zonam superficie aurantiaco puncticulata, punctis minimis, creberrimis, in quincunces dispositis; apertura subquadrata; labro incrassato, intus vi.-dentato; labio exstante, a lirulis circa basim spiralibus indentato. Long. ·3, long. spir. ·17, lat. ·15 poll., div. 40°.

Differs from *Columbella albuginosa*, Rve., in its peculiar and constant painting.

49. *?Nitidella densilineata.*

?*N.* testa ?*N. millepunctatam* forma et indole simulante, sed omnino nitida, anfractibus planatis, suturis indistinctis, striolis circa basim minimis; livida, lineolis aurantiaco-fuscis divaricatis, sæpe ziczacformibus, densissime signata. Long. ·25, long. spir. ·15, lat. ·1 poll., div. 35°.

The opercula of these two species being unknown, their generic position remains doubtful. The same is true of the two following.

50. *?Anachis tincta.*

?*A.* testa parva, turrita, albida, rufo-aurantiaco supra costas tincta; anfr. nucl. lævibus; norm. iv.–v., subplanatis, suturis valde impressis; costulis x. radiantibus, et liris spiralibus transeuntibus, in spira iii. supra costas conspicuis, unaque in sutura, dense insculpta; interstitiis alte cælatis; apertura subquadrata; labro in medio incrassato. Long. ·19, long. spir. ·12, lat. ·08 poll., div. 30°.

51. *?Anachis fuscostrigata.*

?*A.* testa parva, turrita, livida, nitida; zonis rufo-fuscis, subspiralibus, in spira circ. iii., interdum, maxime ad basim, confluentibus, conspicue cincta; lirulis radiantibus subobsoletis, circ. x., prope suturam se monstrantibus; apertura subquadrata. Long. ·13, long. spir. ·095, lat. ·045 poll., div. 20°.

52. *Pisania elata.*

P. testa minore, valde turrita, Latiroidea; alba, rufo-fusco antice et postice varie maculata seu strigata; anfr. nucl. ?. . . .; norm. vi., convexis, suturis impressis; costis radiantibus vi.–viii., obtusis, interstitiis undatis; lirulis spiralibus distantibus, in spira plerumque iii., aliis minoribus intercalantibus; canali angusto, subrecurvato; apertura subovata; pariete postice dentata; columellæ parum contorta. Long. ·68, long. spir. ·37, lat. ·29 poll., div. 38°

D.

CONTRIBUTIONS

TOWARDS A

MONOGRAPH OF THE PANDORIDÆ.

BY

PHILIP P. CARPENTER, B. A., Pɥ. D.

From the Proceedings of the Zoölogical Society of London, pp. 596–603,
November 22, 1864.

(223)

Contributions towards a Monograph of the Pandoridæ.

By Philip P. Carpenter, B.A., Ph.D.

It is remarkable that, notwithstanding the zeal with which most of the old genera have been divided, to meet the wants of modern malacology, the genus *Pandora*, Lam., has been left untouched by Dr. Gray, Messrs. Adams, and their follower, Chenu. Yet the species known to the elder Sowerby present three distinct types of hinge, which were well figured by him in his 'Conchological Illustrations.' Specimens and even species of *Pandora* (except of the well-known N. Atlantic forms) being very rarely seen in collections, it is presumed that naturalists have had but few opportunities of studying them. Mr. Cuming having most kindly allowed me to examine the hinge of all the species in his collection, it has appeared desirable to propose two new genera, and also to group part of the typical species under a subgenus.

It was at one time thought that the presence of an ossicle in the cartilage was a family mark of *Anatinidæ*, to which *Myadora* from *Pandoridæ*, and *Tellimya* from *Kelliadæ*, were consequently removed. One of the new genera of Pandorids, however, possesses a well-developed ossicle; and a small one is seen even in some species of the normal genus.

The most highly organized structure in the family is found in the North American genus *Clidiophora*, which has both clavicle[*] and ossicle; the next is the East-Indian group *Cœlodon*, which wants both clavicle and ossicle, but possesses a tent-shaped dentition in the left valve. The simplest form is the well-known *Pandora*, which has neither clavicle, tent, nor ossicle; but in the subgenus *Kennerlia* the ossicle is present. The genus *Myodora* is quite distinct, but connected with *Pandora* through *Kennerlia*.

Genus Clidiophora[†].

Testa Pandoriformis, ventraliter expansa; valva dextra tridentata, dente postico elongato; valva sinistra sæpius bidentata, dente antico simplici; cartilagine ossiculo firmata; sinu pallii nullo.

1. *Type,* Clidiophora claviculata, Cpr. (*Pandora cl.*) P.Z.S. 1855, p. 228.

---

[*] The word "clavicle" is used (in default of a better) to denote a linear dental process running into the body of the shell, often serving as a support to the cardinal plate, as in *Anatina* and some species of *Placunomia*.

[†] Th. κλειτίον, a clavicle; φέρω.

In the dentition of the right valve this genus resembles *Cœlodon,* except that the posterior lamina is greatly developed, resembling a clavicle. The left valve wants the central tooth and chamber of that genus. This structural deficiency, however, is compensated by the development of an ossicle in the long cartilage. As far as is known, all the species are from North and Central America, and are swollen ventrally.

2. CLIDIOPHORA CRISTATA.

C. *t. securiformi, minus transversa, tenui, subplanata ; umbonibus ad ⅖ longitudinis sitis ; ventraliter maxime excurvata ; marginibus dorsalibus, post. maxime incurvato, ant. hic et illic alalis triangularibus cristato : intus marginibus posticis utraque in valva erectis : v. dextr. dente postico satis longo, cicatrice adductoris tenus haud porrecto ; dente centrali extante ; dente antico a margine separato, usque ad cic. anticam porrecto, haud extante : v. sinistr. dente post. bifido, haud extante, alterum recipiente, fossa cartilaginea contigua ; d. centr. nullo ; d. ant. satis extante, usque ad cicatr. anticam porrecto ; linea palliari a margine valde remota, regulariter in puncta divisa ; radiis ab umbonibus usque ad puncta conspicuis, æqualibus ; ossiculo tenui, elongato.*

Long. 1·0, lat. ·6, alt. ·1 poll.

Hab. in sinu Californiensi ; legit Conway Shipley diligentissimus; sp. un. in Museo Cumingiano.

This species is known from *C. claviculata* by the much greater posterior curvature of the beaks, and anteriorly by the beautiful triangular wing-like serrations of the margin, in which it resembles *Tellidora burneti.* The inside has elegant rays from the umbo to the dotted pallial line.

3. CLIDIOPHORA TABACEA, Meusch. (Mus. Gron.).

Specimens under this specific name are preserved in the Cumingian collection.

3 *a.* CLIDIOPHORA TRILINEATA, Say (*Pandora tr.*), Hanl. Rec. Shells, p. 49.

3 *b.* CLIDIOPHORA NASUTA, Sby. (*Pandora n.*), Sp. Conch. f. 18, 19.

It is probable that these are simply varietal forms of the well-known New England species. Say's name and Sowerby's excellent figure prove that the peculiar hinge of the genus was observed by both authors. Mr. Cuming gives "Philippines" as the habitat of his specimens of *C. nasuta,* probably in error. Mr. Hanley quotes it as a synonym of *C. trilineata.* An examination of a large series from Staten Island proves that the outline varies considerably. The tablet in the Nuttallian collection at the British Museum, marked *Pandora punctata,* belongs to this species. Young shells, when quite perfect, display faint radiating grooves on the prismatic layer of the flat valve, as in *Kennerlia*.

4. CLIDIOPHORA PUNCTATA, Conr.

This very rare species was only known in England by worn left valves in the British Museum, and in Mr. Cuming's and Mr. Hanley's collections. The first perfect specimens were dredged by Dr. J. G. Cooper (Zoologist to the Californian State Survey) at San Pedro. A young shell, sent by him to the Smithsonian Institution, displays a dentition agreeing in the main with *C. trilineata*. In the flat valve, the central and anterior teeth are close together and nearly parallel; the anterior short, nearly obsolete; the middle long and sharp, corresponding with the long, sharp tooth in the convex valve, which points to the outside of the anterior scar, instead of to the middle, as in *C. trilineata*. The (posterior) clavicle-tooth in the flat valve is longer than in the Eastern species, with the cartilage on it for two-fifths of the length. In *C. trilineata* it lies by the side, nearly the whole way. The posterior margin of the convex valve fits between the clavicle and the margin of the flat valve. The ossicle is remarkably long and thin. The punctures are extremely conspicuous even in this young, transparent, and papyraceous specimen; and, what is more peculiar, the dried remains of the animal are covered with minute pearl-shaped grains of shelly matter corresponding with them.

4 a. CLIDIOPHORA DEPRESSA, Sby., = *Pandora d.*, Sp. Conch. f. 11, 12 ; Hanl. Rec. Shells, p. 49.

The "posterior" dilated side of Sowerby is the "anterior" of Hanley. The species was constituted from a "very few specimens, all of them much worn down, as if they had been used as ornaments." The hinge therefore may not have been accurately observed. They were part of the Humphrey collection, and perhaps from the Californian region. Judging from the shape (for no type has been discovered), it may be identical with *C. punctata*, Conr.

5. CLIDIOPHORA ACUTEDENTATA (vice C. B. Ad.).

C. *t. parum " elongata, ovato ; parte postica " haud rostrata, latiore, obtusa; "margine dorsali" postico "subrecto; margine ventrali rotundato," haud tumente; parte antica curtiore; "umbonibus subæqualiter subconvexis, umbone dextro postice angulato": intus, v. convexa dente antico magno, acutissimo, medio parvo, postico valido, maxime elongato; v. planata dentibus antico et postico acutis; ligamento juxta dentem posticum sito.*

"Long. ·7, lat. ·42, alt. ·11 poll."

Hab. in Panama: sp. unicum, postice fractum, legit C. B. Adams deploratus: Museo Coll. Amherstianæ : = *Pandora cornuta* (Gld.), C. B. Ad. Pan. Shells, no. 498, P.Z.S. 1863, p. 368.

Prof. Adams's "appropriate name suggested by Dr. Gould" being calculated to mislead, I have thought it necessary to change it.

Most of the original diagnosis must also be dropped, the parts above quoted being all that it is desirable to retain. The present description is written from notes and drawings made on a careful examination of the broken type. The lines of growth show that, so far from being "cornute," the species is remarkable for the absence of beak, —the margins being more equally rounded even than in *P. obtusa*, which in shape it somewhat resembles. The hinge is almost exactly like that of *C. claviculata*, jun., but differs in the somewhat greater proportionate length of the clavicle, and in the unwonted size and sharp pointing of the anterior tooth. The new name has been chosen to record this peculiarity, rather than follow the modern custom of naming from the author of the mistake. The best naturalists occasionally err; but corrections can be made without affixing a false compliment in perpetuity.

6. ? CLIDIOPHORA DISCORS, Sby. (*Pandora d.*), P. Z. S. 1835, p 99; Sp. Conch. f. 29, 30.

The type has not been discovered; the figure and diagnosis only relate to the outside; and the habitat is not stated. The genus is therefore doubtful; but in shape it resembles the young of *C. claviculata*.

7. ? CLIDIOPHORA ARCUATA, Sby. (*Pandora a.*), Sp. Conch. f. 27, 28; P. Z. S. 1835, p. 93; Hanl. Rec. Shells, p. 49.

The worn valves in the Cumingian collection do not allow of a confident determination of the genus.

Genus CŒLODON *.

Testa Pandoriformis : valva sinistra dentibus duobus, cicatricem adductoris anticam versus radiantibus, lamina infra cavernosa junctis : ossiculo nullo : sinu pallii nullo.

The shells of this group vary considerably in shape and dentition in the different species; but agree in this, that in the left valve there is a kind of tent, formed by a thin laminated roof lying on the top of two diverging teeth. It is hard even to guess what is the use of this (perhaps unique) structure; especially as its opening is not towards the body of the shell, but directly facing the anterior adductor. It is seen at once on opening the typical species, which was well figured by Sowerby, Sp. Conch. f. 22. In the aberrant forms it might easily be overlooked, and a glass is needed to detect it in small specimens; but if it exists, the shell can be supported on a pin thrust into the "hollow tooth." When more species are known, the group may require subdivision, the *C. flexuosus* especially presenting a marked transition to *Clidiophora*. In that genus the posterior part excels in development; in *Cœlodon*, the anterior. - All the known species are from the Eastern seas, but are very seldom seen in collections. An enlarged diagnosis of the type species is offered.

* Th. κοῖλος, hollow; ὀδούν, tooth.

228

1. CŒLODON CEYLANICUS.

Pandora ceylanica, Sby. P. Z. S. 1835, p. 94 ; Sp. Conch. f. 20, 21, 22, = *P. ceylonica,* Hanl. Rec. Shells, p. 50, = *P. indica,* Chenu, Man. Conch. ii. p. 54. f. 214.

C. *t. planata, rostrata, securiformi; ventraliter maxime, antice satis excurvata ; margine postico dorsali valde incurvato : intus, valva dextra, margine postico rectangulatim superstante, dentibus anticis ii. prælongis, satis extantibus, usque ad cicatricem adductoris continuis, dentem cavernosum valvæ alterius amplectantibus ; dente postico curtiore, extante, fossam cartilagineam per totam longitudinem gerente : valva sinistra, margine postico subrectangulatim superstante ; sulco postico dentem v. alt. recipiente ; dentibus anticis usque ad cicatricem adductoris continuis, centrali longiore, plus quam dimidio interstitii lamina tenui tecto, ventraliter arcuato.*

Under this species, of which the correct locality appears in the name, Mr. Sowerby quotes "a single specimen obtained at Island Muerte, W. Columbia, 11 fm., by Mr. Cuming." The hinge may not have been examined. The shell quoted does not now appear in the Cumingian collection, and probably belonged to *Cleidophora claviculata,* which in shape resembles the typical *Cœlodon.*

1 *a.* CŒLODON CUMINGII, Hanl. (*Pandora c.*), P. Z. S. 1861, p. 272.

This agrees with the last species in shape and dentition, and is probably only a variety.

Hab. Philippines (*Cuming*).

2. CŒLODON DELICATULUS, A. Ad. (*Pandora d.*) P. Z. S. (diagn. auct.).

. . . *marginibus dorsalibus ad angulum circ.* 160° *divergentibus : cardine v. dextr. dente postico satis elongato ; centrali curto, ad umbonem valde calloso ; antico longissimo, cicatricem ant. superante, margini contiguo : v. sinistr. dente centrali curto, supra cavernam evecto, in anticum prælongum continuo.*

In this species, the shape of which is not unlike *P. obtusa,* though less transverse, the anterior teeth are enormously developed at the expense of the central. These are short, but prominent ; in the left valve bent over, along the whole length, to form the roof of the chamber, and then drawn on into the anterior tooth.

3. CŒLODON ELONGATUS, n. s.

C. *t. parva, tenuissima, maxime planata ; parte antica minore, excurvata ; ventraliter valde excurvata, postice maxime elongata, rostro angustiore ; dorsaliter valde incurvata : intus, v. dextr. dente post. satis longo ; d. centrali prælongo, postice flecto, cicatricem adductoris parum superante ; d. antico minore : v. sinistr. cartilagine valde elongata, postice sita ; d.*

centrali prælongo, postice flecto; d. antico minore a margine remoto, lamina totius longitudinis ad centralem juncto.

Long. ·65, lat. ·3, alt. ·05 poll.

Hab. in China et Borneo (*Mus. Cuming.*).

This species is the Eastern representative of *P. rostrata*, as is *C. delicatulus* of *P. obtusa.* It has the reverse dentition, the central tooth being very long, and the anterior short, bridged over to meet it at the whole length. In the Borneo shell, which is larger, the anterior tooth is rather longer, with the front margin of the ceiling more incurved; but the differences are probably due to increased age only.

4. CŒLODON FLEXUOSUS, Sby. (*Pandora f.*), Sp. Conch. f. 13, 14, 15; Hanl. Rec. Shells, p. 49 (diagn. auct.),

. . . *cardine v. dextra dente postico prælongo, a margine separato, usque ad cicatr. adduct. porrecto; fossa cartilaginea curta, inter dentes post. et centr. sita; d. centr. curtissimo, maxime extante, retrorsum deflecto; d. ant. minimo, pene obsoleto: v. sinistr. sulco prælongo postico; fossa cartilaginea separata, curtiore; d. centr. extante, curtissimo, supra cavernam pyriformem, in dentem anticum usque ad cicatr. adduct. prolongatum, porrecto.*

This long-known but rare Red Sea species is to *Pandora* what *Trisis* (Gray) is to *Arca.* It is swollen and twisted, and, by its long clavicle, forms an interesting transition to *Clidiophora.*

4 *a.* ? CŒLODON UNGUICULUS, Sby. (*Pandora u.*), Sp. Conch. f. 16, 17; Hanl. Rec. Shells, p. 49.

The type has not been found of this species, which was described from a convex valve only. It clearly belongs to the same section as *C. flexuosus,* and, though the shape is somewhat different, perhaps it is only a variety.

Genus PANDORA, Lam.

It is proposed to limit this genus according to the diagnosis of Sowerby, founded on Lamarck's. Succeeding naturalists have adopted the diagnosis, while they have included in it species to which it did not apply[*]. It presents a very simple type of hinge, as though the Pandorid idea were gradually fading away towards *Myodora.* The *P. wardiana* is the finest species in the group; but it is scarcely typical, having the radiating grooves of the section *Kennerlia.* The Lamarckian type is the *Tellina inæqualis* of Linnæus.

1. PANDORA ROSTRATA, Lam., Forbes & Hanl. et auct. plur.= *P inæqualis,* Linn., Gray, Add.

* Chenu, however (Man. Conch. ii. p. 51), gives an original and extended diagnosis, in which he accredits to the whole genus "une dent triangulaire, aplatie, bifurquée, dont la portion antérieure, plus longue, se prolonge jusqu'à l'impression musculaire antérieure"—a character which only belongs to the section *Cœlodon.*

2. Pandora obtusa, Lam., auct.

3. Pandora brevifrons, Sby., Sp. Conch. f. 25, 26; P. Z. S. 1835, p. 93.

4. Pandora cistula, Gld. Otia, p. 77.

This species is not quoted in the index to the E. E. Moll., but appears in the text (p. 396) and in the Atlas (f. 500). In shape, but not in texture, it resembles *P. oblonga*.

5. Pandora oblonga, Sby., Sp. Conch. f. 10; Hanl. Rec. Shells, p. 49.

The unique type of this species, from Humphrey's collection, has not been found; it was not described in the P. Z. S., and very closely resembles *P. rostrata*.

6. Pandora radiata, Sby., P. Z. S. 1835, p. 24; Sp. Conch. f. 23, 24.

7. Pandora wardiana, A. Ad. P. Z. S. 1859, p. 487.

No ossicle has been observed in any of the above species. If it be found hereafter in living specimens of the grooved *P. radiata* and *P. wardiana*, they should be removed to the subgenus. The group is not local, as appears to be the case with *Cælodon* and *Clidiophora*, being found in both hemispheres and on both sides of the equator.

Subgenus Kennerlia*.

Pandora cartilagine ossiculo tenuiore instructa; lamina exteriore prismatica valvæ planatæ radiis plerumque insculpta.

The typical species have radiating grooves in the exterior prismatic layer of the right valve. These have not been observed in *K. glacialis*, but perhaps the specimens are somewhat decorticated. The essential character is the possession of an ossicle. This is well developed in *K. glacialis*, but so thin in the other species that it is often hidden in dried shells by the contraction of the cartilage. The first species in which it was observed (Dr. Kennerley having sent several fresh specimens, preserved in alcohol, to the Smithsonian Institution) was

1. Kennerlia filosa, n. s.

K. *t. tenui, planoconvexa, maxime rostrata; marginibus dorsalibus rectis, ad angulum circ.* 160° ; *ventrali regulariter et modice excurvato, postice vix sinuato; epidermide olivacea, plerumque erosa, postice corrugata; lamina externa prismatica spongiosa; valva planata radiatim sulcata (quasi filosa), sulcis distantibus; valva convexa, costa obtusissima postice decurrente;*

* Named in grateful remembrance of the services rendered to science by the late Dr. Kenneriey, the naturalist to the American N. Pacific Boundary Survey; whose premature death has interrupted, almost at the onset, our knowledge of the dredging-fauna of Puget Sound

lineis seu undis incrementi conspicuis : intus dente cardinali uno, parvo, extante ; callositate claviculoidea antica, margini contigua ; fossa cartilaginea postice sita ; cicatricibus adductorum rotundatis, margini dorsali contiguis ; linea pallii simplici.

Long. ·8, lat. ·4, alt. ·12 poll.

Hab. in sinu Pugetiano (*Kennerley*).

2. KENNERLIA BICARINATA, n. s.

K. t. "K. filosæ" *simili, sed haud rostrata ; postice latiore ; carinis in valva convexa duabus, in valva planata una, ex umbonibus postice decurrentibus ; lamina prismatica radiatim sulcata, haud spongiosa ; valva convexa tenuiter indentata ; ligamento elongato, tenuissimo.*

Long. ·5, lat. ·25, alt. ·06 poll.

Hab. in insula Catalina, Californiæ ; 40–60 uln., rara (*Dr. J. G. Cooper.* State Geological Survey Coll. no. 1063 ; Mus. Smithsonian Inst.).

The shape and keels at once distinguish this beautiful little species from its Northern ally, with which, in the hinge and threading of the outer layer, it exactly agrees. The ligament in both species is extremely thin, holding the valves together from the umbo to the posterior end. The fossil *Pandora bilirata,* Conr., may prove identical with this recent species ; but the diagnosis, figure, and type specimen are so imperfect that it would be too hazardous to affiliate them.

3. KENNERLIA GLACIALIS, Leach (*Pandora gl.*), Sby. Sp. Conch. f. 4, 5, 6 ; Hanl. Rec. Shells, p. 49 (diagn. auct.).

. . . *valva dextra callo conspicuo fossam cartilagineam firmante ; ossiculo fortiore.*

The known species of *Kennerlia* are thus confined to the North Pacific and the Arctic seas. The diagnosis of No. 1 belongs to a paper on Dr. Kennerley's new species in the Journ. Ac. N. S. Philad. ; and that of No. 2 to a series of papers on Dr. Cooper's new species in the Proc. Calif. Ac. N. S. They are inserted here to complete the monograph, as far as known to the writer. The "*Pandora striata,* Quoy" (Add. Gen. ii. p. 371), is a *Myodora.* The latter genus is so well defined that no alteration is proposed in it.

232

E.

DIAGNOSES

OF

NEW FORMS OF MOLLUSCA

FROM

THE VANCOUVER DISTRICT.

BY

PHILIP P. CARPENTER, B.A., Ph.D.

From the Annals and Magazine of Natural History. Third Series, Vol
XIV. (Nos. 5—37), pp. 423—429, December, 1864. Ibid. Vol. XV
(Nos. 37—56), pp. 28—32, January, 1865.

DIAGNOSES

OF

NEW FORMS OF MOLLUSCA

FROM

THE VANCOUVER DISTRICT.

BY

PHILIP P. CARPENTER, B.A., Ph.D.

THE shells here described were mostly collected by Indian children for their excellent teacher Mr. J. G. Swan, in the neighbourhood of Neeah Bay, W. T. They were presented by him to the Smithsonian Institution, Washington, D.C.; and, in accordance with their liberal policy, the first available duplicates will be found in the British Museum or in Mr. Cuming's Collection. The species are numbered to correspond with the list in the British Association Report for 1863, pp. 626–628; see also pp. 636–664.

5. *Mæra salmonea.*

M. testa parva, solida, compacta, subquadrata; lævi, nitente, epidermide tenui cinerea induta; extus pallide, intus vivide salmoneo tincta; marginibus dorsalibus rectis, ad angulum 120° separatis, umbonibus haud extantibus; marginibus antico et ventrali regulariter late excurvatis; parte postica brevissima, h aud angulata: intus, dent. card. utraque valva ii., quorum unus bifidus; lateralibus v. dextr. æquidistantibus, ant. extante, post. parvo; nymphis rectis, haud conspicuis; cicatr. add. post. subrotundata, ant. subrhomboidea; sinu pallii satis regulariter ovali, per iv. inter v. partes interstitii porrecto. Long. ·57, lat. ·45, alt. ·11 poll.
Variat testa aurantiaca, rarius albida, rosaceo tincta.

Hab. San Francisco (*Pac. Rail. E. E.*); Neeah Bay (*Swan*), plentiful; Monterey, 20 fathoms (*Cooper*).

In shape almost close to *Macoma crassula*, Desh. (Arctic); but that species is thinner, not glossy or salmon-coloured, and has no lateral teeth.

6. *Angulus variegatus.*

A. testa forma *A. obtuso* simili, sed costa interna omnino carent, valde inæquilaterali, solidiore, nitente, rosaceo et flavido subra'

235

tim eleganter variegata ; striis incrementi concentricis, postice ex-
tantioribus; umbonibus postice flectentibus, obtusis : parte antica
prolongata, regulariter excurvata; marginibus dorsali et ventrali
subparallelis, subrectis ; parte postica curtiore, subangulata : intus,
dent. card. utraque valva ii. minutis, quorum alter bifidus ; v.
dext. dent. lat., ant. curto, satis extante, post. nullo ; nymphis
curtis, latis, parum concavis, subito sectis, valvis postea subalatis ;
sinu pallii fere cicatr. ant. tenus porrecto. Long. ·72, lat. ·42,
alt. ·15.

Hab. Neeah Bay *(Swan)*; Monterey and Catalina Island,
20–60 fathoms, rare *(Cooper)*.

Subgenus MIODON*.

Testa Lucinoidea, dentibus cardinalibus, ut in *Cardita*, elongatis ;
laterali antico parvo instructa.

This little group of species is intermediate in character between *Astarte*, *Venericardia*, and *Lucina*. It first appears in
the Great Oolite, where it is represented by *Astarte (Miodon)
orbicularis*, J. Sby. Min. Conch. pl. 444. f. 2, 3. This must' not
be confounded with a second and true *Astarte orbicularis*, by the
same author, pl. 520. f. 2. It appears in Mr. Searles Wood's
Crag-series as *Astarte corbis*. The following is the only recent
species at present known.

9. *Miodon prolongatus.*

M. testa parva, solida, tumida, compacta, albida ; ventraliter antice
valde prolongata, excurvata ; lunula longa, rectiore, haud impressa ;
umbonibus antice inflectis, obtusis, valde prominentibus ; margine
dorsali postico parum excurvato ; costis radiantibus x.–xii. latis,
obtusis, marginem attingentibus, parum expressis, dorsaliter obsoletis, a liris incrementi concentricis, plus minusve distantibus, expressis, hic et illic interruptis : intus, margine a costis plus minusve
obsoletim crenulato ; cardine dentibus v. dextr., uno postico, inter
duas fossas elongato, et lat. ant. lunulari ; v. sinistr., dent. ant. triangulari, post. valde elongato, lat. ant. minimo, obsoleto ; cicatr. add.
subrotundatis, ventraliter sitis. Long. ·23, lat. ·24, alt. ·16.

Subgenus ADULA, Add. (diagn. auct.).

Testa ·inter *Modiolam* et *Lithophagum* intermedia, cylindracea ;
umbonibus obtusis ; parte antica longiore ; ligamento subinterno,
valde elongato ; epidermide haud testacea.

Animal byssiferum, in cryptis affixum ; musculis adductoribus
majoribus, antico ovato.

Constituted by Messrs. Adams for *A. soleniformis*, D'Orb.,
which very closely resembles the young of the Vancouver species :
enlarged to receive the shells of Lithophagoid shape which are

* *Th.* μείων, smaller; ὀδούς, tooth.

moored by byssus, like *Modiola.* The largest known species is
A. falcata, Gld., which is normally straight, but often grows in
a twisted burrow. *A. parasitica,* Desh., and the long-known
A. cinnamomea appear congeneric.

13. *Adula stylina.*

A. testa cylindracea, lithophagoidea, lævi, tenuissima, parum arcuata, subnacrea, albida, postice interdum livido tincta; epidermide nitente, lævi, solidiore, nigro-fusca : testa jun. typice modio-
læformi, umbonibus subanticis, obtusissimis ; margine dorsali
antice (rarissime paululum, testa minima, postice) tenuiter crenulato : testa adulta marginibus dors. et ventr. fere parallelis, ant.
et post. rotundatis ; umbonibus detritis, haud conspicuis, circiter
sextantim antice sitis ; incrustatione haud solida, densissime spongiosa, aream posticam diagonalem tegente, supra valvas prolongata,
appressa ; ligamento interno, postice valde prolongato ; pagina
interna pallida ; cicatr. add. postica tumida, pyriformi, antica
(quoad familiam) maxima, haud impressa, oblonga ; cicatr. pedali
antica magna, circulari, impressa ; callositate subumbonali (testa
jun.) cicatr. pedalem versus conspicua. Long. ·155, lat. ·4, alt. ·5.
Variat t. magis arcuata ; ut in *A. falcata,* antice tumidiore, sub-
    angulata.
Variat quoque testa attenuata.
Variat interdum ventraliter late hiante.

    Hab. Neeah Bay, abundant (*Swan*) ; Monterey (*Taylor*).

    On smashing a large lump of hard clay, bored by Pholads,
Petricolids, &c., large numbers of this species, with a few of *A.
falcata,* of all ages from ·06 onwards, were found *in situ.* Several
struggled for room in a single crypt. The umbos are abraded
by the wide opening of the valves.

14. *Axinæa (?septentrionalis, var.) subobsoleta.*

A. testa *A. septentrionali* simili, parum inæquilaterali, haud tumida ;
umbonibus obtusis, latis, satis prominentibus ; cinerea, rufo-cas-
taneo varie picta ; epidermide copiosa, sublaminata ; marginibus
ventrali et postico valde rotundato, antico parum producto, dorsali recto ; sulcis radiantibus subobsoletis sculpta, dorsaliter sæpe
evanidis : intus, marginibus ventrali valde, ant. et post. parum cre-
natis ; lamina cardinis subangulata ; dentibus paucioribus, validis,
angustatis ; cicatr. add. antica castanea, callosa ; ligamento sul-
cato. Long. ·13, lat. ·12, alt. ·7.

    Hab. Neeah Bay (*Swan*) ; Shoalwater Bay (*Cooper*).

    Middendorff's shell is figured with much stronger ribs, but
may have been described from decorticated specimens.

15. *Siphonaria Thersites.*

S. testa parva, tenui, haud elevata, valde inæquilaterali, dense nigro-
castanea, lævi, seu interdum costulis paucis, obtusis, obsoletis,

radiatim vix ornata; epidermide lævi, tenui, fugaci; costa pulmo-
nali intus et extus valde conspicua, tumente; vertice obtuso,
plerumque ad quadrantem, interdum ad trientem totius longitudinis sito; intus intense nigro-fusco, margine acuto. Long. ·46,
lat. ·33, alt. ·17.

Hab. Neeah Bay (*Swan*).

This genus, which culminates in western tropical America and
at Cape Horn, is not known in California. The Vancouver species resembles *S. lateralis* and its congeners, but differs in having
an enormous lung-rib and no colour-rays.

16. *Mopalia* (*Kennerleyi*, var.) *Swannii.*

M. testa *M. Kennerleyi* typicæ simili, sed jugo fornicato, haud carinato; omnino rubida, sculptura mult minus expressa; areis lateralibus vix definitis; latera versus subgranulata; dorsum versus
lineis jugum versus procedentibus, interstitiis punctatis; sinu
postico latiore; limbo pallii lato, coriaceo, vix piluloso. Long.
2·4, lat. 1·, div. 120°.

Hab. Tatooche Island (*Swan*).

23. *Margarita Cidaris,* A. Ad.

M. testa magna, conica, Turcicoidea, tenui; albido-cinerea, nacreo-
argentato; anfr. nucleosis?...(decollatis), norm. vii., subplanatis;
suturis alte insculptis; superficie spiræ tota valide tuberculosa,
seriebus tribus, alteris postea intercalantibus; peripheria et basi
rotundatis, carinatis; carinis circ. viii., haud acutis, irregularibus,
scabris, haud tuberculosis; lacuna umbilicali vix conspicua; apertura subrotundata; labro tenuissimo; labio obsoleto; columella
arcuata. Long. 1·1, long. spir. ·65, lat. ·75, div. 60°.

Hab. Neeah Bay (*Swan*).

Mr. A. Adams suggested the above expressive name for this
very remarkable and unique shell.

25. *Gibbula parcipicta.*

G. testa solidiore, parva, conica, pallida, purpureo-fusco varie nebulosa et maculata; anfr. v., rotundatis; carinis ii. validis in spira
se monstrantibus, minore intercalante; interstitiis subsuturalibus,
sublævibus, inter carinas obtuse decussatis; lira peripherica definita, sæpe in spira se monstrante; basi valde rotundata; lirulis
basalibus circ. v. rotundatis, subdistantibus; apertura subcirculari;
columella arcuata; umbilico majore, infundibuliformi, haud angulato. Long. ·14, long. spir. ·07, lat. ·13, div. 70°.

Hab. Neeah Bay (*Swan*); Santa Crux (*Rowell*).

26. *Gibbula succincta.*

G. testa parva, subelevata, solidiore; livida, testa jun. strigis angustis,
creberrimis, fusco-purpureis penicillata, testa adulta maculis quoque magnis nebulosa; anfr. v., subquadratis; liris obtusis medianis

et striis subobsoletis cincta, suturis valde impressis ; basi rotun-
aata, obtuse angulata, striis sæpe evanidis spiralibus ornata, tesra
adulta circa umbilicum magnum, infundibuliformem, vix angu-
latum, sæpe tumidiore, medio obtuse impressa ; apertura subquadrata, parum declivi ; columella subarcuata. Long. ·16, long.
spir. ·07, lat. ·16, div. 70°.

Hab. Neeah Bay (*Swan*) ; Lower California, on *Haliot's*
(*Rowell*).

27. *Gibbula lacunata.*

G. testa parva, fusco-purpurea, solidiore ; marginibus spiræ valde
excurvatis ; anfractibus nucleosis normalibus, postea iv. subplanatis, suturis distinctis, apice mamillato ; sublævi, circa basin
vix angulatam striolata, striolis spiralibus distantibus ; apertura
suborbiculari, parum declivi ; labio juxta umbilicum constrictum,
quasi lacunatum, lobato ; columella callositate parva umbilicum
constringente. Long. ·11, long. spir. ·05, lat. ·11, div. 80°.

Hab. Neeah Bay (*Swan*).

28. *Gibbula funiculata.*

G. testa parva, elevata, compacta, fusca ; marginibus spiræ excurvatis ; anfr. vi., haud tumidis, suturis parum impressis ; lirulis
crebris rotundatis undique cincta, quarum v. in spira monstrantur ;
interstitiis parvis ; basi rotundata, haud angulata ; umbilico parvo,
haud carinato ; apertura suborbiculari, parum declivi ; columella
vix arcuata. Long. ·24, long. spir. ·11, lat. ·2, div. 70°.

Hab. Neeah Bay (*Swan*), specimen unicum.

29. *Hipponyx cranioides.*

H. testa valde planata, majore, albida ; vertice nucleoso? ... ; testa
adulta apice interdum subcentrali, sæpius plus minusve postico ;
laminis incrementi confertis, undique rapide augentibus ; striis
radiantibus fortioribus, confertissimis, laminarum margines sæpe
crenulantibus ; margine acuto ; cicatr. musc. angusta, margini
contigua, regione capitis minore, sæpe dextrorsum torsa ; epidermide? ... Long. ·85, lat. ·75, alt. ·3.

Hab. Neeah Bay (*Swan*).

30. *Bivonia compacta.*

B. testa satis magna, sæpe solitaria, purpureo-fusca, spiraliter plerumque satis regulariter contorta, obsoletim cancellata seu sculptura fere evanida ; testis tenacissime adhærente. Long. (plerumque) ·7, lat. ·3, diam. apert. ·1.

Hab. Barclay Sound ; abundant on *Pachypoma gibberosum*
(*Swan*).

Belongs to *Bivonia*, Gray (not Mörch). Has the aspect of
Petaloconchus macrophragma on a large scale, but is entirely
destitute of internal laminæ. One specimen had a faint colu-

mellar thread for two whirls only.   Operculum normal, with thin edge, dark red.

32. *Lacuna porrecta.*

L. testa *L. puteolo* simili, sed multo majore, spira magis exserta; seu omnino fusca, seu zona pallidiore, seu pallida lineolis fuscescentibus tenuissime spiraliter ornata; epidermide tenuiter striata olivacea seu viridescente induta; tenuiore, spiraliter tenuiter striata; anfr. v., vix planatis, rapide augentibus, suturis impressis, vertice mamillato; apertura tumente; labio tenui, vix parietem attingente, intus subrecto; lacuna maxima, elongata, ad basin arcuata; peripheria expansa.   Long. ·52, long. spir. ·2, lat. ·4, div. 80°.

?Var. *effusa*: testa *L. porrectæ* simili, sed multo majore; spira elevata, satis effusa; anfr. tumidioribus, suturis valde impressis; aperturam versus magis expansa.   Long. ·65, long. spir. ·25, lat. ·5, div. 60°.

?Var. *exæquata*: testa *L. effusæ* simili, sed anfr. planatis, suturis parum impressis.   Long. ·5, long. spir. ·2, lat. ·42, div. 80°.

Hab. Neeah Bay (*Swan*).

The form *L. exæquata* is intermediate between the very different *L. porrecta* and *L. effusa*.   The *Lacunæ* vary so much (*vide* Forbes & Hanley *in loco*) that, even with a large multitude of specimens, it is not easy to state what constitutes a species.

33. *Lacuna* (? *solidula*, var.) *compacta.*

L. testa *L. solidulæ*, var., simili; parva, solida, compacta, angusta, subturrita, marginibus spiræ excurvatis: aurantiaca, interdum pallidiore zonata; anfr. subplanatis, suturis distinctis; tota superficie confertissime spiraliter striolata; basi valde angulata, subplanata; apertura subquadrata; columella vix lacunata.   Long. ·23, long. spir. ·1, lat. ·17, div. 60°.

Variat testa elongata: variat quoque columella normaliter lacunata.

Hab. Neeah Bay (*Swan*).

Possibly an extreme form of the very variable *L. solidula*, Lov. (= *L. carinata*, Gld., non A. Ad., = *Modelia striata*, Gabb), yet distinct in all ages.   The young shells resemble small *Litorinæ*.

34. *Lacuna variegata.*

L. testa tenui, plus minusve elevata, soluta, irregulari; adolescente fusco-purpureo; adulta livida, radiatim seu diagonaliter varie irregulariter strigata, strigis fusco-aurantiacis, sæpe ziczacformibus; anfr. vi., quorum primi compacti, apice submamillato; dein solutis, postice planatis, antice expansis; basi rotundata seu angulata; apertura subovata; labro postice porrecto; labio sæpe parietem vix attingente; columella intus recta, extus valde lacunata. Long. ·3, long. spir. ·16, lat. ·17, div. 50°.

Hab. Neeah Bay (*Swan*).

Painted like *L. decorata*, A. Ad., which differs in having a normal growth, with very slight chink.

35. *Isapis fenestrata.*

I. testa *I. oroideæ* forma et indole simili ; carinis ix. acutis (quarum iv. in spira monstrantur) cincta ; interstitiis duplo latioribus, concinne quadratim decussatis, lirulis radiantibus acutissimis ; anfr. postice tumentibus, suturis valde excavatis ; peritremate continuo ; labro a carinis pectinato ; labio parietem parum attingente, medio calloso ; umbilico angusto. Long. ·18, long. spir. ·13, lat. ·19, div. 70°.

Hab. Neeah Bay (*Swan*); S. Diego and Sta. Barbara Island (*Cooper*).

Dr. Cooper's shells are much smaller than those from the Vancouver district, which are white and eroded, varying much in the size of the umbilicus.

36. *Alvania reticulata.*

A. testa parva, subturrita, rufo-fusca, marginibus spiræ rectis ; anfr. nucleosis ii. et dimidio, naticoideis, lævibus, tumentibus, apice mamillato ; norm. iii., tumidis, suturis impressis ; liris angustis, distantibus, spiralibus circ. xii. (quarum iv.–vi. in spira monstrantur), et lirulis radiantibus, supra transeuntibus, haud nodulosis, secundum interstitia incurvatis, eleganter exsculpta ; interstitiis altis, quadratis ; peritremate continuo, subrotundato, acutiore. Long. ·085, long. spir. ·05, lat. ·04, div. 30°.

Hab. Neeah Bay ; two specimens in shell-washings (*Swan*).

37. *Alvania filosa.*

A. testa *A. reticulatæ* indole et colore, haud sculptura, simili ; multo majore, elongata ; anfr. nucl. ?... (detritis), norm. iv. ; striis parum separatis circ. xviii. (quarum circ. xii. in spira monstrantur) cincta ; rugulis radiantibus posticis creberrimis, haud expressis, circa peripheriam evanidis ; peritremate continuo ; columella rufo-purpureo tincta. Long. ·13, long. spir. ·09, lat. ·06, div. 20°.

Hab. Neeah Bay ; one specimen in shell-washings (*Swan*).

38. ?*Assiminea subrotundata.*

?*A.* testa haud parva, lævi, tenui, fusco-olivacea ; anfr. nucl. ?...(decollatis) ; norm. v., rapide augentibus, subrotundatis ; marginibus spiræ rectis, suturis valde impressis ; basi rotundata, haud umbilicata ; apertura rotundato-ovali, intus fuscescente ; peritremate continuo ; labro acuto ; labio parum calloso ; columella arcuata. Long. ·28, long. spir. ·13, lat. ·2, div. 65°.

Hab. Neeah Bay ; one specimen among *Lacunæ* (*Swan*).

May prove to be a large *Hydrobia.*

39. ?*Paludinella castanea.*

?*P.* testa compacta, solidiore, fusco-castanea, marginibus spiræ rec-

tioribus; rugulosa, lineis distantibus spiralibus irregulariter insculpta; anfr. nucleosis?.... (detritis), vertice late mamillato;
norm. iv., rapidius augentibus, tumidioribus, suturis satis impressis; basi regulariter excurvata, vix rimata; apertura suborbiculari, haud continua; labro acuto; labio supra parietem obsoleto,
supra columellam arcuatam intus calloso: operculo, anf. iv. haud
rapide augentibus.   Long. ·21, long. spir. ·09, lat. ·17, div. 70°.

Hab. Neeah Bay; one specimen among *Lacunæ* (*Swan*).

May be an aberrant *Assiminea*.

40. *Mangelia crebricostata.*

M. testa tereti, rufo-fusca, albo zonata; anfr. nucl.?... (decollatis);
norm. v. elongatis, subrotundatis, suturis impressis; costis radiantibus, obtusis, subrectis, circ. xv., spiram ascendentibus; sculptura spirali?... (detrita); apertura pyriformi, antrorsum in canalem brevem attenuata; labro postice parum sinuato; labio conspicuo.   Long. ·54, long. spir. ·3, lat. ·2, div. 28°.

Hab. Neeah Bay; 1 specimen (*Swan*).

41. *Mangelia interfossa.*

M. testa parva, valde attenuata, rufo-fusca, marginibus spiræ parum
excurvatis; anfr. nucl. ii., ut in *Chrysodomo* irregularibus, apice
mamillato; norm. vi., parum excurvatis, haud tabulatis, suturis
distinctis; costis radiantibus circ. xv., angustis, extantibus; costulis spiralibus circ. xv., quarum circ. v. seu vi. in spira monstrantur,
angustis, supra costas transeuntibus, ad intersectiones parum nodulosis; interstitiis altis, quadratis; basi effusa; apertura sub-
pyriformi; labro acuto, postice vix emarginato; labio tenui.
Long. ·38, long. spir. ·22, lat. ·13, div. 25°.

Hab. Neeah Bay; very rare (*Swan*).

42. ?*Mangelia tabulata.*

?*M.* testa parva, solidissima, luride rufo-fusca, marginibus spiræ excurvatis; vertice nucleoso chalcedonico (eroso); anfr. norm. v.,
postice rectangulatim tabulatis, suturis impressis; costis radiantibus circ. xvi., validis, obtusis, circiter basim attenuatam obsoletis;
costis spiralibus in spira iii.–iv. angustis, extantibus, supra cost.
rad. nodosis; interstitiis alte insculptis, subquadratis; costis circa
basim circiter vii., quadratim extantibus, interstitiis a lineis incrementi vix decussatis; canali curta, aperta; labro acutiore, ad angulum posticum vix sinuato; labio tenui; columella obsolete uni-
plicata.   Long. ·45, long. spir. ·26, lat. ·2, div. 35°.

Hab. Neeah Bay; several worn specimens (*Swan*).

The distinct fold near the base of the pillar may require the
formation of a new genus.

43. ?*Daphnella effusa.*

?*D.* testa gracillima, maxime effusa, rufo-fusca ; anfr. angustis, elongatis, suturis impressis ; striis spiralibus crebris a lineis incrementi decussatis ornata ; labro tenuiore, postice vix sinuato. Long. ·65, long. spir. ·45, lat. ·22, div. 30°.

Hab. Neeah Bay ; one broken specimen (*Swan*).

44. *Odostomia satura.*

O. testa magna, alba, lævi, solidiore, satis elevata ; anfr. nucl. ii., angustis, subplanorboideis, valde decliviter sitis, dextrorsum immersis, sinistrorsum extantibus ; norm. v., tumidioribus, regulariter convexis, suturis impressis ; basi rotundata, tumente, quasi umbilicata ; apertura ovata ; labro vix sinuato ; labio tenui, appresso ; plica columellari valida, subantica, parieti haud contigua, transversa. Long. ·26, long. spir. ·14, lat. ·13, div. 40°.

Hab. Neeah Bay ; rare (*Swan*).

Var. *pupiformis* : anfr. primis valde depressis, planatis ; vertice mamillato ; anfr. ult. normali. Specimen unicum, quasi monstruosum. Long. ·19, long. spir. ·1, lat. ·12, div. 45°.

44 b. *Odostomia* (? var.) *Gouldii.*

O. testa solida, alba, ovoidea, marginibus spiræ valde excurvatis ; vert. nucl. decliviter immerso ; anfr. norm. v., subplanatis, suturis valde impressis ; peripheria haud angulata ; basi excurvata, haud tumida ; apertura ovata, postice parum constricta ; labro solido ; labio conspicuo, rimam umbilicalem formante ; plica submediana, solida, extante, haud declivi. Long. ·23, long. spir. ·13, lat. ·1, div. 30°.

Hab. Neeah Bay ; very rare (*Swan*).

Agrees in some respects better with the diagnosis of *O. gravida*, Gould, than do Col. Jewett's shells, from which it is presumed the species was described. These large forms appear very variable.

45. *Odostomia nuciformis.*

O. testa magna, compacta, lævi, solida, alba ; anfr. nucl.? . . . (erosis), vertice submamillato ; anfr. norm. v., subplanatis, subelongatis ; spira brevi, marginibus valde excurvatis ; basi elongata, haud umbilicata ; apertura subovali, postice angusta ; labro solido ; labio tenui ; plica antica, solida, obtusa, transversa, parietem haud attingente. Long. ·3, long. spir. ·14, lat. ·18, div. 70°.

Hab. Neeah Bay ; extremely rare (*Swan*).

45 b. *Odostomia* (? var.) *avellana.*

O. testa *O. nuciformi* indole simili, sed spira valde prolongata. Long. ·32, long. spir. ·16, lat. ·16, div. 50°.

Hab. Neeah Bay ; one specimen (*Swan*).

Like a gigantic form of *O. conoidalis.*

47. *Oiostomia tenuisculpta.*

O. testa ovoidea, subelevata, albida, tenui, diaphana; anfr. nucl. subverticaliter immersis, angustis; norm. iii., parum tumidis, suturis impressis, sulculis spiralibus latioribus haud impressis, distantibus, in spira iii., circa basim rotundatam circ. vi. subobsoletis; apertura ovata; plica acuta, declivi, parva, parieti contigua; labro acuto; labio indistincto; columella antice parum effusa. Long. ·1, long. spir. ·04, lat. ·06, div. 60°.

Hab. Neeah Bay; one specimen (*Swan*).

48. *Scalaria Indianorum.*

S. testa gracili, turrita, alba; anfr. circ. x., rotundatis, parum separatis, lævibus; basi simplici, haud umbilicata; costis viii.–xv. (plerumque xii.), acutioribus, subreflexis, interdum latis, plerumque lineis irregularibus margini spiræ recto parallelis ascendentibus, rarius juxta suturam subnodosis; apertura ovata. Long. 1·05, long. spir. ·8, lat. ·36, div. 28°.

Hab. Neeah Bay (*Swan*).

Strung as ornaments by the Indian children.   Intermediate between *S. communis* and *S. Turtonis*, and scarcely differs from " *S. Georgettina*, Kien.," Mus. Cum. no. 34, Brazil.

48 b. *Scalaria* (? *Indianorum*, var.) *tincta.*

S. ?*Indianorum* costis acutis, haud reflexis; anfractibus postice fuscopurpureo tinctis.

Hab. Cerros Island (*Ayres*); S. Pedro (*Cooper*).

The Lower-Californian shell may prove distinct.   It is like *S. regularis*, Cpr., but without the spiral sculpture.

Subgenus OPALIA, H. & A. Ad. (diagn. auct.).

Scalariæ varicibus obtusis, irregularibus, parum definitis: sculptura basim versus interrupta.

Ex. in Mus. Cum. :—*O. crassicostata*, *O. crassilabrum*, *O. diadema*, *O. funiculata*, *O. crenata*, *O. granulosa*, *O. australis*, *O. bicarinata*, *O. attenuata*, Psc., *O. M'Andreæ*, Fbs., sp. ined. (West Indies).   Other West-coast species are *O. crenatoides* and var. *insculpta*, *O. spongiosa*, and *O. retiporosa*.

The species of this very natural group were arranged by Messrs. Adams partly under *Opalia* and partly under *Cirsotrema*.

49. *Opalia borealis*, Gld.

O. testa *O. australi* simillima, valde elongata; anfr. xii., planatis, suturis parum impressis; testa jun. costis validissimis viii. latis, rotundatis, peripheriam attingentibus, interdum interruptis; testa adulta sæpius obsoletis, ad peripheriam evanidis; circa basim totam usque ad peripheriam angulatam lamina spirali, planata; apertura ovali; tota superficie minutissime spiraliter striolata : operculo pauci-spirali, nucleo ad trientem longitudinis sito, lineis incrementi validis. Long. 1·7, long. spir. 1·3, lat. ·53, div. 20°.

Hab. Puget Sound (*U. S. Expl. Exp.*); Neeah Bay and Tatooche Island (*Swan*).

This species was doubtfully indicated, not described, by Dr. Gould, in the ' E. E. Moll.' p. 207. It appears to be exactly identical with "*crassicostata*, Australia," in Brit. Mus., and is nearly related to *Ochotensis*, Midd. It must not be confounded with *Acirsa borealis*, Beck. One young specimen has the ten ribs of *O. australis*.

50. *Cerithiopsis munita*

C. testa *C. purpureæ* simili, sed angustiore, marginibus spiræ fere rectis; costis spiralibus magis expressis, testa adulta minus nodulosis; basi æqualiter lirulata. Long. ·34, long. spir. ·24, lat. ·11, div. 20°.

Hab. Neeah Bay; common (*Swan*).

51. *Cerithiopsis columna.*

C. testa majore, valde elongata, purpureo-fusca; anfr. norm. ix., planatis, suturis distinctis; seriebus iii. nodulorum spiralibus valde appressorum, creberrimorum, interstitiis parvis, altis; aliis interdum intercalantibus; lira quarta supra suturam haud valde nodulosa, liris duabus haud expressis aream suturalem circumeuntibus; basi planata, haud sculpta, ad peripheriam obtuse angulata; apertura quadrata. Long. ·38, long. spir. 32, lat. ·1, div. 10°.

Hab. Neeah Bay; several worn specimens (*Swan*) : Monterey; rolled fragment of larger shell (*Cooper*).

Easily recognized, even in portions, by the "strung-fig" pattern.

55. *Cancellaria modesta.*

C. testa elata, subrufa, trichotropiformi, marginibus spiræ rectis; anfr. norm. v., rotundatis, postice subtabulatis, suturis impressis; costis spiralibus obtusis, distantibus, in spira circ. iv., circa basim prolongatam circ. vii., aliis minoribus interdum intercalantibus; interstitiis secundum incrementa, decussatis; apertura subquadrata; columella plicis duabus declivibus anticis et costulis basalibus ornata; labio nullo. Long. ·68, long. spir. ·34, lat. 34, div. 50°.

Hab. Neeah Bay; one specimen and fragment (*Swan*).

56. *Velutina prolongata.*

V. testa majore, subplanata, tenuiore, carnea, spira minima; anfr. iii.

et dimidio, rapidissime augentibus; vertice vix conspicuo; anfr. ult. antice valde porrecto; regione columellari incurvata; labio valido; axi haud rimata; epidermide tenui, rugis incrementi ornata, spiraliter haud striata.   Long. ·1, long. spir. ·15, lat. ·95, div. 140°.

Hab. Neeah Bay; rare (*Swan*).

246

F.

DIAGNOSES

OF

NEW FORMS OF MOLLUSCA

FROM

THE VANCOUVER DISTRICT.

BY

PHILIP P. CARPENTER, B. A., Pʜ. D.

From the Proceedings of the Zoölogical Society of London, pp. 201–204,
February 14, 1865.

(247)

Diagnoses of New Forms of Mollusca from the Vancouver District. By Philip P. Carpenter, B.A., Ph.D.

Tebebbatula unguicula, n. s.

T. *t. juniore* "Terebratulinœ capiti-serpentis" *simillima, sed latiore, subtriangulata ; punctis valde conspicuis ; costis conspicuis, interdum obtusioribus, aliis intercalantibus ; intus, amento suboctiformi, postice aperto, cruris diagonalibus cardini affixis : testa adulta valva inferiore subrotundata, marginem versus haud planata ; umbone valde tumente, latiore ; striis radiantihus, ut in* "T. capite-serpentis" *conspicuis ; marginibus crenulatis, haud undatis ; intus amento majore, bisinuato, dorsaliter haud continuo, calcaribus duobus munito.*

Long. ·6, lat. ·5, alt. ·3 poll.

Hab. San Diego, 6 fm.; Monterey, not rare in 20 fm., (in California State Geological Survey) *Cooper.* Neeah Bay (valve), *Swan.* Vancouver, *Forbes.*

The specimens sent by Dr. Cooper were all of small size, and, from the intercalation of riblets near the margin, clearly immature. They presented the incomplete loop of the restricted genus to which Dr. Cooper affiliated them. Notwithstanding, as both Davidson and Woodward state that the young of the British species has the loop similarly open, it remained doubtful whether this might not prove conspecific. Messrs. Reeve and Hanley unhesitatingly pronounced them to be "*caput-serpentis*, jun.," the latter gentleman stating that they presented the peculiar form of that species which belongs to the Mediterranean examples. Dr. Forbes, however, was fortunate enough to

249

obtain an adult shell, which passed into the Cumingian Collection
Having removed the animal matter with great care, the loop was
found to retain the form seen in the young shell, only perhaps still
more open.   This is the first recent species of the genus which has
been discovered with a sculptured surface, and affords an instructive
lesson not to rely on external characters.

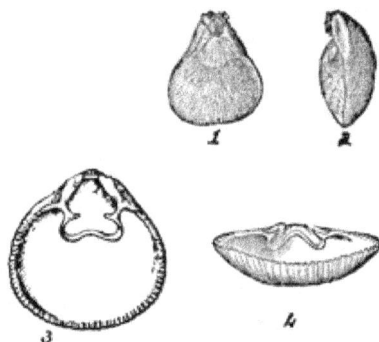

Terebratula unguicula: 1, 2, outside views of Mr. Cuming's adult specimen,
natural size : 3, 4, inside views of the upper valve, slightly magnified.

The outline of the adult is much rounder, and the margin blunter,
than in *T. caput-serpentis*.   Inside, the noncompletion of the somewhat ω-shaped loop is a very obvious character.   This is large in
proportion, extending to about two-fifths of the length and one-
third of the greatest breadth of the shell.   It is bent upwards in the
middle, as seen from the partly opened valves ; with a double wave at
the sides, as seen from the direction of the opposite valve.   Two spurs
ascend from the crests of the side waves, as though preparing to
complete the loop.   The similar *Terebratella angustata* from Japan,
when of the same size as Dr. Cooper's specimens, has the loop quite
continuous *.

Subgenus NETTASTOMELLA†.

*Pholadidea: valvis postice in calycem testaceum planatum pro-
longatis; calyce coriaceo nullo.*

NETTASTOMELLA DARWINII, Sby. (diag. auct.).

N. *t. minore, elongata, tenuissima ; parte postica costis radiantibus acutioribus circ. vii. et laminis concentricis acutissimis
distantibus, antice continuis, elegantissime ornata; rostris pla*

* Dr. Cooper having forwarded for my inspection a large and beautifully perfect specimen of the true *Waldheimia californica*, I have compared it with the
series of the very variable *W. globosa* in the Smithsonian Museum, undoubtedly
from Orange Harbour. The California shell, however, has a strong brownish-
red tinge, and does not display the beautiful veining of the Maghellan species.

† Th. νῆττα, a duck, στόμα, mouth. The name *Netastoma*, given in the
‘ Brit. Assoc. Report,’ 1863, being preoccupied in another subkingdom, according
to Dr. Cooper, it is thought necessary to vary the termination.

natis, postice divergentibus, striis incrementi crebris acutis, aliter haud sculpta ; parte antica t. jun. aperta, adultæ clausa ; clausis tenuissimis, secundum incrementa undulatis, super umbones prolongatis, umbilicos postice formantibus ; epidermide fugaci, tenui, pallide viridi.

Hab. Monterey, *Rich.* ; Vancouver, *Lord* ; S. Diego, *Cooper.*

= *Pholas darwinii,* Sby.

= *Jouanettia darwinii,* Mus. Cuming.

= *Parapholas penita,* Tryon, Mon. Phol.

This remarkable shell differs from *Jouanettia* in having both valves equal ; from *Pholadidea* proper in having no coriaceous cup, its place being supplied by a flattened prolongation from each valve, like a duck's bill in miniature. In Mr. Lord's specimen (preserved in the British Museum), though the valves are closed, the prolongations are widely divergent, as when the bird utters its cheerful "quack." The loose, thin epidermis appears to have covered the bill as well as the valves. Mr. Tryon had probably not seen a specimen, else he could hardly have affiliated so very different a shell to *Pholadidea penita.* The original specimen is said to have come from Chili.

DARINA DECLIVIS.

D. *t. tenuissima, planata, elliptica, Machæræformi, utroque latere hiante ; cinerea, epidermide fortiore induta ; marginibus regulariter excurvatis ; umbonibus haud conspicuis, ad duas inter quinque partes longitudinis postice sitis : intus cartilagine spathula elongata, dorsum versus utraque valva decliviter sita, a ligamento lamina extante tenuissima separata ; dente cardinali laminato, extante, curtiore ; lateralibus vix conspicuis ; sinu pallii ovali, fere ad medium porrecto.*

Long. 1·77, lat. ·85, alt. ·34 poll.

Hab. Vancouver's Island (*Forbes*).

The only other species of *Darina* known is from the Straits of Maghellan. The northern shell may have been passed over as the young of *Machæra patula,* to which it bears a strong external resemblance.

SAXIDOMUS BREVISIPHONATUS.

S. *t. subovali, tenuiore, subplanata, albida, epidermide pallide olivacea induta ; tota superficie rugis concentricis, crebris, valde obtusis, et undis incrementi interdum majoribus, ornata ; marginibus subæqualiter excurvatis, maxime ventrali : intus cardine tenuiore, dente antico elongato ; sinu pallii parvo, ad trientem interstitii porrecto, latiore.*

Long. 2·65, lat. 2·05, alt. 1·15 poll.

Hab. ?Vancouver, ?Japan (*Mus. Cuming*).

A very distinct species, in shape and hinge not unlike *Callista,* but without lunule. It is more rounded and flatter than the three typical Californian species, and known at once by the very small mantlebend. From four to six blunt riblets are seen on each of the very blunt waves of growth. The shell was sent me as from Dr. Forbes's Vancouver collections, and is so quoted in the Br. Assoc. Rep. 1863, p. 607 ; but Mr. Cuming subsequently stated his belief that it came from Japan. It may be allowable to state that many of the species included in *Saxidomus* by authors are more correctly rough forms of *Tapes*, of the *decussata*-type ; the true *Saxidomi* differing from that genus (as *Callista* does from *Venus*) in having an additional pseudo-lateral anterior tooth. This is very evident in the young shell, which has a much rounder outline than the adult, and can scarcely be distinguished from *Callista*, except by the absence of lunule.

252

G.

DIAGNOSES

OF

NEW SPECIES AND A NEW GENUS OF MOLLUSKS,

FROM

THE REIGEN MAZATLAN COLLECTION;

WITH AN ACCOUNT OF ADDITIONAL SPECIMENS PRESENTED TO
THE BRITISH MUSEUM.

BY

PHILIP P. CARPENTER, B.A., PH. D.

From the Proceedings of the Zoölogical Society of London, pp. 263-273,
March 14, 1865.

(253)

DIAGNOSES OF NEW SPECIES AND A NEW GENUS OF MOLLUSKS FROM THE REIGEN MAZATLAN COLLECTION: WITH AN ACCOUNT OF ADDITIONAL SPECIMENS PRESENTED TO THE BRITISH MUSEUM. BY PHILIP P. CARPENTER, B.A., PH.D.

After the publication of the British Museum Mazatlan Catalogue, the backs of several fresh *Spondylus*-valves were examined by Mr. R. D Darbishire and myself. Among the specimens were several which were deemed worthy of being added to the national collection; they were deposited there, with a MS. appendix to the Catalogue, in 1858. As it is not judged necessary to print this separately, I have (with the permission of Dr. Gray) transcribed what should be placed on record, in hopes that it may not be judged out of place in the 'Proceedings.' Those who use the Mazatlan Catalogue are requested to observe not only the corrections in the Appendix, pp. 547–552, but also those made in the Review of Professor C. B. Adams's Panama Catalogue, P Z. S. 1863, p. 339; and in the British Association Reports, 1863, pp. 543 *et seq.* The numbers, both of species and of tablets, are continued from the Mazatlan Catalogue, and correspond with those in the Report. The student of the Gulf fauna should also consult the account of Mr. Xantus's

Cape St. Lucas shells in the 'Annals Nat. Hist.' 1864, and in the Report, pp. 616–626 *.

704. CELLEPORA AREOLATA, Busk†.

Tablet 2540 contains a specimen on *Omphalius ligulatus.*

705. MEMBRANIPORA ? FLEMINGII, Busk†.

Tablet 2541 contains a group on *O. ligulatus.*

---

* The following additional specimens from the Reigen Collection have been presented to the British Museum.—

Tablet.

12*. A group on *Omphalius ligulatus.*

13*. *Lepralia adpressa* and *Membranipora*, sp. ind., on ditto.

42. Young opposite valve of *?Solecurtus*, perhaps conspecific.

201*. Four young valves (smallest ·05 by ·034) probably of this species.

266*. Minute transparent valve, ·028 across, teeth unformed; perhaps of this species.

358*. Two specimens; margin irregular.

504*. Several specimens in *Uranilla unguis*; one, not having room within, has made a case for itself outside the *Uranilla.*

642*. A pair, ·3 by ·15; probably an older state of the same species, *Barbatia alternata.*

60*. A minute, transparent valve, ·045 by ·024, without teeth; resembling "? *Saxicava fragilis*, Nyst," Jeffr., in 'Ann. Nat. Hist.,' Aug. 1858.

486*. A young shell, ·06 across, laid open; crowded inside, especially near the umbones, with a pinkish mass of young ones, about ·0018 in length.

500. A younger pair, much more transverse, transparent, without concentric ridges, the lateral teeth in one valve being simply the raising of the dorsal margins.

833*. Two young specimens, nestling among Nullipore on *Fissurella alba.*

869*. Two specimens, with egg-cases arranged in pattern like *Orbitolites.*

876*. One specimen, curiously mended after fracture.

877*. One specimen, with columella curiously contorted.

1023*. One specimen, with ribs rounded and aspect of *Siphonaria lecanium*; probably a distinct species.

1058*. One young specimen, probably conspecific, though only ·07 by ·047; there is no trace of spire.

1059*. Three specimens; broad form.

1468*. Fragment of *Spondylus calcifer*, with basal supports of *Hipponyx ?serratus*, in burrow of *Lithophagus plumula.*

1795*. Two specimens with five intercalary teeth.

1834*. One specimen with the canal bent back, as in *Cassidaria.*

2221*. One specimen, mended after severe fracture.

2223*. One specimen; columellar fold bifid.

2224*. Two specimens; columella bent and straight.

2225*. One specimen; labrum thin.

2226*. One specimen; ribs close.

2376*. One specimen, dwarf form; nodulous, as in *N. nodulifera*, Phil.

2516. An opposite larger valve, since found, in which there is only one distinct posterior tooth, and the anterior hooked tooth is separating into two.

[2534. One specimen of *Vitrinella ?tricarinata*, jun., of which the ribs are nodulous in the young state. If rightly determined, this adds no. 710 to the list of species.]

2536. A nuclear shell, ·046 across, of Naticoid shape, very finely striated in each direction. It is probably a young *Hipponyx*

† Both of these species were kindly identified by Mr. G. Busk.

Genus CYCLADELLA.

Testa bivalvis, tenuis, æquilateralis, æquivalvis, haud hians, um-bonibus planatis. Ligamentum tenuissimum, externum. Cardo linea curvata, dent. lat. distantibus, card. transversis, haud radiantibus.

56. CYCLADELLA PAPYRACEA, n. sp.

C. *t. tenuissima, subdiaphana, epidermide tenui induta, planata, suborbiculari; concentrice fortiter lirata, liris rotundatis, intus excavatis; tota superficie lineis granulosis radiantibus creber-rimis minutissime cælata; dent. card. i.–ii. transversis, mar-gini dorsali subparallelis; dent. lat. validis.*

= "*Tellina ? eburnea,* Hanl." (fragments only), Maz. Cat. no. 56.

Mr. Hanley kindly sent for my inspection a perfect pair (as "*Lepton*"), which he had found nestling in a burrow in *Spondylus.* The hinge more resembles *Cyclas* (Lam.) than any other known genus. Its great peculiarity is, that the cardinal teeth, instead of radiating from the umbo, fall in the curve of the hinge-line, as though uniting the lateral teeth. The shell is too thin (being deeply indented within by the concentric waves) to make out the pallial line; but no trace of sinus is visible. It may therefore rank, provi-sionally, under *Kelliadæ,* although in other respects its affinities appear to be with *Œdalia* and *Cooperella.* The ligament appears little more than a prolongation of the epidermis. Beside the trans-verse cardinal teeth, there is in each valve a curved line, slightly raised. like the end of a finger-nail, which bounds what would be the lunule in other shells.

Long. ·1, lat. ·123, alt. ·045.

Hab. Mazatlan; one perfect specimen from Havre Collection (*Mus. Hanl.*); fragments, Liverpool Collection.

706. ? MONTACUTA OBTUSA, n. sp.

?M. *t. planata, valde inæquilaterali, subrhomboidea; subdia-phana seu chalcedonica, haud punctata, lævi; marginibus ple-rumque regulariter excurvatis, dorsali recto, umbonibus haud prominentibus; cardine, utraque in valva, dente uno cardinali et fossa ligamentali; dent. lat. altera valva elongatis, rectis, altera vix conspicuis.*

Differs from ? *M. dionæa* in the elongation of the lateral teeth, and in the possession of a distinct cardinal tooth in each valve.

Long. 047, lat. ·06, alt. ·01.

Hab. Mazatlan; two fresh specimens, Liverpool Collection.

Tablet 2530 contains the larger specimen; the other is trans parent.

696. PECTUNCULUS, sp. ind.

Tablet 2531 contains a minute valve, ·033 across; outside with close, prominent concentric ridges, foliated by about twenty-four

rounded ribs, which are evanescent near the umbo.   Inside with a
very few strong teeth, developed in a curved line.

698. SCISSURELLA RIMULOIDES, n. sp.

S. *t. rapide augente, albida, tenuissima; apice celato; anfr.
iii., radiatim liratis, liris subdistantibus, acutis, obliquis; umbilico magno; labro declivi, haud fisso, sed apertura postica,
ut in* "Rimula" *formata, subquadrata, elongata; liris transversis gradus testæ increscentis definientibus; peritremate continuo, obliquo.*

Only one specimen was found of this beautiful little species, the
first known from America. It looks like a *Velutina* crossed by
sharp ribs in the direction of the slanting mouth. In the first whorl
the ribs are very close. It then assumes its normal sculpture, but
there is nearly a whorl before there is any trace of incision. This
appears to have begun as a slit, which was afterwards closed up. A
band, marked off by ten transverse ribs showing stages of growth,
encircles the shell as far as the hole, which is long and somewhat
rectangular; but there is no band between the hole and the outer
lip. The shell furnishes a complete transition to *Rimula*. It is
preserved on tablet 2532.

Long. ·023, long. spir. ·003, lat. ·03; div. 140°.
Hab. Mazatlan; off *Spondylus calcifer*; Liverpool Collection.

699. VITRINELLA ORNATA, n. sp.

V. *t. subdiscoidea, diaphana, tenuissima; anfr.* iv., *quorum* iii.
*primi nucleosi, insculpti; ultimo carina maxima circa periphe-
riam; postice subangulata, rugis radiantibus et striolis spiralibus ornata; antice carinata, carina nodosa; basi carina
altera et rugis radiantibus ornata; umbilico angulato, satis
magno; labro a carina indentato.*

Long. ·015, lat. ·028–·035; div. (circ.) 175°.
Hab. Mazatlan; one specimen off *Spondylus*, on tablet 2533;
Liverpool Collection.

700. VITRINELLA TENUISCULPTA, n. sp.

V. *t. planata, diaphana, tenuissima; anf.* iii. *et dimidio, quorum*
iii. *nucleosi; striis elevatis, spiralibus, quarum una magna,
quasi carina prope suturam sculpta; peripheria haud angulata; basi bis angulata, interdum rugis radiantibus distantibus
ornata; umbilico satis magno, carinato; apertura undata, subquadrata.*

The sculpture is not uniform over the last whorl. The principal
diagnostic features are the biangulated base, the infrasutural keel,
and the rounded periphery.

Long. ·016, long. spir. 0, lat. ·023–·03; div. 180°.
Hab. Mazatlan; one specimen off *Spondylus*, on tablet 2534;
Liverpool Collection.

701. ? VITRINELLA, sp. ind.

Tablet 2535 contains a fragment, ·085 across, of what was probably a gigantic species of this genus or of *Cyclotrema*, strongly keeled.

492. DIALA PAUPERCULA, C. B. Ad.

= *Cingula paupercula*, C. B. Ad. Pan. Shells, no.   : *diagnosi mutata.*

= ? *Odostomia mamillata*, Maz. Cat. no. 492: *diagnosi aucta.*

D. *t. nitida, solida; vert. nucl. anfr. iv., lirulis spiralibus et radiantibus tenuiter decussato; t. adulta decollata, ve.·tice mamillato; anfr. norm. iv.; peritremate continuo; basi obtuse angulata, lacuna umbilicali a labio separato formata.*

Long. ·085, long. spiræ ·055, lat. ·05; div. 34°.

The fortunate discovery of a perfect young specimen and some adult shells in the shell-washings of Professor Adams's collection enables us to explain the anomalies described in the Mazatlan Catalogue, where the solitary dead shell was referred, with doubt, to *Odostomia*, in consequence of its truncated apex. It was not possible to recognize in it Professor Adams's "*Cingula*," since that was described as having the apex "subacute," and the angular base and continuous peritreme were not mentioned. The nuclear whorls are sculptured as in *Alaba supralirata;* but the vertex, instead of being persistent as in that genus, appears to be always decollated in the adult. The shell has the peculiar glossy texture of *Diala*.

702. MANGELIA SULCATA, n. sp.

M. *t. subturrita, albida, apice obtuso; anfr.* vii., *tumidioribus, liris* vii., *obtusis, rectis, vix angulatis; sulcis spiralibus creberrimis, circa basim continuis; labro?* ... [*fracto*].

Long ·2, long. sp. ·12, lat. ·07; div. 35°.

Hab. Mazatlan; one specimen off *Spondylus*, on tablet 2538; Liverpool Collection.

703. ? TORINIA, sp. in.

Tablet 2539 contains a small shell, ·035 across, consisting of 3½ smooth, flattened, sinistral whorls; with a distinct suture, but not umbilicated. In a larger specimen (unfortunately lost), under the microscope this sinistral vertex appeared turned completely upside down, with more than half a whorl of an orbicular shell, white, sculptured like *Vitrinella*, with a very strong peripherical keel, and other smaller keels, decussated by radiating rugæ. This mode of growth is exactly as in the young *Torinia*; but the adult must have been very distinct from any known species, and perhaps did not belong to any described genus.

550. MUCRONALIA INVOLUTA, n. sp.

M. *t. parva, tenui, albida, irregulari, marginibus spiræ valde excurvatis; vertice declivi: anf. norm.* vi. +.... *satis excur-*

259

*vatis, suturis valde impressis ; basi prolongata, obtusa ; aper-
tura ovali, postice angusta ; labro acuto ; labio tenuissimo.*
Long. ·105, long. spir ·068, lat. ·033 ; div. 20°.
=*Leiostraca ?recta*, Maz. Cat. *in loco* : non C. B. Ad.

551. LEIOSTRACA PRODUCTA, n. sp.

L. *t. parva, albida, subfusiformi, marginibus spiræ rectis; vertice
acutiore, recto ; anfr. norm.* ix., *planatis, suturis vix conspicuis ; peripheria satis rotundata ; basi rapide angustata, postea
producta ; apertura subrhomboidea, axi antice acuta, angulata;
labro acuto ; labio tenui.*
Long ·123, long. spir ·08, lat ·046 ; div. 23°.
= *Leiostraca ! solitaria*, Maz Cat., *in loco* : non C. B. Ad.
This species is easily recognized by its very peculiar sharply-
pointed beak ; in shape like a young *Rostellaria*, without the canal.

652. ANACHIS TÆNIATA, Phil.

Columbella tæniata, Phil. in Zeit .·. Mal. 1846, no. 26 (non Ad.
& Rve. in Voy Samarang)
= *Anachis Gaskoini*, Cpr. in Maz. Cat p. 510, no. 652.
Variat *lineis spiralibus fuscis* viii., *quarum* iii. *in spira mon-
strantur ; maculis alternatis inter secundam et tertiam sitis.*
Variat quoque *maculis evanescentibus.*

Hab. Callao (teste *Gaskoin*) ; Mazatlan (*E. B. Philippi, Reigen*);
Cape St. Lucas (*Xantus*)
It appears that Mr. Gaskoin was not acquainted with Philippi's species. which had not then reached the Cumingian Collection ; as he pronounced M. Reigen's specimen to be new, and suggested the specific name in the Mazatlan Catalogue.   It would have
avoided a double synonymy, could the name *tæniata* have been retained for the Samarang shell, and Mr. Gaskoin's for this.   The
Cape St. Lucas shells vary as above in licated.

650. ?ANACHIS SERRATA, Cpr.

Maz. Cat. no. 650, p. 509.   Perfect specimens of this singular
species having been found at Cape St. Lucas by Mr. Xantus, the
diagnosis may be thus completed :—
*Epidermide fimbriata, lirulas spirales eleganter decussante ; labri
denticulis variantibus, interdum subobsoletis.*
Long. ·28 long. spir 15. lat ·13 ; div. 40°.
With the sculpture and general aspect of a small *Cantharus*, it has
the mouth of an *Anachis*. The operculum, and therefore the generic
relations, are not yet known *.

* The following additions and corrections may be useful to the students of
the British Museum Catalogue :—
Species 181 *Arca multicostata* further differs from *A. grandis* in the epidermis being soft and very finely hairy.

223. The length should be 1·1.

319. For "*labio nullo*" read "*tenuissimo*"

390. The nuclear shell has two whorls, *Ampullaria*-shaped.

. 367. Add to diagnosis, "*operculo concavo, linea elevata suturam definiente.*"

368. Add to diagnosis, "*operculo vix concavo, suturis minus definitis.*"

373. Add to diagnosis, "*operculo concavo, suturis distinctis, peripheriam versus linea elevata instructis.*" The species was found living among the *sinul Olivellæ.*

376. Add to diagnosis, "*operculo concavo, suturis vix definitis.*" Living among *Olivellæ.*

501 Instead of the specimen from which the description in the text wa written, tablet 1966 contains a much finer shell, since found, which al'ows of th following additions to the diagnosis:—" *vert nucl. parvo, satis extante, di clt citer sito ; anfr. norm.* v ; *interstitiis carinarum transversim rugulosis ; labr solidiore.* Long. 087, long. spir 037, lat. ·038."

510. A very beautiful shell, found in the refuse of Professor Adams's Panam collection, is probably of this species, though the sutural cancellations are close It has one more whorl · vertex Chemnitzoid, of three Helicoid whorls, scarcel projecting ; apex hidden

650. From perfect Cape St. Lucas specimens, add the following to diagnosis —" *epidermide fimbriata, lirulas spirales eleganter decussante.*"

Page 312. Add to the diagnoses of opercula of *Vermetidæ* :—

"(*h.*) *Operculum corneum, intus convexum, nitidum, umbone magno extante extus concavum, paucispirale, lamina extante suturas definiente.* Diam. ·045. Tablet 2537 contains the only specimen found, resembling *Siphonium*, fror the *Spondylus*-washings.

Tablet 447 is *Liocardium apicinum*, which should stand as species 700.

Page 314, note * (*et seq.*), for "*Inflatulum*" read "*Mioceras.*"

Page 350, line 18, *for* "regular" read "irregular."

H.

DESCRIPTIONS

OF

New Species and Varieties of Chitonidæ and Acmæidæ,

FROM

The Panama Collection of the late Prof. C. B. Adams.

BY

PHILIP P. CARPENTER, B.A., Ph.D.

From the Proceedings of the Zoölogical Society of London, pp. 274-277,
March 14, 1865.

(263)

DESCRIPTIONS OF NEW SPECIES AND VARIETIES OF CHITONIDÆ AND ACMÆIDÆ, FROM THE PANAMA COLLECTION OF THE LATE PROF. C. B. ADAMS. BY PHILIP P. CARPENTER, B.A., PH.D.

LEPIDOPLEURUS ADAMSII.

L. *t.* " L. dispari" *simili; pallide rufo-fusca, colore intensiore irregulariter strigata seu maculata; sæpius maculis albidis regione diagonali ornata; jugo vix acuto; areis centralibus et valvis terminalibus conspicue granulosis; areis lateralibus irregulariter verrucosis, verrucis plerumque lobatis; mucrone antico, vix conspicuo: intus, valvis centralibus uni-, terminalibus* viii.–x.-*fissis; subgrundis parvis, dentibus acutis; suturis medianis postice rectis, antice laminas haud attingentibus, sinu planato, latissimo: limbo pallii imbricatim squamoso.*

Long. ·6, lat. ·3 poll. ; div. 110°.

Variat *verrucis minus expressis, simplicioribus.*

= *Chiton dispar,* C. B. Ad. no. 373, par.

= *Lophyrus adamsii,* P. Z. S., 1863, p. 24.

Unfortunately for those who do not like to remove the non-testaceous portion from their Chitons, as they do from their other shells, the mantle-margin by no means affords a safe clue to the structure of the valves. Among the species of the genus *Ischnochiton,* Gray,

265

(=*Lepidopleurus*, Add.,) known by the sharp incisor-teeth lying within a projecting lip, there are three types of mantle-margin, which may be conveniently separated as subgenera, to aid in the difficult task of describing and identifying species. The typical forms, for which the name *Ischnochiton* should be retained, have the scales somewhat chaffy, and very finely striated. *I. magdalensis* and *I. sanguineus* well represent the group. But another series have the mantle-scales imbricate and strong, as in *Chiton*, Gray, (=*Lophyrus*, Add.,) from which they cannot be distinguished without dissection. For this Messrs. Adams's name *Lepidopleurus* may be retained in a restricted sense. It is uncertain what Risso's original genus was meant to include: his diagnosis applies to all Chitons with distinct side-areas and scaly margins.

A third group, separated by Dr. Gray in his 'Guide,' p. 182, as having the "mantle-scales minute, granular," has been named *Trachydermon*: it abounds in the Californian region.

The specimens of *L. adamsii* were found among the duplicates named *Chiton dispar* by the Professor; one was attached to *Discina cumingii*.

LEPIDOPLEURUS TENUISCULPTUS.

L. t. " L. adamsii" *simili; olivacea, colore pallido seu intensior-minute variegata; tota superficie minute granulosa; areis lateralibus vix definitis; suturis plerumque albido maculatis; mucrone antico, satis conspicuo, parte postica concava : intus, ut in* " L. adamsii" *formata.*

Variat: *t. pallidore, ad jugum rufo-tincta.*

=*Chiton dispar*, C. B. Ad. no. 373, pars.

The outside of this shell so much resembles the young of *Chiton (Lophyrus) stokesii*, that specimens may have been distributed under that name. Very few individuals were found.

ISCHNOCHITON ELENENSIS (diagn. auct.).

Extus areis centralibus clathris parallelis circ. xx. decussatis, ar. lat. costis ii., validioribus, tumidis, tuberculosis : intus marginibus suturalibus posticis reflexis, tuberculatis, sinu ad jugum parvo; laminis insertionis unifissis, ad laminas suturales anticos junctis, sinu latissimo. Valva antica extus costis xii., haud validis; intus fissuris x., dentibus acutis, subgrunda parva. Valva postica mucrone subpostico, depresso; parte postica expansa, concava, costis circ. xi. subobsoletis; intus lamina insertionis circ. ix.-fissa, dentibus curtis, subgrunda parva, intus callosa.

The central valves in this species are normal; but the posterior valve offers a transition towards *Callochiton*, the outside being concave posteriorly, the insertion-teeth short and the eaves callous.

ISCHNOCHITON (? var.) EXPRESSUS.

I. t. "I. elenensi" *simili, sed carnea; areis centr. clathris x.,*

*distantibus, crebre decussatis, jugo acuto; ar. lat. costis ii.,
validissimis, angustis, tuberculis angustis : intus marginibus
suturalibus posticis planatis, haud tuberculosis, haud sinuatis;
lam. insert. ut antea, sinu angusto, ad jugum angulato. Valva
antica costis x., validis, angustis : intus ut antea, sed fissuris
viii. Valva postica mucrone postico, planato; parte postica
expansa, haud concava, costis circ. vii. validissimis : intus
lamina circ. vii.-fissa, subgrunda planata.*

With a strong general resemblance to *I. elenensis*, the differences
in detail in the only two specimens examined, as above stated, appear of specific importance. If only varietal, it is equally important
to notice how much change is tolerated by the habits of the animal.
It may be the shell called *Chiton clathratus* by Prof. Adams, of which
there were no duplicates to compare. It offers a still more marked
transition to *Callochiton*, the margin of the posterior valve being
somewhat pectinated by the great projection of the ribs.

"Callochiton" pulchellus : diagn. auct.

*Extus areis centr. lincis interdum parallelis, interdum radian-
tibus, rugose scrobiculatis; ar. lat. costis ii., validissimis, im-
bricato-nodosis : valva antica costis similibus circ. ix. : v.
post. area centrali lata; mucrone subpostico, planato; parte
postica costis vii. similibus, medianis curtissimis, excurvatis :
pallio squamulis minutis imbricatis. Intus v. ant. subgrunda
(ut in* Ischnochitone) *munita, sed a costis pectinata ; dentibus
acutis, intus linea undulata secundum costas instructa, extus
concavis, parte convexa costarum incisis : v. medianis similiter
pectinatis, laminis secundum costas diag. uniscissis : laminis
suturalibus medio continuis, late sinuatis; suturis posticis a
sculptura externa granulatis : v. post. vii.-lobata, marginibus
planatis, laminis dense compressis incrassatis ; dentibus obtusissimis, appressis, haud extantibus, subobsoletis, extrorsum
planatis, ut in v. ant. fissis; interdum fissuris quoque in par-
tibus concavis.*

As I have seen no published diagnosis of the very peculiar type of
insertion-plates observed in this species, which has hitherto been too
rare to allow working naturalists an opportunity of dissection, I have
given a minute description. The plates of insertion, as well as the
exterior caves, are scalloped by the strong ribs, and alternate with
them. In the posterior valve the caves are flattened outwards, in
closely appressed layers, the blunt, ill-developed insertion-teeth
lying flat upon them. The valves easily separate from the mantle,
when immersed in water. Outside, the species is easily recognized
by the two strong ribs of the diagonal areas, the central pitted in
somewhat branching rows, and the ribs on the curiously flattened
posterior valve resembling a clenched fist.

Acmæa (? floccata, var.) filosa.

A. t. "*A. mesoleucæ*" *forma et indole simili; sed sculptura multo tenuiore ; t. jun. lævi ; dein lirulis delicatulis, acutis, haud granulosis, valde distantibus, interdum obsoletis, filosa ; inter-stitiis latis, lævibus ; tenui, planata, ovali, subdiaphana ; nigro-fusco, corneo radiatim strigata, seu varie maculata : intus livida seu albida, coloribus externis transeuntibus ; limbo lato, acuto.*

Long. ·7, lat. ·56, alt. ·12.

= *Lottia ? patina*, C. B. Ad. Pan. Shells, no. 367.

Hab. Panama (*C. B. Adams*).

There is no described west-tropical species to which these shells can be affiliated, unless they prove to be a very delicate variety of *A. floccata*, Rve. Unfortunately the Panama limpets have never been collected in sufficient numbers to make out their specific limits satisfactorily. The names here given may stand as species or va-rieties, according to future elucidation. In shape and texture, but not in colour or sculpture, these shells resemble *A. fascicularis* ; in the latter respects, *A. strigatella*. They were named " *tenera*, Ad." by Dr. Dohrn, but are sufficiently distinct from that West-Indian species.

ACMÆA (? FLOCCATA, var.) SUBROTUNDATA.

A. t. " A. var. filosæ" simili, sed subrotundata, magis elevata, vertice subcentrali ; colore intensiore, lineis corneis crebrioribus, angustis ; t. jun. sæpe pallidiore, radiis duobus postice trian-gulata : intus collo livido, tenuiore.

Long. ·53, lat. ·45, alt. ·15.

= *Lottia*, sp. ind. *a*, C. B. Ad. Pan. Shells. no. 368.

Hab. Panama (*C. B. Adams*).

ACMÆA (? var.) VERNICOSA.

A. t. parva, subrotundata, depresso-conica, apice ad duas quintas partes sito ; albido-viridi, strigis paucis rufo-fuscis hic et illic ornata, sæpius radiis duobus candidis, postice triangulata ; extus lineis acutis radiantibus, valde distantibus, sæpe obsoletis vix sculpta : intus livida, callosa, sæpius spathula candida or-nata ; basi subplanata, limbo angusto.

Long. ·3, lat. ·24, alt. ·1.

Hab. Panama (*Jewett, C. B. Adams*).

= *Lottia*, sp. ind. *b*, C. B. Ad. Pan. Shells, no. 369.

Had this form been brought from the China Seas, it might have been taken for the young of *A. biradiata*, Rve. From its solidity, however, its rough exterior, and its callous interior, it appears to be adult. It is barely possible that it may develope into *A. vesper-tina*. It differs from the young of *A. subrotundata* in being much thicker and less spotted with the green tint.

I.

DIAGNOSES

OF

NEW SPECIES OF MOLLUSKS,

FROM

THE WEST TROPICAL REGION OF NORTH AMERICA,

PRINCIPALLY COLLECTED BY THE REV. J. ROWELL, OF SAN FRANCISCO

BY

PHILIP P. CARPENTER, B. A., Ph. D.

From the Proceedings of the Zoölogical Society of London, pp. 273–282, March 14, 1865.

DIAGNOSES OF NEW SPECIES OF MOLLUSKS, FROM THE WEST TROPICAL REGION OF NORTH AMERICA, PRINCIPALLY COLLECTED BY THE REV. J. ROWELL, OF SAN FRANCISCO. BY PHILIP P. CARPENTER, B.A., PH.D.

Of the new species quoted in the "Supplementary Report on the Present State of our Knowledge of the Mollusca of the West Coast of North America," published in the Transactions of the British Association, 1863, pp. 517-686, the principal portion (namely, those dredged by Dr. J. G. Cooper, Zoologist to the Californian State Geological Survey) are described in the ' Proceedings of the California Acad. Nat. Sciences,' for 1864-65; those dredged in Puget Sound, during the U. S. North Pacific Boundary Survey, by the late Dr. Kennerley, are described in the 'Journal of the Philadelphia Acad. Nat. Sc.' for the present year. The species obtained by the naturalists of the British Survey are described in three papers by Dr. Baird and myself, P. Z. S. 1863-65. The new species sent by Mr. J. Xantus from Cape St. Lucas, and by Mr. J. G. Swan from Neeah Bay, appear in the 'Ann. and Mag. Nat. Hist.,' 1864-65. In the same Journal are described the new species which I found in Col. Jewett's collection. Those sent to Dr. Gould from the same collection had been previously analyzed in the ' Proc. Zool. Soc.' 1856. The above are the principal sources of fresh knowledge; but a number of species from the Californian province, which do not range under any of these heads, will be found in the 'Journal de Conchyliologie' for the current year.

In separate papers communicated to the Zoological Society are the diagnoses of additional species from Prof. Adams's Panama and from M. Reigen's Mazatlan collections. The remaining species, from the tropical province, are embodied in the present paper. The types (unless otherwise stated) are in the Museum of the Smithsonian Institution.

(TELLINA) ANGULUS DECUMBENS.

A. t. tenui, subplanata, alba seu rosacea; lævi, striolis incrementi insculpta; epidermide pallide straminea induta; antice et ventraliter valde producta; postice truncata, angulata; umbonibus acutioribus, vix prominentibus; marginibus dorsalibus postico recto, antico ad angulum parum excurvato, antico et ventrali valde et regulariter excurvatis; parte postica v. dextr. subito angulata, v. sinistr. parum sinuata; nymphis angustis, elongatis, cartilagine omnino externo : dent. card. minimis; dent. lat. v. dextr. antico satis conspicuo, postico obsoleto; v. sinistr. nullis; cicatr. adduct. posticis subrhomboideis, anticis valde elongatis, angustis; sinu pallii maximo, subtriangulari, usque ad cicatricem alteram utraque valva porrecta.
Long. 1·7, lat. 1·2, alt. ·68 poll.
Hab. Panama (teste Rowell, Pease).
This shell was affiliated by Mr. Hanley to the W. African T.

271

nymphalis, but differs in the internal scars. Externally it resem-
T. dombeyi, Lam. (= *Scrobicularia producta*, Cpr. P. Z. S. 1855,
p. 230), but is easily recognized by the strictly Tellinoid ligament
and anterior lateral tooth, by the posterior portion being pinched
instead of waved, and by the junction of the pallial sinus with the
opposite scar. By the same characters it is distinguished from *T.
tersa*, Gld., which closely resembles *S. dombeyi*, var., in Mus. Cum.
Like many other Tellens, it has a white and a pink variety. The
name was printed by an oversight in Brit. Assoc. Rep. 1863, p. 669,
as *A. amplectans*; but as it was unaccompanied by a diagnosis, and
does not describe the shell, no confusion will arise from reverting
to the name first given.

LUCINA UNDATA.

L. *t. convexa, tenuiore, albida; tota superficie lirulis concentricis
creberrimis, compressis, haud acutis ornata, interstitiis minimis; parte ventrali costis radiantibus* iii., *obtusis, latis, validissimis, interstitiis parvis; lunula maxima, a sulco bene definita, sub umbonibus incurvatis fossa alta minuta indentata;
parte postica alata; margine a costis valde undato, minute
crenulato; ligamento quasi interno : intus dent. card. parvis,
a fossa lunulari intortis; lat. curtis, obtusis; cicatr. adduct.
antica irregulari, postica subovali; linea palliari prope marginem sita, undata.*
Long. ·45, lat. ·44, alt. ·3.
Hab. Gulf of California (teste *Rowell*).
The outline somewhat resembles *Cryptodon*; but the aspect
is more that of *Verticordia*, while the minute subumbonal pit
is suggestive of *Opis*. The shell is sexpartite; the portion between
the anterior rib and the lunule resembles a fourth rib, while the
projecting lunule and the posterior wing are quite distinct from the
body of the shell. The specimen sent by Mr. Rowell to the Smithsonian Institution was completely smashed. The diagnosis is written
from a perfect shell sent by Dr. Newcomb to Mr. Cuming.

CALLIOSTOMA (? LIMA, var.) ÆQUISCULPTA.

C. *t.* "C. limæ" *simili; sed anfr. planatis, suturis haud distinctis; sculptura regulari; jun. monilibus spiralibus inter se
æqualibus; t. adulta majore et minore alternantibus; co'ore
rufescente, granulis interdum rufo-fusco maculatis.*
Hab. Acapulco (*Newberry*).
Dr. Newberry's specimens agree in most essential respects with
" *Trochus lima*, Phil.," in C. B. Ad. Pan. Shells, no. 276, which
appears identical with the shells marked " *Ziziphinus antonii*, Koch,
N. Zealand," in Mus. Cuming. The Acapulcan shells are quite
flat, while those from Panama are for the most part shouldered as
in *C. eximium*, Rve. (= *C. versicolor*, Mke. Maz. Cat. no. 289).
However, there is no little variation among the Professor's specimens of *C. lima*, and some are so slightly shouldered that the Acapulcan form may be a local variety.

NARICA INSCULPTA.

N. *t.* " N. apertæ" *simili, sed magis compacta ; paullum angustiore, umbilico tamen majore; lineis spiralibus circ.* xxvi. *distantibus insculptis cincta, quarum* x. *in anfr. penult. monstrantur ; postice lineis incrementi vix conspicuis.*

Long. ·3, long. spir. ·08, lat. ·28 ; div. 100°.

Hab. Acapulco, on *Ostrea iridescens*, Rowell.

The Cape St. Lucas species (*vide* Ann. Nat. Hist. 1864, xiii. p. 476) has the sculpture in irregularly raised lirulæ, while this has minute grooves chiselled out of a smooth surface. It appears that the San Franciscans import the huge tropical oysters in large quantities, their own species having the coppery flavour which Americans dislike in the British species. From the outside of the valves, Mr. Rowell obtained this and many other interesting species.

DRILLIA EBURNEA.

D. *t. turrita, carneo-albida, tenuiore, lævi, maxime nitente; marginibus spiræ rectis ; anfr. nucl.?* . . . [*decollatis*] ; *norm. circ.* ix., *postice planatis, supra suturas appressis, medio satis excurvatis ; hic et illic rugis radiantibus, obsoletis, irregularibus exsculpta ; basi prolongata, canali conspicuo, aperto; sinu postico minore, in sulco lato, haud definito, spiram ascendente sito ; labro acuto ; labio indistincto ; columella planata.*

Long. 1·3, long. spir. ·8, lat. ·45; div. 30°.

Hab. Near Gulf of California (teste *Rowell*).

Easily recognized by its smooth glossy aspect and French-white colour ; the notch lying along a broad spiral channel, which throws the junction of the whorl as it were up the suture.

MANGELIA ALBOLAQUEATA.

M. *t. solida, turrita, alba, rudi, marginibus spiræ rectis ; anfr. nucl.?* . . . [*decollatis*] ; *norm. circ.* ix. *subrotundatis, costis circ.* xi.–xv., *declivibus, satis angustis, postice obsoletis, lineis subregularibus spiram ascendentibus ; lirulis spiralibus anticis crebris, postice obsoletis ; basi elongata ; labro?* . . . ; *labio calloso ; sinu postico majore, suturam attingente.*

Long. ·88, long. spir. ·55, lat. ·34; div. 30°.

Hab. Panama (teste *Rowell*).

Described from an imperfect and worn specimen, but easily recognized by its ivory-white colour, and ribs in slanting rows, as though the creature were roofed with white tiles. It was erroneously quoted in the Brit. Assoc. Rep. 1863, p. 669, as a *Drillia.*

EULIMA FALCATA.

E. *t. valde tereti, valde curvata, alba, politissima, solidiore, marginibus spiræ meniscoideis ; anfr. nucl.?* . . . [*detritis*] ; *norm. circ.* x., *planatis, lente augentibus ; axi hamata ; suturis indistinctis ; basi elongata, haud tereti ; apertura pyriformi, antice latiore ; labro acuto ; labio tenui, appresso.*

18   273

Long. ·31, long. spir. ·21, lat. ·09 ; div. 12°.
Hab. Acapulco, on *Ostrea iridescens*, Rowell.
The spire-outlines are scythe-shaped. It is much larger and more
solid than *L. distorta* and (?var.) *yod.*

CERITHIOPSIS INTERCALARIS.

C. t. *valde elongata, rufo-fusca, marginibus spiræ rectis, suturi.
impressis; anfr. nucl.* iii. +? . . . *(decollatis), radiatim dis-
tanter liratis; norm.* x., *planatis; costis radiantibus primum*
xii., *dein circ.* xxii., *angustis, haud extantibus, ad peripheriam
continuis, interstitiis quadratis; carinis spiralibus primum* ii.
nodulosis, dein alteris ii. *minoribus inter eas intercalantibus;
carina postica suturali haud nodulosa, secunda valde nodulosa,
tertia intercalante æquante sed haud nodosa, quarta antica
valde nodosa, quinta circa peripheriam, primæ et tertiæ simili,
haud nodosa, alteraque contigua, minima, inter quas sutura
gyrat; basi concava, lævi; columella valde contorta; canali
brevi, aperto; labro?* . . . *

Hab. Guacomayo.

This beautiful species comes nearest to *C. bimarginata*, C. B. Ad.,
of which, indeed, the type does not agree with the diagnosis so well
as does this specimen. It differs in having other spiral ribs inter-
calating between the two principal ones, and in the radiating sculpture being continued to the periphery. One specimen only was
found in the shell-washings, not perfect at the mouth.

COLUMBELLA HUMEROSA.

C. t. *parva, turrita, alba, linea seu maculorum serie fusca interdum spiram ascendente; marginibus spiræ parum excurvatis;
anfr. nucl.?* . : . *[detritis]; norm.* vi., *convexis, postice tumentibus, suturis valde impressis; costis radiantibus* vii.–viii., *distantibus, validissimis, rotundatis; interstitiis late undatis;
lirulis validis spiralibus extantibus, interstitiis eas æquantibus,
costas et harum interstitia transeuntibus; basi angusta; labro
rix raricoso, postice emarginato, intus solidiore, dentibus circ.*
iv. *munitis; apertura late undata, compacta.*

Long. ·26, long. spir. ·15, lat. ·13 ; div. 38°.
Hab. Acapulco, on *Ostrea iridescens*, Rowell.

The sculpture resembles that of *Rhizocheilus*, and the tall spire that
of *Anachis*; yet it appears to belong to the restricted typical genus.

MURICIDEA DUBIA, var. SQUAMULATA.

Variat *t. omnino albida; sculptura tenuiore; spira elevata; tota
superficie minute squamulata, squamulis imbricatis.*
Hab. Cape St. Lucas (*Xantus*).
The opercula in the beautiful specimens sent by Mr. Pease are

* I forgot to measure the specimen before returning it to the Smithsonian
Inst.; but it is about the size of *C. assimilata.*

typically Muricoid. The essential features are those of *M. dubia*;
the pale colour and delicate sculpture and imbrication may arise
from a deep-water station, as is seen in similar European shells.
Mr. Cuming, however, regards it as distinct.

K.

DIAGNOSES

OF

NEW FORMS OF MOLLUSCA,

FROM

THE WEST COAST OF NORTH AMERICA,

FIRST COLLECTED BY COL. E. JEWETT.

BY

PHILIP P. CARPENTER, B.A., Ph. D.

From the Annals and Magazine of Natural History. Third Series, Vol. XV., pp. 177–182 (Nos. 373–386), March, 1865. Ibid., pp. 394–399 (*Mangelia variegata* to end), May, 1865.

(277)

DIAGNOSES

OF

NEW FORMS OF MOLLUSCA

FROM

THE WEST COAST OF NORTH AMERICA,

FIRST COLLECTED BY Col. E. JEWETT.

BY

PHILIP P. CARPENTER, B.A., Ph.D.

An account of Col. Jewett's shells will be found in the British Association Reports for 1856 (pp. 226–231) and 1863 (pp. 534–539). The exact localities are often uncertain; but many of them have been fixed by subsequent explorers. Being generally worn beach-specimens, the diagnoses have been written (whereever practicable) from perfect shells, and especially from the beautiful series dredged by Dr. J. G. Cooper, in the Californian State Survey. The types belong to Mrs. Boyce, of Utica, N.Y., and are at present in my keeping. The numbers, in the species from the temperate fauna, refer to the table in the British Association Report for 1863, pp. 636–664.

37 b. Solen (? sicarius, var.) rosaceus.

S. testa S. sicario simili, sed minore; multo angustiore, elongata, recta, extus et intus rosacea; epidermide tenui, valde nitente. Long. ·27, lat. ·5, alt. ·32 poll.

Hab. Sta. Barbara (Jewett); S. Pedro (Cooper).

74. Subgenus AMIANTIS*.

Callista: dente postico utraque valva ruguloso.

Type: Amiantis callosa, = Cytherea callosa, Conr., = Dosinia

* Th. ἀμίαντος, ὁ καὶ ἡ, unpolluted.

callosa, Brit. Assoc. Rep. 1857 (from fragments) : non *Venus callosa* (as of Conr.), Sow., Rve., Desh.

Hab. Sta. Barbara (*Nuttall, Jewett*) ; S. Pedro (*Cooper*) ; Cape St. Lucas (*Xantus*).

This section differs from the typical *Callista* as does *Mercenaria* from *Venus.* Whether the other peculiarities of the species (redescribed by Reeve as *Cytherea nobilis*) are coordinate, cannot yet be stated, as it stands alone. In sculpture and colour it resembles *Dosinia* ; in its ponderous growth, *Pachydesma.*

110. *Lazaria subquadrata.*

L. testa extus *Carditæ variegatæ* jun. simili ; pallida, castaneo tincta; subquadrata, antice truncata, subregulariter ventricosa, dorsaliter tumida ; costis radiantibus circ. xiv.–xvi., tumidis, nodosis, diagonalibus majoribus; interstitiis plus minusve insculptis : intus, valva dextra dente cardinali triangulari, inter duas fossas sito, haud elongato ; dent. lat. a cardine separatis, ant. extante, post. obsoleto, calloso : v. sinistrali dent. card. ii. angustis, subæqualibus, radiantibus ; lat. ant. et post. extantibus : cicatr. adduct. subrotundatis. Long. ·37, lat. ·25, alt. ·34.

Hab. Sta. Barbara (*Jewett*) ; Monterey, and along the coast to S. Pedro (State Coll. no. 403) (*Cooper*).

The outside of this remarkable little species is typically Carditoid; the hinge is intermediate between *Lazaria* and *Cypricardia.*

132. *Modiola fornicata.*

M. testa curta, lævi, latiore, maxime fornicata ; pallide carnea, epidermide rufo-fusca, rugis incrementi et incrustatione densissime pilosa induta ; umbonibus maximis, spiralibus, antice torsis, per tres quadrantes totæ latitudinis devectis ; area ligamentali curtissima, arcuata ; margine dorsali antice nullo, postice longo, arcuato; margine ventrali recto, vix propter byssum hiante ; postico lato, antico angusto ; altitudine dorsaliter valde elevata, ventraliter plane declivi, cuneiformi ; umbonibus trans marginem anticum per sextantem totius longitudinis excurrentibus : intus, sub umbonibus excavata ; cicatr. adduct. ant. ventraliter sita. Long. 1·4, lat. ·76, alt. ·95.

Hab. Sta. Barbara (*Jewett*) ; Monterey (*Taylor*).

160. *Pecten* (? var.) *æquisulcatus.*

P. testa *P. ventricoso* simili, sed tenuiore, minus ventricosa ; costis pluribus angustioribus xx.–xxi. ; interstitiis (præcipue valva superiore) fere æqualibus ; auriculis magis productis, acutis ; sinu serrato : testa jun. interstitiis alte insculptis, laminis concentricis crebris, vix extantibus, interstitia, costas auriculasque transeuntibus. Long. 3·2, lat. 3·35, alt. 1·5.

Hab. Sta. Barbara (*Jewett*); S. Diego (*Cassidy, Newberry, Cooper*).

Intermediate between the tropical *P. ventricosus* and the Atlantic *P. irradians.*

161. *Pecten paucicostatus.*

P. testa subconvexa, vix æquilaterali; castaneo seu rubido seu electri∴ ; ¡ ∴ta; costis xi.–xv., validis, angustis, rotundatis; interstitus multo latioribus. subplanatis; tota superficie minutissime concentrice striata; auriculis latis, haud æqualibus, lirulis circ. vi. ornatis; sinu paucidentato: intus pallidiore, linea cardinis costata, ad suturas auricularum tuberculosa; fossa ligamentali curta, transversim lata. Long. 1·7, lat. 1·84, alt. ·56.

Hab. Sta. Barbara (*Jewett*); Sta. Barbara Island (*Cooper*).

Pecten (? var.) *squarrosus.* (Page 536.)

P. testa orbiculari, æquilaterali, rubida, albido maculata; valva dextra convexa; costis xviii., æqualibus, testa jun. approximatis, testa adulta interstitiis æqualibus; costis et interstitiis regulariter undatis, striis crebris squamosis radiantibus ubique ornata; auriculis magnis, latissimis, subæqualibus; antica anguste fissata, serrata, postica sinuata; auriculis ambabus et regione contigua scabroso striatis: intus alba, linea cardinali alte sulcata. Long. 1·82, lat. 1·79, alt. ·9.

Hab. "Sta. Barbara," teste *Jewett.*

Resembles a shell in Mus. Cuming., marked "*exasperatus,* var.," but does not agree with the diagnosis of that species. All Col. Jewett's valves were dextral. The locality needs confirmation.

183. *Volvula cylindrica.*

V. testa cylindracea, alba, nitente, striis spiralibus distantibus cincta; medio planato, marginibus fere parallelis; antice satis effusa, postice subito angustata; canali brevissimo; labro acuto; labio indistincto; plica columellari parva, valde declivi. Long. ·17, lat. ·07.

Hab. Sta. Barbara (*Jewett*).

265. *Phasianella* (? *compta,* var.) *punctulata.*

P. testa *P. comptæ* simili, sed elatiore; suturis impressis; anfractibus tumentibus; omnino minutissime fusco punctata; columella lacunata. Long. ·24, long. spir. ·12, lat. ·14, div. 50°.

Hab. S. Diego (*Jewett*).

265 *b*. *Phasianella* (? *compta*, var.) *pulloides*.

P. testa *P. pullo* simillima; solida, compacta, spira breviore; suturis distinctis. Long. ·2, long. spir. ·1, lat. ·13, div. 55°.

Hab. Sta. Barbara (*Jewett*); Monterey, 20 fathoms (State Coll. no. 353). Smaller var., 8–10 fathoms, Catalina Island (*Cooper*).

265 *c*. *Phasianella* (? *compta*, var.) *elatior*.

P. testa perparva; spira elongata, ut in *P. pullo* picta; anfractibus subplanatis; suturis haud impressis; columella haud lacunata. Long. ·19, long. spir. ·12, lat. ·11, div. 40°.

Hab. Sta. Barbara (*Jewett*).

P. compta, with a large proportion of the small shells of the genus, is included under *P. pullus* in Mr. Reeve's monograph. In so difficult a tribe, it is judged better to name the distinct forms, and those from separated localities, until more is known.

276. *Trochiscus convexus.*

T. testa parva, subelevata, purpureo-fusca, tenuiter sculpta; anfr nucl. ? sinistralibus, vertice quasi decollato; norm. iv., convexis, suturis impressis; obtusissime bicarinatis, striolis confertissimis, minimis, subobsoletis cinctis; umbilico majore, costis duabus cincto, quarum interior acuta, exterior rotundata, crenata; apertura circulari. Long. ·15, long. spir. ·06, lat. ·15, div. 90°.

Hab. Monterey (*Jewett*).

The nuclear whorls in this unique little shell and in the typical species appear sinistral, as in Phoridæ and Solariadæ. The operculum also resembles that of *Solarium* rather than of *Trochus*. The genus may prove to belong to the Proboscidifers, notwithstanding its nacreous texture.

317. *Hipponyx tumens.*

H. testa normaliter fornicata, rotundata, albida; epidermide rugulosa, interstitiis pilulosa; vertice nucleoso nautiloideo, lævi, parum tumente, apice celato, interdum persistente; dein rapidissime augente, expansa, undique regulariter arcuata; liris acutis, subelevatis, distantibus, spiralibus, aliis intercalantibus; lineis incrementi minoribus decussantibus; margine acuto; apertura plerumque rotundata; cicatrice musculari a margine parum remota, regione capitis valde interrupta. Long. ·7, lat. ·46, alt. ·33, div. 90°.

Hab. Sta. Barbara (*Jewett*); S. Pedro (*Cooper*).

="*H. ?subrufa*" + "*Capulus*, 213," Brit. Assoc. Rep. 1857, p. 230.

329 *b*. *Bittium* (? var.) *esuriens.*

B. testa *B. filoso* simili, sed multo minore, graciliore, interdum valdè attenuata ; sculptura testæ jun. ut in *B. filoso,* testæ adultæ sub obsoleta ; interstitiis haud insculptis. Long. ·3, long. spir. ·21 lat. ·11, div. 25°.

Hab. Sta. Barbara (*Jewett*) ; Neeah Bay (*Swan*) ; Monterey (*Cooper*).

334. *Bittium fastigiatum.*

B. testa parva, gracili, pallide rufo-cinerea, marginibus spiræ vix excurvatis ; anfr. nucl. iii., lævibus, tumidis, apice acuto ; norm. ix., planatis, suturis alte impressis ; anfr. primis iii. carinatis, postea costis radiantibus circ. xiii., obtusis, satis extantibus, ad suturas interruptis, interstitiis undatis, liris spiralibus iv. in spira se monstrantibus, costas undatim superantibus, quarum antica in testa jun. plerumque extat ; anfr. ultimo parum contracto, basi elongata, liris spiralibus vi. contiguis ornata ; apertura gibbosa ; labro acuto, interdum varicoso, antice angulatim emarginato ; labio tenui. Long. ·25, long. spir. ·19, lat. ·09, div. 20°.

Hab. Sta. Barbara (*Jewett*).

Genus AMPHITHALAMUS*.

Testa Rissoidea, nucleo magno ; apertura labio producto, labro subpostice juncto, subito in adulta contracto.

355. *Amphithalamus inclusus.*

A. testa minuta, lata, solidiore, pallide rufo-fusca ; vertice mamillato ; anfr. nucl. uno et dimidio, quoad magnitudinem permagnis, minutissime et confertissime spiraliter et radiatim striolatis ; anfr. norm. iii.. lævibus, subplanatis, suturis impressis ; basi subangulata ; costa peripherica rotundata, haud extante, interdum in spira se monstrante ; costa altera circa regionem pseudo-umbilicarem ; labro acuto, haud contracto : labio testa adolescente normali, dein a pariete separata, sinum posticum suturam versus formante, t. adulta valde separata, regionem quasi umbilicarem magnam formante ; ad labrum subito fere perpendiculariter, subpostice juncto : operculo tenuissimo. Long. ·04, long. spir. ·02, lat. ·03, div. 60°.

Hab. Sta. Barbara (*Jewett*) ; S. Diego (*Cooper*).

This very remarkable little shell bears the same relation to *Rissoa* that *Stoastoma* does to *Helicina.* The peritreme resembles a figure **6** inverted, as on the face of the type. In the disproportionate size of the nuclear whorls it resembles *Vitrinella.*

373. *Drillia mæsta.*

D. testa acuminata, lævi, dense olivaceo-fusca, epidermide lævi adhærente induta ; anfr. nucleosis ?...(decollatis) ; norm. viii., parum

* Th. ἀμφὶ, θάλαμος, having a chamber on both sides.

excurvatis, suturis parum distinctis ; testa adolescente costis radiantibus circ. x., subobsoletis, elongatis, arcuatis, sinum versus interruptis, postice nodosis ; anfr. ult. sculptura nulla ; apertura
elongata ; canali brevi, aperto ; columella recta ; labio tenui ;
labro acuto, suturam versus sinuato, sinu parvo, expanso ; operculo
normali.   Long. 1·1, long. spir. ·65, lat. ·36, div. 27°.

Hab. Sta. Barbara (*Jewett*) ; S. Pedro (*Cooper*).

386. *Mitromorpha filosa.*

M. testa parva, solidiore, atro-purpurea, subconiformi, antice et postice subæqualiter tereti ; anfr. nucl. ii., albis, lævibus, apice
mamillato ; norm. iv., planatis, suturis haud distinctis ; omnino
æqualiter spiraliter lirulata ; lirulis acutioribus, in spira iv., anfr.
ult. circ. xx., interstitiis majoribus ; apertura lineata ; labro parum
inflexo, rotundato, postice vix sinuato, intus circ. xii.-dentato ;
labio inconspicuo ; columella arcuatim truncata.   Long. ·26,
long. spir. ·1, lat. ·12, div. 45°.

Hab. Sta. Barbara (*Jewett*) ; Lower California (teste *Trick*, in
Mus. Cuming.).

=?*Daphnella filosa*, Brit. Assoc. Rep. 1863, p. 658, note †.

Mr. A. Adams obtained two similar species from Japan ; and
as the shells do not rank satisfactorily under any established
group, he proposes the above genus for their reception. M. Crosse
suggests that *Columbella dormitor*, Sby., may be congeneric.

Mangelia variegata.

M. testa valde attenuata, tenui, parva, pallide carnea, rufo-fusco
normaliter bizonata, interdum unizonata, seu zonis interruptis ;
vertice nucleoso conspicuo, anfr. uno et dimidio, apice mamillato ;
anfr. norm. vi., subrotundatis, suturis valde impressis ; costis
radiantibus ix., angustis ; costulis spiralibus crebris, validioribus,
in spira circ. x., costas superantibus ; apertura valde elongata ;
canali brevi, aperto ; labro tenui, juxta suturam conspicue arcuato ;
labio tenui.   Long. ·31, long. spir. ·17, lat. ·1 poll., div. 22°.
Variat costis crebrioribus, sculptura minus expressa.

Hab. Sta. Barbara (*Jewett*).

Mangelia (? variegata, var.) nitens.

M. testa *M. variegatæ* simili, sed nitentiore, fascia alba et altera
rufo-fusca attingente spiram ascendentibus.   Long. ·25, long.
spir. ·15, lat. ·08, div. 20°.

Hab. Sta. Barbara (*Jewett*), rare.

Mangelia angulata.

M. testa parva, rufo-purpurea, vix gracili, epidermide tenui fugaci ;
anfr. nucl. iii., helicoideis, primum lævibus, dein cancellatis, apice

mamillato; anfr. norm. iv., convexis, suturis impressis, in medio spiræ obtusangulatis; costis radiantibus circ. xii., acutioribus; costula spirali circa angulum, inter costas subobsoleta; tota superficie tenuiter spiraliter crebrisulcata, sulculis sub lente sæpius bifidis; apertura pyriformi, canali longiore, recto, aperto; labro acuto, postice conspicue sinuato; columella haud contorta; labro obsoleto. Long. ·35, long. spir. ·18, lat. ·13, div. 30°.

Hab. Sta. Barbara (*Jewett*).

Myurella simplex.

M. testa rufo-cinerea, minore, minus tereti, epidermide tenui; anfr. xii., planatis; fascia suturali valida, nodosa, tuberculis ovalibus crebris validioribus (anfr. penult. circa xv.) ornata; testa adolescente costulis radiantibus, postea evanescentibus; striolis antice et postice spiralibus, circa peripheriam sæpe obsoletis; basi rotundata; canali brevissimo, alte emarginato; carina supra canalem acuta, columellam plicante; labro acuto, vix undato. Long. 1·03, long. spir. ·76, lat. ·27, div. 20°.
Variat tuberculis subobsoletis.

Hab. Sta. Barbara (*Jewett*); S. Pedro (*Cooper*).

Odostomia inflata.

O. testa majore, tenui, pallide cinerea, epidermide cinerea induta; vert. nucl. subito immerso; anfr. norm. iv., rapidissime augentibus, subplanatis, suturis impressis; tota superficie minutissime et confertissime spiraliter striolata; umbilico nullo; basi et apertura valde elongatis; labro acuto; labio tenuissimo; plica acuta, transversa, parietem attingente; columella valde arcuata, antice effusa. Long. ·26, long. spir. ·09, lat. ·14, div. 60°.
Variat spira elatiore. Long. ·24, long. spir. ·11, lat. ·13, div. 45°.
Variat quoque striolis subobsoletis.

Hab. Sta. Barbara (*Jewett*); Farralcone Islands, in cavities, on *Haliotis* (teste R. D. Darbishire); near San Francisco (*Rowell*); Neeah Bay (*Swan*).

Chemnitzia crebrifilata.

C. testa satis tereti, subalbida, haud regulari; anfr. nucl. ii., helicoideis, decliviter sitis, margines spiræ parum excurvatos paullum superantibus; norm. viii., quorum primi subrotundati, ultimi vix planati; suturis valde distinctis; cost. rad. circ. xxiv., subrectis, acutioribus, angustis, interdum attingentibus, anfr. ultimo crebrioribus minus expressis, circa basim prolongatam haud subito evanescentibus; lirulis spiralibus, in spira circ. viii., rotundatis, expressis, anfr. ult. supra costas subnodulosis, circa basim crebrioribus; peritremate continuo; columella vix torta, haud plicata; labio distincto. Long. ·22, long. spir. ·17, lat. ·07, div. 18°.

Hab. Sta. Barbara, 1 specimen (*Jewett*).

403 *b*.   *Chemnitzia* (?*torquata*, var.) *stylina*.

C. testa *C. torquatæ* simili, sed valde teretiore, gracillima, interdum subdiaphana; anfr. nucl. ii., decliviter sitis, margines spiræ fere parallelos vix superantibus; norm. xii., angustis, subplanatis, suturis distinctis; costis radiantibus circ. xxiii., latis, declivibus, testa juniore continuis, adulta fascia haud sculpta suprasuturali separatis; interstitiis parvis, haud sculptis; basi rotundata, haud sculpta; columella parum torta. Long. ·32, long. spir. ·27, lat. ·8, div 10°.

Hab. Sta. Barbara (*Jewett*); Monterey (*Cooper*).

Chemnitzia Virgo.

C. testa parva, alba, gracili, stylina; anfr. nucl. ii., decliviter sitis, margines spiræ subparallelos haud superantibus; norm. viii., subrotundatis, suturis distinctis; costulis radiantibus circ. xviii., angustis, acutioribus, sæpe attingentibus, circa peripheriam haud subito evanidis, interstitiis subæqualibus alte spiraliter sulcatis, sulcis circ. viii., latera costarum crenulantibus, costas haud superantibus; basi valde rotundata, curta, haud sculpta; axi lacunato; peritremate vix continuo; columella recta. Long. ·18, long. spir. ·14, lat. ·05, div. 12°.

Hab. " Sta. Barbara," 1 specimen (*Jewett*).

Dunkeria laminata.

D. testa satis elevata, rufo-fusca, fasciis pallidioribus interdum cincta; anfr. nucl. ii., helicoideis, valde decliviter sitis, margines spiræ subrectos haud superantibus; norm. viii., subrotundatis, suturis impressis; costis spiralibus rotundatis, in spira iv., aliisque suturalibus vix rotundatis, interstitiis minoribus impressis; super eas laminis radiantibus acutioribus circ. xxx., circa basim rotundatam tenuiter continuis; liris spiralibus basalibus circ. viii., obtusis, columellam versus subflexuosam obsoletis; peritremate continuo; labio appresso. Long. ·25, long. spir. ·18, lat. ·07, div. 20°.

Hab. Sta. Barbara (*Jewett*); San Diego (*Cooper*).

This beautiful Fenelloid species may be regarded as the type of the group *Dunkeria*.

Eulima Thersites.

E. testa parva, curtissima, albida, arcuata, valde distorta; marginibus spiræ dextro subrecto, sinistro valde excurvato; anfr. nucl. ?.. (decollatis); norm. vi., lævibus, subplanatis, suturis distinctis; basi valde arcuata; apertura subovali, dextrorsum producta; peritremate continuo, valde calloso; labro sinuato. Long. ·21, long. spir. ·13, lat. ·09, div. 40°.

Hab. Sta. Barbara, 1 specimen (*Jewett*).

Preeminent for aberration among the distorted Eulimidæ. A second specimen occurred from an uncertain source.

Opalia bullata.

O. testa minore, alba, subdiaphana, turrita, gracili; marginibus spiræ subrectis; tota superficie minutissime et creberrime spiraliter striolata; vertice nucleoso declivi, celato; dein anfr. ii., globosis, radiatim haud sculptis; dein v. normalibus, pianatis, suturis vix impressis; lirulis radiantibus circ. xxvi., haud nisi in anfr. primis expressis, circa basim irregu ariter rotundatam ad axim continuis; serie bullularum suturalium anfr. primis e lirulis extantibus formata, postea lirulis haud convenientibus, anfr. penult. circ. xvii., planatis, super suturas parieti appressis, interstitiis haud infossis; basi subangulata, haud costata; apertura subovali, sinistrorsum subplanata; peritremate continuo, calloso; labro haud sinuato. Long. ·3, long. spir. ·21, lat. ·09, div. 20°.

Hab. Sta. Barbara, one specimen (*Jewett*).

422. *Cerithiopsis purpurea.*

C. testa compacta, haud gracili, marginibus spiræ parum excurvatis; purpurea seu fusco-purpurea, circa peripheriam pallidiore; anfr. nucl. ? ii., lævibus; norm. vii., planatis, suturis impressis; scriebus iii. nodulorum minorum supra costulas spirales minores, ad intersectiones costularum radiantium circ. xxiii., lineis fere rectis, ad suturas interruptis, spiram ascendentium sitis; interstitiis impressis, quadratis; costulis suturalibus ii. haud nodulosis; basi rotundata, antice lirulis paucis expressis inter eas et costulas suturales vix sculpta; apertura subquadrata; columella torta, emarginata. Long. ·29, long. spir. ·19, lat. ·1, div. 20°.

Hab. Sta. Barbara (*Jewett*); Monterey, San Diego (*Cooper*).

423. *Cerithiopsis fortior.*

C. testa *C. purpureæ* simili, sed sculptura multo fortiore, basi pallida; seriebus nodulorum spiralibus testa adolescente ii., postea iii.; costis radiantibus circ. xiii., interstitiis magnis; costis suturalibus validis, subnodosis; costa basali valida. Long. ·3, long. spir. ·2, lat. ·11, div. 26°.

Hab. Sta. Barbara, 1 specimen (*Jewett*).

439. *Marginella subtrigona.*

M. testa *M. Jewettii* simili, sed multo curtiore, latiore; antice valde angustata, postice valde tumente; labro postice minus prolongato; plicis iv., validioribus, parietali una. Long. ·14, long. spir. ·01, lat. ·11, div. 130°.

Hab. Sta. Barbara (*Jewett*).

440. *Marginella regularis.*

M. testa *M. Jewettii* simili, sed multo minore, paullum angustiore; tenui, nitidissima, crystallina, omnino diaphana; labio magis calloso. Long. ·13, long. spir. ·01, lat. ·09, div. 120°.

Hab. Sta. Barbara (*Jewett*); coast of California south from

Monterey, beach to 20 fathoms; Catalina Island, 10–20 fathoms, State Coll. no. 398 *a* (*Cooper*).

453. *Amycla tuberosa.*

A. testa *A. minori* simillima, sed vertice nucleoso tuberoso; anfr. iv., tumidis, rapide augentibus; apice minimo, marginus spiræ rectos parum superante, interdum subdecliviter sito; testa adulta interdum unicolore, livida seu aurantiaca; plerumque albida, rufo-fusco varie picta, seu maculata, seu nebulosa, seu strigata strigis radiantibus seu flexuosis, seu varie penicillata, sæpe fascia tessellata subsuturali; anfract. norm. v., planatis, suturis distinctis; basi subangulata; apertura pyriformi, canali satis prolongato, arcuato; labro intus acuto, deorsum quasi tumidiore, postice sinuato, intus circ. octodentato; labio parum conspicuo, vix rugulato; columella torta, axi antice striato; superficie lævi, seu interdum minutissime sub lente radiatim striolata; epidermide cornea, tenui, subdiaphana, spiraliter sub lente minutissime striolata: operculo Nassæformi, parvo, marginibus irregulariter serratis, cicatrice bilobata. Long. ·32, long. spir. ·18, lat. ·14, div. 30°.

Hab. Sta. Barbara, recent and fossil (*Jewett*); coast of California north to Monterey; Catalina Island, 8–10 fathoms (*Cooper*).

As this belongs to a group of closely allied species of Nassoid Columbellæ, a minute diagnosis is given. The fossil specimens are larger, and have the remarkable nucleus more perfect, than any of the recent shells yet seen. In appearance it scarcely differs from the small variety of the Mediterranean *A. minor*, Scac.; but that (with *A. corniculata*) has a Chrysodomoid nucleus, the Californian an Alaboid.

? *Anachis penicillata.*

?*A.* testa parva, Metuloidea, turrita, albida, rufo-fusco plus minusve penicillata; anfr. nucleosis ii., tumidis, helicoideis, apice mamillato; norm. vi., tumidis, suturis valde impressis; costis radiantibus circ. xii., angustis, expressis; lirulis spiralibus extantibus, in spira plerumque vi. supra costas transeuntibus; apertura pyriformi, antice effusa; labro postice sinuato. Long. ·21, long. spir. ·13, lat. ·08, div. 25°.

Hab. Sta. Barbara (*Jewett*); S. Diego, Catalina Island, shore to 10 fathoms (*Cooper*).

Neither of the specimens sent is quite mature. The mouth is that of an adolescent *Anachis*, but the sculpture is Metuloid.

Siphonalia fuscotincta.

S. testa minima, turrita, albida, apicem versus fusco tincta; anfr. nucl. ii., compactis, subplanatis, apice mamillato; norm. iv., convexis, suturis impressis; costis radiantibus rotundatis, tumentibus, basim versus evanidis, interstitiis undulatis, subæquantibus; lirulis crebris spiralibus, costas superantibus; apertura pyriformi, in canalem brevem apertum contortum producta; labro acuto; labio haud conspicuo; columella canalem versus valde contorta. Long. ·17, long. spir. ·1, lat. ·08, div. 32°.

Hab. Sta. Barbara (*Jewett*).

The unique specimen is like a minute edition of *Siphonalia Kellettii*, but does not accord with the young of that or of any other species known in the region. It is probably not mature.

19 289

L.

DIAGNOSES

OF

NEW FORMS OF MOLLUSCA,

COLLECTED BY COL. E. JEWETT

ON THE

WEST TROPICAL SHORES OF NORTH AMERICA.

BY

PHILIP P. CARPENTER, B.A., Ph.D.

From the Annals and Magazine of Natural History. Third Series, Vol. XV., pp. 399—400, May, 1865.

(291)

DIAGNOSES

of

NEW FORMS OF MOLLUSCA

COLLECTED BY Col. E. JEWETT

on

THE WEST TROPICAL SHORES OF NORTH AMERICA.

BY

PHILIP P. CARPENTER, B.A., Ph.D.

Rissoina expansa.

R. testa magna, lata, tenuisculpta, alba, nitente, subdiaphana; marginibus spiræ parum excurvatis; anfr. nucl. lævibus, vertice mamillato ; norm. v., planatis, suturis distinctis ; costulis radiantibus circ. xxiv., obtusis, haud extantibus, interstitia æquantibus, peripheriam versus evanidis ; circa basim productam striis spiralibus expressis ; medio lævi ; apertura valde expansa, semilunata ; labro subantice producto, varicoso, antice et postice alte sinuato ; labio calloso.   Long. ·35, long. spir. ·18, lat. ·17 poll., div. 30°.

Hab. Mazatlan (teste *Jewett*).

This fine species is the largest known in the fauna.   It most resembles *R. infrequens,* C. B. Ad., which was described from a dead shell.

Mangelia hamata.

M. testa carneo-aurantiaca, satis turrita, marginibus spiræ excurvatis ; anfr. nucl. ii. globosis, tenuissime cancellatis, apice mamillato ; norm. vi., subelongatis, in spira tumentibus, subangulatis, suturis impressis ; costis radiantibus x.–xii., acutioribus, validis, circa basim prolongatam continuis ; interstitiis concavis ; lirulis spiralibus filosis, distantibus, supra costas transeuntibus, in spira iii.–iv. ; apertura subelongata, quasi hamata, intus lævi, intense colorata ; labro

293

acuto, dorsaliter varicoso, postice valde sinuato. Long. ·24, long. spir. ·13, lat. ·1, div. 25°.

Hab. Panama (teste *Jewett*).

This very beautiful species is easily recognized by the varicose lip, sloping off to a sharp edge; by the deeply cut posterior notch, giving the smooth mouth a hooked appearance; by the sharp ridges, traversed by distant spiral threads; and by the flesh-tinted orange colour.

Mangelia cerea.

M. testa *M. hamatæ* simili, sed textura cerea, aurantiaca, graciliore, anfractibus tumidioribus, haud angulatis; anfr. nucl. lævibus; normalibus v., costis radiantibus haud acutis, interstitia æquantibus; liris spiralibus validioribus, haud filosis, supra costas nodulosis, in interstitiis subobsoletis; apertura, testa adulta, ?.... Long. ·25, long. spir. ·14, lat. ·1, div. 28°.
Variat testa rufo-fusca.

Hab. Panama (teste *Jewett*).

Col. Jewett's unique specimen is not mature. It is distinguished from *M. hamata* by the smooth nucleus, waxen texture, rounder whorls, more equal distribution of the contour between ribs and interstices, and especially by the spiral sculpture, which is faint in the hollows, but nodulose on the ribs. Mr. Cuming has a specimen with the same texture, but of a rich brown colour.

Chemnitzia cælata.

C. testa satis magna, cinerea, elongata; anfr. nucl. ?...; norm. xiii., planatis, suturis vix impressis; costis radiantibus xx.–xxviii., rectis, haud semper convenientibus, subacutis, ad peripheriam subito truncatis; sulcis spiralibus in spira iv.–v., valde impressis, interstitia et costarum latera transeuntibus, juga haud superantibus; basi subito angustata, angulata, lirulis spiralibus circ. vi. ornata; apertura subquadrata; columella satis torta. Long. ·35, long. spir. ·3, lat. ·09, div. 13°.

Hab. West coast of North America (*Jewett*).

This beautiful and unique shell was probably from Panama; but there was no locality-mark. It is remarkable for its deep furrows and the suddenly shortened and spirally sculptured base. It is much larger and broader than the northern *C. Virgo,* and differs in details of sculpture.

M.

DIAGNOSES

DES

MOLLUSQUES NOUVEAUX

PROVENANT DE CALIFORNIE,

ET FAISANT PARTIE DU MUSÉE DE L'INSTITUTION SMITHSONIENNE.

BY

PHILIP P. CARPENTER, B. A., Ph. D.

From the Journal de Conchyliologie, Vol. XII. (Third Series, Vol. V.), pp. 129-149, April, 1865.

(295)

Diagnoses de **Mollusques nouveaux** provenant de **Californie** et faisant partie du **musée** de l'**Institution Smithsonienne**,

par Philip P. Carpenter, B. A., Ph. D.

I.

D'après les lois des États-Unis, tous les objets d'histoire naturelle recueillis dans le cours des expéditions faites par

les États deviennent la propriété de l'institution Smithsonienne, qui est autorisée, de plus, à échanger les doubles.
Cette institution, si bien dirigée par le professeur Henry,
qui en est le secrétaire, n'a pas pour objet principal son
seul agrandissement; elle est établie pour « l'accroisse-
ment et la propagation de la science *parmi les hommes,* »
c'est-à-dire qu'elle embrasse toutes les nations. Dans l'é-
change des doubles, on n'a pas pour but d'obtenir un *quid
pro quo,* mais plutôt d'envoyer les échantillons à quelque
endroit où ils seront plus utiles pour l'avancement de la
science. Le revenu de l'institution ne suffisant pas pour
avoir à poste fixe des naturalistes chargés de classer et de
décrire au besoin les objets d'histoire naturelle de ce
musée, on envoie ces objets en communication à des naturalistes des États-Unis ou d'autres pays, selon leur spécia-
lité, en vue d'arriver à déterminer les espèces et de faire
choix des échantillons pour leur collection permanente et
pour les échanges. En conformité de ce principe, les di-
recteurs de l'institution m'ont transmis en Angleterre
toutes les coquilles recueillies sur la côte ouest d'Amérique. Je les ai soigneusement comparées avec les types
de la collection Cuming et du musée britannique; et, par
suite de cet examen comparatif joint à celui de mes
propres matériaux, je me suis trouvé dans la nécessité de
décrire à peu près trois cents espèces ou variétés locales,
en dehors de celles que j'ai publiées antérieurement dans
mon catalogue des coquilles de Mazatlan.

On trouvera des renseignements sur ces espèces et sur
toutes les sources originales d'information concernant le
même sujet, dans mon «*Supplementary Report on the
present state of our knowledge of the Mollusca of the
West coast of N. America.*» écrit à la demande de l'Association britannique pour l'avancement de la science, et

publié dans ses *Transactions* pour l'année 1863 (p. 517-686). Aux pages 636-664, on peut consulter une table disposée de manière à faire voir d'un coup d'œil toutes les espèces de la région de Vancouver et de Californie, jusqu'ici très-peu connues, avec tous les endroits où on les a recueillies, d'après les renseignements fournis par les principaux collecteurs. Dans les mêmes pages on trouvera une description très-succincte des espèces qui sont nouvelles ou peu connues : quant aux diagnoses latines, elles ont été publiées dans divers journaux scientifiques, selon la source de provenance des espèces qu'elles concernent. Ainsi, par exemple, on doit en chercher le plus grand nombre, qui ont été draguées par le docteur Cooper, lors du *Geological Survey* de l'État de Californie, dans les *Proceedings of the California Academy*, 1864-5. Les espèces draguées par le docteur Kennerley au *Puget-Sound* se trouvent décrites dans le *Journal of the Philadelphia Academy*, 1863. Les espèces trouvées par le colonel Jewett, en Californie, ont été publiées dans les *Annals of natural History*, 1864-5 ; celles qui ont été recueillies par M. Swan et les jeunes Indiens, de l'instruction desquels il est chargé, à la baie de Neeah (vis-à-vis l'île de Vancouver), et par M. Xantus, au cap St.-Lucas, se trouvent décrites dans le même recueil périodique (1864). Dans les *Proceedings of the zoological Society* (1863, p. 339-369), on trouvera un examen critique du *Panama catalogue* du professeur C. B. Adams, fait d'après ses échantillons typiques ; et, pendant le cours de la présente année, le même journal doit publier les espèces nouvelles de la région tropicale, recueillies par MM. Reigen, C. B. Adams, etc.

Profitant de la bienveillance avec laquelle l'éditeur du *Journal de Conchyliologie* a bien voulu m'ouvrir les co-

lonnes de son recueil scientifique, je me propose de donner, dans cet article, les diagnoses des espèces nouvelles
de Californie, qui ne se trouvent pas décrites dans les mé-
moires cités plus haut. Je me trouve dans l'impossibilité
d'en donner en même temps les figures, attendu que j'ai
déjà restitué les échantillons typiques à l'institution Smithsonienne; mais cette absence de figures est moins regret-
table, si l'on considère qu'elle n'est que momentanée, et
que les espèces en question doivent être prochainement
dessinées et gravées sur bois par le savant artiste, M. le
Dʳ W. Stimpson, pour le *Manuel des Mollusques de la côte
ouest d'Amérique*, que je prépare en ce moment, à la demande de l'institution Smithsonienne (1). Lorsqu'il existe
des doubles de ces diverses espèces, on les trouvera ou
dans le *Musée britannique* ou dans la collection Cuming.

Warrington (Angleterre), 15 février 1865.

II.

1. Angulus Gouldii.

*A. t. parva, alba, tenui, tumida, subdiaphana, subqua-
drata; epidermide pallida, tenuissima, induta; lævi, lineis incrementi haud exstantibus; antice et ventraliter inflata , marginibus regulariter excurvatis; parte postica
minima, haud angulata; umbonibus prominentibus : intus, dentibus cardinalibus utraque valva uno simplici
unoque bifido, validis, obtusis; laterali antico valva dex-*

(1) Je prie les naturalistes qui trouveraient des erreurs dans
mes ouvrages déjà publiés, ou qui posséderaient de nouveaux
matériaux relatifs aux *Mollusques* de la côte ouest d'Amérique,
de vouloir bien me communiquer leurs renseignements, en me
les adressant chez M. le professeur Henry, Smithsonian institution, Washington, D. C., États-Unis, afin que je puisse rendre ce
Manuel aussi complet et aussi exact que possible.   P. C.

tra curto, valido, exstante; postico obsoleto; valva sinis-
trali nullis; nymphis rectis, inconspicuis; sinu pallii
maximo, subtriangulari, fere cicatricem alteram tenus
porrecto; cicatricibus adductoribus postica subquadrata,
antica elongata. — Long. ·48, *lat.* ·4, *alt.* ·1 *poll.* (1).

Hab. San Diego, *Cassidy.* l.'île de Cerros, dans la basse
Californie, *Ayres.*

Cette petite coquille porte le nom de « *Mæra Gouldii,*
Hanl., » dans le musée Cuming et dans les *Genera* de
MM. Adams (t. II, p. 396), mais je n'ai pu parvenir à en
trouver de diagnose publiée. Sur quelques-uns des échantillons, on peut trouver le commencement d'une dent la-
térale postérieure. Ainsi la différence entre les sous-
genres *Mæra* et *Angulus* de MM. Adams est de très-peu
d'importance. Cette espèce offre l'aspect de l'état jeune du
Lutricola Dombeyi, Lamarck (2), mais elle en diffère par
la charnière.

(1) Les dimensions des espèces sont données en pouces an-
glais, dont chacun = 2.53 centimètres.

(2) Pour cette section de *Scrobicularia,* MM. Adams proposent
le vocable *Capsa;* ce qui fait grandement confusion, *Capsa* étant
un nom de Lamarck, synonyme, il est vrai, d'*Iphigenia,* Schuma-
cher, mais néanmoins très-usité. Je propose de reconstituer le
genre ancien *Lutricola,* de Blainville, pris dans un sens restreint,
pour ce groupe, intermédiaire entre les vrais *Scrobicularia* et les
Macoma, ainsi qu'il suit :
  Sous-genre *Lutricola.*
  = *Lutricola,* Blainv. pars.
  = *Capsa,* H. et A. Ad., non Lam.
  = *Scrobicularia,* seu *Macoma,* seu *Tellina,* pars, auct.
  Testa tumida, sæpe inæquivalvis, irregularis, subquadrata seu
antice producta; pars postica undata seu truncata; cartilago fossa
subinterna sita, ligamento curtiore contigua : dentes cardinales
utraque valva duo, laterales nulli.
  Ex. *Lutricola ephippium,* Solander, *L. alta,* Conrad; *L. Dom-*
beyi, Lamarck, etc.

OEDALIA, n. g.

Étym. οἰδαλεα (une coquille) renflée.

Testa inflata, tenuis, æquivalvis, æquilateralis, cycla-
diformis : margo haud hians, haud sinuatus : ligamentum
et cartilago externa : dentes cardinales 3-2, bifidi, late-
rales nulli : sinus pallii magnus.

2. OEDALIA SUBDIAPHANA.

OE. t. albida, tenuissima, subdiaphana, submargarita-
cea, tumente; lævi, striulis incrementi exillimis; epider-
mide pallide straminea, tenuissima, induta; suborbiculari,
umbonibus tumentibus, prominentibus; marginibus om-
nino satis excurvatis, antico rotundato, postico paululum
porrecto, lunula nulla : intus, valva sinistrali dentibus
cardinalibus 3 bifidis, radiantibus, quorum centralis ma-
jor, valva dextra 2 bifidis, intercalantibus; nymphis par-
vis, curtis, tenuibus; ligamento circa umbones excurrente;
lamina cardinali dorsaliter parum claviculata; cicatrici-
bus adductoribus parvis, marginem dorsalem versus sitis,
antica ovali, postica subrotundata; sinu pallii regulariter
ovali, per duas trientes interstitii incurrente, longitudi-
naliter tenuissime corrugato; linea pallii antice a mar-
gine remota, diagonaliter reflexa. — Long. ·52, lat. ·44,
alt. ·26, poll.

Hab. San Diego, *Cassidy.*

Je n'ai vu qu'un seul échantillon de cette coquille fort
remarquable. Après l'avoir examinée pour la seconde fois
et avec beaucoup de soin au microscope, pour caractéri-
ser l'espèce et pour comparer ses caractères avec ceux du
Cooperella scintillæformis, j'ai eu le malheur de le laisser
tomber à terre et de le briser : mais je puis attester l'exac-
titude de la description. Cette espèce a l'aspect externe

d'un *Kellia suborbicularis*; l'inflexion palléale d'un *Semele*; le ligament circumumbonal des *Circe* et des *Psephis*; et une charnière très-complexe, contenant cinq dents, toutes bifides. Avec le sous-genre *Cooperella*, qui en diffère comme les *Lutricola* et les *Macoma* (le cartilage étant semi-interne) et peut-être avec les *Cycladella*, elle constitue un groupe particulier des *Tellinidæ*

3. Psephis tellimyalis.

Ps. t. valde transversa, subquadrata, tumidiore, valde inæquilaterali; umbonibus obtusis, vix prominentibus; pallide carneo–lutescente, purpureo (maxime circa marginem dentesque) tincta; epidermide tenuissima induta; tota superficie creberrime concentrice striata; marginibus, dorsali et ventrali subparallelis, antico rectiore, postico rotundato; lunula inconspicua : intus, dentibus centralibus minimis, anticis elongatis, posticis valde elongatis; sinu pallii vix sinuato. — Long. ·09, lat. ·07, altit. ·04, poll.

Hab. Californie (sur la partie dorsale d'une *Haliotide*, *Rowell*).

Le sous-genre *Psephis* se compose de très-petites coquilles vénériformes, dont l'animal est ovivipare, comme celui des *Cyclas*, etc., des eaux douces, et des *Bryophila* parmi les *Lamellibranches* marins. La charnière porte trois dents; quelquefois elles ressemblent à celles des *Chione*; mais ordinairement les dents antérieures et postérieures se prolongent. Le *Psephis tellimyalis* se trouve sur les limites extrêmes du groupe. Il a l'aspect extérieur d'un *Tellimya bidentalis* et quelque chose aussi de sa charnière, à cause du très-grand développement des deux dents terminales aux dépens de la dent centrale. Je n'en ai

vu qu'un seul échantillon, qui appartient au révérend
J. Rowell, pasteur à San Francisco.

4. TAPES LACINIATA.

T. t. « *T. stamineæ* » *simili, sed majore, fragili, multo
tenuiore; satis tumida, subovali, regulariter excurvata,
cinerea; lunula linea impressa, parum definita; marginibus, postico vix subquadrato, antico producto; ligamento
haud prominente; costis radiantibus acutis, distantibus,
ventraliter dimidium interstitiorum æquantibus, postice
parvis, crebris, antice latis; laminis concentricis creberrimis, vix erectis, costas transeuntibus, a costis et interstitiis eleganter undatis, haud nodosis : pagina interna albida; dentibus cicatricibusque ut in «T. staminea» forma-
tis; sinu pallii paulum longiore, acutiore.* — Long. 2· 4,
lat. ·2, alt. 1·4, poll.*

Hab. San Diego, *Rich, Blake, Cooper.*

Cette espèce est remarquable, en même temps pour la
délicatesse de sa sculpture, et pour les caractères particu-
liers de sa texture. Elle appartient au même groupe que
les *T. Adamsii*, Reeve, *T. tenerrima*, Carpenter (décrit
d'après un individu très-jeune) et *T. staminea*, Conrad.
Cette dernière espèce compte parmi ses variétés les *V. Pe-
tilii* et *V. ruderata*, Deshayes, *V. mundulus*, Reeve (= *T.
diversa*, Sowerby) et *V. tumida*, Sowerby. Mais elle se distingue facilement de toutes ces formes par ses lames con-
centriques, disposées au-dessus des rayons et de leurs interstices bien prononcés, et laciniées au sommet fort
élégamment.

5. KELLIA (LAPEROUSII, var.) CHIRONII.

K. t. « *K. Laperousii*» *simili; sed tenuiore, minus transversa, ventraliter excurvata; epidermide pallidiore; um-*

bonibus angustioribus : dentibus multo minoribus, haud exstantibus. — *Long.* ·76, *lat.* ·62, *alt.* ·41, *poll.*

Hab. Neeah Bay, **Swan** ; San Pedro, *Cooper.*

· Cette variété est assez distincte de la forme typique du **K.** *Laperousii;* mais la suite d'individus que j'ai eu occasion d'examiner comparativement m'a permis de me convaincre que l'espèce variait beaucoup.

6. Kellia rotundata.

K. t. *tenuissima, orbiculari, satis convexa, œquilaterali, lœvi; epidermide subnitente, pallide olivacea; umbonibus angustis, satis prominentibus; marginibus omnino regulariter excurvatis : intus, dentibus cardinalibus* 2 *tenuibus, satis conspicuis, clavicula haud exstante; dentibus lateralibus satis elongatis.—Long.* ·6, *lat.* ·5, *alt.* ·28, *poll.*

Hab. Monterey, *Taylor.*

Cette espèce est beaucoup plus grande, mais moins renflée que le **K.** *suborbicularis,* et se distingue facilement par sa forme presque complétement arrondie.

7. Ostrea lurida.

O. t. *irregulari, suborbiculari, ellipsoidea, seu producta; superficie interdum laminata, purpurea seu squalide grisea, haud costata : intus olivacea, interdum purpureo tincta, seu omnino purpurea, submargaritacea; cardine recto; umbonibus haud conspicuis, haud excavatis; margine interno, cardinem versus sœpe crenulato.*

Animal flavore cupreo tinctum.

Var. *laticaudata,* Nutt, *ms.* : *t. omnino purpurea, margine producto, undato; cardinem versus, denticulis conspicuis instructo.*

Hab. Vancouver Is., à 2-3 toises sur fond de vase, *Lord ;*

Shoalwater Bay, *Cooper*; Neeah Bay et Tatooche Is.,
Swan (Var.) Monterey, *Nuttall*.

?Var. *expansa* : *t. omnino planata, per totam superfi-
ciem affixa ; extus, marginem versus laminata, purpureo
radiata ; intus, olivaceo-rufa, ligamento parvo, in medio
undato, solidiore.*

Hab. S. Pedro, *Cooper.*

?Var. *rufoides* : *t.* « *O. Virginicæ* » *jun. simili ; sed tenuissima, luteo-rufa, intus rufo tincta ; umbonibus concavis.*

Hab. S. Diego, *Cassidy*, *Cooper*. Fossile à San Pablo,
20 pieds au-dessus de la haute marée, *Newberry*.

Les *Huîtres* de Californie, dans leur état ordinaire,
comme on les trouve au Shoalwater Bay (Orégon), ont à
peu près la couleur et l'aspect de petites *Éthéries*. Les
individus des mers plus chaudes ont l'air d'être très-dis-
tincts ; mais, d'après le docteur Cooper, qui a une grande
expérience de la matière, ce ne sont que des variétés. Je
ne pouvais pas prendre pour nom spécifique celui que le
professeur Nuttall avait donné en manuscrit à une forme
accidentelle. Quant aux autres formes, assez constantes
dans leurs diverses localités, je leur ai donné des noms
qui pourront servir à les désigner soit comme espèces,
soit comme variétés, lorsque, plus tard, la connais-
sance d'un plus grand nombre d'individus permettra
d'avoir une opinion définitive en ce qui les concerne. La
variété *rufoides* a beaucoup de l'aspect de l'*O. Virginica*
(Maz. Cat., n°. 212). Elle était désignée sous le nom « *O.
?rufa* » par le docteur Gould ; mais je suis porté à croire
que l'espèce de Lamarck est une variété des Huîtres atlan-
tiques, attendu que les coquilles de la haute Californie
n'étaient pas connues à l'époque où il a écrit.

— 139 —

8. TORNATELLA PUNCTOCÆLATA.

T. t. tenui, satis elongata, ovoidea; cinerea, fasciis duabus latis fuscis ornata; vertice nucleoso decliviter cœlato; anfractibus normalibus 4 vix convexis, suturis distinctis; tota superficie sulcis subdistantibus cœlata, punctis impressis seriatim dispositis, quarum 7-9, in spira monstrantur; basi ovali; apertura latiore; labro acuto, antice sinuato; labio indistincto; plica acuta declivi juxta parietem, haud exstante; columella antice torta. Long. ·2, long. spir. ·06, lat. ·09, poll.: div. 50°.

Hab. Santa-Crux, *Rowell*. — San Diego, *Cooper*.

Cette espèce est un peu aberrante, à cause de son ouverture large, de son pli reporté près du bord pariétal et de sa columelle tordue comme celle des *Bullina*. La ciselure des tours ressemble aux impressions que laisserait une série de petits colliers.

9. CYLICHNA PLANATA.

C. t. parva, cylindracea, subelongata, alba, lævi, epidermide straminea induta; marginibus fere parallelis; spira planata, haud umbilicata, haud mamillata; anfractibus 4 convolutis, suturis parum impressis; basi modice effusa; labro tenui, in medio satis producto, antice late arcuato, postice parum sinuato, haud canaliculato, suturam versus satis rotundato; labio distincto, postice subcalloso; columella plica satis exstante, axi basim circumgyrante. Long. ·11, lat. ·055, poll. : div. 180°.

Hab. San Diego, *Cassidy*.

On n'a trouvé qu'un seul échantillon de cette petite espèce, qui est intermédiaire entre les *Cylichna* et les *Tornatina*.

307

Genus LOTTIA.

= *Lottia*, *Gray*, pars.

= *Acmœa*, seu *Tectura*, seu *Patella*, pars, *auct.*

= *Tecturella*, Cpr. Brit. Assoc. Rep. 1861, p. 157; non Stimpson, Invert., Grand-Manan.

Testa Patellis quibusdam seu Helcioni similis; ple-rumque planata, solida, apice anteriori.

Animal margine pallii intus papillis lamellosis circa dorsum lateraque instructo, regione capitis interruptis; pede elongato, ovali, planato; branchia minima.

Ce genre est intermédiaire entre les *Acmœa* et les *Scurria*. Dans les *Acmœa*, le manteau est simple ; dans les *Scurria*, il est garni, sur toute sa circonférence, de papilles qui, à première vue, offrent l'apparence des branchies des vraies *Patelles*; chez les *Lottia*, on trouve ces papilles sur le corps, mais non sur la tête de l'animal. De plus, la branchie, qui est ordinairement allongée et en forme de plume chez les *Acmœa*, et triangulaire chez les *Scurria*, est très-petite dans le genre qui nous occupe. Il serait prématuré de vouloir fixer définitivement les caractères conchyliologiques du genre *Lottia*, quoique le type soit très différent des *Patelles* ordinaires ; car il est possible que quelques-unes des espèces que l'on considère actuellement comme des *Patelles* se trouvent être des *Lottia*, lorsqu'on aura eu l'occasion d'observer leurs animaux.

On sait qu'il y a quatre noms employés pour désigner les *Patelles* à branchie de petite dimension. *Acmœa* est le premier en date, ayant été publié dans l'appendice du voyage de Kotzbue. J'aurais voulu conserver pour ce groupe le vocable générique *Tectura*, employé (après Milne Edwards) par Gray et MM. Adams : mais je trouve que Sowerby sen., dans son *Genera*, a figuré l'espèce originale comme type de son « *Lottia*, Gray. »

C'est le docteur Cooper qui, le premier, a observé et signalé les particularités de l'animal ; mais la diagnose que je viens de donner est le résultat des études du docteur Alcock, qui a succédé au capitaine Brown comme curateur du Musée de Manchester. Il a fait l'anatomie de presque toutes les *Patelles* de la côte ouest d'Amérique ; mais je ne veux pas anticiper sur ses découvertes. Voici la diagnose de l'espèce typique.

10. Lottia gigantea, *Gray.*

L. t. magna, crassiore, planata, expansa, textura sæpius extus spongiosa; nucleo minore, corneo, nigro-fusco, ancyliformi, vertice mamillato, subelevato; dein elongata, postice grisea, undulata; t. adolescente verrucosa, radiis obscuris, antice haud verrucosis; t. adulta plus minusve lata, plus minusve radiata seu verrucosa; apice plus minusve a margine remoto; parte antica seu haud exstante, seu circiter per quintam totius longitudinis projiciente, parte postica plus minusve elevata, convexa; extus ut in « Acmæa pelta » picta, albido-grisea, fusco-olivaceo copiose irregulariter strigata : intus, plerumque testudinaria, margine lato, nigro; spectro definito, seu rarius albido, cicatrice musculari fortiore, interdum purpureo seu violaceo tincta.

Long. (sp. normalis) 2·6, *lat.* 2·05, *alt.* ·7, *poll. A.*

Long. (sp. variantis) 2·95, *lat.* 2 35, *alt.* ·8, *poll. B.*

On mesure de l'*apex* jusqu'au bord antérieur, dans le sp. A, ·45.

On mesure de l'*apex* jusqu'au bord antérieur, dans le sp. B, ·05.

L'altitude de l'*apex* en sp. A est de ·6.

L'altitude de l'*apex* en sp. B n'est que de ·35.

= *Tecturella grandis*, Cpr. Brit. Assoc. Rep., loc. cit., où l'on peut voir quelques détails sur les variations de cette espèce remarquable.

11. Bittium (?var.) esuriens.

B. t. « B. filoso » simili, sed multo minore, graciliore, interdum valde attenuata; sculptura t. juniore ut in « B. filoso; » sed t. adulta subobsoleta, interstitiis haud insculptis. Long. ·27, long. spir. ·19, lat. ·085, poll. : div. 25°.

Hab. Neeah Bay, *Swan.* Sta.-Barbara, *Jewett.* — Monterey, San Pedro, *Cooper.*

Bien que j'aie vu beaucoup d'individus de cette forme, et un plus grand nombre encore du *B. filosum*, Gld. (= *Turritella Eschrichti*, Midd. = *Acirsa Eschrichti*, Adams, *Genera*), je ne puis pas décider avec une certitude complète si c'est une véritable espèce, ou seulement une variété dégradée et, pour ainsi dire, affamée (*esuriens*) du *B. filosum*, qui, d'ailleurs, ne varie pas. Comme le *B. filosum* ne s'étend pas aussi loin au sud, il est probable que les échantillons californiens doivent être considérés comme distincts, tandis que les individus de la région Vancouvérienne peuvent être réunis au *B. filosum*. Tous les individus qu'on a envoyés étaient très-roulés.

12. Bittium attenuatum.

B. t. valde gracili, attenuata; anfr. nucl... (detritis); normalibus 10 *planatis, suturis haud impressis; t. juniore lirulis spiralibus* 2 *anticis conspicuis, aliis posticis parum conspicuis, supra costulas circiter* 11. *radiantes transeun-*

tibus; t. adulta costulis et lirulis anticis obsoletis; lirulis
2. suturalibus ; basi prolongata, striis circiter 6 ornata;
apertura ovali; colum·lla intorta, parum emarginata.
Long ·4, long. spir. ·31, lat. ·11, poll. : div. 18°.

Hab. Monterey, *Taylor.* — Neeah Bay, *Swan.*

Je n ai vu qu'un seul échantillon en bon état de cette
espèce. Elle a la taille du *B. plicatum, A. Ad.*, mais la
sculpture de la base est différente.

13. ?Bitticum quadrifilatum.

?B. t. satis tereti, pallide cinerea, tenuisculpta; anfr.
nucleosis,primo omnino cœlato,?sinistrali, dein 2 lævibus,
rotundatis, apice quasi mamillato; anfr. normalibus 7
subplanatis; suturis valde impressis, haud sculptis; cos-
tulis radiantibus circ. 16-22, angustis, subrectis, anfr.
ult. crebrioribus, suturam versus evanidis; filis spiralibus
semper æqualibus, supra spiram 4 angustis, expressis,
costulas transeuntibus, haud nodulosis; filis duabus alteris,
inter quas sutura sita est; basi tenue striata; columella
intorta, parum effusa; apertura ovata; labio parvo, labro
tenui, parum arcuato. Long. ·26, long. spir. ·18, lat. ·09,
poll.: div. 25°

Hab. S. Pedro, *Cooper.* — S. Diego, *Cassidy.*

Dans cette espèce et dans quelques autres très voi-
sines, les *B. asperum* et *B. armillatum*, par exemple, le
nucléus est très-différent de celui des *Bittium* typiques.
Il est probable qu'elles n'appartiennent pas au même
genre.

14. Barleeia subtenuis.

B. t. parva, tenui, interdum subdiaphana, rufo-cornea,
anfr. nucleosis normalibus, apice submamillato; normali-
bus 4, planatis, suturis distinctis; basi rotundata; aper-

*tura subovata, peritremate continuo; labro acuto; labio
distincto, lacunam umbilicalem formante; columella subangulata operculo semilunato, dense rufo-vinoso, subho-
mogeneo, haud spirali, rudi; apophysi prælonga antice
columellam versus exstante. Long.* ·11, *long. spir.* ·07,
lat. ·06, *poll.: div.* 40°.

Hab. S. Diego, *Cassidy*; sur l'herbe, *Cooper.* — Cape
St.-Lucas, *Xantus.*—Mazatlan, *Reigen.*

Si l'on juge seulement d'après la coquille, on ne peut
guère séparer cette espèce des petites variétés dégradées de
l'*Hydrobia ulvæ* d'Europe. J'avais rapporté à cette espèce
quelques individus, en très-mauvais état, de la collection
Reigen (Maz. Cat., n° 417). Mais les individus frais qui
ont été recueillis, grâce au zèle du docteur Cooper, pos-
sèdent l'opercule remarquable des *Barleeia.*

15. BARLEEIA (?SUBTENUIS, VAR.) RIMATA.

B. t. • *B. subtenui* • *simili; sed paulum tumidiore;
anfractibus minus planatis; rima umbilicali conspicua.*

Hab. S. Diego, *Cassidy, Cooper.*

Peut-être cette forme se trouvera-t-elle constituer une
espèce distincte, lorsqu'elle sera mieux connue.

16. BARLEEIA HALIOTIPHILA.

*B. t. parva, turrita, lævi, angusta, tenui, rufo-fusca;
marginibus spiræ subrectis; anfr. nucleosis normalibus,
vertice submamillato; norm.* 5 *subplanatis, suturis distinctis; basi subplanata, obsolete angulata; apertura ovata,
peritremati haud continuo; labro tenui; labio parum calloso; columella vix arcuata; operculo ut in* • *B. subtenui* •
Long. ·4, *long. spir.* 06, *lat.* ·05, *div.* 30°.

Hab. Basse Californie, sur la partie dorsale d'une *Haliotide, Rowell.*

312

Cette espèce est voisine du *B. subtenuis;* elle s'en distingue par sa taille beaucoup plus petite, et sa forme plus élancée.

17. DRILLIA TOROSA.

D. t. acuminata, lævi, aurantio-fusca, epidermide aurantio-olivacea induta; anfr. nucleosis ?...(detritis); normalibus 7 tumidioribus, suturis planatis; serie una tuberculorum validorum, subrotundatorum, anfractu penultimo 8, anfr. ultimo haud obsoletis; regione sinus parvi, rotundati paulum excavata; regione suturali haud sculpta; canali longiore; columella recta; labio tenui; labro acuto, postice sinuato. Long. ·95, long. spir. ·55, lat. ·3, poll. : div. 30°.

Hab. Monterey, *Taylor, Cooper.*

Cette espèce, ainsi que d'autres *Pleurotomidæ* californiens, appartient à un groupe particulier, dont le *D. inermis,* Hinds, peut être considéré comme le type. Peut-être ces formes seraient-elles mieux placées dans le sous-genre *Clionella,* qui est vraiment marin, d'après les observations du docteur Stimpson sur les espèces du cap de Bonne-Espérance, et non pas Mélanien, comme l'a supposé le docteur Gray, et comme l'ont dit, après lui, MM. Adams et Chenu.

18. DRILLIA (?TOROSA, *var.*) AURANTIA.

D. t. « D. torosæ » simili, sed aurantia ; linea suturali expressa; interdum spiraliter sculpta. Long. ·6, long. spir. ·32, lat. ·28, poll.: div. 38°.

Hab. San Diego, *Cassidy.* — San Pedro, *Cooper.*

Les individus des localités méridionales étaient tous en mauvais état, et je ne suis pas encore convaincu qu'ils appartiennent à la même espèce.

19. Drillia penicillata.

D. t. • D. inermi • forma et indole simili; sed cinerea, rufo-fusco dense penicillata; lineolis creberrimis, interdum diagonalibus, seu zic-zacformibus, seu varie interruptis; anfractibus planatis, plicato-costatis, costulis circiter 14, regione sinus minimi, lati, expansi interruptis, postice nodosis; canali effusa.—Long. 1·35, long. spir. ·75, lat. ·42, poll. : div. 25°.

Hab. Cerros Is., basse Californie, *Veatch.*

Tous les individus que j'ai vus de cette espèce étaient excessivement roulés, mais on peut la reconnaître très-facilement à sa coloration élégante.

20. ? Daphnella aspera.

? D. t. parva, tenui, rufo-fusca, gracili, angusta, fusiformi, epidermide tenui induta; anfr. nucleosis 2 lævibus, vertice contorto; normalibus (t. adolescente) 4 elongatis, fenestratis, suturis distinctis; costulis radiantibus circiter 13 angustis, acutis, et costulis spiralibus, in spira 3, anfractu ultimo circiter 10, angustis, acutis, radiantes superantibus, eleganter decussata; intersectionibus subnodulosis, interstitiis quadratis; apertura elongata, angusta, antice effusa; labro postice vix sinuato. — Long. ·11, long. spir. ·09, lat. ·08, poll.: div. 35°.

Hab. Monterey, *Taylor.*

Je n'ai vu de cette charmante petite coquille qu'un seul échantillon très-frais, mais incomplétement adulte. Peut-être se trouvera-t-elle mieux placée dans le genre *Mitromorpha,* A. Adams?

21. Odostomia straminea.

O. t. • O. inflatæ, var. elatiori • simili, sed multo ela-

tiore; haud inflata, epidermide straminea, haud striu-
lata. — Long. ·18, *long. spir.* ·08, *lat.* ·1, *poll.* : *div.* 40·.

. Hab. basse Californie (sur la partie dorsale d'une *Ha-*
liotide), *Rowell.* — Cap St.-Lucas, *Xantus.*

On peut facilement distinguer cette espèce de celles du
Nord par sa spire allongée et son épiderme d'un jaune
de paille.

22. CHEMNITZIA TRIDENTATA.

Ch. t. (quoad genus) magna, compacta, latiore; casta-
nea, interdum fasciis pallidioribus; anfr. nucleosis 3 heli-
coideis, apice conspicuo, marginibus spiræ rectis parum
superantibus; normalibus 11 *subplanatis, suturis' distinc-*
tis; costis rectis acutis, interdum 19, *interdum* 24 *tenus,*
haud attingentibus, circa peripheriam haud subito evani-
dis; interstitiis undatis, eleganter spiraliter sulcatis;
sulculis circiter 8-10, *costis haud superantibus; apertura*
subquadrata; labro intus tridentato; columella tortuosa;
basi rotundata.—Long. ·45, *long. spir.* ·35, *lat.* ·12, *poll.:*
div. 16°.

Hab. Santa Barbara, *Jewett.* — Puget Sound, *Kenner-*
ley. — Monterey, San Pedro, *Cooper.*

Les trois dents de cette belle espèce, cachées tout à fait
à l'intérieur de l'ouverture, comme dans plusieurs espèces
du genre *Obeliscus*, ont été, pour la première fois, ob-
servées sur un individu cassé et roulé de Santa Barbara.
Celui-ci a 22 côtes; celui de Monterey, 20; celui du nord,
19; et ceux de San Diego, 24.

23. CHEMNITZIA (? *var.*) AURANTIA.

Ch. t. « *Ch. chocolatæ* » *simili, sed multo minore, latiore,*
haud tereti, aurantia; anfr. nucleosis ?... (detritis); nor-
malibus 7 *planatis, suturis impressis; costulis radianti-*

bus circiter 26, *haud expressis*, *ad peripheriam evanidis,
interstitiis late undatis ; lineolis spiralibus castaneis creberrimis tota superficie ornata ; basi subrotundata ; columella parum torta ; apertura ovata ; labro tenui, acuto ;
labio haud conspicuo.—Long.* ·23, *long. spir.* ·16, *lat.* ·07,
poll.: div. 20·.

Hab. Santa Barbara, *Jewett.*—Puget Sound, *Kennerley.*

Il est possible qu'on reconnaisse plus tard que cette
espèce est le jeune âge du *Ch. tridentata :* elle est intermédiaire entre elle et le *Ch. chocolata.*

24. VOLUTELLA PYRIFORMIS.

V. t. parva, « *V. margaritulæ* » *simili, sed aurantiaco
pallide tincta ; antice angustiore, magis elongata ; labio
conspicuo ; labro postice parum sinuato, intus denticulis
minus expressis ornato; plicis columellaribus normalibus,
acutioribus.—Long.* ·1, *lat.* ·065, *poll.*

Hab San Diego, *Cooper.* —California, « *Pacific Railway exploring Expedition.* »

Cette espèce ressemble au *V. margaritula* (Maz. Cat.,
n· 589), mais elle est plus allongée en avant. Le genre
Votutelia, Swainson (non d'Orbigny), correspond au genre
Closia de Gray.

25. OCINEBRA POULSONI (Nutt. ms.).

*O. t. turrita, solida, luteo-albida, rufo-sanguineo spi-
raliter lineata ; vertice nucleoso parvo, lævi, parum tumente : t. juniore rhomboidea, haud varicosa, spira planata, peripheria subangulata, canali recta, longiore, labro intus dentato, labio distincto, subcalloso : t. adulta,
anfr.* 7 *primis planatis, posticis tumidis ; suturis planatis, sed area postica concava ; costis subvaricosis crebris,*

*tumentibus, irregularibus, anfractu ultimo 7, circiter
quinquies subnodosis; tota superficie spiraliter crebre insculpta ; sulcis punctatis, rufo sanguineis ; apertura ovali;
labro acutiore, dorsaliter tumido, varicoso, intus dentibus
validis circiter 6 munito ; labio solido, sub suturam dente
valido parietali munito, super columellam calloso; canali
breviore, aperto. — Long.* 1·85, *long. spir.* ·96, *lat.* ·93,
poll. : div. 38°.

Hab. San Diego, *Nuttall.* — Cerros Is., *Veatch.* —
Santa Barbara, *Jewett.*

Je n'ai vu que trois individus de cette belle espèce :
l'un·d'eux, qui est typique, porte le nom de « *Buccinum
Poulsoni* » dans la collection Nuttall qui fait partie du
Musée britannique : un second, très-jeune, et d'un aspect fort particulier, bien qu'il appartienne évidemment
à la même espèce, a été recueilli par le colonel Jewett,
probablement à Santa Barbara (mais, d'après son étiquette,
à Panama) : enfin celui du docteur Veatch provient de la
basse Californie, et il est en très-mauvais état. Le premier
a été dessiné sur bois pour l'institution Smithsonienne
par M. Sowerby. Comme cette espèce intéressante est
presque inconnue en France, j'ai cru devoir en donner
une description suffisamment précise.   P. P. C.

N.

ON

THE PLEISTOCENE FOSSILS

COLLECTED BY

COL. E. JEWETT, AT STA. BARBARA, CALIFORNIA;

WITH

DESCRIPTIONS OF NEW SPECIES.

BY

PHILIP P. CARPENTER, B.A., Ph.D.

From the Annals and Magazine of Natural History. Third Series, Vol. XVII., pp. 274—278, April, 1866.

(319)

[*From the* ANNALS AND MAGAZINE OF NATURAL HISTORY
for April 1866.]

ON

THE PLEISTOCENE FOSSILS

COLLECTED BY Col. E. JEWETT AT Sta. BARBARA, CALIFORNIA;

WITH

DESCRIPTIONS OF NEW SPECIES.

BY

PHILIP P. CARPENTER, B.A., Ph.D.

THE study of the recent and tertiary mollusks of the west coast of America is peculiarly interesting and instructive, for the following reasons. It is the largest unbroken line of coast in the world, extending from 60° N. to 55° S., without any material salience except the promontory of Lower California. Being flanked by an almost continuous series of mountain-ranges, the highest in the New World, it might reasonably be supposed that the coast-line had been separated from the Atlantic from remote ages. The almost entire dissimilarity of its faunas from those of the Pacific Islands, from which it is separated by an immense breadth of deep ocean from north to south, marks it out as containing the most isolated of all existing groups of species, both in its tropical and its temperate regions. When we go back in time, we are struck by the entire absence of anything like the boreal drift, which has left its ice-scratchings and arctic shells over so large a portion of the remaining temperate regions of the northern hemisphere, and also by the very limited remains of what can fairly be assigned to the Eocene age. The great bulk of the land on the Pacific slope of North America (so far as it is not of volcanic origin) appears to have been deposited during the Miocene epoch. Here and there only are found beds whose fossils agree in the main with those now living in the neighbouring seas. To trace the correspondences and differences

21   321

between these and their existing representatives may be expected
to present results analogous to those now being worked out
with such discerning accuracy from the various newer beds of
modern Europe.

The first collection of Californian fossils seen in the east was
made near Sta. Barbara by Col. E. Jewett in 1849; but no account was published of them before the list in the British Association Report (1863), p. 539. They consist of forty-six species,
of which twenty-nine are known to be now living in the Californian seas, and others may yet be found there. The following
ten are Vancouver species, some of which may travel down to
the northern part of California :—

Margarita pupilla,	*Priene Oregonensis,*
Galerus fastigiatus,	*Trophon Orpheus,*
Bittium filosum,	*Chrysodomus carinatus,*
Lacuna solidula,	*C. tabulatus,* and
Natica clausa,	*C. dirus.*

Some of these are distinctly boreal shells, as are also *Crepidula
grandis* (of which Col. Jewett obtained a giant, $3\frac{1}{2}$ inches long,
and which now lives on a smaller scale in Kamtschatka) and
Trophon tenuisculptus (whose relations will be presently pointed
out). So far, then, we have a condition of things differing from
that of the present seas, somewhat as the Red Crag differs from
the Coralline. But in the very same bed (and the shells are in
such beautiful condition that they all appear to have lived on
the spot, which was perhaps suddenly caused to emerge by
volcanic agency) are found not only tropical species which even
yet struggle northwards into the same latitudes (as *Chione
succincta*), but also species now found only in southern regions,
as *Cardium graniferum* and *Pecten floridus*. Besides these,
the following, unknown except in this bed, are of a distinctly
tropical type, viz. :

Opalia, var. *insculpta.*	*Pisania fortis.*
Chrysallida, sp.	

From a single collection made only at one spot, in a few
weeks, and from the very fragmentary information to be derived
from the collections of the Pacific Railway surveys (described by
Mr. Conrad, and tabulated in the Brit. Assoc. Report, 1863,
pp. 589–596), it would be premature to draw inferences. We
shall await with great interest the more complete account to be
given by Mr. Gabb in the Report of the California Geological
Survey. With the greatest urbanity, that gentleman has sent
his doubtful Pleistocene fossils to the writer, to be compared
with the living fauna; but it would be unfair here to give any

account of them, except that they confirm the foregoing statements in their general character.

The following are diagnoses of the new species in Col. Jewett's collection.

Turritella Jewettii.

T. testa satis tereti, haud tenui, cinerea rufo-fusco tincta; anfr. subplanatis, suturis distinctis; lirulis distantibus (quarum t. jun. duæ extantiores) et striolis subobsoletis spiralibus cincta; basi parum angulata; apertura subquadrata; labro tenui, modice sinuato.

Hab. Sta. Barbara, Pleistocene formation (*Jewett*). San Diego, on beach (*Cassidy*).

This species comes nearest to *T. sanguinea,* Rve., from the Gulf, but differs in the faintness of the sculpture. Mr. Cassidy's specimens may be washed fossils, or very poor recent shells.

Bittium ?asperum.

B. testa *B. quadrifilato* forma, magnitudine, et indole simili, sed sculptura intensiore; eodem vertice nucleoso abnormali; sed, vice filorum, costulis spiralibus costas spirales superantibus, subnodulosis; t. jun. costulis ii. anticis majoribus, alteris minimis; postea plerumque iv. subæqualibus, interdum iii. interdum aliis intercalantibus; sculptura basali intensiore; costis radiantibus subarcuatis.

? = *Turbonilla aspera,* Gabb, in Proc. Acad. Nat. Sc. Philadelphia, 1861, p. 368.

Hab. Sta. Barbara, fossil in Pleistocene beds; abundant(*Jewett*). S. Pedro, S. Diego, Catalina Is. 30–40 fms. (*Cooper*), State Col. no. 591 c.

Mr. Gabb informs me that his *Turbonilla aspera* is a *Bittium.* Unfortunately the type is not accessible; and as the diagnosis would fit several closely allied species, it cannot be said with precision to which it rightfully applies. As this is the commonest of the group, it is presumed that it is the " *Turbonilla* " intended. Should the type, however, be recovered, and prove distinct, this shell should take the name of *B. rugatum,* under which I wrote the diagnosis, and which was unfortunately printed in the Brit. Assoc. Report, p. 539. The fossil specimens are in much better condition than the recent shells as yet discovered.

Bittium armillatum.

B. testa *B. aspero* simili; anfr. nucl. ii. lævibus, tumentibus, vertice declivi, celato; dein anfr. ix. normalibus planatis, suturis impressis; t. adolescente seriebus nodulorum tribus spiralibus extantibus, supra costas instructis; costis radiantibus circ. xiii. fere parallelis, seriebus, a suturis separatis, spiram ascendentibus; t. adulta, costulis spiralibus, interdum iv., intercalantibus; costulis radiantibus creberrimis; costis suturalibus ii. validis, haud nodosis; basi effusa, liris circ. vi. ornata; apertura subquadrata; labro labioque tenuibus; columella vix torsa, effusa, vix emarginata.

Hab. Sta. Barbara, Pleistocene, 1 sp. (*Jewett*). S. Pedro, S. Diego (*Cooper*).

The sculpture resembles *Cerithiopsis*; but the columella is pinched, not notched.

Opalia (?*crenatoides*, var.) *insculpta*.

O. testa *O. crenatoidei* simili; sed costis radiantibus pluribus, xiii.–xvi., in spira validis; anfr. ult. obsoletis; sculptura spirali nulla; punctis suturalibus minus impressis, circa fasciam basalem lœvem postice, non antice continuis.

Hab. Sta. Barbara, Pleistocene, 1 sp. (*Jewett*).

Very closely related to *O. crenatoides*, now living at Cape St. Lucas, and, with it, to the Portuguese *O. crenata*. It is quite possible that the three forms had a common origin.

Trophon tenuisculptus.

T. testa *T. Barvicensi* simili, sed sculptura minus extante; vertice nucleoso minimo; anfractibus uno et dimidio lœvibus, apice acuto; normalibus v., tumidis, postice subangulatis, suturis impressis; costis radiantibus x.–xiv., plerumque xii., haud varicosis, angustis, obtusis; liris spiralibus majoribus, distantibus, quarum ii.–iii. in spira monstrantur, aliis intercalantibus, supra costas radiantes undatim transeuntibus; tota superficie lirulis incrementi, supra liras spirales squamosis, eleganter ornata; canali longiore, subrecta, vix clausa; labro acutiore, postice et intus incrassato, dentibus circ. v. munito; labio conspicuo, lœvi; columella torsa.

Hab. Sta. Barbara, Pleistocene formation (*Jewett*).

This very elegant shell is like the least-sculptured forms of *T. Barvicensis*, from which it appears to differ in its extremely small nucleus. It is very closely related to *T. fimbriatulus*, A. Ad., from Japan, but differs in texture, and is regarded by Mr. Adams as distinct. It stands on the confines of the genus, there being a slight columellar twist, as in *Peristernia*.

Pisania fortis.

P. testa *P. insigni* simili, sed solidiore; crassissima, sculptura valde impressa; anfr. norm. v., parum rotundatis, suturis distinctis; costis radiantibus t. juniore circ. xii., obtusis, parum expressis, postea obsoletis; liris spiralibus validis, crebris (quarum t. juniore v., postea x., in spira monstrantur), subæqualibus, anticis majoribus; canali recurvata; lacuna umbilicali magna; labro intus crebrilirato ; labio conspicuo, spiraliter rugose lirato.

Hab. Sta Barbara, Pleistocene formation (*Jewett*).

Col. Jewett's single specimen is in very fine condition, and is confirmed by a fragment obtained by Mr. Gabb, the palæontologist to the California State Survey. Although resembling *Purpura aperta* and congeners in the irregular rugose folds of the labium, and *Siphonalia* in the strongly bent canal, Mr. H. Adams considers that its affinities are closest with the *Cantharus* group of *Pisania.* That genus is extremely abundant in the tropical fauna, but does not now live in California. It is the only distinctly tropical shell in the whole collection; and its presence, along with so many boreal species and types, appears somewhat anomalous, like the appearance of *Voluta* and *Cassidaria* in the Crag fauna. It is distinguished from the extreme forms of *P. insignis* by having the spiral liræ pretty equally distributed over the early whorls, by the close internal ribbing of the labrum, by the absence of the stout posterior parietal tooth, and by the great development of the columellar folds.

Note.—Unfortunately, during the long interval which has elapsed between the transmission of the MS. and receipt of the proof, the types have been returned to the owner, and (with the remainder of Col. Jewett's invaluable collection of fossils) have become the property of a college in New York State. As they are packed in boxes, and at present inaccessible, I am unable to give the measurements; but the unique specimens were drawn on wood by Mr. Sowerby for the Smithsonian Institution.—P. P. C., Montreal, Feb. 22, 1866.

INDEX OF SPECIES.

(13)

Cerithium

corallium, O 170.

famelicum, 36, 185, O 256, O 272, O 282, P 334, P 335.

filosum, 17, 185, O 209, O 212, O 295.

fragraria, 7, O 170.

Gallapaginis, 32, 63, 185, O 189, O 256, O 272, O 325, P 338.

gemmatum, O 272, P 339.

granosum, 7, O 170.

Guinaicum, P 333.

Hegewischii, O 295, P 345.

interruptum, 24, 32, 36, 45, 63, 108, 155, 185, O 189, O 226, O 238, O 256, O 272, O 325, O 360, P 337, P 338, P 542.

iostoma, P 345.

irroratum, 17, 32, 36, 45, 185, O 189, O 209, O 256, O 272, O 283, O 325, P 337.

Largillierti, P 343.

lima, O 170, O 222.

literatum, O 170.

maculosum, 7, 24, 27, 108, 185, O 189, O 230, O 238, O 256, O 272, O 282, O 293, O 325, O 360, O 366, P 333, P 339, P 340, P 542.

mediale, O 367.

var. mediolæve, 24, 35, 108, 185, O 256, P 334.

Menkei, P 338.

Montagnei, O 190, O 239, P 342, P 343, R 345, P 542.

musicum, 7, O 170, O 171, O 256, O 325, P 335.

nebulosum, O 189, O 256, O 325, P 333.

neglectum, 185, O 272.

obesum, 17, 32, 185.

ocellatum, 45, O 189, O 236, O 238, O 256, O 296, O 325, O 366, P 337, P 536, P 542.

Pacificum, 48, 185, O 170, O 272, O 325.

Cerithium

pauperculum, 186, O 272.

Peruvianum, P 442.

pulchrum, 186, O 256, O 272, P 343.

Reevianum, 186, O 256, O 272, P 343.

reticulatum, 6.

sacratum, O 209, U 206, V 226.

stercusmuscarum, 17, 27, 32, 36, 108, 152, O 170, O 209, O 233, O 236, O 238, O 256, O 272, O 282, O 325, O 360, O 366, P 337, P 339.

terebellum, O 289.

trilineatum, O 289.

umbonatum, O 256, P 335.

uncinatum, 24, 63, 108, 151, 185, O 256, O 272, O 285, O 325, O 364, P 334, P 335.

validum, 186, O 163, O 257, O 272, P 344.

varicosum, 7, 48, O 170, O 189, O 190, P 343, P 344.

vulgatum, O 170.

Cerithidea

albonodosa, 153, 186, O 228, O 283, O 325, O 351, U 205.

Californica, 141.

fuscata, 79, O 228, O 233, P 345.

Lavalleana, O 364.

Mazatlanica, 108, 141, 186, O 233.

Montaguei, 24, 27, 151, 186, O 230, O 256, O 272, O 325, P 342, P 343.

pulchra, O 325.

pullata, 141, 151, O 325, O 351.

Reeviana, O 325.

sacrata, 23, 79, 141, O 200, O 228, O 230, O 233, O 325, O 351, P 345, U 206, V 226.

(?sacrata, var.), fuscata, U 206.

solida, O 230.

valida, O 230, O 325.

Chiton
regularis, 40, O 287, O 318, Q 232.
retusus, O 180.
sanguineus, 63, O 364, P 194.
scaber, O 229, O 290, O 317.
scabriculus, O 180, O 318.
scrobiculatus, 19, O 215, O 224.
setiger, O 214.
setosus, 18, O 178, O 180, O 214, O 215, O 318.
Simpsonii, O 208.
Sitchensis, 19, O 192, O 214, O 223, O 229, O 290.
Stelleri, 19, O 194, O 214, O 223, O 229.
Stimpsonii, 72.
Stokesii, 38, 153, 198, 266, O 180, O 229, O 277.
submarmoreus, 84, 214, O 219, O 223.
sulcatus, 9, O 187.
textilis, 35.
tunicatus, 9, 84, O 178, O 192, O 214, O 223, O 288.
vespertinus, 16, O 210.
vestitus, O 175, O 223, O 296.
Wosnessenskii, 19, 92, O 214, O 318.

Chlorostoma
aureotinctum, 28, 138, 152.
brunneum, 27, 138.
funebrale, 19, 23, 27, 40, 49, 79, 113, 138, 170, O 287, O 297.
gallina, 138, 152.
maculosum, 21, O 227.
marginatum, 79.
moestum, 49, 170.
nigerrimum, 28, 138.
Pfeifferi, 23, 27, 138.
var. pyriforme, 138.
rugosum, P 233.
——— var. O 283.
var. subapertum, 113, 138.

Chondropoma
rubicundum, 45.

Choristodon
typicum, 29, O 244, O 364, P 447, P 529.

Chorus
Belcheri, 60, 149, 151.

Chætopleura
muscosa, 16.
dentiens, 16.

Chrysallida
acuminata, O 273, O 334.
angusta, 104, 219.
cancellata, O 364.
cincta, 99, 145.
clathratula, 36, 187, O 259, O 273, O 334, P 424.
clausiliformis, O 260, O 334, P 367, P 369, P 370, P 426.
communis, 36, 110, 187, O 273, O 334, O 357, O 364, P 408, P 419, P 421, P 423.
convexa, O 260, O 334, P 422.
crebristriata, T 170.
effusa, 36, 39, 187, O 259, O 334, P 422.
fasciata, 39, O 259, O 334, P 417, P 423.
indentata, O 260, O 334, P 425.
marginata, O 273, O 334, P 423.
nodosa, O 259, O 334, P 369, P 417.
oblonga, O 259, O 334, P 418.
ovata, O 259, O 334, P 417, P 418.
paupercula, 36.
Photis, O 260, O 334, P 425.
pumila, 99, 145.
Reigeni, O 259, O 334, P 422.
rotundata, O 259, O 334, P 418, P 419.
telescopium, 36, 39, 187, O 259, O 334, P 418, P 421, P 422.

Chrysodomus
antiquus, 69, 70, 83, 166, 183, O 343.
Baeri, O 343.
Behringii, O 343.

Diala

  mamillata, 33, P 412.

  marmorea, 99, 143.

  paupercula, 259.

Dione

  affluis, O 305.

  alternata, O 363.

  aurantia, O 246, O 305, P 56
  P 63.

  aurantiaca, O 282.

  biradiata, O 232, O 305, P VI.

  brevispina, 57.

  brevispinata, 57, O 281, P 69.

  brevispinosa, O 247, O 305, O
  358, P 69.

  chione, O 366, P VI., P 63, P
  65.

  chionæa, O 226, O 232, O 234,
  O 246, O 282, O 305, O 352,
  O 366, P VI , P 63, P 64, P 65,
  P 70.

  chionæa, *var.* O 364.

  circinata, 58, O 232, O 247, O
  305, O 363, P 69.

  concinna, O 247, O 305, P 69.

  consanguinea, O 305.

  dione, O 232, O 364.

  elegans, P VI.

  exspinata, 58.

  lepida, O 234.

  lupinaria, 57, O 232, O 246, O
  265, O 297, O 305, O 358, O
  O 364, P 67.

  maculata, 57, O 364, P 65.

  multispinosa, 57.

  nobilis, 57.

  pannosa, 58, 211.

  prora, 58.

  ———— *var.* 210.

  puella, 21.

  rosea, O 232, O 234, O 246, O
  305, P 66.

  semilamellosa, 57, 58.

  squalida, O 305, P VI., P 64.

  tortuosa, O 305.

  unicolor, 58, O 305.

Dione

  Veneris, 57, P 67.

  vulnerata, O 246, O 305, P 68.

Diplodonta

  calculus, 106, O 308.

  circularis, O 366.

  obliqua, O 224, O 248, O 308,
  P 103, P 534.

  orbella, 12, 22, 26, 113, 129, O
  197, O 232, O 308, O 349,
  O 351, O 352, U 202, V 218.

  semiaspera, 30, 154, O 197,
  O 224, O 229, O 248, O 297,
  O 308, O 363, O 366, P 102.

  ———— *var.* O 227, U 202.

  semiaspera, *var.* discrepans,
  O 248, P 103.

  serricata, O 248, P 104.

  subquadrata, 106, O 287, O 308,
  Q 230.

  trigonula, P 103.

  undata, P 103.

Discina

  Cumingii, 37, 105, 155, 194, 205,
  266, O 244, O 298, O 366, P 7.

  Evansii, 55, 102, O 298, O 349.

  striata, O 366.

  strigata, 54.

Discopora

  trispinosa, P 3.

Discus

  Vancouverensis, 157.

Dispotæa

  Byronensis, 10.

  dentata, O 3, P 287.

  spinosa, O 239, P 546.

  striata, Q 234.

Distortio

  anus, O 171.

  constrictus, 182.

Ditrupa

  gadus, X 413.

Dolium

  crassilabre, O 238, P 543.

  dentatum, 8, O 238, P 543.

  latilabre, O 238.

4

Leda
  eburnea, 46.
  Elenensis, 24, 200, O 249, O 311,
    P 145, P 530.
  fossa, 88, 91, 130.
  foveata, 91.
  gibbosa, O 311.
  hamata, 98, 130.
  Hindsii, 41.
  impressa, O 367.
  inornata, 130.
  lyrata, 46.
  minuta, 71, 89, 130, 169.
  minuta, var. 71.
  pernula, 130.
  polita, 24, 200, 311.
  Sowerbiana, 46.
  Taylori, 41, 46.

Leiosolenus
  spatiosus, O 249, O 310, P 130,
    P 550.

Leiostraca. *See* **Liostraca.**

Leiostracus
  Mexicanus, P 177.
  Ziegleri, P 177.

Lepas
  alba, P 297.

Lepeta
  candida, 71.
  cæcoides, 89, 137, 169.

Lepidopleurus
  Adamsii, 37, 265, 266.
  Beanii, O 252, O 317, P 197.
  bullatus, O 252, O 317, P 195.
  ———— *var.* calciferus, O 252,
    P 196.
  clathratus, O 252, O 317, P 195.
  limaciformis, O 317.
  MacAndrew, O 252, O 317, P
    196, P 197.
  Magdalensis, O 317.
  Mertensii, 89, 135.
  pectinatus, 89, 135.
  regularis, 135.
  sanguineus, O 252, O 317, P 194,
    P 195, P 196.

Lepidopleurus
  scabricostatus, 98, 135.
  tenuisculptus, 37, 39, 266.

Lepralia
  adpressa, 256, O 244, O 298, P
    5.
  atrofusca, O 243, O 298, P 3.
  cucullata, P 3.
  hippocrepis, O 244, O 298, P 4.
  humilis, O 244, O 298, P 5.
  marginipora, O 244, O 298, P 4.
  Mazatlanica, O 243, O 298, P 3.
  rostrata, O 243, O 298, P 4.
  trispinosa, O 243, O 298, P 3.

Leptinaria
  Elisæ, 44.
  Emmelinæ, 44.

Leptochiton
  cinereus, 92.
  interstinctus, 16.
  lividus, O 317.
  Mertensii, O 317, O 349.
  nexus, 98, 136.
  proprius, O 317.
  scrobiculatus, O 317, O 349.

Leptoconchus
  monodonta, 63.

Leptoconus
  gladiator, P 405.
  puncticulatus, P 404.
  purpurascens, P 402.
  regularis, P 402.
  regalitalis, P 403.

Lepton
  clementinum, O 248, O 308, P
    110, P 111.
  dionæum, O 248, O 308, P 111.
  meroëum, 97, 129.
  placunoideum, P 111.
  umbonatum, O 248, O 308, P
    111.

Leptonyx
  bacula, 98, 138.
  sanguineus, 113, 138.

Leptoxis
  fusca, 163.

6

Onychoteuthis
Bergii, O 218, O 223, O 345.
fusiformis, 99, 118, 119, 150.
Kamtschatica, O 218, O 223.

Opalia
attenuata, 244.
australis, 244, 245.
bicarinata, 244.
borealis, 18, 99, 114, 146.
bullata, 23, 146, 287.
crassicostata, 244, 245.
crassilabrum, 244.
crenata, 105, 220, 244, 324.
crenatoides, 105, 220, 244, 324.
(———— var.) insculpta, 25, 105, 146, 214, 322, 324.
diadema, 244.
funiculata, 37, 244.
McAndreæ, 244.
Ochotensis, 114, 245.
retiporosa, 99, 146, 244.
spongiosa, 99, 146, 244.

Orbicula
Cumingii, 54, 205, O 280.
Evansii, 55, O 287.
Norvegica, 55.
ostreoides, 55.
striata, 55.
strigata, 54.

Orthalicus
livens, 59, O 251, P 176.
Mexicanus, O 250, P 177.
princeps, P 177.
undatus, 158, O 363, P 176.
zebra, 93, 158, O 170, O 363, P 176.
Ziegleri, O 251, P 177.

Orthocera
glabra, X 436.
imperforata, X 425.
trachea, X 414, X 423.

Oscilla
exarata, 33, 110, P 415.
terebellum, 110.
ziziphina, 33, P 416.

Osilinus
ater, O 321, O 348, O 351.
gallinus, O 321.
———— var. U 204.

Osteodesma
bracteatum, 17, O 209, O 210.
Californicum, O 231.
corbuloides, O 222.
diaphanum, O 287, Q 228.
hyalinum, 119, O 209, O 210, O 222.
nitidum, 17, O 226, O 228, U 199, Q 229.

Ostrea
æquatorialis, O 191, O 250, P 157.
amara, 27, 38, 107, 152, 199.
bicolor, P 161.
borealis, 74.
Bourgeoisii, 119.
Canadensis, P 160, P 550.
Columbiensis, 107, 132, O 186, O 226, O 250, O 277, O 312, P 161.
conchaphila, 38, 78, 132, 151, 152, 199, O 198, O 233, O 250, O 277, O 282, O 312, O 351, O 353, O 365, P 159, P 161, P 163, P 352, P 482, V 220.
Cumingiana, O 250, O 312, O 352, P 163.
edulis, 85, 132, 198, P 159, P 161.
var. expansa, 101, 132, 306.
frons, 6.
gallus, 14.
Heermanni, 76.
iridescens, 107, 117, 198, 273, 274, O 162, O 226, O 250, O 312, O 365, P.157, P 162, P 164.
var. laticaudata, 101, 132, 305.
longirostris, P 160.
lurida, 85, 92, 101, 132, 305.
———— var. 76.
margaritacea, O 250.

Patula

Cooperi, 157.

Mazatlanica, 157.

sportella, 157.

strigosa, 157.

Pecten

adspersus, O 236, P 538.

(*?var.*) æquisulcatus, 22, 26, 78, 85, 131, 155, 170, 280.

altiplicatus, 81.

aspersus, 199, O 277

catilliformis, 77.

caurinus, 73. 85, 131, O 311, O 348.

circularis, 40, 45, 76, 107, O 250, O 285, O 290, O 352, P 152.

dentatus, O 233, O 311, O 352.

deserti, 76, 81.

Dieffenbachii, 73.

digitatus, O 207.

discus, 81.

excavatus, 14.

Fabricii, 60, O 211, O 218.

fasciculatus, O 207, O 311.

floridus, 25, 322, O 207, O 311, O 351.

hastatus, 14, 18, 22, 81, 92, 131.

hericeus, 18, 92, 131, O 212, O 311, O 348.

Hindsii, 60, 92.

inca, 199, O 277, O 311

intermedia, 80, 107.

irradians, 281.

Islandicus, 4, 20, 60, 70, 92, 131, O 218, O 223.

Jeffersonius, 81.

lætus, 73.

laqueatus, O 288.

latiauritus 22, 45, 60, 131, O 198, O 229, O 233, O 234, O 311, O 349, O 351, V 219.

Madisonius, 77.

magnificus, O 185, O 311, O 359.

magnolia, 81.

Pecten

Meekii, 81.

mesotimeris, 45.

monotimeris, 26, 78, 131, 151, O 198, O 229, O 233, O 234, V 219.

Nevadanus, 77.

nodosus, O 233, O 234, O 311, O 352.

nucleus, *var.* O 290.

Pabloensis, 80.

paucicostatus, 22, 100, 131, 281.

Pealii, O 218.

pomatia, 14.

propatulus, 165, O 367.

purpuratus, 102, O 233, O 284, O 351.

pyxidatus, 153.

rastellinus, 14.

rubidus, 4, 20, 92, 131, O 207, O 218, O 223, O 311.

senatorius, 40, 73, O 282.

sericeus, O 207, O 311.

(*?var.*) squarrosus, 22, 281.

subcrenatus, 153.

subnodosus, 24, 27, 107, 151, O 185, O 311.

Townsendi, 18, O 213, O 311, O 348.

Tumbezensis, 199, O 277, O 311.

tumidus, 35, 78, 85, O 185, O 187, O 277, O 290.

tunica, 60, 131.

varius, O 222, P 532.

ventricosus, 14, 24, 27, 40, 45, 54. 78, 85, 107, 131, 151. 152, 170, 199, 280, 281, O 187, O 233, O 234, O 277, O 282, O 290, O 311.

———— *var.* 22.

Yessoensis, 70, 74.

Pectunculus

assimilis, 200, O 182, O 229, O 233, O 249, O 277, P 144.

bicolor, O 285, O 290, O 310.

Californicus, O 192.

7

Recluzia
Rollandiana, 62, O 297, O 316.

Rhinoclavis
geminata, 7, 24, 108, 152, 185.

Rhizochilus
asper, O 287, O 297, O 340.
Californicus, 35, 111, 180, O 262, O 287, P 484.
distans, 34, 35, 180, P 484.
foveolatus, O 340.
gibbosus, P 485.
madreporarum, 155.
niveus, P 484.
nux, 25, 34, 35, 111, 180, O 262, O 269, O 340, P 484.

Rhodea
Californica, 158.

Rhynchonella
lucida, 72.
psittacea, 71, 93, 122, 168.

Ricinula
alveolata, O 187, O 293.
arachnoidea, O 176.
carbonaria, 181, O 231, O 270.
contracta, O 187.
elegans, O 176.
heptagonalis, O 187.
jugosa, 181, O 270.
Reeviana, 181, O 270.
zonata, O 187.

Rimula
cucullata, O 209, O 213.
galeata, O 209.
Mazatlanica, 108, O 252, O 320, P 222.

Rissoa
acutelirata, 99, 142.
albolirata, 104, 216.
arctica, O 220.
bryerea, P 357.
clandestina, 189, O 273, P 257.
compacta, 89, 142.
firmata, 361, 89, O 273, P 357.
fortis, O 273, P 356.

Rissoa
glabra, O 220.
incouspicua, 32, 33, 36, 189, 190, O 273.
infrequens, 189, O 273, O 327.
Janus, 189, O 273, O 327.
lirata, P 358.
notabilis, 33, 36, 189, 190, O 273, O 327.
proxima, P 437.
saxatilis, O 220.
scalariformis, 36, 189, O 273, O 327.
striata, O 238, P 356, P 542.

Rissoina
ambigua, 230.
Catesbyana, O 364.
Clandestina, 109, O 327.
expansa, 24, 293.
infrequens, 109, 293.
interfossa, 99, 142.
firmata, 24, 32, 109, 189, O 327.
fortis, 24, 109, O 327.
Janus, 24.
pyramidata, P 356.
scalariformis, 32.
striata, 24, 109, O 257, O 327, P 356.
Woodwardii, 24, 189, O 257, O 327, O 364, P 356, P 357.

Rocellaria
ovata, 121.

Rostellaria
indurata, O 367.

Rotella
lineata, O 222.

Rupellaria
Cordieri, 127.
exarata, O 244, O 299, P 20.
foliacea, 154, O 299.
lamellifera, 22, 25, 26, 127, O 299, O 349, V 214.
lingua-felis, 106, O 244, O 299, P 20.
paupercula, O 299.

Sphænia
Binghami, P 16, P 24.
Californica, 78, 87, O 194, O 211, O 284, O 301, O 349, O 351, V 210.
fragilis, 29, 39, 105, O 244, O 300, P 24, P 530.
luticola, 29.
ovalis, 168.
ovoidea, 88, 123.

Sphærella
tumida, 30, 129.

Sphærium
dentatum, 164.
lenticula, 165.
meridionale, 165.
nobile, 165.
occidentale, 116, 165.
ovale, 165.
patella, 165.
Spokani, 91, 165.
striatinum, 116, 164.
subtransversum, 165.
tumidum, 91, 165.

Spiraxis
Cobanensis, 44.
Lattrei, 44.
Shuttleworthii, 44.

Spiroglyphus
albidus, 43.
lituella, 27, 108, 140.

Spisula
fragilis, P 51.

Spondylus
calcifer, 24, 107, 199, 256, 258, O 241, O 250, O 277, O 312, P 547, P 548, P 550.
crassisquama, O 233.
dubius, O 182, O 312, P 153.
ducalis, P 153.
Estrellanus, 81.
Lamarckii, 199, O 250, O 277, P 153, P 547.
limbatus, 43, O 290, O 312.
pictorum, O 233, O 234, O 265.
——— var. P 153.

Spondylus
princeps, O 312.
——— var. O 182.
radula, O 290, O 312.
varians, O 233.
Victoriæ, 41.

Standella
Californica, 22, 99, 113, 126, 151.
falcata, 126.
fragilis, 27, 106.
nasuta, 12, 99, 126.
planulata, 99, 126.
velata, 204.

Stenotrema
germana, 157.

Stephopoma
var. bispinosa, 42.
pennatum, 42.

Stoa
ammonitiformis, 42.
subcrenata, 44.

Stomatella
inflata, 37, 194, O 275, O 320.

Stramonita
petrosa, 76.

Strategus
inermis, 94, 95.

Strebloceras
anellum, 43.
cornuoides, X 441, X 443.
solutum, X 441, X 443.

Strephona
incrassata, P 464.
Pedroana, 76.

Strigatella
effusa, O 339.
tristis, 24, 110, 151, 177, O 261, O 339, P 461.

Strigilla
carnaria, 23, 27, 102, 151, 154, O 195, O 224, O 227, O 228, O 245, O 303, O 350, O 353, O 363, P 39, P 40, U 200.
dichotoma, O 224, O 303.
disjuncta, 40, O 284, O 303, S. 160.

Tellina

Panamensis, O 295, O 303.
Pedroana, 75.
perna, O 366.
petalum, O 170, O 302.
pisiformis, 60, O 224, P 102.
plebeia, O 186, O 302.
princeps, 154, O 186, O 282, O 302.
prora, 202, O 279. O 303.
proxima, O 178, O 221.
puella, 23, 38, 202, O 245, O 279, O 302, P 37.
punicea, 8, 23, 154, O 245, O 279, O 302, O 363, P 35.
pura, 21, 29, 40, O 227, O 232, O 302, O 351, U 199.
purpurea, 29, P 33.
regia, O 186, O 232, O 302.
regularis, O 245, O 302, P 36.
rhodora, O 284, O 303.
rosea, 35.
rubella, 23.
rubescens, 105, 202, O 186, O 282, O 302, P 32.
rufescens, 47, O 208, O 246, O 296, O 302, O 363, O 366, P 32.
rugosa, 9.
siliqua, 202, O 279, O 303.
similis, O 364.
solidula, 20, O 170, O 219, O 221, O 223, O 301.
sordida, O 221.
straminea, O 245, O 287, O 302, P 34.
striata, 155, P 35.
suborbicularis, P 105.
tersa, 20, 272, O 226, O 228, O 303, U 199.
triangularis, 221.
vicina, 12, 38, 78, 126, 203, O 232, O 279, O 284, O 302, O 351, O 363, U 201.
virgo, O 189, O 302.

Tellimya

bidentalis, 303.

Tellimya

lactea, P 105.
suborbicularis, P 105.
tenuis, P 105.
tumida, 88, 97, 129.

Tellinides

purpureus, O 175, P 32.

Terebra

aciculata, O 185, O 285, P 388, P 389.
Africana, 51, 61, O 285, O 288, P 384.
albocincta, 51, O 226, O 258, P vi., P 384, P 386.
arguta, O 228, O 233, O 258, P 388, U 206.
armillata, 51, O 206, O 239, O 258, O 366, P 384, P 545.
aspera, 51, O 185.
Belcheri, O 296.
castanea, 51.
cinerea, 51, O 364.
dislocata, 51.
elata, 177, O 185, O 267.
elongata, 51.
flammea, 41, 51, 61, O 207.
formosa, 41.
frigata, O 189.
fulgurata, O 225, O 228, O 233, O 236, O 352, P 535, P 537, P 552.
Hindsii, 51, O 258.
Hupei, 51.
incomparabilis, 41.
insignis, 41.
interstincta, O 366.
intertincta, 51, P 384.
Jamaicensis, 51.
larvæformis, 41, 177, O 267.
laurina, 51.
lingualis, 109, O 206, O 330.
Loroisi, 51.
luctuosa, 51, 63, O 206, O 239, O 364, P 387, P 545.
marginata, 51.
ornata, O 185, O 207, O 330, O 360.

8

Trophon

. triangulatus, 99, 149.

Truncaria

corrugata, 25, 148.

eurytoides, 104, 220.

modesta, 25, 180, O 231, O 270, O 342.

Truncatalla

assiminea, O 275.

Bairdiana, 154, 194, O 275, O 326.

Californica, 60, 100, 143, 156.

dubiosa, 37, 194, O 275, O 326.

gracilenta, 156.

Montagui, P 363, P 364.

Turbinella

acuminata, 48, O 271, O 292.

ardeola, O 171, O 261, O 338, P 456.

armata, O 182.

cæstus, 27, 183, O 171, O 238, O 261, O 271, O 338, P 456, P 458, P 544.

callosa, O 269.

castanea, 183, O 177, O 271, O 292.

cerata, 61, 183, O 177, O 271, O 292, O 294, P 457.

cingulata, O 294, P 457.

muricata, P 436.

nodata, O 188.

rigida, 10, O 177.

rudis, 183, O 271.

spadicea, 183, O 271.

tectum, O 292.

tubercularis, 61, O 294.

tuberculata, O 182.

varicosa, 10, O 188.

Turbo

bicarinatus, 61, O 174.

Buschii, 36, 192, O 274.

carneus, O 216.

cinereus, O 216.

coccineus, 3.

digitatus, O 203, O 253, P 229.

eximius, 31.

Turbo

fluctuatus, O 192, O 253, P 223.

————, var. O 293, Q 234.

————, var. depressus, Q 234.

fluctuosus, O 179, O 233, O 236, O 237, P 223, P 536, P 541.

Fokkesii, 19, 60, O 216, O 233, O 253, O 351, P 223.

funiculosus, O 288, O 293, P 223.

margarita, O 216.

marginatus, 49, O 200, O 291.

mœstus, 49.

muriaticus, O 220.

pellis-serpentis, O 170.

petholatus, 63.

phasianella, 31, 36, 63, 192, 214, O 274.

pulcher, 48.

pustulatus, O 230.

rotelliformis, O 200.

rutilus, 37, 192, O 274, O 320.

sanguineus, 3.

saxosus, 10, 192, O 179, O 186, O 230, O 274.

squamiger, O 187, O 230, O 360.

var. striulatus, 36.

tessellatus, O 230, O 291.

ulvæ, O 220, P 361.

unguis, P 229.

variegatus, 36.

ventrosus, O 220.

Turbonilla

aspera, 118, 323.

Turris

funiculata, P 390.

Turritella

altilira, 80.

Banksii, 36, 154, 186, O 256, O 272, O 291, O 325, P 330.

biseriata, 77.

Broderipiana, O 190, O 256, P 330.

Californica, P 330.

Cooperi, 98, 141..

Cumingii, O 256, O 291, P 332.

www.ingramcontent.com/pod-product-compliance
Lightning Source LLC
Chambersburg PA
CBHW032259280326
41932CB00009B/625